D1498478

PNEJAD@HOTMAIL.COM
PARISA NEJAD

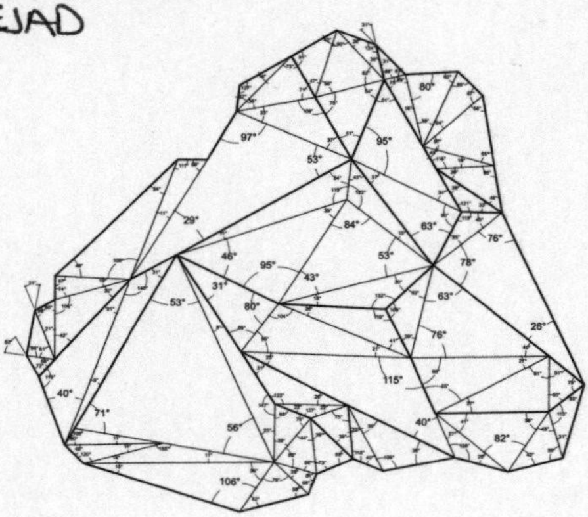

GEO LOGICS

Geography Information Architecture

VICENTE GUALLART

The research presented in this book condenses the work carried out over the last ten years, oriented toward the development of architecture projects. Our practice encompasses multiple scales, from the territorial project, the creation and reform of cities, the design of neighbourhoods, landscape, the buildings, the homes, the objects that inhabit it and the informational relationship between them. 'From bits to geography.'

This multiscale approach is prompted by a recognition of the need to think and create ecosystems in their entirety rather high-profile one-off actuations isolated from the city and the territory. A process oriented toward creating conditions of habitability in the territory more than constructing buildings. We are, then, more interested in the systemic character of the architecture than in its iconic character per se.

There would be no need for architecture if human beings were content to live in caves or in trees.
Architecture is necessary to create conditions of habitability that are not dependent on the time of day or the time of year, on the climatic conditions of the environment anywhere in the territory. Architecture, then, must emerge in specific places, at particular moments in history, in a continuous process of re-foundation of the territory.

Geography is the science that deals with the mapping of physical, economic or social phenomena on the territory. It deals with mountain ranges, trade flows and social interactions. Every architectural project is thus a manipulation of the geographic parameters of a place.

GeoLogics are the logics of the Earth. They are the mechanisms we use to interact with a place in accordance with its own essential rules. They are processes that we define, based on our recognition of the various systems to be acted on, in order to implant habitable structures that follow a natural order. We understand a natural order as one that emerges from the nature of things, from their basic principles, following patterns that tend to the generation and conservation of life.

Architecture is thus a process that adds new layers of history to places. If it knows how to interpret the values of the site, it will be capable of producing a richer and more complex place and leave it open to life and t o its transformation and evolution.

Architecture is a re-active activity.
Our generation, which is the first to operate in a global context, needs to be able to redefine the modes of construction on the Earth so as to ensure that the fact of inhabiting it does not transform the basic parameters of the environment itself in such a way as to make it inhabitable.

And in the light of this, the knowledge of the medium in which we operate and the definition of strategies of interaction with it define new ways of doing for the science of the construction of inhabitable locales that is architecture.

Architecture has managed to respond to the social, technological and cultural conditions of each successive era throughout history. The logics presented here thus encompass a range of issues—structural, formal, physiological, relational—that have to do with the physical aspects of the territory and the elements that compose it and with the actual structural relationships of living beings.

The buildings that we construct today and the cities we inhabit are the products of an accumulation of knowledge over the course of our history. But still, the most rudimentary living being on the planet is more complex and more intelligent than any building constructed at any time in history. Architecture and urbanism need to learn from nature in a structural way, in order to integrate the principles and values of environmental processes, of the logics of natural ecosystems, of the anatomy or physiology of living beings and of their material properties, which in their totality have demonstrated their capacity for survival throughout their evolution process.

And to accumulate this knowledge of all the values that the discipline of architecture has generated in the course of its history.
This constitutes an incredible opportunity for architecture, which down through the ages has defined its field of action in terms of the challenges and aspirations of the societies and cultures that construct it.

In this way, architecture expands its areas of action and its materials for its project of habitability of and in the world. In doing so it must define new codes of actuation, new principles with which to set an architectural project in motion that are grounded in their connection with the energy and the potentials of the place and that, on completion, enable us to leave there open conditions in which life can operate. Just as when a tree is planted.

In the pursuit of an architectural project that is more than an object on a background, an affirmation of personal identity on the landscape or a phenomenon on a cultural context, the human actuation must be a nature in itself capable of possessing differing degrees of artificiality both in its gestation and in its operation.

In this situation, architecture itself must operate on the basis of logics that are no longer confined to the traditional functional typologies or to simple exercises of formal manipulation of the material for a manifestly iconic purpose; what is needed is a logic that responds to the processes and conditions that obtain where it is to be inserted.

In fact, taking the world as a system of ecosystems that interact in a scalar form, every architectural project should seek to integrate itself into that habitat, whether by literally resonating in tune with the energy wavelength of the place, or by acting in the territory as a transformative element, detecting the potentials for modification produced by the new operating conditions on site.

For this to be possible, the informational processes linked to design, visualization or manufacture using digital systems can be seen as key tools in the development of new construction techniques and processes for this new hybrid reality. This means that the practice of the architect is transformed: from being an actor that interprets initial conditions, generates a design that will subsequently be developed and will be constructed by mechanisms more or less linked to the economy and to the techniques of material manufacture and industry, she will be an operator producing information that in the current state of production permits a personalized fabrication in every aspects of the architecture.

This research extends over a considerable period of time in which some of the initial lines of work have been consolidated as precise forms of actuation, while in other cases new lines of work have been marked out for consolidation in the future. In many cases it has been necessary to redefine the team with which the architect works. The incorporation into the projects of external specialists from fields such as geology, anthropology, sociology, engineering, software and interface design, ecology, art, economics or biology enables these projects to encompass records registers that in other conditions would be impossible. In this way, the actual definition of the working group —as in the case of a chamber group, a jazz combo or a symphony orchestra— efficiently reveals the different areas, intensities and registers of interpretation of a project.

We understand the practice of architecture as an activity that sets processes in motion rather than simply surfing the conjunctural waves that periodically invade the territory. In this way, when new spaces are opened up for action, it is able to define its own rules of actuation. This is especially relevant when operating in relation to mechanisms such as the production of the city, where practices based on purely economic problems have produced in the territory places of low environmental or social stimulus. Our practice's approach rests on processes associated with the investigation of new conditions and with principles that we start off intuiting and in most cases go on to establish as crucial for the next years.

A number of the projects are explained in terms of various logics that can operate at different scales or by way of multilayer systems.

We seek to ensure that the logics we present act as dynamical rational systems that go beyond the development of a project on the basis of an 'idea', a purely formal response or an economic discourse. The projects in this book follow a logic that embraces everything from the interaction with natural elements such as mountains, rocks or trees, the transformations of urban areas, and social organizations through to the projects' interaction with the digital world.

Any architectural practice that it seeks to act according to these principles must devote a significant amount of its time to research. In view of this, over the past few years we have created various architectural platforms that make it possible to engage in what we have come to call R+3D (research plus development, teaching [docencia] and diffusion), in order to create and participate in knowledge networks as a means of developing the principles and the technologies with which to achieve these goals.

The Metapolis group, the Institute of Advanced Architecture of Catalonia and the Fab Labs and other structures that may be created in the future are oriented toward stimulating the progress of architecture in an open, collective way. The processes of socialization of the information technologies in the last years permit now mean that all of this open system of organizing the world on the basis of open knowledge networks is diluted in the physical world and transforms it.

We work in this way to produce an architecture which develops the potentials that the information society offers for constructing a more natural world.

THANKS

This book represents, at last, the beginning of a new cycle in our architectural practice, in which many of the questions outlined here should be corroborated, with projects in the next few years which demonstrate that this new hybrid mentality that supplies more human, social and environmental energy to a place can contribute to improving the way we create our habitats.

The majority of these projects have been developed by a team whose members and associates have continually changed over the years. The perception that something we intuited was beginning to be produced as a project, as reality, only became possible when we managed to create an multidisciplinary team to approach the project of habitability from a range of different registers, rhythms and intensities. In chronological order of interaction, the following have been crucial for many of the concepts behind the projects: the artist Nuria Díaz, the anthropologist Artur Serra, the urbanist and sociologist José Miguel Iribas, the geologist Albert Soler, the biologist and agronomy engineer Manel Corominas, the strategist Ignacio Jiménez de la Iglesia, the architect-structural engineer Robert Brufau, the webmaster Lucas Cappelli, the engineer Andreu Ulied and the physicist Neil Gershenfeld, the architect Marta Malé-Alemany. The years of apprenticeship with Jose Luis Mateo were fundamental in defining a practice simultaneously linked to the precise construction of buildings and places and to understanding architecture as a form of knowledge of the world. A number of architects have shared in the design of the projects presented here. María Díaz, current partner in the firm, has played a crucial role, and vital contributions to various projects have been made by Christine Bleicher, Max Sanjulián, Laura Cantarella, Marian Albarrán, Ana Cabellos, Esther Rovira, Jordi Mansilla, Fabián Asunción, Ignacio Toribio, Daniela Frogheri, Fernando Meneses, Daniel Ibáñez or Rodrigo Rubio. All of the partners in the various research platforms with which I have been involved, and a long list of architecture students have been of fundamental importance in the processes of intellectual feedback. The projects could not have been developed without the impetus of the developers, the leaders of organizations and companies and the politicians from whom I have learnt and with whom I have interacted more as partners than as clients.
To all of them, our thanks.

Vicente Guallart

Geography, Geometry, Logic and Structure

The present document could easily have generated two publications: one general and theoretical, setting out the 'geographical logics' on the basis of which we operate, and the other a monograph of projects, ranging all the way from the territorial scale to software design. However, we wanted to present this work in the same way that we work: that is to say, using each project as an opportunity to draw out general principles with which to act in the world.

In various projects carried out in recent years in various places around the world we discovered that our work had more to do with reacting to a natural phenomenon—in many cases a physical geographical phenomenon—than with the insertion of structures of a formal technological or contextualist regionalist order. Our interest in geography comes from the re-foundational nature of architecture, its capacity to transform a site in keeping with the deep values of the place, which are very often prior to the architecture. This led us to develop a method for engaging with the project that is grounded in the recognition of the reality in which we act.

The first thing was to recognize the geographic values of the location in which we were operating. Traditionally, intervening in a city starts with a general plan of the fabric the project is being inserted in and drawing the adjacent buildings. But when it comes to operating in a larger area or a natural setting, the environment to be reacted to will not always be an architectural or urban element, but of a natural order. Recognition here involves measuring, using various techniques, the physical or relational elements we are interested in: in many cases this has only been possible thanks to the input of specialists—geologists, biologists or sociologists—whose interventions enabled us to perceive the rules or the geometry of the object of our study. From these analyses we derived a series of operational rules that could engender the key elements which enabled us to organize a project. And in this way we arrive at a structure that allows us to develop the project.

This research therefore seeks to order these basic logics, which have been brought to bear in one or more projects, and are in fact basic general processes that can be developed as strategies, tactics or techniques to be used in architectural projects. The projects presented below make special reference to these logical processes and to the environments in which they are inserted and develop, and have been grouped according to the types of geography to which they react, from the physical to the more relational or technological.

120

Denia Mountain

121

GEOGRAPHY

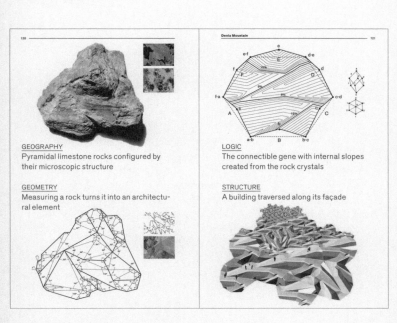

Pyramidal limestone rocks configured by their microscopic structure

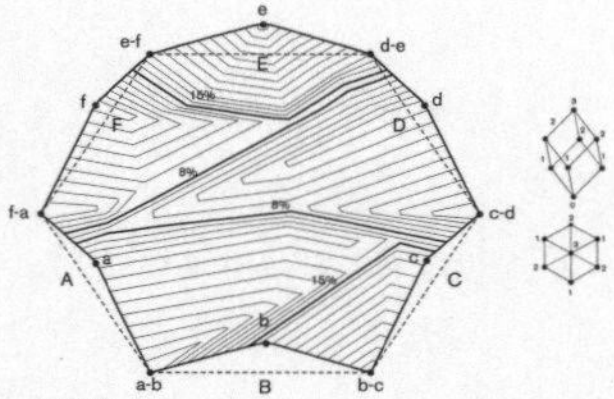

LOGIC

The connectible gene with internal slopes created from the rock crystals

GEOMETRY

Measuring a rock turns it into an architectural element

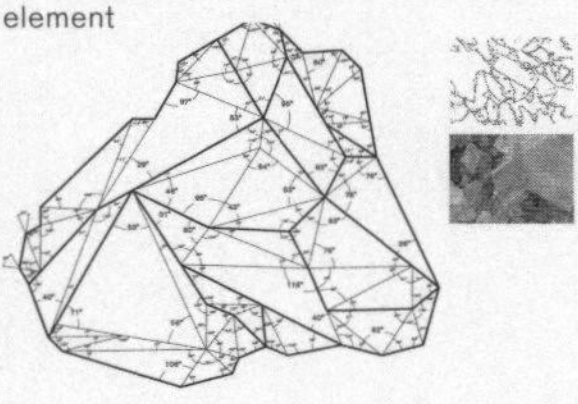

STRUCTURE

A building traversed along its façade

GEOGRAPHY

Any trace on the territory—be it physical, economic or social—has a geographic character. The most basic geographies, predating human action, consist in the physical elements of the territory. Geography deals with phenomena that have a multiscale condition and form complete complex ecosystems. A mountain range and an eroded stone are part of the same geographic phenomenon, as are the relational networks of a city or a personal encounter. Any architectural action operates on multiple geographic factors.

GEOMETRY

Any geographic event can be measured using specific techniques, according to category.

Going beyond traditional Euclidean geometry, fractal geometry makes it possible to draw the self-similar and multiscale natural elements found in any location. Statistical mathematics can make visible basic relationships between elements – in particular, groups of people. Geometry generates maps and relations which in themselves are preformative materials that can give rise to a project.

LOGIC

Logics are the relations, phenomena, conditions or situations that define the physical or relational structures of the various geographic elements which we study. The logics extracted may pertain to strategic, functional, relational or formal questions, which can be applied to engender projects. Projects can be developed in terms of a single logic or multiple logics. The logics that we are interested in have a humanistic, not a speculative value.

STRUCTURE

Structures are the mechanisms—physical, spatial or relational—that allow an architectural project to work. The structure embodies the basic pattern from which the various fabrics and systems of a project will be developed. A structure can be developed strategically (by defining the basic criteria of action), tactically (by defining the mechanisms to be implanted, linking the different parts) or technically (through the specific treatment of its construction elements).

GLOBAL

FE

SE

SE

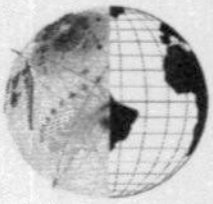

S

REGIONAL

FE

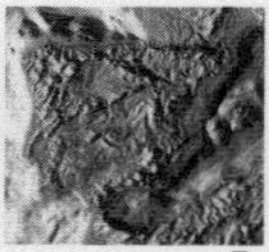

F

FSE

F

METROPOLITAN

FE

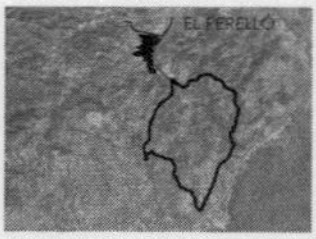

F

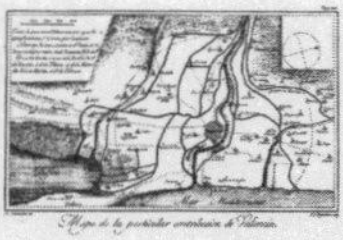

FE

FSE

URBAN

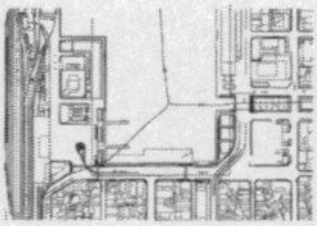

FSE

FSE

FSE

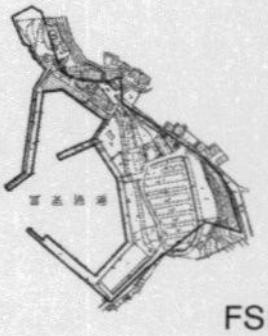

FSE

HABITAT

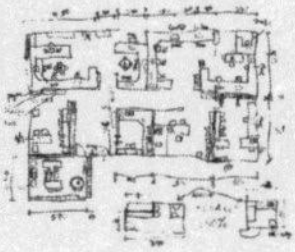

SE

S

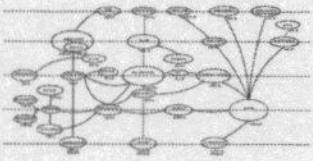

SE

FS

MATERIAL

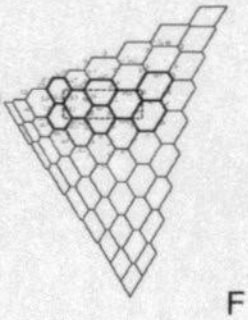

F

F

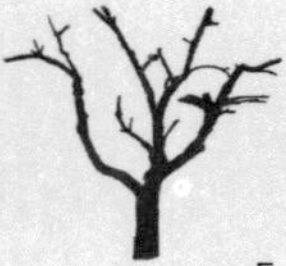

F

F

Geographies

F–**Physical** S–**Social** E–**Economic**

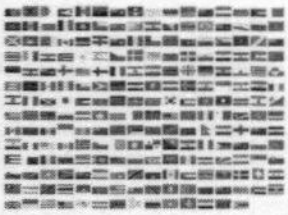

SE

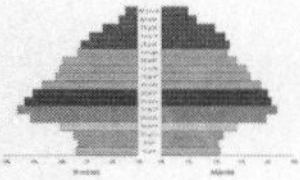

S

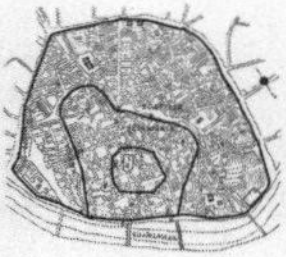

F

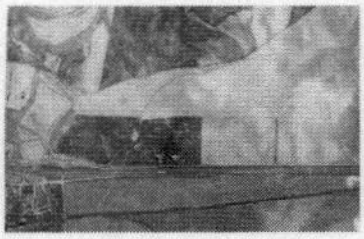

F

F

F

FSE

F

F

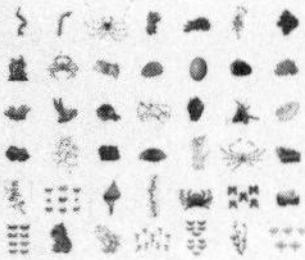

F

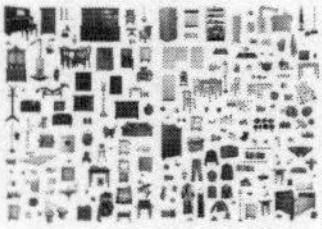

S

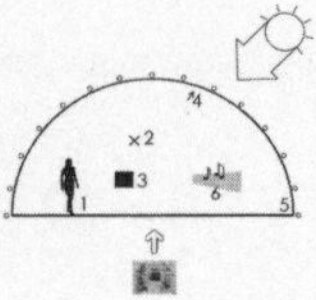

FS

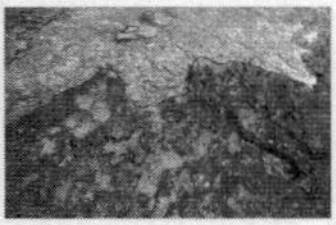

F

F

F

ENVIRONMENTS

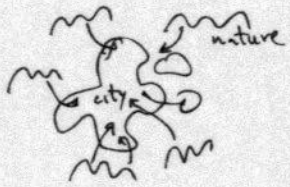

Re-naturalizing

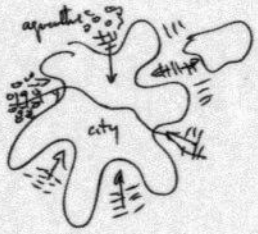

Rurbanizing

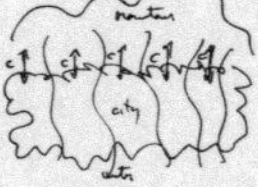

Re-connecting

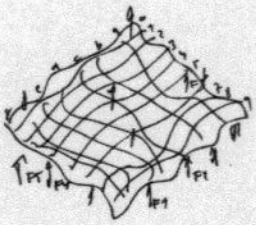

Topographying

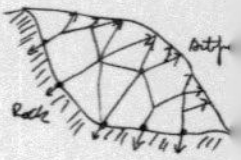

Geomorphosis

REACTING

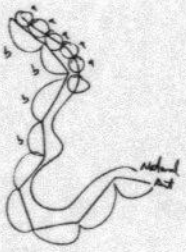

Measuring

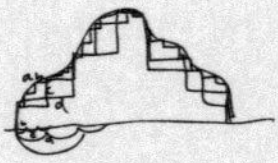

Resolution

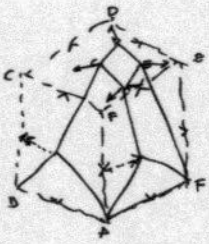

Parametrizing

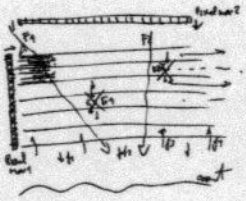

Automaton Pattern

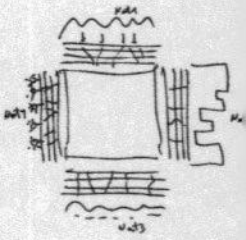

Reflecting

NETWORKS

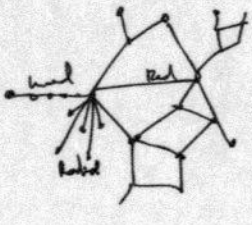

Netting

Urban re-cycling

Re-programming

Re-urbanizing

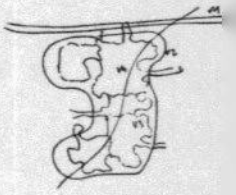

Multivelocity

PROTOCOLS

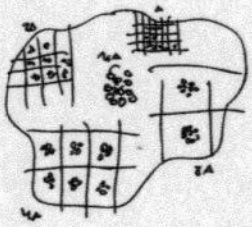

Sharing out

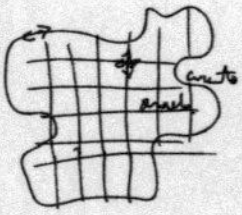

Ringing

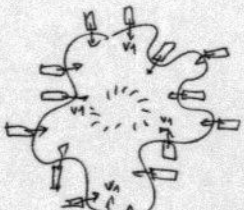

Democratizing

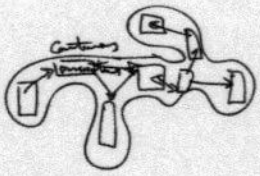

Discontinuity

Multiscalar

Logics

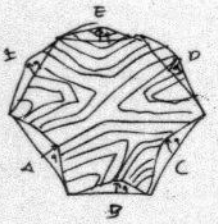

Microtopography

Biomimesis

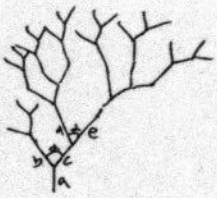

Arborescence

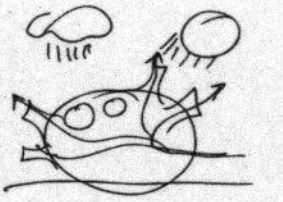

Re-acclimatizing

Programmatic Crystallization

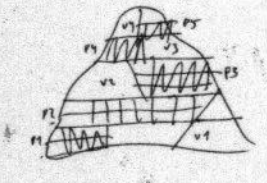

Accumulating

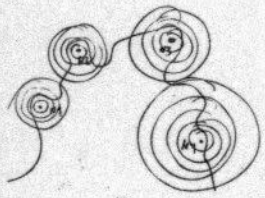

Resonance

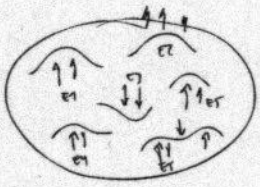

Bulging

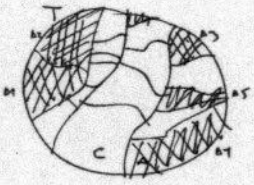

Re-cognition

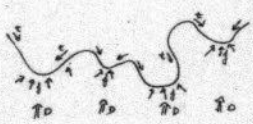

Positioning

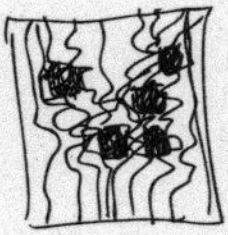

Enmeshing

Humanizing

Icons

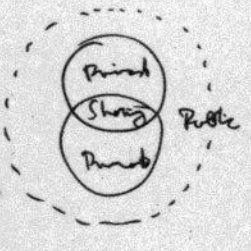

Sharing

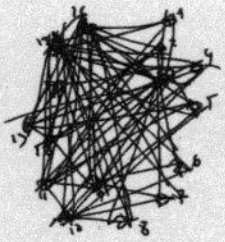

Emergence

Self sufficiency

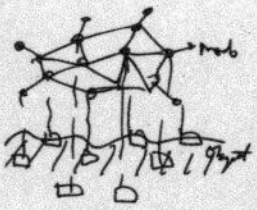

Hypermedia

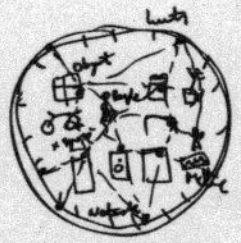

Re-informing

Logics

ENVIRONMENTS

REACTING

NETWORKS

PROTOCOLS

Re-naturalizing

re-, interaction, hybridizing, landscape, nature, centripetal

Transformation of the physical reality produced by human beings, on the basis of the fundamental principles of natural phenomena and natural processes.

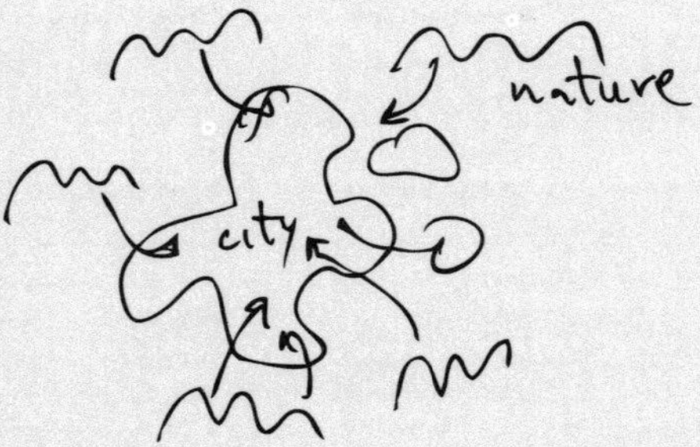

GEOLOGICS	PAGE	PROJECT
Re-naturalizing /01	**98**	**HyperCatalunya**
	108	**Denia Mountain**

After a continuous process of expansion of human construction on the territory over thousands of years, from the first stable settlements to the contemporary megapolis, we are now addressing a 'Re-' process on the territory. Re-cycling, re-forming, re-information, re-naturalization. Every human action on the territory is a manipulation of some sort of matter, that is seated on other matter. It uses a place's energy or potential to generate a new condition of energy and potential. The traditional distinction between urban and rural, between city and country, between natural and artificial does not exist.

If we understand the world as a continuum of energy and information that interacts in ecosystems of various kinds, then the landscape, the topography and the unbuilt territories cease to be a mere ground on which to create an event: rather, they are the project itself.

We could imagine that after millennia of expansion of the artificial over the natural, the basic elements of a territory—its geology, its topography, its botany, its climate—are now a performative material capable of being developed in the opposite direction and of acting both by transforming the historically constructed artificial ecosystems (cities and networks) and by creating new hybrid natures that emerge according to a natural logic.

We understand the idea of the natural as something that goes beyond a compendium of systems associated with the life sciences or geology. We use the idea of the natural to refer to the basic principles of things or places, which are in many cases related to geological or biological processes, and in others to relational, social or cultural issues governed by logics that we find in nature.

The re-naturalizing process thus proposes to operate on the basis of a material that is somewhere between organic and geological, by way of a set of strategies that range from the reform of cities and built territories and the creation of new settlements on the basis of natural logics to actuation by omission, valorizing and integrating into the global processes of inhabitation parts of the territory of high environmental, landscape or heritage value.

Rurbanizing

connecting, opening up the city, rurbanism

Creation of an urban edge in a city, maintaining an open structure that connects with the natural networks of the environment which penetrate the city.

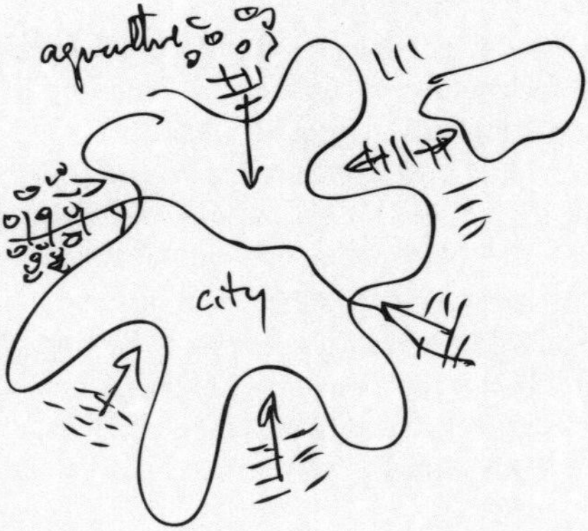

Urbanism as a science developed in the 19th century, and one of its paradigms is the work of Ildefons Cerdà in the city of Barcelona. Urbanism defined the processes by which a rural or natural space is transformed into an urban space capable of accommodating all the functions of the city and organizing the social interaction between citizens.

Urbanizing means literally burying, both physically and conceptually, the agricultural land in order to implant the functional systems needed to provide mass mobility, the space for the commerce and high-density housing while also creating public spaces for encounter and exchange.
Low-density urbanizing systems employ phenomena such as the garden city to locate housing in spaces with more natural attributes, at the cost of consuming a greater quantity of land and significant resources for the transport of people, goods and energy, which at their upper limit have developed in line with the American model of the suburb, thereby conurbating large areas of territory.

Many areas of Central Europe and the northern Mediterranean coast effectively form a built-up territorial continuum.

In part, the predatory consumption of land by the urbanization process—that is to say, the transformation of non-urban land into urban land—is the result of the drastic difference between what is city and what is country; between what is urban and what is rural. The absence of a transitional space between the city and the country means there is great pressure on the space adjacent to those cities in need of land to grow on. Rurbanizing means the inhabiting of a rural space with a urban activity, but without adopting a traditional form of city. A rurban space can be a place of transition between the city and the country. A pre-park between a dense city and natural or agricultural spaces, which need to be conserved for landscape and environmental reasons, to provide a break in continuity between built-up nuclei.

Re-connecting

limit, edge, connection, open, relation

Active definition of the border between urban space and natural space to activate them functionally.

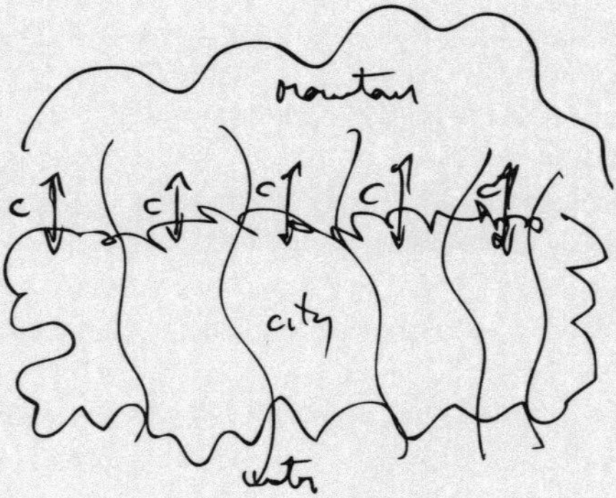

GEOLOGICS
Re-connecting /03

PAGE
176

PROJECT
Cultural gate to Alborz

The logic of the urban calls for a setting of limits on the territory in which city can be constructed, in contradistinction to natural terrain with a certain environmental or landscape value. In scores of large urban agglomerations the 'red lines' laid down to limit the advance of the built fabric have resulted in undefined boundaries between the city and nature: designed to prevent the uncontrolled occupation of the territory, they have failed to propose an intelligent dynamic interaction between two different systems.

They are spaces of fear of the unknown. Now, however, we are facing a new process in the territory, a process in which natural areas outside of the cities—agricultural, woodland or mountain—are acquiring a strategic territorial value. The non-urban is no longer a remainder but a potentially active territory capable of being transformed into large metropolitan parks, and as such it needs to be structured, not only to protect it but to activate it.

This gives these boundary spaces a crucial role in defining the value of the transition, and the potential to define hubs of connection between the urban and the natural, areas of access to spaces for sports, culture, leisure and relaxation, 'green lines' in the territory, connective flows that open up relations with and make use of spaces rich in natural attributes, used by city dwellers as macro parks, conceived on a regional scale.

Topographying

displacement, matrix, mesh, triangulating, topography, resolution

Definition of new formal models of architecture on the basis of geometries that emerge from the forms of the territory.

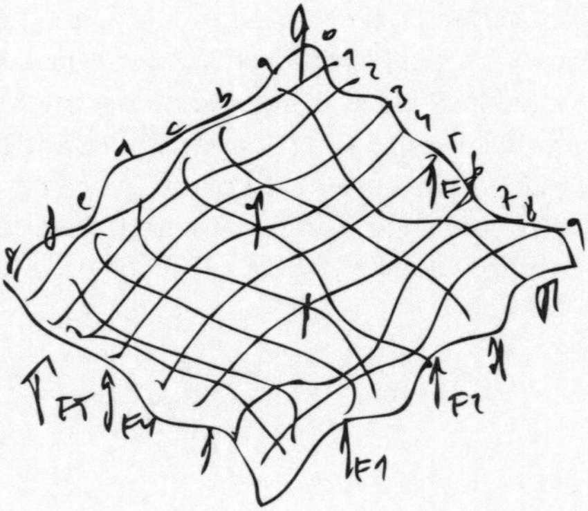

GEOLOGICS	PAGE	PROJECT
Topographying /04	**98**	**HyperCatalunya**
	108	**Denia Mountain**
	146	**Wrocław Expo**

The creation of the networks or matrices needed to appropriate a landscape by means of agriculture is similar to the process of constructing a topography inside a computer. The representation of creased, folded or curved surfaces inside a computer is based on the creation of mesh surfaces with control points at different degrees of resolution. These points are used to triangulate and construct any kind of surface.

Down through the centuries human beings have appropriated a large part of the planet's surface in the form of agriculture in order to produce food, developing processes and techniques for acting on the land by way of plantations, irrigation systems and terraces, all of which demonstrate a very precise control of the geometry and the geography of the environment. Many of these actuations can be taken as paradigms for those models of manipulation of the now anthropized landscape which superpose transforming layers that give it added value. The combination of an unmanipulated landscape and the manipulations of that terrain according to the internal rules of the place being acted on configures—or has configured—a great deal of the agricultural landscape we know.

Only that which can be represented can be built constructed.
The ideal Euclidean solids are no longer the limit for the definition of forms of architecture. We can now define with great precision any kind of surface, fold or erosion and they can be directly fabricated from a digital drawing using numeric control machines. In this way, the topographies that can be recognized in the landscape, connecting the form with energy that emanates from the land, can now provide a structural referent for the construction of new structures on the landscape.

Geomorphosis

regenerating, natural reconstruction, naturalizing, structure, fractal, multiscalar

Reconstruction of a natural space by means of structures that use the structural and formal logic of the existing geology for its regeneration.

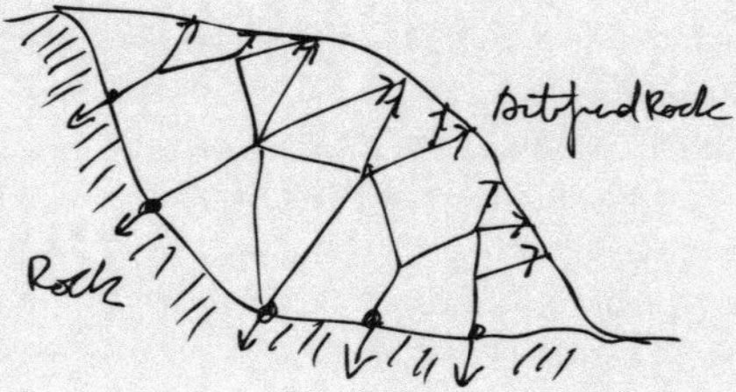

GEOLOGICS	PAGE	PROJECT
Geomorphosis /05	**108**	**Denia Mountain**
	194	**Batoutz Harbor**

Can a mountain be reconstructed? According to the traditional logic associated with architecture, no. A building is different from a natural element. The classic patterns and orders of construction of a building pertain to the logic of the geometry of the functional and circulation structure and the structure of representation.

The mountain is the paradigm of a construction fashioned by the forces of nature. It possesses an internal structure that is coherent with the materials and the internal forces that created it, the erosive processes that have moulded it and the biological settlements that inhabit it.

In his study of the Alps, Viollet-le-Duc declared that 'God could not have invented the mountains without geometry'. In his analyses of the topography of the Alps for the purpose of mapping them he explored the internal structure of the rocky massifs in order to discover the inner laws of the geometry that had given rise to those pyramidal peaks.

The reconstruction of a mountain—or a quarry—is a process that has arise out of new structural forces that connect the existing massif with a new structure, which will have to be stratigraphically coherent with the existing structure. In other words, a calcareous massif or a volcanic massif emerge as a result of different tectonic processes, and potentially should therefore be regenerated on the basis of different structures.

An architecture that obeys a geomorphic logic should be capable of defining simultaneously its structural principles and its epidermal resolution, in a multiscalar process.

Microtopography

fold, gene, incline, fractal, resolution, edge, chain, multiscalar

Definition of the epidermis of a construction on the basis of a microtopography containing precise folds defined in terms of the functional and material principles of the overall structure.

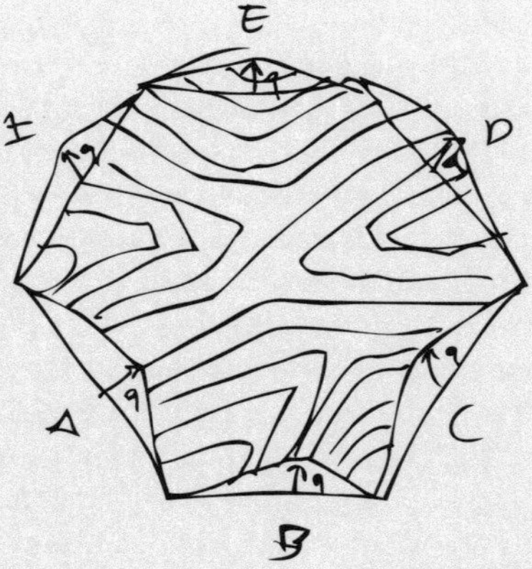

GEOLOGICS
Microtopography /06

PAGE
108

PROJECT
Denia Mountain

Every living being or geographic element has certain surface features or properties that define its interaction with the external environment. The definition of the limits of any architectural project should emerge from its external structures, its material properties and the need for exchanges between its internal life and the external environment.

A project for the surface of a mountainous topography must reconcile the properties of the micro scale of a rock or a mineral and the functionality on the macro scale of its overall structure.

If the part is self-similar to the whole, according to Benoît Mandelbrot, the father of fractal geometry, a stone must be self-similar to the mountain it comes from. Thus, by analysing the geometry of a stone we can arrive at the basic geometric rules with which to construct the surface of a similar mountain or to reconstruct the voids that may have been excavated by quarrying. These surfaces, their materiality and their geometry must be redefined on the basis of the functional principles that are to be attributed to them and their materiality.

The construction of an uneven surface can make use of a variety of construction strategies involving the creation of surfaces with a free geometry formed of non-repetitive elements, or by defining basic geometric units whose grouping and variation—parametric or not—can generate a surface of great formal and spatial diversity.

Traditionally, the primary function of the epidermis of a building is to insulate the exterior, making it possible to create stable climatic conditions in the interior while permitting natural lighting and ventilation. In habitational structures hybridized with the landscape, the function of mobility inherent in natural surfaces must be incorporated into the architectural project through the creation of microtopographies capable of permitting human mobility.

Biomimesis

metabolism, nature, energy, structure, flows, organic

Creation of structures that follow the logical processes of functioning of biological elements.

GEOLOGICS
Biomimesis
/07

PAGE
286

PROJECT
Cristóbal de Moura street

The action of nature over million of years resulted in the creation of living beings of great diversity and, in many cases, complexity, the maximum expression of whose development is the human being.

Human beings, too, have acted as creators of functional structures to improve their habitability on the Earth—structures that nowadays range from computers to cities. The history of evolution shows us how different living beings have managed to adapt to environmental and climatic conditions by transforming, varying their physiology to become more efficient organisms. Bigger leaves, a thicker skin, lighter materials or more intelligent structures are natural creations of the organism's adaptation to its environment—adaptations that enhance its resistance to external agents.

Human beings, however, have always preferred to develop technologies to transform the environment rather than transform themselves. And this process, which took place as local transformations of matter through which to inhabit nature, has gone on to create a global economic ecosystem that has transformed the behaviour patterns of the climate itself on the global scale. At the micro scale, however, the human brain is still more intelligent than the most intelligent computer, the trees create energy and have a more efficient metabolism that the most efficient buildings, certain animals are able to regenerate some of their limbs and there are intelligent and reactive natural materials more efficient than any made by humans. All of this means that we need to study nature in order to understand more clearly how it creates materials, how it organizes their internal processes, and thus learn how to produce artificial structures that are more efficient in their process of implantation as well as in their operation. By means of architecture the functional logical processes of biological elements can be reproduced.

Arborescence

generation, growth, system, L-system, parameters, family, tree

Development of a system of parametric arboreal structures on the basis of fractal geometry which can be grouped in forest-like structures.

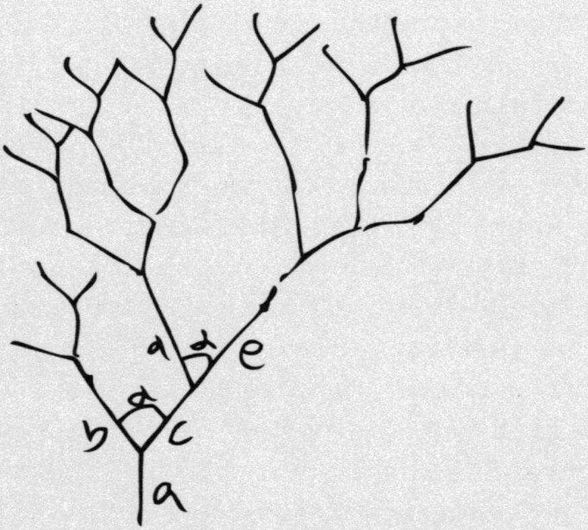

GEOLOGICS
Arborescence
/08

PAGE
162

PROJECT
Expo Shangai 2010

The oldest living thing on the face of the Earth is to be found in California, USA: a tree, of the species Pinus longaeva, which is almost 2150 years old. Much older, then, than any animal specie.

Trees, like all living beings, are natures that have developed and evolved in relation to local geographical conditions. There are as many types of tree as there are climates, landscapes and territories on the Earth. Morphologically, a tree is formed of three differentiated parts: the roots, the trunks and the crown.

As a paradigm example of self-similarity at different scales, trees have been a special object of study for fractal geometry. These principles provided Lindenmayer with the basis for the L-system, in which automata are developed through the application of elementary rules to lines in a two- or three-dimensional space. Various arborescent structures are found in nature, such as those of the pulmonary system, the structure of a river or the electric network.

The geometry of a tree is worked out on the basis of the position of its point of origin, going on to determine the distance and the angle at which the next node is situated, and the number of units into which it branches and their respective angles.

The arboreal structure is the natural form that can cover the greatest area from a single point of origin. An arboreal structure can also be inverted to create a structure of great stability, with multiple points of support underpinning a single vertical element.

The proliferation of a number of arboreal structures can create forest-like structures, distributed in regular or irregular plots, out of which life can emerge.

Re-acclimatizing

flow, tree, microclimate, surroundings, environment, air, natural

Creation of microclimates on the basis of the reproduction of models of natural physical phenomena.

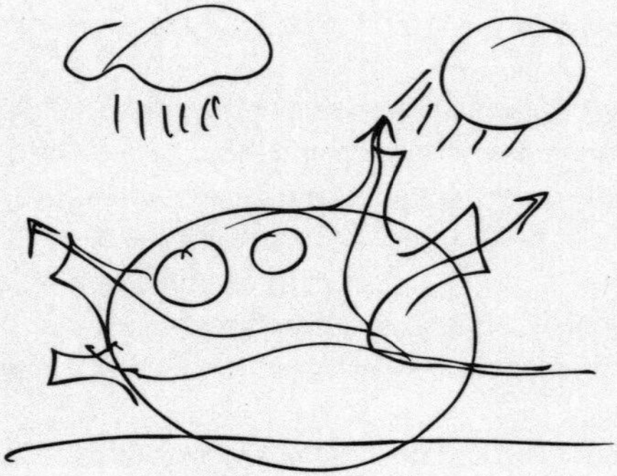

GEOLOGICS
Re-acclimatizing
/09

PAGE
220

PROJECT
Fugee Port

Every territory has a particular set of environmental and climatic conditions, and we human beings have always sought to make the territory inhabitable by means of an architecture that responds to those conditions. Modernity and the machine age have allowed us to transgress those conditions and generate artificial microclimates based on air conditioning systems that expel hot air into the atmosphere, in many cases aggravating the initial conditions.

Volcanic eruptions are the geological phenomena that have the greatest immediate impact on a territory. These are moments of instant creation of geographies, in which the material that emerges from beneath the Earth's surface is transformed with great speed, changing from one state to another, with the interaction of matter in different states (solid, liquid and gas).

If we analyse a stone from a volcanic island, what we see at first sight is chaos. However, a precise geometrical analysis serves to reveal patterns in the spaces in the material. Pumice or pumicite is an extrusive volcanic rock that has lost its gas content in the process of cooling and hardening. The simultaneity of these two processes—expulsion of gases and solidification—generates a geometrical structure with a composition of microbubbles, empty spheres with a 180° geometrical relationship to one another, in the attempt to produce the maximum empty volume with a minimum of surrounding matter.

The transformation of a place's climatic conditions from one state to another more appropriate for human beings is one of the fundamental objectives of the architecture.

The recognition of the processes of configuration of a certain natural element can make it possible to define architectural structures which, in accordance with this model, serve to engender similar physical phenomena. To construct trees on the basis of stones.

Programmatic crystallization

re-programming, boolean, discontinues, aggregation, saturation, crystallization, void

Functional precipitation of activities in the interior of an artificially constructed massif, on the basis of the geometrical rules of growth of the crystals of which it is composed.

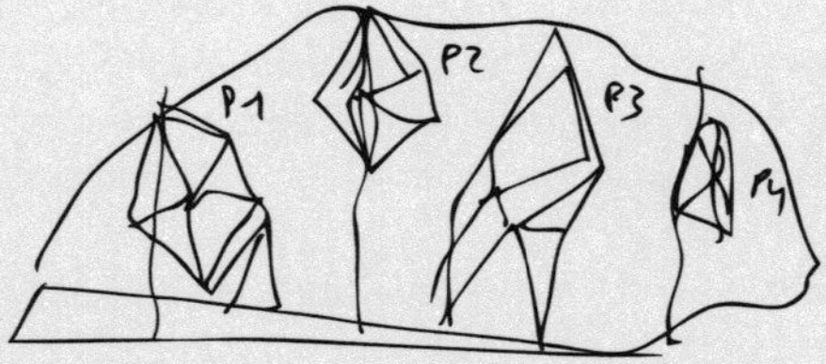

GEOLOGICS
Programmatic crystallization /10

PAGE
108

PROJECT
Denia Mountain

Any construction in the territory emerges out of the crystallization of the desires of people or organizations to transform the place with new activities. Thus by means of architecture there is instantly produced a discontinuous accumulation of material, result of the collaboration of multiple agents, which produce a process of artificial crystallization that creates a new geographical event. In nature this occurs over long periods of time.

The continuity between the properties of the interior and the exterior of a massif is guaranteed by the coherence of its process of formation. The fissures run outward from the interior, the folds of the earth extend through the territory. At the micro scale, the movement of water in rock produces chemical precipitations that eventually form crystals. There can be few more thrilling sights than to see how certain chemical compounds are transformed, in the course of time, and under the right conditions, into crystals. The minute laws of the things bloom in the visible world. Once again, the magic of geometry occurs in the nature.

In this way, in a potential regeneration of a rocky massif the functional attractors of its interior can be crystallized from the growth of the crystalline void that grows on the basis of the geometry and the rules of the defined structure. In this way, the lines of force of the structure with virtual supports of mineral growths follow the geometrical properties of the mineral family of the rock they reconstruct. The crystals, as Euclidean solids, grow by way of simple geometrical processes on the basis of the specific rules that govern each mineral.

Accumulating

concentrating, superposing, form

Accumulation of functional information on the basis of the superposing of various activities as a product of a place's capacity to concentrate social or economic processes.

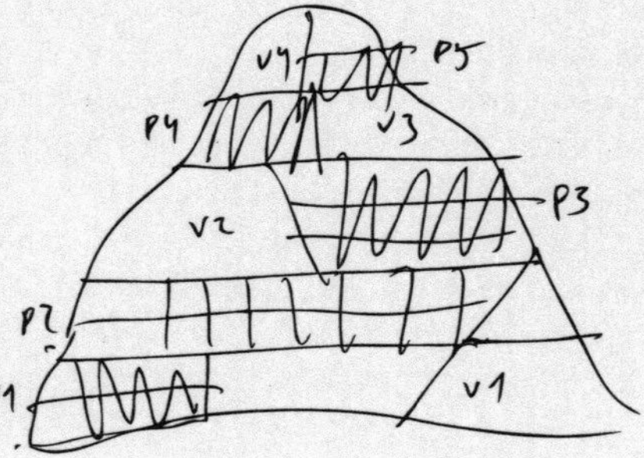

GEOLOGICS
Accumulating
/11

PAGE	PROJECT
146	**Wrocław Expo**
366	**Hortal House**

A high-rise building is the crystallization of an accumulation of functions which it has been decided to locate in that place.

The first human settlements were made by erecting walls and roofs on a place in the territory. But people soon recognized the potential of building spaces one on top of the other in order to multiply the volume of activities that could be accommodated on a given area of land.

This functional accumulation is one of the essences of architecture and of the city.

Is the cuboid form with discontinuity between levels the most natural structure for a building? The cuboid form is determined primarily by urbanistic considerations, the result of the building being developed inside a square or rectangular plot, and constrained not to project into the adjoining properties. There are also environmental considerations, in the matter of the equal distribution of access to elements such as light and air, especially in monofunctional buildings entirely occupied by housing or offices. However, nowadays a home or a building has the potential to accumulate all the functions of an entire city, on a smaller scale.

The need to reduce the time we spend commuting between our place of residence, workplace and leisure places, and the interest in conserving for as long as possible the non-urbanized space around the urban nucleus means that our cities have to grow in height, with constructions that ensure a functional accumulation of various activities. The concentration of functional diversity in a building makes it possible to create urban and social diversity, with entities that function throughout all the day, operating according to the same logic as a micro-city. Functional diversity makes it possible to organize buildings as stratigraphic systems, locating close to the ground those spaces with a priority need for ready access and a lesser need for sunlight and fresh air, and the more private or less multitudinous functions on the upper levels, which have the advantage of fresh air, sunlight and the best views.

Every building has a certain formal potential in relation to its implantation, its structure or its function that is very different from the cubic form that emerges in the traditional city.

Measuring

discontinuity, re-cognition, scaling, tracing, natural-artificial, process, writing

Recognition of the potentials for actuation in a place on the basis of the differences or spaces of opportunity that exist between a natural geometry and an artificial geometry (the space between nature and its recognition by means of Benoît Mandelbrot's fractals).

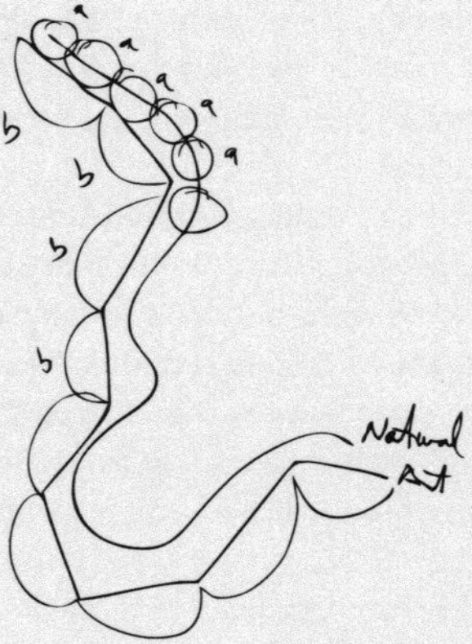

GEOLOGICS	PAGE	PROJECT
Measuring /12	188	**New Taiwan by design**
	194	**Batoutz Harbor**
	220	**Fugee Port**
	246	**Keelung Port**

We can only construct what we can represent. We can only represent what we can measure. In *Fractals: Form, Chance and Dimension*, first published in 1977, Benoît Mandelbrot demonstrated the possibility of describing, by means of various mathematical formulations, elements of nature whose irregularity of form means they are not among the perfect solids of Euclidean geometry. In this way, mountains, clouds, rivers, trees and other natural elements could be described, represented and subsequently reproduced by computer programmes using fractal geometry.

The measurement of the length of a coastline is a paradigm case here. In his early paper 'How Long is the Coast of Britain?' Mandelbrot concluded that the length depends on the length of the ruler used to measure it. In other words, the dimensions of a given reality are dependent on how we approach it. The measuring of natural objects generates data and formulae that, given the self-similar character of many of them, present a multiscalar formula rather than a closed, defined object. If nature is no longer the ground on which human structures stand, as we come more and more to approach the project of the construction of reality as an actual process of the construction of natures or of their artificial-natural hybridization, the way this reality is measured constitutes the basis of the project that sets out to transform it. As a result, the open and dynamic character of fractal geometry suggests that the architectural project itself can be approached in this way, creating open patterns rather than closed structures.

The measurement of natural objects and the systems we use to draw and represent nature are in themselves a project material.

Resolution

density, curve, potential, relational, emergence, rebounding, feedback

Potential development of the project for a building through the modification of its geometry via the concentration of information per unit of measurement.

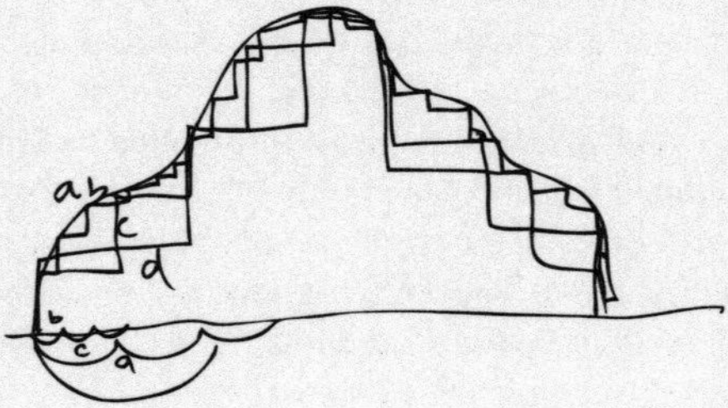

GEOLOGICS	PAGE	PROJECT
Resolution /13	**108**	**Denia Mountain**
	146	**Wrocław Expo**
	366	**Hortal House**

Resolution is the measure of the quantity of information that something possesses per unit of area or volume.

The objects with the highest resolution are those constructed by nature. Any curved surface is constructed with a given resolution, according to the techniques and the materials used for its production. Resolution is one of the basic properties of the materialization of non-regular surfaces and natural forms. Mandelbrot indicates the infinite resolution and the self-similarity of fractal elements.

Antoni Gaudí designed the façade of La Pedrera ['the stone quarry'] in Barcelona as a topographic surface with large curving surfaces. For its execution, he first constructed the façade at low resolution on site with large stone blocks. He then made a 1:10 scale model of the façade in plaster, sectioned it up and distributed the pieces over the scaffolding so that the masons would know what the final form was to be. Over the course of two years the builders gradually increased the resolution of the façade on site, achieving a high degree of precision on the basis of elementary construction systems.

Toward the end of the 20th century, the construction of the façade of the Guggenheim Museum in Bilbao used digital technologies to enable each piece to be independently computerized and digitally manipulated using CNC milling. Digital manufacturing techniques permit a great deal of freedom in the production of different kinds of surface.

A warped surface reconstructed on a computer by means of similar triangles would have a potentially infinite number of forms, depending on the length of side of the triangle used. All of the surfaces would be based on the same mathematical description, but with a different degree of resolution. With traditional construction methods, curved or warped surfaces are more expensive to produce.

The development of parametric fabrication means that the resolution of a building could be defined without a direct relationship with the cost of the same. Given the same geometrical and conceptual base, a building can acquire a particular form by virtue of the technologies available.

Parametrizing

system, formulating, generating, re-materializing, family, genetic

Extraction of the basic geometrical principles of a natural element from a study of its geometry, and the search for growth systems that can be generalized to all similar elements.

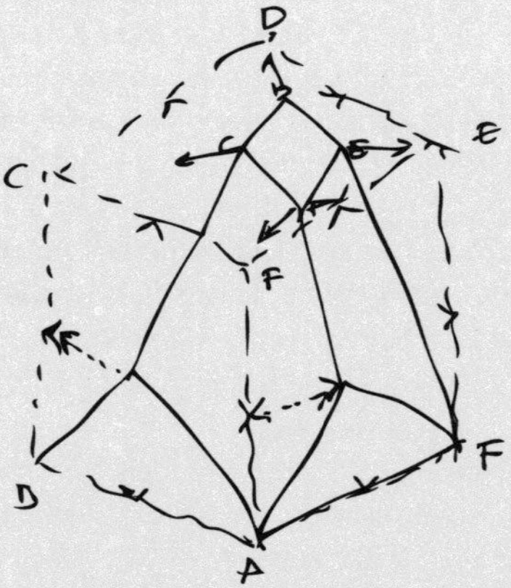

GEOLOGICS
Parametrizing
/14

The members of any family of elements originating in nature have at one and the same time a similarity in their basic physiological and geometric characteristics and a certain formal diversity. From the great complexity of human beings, to all the trees in a forest, or the simplicity of a pebble in a river, to be natural means to be at once equal and different.

Parametrizing serves to define the geometrical characteristics of a family of elements and to define the properties that permit their formal variability.

In order to parametrize an element of nature it is necessary to define a series of basic geometrical principles that define the essence of the element being studied. On the basis of these principles we can then define the variables and formulae with which the variations are produced to ensure that while the resulting elements share certain common characteristics they are nonetheless all different. Their reprogrammability means that having defined a certain parametric set, could be modified a project in real time if appear new conditions that modify it, unchanged their its basic characteristics.

The fabrication of a series of parametric objects, or the pieces that form a surface or a parametric structure is possible only where the production processes use machines such as laser cutters, three-dimensional printers or digital milling machines to manipulate the material directly, from the computer files used to draw up the project.

Automaton Pattern

re-tracing, re-informing, memory, cellular automaton, re-compiling, reading and building, scanning

A system for reading an urban site in terms of a basic pattern of a cellular automaton type that will thus be able to create a pattern that can be transferred to a project, which will materialize a certain memory of the place.

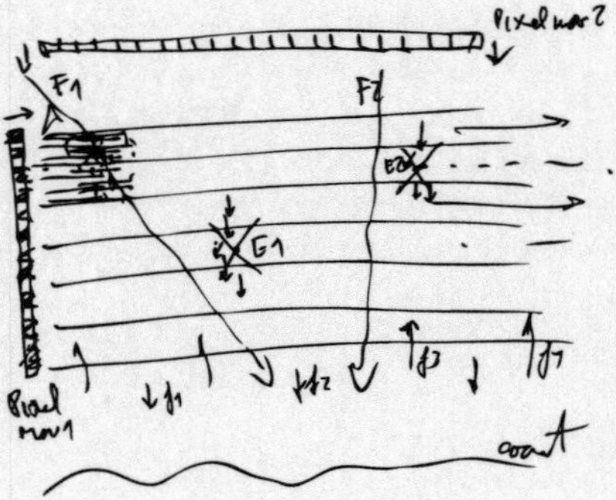

GEOLOGICS
Automaton Pattern /15

PAGE
308

PROJECT
Vinaròs Promenade

To read the territory and to construct it in the same process, on the basis of mathematical patterns. A cellular automaton is a system that grows by a binary process, on the basis of certain basic rules that are repeated in an iterative way. These rules may refer to conditions inherent in the systems themselves, they may be deliberately arbitrary, or they may respond to initially defined local conditions.

When an urban reality or a built volume is earmarked for reform, the actuation always has to address the question of what part of this system is of sufficient value to merit conservation and which elements are to be erased absolutely from the memory of the place.

The functionalist tradition in architecture was based on the premise that architecture is a response to previously established functions, which should be manifested by way of the elements that define the external appearance. Now, however, the patterns that are applied to a place serve rather to bring out and relate key aspects of the area to be acted on.

The application of a pattern whose rules of proliferation are based on the X-ray of the place to be inhabited in relation to people's movements, to the presence of geographical features and the existence of architectural or other elements instantly generates a micro-history of the place that simultaneously offers a reading of a moment of the history that is mapped in the place itself by the construction elements with which the pattern is elaborated.

In this way the action on a place, understood as a relational reading of the site, transforms it on the basis of its own functional, structural or formal rules.

Reflecting

reacting, colour, mimesis, landscape

Configuration of the epidermis of an architectural element on the basis of the reflection of the landscape conditions of its environment.

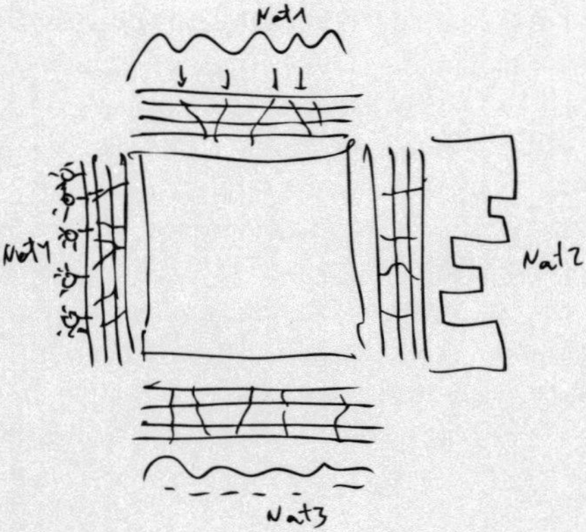

GEOLOGICS
Reflecting
/16

PAGE
346

PROJECT
Apartments in Cambrils

Colour is a function of the breaking down of the light that is the visible part of the radioelectric spectrum to which our eyes are sensitive.

Colour is a fundamental attribute of any landscape, and we perceive it because the sun's light is reflected from objects in different wavelengths. A number of living beings have evolved the capacity of mimetic assimilation with their environment, effectively camouflaging themselves, on the basis of their form, texture or colour.

A building, as an artificial system inserted in a specific place with certain conditions of landscape, environment and culture, can seek to interact with its setting through a reading of the colour of the elements around it.
Light cristallization.

Resonance

measuring, dimension, fractal, roughness, geography, wave

Locating in a place by means of structures that utilize the same wavelength as the place.

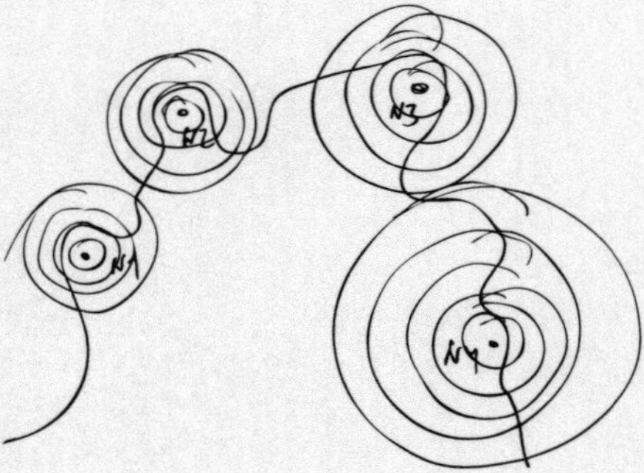

GEOLOGICS
Resonance
/17

PAGE
270

PROJECT
Vinaròs Microcoasts

With our processes of appropriating the territory, we human beings have continually tried to transform the conditions of a place's habitability in order to enjoy they. 'Nature is a mistake,' the sociologist-urbanist and expert on tourism José Miguel Iribas has said, in reference to the fact that nature alone does not define the economy of tourism, because artificial structures are necessary conditions for access to and enjoyment of a place.

Any intervention in a place of special beauty and environmental quality should set out not to promote its appropriation through artificial structures that trumpet this action as a conquest but to encourage an implantation that directly expresses the geometrical and environmental principles of the place.

How big does a geographical feature have to be for it to have a name? The analysis of a great number of stretches of coastline has made it possible to map micro-places of more than sufficient identity to deserve a name, thus breaking with the logic that a territorial event has to be big to be beautiful or worth naming.

The best actuation in the natural environment is that which adds certain properties of habitability while conserving all the attributes of the natural place. The best actuation would be that which literally entered into resonance with the place, which acted by stimulating the wavelength of the landscape or environmental values, through an implantation based on the use of a geometry or a materiality similar to that of the territory in which it is integrated.

Constructing as a process that serves to extend the duration of the vibration of a wave. Inhabiting as a process of recognition of the territory.

Bulging

bulging, reacting, generating environment, re-naturalizing, patterns, environment, reaction, interaction, mountain, material, crystal glass, cell, black, light, optics

Reaction to the presence of entities (human or material) on the basis of the deformation of a material.

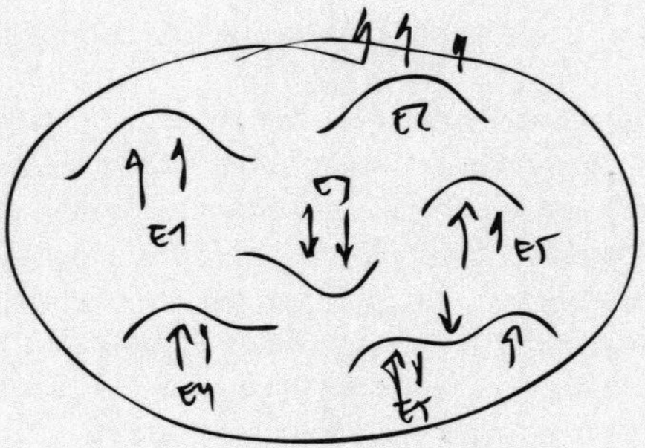

GEOLOGICS
Bulging
/18

PAGE
376

PROJECT
Avignon Expo 2000

Bulging is a phenomenon that is produced as a reaction to certain forces that interact on a particular material, in which, instead of breaking, the material is continuously distorted. The bulge capacity of a material is a function of its nature and the system of its fabrication.

The glass that is created from the liquefaction of silica sand, sodium carbonate and limestone is a material that has been used in architecture in plane form for the construction of façades.

As a result of the application of heat and the creation of certain limiting structures it can be given the desired form with the required degree of precision, due to its system of fabrication.

The construction of an aura.

Re-cognition

systems, networks, protecting, history, knowledge

Transforming a place through the conservation of part of the history that emanates from it.

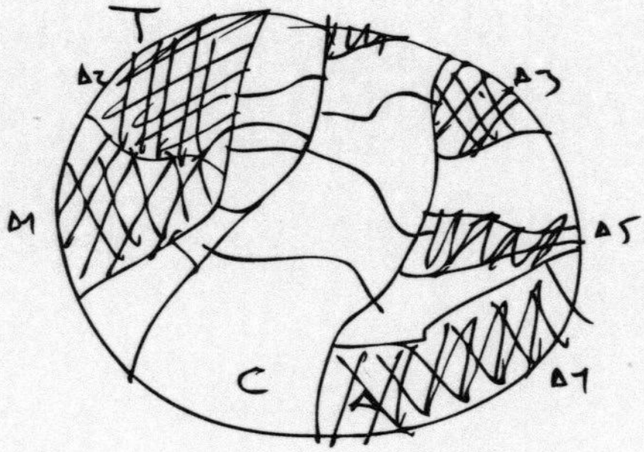

GEOLOGICS
Re-cognition
/19

PAGE
428

PROJECT
Sociopolis Master plan

Every place has a geological history, a biological history, and a cultural history. Every time we act on any place on Earth, whether it be in a desert, a jungle, a city or agricultural land, we act in continuity with its history.
Places, like organizations, have know-how. History has shown us how the growth of our cities has proceeded, in general, by ignoring the cultural and ecological traces of the site. But now, recognizing as we do that any action on the territory has an impact on the planet, such wilful ignorance no longer makes sense.

According to the ecologist Ramon Margalef, the more mature the system, the more numerous the testimonies of its past—including supplementary information—the place will tend to preserve.

The best projects are those that even as they construct new realities are also actively incorporating the genetic code of the place into the project. The know-how of the place. Perhaps traces of mobility, perhaps historical constructions, landscape or environmental elements or any relational element. Nowadays building and protecting are carried out in the same process.

Heritage or ecological sanctuaries are all very well, but the best way of conserving something is to act on it. That which might seem to lead to the destruction of a place may be precisely what enables it to exist in history, and as such to be open to a new encoding.

Positioning

positioning toward history, re-orienting, looking, confronting

Reutilization of strategies or tactics with military, social or cultural uses in order to orient the positioning of an architectural project.

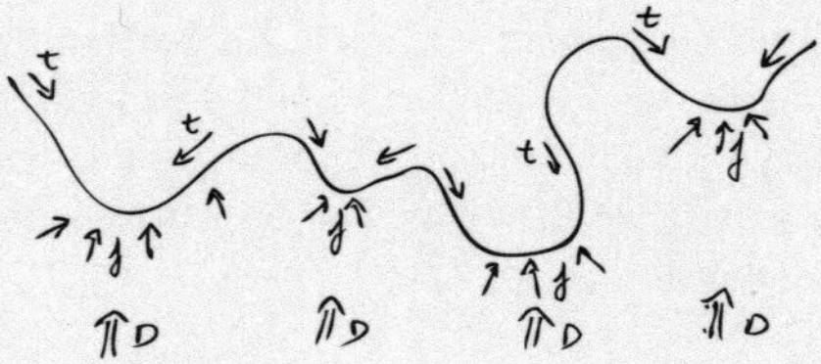

An architectural project is similar to a battle in the sense that strategies, tactics and techniques are essential to its development.

Every place deserves a project, which may or may not coincide with the initial premise of a hypothetical development.

An architectural project is not a linear, unidirectional, finite and irrevocable fact. One way of guaranteeing a building's survival in time is for it to be very beautiful, and for the people who inhabit it to be aware of this; for it ultimately to develop all of the potentials offered it by the technology and the cultural and economic energy of its time, and, once this time is past, for it to become part of the genetic code of the place.

The most intelligent cities and organizations are those capable of valorizing a place's potentials by means of architectural and urban planning projects. The writers, producers and directors of a project must evaluate all possible points of view, in order to take up the optimum position in relation to a place, just as an army does on a field of battle. Any place has multiple potentials and argument lines on which one can act.

Enmeshing

Recognizing, traces, cluster, structure, networks, element, reaction

Creation of an informational matrix out of the recognition of the elements that exist in a territory

GEOLOGICS
Enmeshing /21

PAGE
386

PROJECT
Clothing Museum

The re-action to inhabited territories that have generated material history in time (cities, buildings, places, spaces) makes it possible to define structuring meshes on the basis of the recognition of the elements of a place. A regular recognition pattern that is configured in the space on the basis of precise instructions of re-action is capable of generating a map on the basis of the re-reading of a series of built entities. In this way the history of a place can be transferred to a geometric pattern capable of setting a project in motion, as a process of spatial re-coding. A mesh that generates a structure. A mesh that gives rise to a construction process. In this way a structuring mesh is no longer regular, abstract, generic or universal, but specific, concrete, localized, reactivating precise phenomena of the material history of a place. To build on the specific.

Netting

net, node, connection, link, discontinuity, territory

Creation of networks of cities that participate of the creation of discontinuous urbanities.

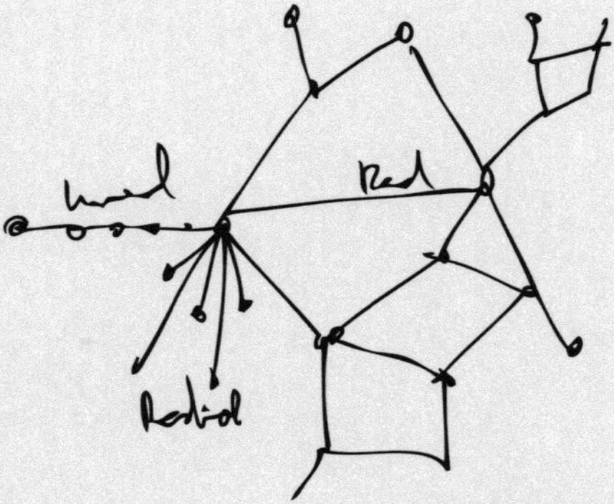

GEOLOGICS	PAGE	PROJECT
Netting /22	406	**Bioclimatic Villages**
	414	**Eco tropical Neighbourhood**
	420	**Sociopolis I**

Cities are to the territory much as computers are to the net: nodes of accumulation of information, territorial IP numbers, points of concentration that have to be absolutely efficient in order for the system to function. If not—and, again, like the Internet—the information flows are diverted and reach their destination by other routes. The cities are entering a state of decadence.

Traditionally, urban nuclei have emerged in two ways; either at the junctions of roads, as places of encounter, as points of great territorial accessibility, or along the length of a road, as intermediate stopping points for the transport systems of the time. In both cases, the primary objective of a city throughout its history—social and military circumstances permitting—has been to grow. The urban model produced by the evolution of the medieval city up to our own day has been the great metropolis. But this model has a limit, the point at which accumulation begins to be inefficient. When its constituent parts lose identity. When their relationship to the environment disappears.

When one city absorbs another it loses efficiency. It is as if one computer absorbed another, but were unable to digest it, because they probably use mutually incompatible operating systems and architectures. In contrast to this model appear the organizations of city networks. Of metapolises, of discontinuous metropolises that represent in a real form the inhabitable space of contemporary society.

The speed of a network is always the speed of the slowest node.
In this situation, the territorial webmasters are of crucial importance, to the extent that they are able to manage an increasingly complex discontinuous reality, which in many cases goes beyond the political limits of decision-making, and the associated complexes—continuity, order and formality, among others—of traditional urbanity.

The capacity to detect the processes that redirect flows toward certain nodes and the potentials linked to the management of centralities associated with logistics or with physical or informational mobility and to the development of emerging territories is vital to a discontinuous global habitability.

Urban Re-cycling

centre, impulsion, metapolis, centrality, geography, refoundation, recycling, hypercity

Strategy for reorienting urban developments on the centre of the city, facilitating the concentration of key activities in the vicinity of its foundational settlement.

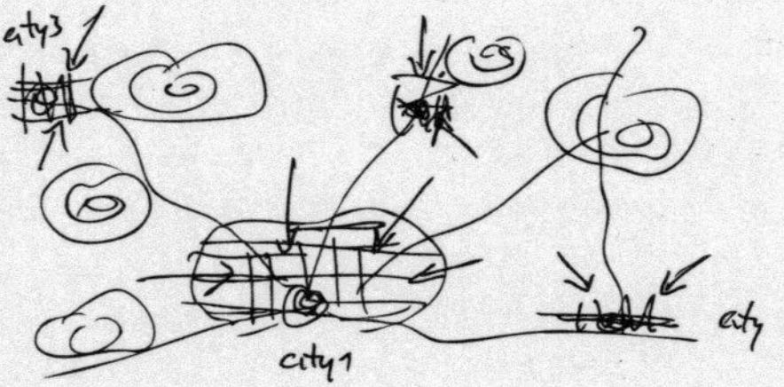

Our cities have developed a process of expansion in the territory throughout history by means of settlements based on strategic criteria: proximity to trade routes, access to water and food, contact with the sea, defensive capacity, etc. Cities as organisms evolve and progress or decline into decadence according to whether or not they know how to respond to the structural changes in the society around them. Meanwhile, other cities have sprung up thanks to the development of new economic phenomena in the territory—the resort cities, for example, or centres for the production of new technologies.

However, there is now a great number of cities that no longer have territory in which to grow: cities whose boundaries are already colliding with those of their neighbours, or conurbations on whose extension is so great as to make them inhabitable.

In this situation there is a pressing need for the strategic definition of where and how to grow. In the face of the potential territorial drift of the big cities, expanding across the territorial magma, what is needed are clear centralities on the territory, primarily in connection with the functional geographical centres of the cities, in many cases developed around physical communications interchanges or centres of economic, political or cultural power. A potent, well-defined and dynamic centre which responds to the changing conditions of its society, and is able to incorporate new functions, is the attractor best equipped to avoid the emergence of an infinite periphery. This process of growing toward the interior will on occasion mean growing in height due to the shortage of available land, or growing down into the subsoil, or promoting functional compatibility at different times of the day, the week or the year.

This strategy simultaneously serves to protect territories and landscapes of untold value—where these are in close proximity to the city or when they finally disappear and instantly become history as a result of their occupation—and to create nodes of centrality on the territory.

Re-programming

re-inhabiting, sound automaton, gram, formulating

Establishment of functional nodes in the territory, in order to generate an urban rhythm.

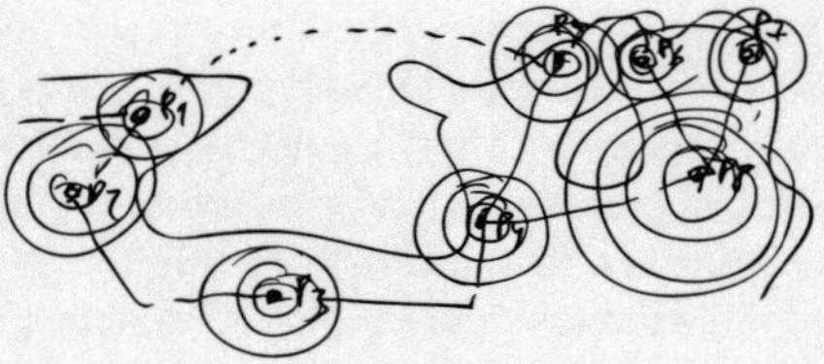

GEOLOGICS	PAGE	PROJECT
Re-programming /24	194	**Batoutz Port**
	220	**Fugee Port**
	420	**Sociopolis I**

The establishment of functional programmes in a particular territory—a city, a port, a street, a house—by means of constructions or actuations in the space endows it not only with a spatial structure relative to the project itself but more also a temporal structural related to the activation of a point in the territory throughout the day.

A sequence of functional nodes will produce the temporary activation of a place in such a way that from that moment on the tension created among a series of sequentially related activities establishes an urban rhythm.
The urban rhythm structures the activity of the city in space and in time.
The best cities are those that have the greatest diversity of activities so that their activity is almost continuous.

The programming of the city must incorporate sequences of activity during the course of the day, the week, the month and the year, and recognize the ages of its users and their condition as residents or visitors.

The ecologist Salvador Rueda has attempted to establish the degree of organization of a territory—for example, a neighbourhood—and its potential for the exchange of information; in part, through an analysis of the diversity (H) of information bearers. Ramon Margalef determined that diversity (H) on its own is a poor index of organization; its scale is increased and completed if two other notions are taken into account—namely, those of persistence and spectrum, the first being related to time and the second to space.

The programming of the city makes it possible to create an open structure of activities and potential human relationships, which are those that foster social interaction and thus, in the best of cases, a change of scale in the city's social relations and economic activity, which is ultimately what creates an urban consciousness or intelligence.

Re-urbanizing

programme, paradigm, cycle, information, hybridization, locale, interaction, social, sport

Transformation of the public space of the city through the incorporation of new functions and locales.

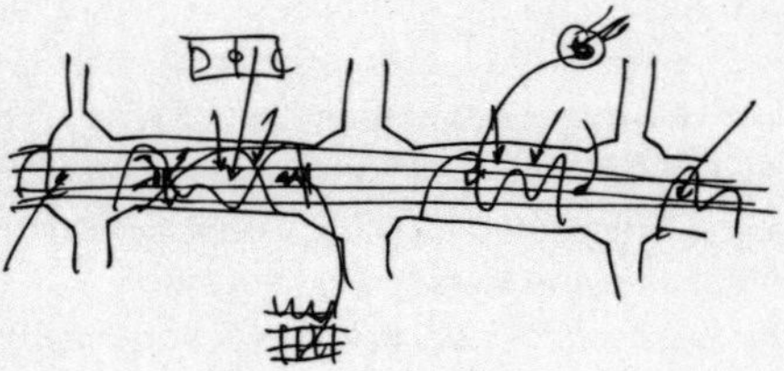

GEOLOGICS	PAGE	PROJECT
Re-urbanizing /25	**286**	**Cristóbal de Moura street**
	414	**Eco tropical Neighbourhood**

The public space of the city is the key to the definition of the quantity and quality of interaction between the people that inhabit it. Its open and continuous character make it the element best able to integrate the multitude of social profiles and personalities that come together in a city.

It is the place that stimulates or restricts the creation of urban intelligence networks, associations, and places for the recognition and expression of the order above that of the individual subject bounded by the house. However, the principal processes of urbanization of the city's public spaces are in most cases geared to the simple functional adaptation of a space in terms of a generic way of life.

The public space is literally an extension of the home. Every city and every society has a public space directly related to its ways of life. Re-urbanizing the city makes it possible to introduce new ways of using the space, and these in turn transform the ways of life of its neighbourhoods and the social interaction within them.

The programmes with the most re-urbanizing values are those that serve to integrate a greater diversity of social profiles and age groups and can be used in different ways at different times of the day.
Systems oriented toward the direct management of the public space by the citizens, such as urban allotments or sports facilities ensure that the inhabitants are the protagonists of the action, rather than mere spectators.

Multi-velocity

space, time, rhythm, node, sequence, foot, times, techno-agricultural

Creation of cities that operate simultaneously at multiple speeds.

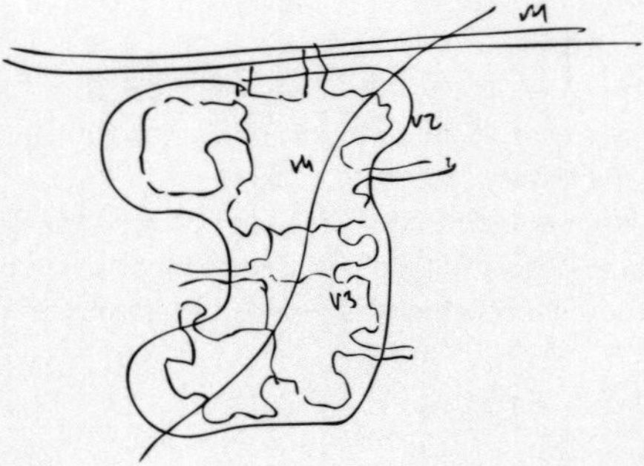

GEOLOGICS	PAGE	PROJECT
Multi-velocity /26	**286**	**Cristóbal de Moura street**
	400	**New Settlements**
	428	**Sociopolis Masterplan**

Speed is a parameter that relates space and time. In the information society the design of the inhabitable space is concerned with organizing the use of the things in both space and time. A self-sufficient neighbourhood should be a neighbourhood designed to be inhabited at multiple speeds.

Out of the 20th-century city, developed on the principles of the industrial economy, posited on individual mobility and constructed to the scale of the motor car, the information society is fashioning a city that functions at multiple speeds. A potential multi-velocity city would foster the construction of local environments, locales of very good environmental quality, sited next to vitally productive agricultural lands to be lived at very low speed, simultaneously connected with the world in real time via high-speed information networks.

These places would be physically connected with the rest of the world by high-speed trains and planes. The information technologies have facilitated not only spatial discontinuity but also temporal discontinuity, insofar as the people who work in networks and on the Net can do so independently of one another, sharing a common work rhythm, but having no need of simultaneity. Our cities should make it easier for us to work close to home, so that our daily lives need not involve long journeys, thus saving time and energy. Natural spaces in close proximity to housing are an extension of the home, and can, in the best of cases, encourage an urban velocity adapted for pedestrians and cyclists, and, with luck, provide the opportunity to benefit from the proximity of agricultural activity to people's homes. Agricultural velocity, industrial velocity and digital velocity, superposed on one another. Multi-velocity.

Humanizing

appropriation of the city, pedestrianizing, extending, creation of public space

Transformation of cities toward qualitative rather than quantitative models.

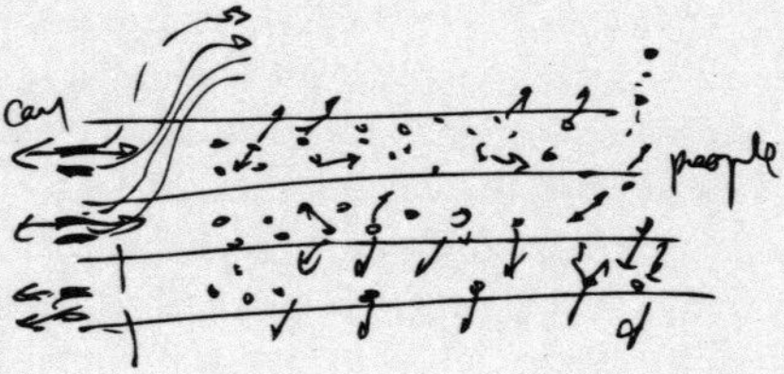

GEOLOGICS
Humanizing
/27

PAGE
246

PROJECT
Keelung Port

Finally, the right to inhabit the city. The accumulation of history, of energy, of functionality in the cities has meant that we sometimes lose sight of the fact that this is an artificial ecosystem created by human beings in order to organize life better.

The economic history of our societies shows there have been plenty of occasions when quantitative development has taken precedence over qualitative development. Anything that happens somewhere has already happened somewhere else. Or will happen.

Innovation is a supreme and far from frequent occurrence. But when it does occur, it is the catalyst of multiple transformations in many places. Finally, we always come back to the city. To habitability, to the humanization of spaces, in some cases given over to functional structures in an apparent search for an instant progress that almost never occurs.

If, as Jaime Lerner claims, the cities are not the problem, but the solution, the new cities are waiting to be made. Each generation has a way of building its territory, and must strive to transform what it has inherited from the past in such a way that all of its potential are developed in accordance with the new ways of inhabiting. But the city can also be created from scratch. And for this to happen we need to engage in structural reflections guided to determining how we can create habitable environments in which human beings, in interaction with their surroundings, will be happy.

Icons

iconizing, icon, symbol, form, concentration, architecture, city, time, memory.

Creation of a recognizable symbolic construction that connects with the geography, the history and the culture of a place by way of a universal event related with the spread of the city.

GEOLOGICS
Icons
/28

PAGE
146

PROJECT
Wrocław Expo

The construction of the city must be understood as a systemic process rather than an iconic concentration. The cities seem to have renounced urbanism, on account of the complexity of managing it and the great burden of social and/or economic pressures bearing on it that are impediments to planning in the medium and long term. As a result, the cities of the early 21st century are developing more on the basis of economic conjunctures and of concrete projects than of long-term strategies. Formal or functional icons are concentrations of urbanity that establish rhythms in a city that would otherwise be devoid of intensity.

Urban icons have proved to be of great utility in cities that have sought to set in motion the reform or the development of certain areas, while at the same time projecting a message of optimism for internal consumption and of euphoria toward the exterior. They are symbols of moments of the city's progress.

In a globalized economy, cities compete with one another, just as companies and organizations do, to attract the attention of the media and/or of capital. A city has to be able to create a coherent urban structure in the medium and long term, while at the same time exploiting the opportunities offered by the flows of regional economic development that characterize the global economy. And in this situation the cities promote events capable of attracting economic and media attention: events that, if they are successful —essentially because they were put together in order to be successful from a social and economic point of view—can create a structure for a ongoing, sustained development.

The Expos and Olympic Games are paradigms of this mediatic concentration that does not have any predefined image of its own. Architecture thus has a fundamental role to play, in the sense that it can generate—by means of the icons that represent the event—an image of something that we already know in functional terms but that more rather than needs to renew its imaginary in each new staging.

Sharing out

regrouping, dividing, structure, part, territory

Appropriation of a territory by a number of functional units, creating groups based on the discontinuous protection and use of the territory.

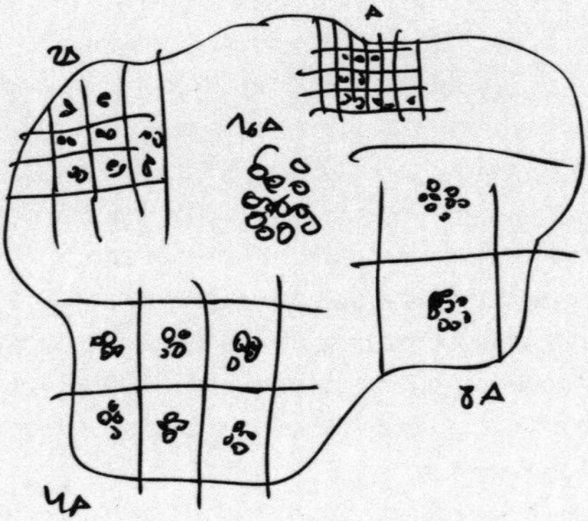

GEOLOGICS
Sharing out
/29

PAGE
400

PROJECT
New Settlements

In the history of human settlement there is a great tradition of sharing out land among the victors of wars and other conflicts. Every model or form of sharing out property, or of concentration or dispersion strategy in the territory has an impact on the vital and functional structures that are established in the territory.

On a hypothetical terrain of area A, on which N number of people (or activities) are to be implanted, the two possible extremes would be to have a single concentration in which N people were settled, creating a town or village and managing a single system of unbuilt land, or to have N units of area A/N.

One of the questions to consider is that of the minimum unit of population in a territory that would constitute a town or village. What size is the smallest settlement in the world? What attributes distinguish a village from a house or a group of houses? When the King James I undertook the process of reconquering the territories of the Mediterranean coast he had to decide which concentrations qualified as a town and which did not. He decreed that those built nuclei that comprised at least 16 'households' would be a town.

The creation of extended networks of settlement on the territory, instead of a few dense concentrations surrounded by large tracts of unoccupied land, is a valid strategy for acting on large areas of non-urbanized agricultural terrain, in which the intention is that the territory should be inhabited and that the impact of the built fabric on it should be limited.

Ringing

re-, orienting, network, circuit, occupying, tracing, grouping, re-participating

Occupation and ordering of a territory on the basis of a system of mobility based on circuits rather than grids.

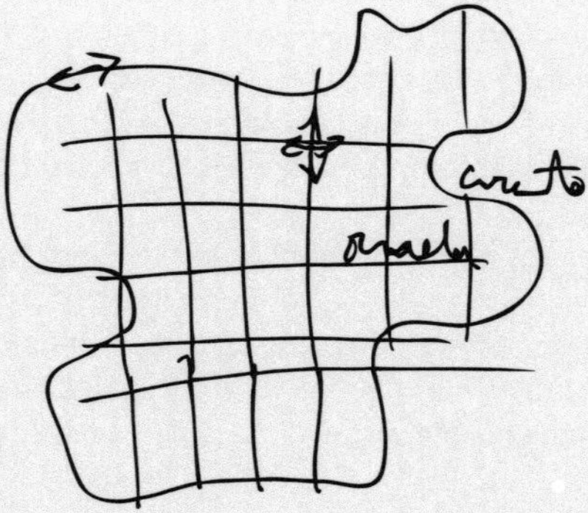

GEOLOGICS	PAGE	PROJECT
Ringing /30	**406**	**Bioclimatic Villages**
	420	**Sociopolis I**

Any settlement in the territory requires a road structure, which guarantees the accessibility of any point within it. Traditionally, our cities have been constructed on the basis of grids, generally orthogonal, with the potential for unlimited growth. This was the option favoured by the Greeks and the Romans, and for many of the 'new town' expansions of European and American cities.

However, on the basis of a process of reading the territory in which the values of the landscape or of certain natural features are regarded as especially important, the reduction of the area devoted to mobility as well as the equidistance to certain points of the territory means that structures based on circuits or ring-road systems are potentially a good strategy for implantation. A circuit makes it possible to concentrate in a single directrix the set of networks (transportation, water, electricity, etc) that the urbanization of a territory implies.

Democratizing

systems, networks, protecting, history

Urban development on the basis of ensuring equitable access to the best views and the best urban location.

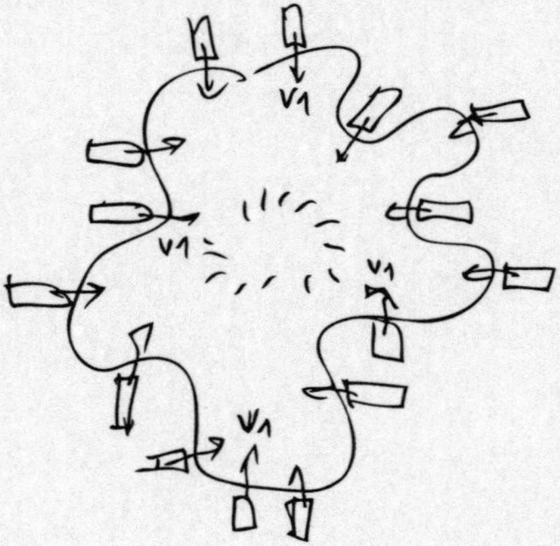

GEOLOGICS
Democratizing
/31

PAGE
428

PROJECT
Sociopolis Master plan

If a settlement is established in order to take advantage of elements of great natural value such as a sea coast or a fine landscape, or certain monumental elements, the sharing out of access to these elements among the greatest possible number of people would seem to be a necessary point of departure.

Good views, fresh air, access to services or proximity to a node of communication are among the values that should be distributed equitably among the inhabitants of a neighbourhood, a town or a city. This means that we need to promote strategies of volumetric implantation that favour the equitable allocation of these goods. The case of the town of Benidorm on Spain's Mediterranean coast seems paradigmatic here. A simple urbanistic decision about spatial ordering that allows the construction of towering high-rise blocks in place of the traditional compact grids of buildings of conventional height has led to the greatest concentration of skyscrapers in Europe, so that most apartments in the town, no matter how far from the shore, have views on the sea.

In other cases, the panoptic character of certain constructions with specific functions determines a specific form of the architecture in the same way that a natural form can be determined by a certain environmental process. All of this means that in the face of certain generic forms of appropriation and use of the territory by human beings we need to reflect in each individual case on the systemic requirements that determine whether any place in the world can or should be different from any other.

Discontinuity

topographies, fractal, part, sequence, relationship

Promotion of spatial continuity on the basis of physical discontinuity, by means of levels or precincts.

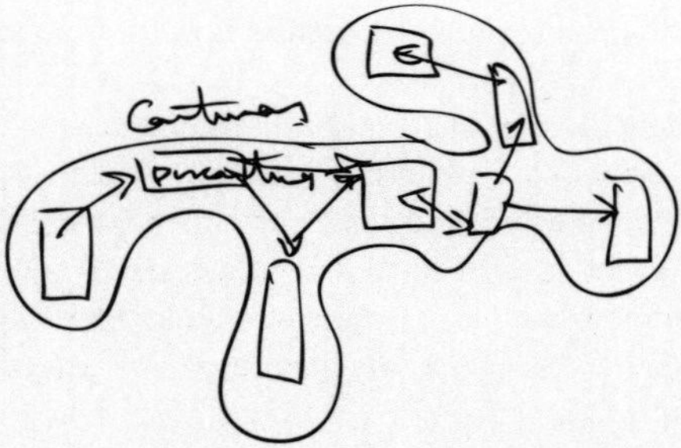

GEOLOGICS
Discontinuity
/32

PAGE
482

PROJECT
Kim Hygn Yoon Editing Co.

The repetition of the floor plan in order to accommodate more activity on a given area of land has been common practice since cities were first established. This process was amplified when certain technical inventions such as the elevator or reinforced concrete made the construction of even taller buildings practicable, in such a way that the discontinuity of the accumulation of floors was compensated by a mechanism that equalized the relative effort involved in getting to the floors closest to and furthest away from the ground. This process has become a generally accepted practice, over and above the analysis of the potentials of the dividing up of the floor plan as a way of achieving spatial or functional relations that may be more useful for an organization.

This being so, the floor plan need not be discontinuous from one floor to the next. If we think of the entire area of a construction as a field on which organizations or groups of activities are implanted, the way this field is divided up and the way different parts or units of a building are connected is part of the very essence of the act of building multiple levels of roofs on a given plot of land.

A fragmented, locally discontinuous system can permit complete continuity at the global level. The degree of discontinuity of a system and the way in which its the parts recombine to form a whole are part of the essence and nature of that system. They define its formal and functional structure.

Multiscalar

node, unit, network, connection, resolution

Relation of units at different scales of habitability, in order to define complete and complex inhabitable environments.

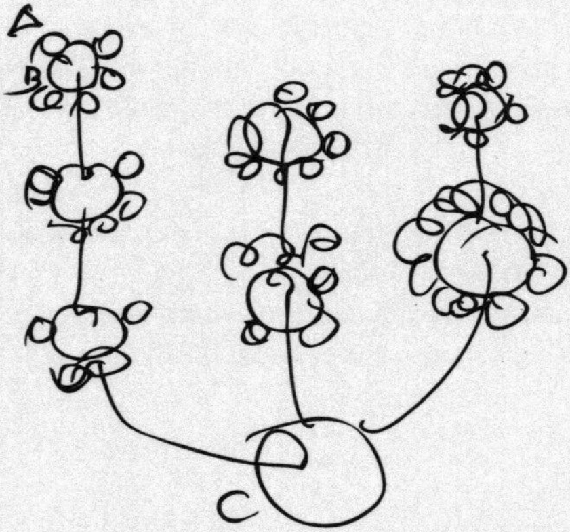

GEOLOGICS
Multiscalar
/33

PAGE
474

PROJECT
University Housing

The objective of constructing neighbourhoods and cities is to create a complete habitat for human beings in which the needs of habitability can be satisfied. In the light of this, the redefinition of the scale on which certain activities that form part of people's daily lives are implanted is crucial to determining one way of living or another.

We could define the sequence of 1, 10, 100, 1000, 10,000, 100,000, 1,000,000, 10,000,000,000, 100,000,000, 1,000,000,000 and 10,000,000,000 people as referring in a simplified way to the scales of apartment, floor, building, city block, neighbourhood, district, city, metropolis, country, continent and planet.

Any object present in a person's home forms part of a multiscalar network that can be identified with elements on all these scales. From a crucifix to the Vatican. From a plant to the Amazon. From a toilet to a sewage farm. From a book to the Library of Congress.
There are scales at which certain solutions make no sense at present. A nuclear power plant for a neighbourhood, for instance.

Industrial society began the process of replacing a great number of spaces with objects. More and more human functions can be performed by objects. Objects replace spaces, and at the same time lead to other spaces being resignified with new functions. The home has been converted into a micro-city, in which we can work, have fun, shop and rest.

The definition of the resolution of certain functions on one scale or another—from the apartment to the building to the neighbourhood to the city—and the way these are grouped, is what determines different models of settlement. In so far as the construction of a neighbourhood, its buildings, and its individual homes are undertaken simultaneously, it is possible to reprogramme which activities are carried out individually, jointly or publicly.

Sharing

parts, relationship, interaction, division, connection, architecture, physical

Utilization in the physical world of the principles that govern the sharing of resources in the digital realm, creating a sequence between private spaces and spaces for sharing in proximity.

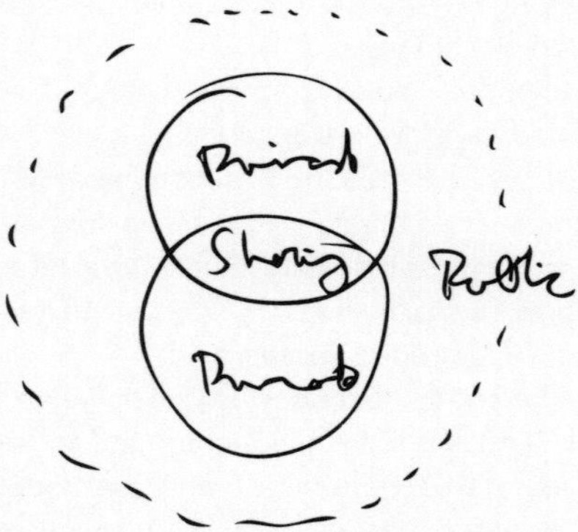

GEOLOGICS	PAGE	PROJECT
Sharing	**458**	**Sharing Tower**
/34		
	474	**University Housing**

The physical world recognizes the private or public value of any given place. The decentralized nature of the information society has enabled the creation of systems for sharing resources through networks. Peer-to-peer systems allow large numbers of individual entities to share informational resources, in order to gain access to more resources without actually owning them. This ties in with the strategy advocated in the book *Factor Four: Doubling Wealth, Halving Resource Use, a report to the Club of Rome* by Jeremy Rifkin, as a means of obtaining twice the benefit from half the resources in areas such as energy consumption or the occupation of the land.

In the physical world, resources such as land can be shared on the basis of an agreement between individual owners who are willing cede part of their property in return for more resources and improved efficiency.
But at what point does a thing cease to be 'shared' and become public? How many people have to use the same car to travel to and from work for us to think of it as shared? If forty people are using the same vehicle, it takes on the character of a public space. Eight people sharing a kitchen and a dining room is a number in which we recognize the scale of the space as a family scale. A kitchen and a dining room for eighty people have a dimension such that the space no longer has the character of an extension of a private property and becomes a public space.

The home is a physical space that in many cases is shared despite not having been designed for this. We can imagine the sharing of resources inside a house, between two neighbouring houses, between all the houses on the same floor, between the floors of a building, or between the buildings in a neighbourhood. Each of these situations offers various possibilities for extending habitability beyond the relationships within a family and the confines of the home.

Emergence

interaction, nodes, relation, connection

The promotion of spatial continuity on the basis of physical discontinuity, by means of levels or precincts.

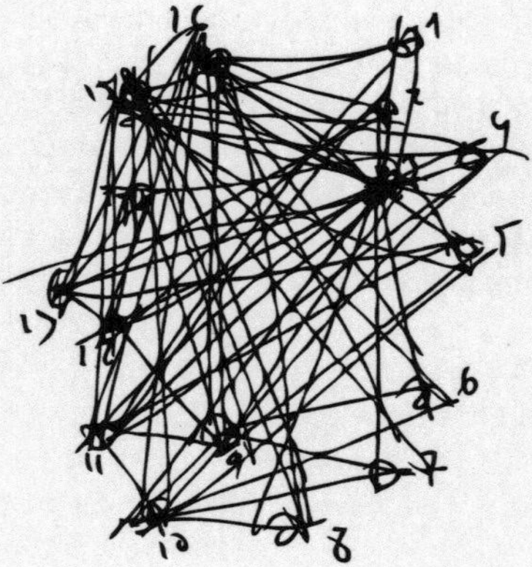

GEOLOGICS
Emergence
/35

PAGE	PROJECT
428	**Sociopolis Masterplan**
458	**Sharing Tower**

Marvin Minsky, one of the pioneers of artificial intelligence, was once asked how it was possible for intelligence to arise from the relationship of millions of non-intelligent elements such as neurons.

Emergence occurs when the simple (or complex) interaction of elements of the same category generates a new category with a consciousness superior to that of the sum of the first.

A brain's intelligence depends on the number of different connections that exist between the neurons.

The strongest societies and the strongest cities are those with the greatest diversity. The fundamental goal of every living being and every ecosystem is survival. And the better able it is—on the basis of the elements that constitute it—to create structures that can withstand unexpected events, and the better able it is to transform and organize itself in the most effective ways, the more likely it will be to achieve this goal.

The city is the paradigm system of systems, in which dozens of relational structures intersect and, in their interaction with others, create new and more complex, potent and evolutive systems.

Those cities that are able to mutate fastest, to innovate in processes and systems, to attract other elements that contribute intelligence and relational capacity to the system, are the cities with the best chance of success in a highly competitive global economy.

The design of a building, a city, a territory, in so far as it defines the relational capacity of individuals or organizations and stimulates or impedes the neuronal connections between elements, is the key to enhancing the intelligence of the territory.

Self-sufficiency

energy, creation, interaction, connection, environment

Development of systems that enable units of habitation to establish a balance between the resources they put into and take out of a system.

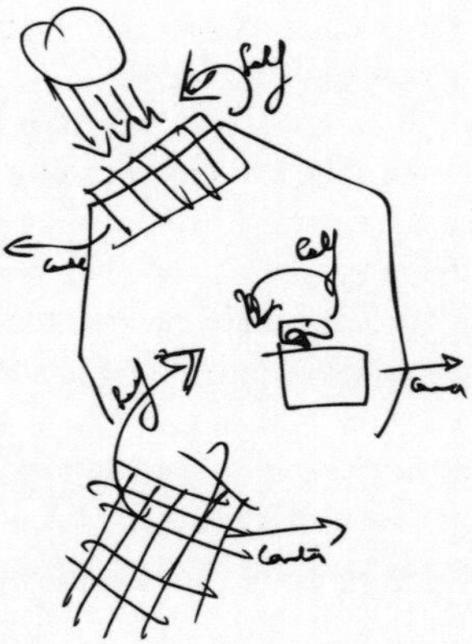

GEOLOGICS	PAGE	PROJECT
Self-sufficiency /36	**406**	**Bioclimatic Villages**
	428	**Sociopolis Masterplan**
	520	**Hyperhabitat**

The new limit—of the apartment, the building, the neighbourhood or the city—is self-sufficiency, just as it is for a tree in a field, which has to be capable of capturing and processing the energy it consumes, of drawing resources from its environment and releasing others that its environment can use; capable of bearing fruit and nurturing life. And of taking part in the complete and complex ecosystems that foster life.

Jeremy Rifkin's book *The Hydrogen Economy* looks at how the storage capacity of small entities such as homes, buildings or neighbourhoods could create new economic systems based on the exchange of energy. In effect, the kind of transformation Internet has brought about in the way information is distributed, with a centralized system like television giving way to a distributed system thanks to computers' capacity for storing and sharing information, can also take place in energy, if no political impediments are put in its way. The storage of energy in the form of hydrogen could be the basis for an 'Energy Internet', with a distributed system for generating and sharing it far surpassing the traditional centralized systems of the industrial era. The richest will be those who save most energy and are therefore able to profit from their surplus.

As with almost all contemporary energy-management resources, the exchange of energy between millions of producers and consumers is bound up with the development of new businesses and economies.

Hypermedia

bits, information, interface, pixels, sensor, computer

Creation of physical spaces with continuity in digital space, so that each is necessary for the functioning of the other.

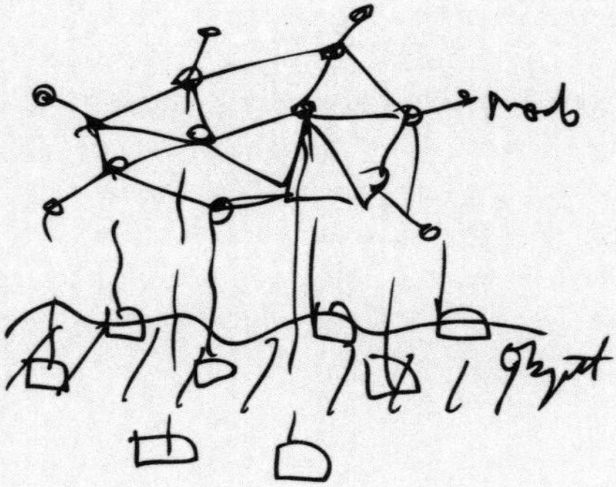

GEOLOGICS
Hypermedia
/37

PAGE	PROJECT
500	**Media House**
494	**Web Hotel**
520	**Hyperhabitat**

The development of the digital world has introduced us to the spaces, compartments, relationships and images of a new technology that has generated a whole sensorial culture, effectively expanding that which exists in the physical world of the senses.

The immersion characteristics now being developed could make it possible for the digital world to be enjoyed as a full-colour, dynamic, changing, configurable-reactive, instant, fast-moving environment, with the physical world seeming slow, heavy and resistant to the change.

However, having got to know the all but magical properties of the digital world, we need to promote the hybridization of the two worlds through the insertion of a logical infrastructure in the development of physical elements. We are currently witnessing the miniaturization of computers and their implantation in a whole range of elements in our daily lives, transforming these into nodes with their own IP address, capable of reacting simultaneously in the hybrid space of the hypermedia.

The computers are vanishing, the screens are expanding to the size of any space you choose.

The best interface for access to the digital world is not a keyboard or a screen but the actual physical world itself.

Re-informing

neuron, Internet 0, media, distributed, infinite

The transformation of architecture as inert space into intelligent reactive space through the introduction of distributed computing systems.

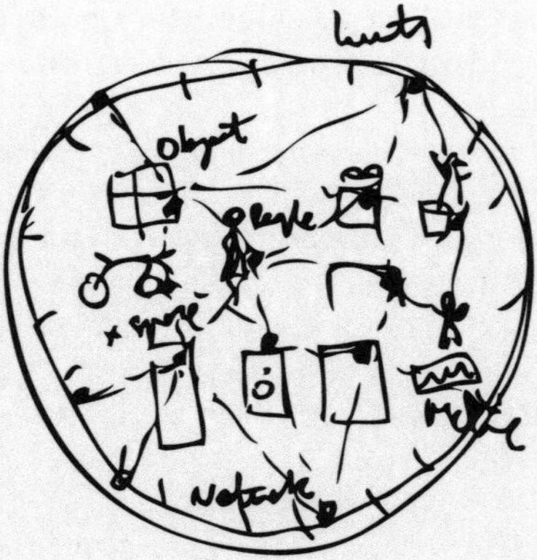

GEOLOGICS	PAGE	PROJECT
Re-informing /38	**500**	**Media House**
	494	**Web Hotel**
	520	**Hyperhabitat**

If buildings are to behave in a more natural way they need to be more intelligent. They will need, like living beings, to have those properties that allow them to respond to specific internal and external stimuli and to modify their form or their behaviour accordingly.

The last few years have seen the introduction of building control systems in which a centralized computer is used to reconfigure some of the building's parameters.

A built space has, from the physical point of view, six categories of entity: living beings, objects, networks, bounds, space and contents. Each of these has its own particular properties.

In order to develop the potential of a system made up of such diverse elements, in which there can be a great variety of functional relations between its various constituent parts, its intelligence needs to be organized in much the same way as that of a human brain, via the interrelation of millions of neurons, which are not in themselves intelligent. The Media House project effectively related a series of microservers connected to one another in a simplified version of the IP protocol, enabling the physicist Neil Gershenfeld to define the concept of Internet 0, as a system capable of relating infinite microservers, each handling a very small amount of information, but their relation,on the basis of algorithms allows them to perform in a decentralized way and permit the emergence of something akin to intelligence. In this way, intelligence is dissolved in spaces, which will never again be inert. We do not build a house with a computer.
The house is the computer.

If Web 1.0 was the network of information and trade, and Web 2.0 was that of social networks, Web 3.0 is the internet of things, through the dissolving of digital systems into them, creating new categories of technology, of systems of fabrication and production, and of the creation of natures.

Projects

Hyper Catalu-nya

Barcelona. Spain. 2003
MACBA Exhibition

Re-naturalizing
/01

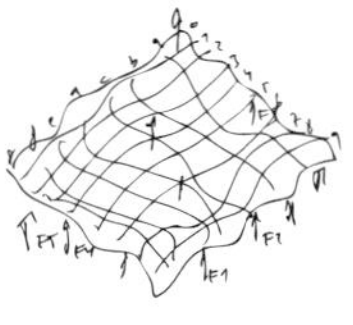

Topographying
/02

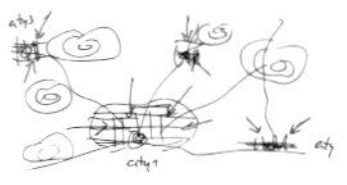

Urban Re-cycling
/23

In 2003 we carried out a study called HyperCatalunya, which sought to identify the potentialities of Catalonia as city. The project was undertaken in conjunction with specialists in the different strata of information that configure the territory (nodes, networks and environments) with the aim of discovering new categories of projects with which to address the habitability of a territory in the process of urbanization.

If our cities have grown over the centuries without acknowledging any limit to their growth, in the last forty years Paris and London—and Barcelona to a lesser degree—have discovered that there is no longer any vacant land on which to expand. Our research revealed that if the accelerating urbanization of Catalonia continued at the present rate there would be no more land to build on anywhere in the country by 2375.
Projects that once seemed infinitely extended in time eventually reach completion: Barcelona's Eixample 'new town' was built in 60 years, and the metropolitan area in 80. This being so, there should be a plan to design, occupy and manage ever larger territories – cities, countries and continents.

Why should our cities, including even those areas most deficient in urban structures, be conserved as they are today? What percentage of the beauty of a city that attracts tourists from around the world are we willing to gamble in transforming it, in exchange for what percentage of increased efficiency and capacity to attract contemporary global functions into our city centres? Constructing the city on itself must be part of a new strategic project, willing to learn from the founding geographic and environmental values of the city. The material from which our cities are constructed can no longer be the same in an era in which there is no longer a virgin natural environment from which to extract raw materials.

We therefore consider that inhabiting the territory should be based on a process of landscape engineering, a hybridizing of natural and artificial structures to create new materialities. Buildings are thus more an eruption of a preformative magma capable of being inhabited than an inert structure that needs to draw energy from its environment to survive. If architecture is landscape, buildings are mountains.

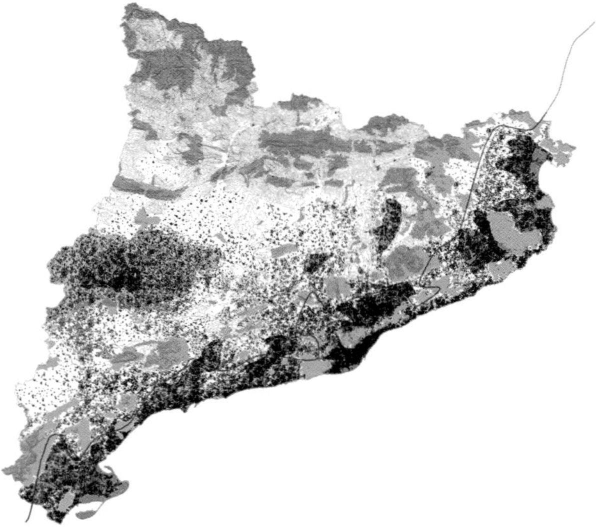

GEOGRAPHY

Catalonia 2003

GEOMETRY

Density of occupation of the Barcelona Eixample in 65 years

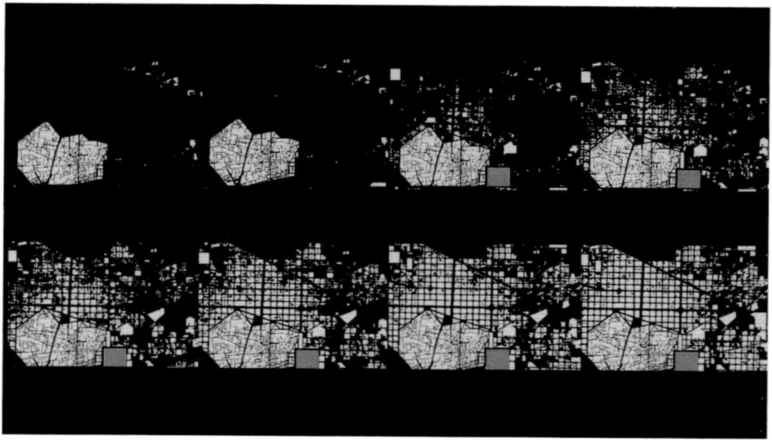

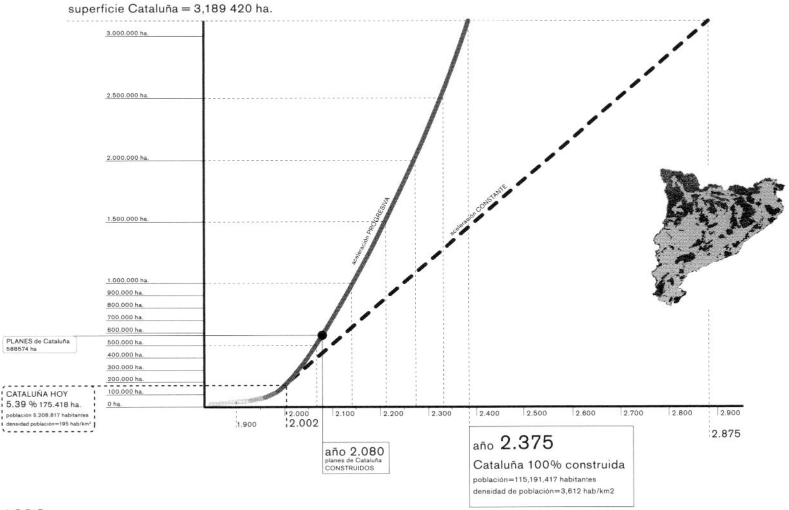

LOGIC

Projection of occupation of the territory according to the urban growth rate

STRUCTURE

Urban recycling strategy

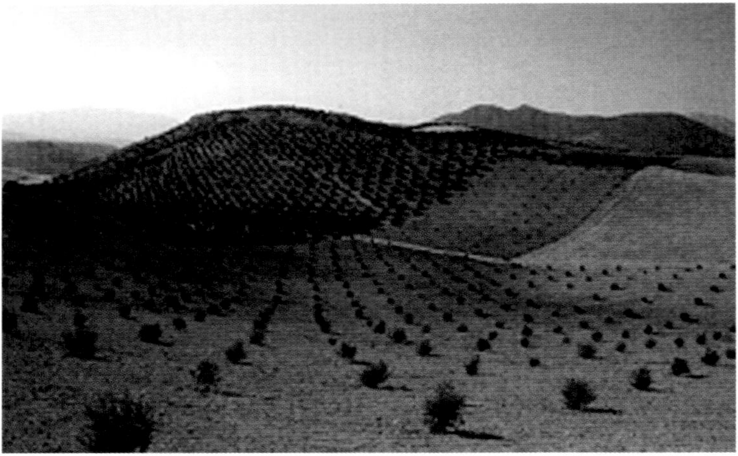

GEOGRAPHY

Matrix of natural nodes that measure a surface

GEOMETRY

Matrix of digital nodes that create a surface

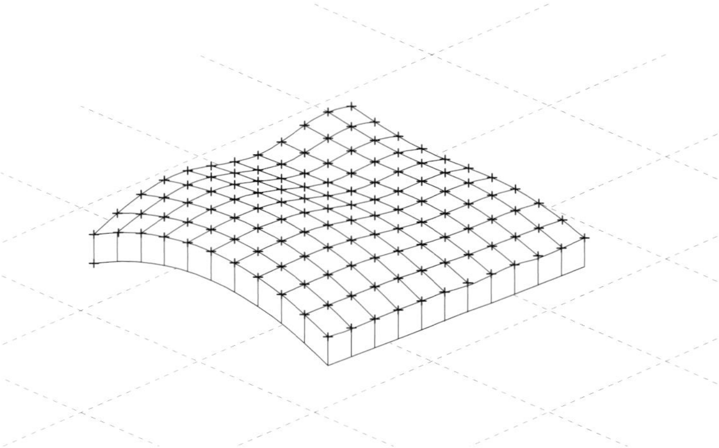

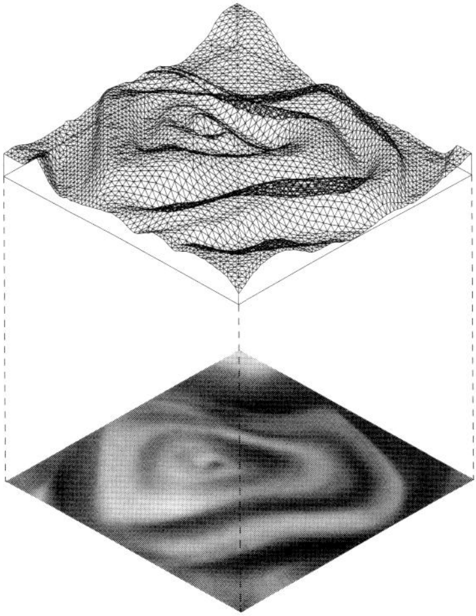

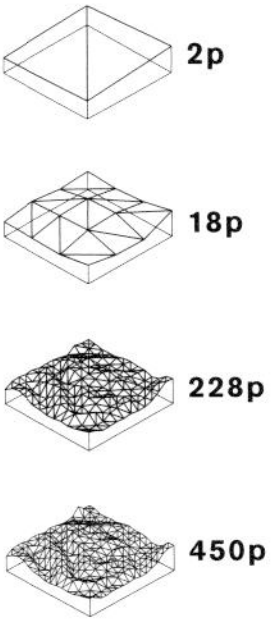

LOGIC

Shifting topography with precise resolution

STRUCTURE

Topographical mesh

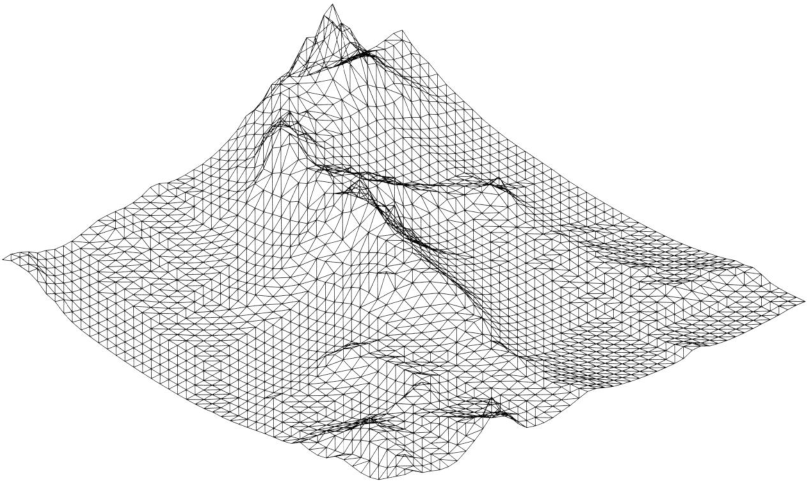

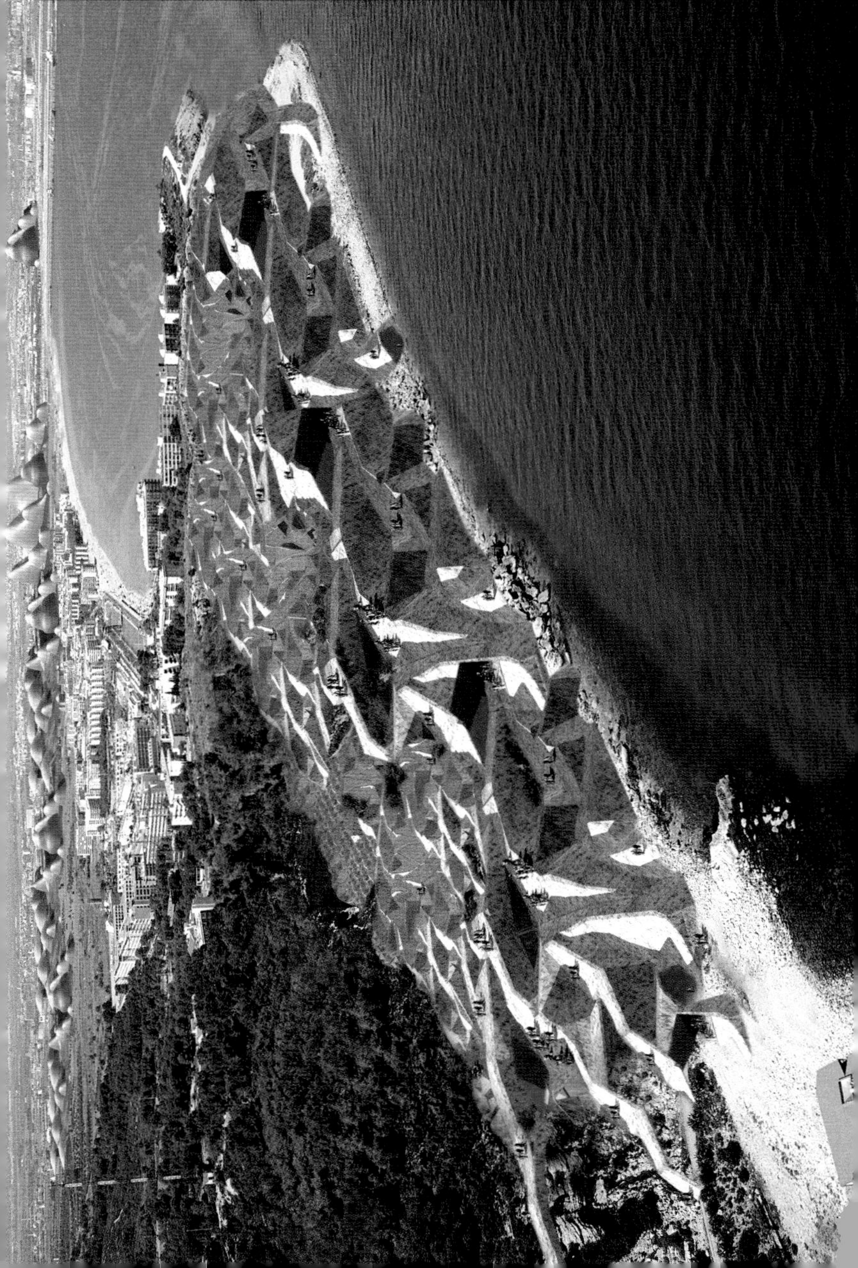

Denia Mountain

Denia, Alicante. Spain. 2002—
Geometry of the façade with Max Sanjulián

1st Prize national competition

Re-naturalizing
/01

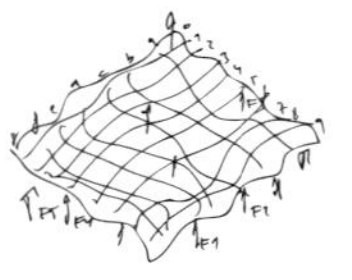

Topographying
/04

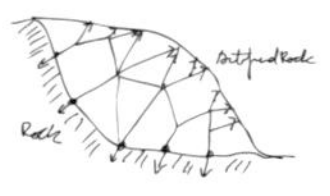

Geomorphosis
/05

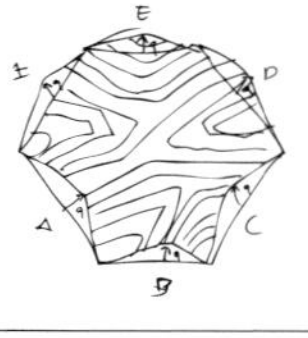

Microtopography
/06

Biomimesis
/07

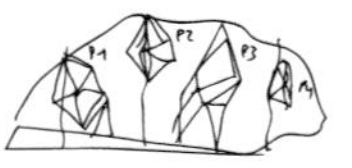

Programmatic cristallization
/10

Resolution
/13

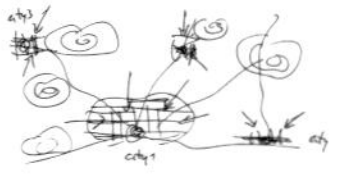

Urban re-cycling
/23

The mayors are the great urban ecologists, embodying as they do all of a town's economic, social, human and cultural information. As managers of the artificial ecosystem that is a city, they have a key role in its development. The discourse in the urban development of the Mediterranean is centred on environmental issues relating to the vertical or horizontal growth of the cities in order to preserve the ever smaller territories of special environmental and landscape quality. However, all too often this discourse neglects the social or economic factors that are essential to ensuring the viability of the continued influence of a population in its territorial environment or beyond. In effect, then, decisions of a strategic order in relation to the implanting of new activities in the territory, the product of present-day needs in terms of a town's economic and social fabrics, are key factors in orienting social and economic flows within the territory.

The project for the quarry in Denia is fruit of a very intelligent strategic decision by a town committed to concentrating the key activities in the centre, in order to guarantee that the centre continues being the most interesting and dynamic part of the territory, and in this way to attract the energy of urban, social and economic development there.

The largest tourist town in Europe is on the Mediterranean coast: Benidorm is a potent machine of the tourist industry whose success is the result of creating spaces for leisure in a dense, high-rise form, so that all of the buildings, however far they may be from the beach, have views of the sea. However, this model of concentration on the coast, which implied the protection of the empty territory of the interior, is being modified by theme parks, low-rise housing and other extensive non-urban mechanisms, of low social and environmental value.

Denia, situated between Alicante and Valencia, represents another model of tourist development based on a medium density; this has traditionally functioned on the basis of attractions such as the port (with ferries to Ibiza), or the quality of its beaches and rocky coves and its magnificent gastronomy. However, the real-estate processes linked to the development of holiday-home tourism had already begun in the 1960s to transform the slopes of the Montgó, an imposing massif that has now been declared a natural park. With those slopes fully occupied, real-estate development turned to the coast north of the town, creating a built continuum of very poor urban quality several kilometres long.

Accordingly, given this process in which real-estate pressure has already affected the environs of the natural park and the beaches to the north, the coves to the south and the agricultural land in the interior, the wisest decision would be to go back to concentrating the activities that energize the economy and contemporary culture in the centre of the town, thus continuing a process of urban refoundation.

Many Mediterranean towns and cities (such as Sagunto) were founded by the Romans on relatively low hills on or near the coast, with a command of the sea that enabled them to protect themselves more easily. Roman Dianium was established to the north of a small massif overlooking a natural harbour in a strategic part of the Mediterranean. The Moors built a castle on the upper flank, and after the Christian reconquest in the 14th century the population settled there. The War of the Spanish Succession resulted in the levelling of the interior of the fortress, and it was used as a military fort until the middle of the 19th century. When all over Europe the old city walls were being demolished, the old fortress was sold for agricultural use, and the stones of the Christian town served to construct terraces to cultivate grapes to produce raisins. At the beginning of the last century the north face, outside of the walled enclosure, was exploited to obtain stone to reinforce the harbour wall. During the Spanish Civil War a network of tunnels was dug in the interior of the massif to provide air-raid shelters, and this has since served to communicate the north and south sides of the crag. In the 1950s the castle was expropriated, a park was laid out and a secondary school was built in the quarry.

After this intense history, in the year 2002 we started work on the Plan for the protection of the castle and its environs including the creation of a major new amenity comprising cultural and urban services, which was considered crucial by the town council.

The town council proposed to locate in the quarry of the castle a great car park connected with the new ring road that would provide access to the town centre by way of the Civil War tunnels, together with a cultural facility and a theatre-auditorium or a conference centre. In order to finance and operate this, it was decided to incorporate profit-making activities of a social character for public use such as a cinema complex, additional cultural spaces, a shopping zone and a hotel, with a resort based on the German model of publicly owned tourist resorts.

It was subsequently decided that it would be necessary to seek the agreement of the participative civic forums of Agenda 21 on the various uses that were to be incorporated into the multifunctional complex in the quarry. To date this consultation process has been very slow, due in part to the development of the new urban plan for the municipality as a whole, and the project is currently awaiting the conclusion of this process to resolve the future of the site.

During the development of the project we became aware that the greatest threat to territorial cohesion was that some of the activities that were envisaged for this site and embraced a logic of concentration of new urban functions in order to attract the population into the centre and thus facilitate urban compactness would end up being implanted in other parts of the territory that were quicker at taking the initiative.

Ondara, a town in the interior, just off the motorway that runs the length of the Mediterranean coast, decided to develop a leisure and shopping centre on a site that is highly accessible not only for the local area but for the whole region, and to capture part of the commercial and leisure market that has traditionally been drawn to the centre of Denia — both from the town itself and from the surrounding area. The systems of territorial delocalization have in this case attained their maximum expression in obtaining, by means of municipal initiatives, the transformation of the traditional compact model of the Mediterranean town into a system of growth based on functional islands that float around the territory, connected by the high-speed transport networks.

The plot intended for an exercise in urban renaturalization that concentrates key activities for the identity of the town in its centre while at the same time undertaking an exemplary operation of landscape restoration still exists in the quarry of Denia.

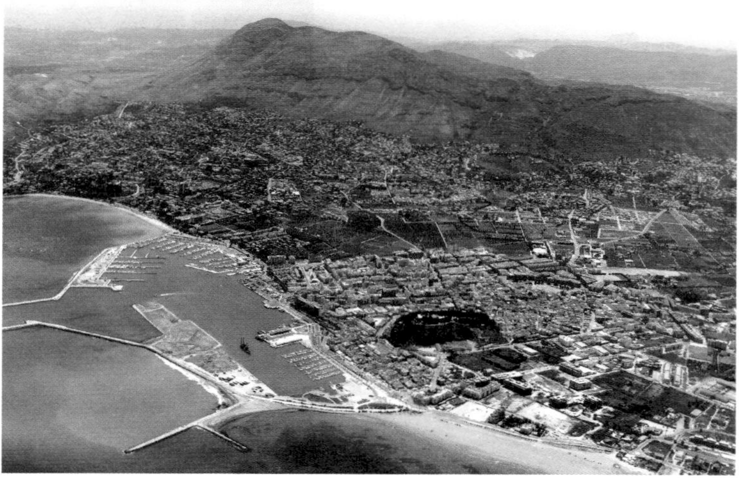

GEOGRAPHY

A historic town overwhelmed by tourism development

GEOMETRY

Position relative to geographic landmarks

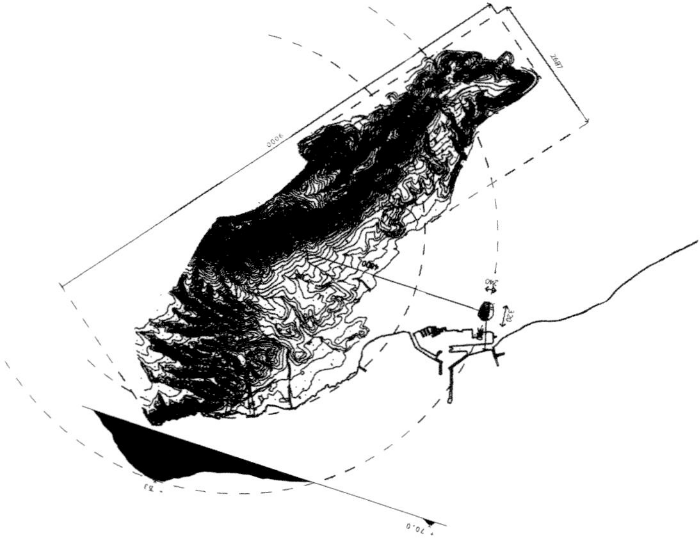

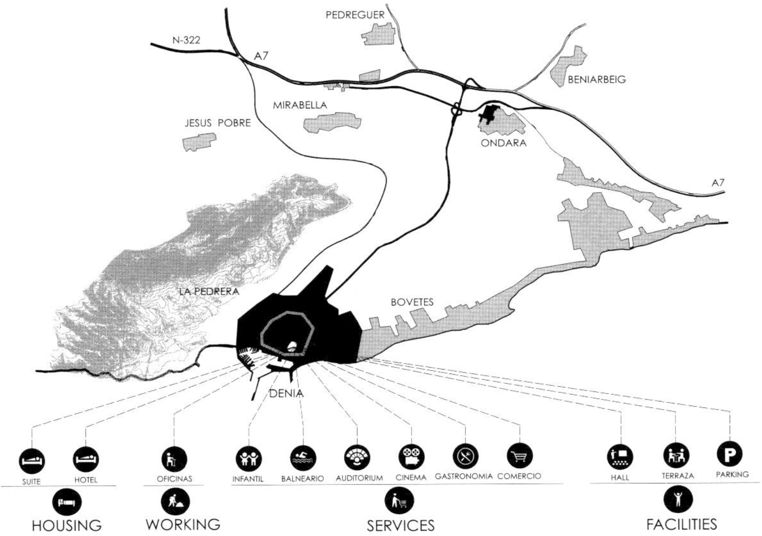

LOGIC

Concentration of valuable activities in the geographic centre

STRUCTURE

Radial structure of territorial development versus occupation of the coastline

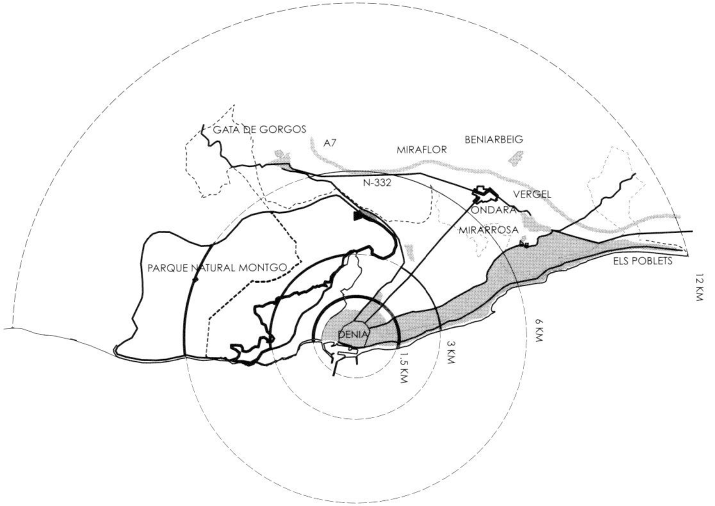

Historic evolution

Roman times

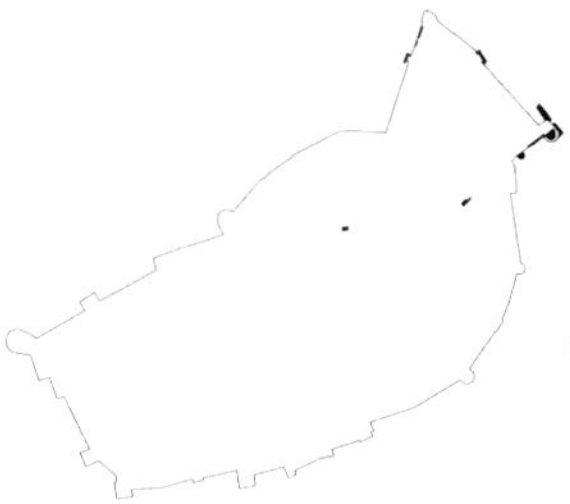

Al-Andalus times

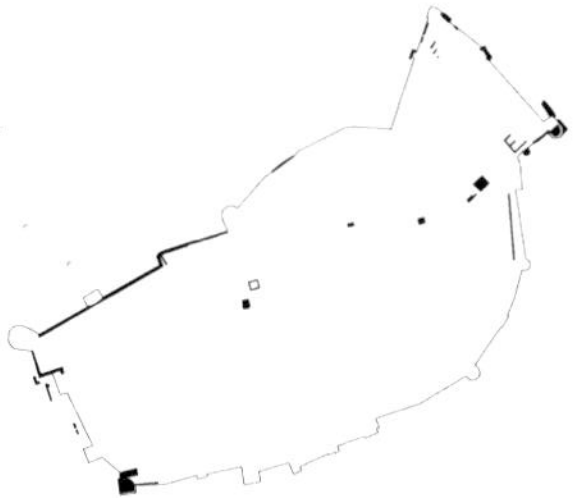

1244–1500

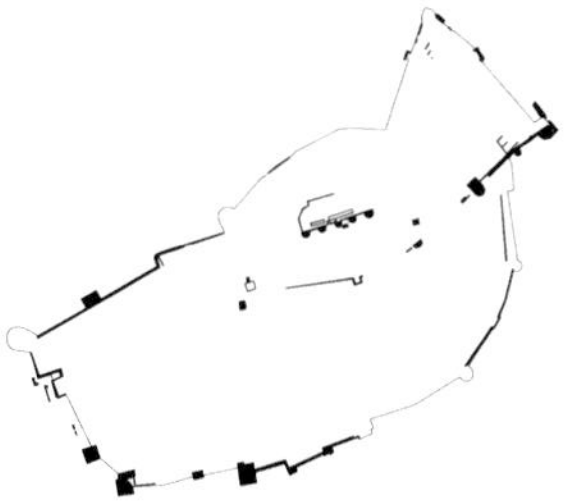

1500–1575

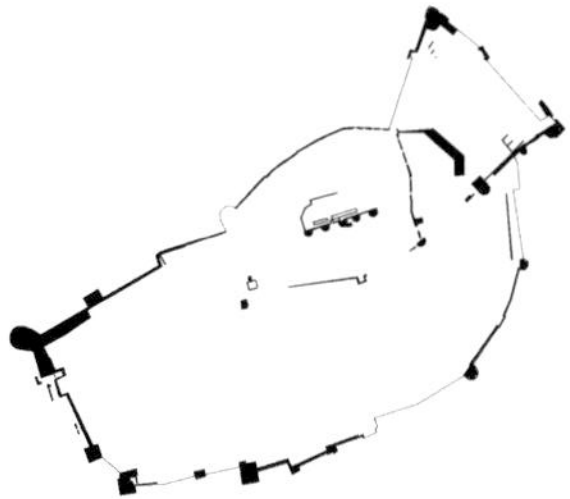

1575–1705

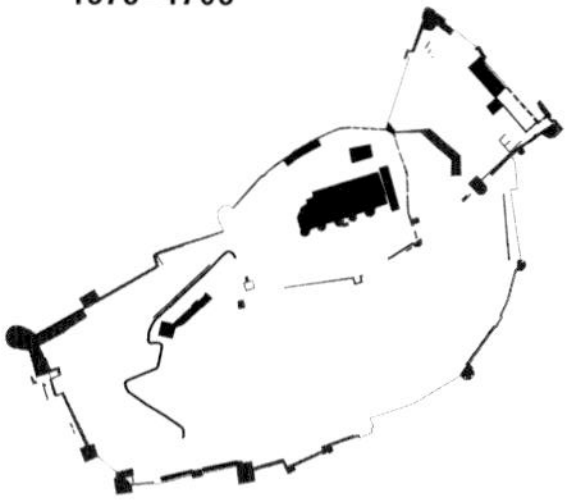

1705–1808

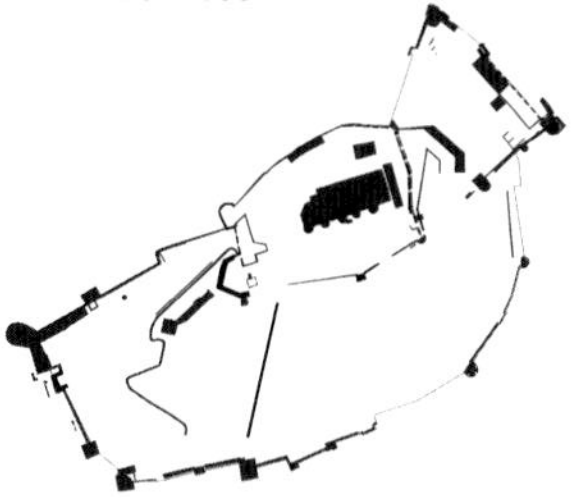

1808–1859

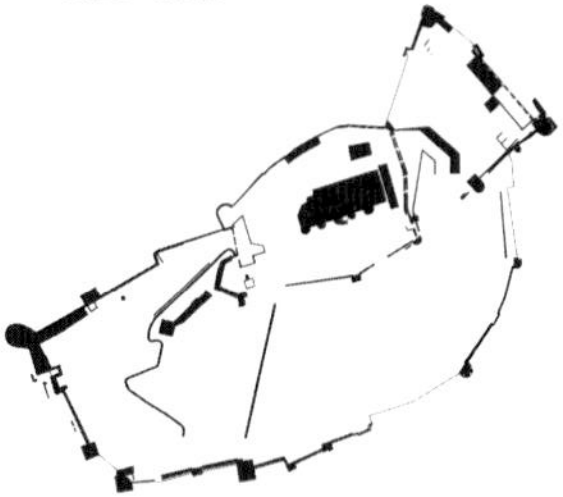

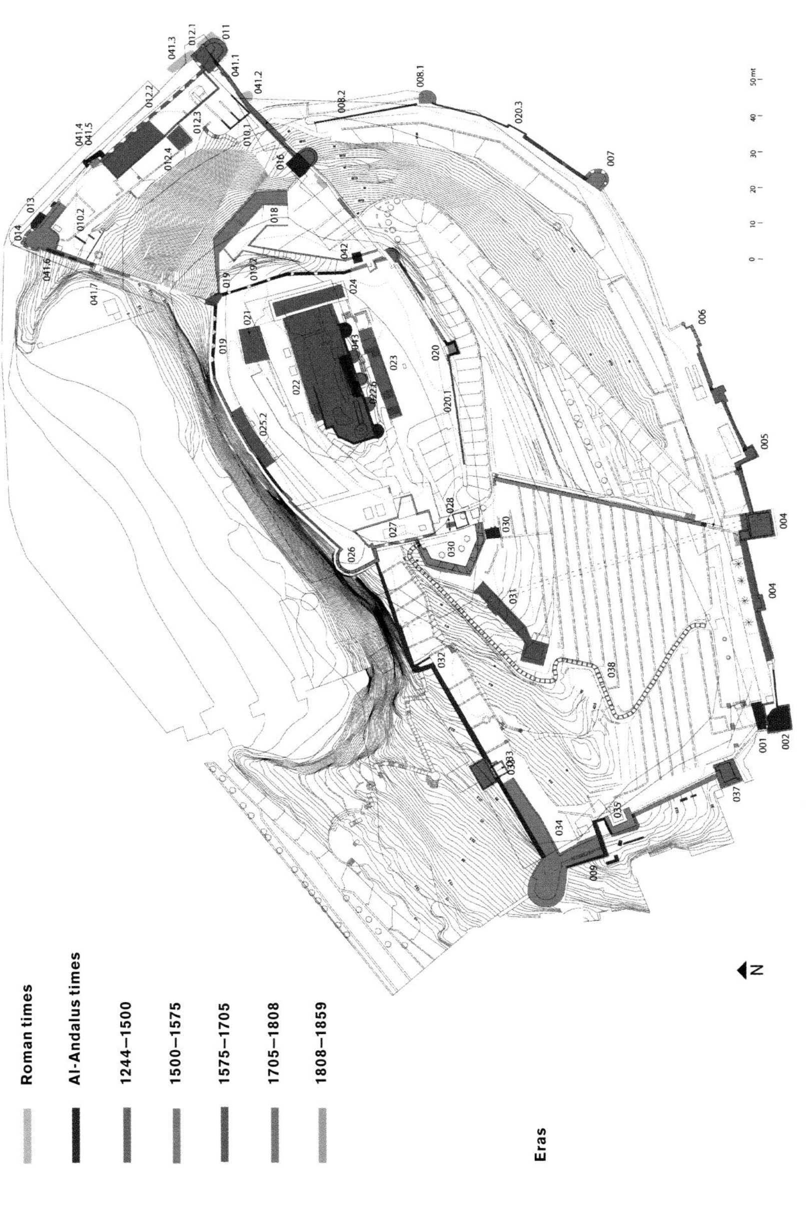
Eras
Roman times
Al-Andalus times
1244–1500
1500–1575
1575–1705
1705–1808
1808–1859
N
0
10
20
30
40
50 mt
001
002
004
005
006
007
008.1
008.2
009
010.1
010.2
011
012.1
012.2
012.3
012.4
013
014
016
018
019
019.2
020
020.1
020.3
021
022
022.6
023
024
025.2
026
027
028
030
031
032
033
034
035
037
038
041.1
041.2
041.3
041.4
041.5
041.6
041.7
042
043

In what category does an artificial mountain belong?

The project for Denia emerges as the possibility of concentrating in a place of exceptional historical, social and cultural value previously expressed intuitions in relation to the possibility of converting the act of construction into a landscaping operation, in which the resulting structure follows the structural and formal logic of a mountain. In this way, this project posited the challenge of proposing a structure that responded to the scale of the great void that is the legacy of the material interventions in the place in the course of its history. And this being so, the first question to be answered is that of the category to which the actuation to be carried out belongs: if this is to be an epidermis actuation in which a series of activities organized as superposed planes are 'covered' by a sculptural skin; if the building is to be implanted outside of the originally excavated volume, proposing new formal codes to respond to the place; or if, on the contrary, we assume the challenge of reconstructing the mountain in terms of the logic of its geological structure. The three-dimensional void has a length of one hundred and twenty metres, with a relatively constant triangular section with a height of forty metres up to the foot of the castle wall, and a base of fifty metres, with an approximate gradient of three in ten. The first decision was assumed the essential logic of the project, in which their its surface as well as their its functional organization would be based on an only structural logic emerged on the basis of an act of regeneration of the own mountain. We would act here as nature does in the case of certain animals, which are capable of regenerating a member in the event of amputation. Initially, at the intermediate scale, the limestone rock of the front of the quarry presented various fissures and folds that did not determine any specific rules of actuation.

We carried out numerous analyses of the surface of Mediterranean mountains, characterized by their having very little soil and a great quantity of loose rocks and an abundance of low scrub and brushwood. This involved measuring the various elements of which this terrain is composed, and in one of these surveys we studied a pyramidal stone, which surprised us with its formal clarity, defined by faces whose geometry consisted of crumpled triangles with different degrees of resolution. According to the theory of fractal geometry, many natural elements, which can be reconstructed on the basis of such a geometry, have self-similarity at various scales of magnitude. A branch is self-similar to the tree to which it belongs. A fragment of coastline is self-similar to the whole coast. And in this case, in theory a stone ought to be self-similar to the whole mountain. However, our attempts at translating the triangular systems of the skin of the rock to the skin of the mountain failed to provide the necessary consistency, and in our search for the logic of the triangulate form of the stone we decided to incorporate a new expert into the team, who would be able to make a microscope study of the interior of a similar rock. And in those microscopic photographs, which revealed an arrissed geometry of the various parts of the limestone rock, as well as rhomboidal crystals in the rocks where water circulated in the interior of the massif, we perceived the reason for the arrissed break of the rock and understood that the regeneration of the mountain would have to emerge through its re-crystallization, reproducing the characteristic rhombohedric structure of the limestone crystals.

Thus, the first step was to define a large-scale structure that rested on the floor of the quarry and on its front, in such a way that the foundation of the structure is supported on both the vertical and the horizontal plane. If the horizontal projection of the rhombohedron is hexagons, we decided that the surface of the mountain should be constructed on the basis of three different-sized hexagons in such a way that the one closest to ground would be the largest, so that the topography that emerged from it would permit the movement of people in larger spaces.

The programme proposed in the project was organized around the creation of three large voids that act as poles of attraction for the contents associated with the programme. The geometry of these programmatic crystals is defined through the overlapping, aggregation or linkage of various types of calcite crystals. These voids make it possible to preserve the quarry intact at several relevant key points in the project.

The intention is to construct an urban agora by the exit of the existing tunnel, located between the new rhomboidal structure and the wall of the quarry, with various recreational or commercial activities deployed around it. The auditorium, located in the centre of the new mountain, will have access from the car park and from the exterior of the mountain, by way of a lobby beneath the orchestra pit. The auditorium itself is like the interior of an instrument, with a precise geometric definition that ensures excellent acoustics. At the east end of the auditorium an interior void will accommodate saltwater swimming pools at the base of the quarry, with natural overhead lighting thanks to a geometry that connects with the complexity and wealth of the spaces bequeathed by the Moorish culture that helped create the personality of this territory. The surface of the mountain can also be used for music events, and is laid out with a botanical garden of Mediterranean plants. During the development of the project we discovered Viollet-le-Duc's assertion, in his writings on the Alps, that 'God could not have invented nature without geometry.' Viollet-le-Duc used the same geometry that we have used to reconstruct the quarry of Denia, as the basic structure of the pyramidal massif of the Alps.

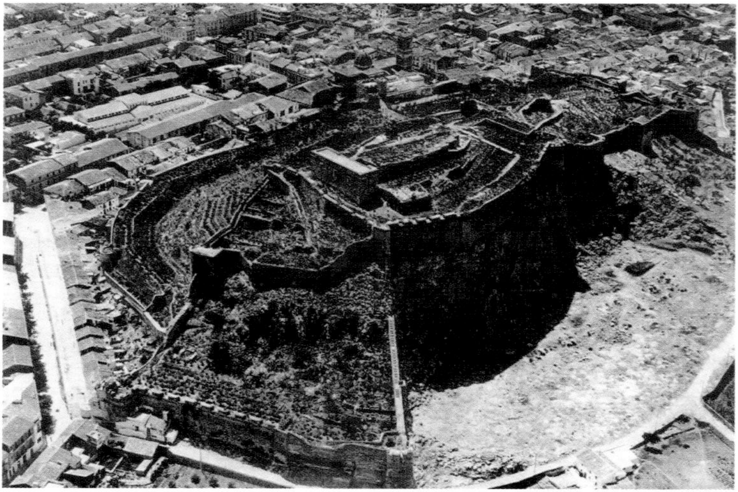

GEOGRAPHY

The quarry in Denia beneath the walls of the mediaeval castle

GEOMETRY

A three-dimensional plot

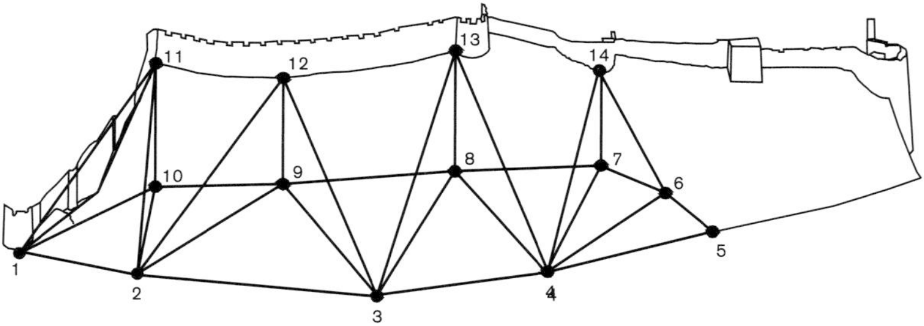

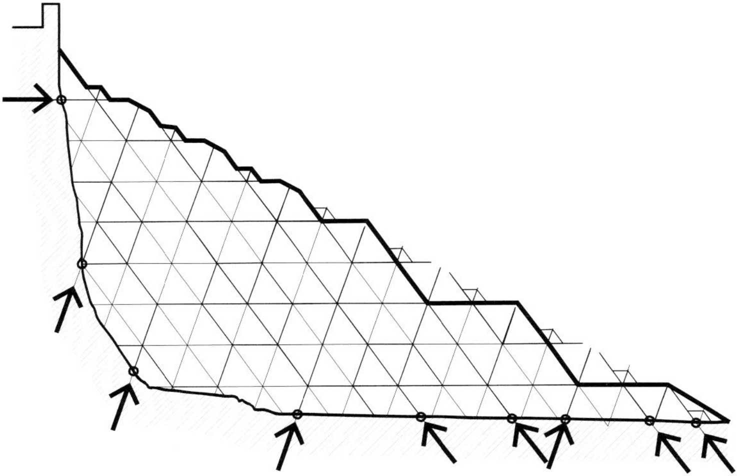

LOGIC

Regeneration of the volumetry on the basis of the internal forces

STRUCTURE

The multiscale surface emerges from the structure

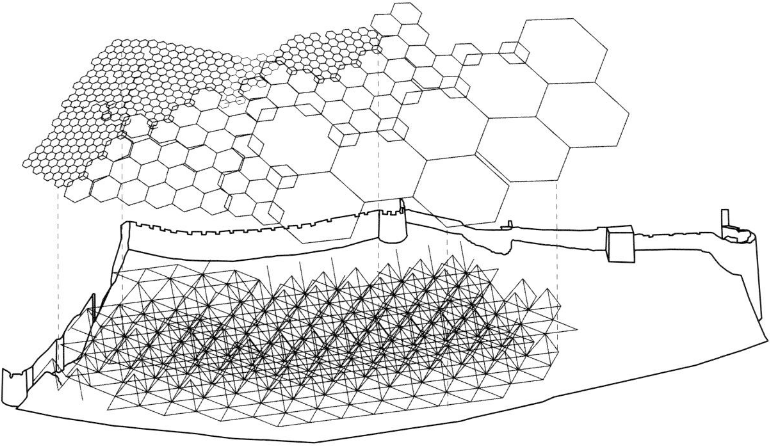

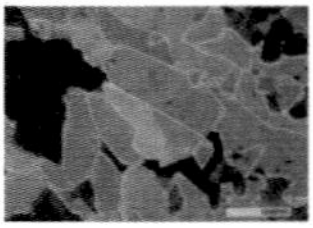

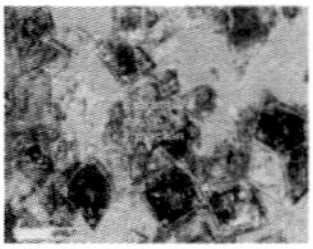

GEOGRAPHY

Pyramidal limestone rocks configured by their microscopic structure

GEOMETRY

Measuring a rock turns it into an architectural element

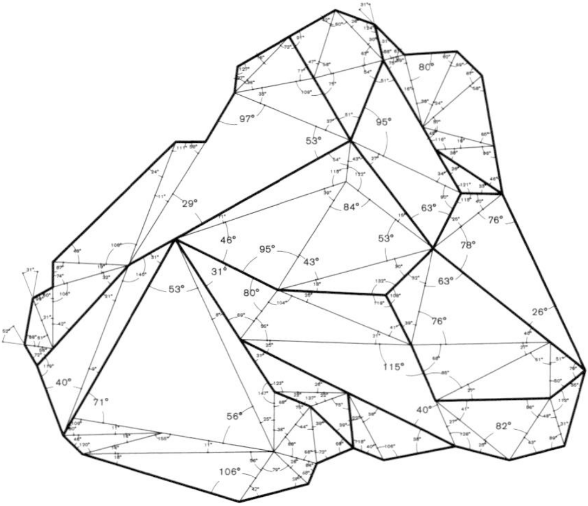

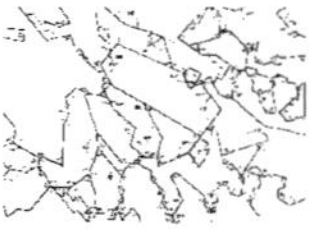

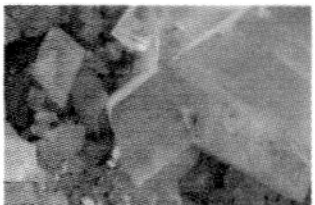

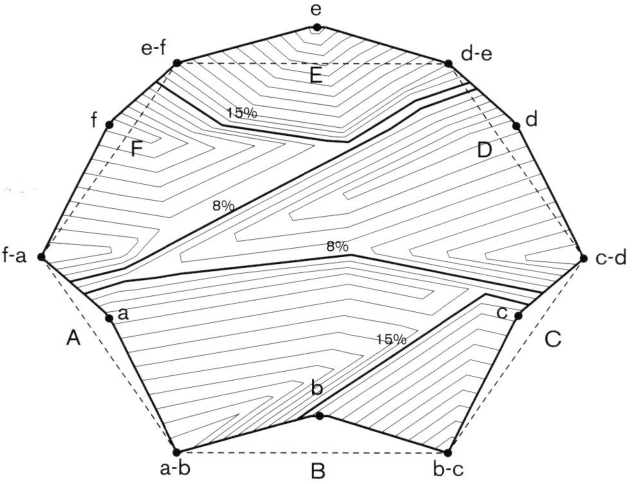

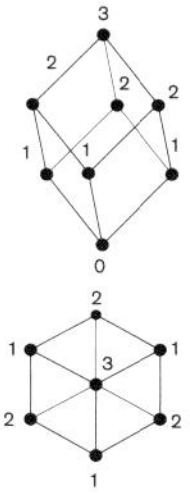

LOGIC

The connectible gene with internal slopes created from the rock crystals

STRUCTURE

A building traversed along its façade

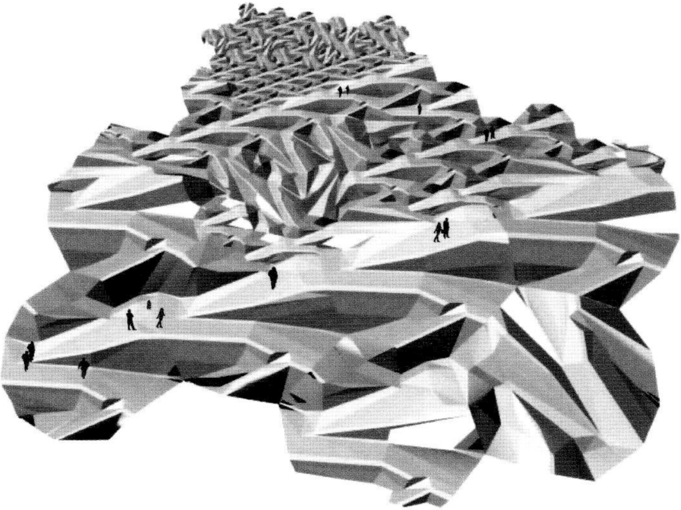

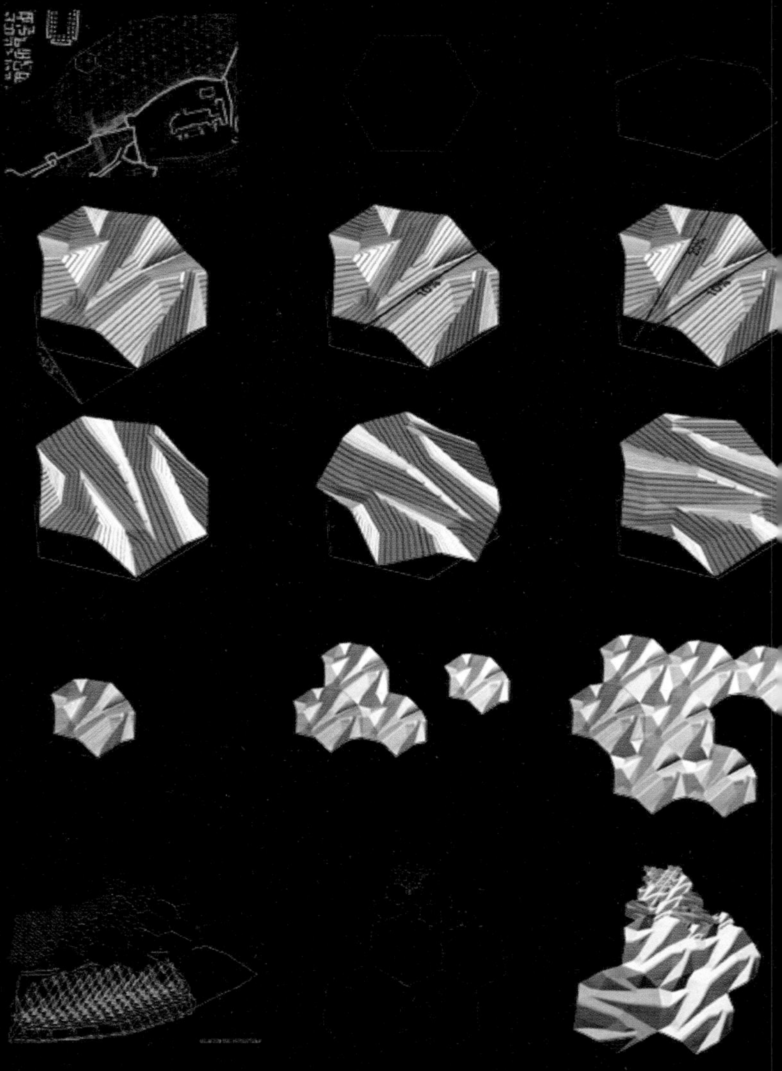

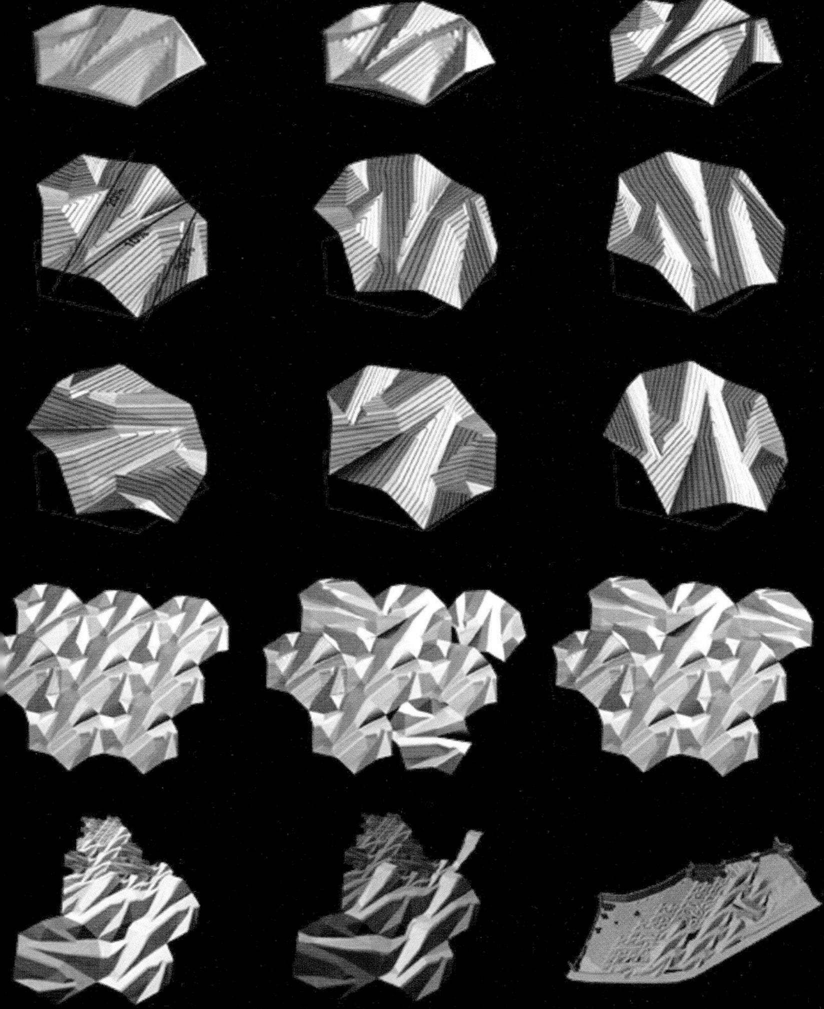

The skin is the path.

The last act of the quarry will be to reconstruct itself. For this reason the surface of the new construction must be of stone and facilitate the regeneration of the natural systems, both organic and inorganic, that are found in the Mediterranean mountains.

The project for the surface of the reconstructed mountain posited the question of whether to create an amorphous surface where the materiality would be precise, and on which mobility would be on roads dug out of the defined surface, in keeping with the model of the hermitages found on the tops of hills in various parts of the region. However, this approach did not seem valid, given that the opportunity of defining the geometry of this surface would serve to merge those places where human circulation is possible thanks to the gentle slope and others where access is more difficult. In order to rationalize the construction process, it was decided to work with the hexagon, supported on the underlying rhombohedric structure, as the basic unit on which to create a microtopography that would allow pedestrian circulation. This element would have a gradient of 30 degrees (similar to that of the original mountain) and would permit circulation on gradients varying from 8%, accessible to handicapped visitors, to the 30% of a stepped ramp. Like a natural system, the system to be developed had to permit a form of proliferation that was not modular, but more akin to the complex surfaces found in nature. The proposed solution is a piece in which all of the sides connect with one another, thereby creating interior micro routes whose gradients vary according to the position of the pieces. The pieces that permit a change of the scale have a special geometry. In this way the surface of the mountain emerges from the rhomboidal structure of its interior and invites a form of circulation similar to that of the Mediterranean mountains, in which each individual traces his or her own path.

Unit organization and position

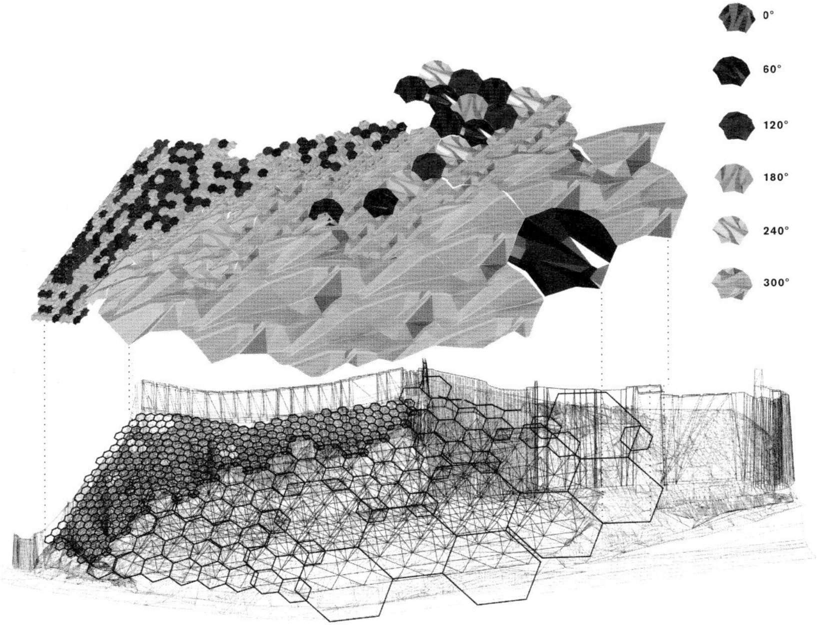

Material variation of units

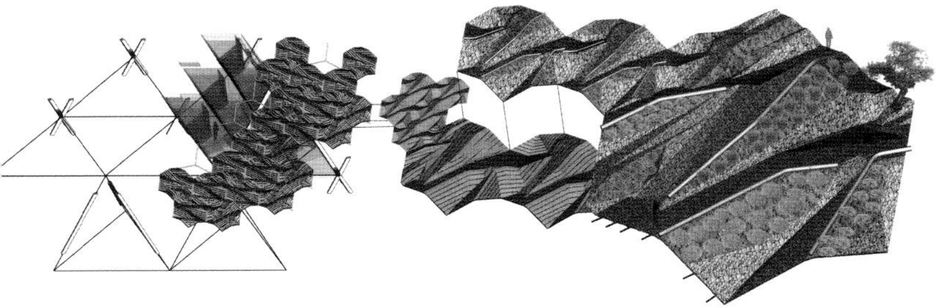

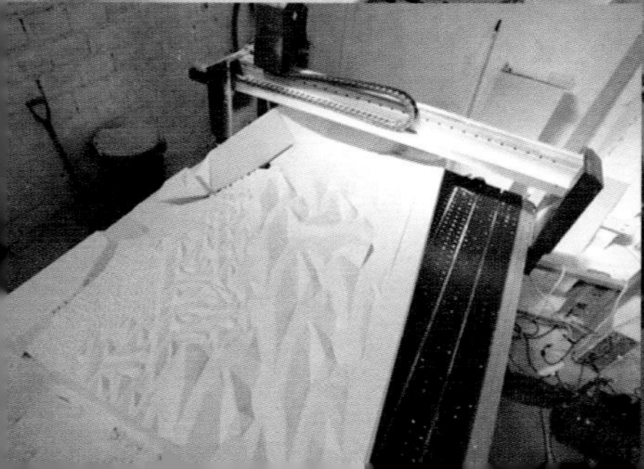

Denia Mountain

CNC milling machine

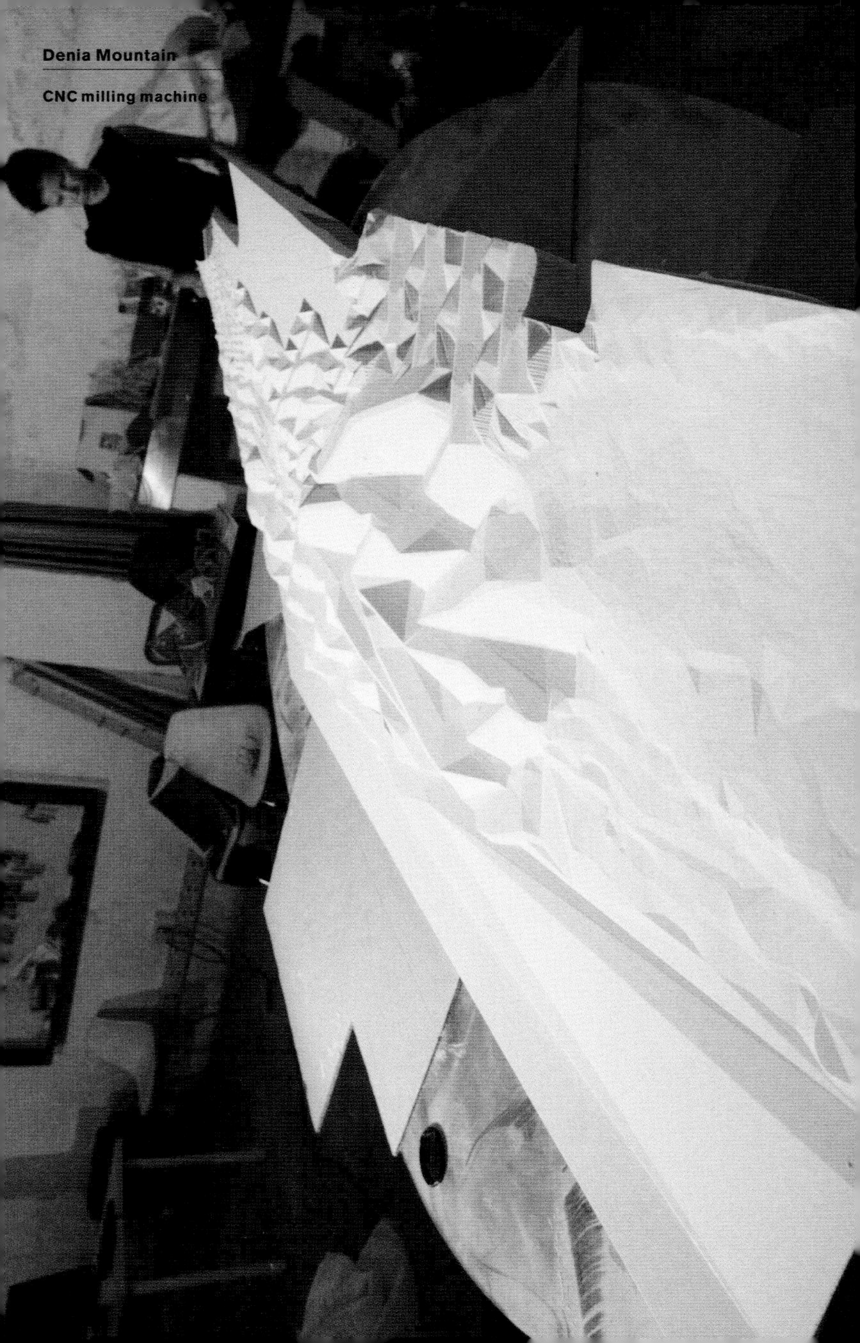

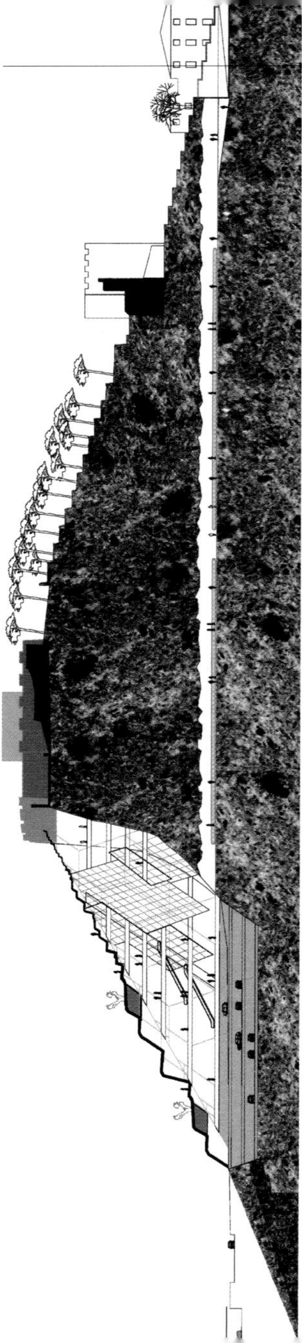

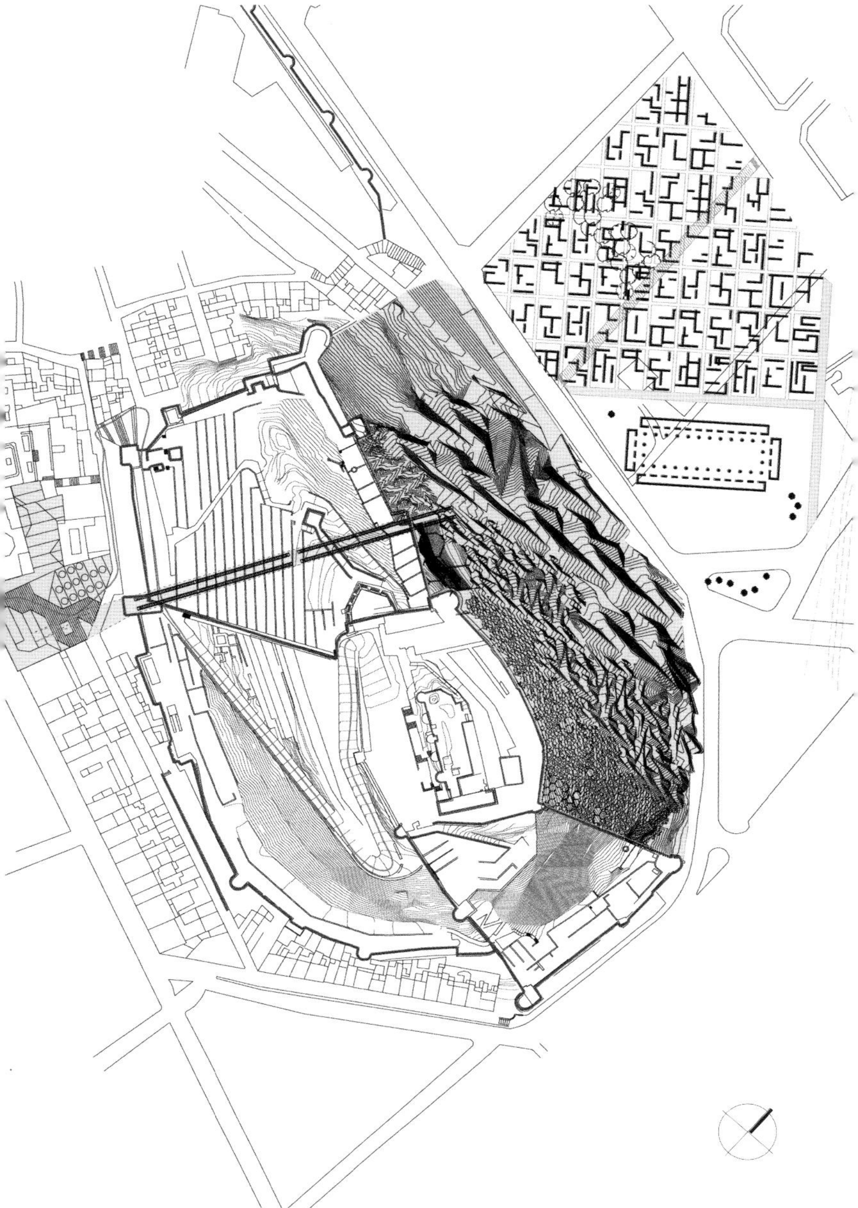

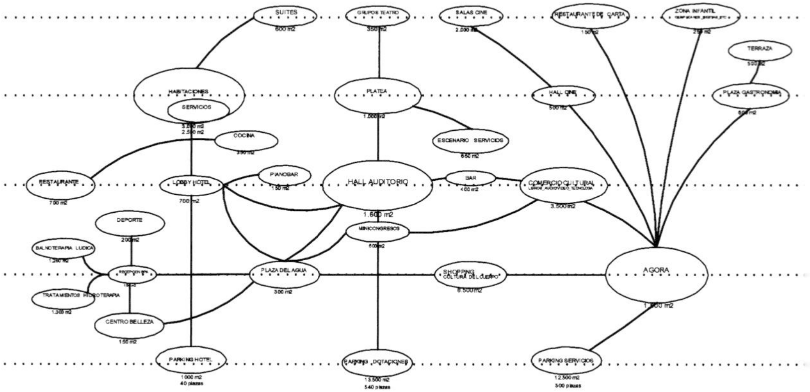

GEOGRAPHY

Programme organized according to functional relations

GEOMETRY

Implantation of a programme in an irregular space

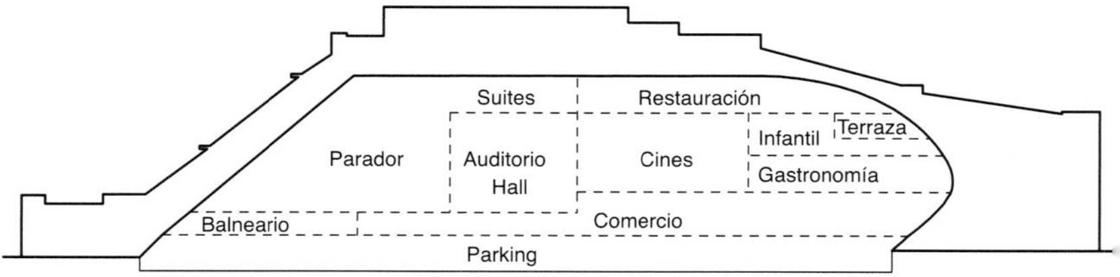

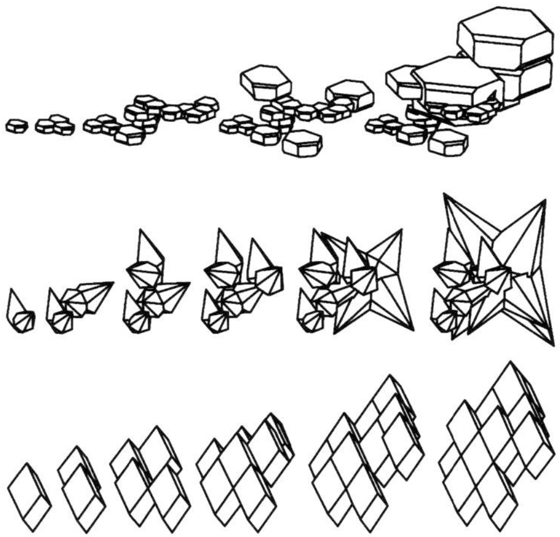

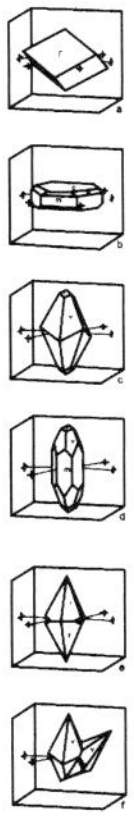

LOGIC

The rock's systems of crystallization define the construction of the space

STRUCTURE

Three crystalline voids structure the quarry in functional terms

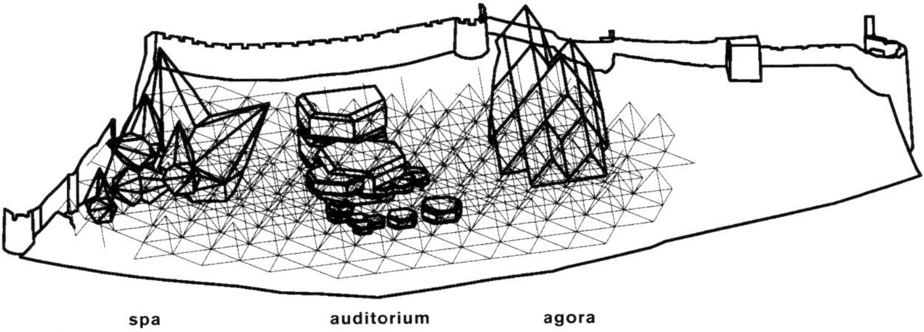

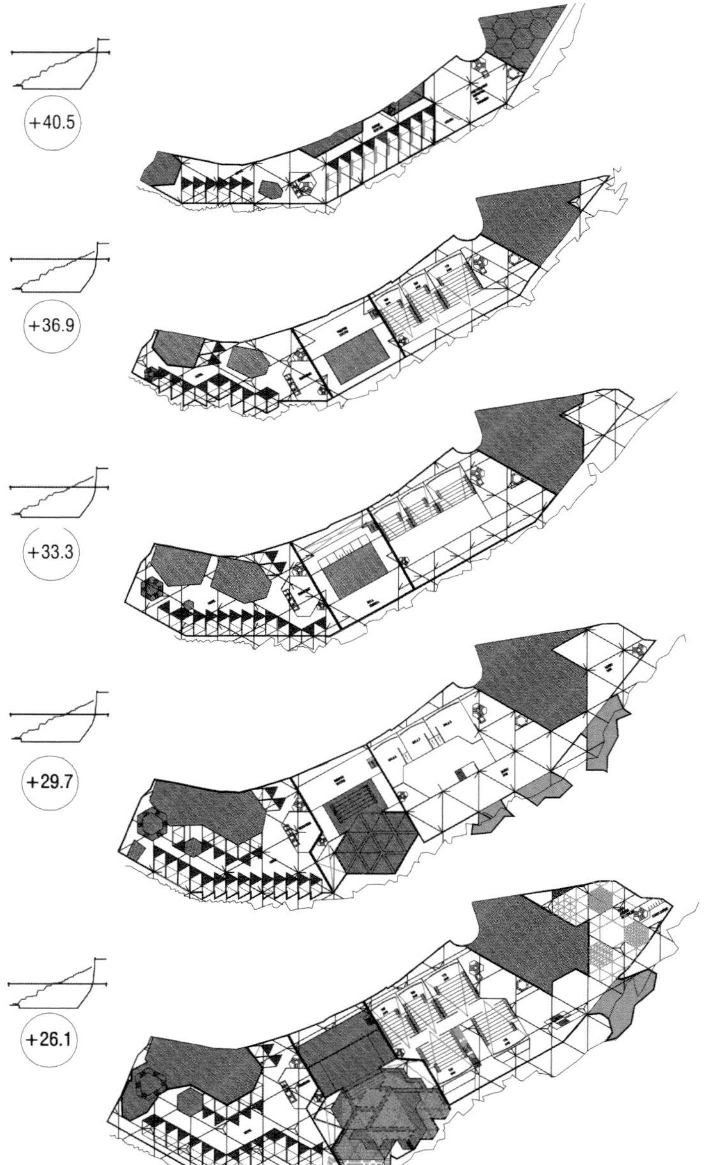
+40.5
+36.9
+33.3
+29.7
+26.1

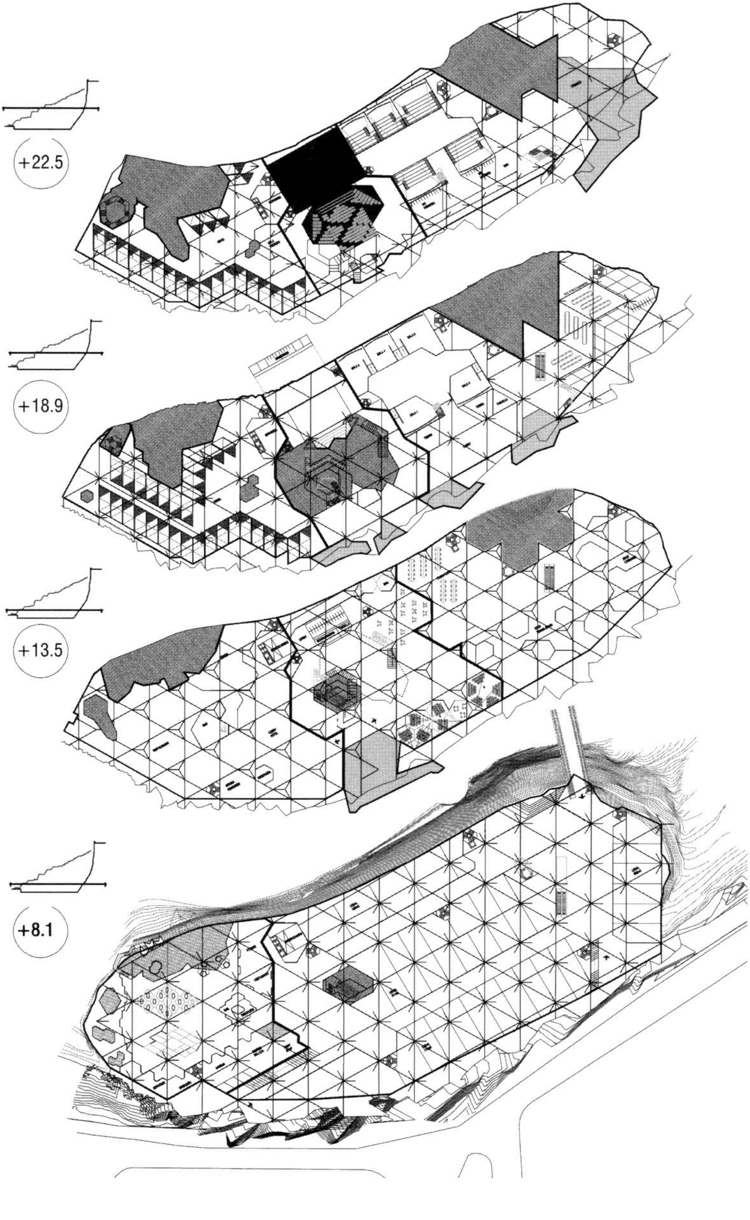
+22.5
+18.9
+13.5
+8.1

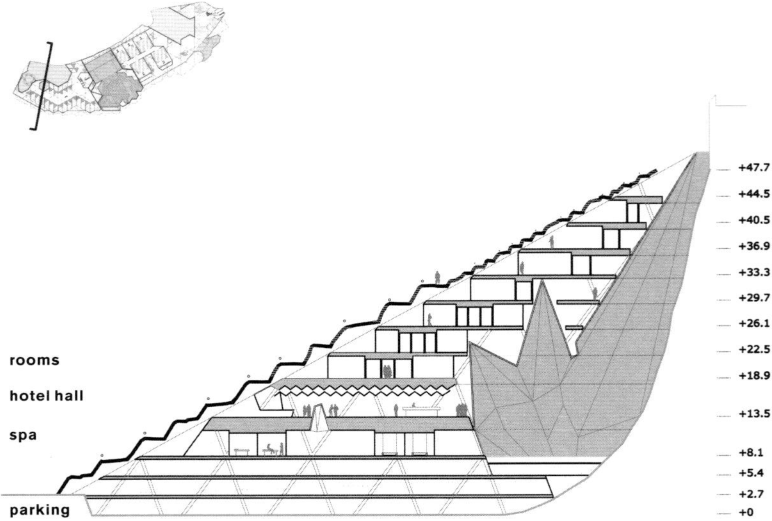
rooms
hotel hall
spa
parking
+47.7
+44.5
+40.5
+36.9
+33.3
+29.7
+26.1
+22.5
+18.9
+13.5
+8.1
+5.4
+2.7
+0

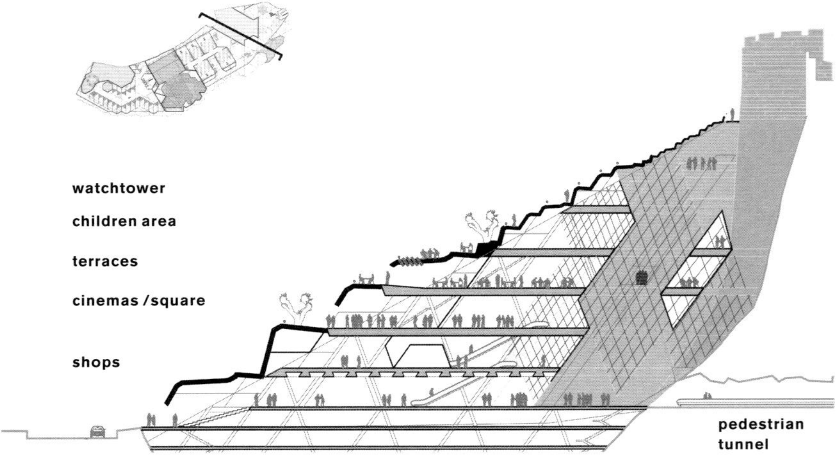
watchtower
children area
terraces
cinemas /square
shops
pedestrian
tunnel

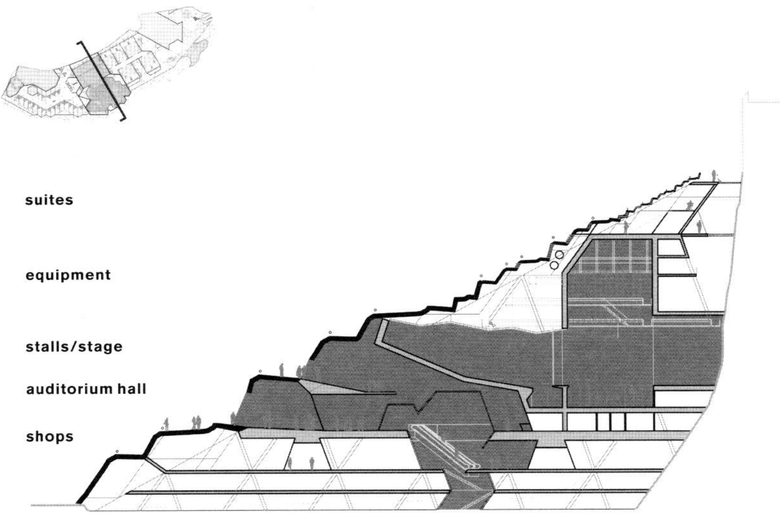
suites
equipment
stalls/stage
auditorium hall
shops

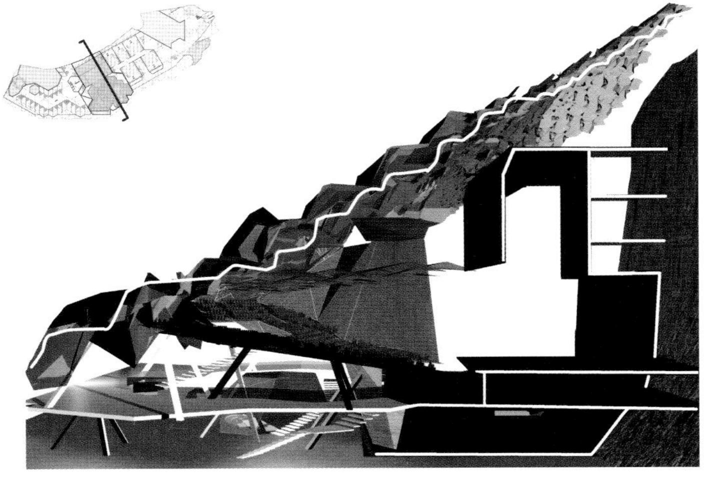

The PHANTOM of the OPERA
MAJESTIC THEATRE

Wrocław Expo

Wrocław, Poland. 2007

International competition

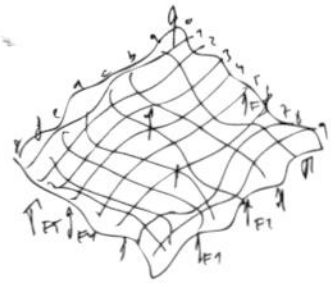

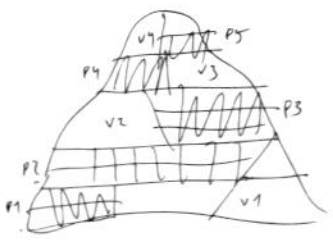

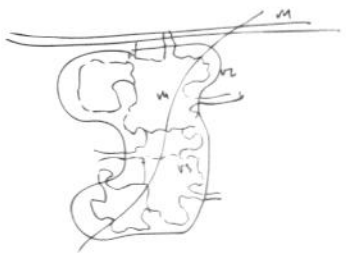

The Universal and International Expositions, like the Olympics, are events that tend to be staged either in emerging countries that are consolidating a position in the international panorama primarily in political or economic terms, or in central locations engaged in reasserting their international leadership. Wrocław, in the south of Poland, near the German border, belongs to the first category, as a place that is undergoing major political and economic transformation and hopes to attract the world's attention with a great event. In this endeavour it is competing with Tangiers in Morocco and Yeosu in Korea to host the forthcoming Expo 2012. In order to choose the master plan for the laying out of its Expo and a scheme for an emblematic building, the city organized an international competition, in which our proposal was selected for the design of the building. An Expo is an event that has no real identity in its own right. This being so, the ones that have gone down in history are those that have been very clearly symbolized by a landmark building that has come to constitute an icon of the city, such as Paxton's Crystal Palace in London, the Eiffel Tower in Paris, the Atomium in Brussels or Buckminster Fuller's Dome in Montreal.

Wrocław stands at a crossroads, a territory occupied throughout the course of history by different cultures and empires, in which the rivers Oder and Olawa meet. In the light of this we saw crossing and cross-fertilization as fundamental attributes of the icon of this Expo, the key theme of which will be 'the culture of leisure in the world's economies.' Two of Poland's outstanding buildings of the 20th century are the Hala Ludowe or Centennial Hall by Max Berg in Wrocław (completed in 1914, and in its day the largest concrete dome in the world) and the Tower of Culture and Science in Warsaw, a potent symbol of a foreign power in the centre of Warsaw that nevertheless represents a surprising typology of high-rise, containing cinemas, exhibition spaces and events venues, offices and other culture-related services. The Centennial Hall was built under German dominance, and the Warsaw Tower under de facto Soviet occupation.

Poland is starting on a new phase with its full integration into the European Union, and is due to receive a massive amount of funds with which to construct infrastructures and amenities. In view of this, this Expo, its urban setting and its principal buildings are an important opportunity to define the identity of a new turn, political, economic and social, just as previously occurred in countries such as Spain. Our building is located, volumetrically speaking, between the Centennial Hall and the Tower of Culture and Science in Warsaw. In its initial phase it was conceived as an accumulation of generic and as yet imprecise programmes that could include offices, an auditorium, a leisure centre and exhibition spaces that generated its identity on the basis of its mountain-like form. The building's activities would be allowed to expand onto exterior terraces, created directly by the topography of the building, and onto its roof, directly accessible by way of a cable car from the park in which the building stands. The topography of the mountain is such that its south face forms an angle to accommodate a bank of photovoltaic panels on the façade which will generate part of the energy consumed by the building.

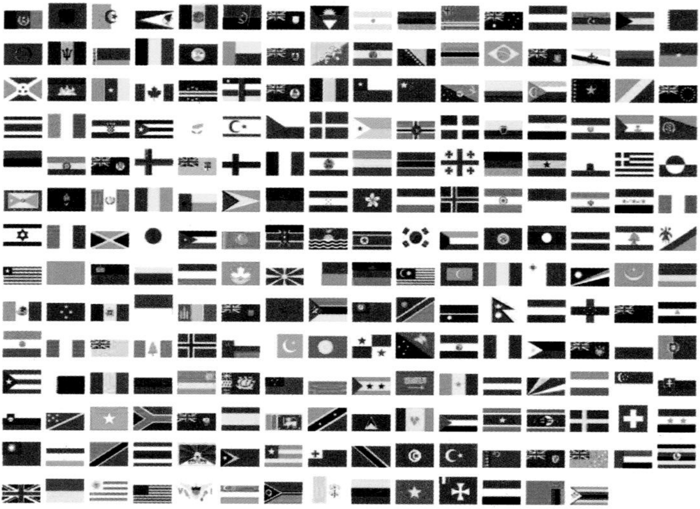

GEOGRAPHY

A world of flags

GEOMETRY

Sequence of Expos around the world

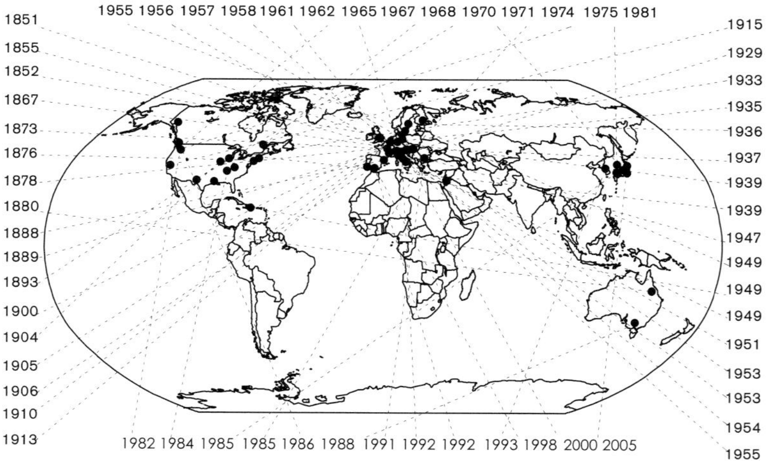

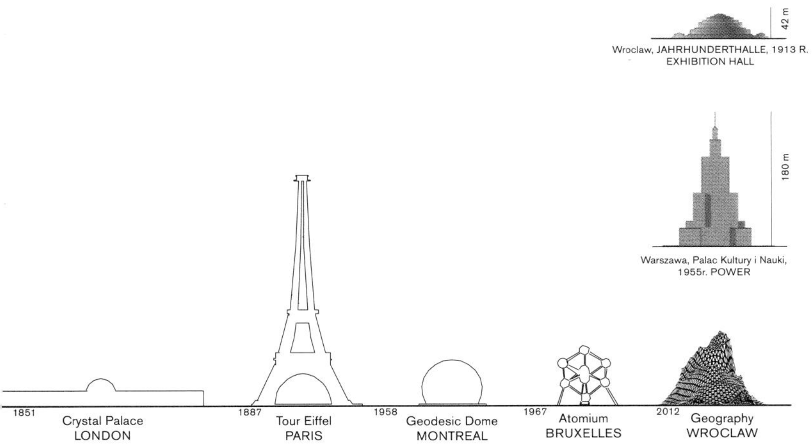

LOGIC

An Expo does not have an identity: its icons create one

STRUCTURE

Iconic structure based on functional accumulation

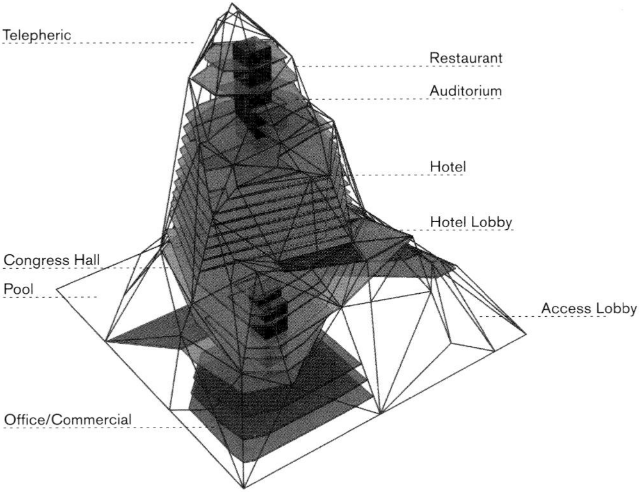

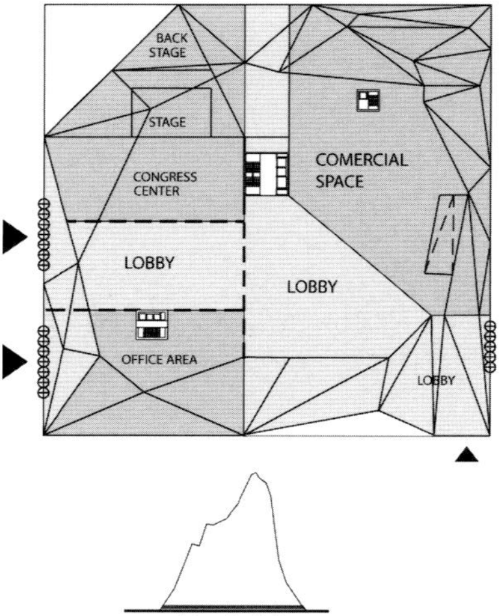

N± 0.00

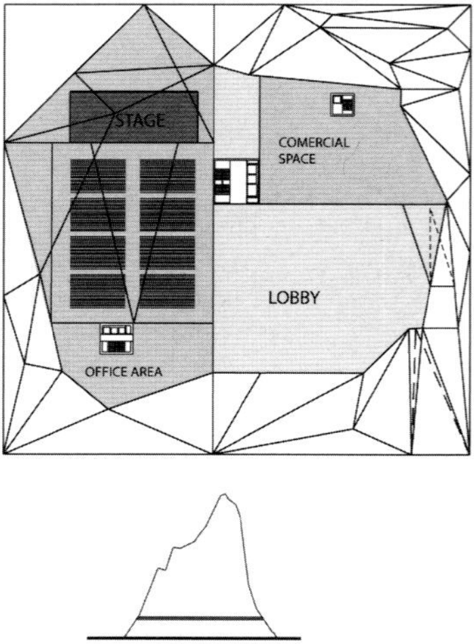

N +12.00

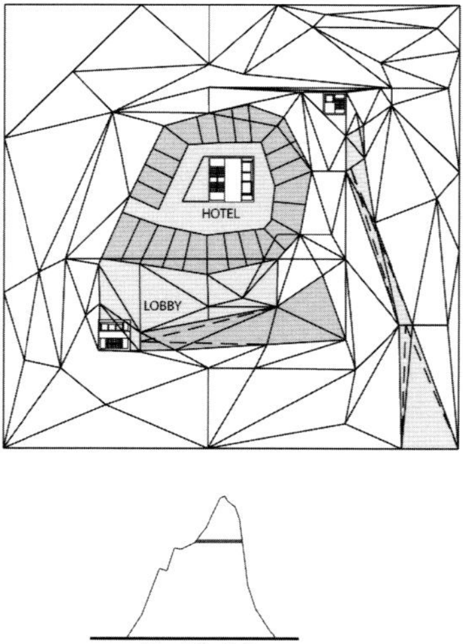

N+65.30

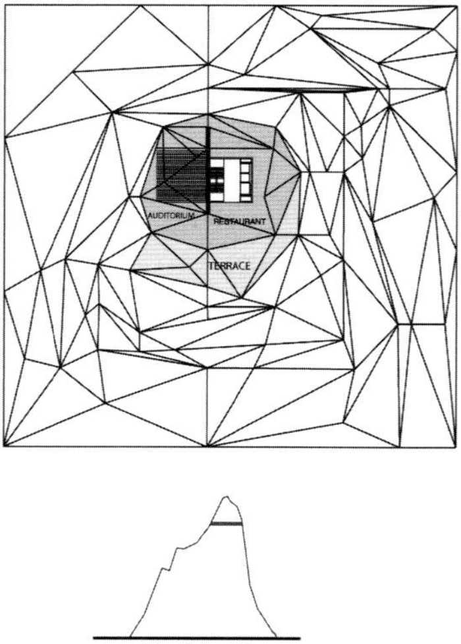

N+76.40

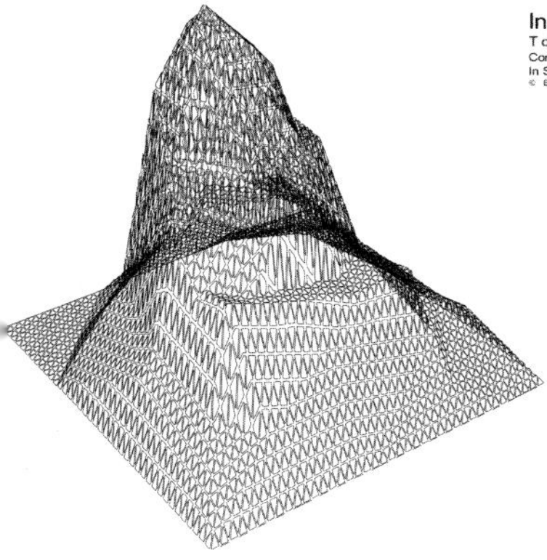

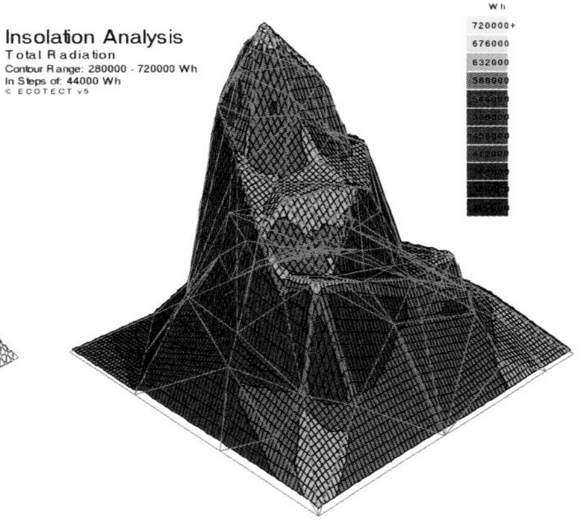
Insolation Analysis
Total Radiation
Contour Range: 280000 - 720000 Wh
In Steps of: 44000 Wh
© ECOTECT v5
Wh
720000+
676000
632000
588000

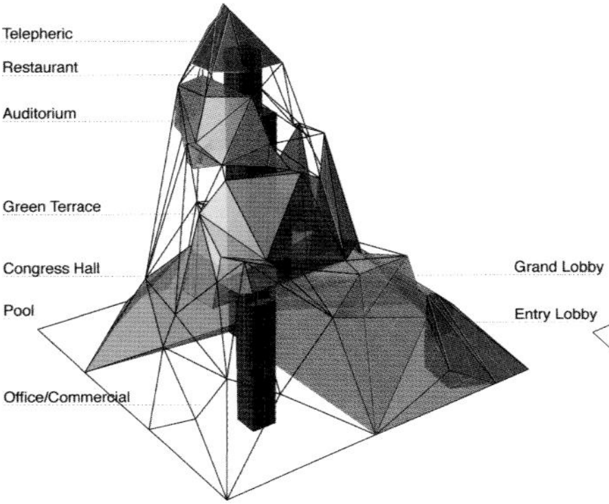
Telepheric
Restaurant
Auditorium
Green Terrace
Congress Hall
Pool
Office/Commercial
Grand Lobby
Entry Lobby

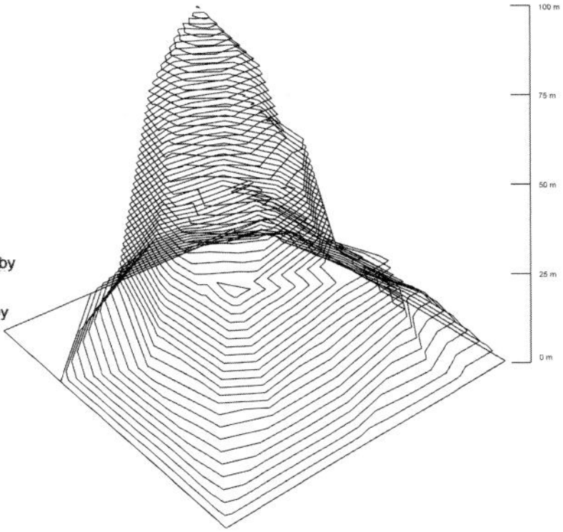
100 m
75 m
50 m
25 m
0 m

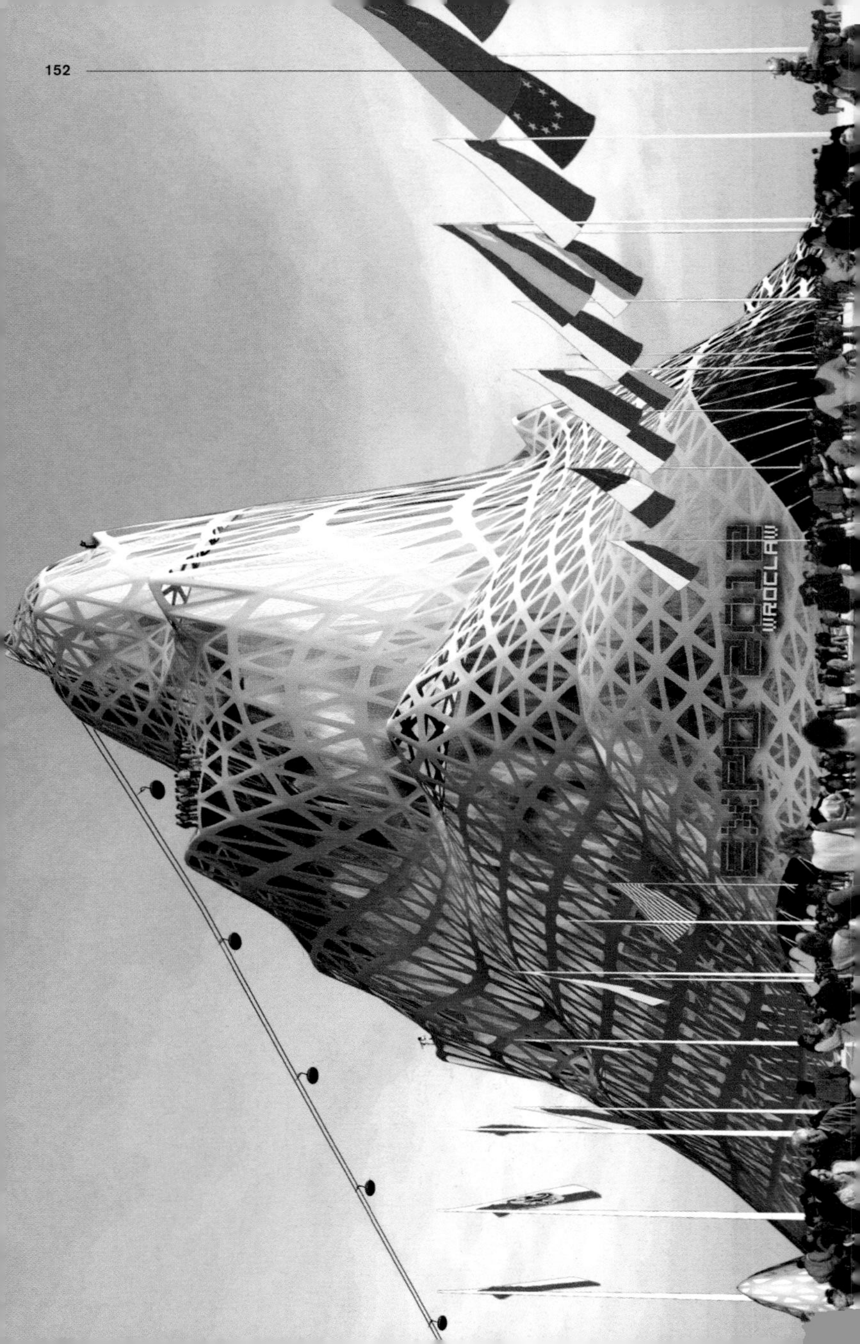
EXPO 2012
WROCLAW

EXPO 2012
WROCLAW

Expo 2012
WROCLAW 2012
Kultura Czasu Wolnego
w Gospodarkach Świata
The Culture Of Leisure
In World Economies

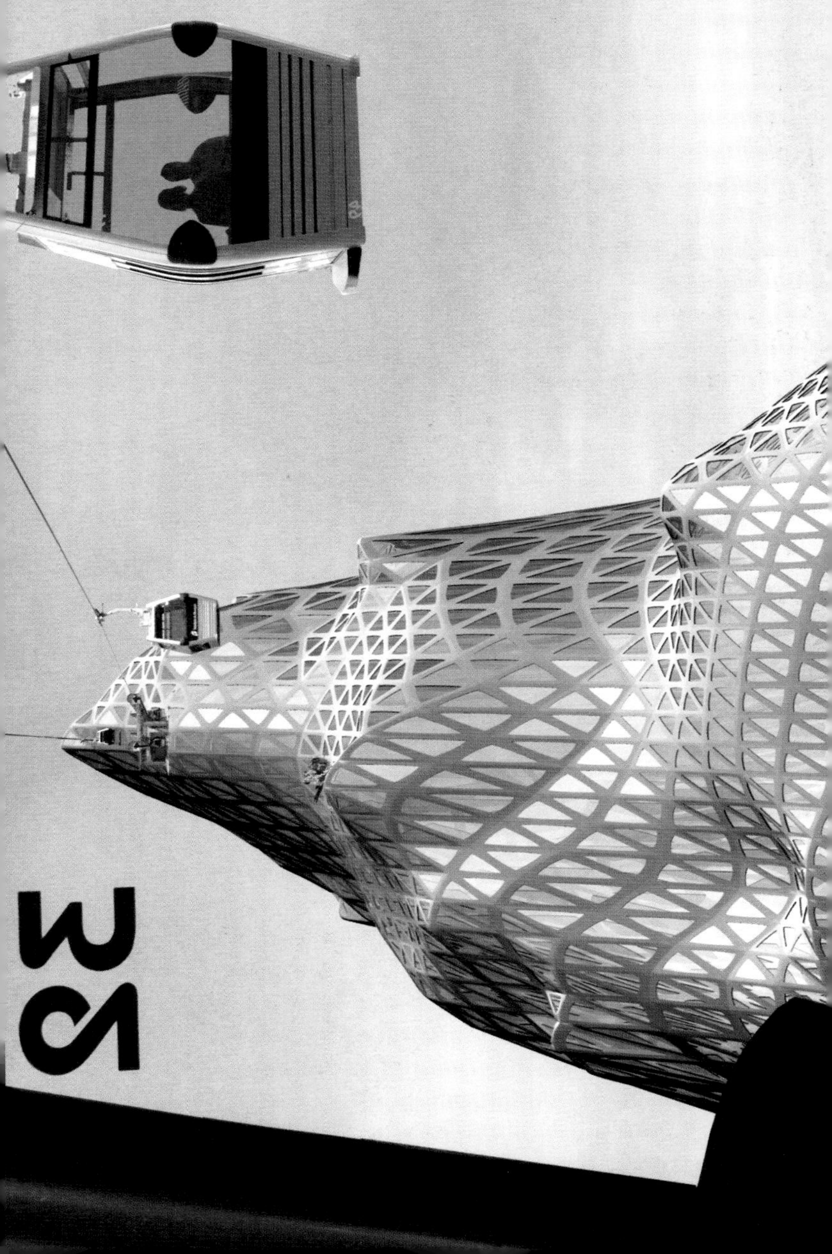

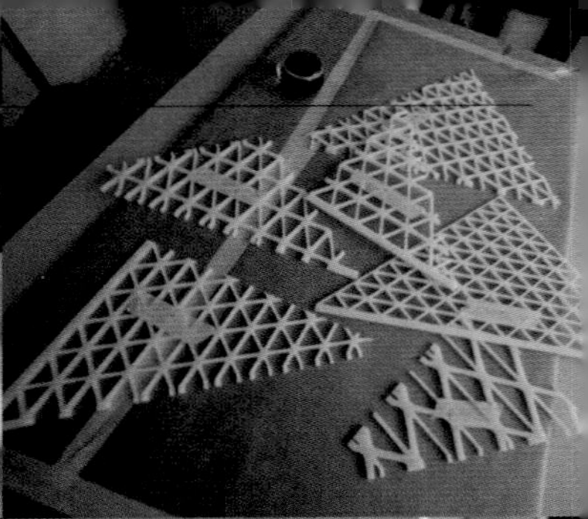

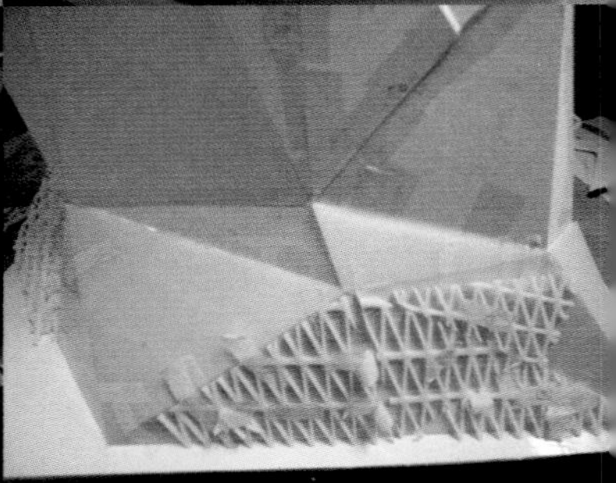

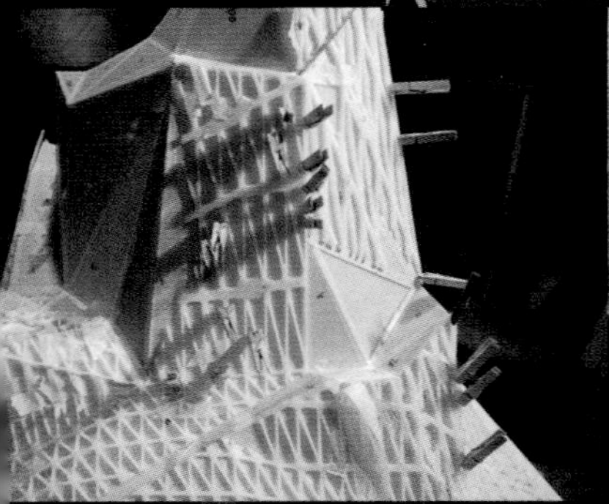

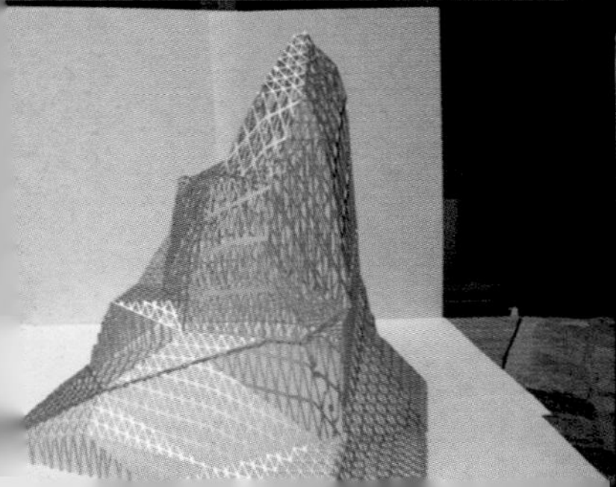

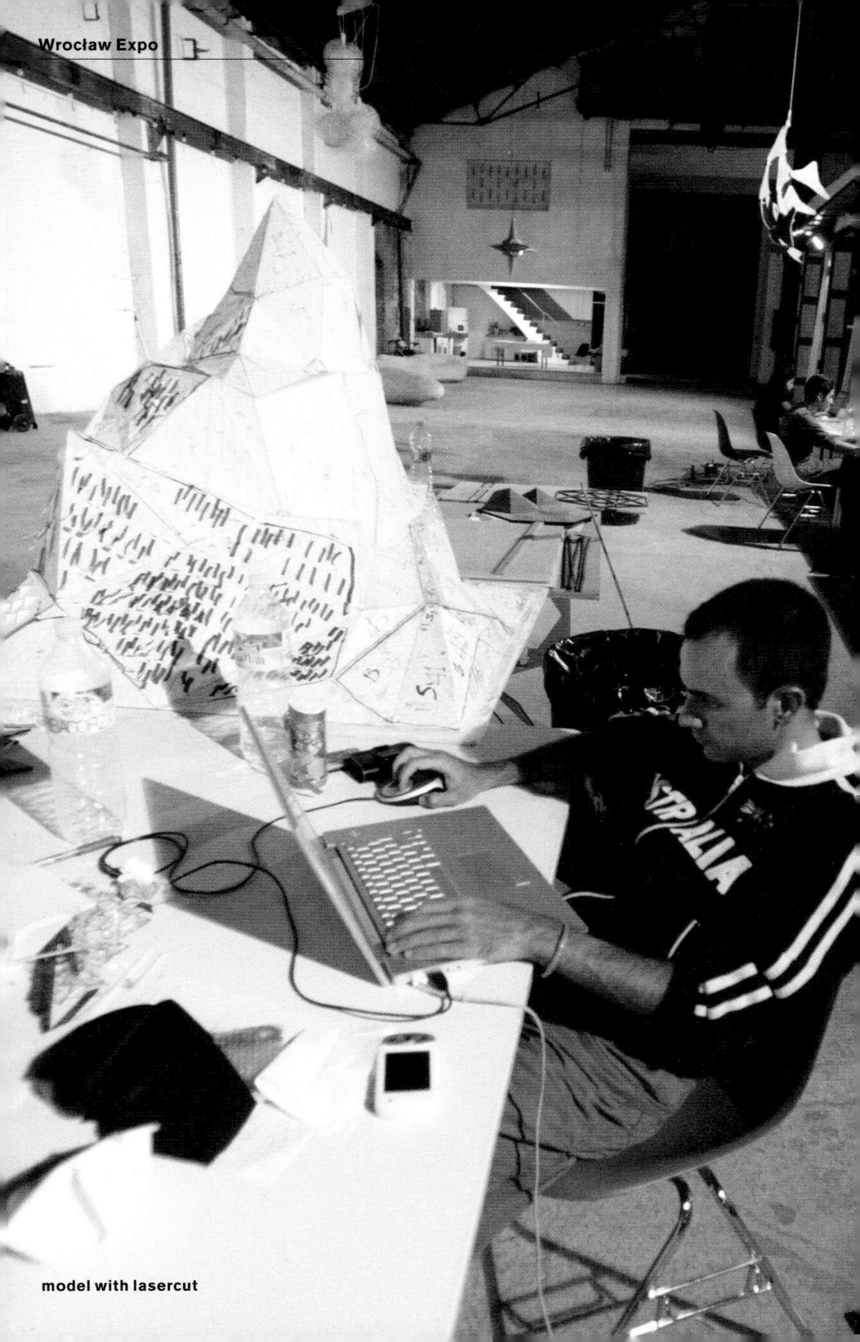

model with lasercut

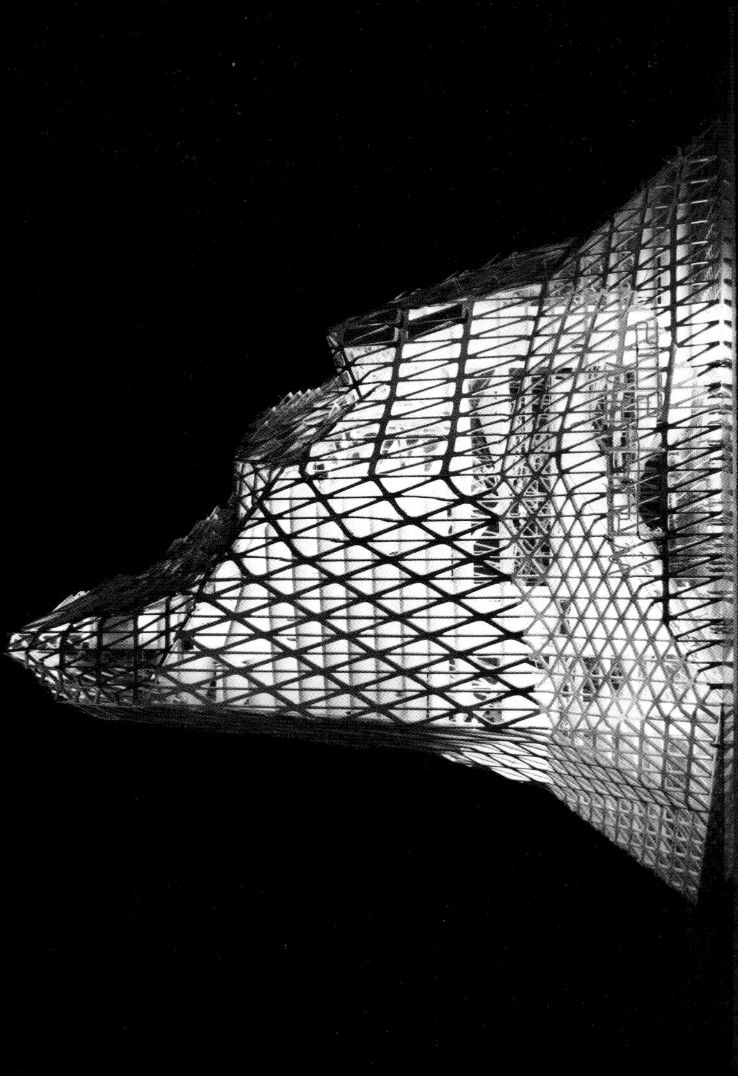

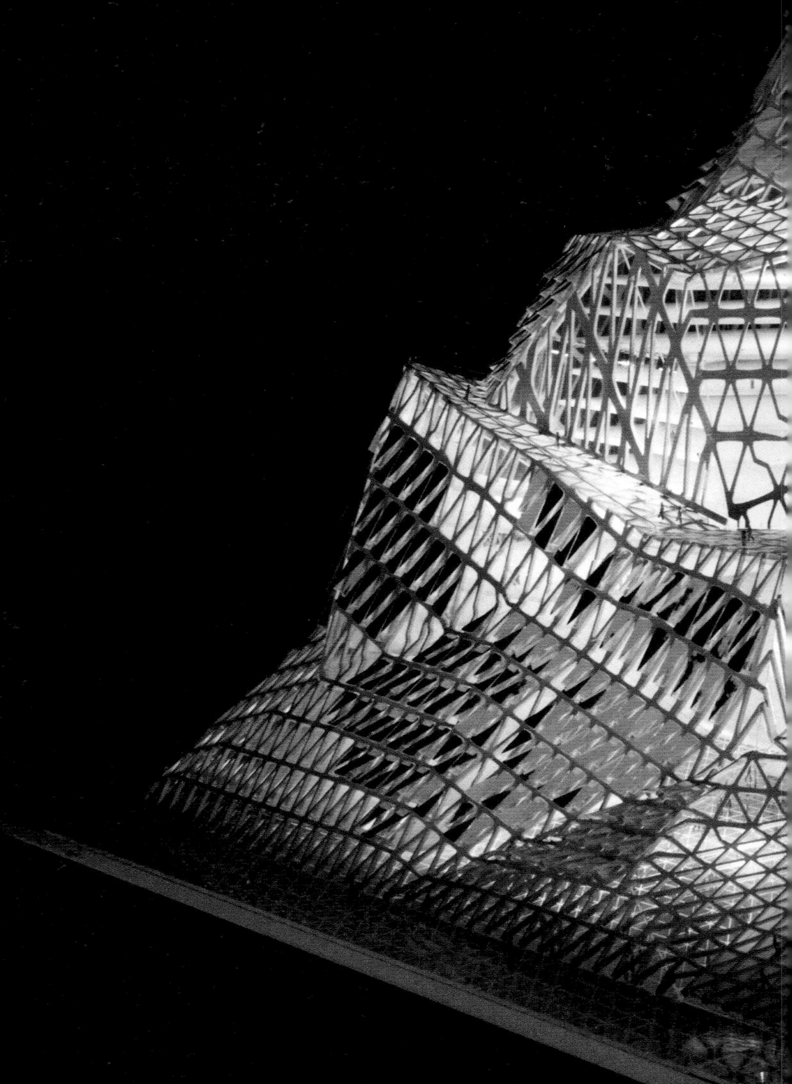

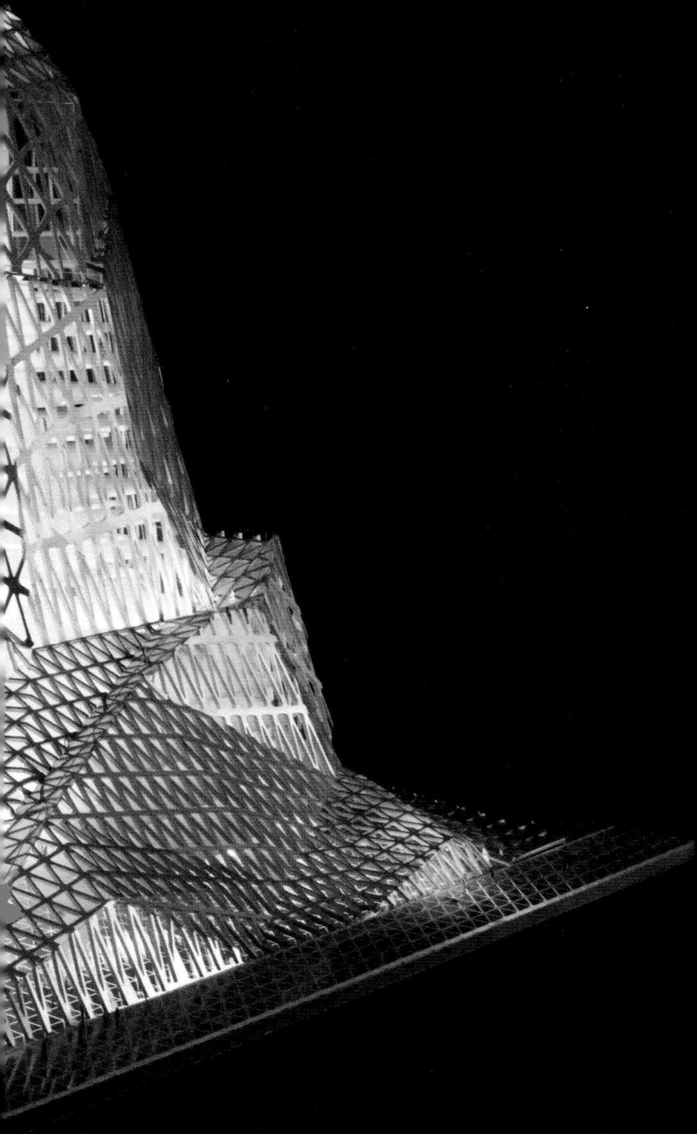

Shanghai Expo 2010

Spanish Pavilion
Shanghai. China

3rd Prize national competition
Project. 2007

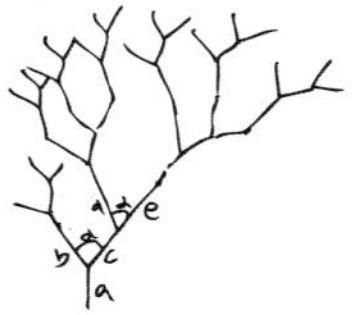

Arborescence
/08

The Spanish Pavilion for the Shanghai Expo projects itself as a recognizable space which connects with the culture of Spain and generates synergies in the Chinese context. The pavilion is clearly iconic and develops the theme of Expo —'Better city, Better Life'— to propose that cities be developed on the basis of a formal and functional hybridization of the natural and the artificial. The scheme creates a plantation of artificial trees, surrounded by the fruits of Spanish agriculture, especially orange and lemon trees. The trees, of laser-cut sheet metal, will constitute the physical structure of the building, and will also contain its metabolic systems. Photovoltaic panels on the tops of these trees will provide the building with energy, which will be distributed through the structural elements to the spotlights that will indirectly illuminate the interior spaces. The dimensions of the structure (which in places reaches an internal height of five metres) are sufficient to house the air conditioning and water vapour systems. The elevators are also incorporated into these structures. This makes it possible to create large empty spaces to accommodate the activities of the Expo. The same principle has been applied to a series of smaller pavilions to be constructed all over Spain.

The project serves to explore the development of a parametric arboreal structure based on the L-system in which a constant section is applied to the three-dimensional structure. The proliferation of trees is sufficient to allow them to be grouped into a hypostyle structure.

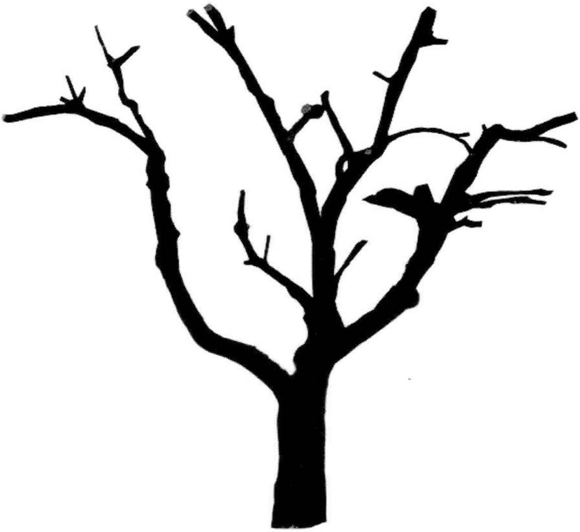

GEOGRAPHY

Natural arboreal structure

GEOMETRY

Order of development

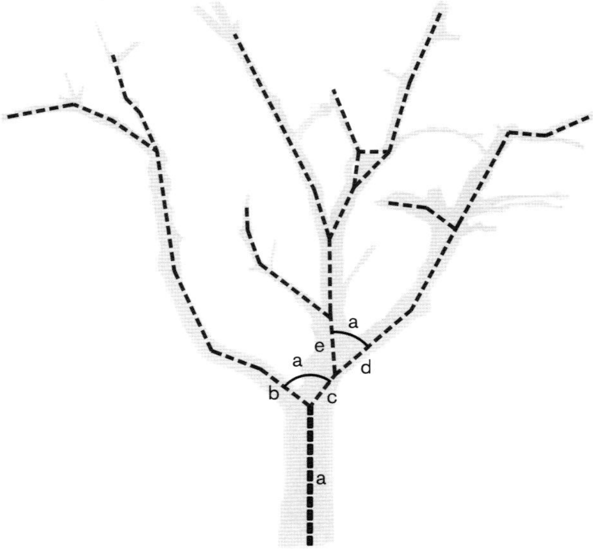

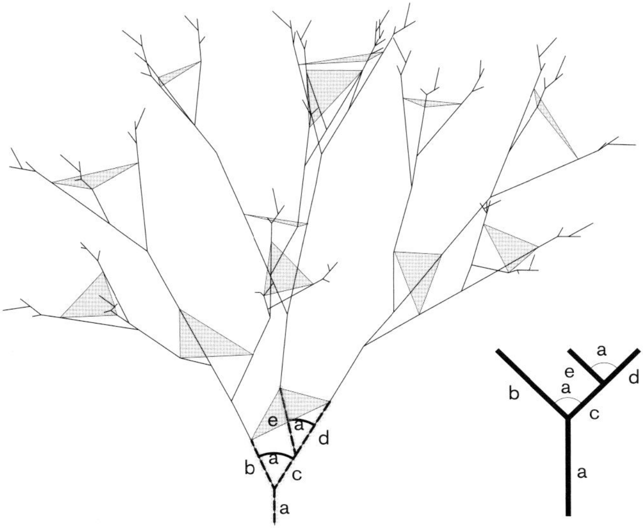

LOGIC

A geometric growth pattern

STRUCTURE

An artificial arboreal structure

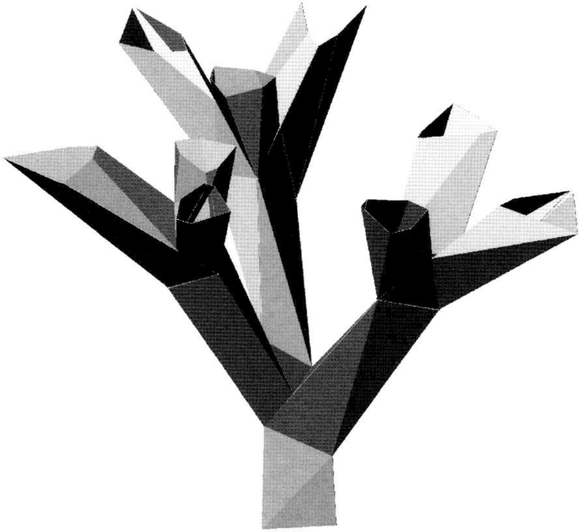

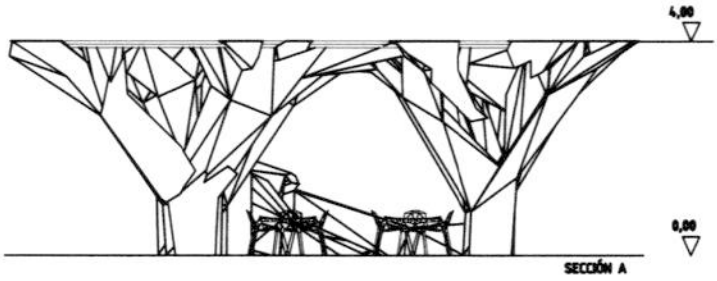
4,00
0,00
SECCIÓN A

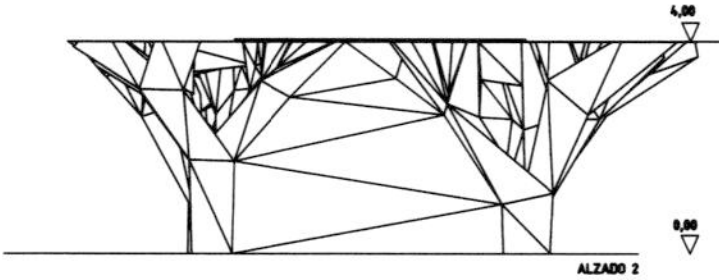
4,00
0,00
ALZADO 2

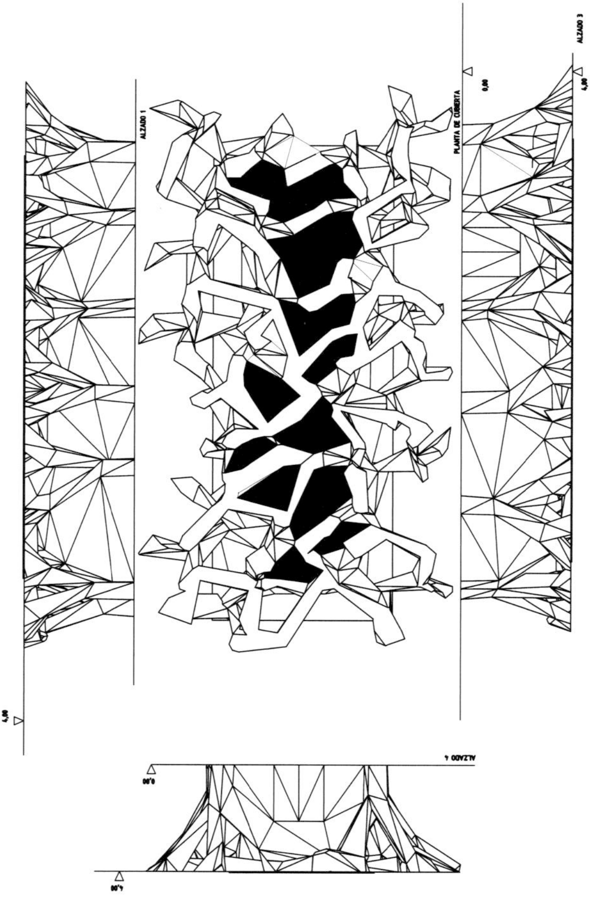
ALZADO 1
PLANTA DE CUBIERTA
0,00
ALZADO 3
4,00
4,00
ALZADO 4
0,00
4,00

3D print

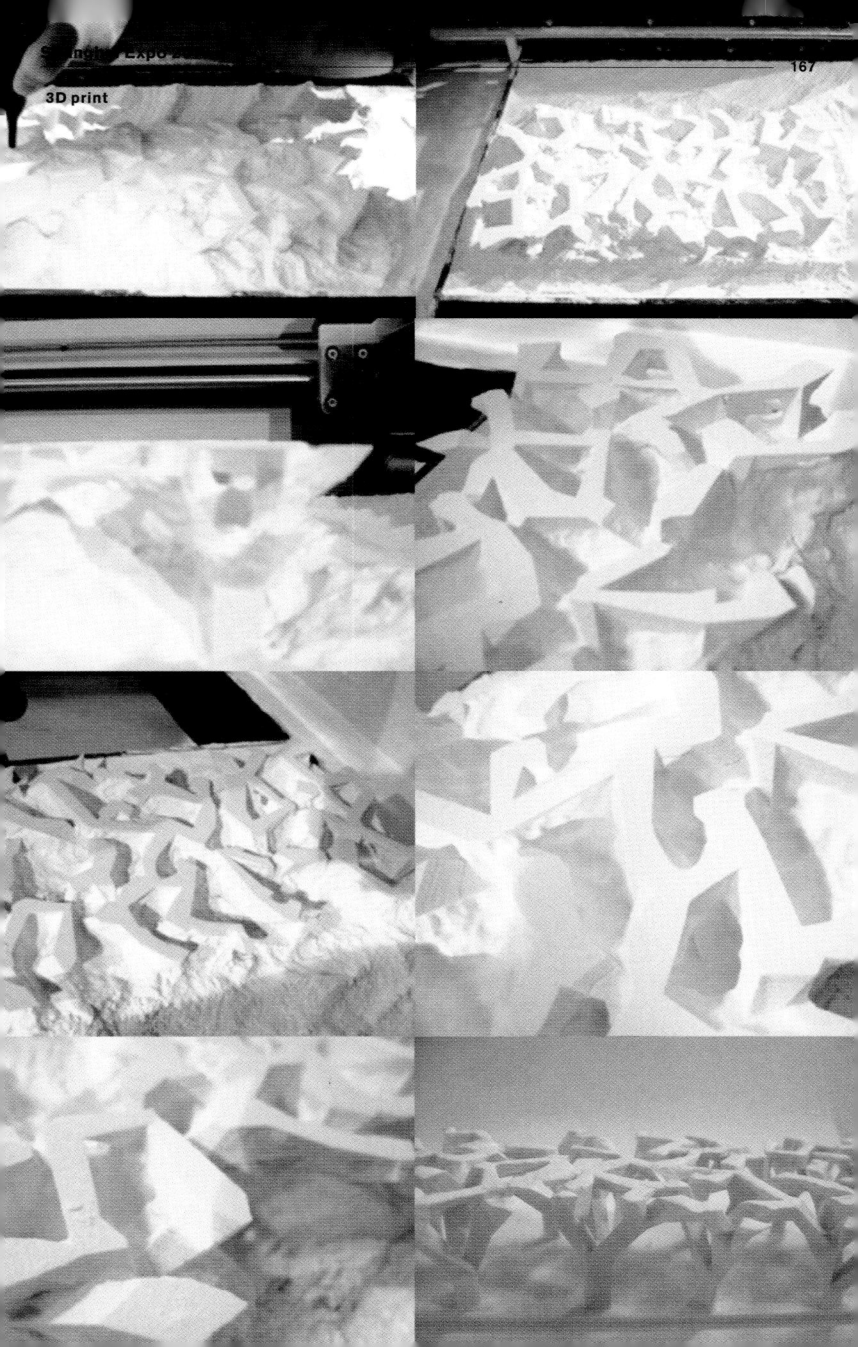

A **B** **C**

A1

a=5.1620
b=3.6870
c=0.9830
d=2.9500
e=2.2120
α=52.9192°

B1

a=5.1620
b=4.9160
c=3.4410
d=2.2120
e=1.4750
α=52.9192°

C1

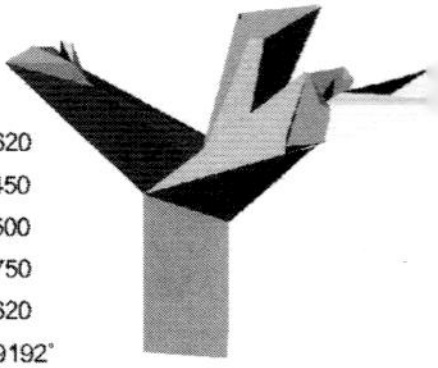

a=5.1620
b=6.1450
c=2.9500
d=1.4750
e=5.1620
α=52.9192°

A2

a=3.7470
b=6.2450
c=2.9140
d=1.8740
e=1.2490
α=49.3353°

B2

a=4.4250
b=6.1450
c=2.9500
d=1.4750
e=5.1620
α=49.3353°

C2

a=4.4250
b=4.9160
c=2.4580
d=5.1620
e=4.4250
α=49.3353°

A3

a=3.4940
b=5.8230
c=2.7950
d=1.3970
e=4.8910
α=45.5730°

B3

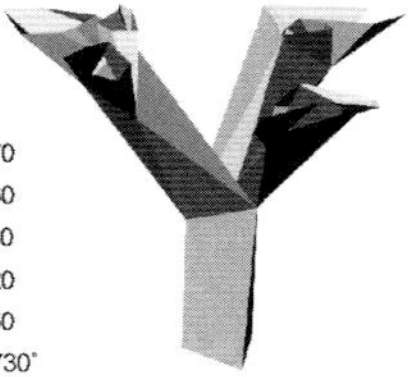

a=3.6870
b=4.9160
c=2.4580
d=5.1620
e=4.4250
α=45.5730°

C3

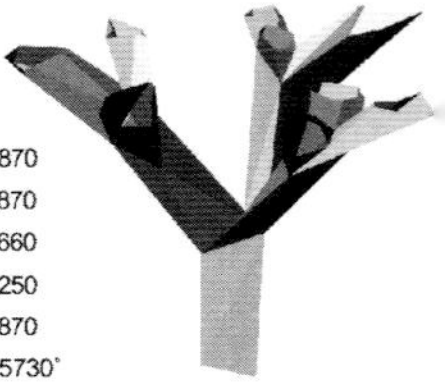

a=3.6870
b=3.6870
c=1.9660
d=4.4250
e=3.6870
α=45.5730°

A4

a=2.9500
b=4.9160
c=2.4580
d=5.1620
e=4.4250
α=41.6342°

B4

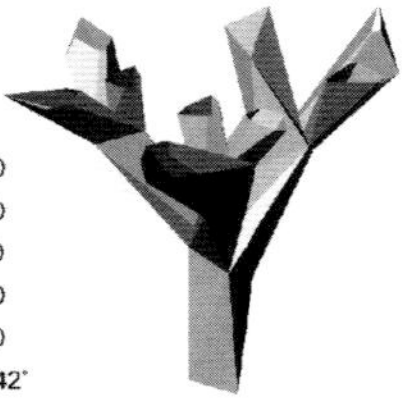

a=2.9500
b=3.6870
c=1.9660
d=4.4250
e=3.6870
α=41.6342°

C4

a=3.8370
b=3.1970
c=1.9180
d=4.7960
e=3.8370
α=41.6342°

A **B** **C**

A5

a=2.4680
b=4.1130
c=2.1940
d=4.9360
e=4.1130
α=37.5235°

B5

a=2.6230
b=2.9150
c=1.7490
d=4.3720
e=3.4980
α=37.5235°

C5

a=1.4750
b=4.9160
c=4.9160
d=2.9500
e=3.6870
α=33.2482°

A6

a=1.9170
b=3.1950
c=3.1950
d=4.7930
e=3.8340
α=33.2482°

B6

a=1.9290
b=4.8230
c=2.5720
d=5.7880
e=4.8230
α=33.2483°

C6

a=1.4750
b=4.9160
c=4.9160
d=2.9500
e=3.6870
α=33.2482°

A7

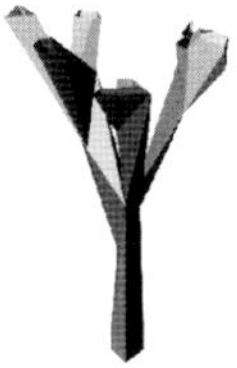

a=4.6010
b=1.9170
c=1.5340
d=4.6010
e=3.4510
α=28.8190°

B7

a=3.6250
b=3.0200
c=2.7180
d=3.6250
e=1.8120
α=28.8190°

C7

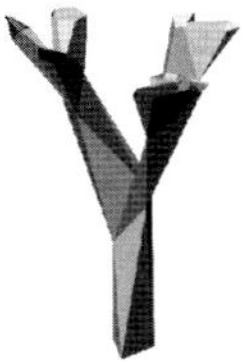

a=2.9500
b=3.6870
c=4.4250
d=2.9500
e=3.4890
α=28.8190°

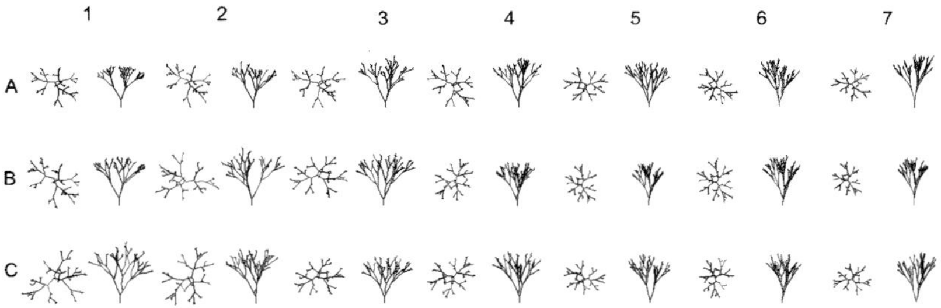

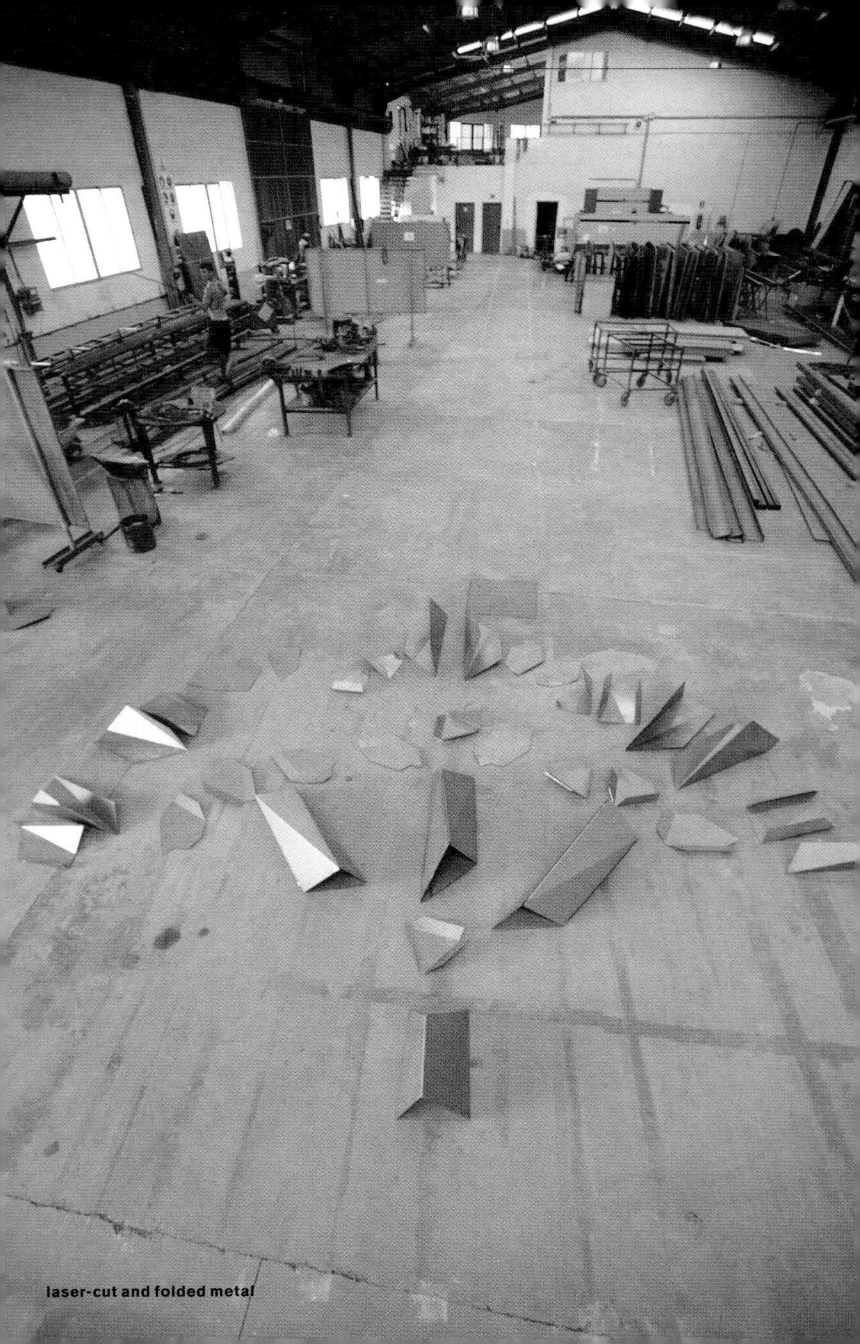

laser-cut and folded metal

西班牙

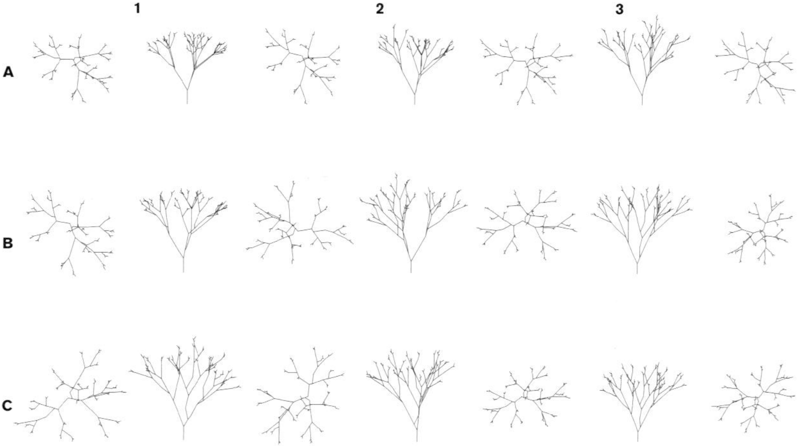

4

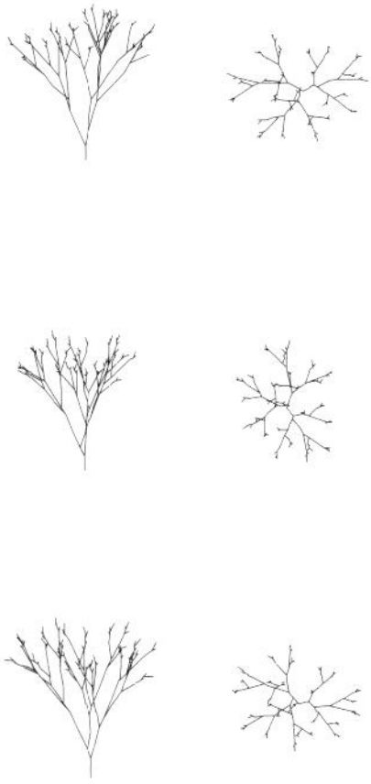

5

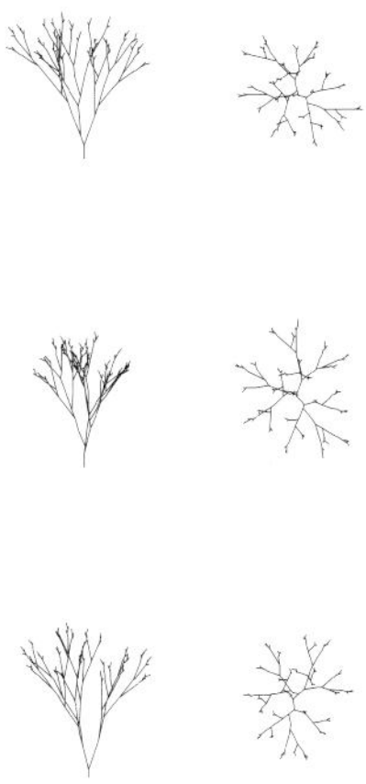

6

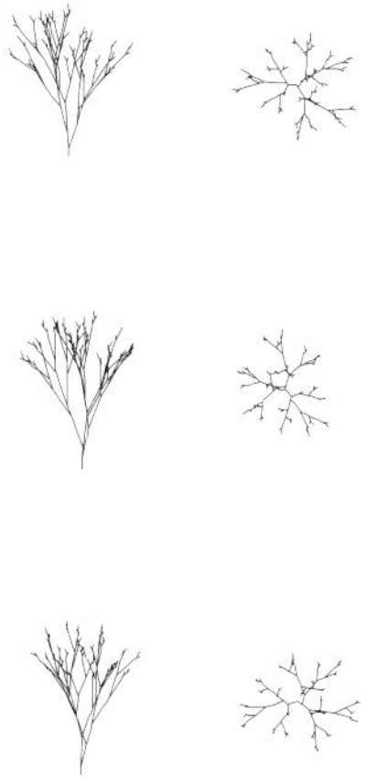

7

Cultural Gate to Alborz

Tehran. Iran
Local partner: Bonsar Architecture Studio
Project. 2008—

Re-connecting
/03

The project 'The Seven Gates to Alborz' is an opportunity to redefine the relationship between Tehran, a major global metropolis, and the mountain range to which it owes its foundation. The project proposes to create focal points of attraction between the edge of the city and the mountains that will act as a monumental gateway, creating a virtual boundary between city and nature. The 'gateways' are on the urban periphery, near the residential buildings, making them readily accessible by public transport. Each gateway is flanked by two parks that are laid out on historic water courses, thus creating a new urban landmark and serving to establish a rhythm in the relationship between the city and its mountains. Each of the constructions will unite and separate, both a gateway and a bridge: a platform from which to contemplate the city from a privileged location by a 30-kilometre walking path that will pass through the gateway-bridge.

Uses

A city has homes, workplaces, services and amenities. The seven gateways to the Alborz should primarily contain urban amenities. If a Master Plan is drawn up for all the new urban nodes, it must be decided whether they all have the same uses or each one has different uses so that the sum of and relationships between them all generate an entity of a higher order.

We propose to create seven gateways, each with a distinctive principal use related to culture, art and science, and a range of leisure uses. Each use will be strategically sited in relation to its position in the city: on the western edge a gateway for adventure; the second will be for science, next to the University; then culture, health, sports, art and finally a centre for sports with animals. Each gate should have a distinctive main use and other secondary uses which will be present in all seven — places for reading and exhibition spaces, urban services and landscaped areas.

The cultural gate to Alborz is on the edge of the city between the Kan and Sowhanak parks. The project consists of:

- A new car park for 436 cars and 16 buses, connected to the amenity.
- Pedestrian access to and from the public transport bus stop by way of a park.
- A gateway-bridge dedicated to culture with a library, mediatheque, exhibition rooms and lecture halls.

The park will be laid out on the basis of a connectible topographical system, which will combine wooded areas, walks, water channels and rest areas.

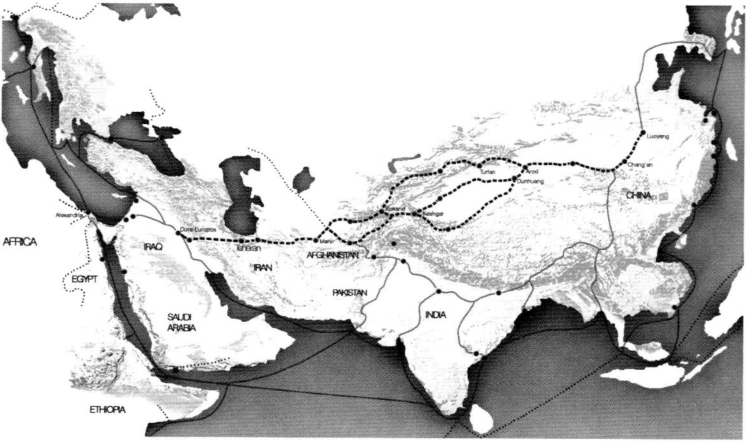

GEOGRAPHY

Settlement on the historic Silk Route

GEOMETRY

The city's water comes from the Alborz

Alborz

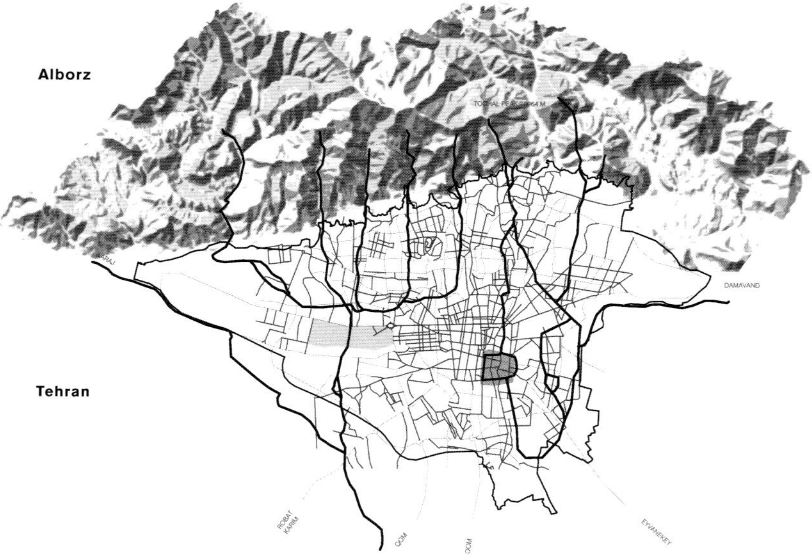

Tehran

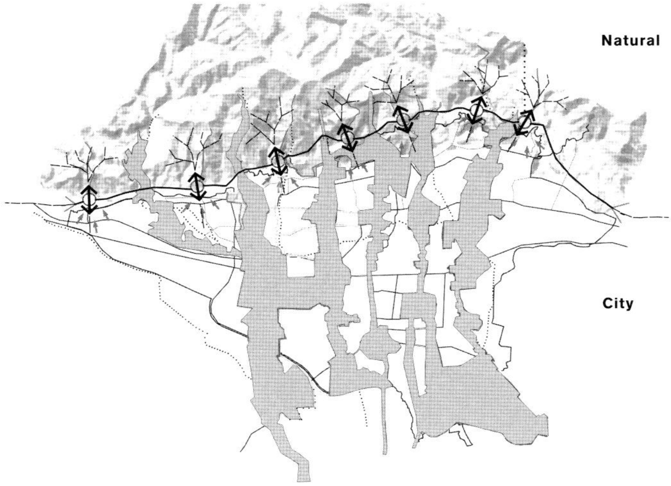

LOGIC

A well-defined city/mountains relationship

STRUCTURE

A gateway-bridge

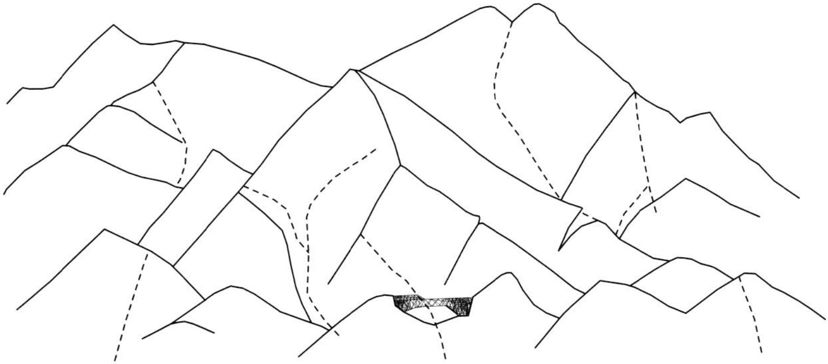

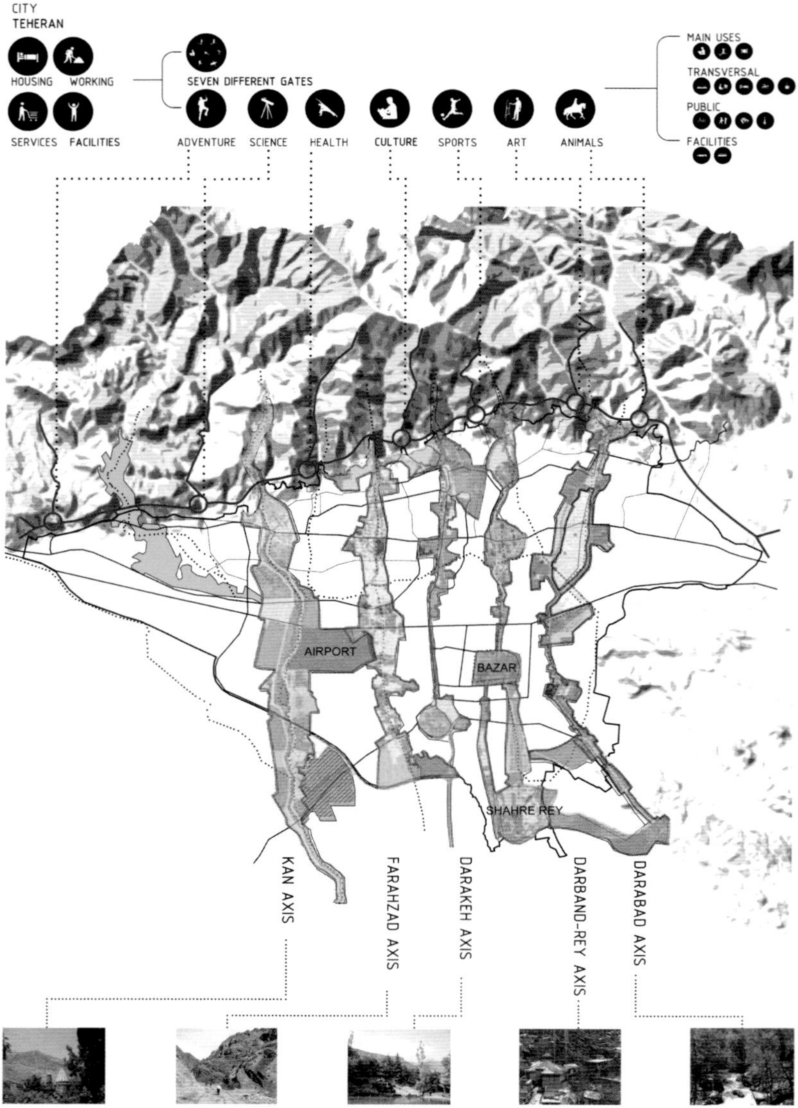

CITY
TEHERAN
HOUSING
WORKING
SERVICES
FACILITIES
SEVEN DIFFERENT GATES
ADVENTURE
SCIENCE
HEALTH
CULTURE
SPORTS
ART
ANIMALS
MAIN USES
TRANSVERSAL
PUBLIC
FACILITIES
AIRPORT
BAZAR
SHAHRE REY
KAN AXIS
FARAHZAD AXIS
DARAKEH AXIS
DARBAND-REY AXIS
DARABAD AXIS

FORM & GEOMETRY

هفت دروازه به سوی البرز

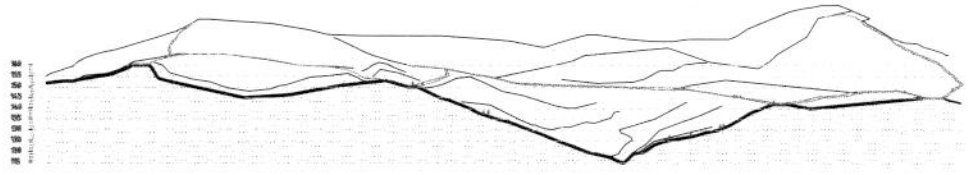

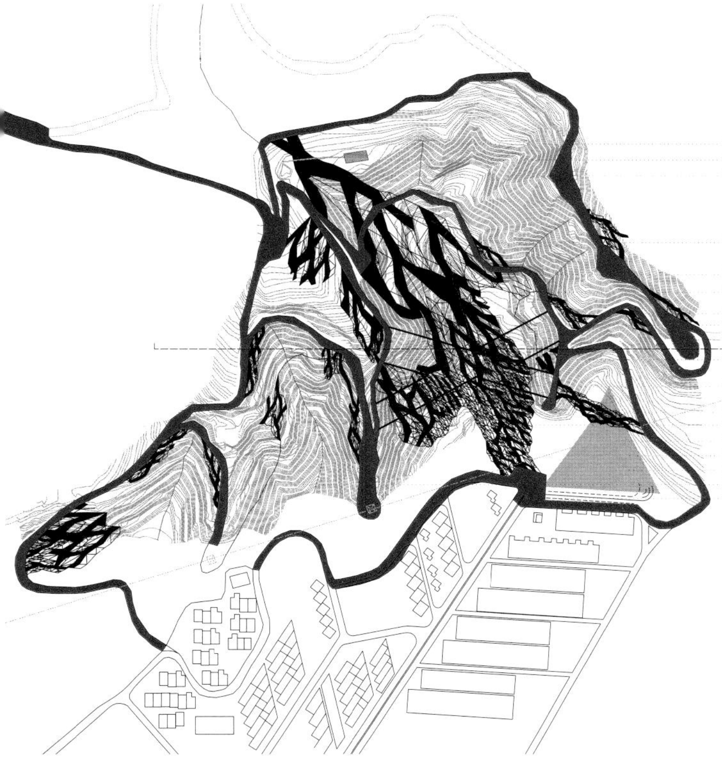

	00:00	01:00	02:00	03:00	04:00	05:00	06:00	07:00	08:00	09:00	10:00	11:00	12:00	13:00	14:00	15:00	16:00	17:00	18:00	19:00	20:00	21:00	22:00	23:00	24:00
WATER								X	X	X	X	X	X	X	X	X	X	X	X	X	X				
KIOSK					X	X	X	X	X	X	X	X	X	X	X	X	X	X	X	X	X	X	X		
BOTANICAL GARDEN										X	X	X	X	X	X	X	X	X	X	X	X	X			
WATER								X	X	X	X	X	X	X	X	X	X	X	X	X	X				
BIKE										X	X	X	X	X	X	X	X	X	X	X	X	X			
KIOSK					X	X	X	X	X	X	X	X	X	X	X	X	X	X	X	X	X	X	X		
LIBRARY										X	X	X	X	X	X	X	X	X	X	X	X	X			
BOOK SHOP										X	X	X	X	X	X	X	X	X	X	X	X	X			
BELVEDERE					X	X	X	X	X	X	X	X	X	X	X	X	X	X	X	X	X	X	X		
EXHIBITION								X	X	X	X	X	X	X	X	X	X	X	X	X	X				
COMPUTER ROOM								X	X	X	X	X	X	X	X	X	X	X	X	X	X	X			
OUTDOOR THEATER								X	X	X	X	X	X	X	X	X	X	X	X	X	X				
RESTAURANT									X	X	X	X	X	X	X	X	X	X	X	X	X				
PARKING							X	X	X	X	X	X	X	X	X	X	X	X	X	X	X	X	X		
BUS							X	X	X	X	X	X	X	X	X	X	X	X	X	X	X	X	X		
BIKE										X	X	X	X	X	X	X	X	X	X	X	X	X			
SWIMMING										X	X	X	X	X	X	X	X	X	X	X					
BUS								X	X	X	X	X	X	X	X	X	X	X	X	X	X				

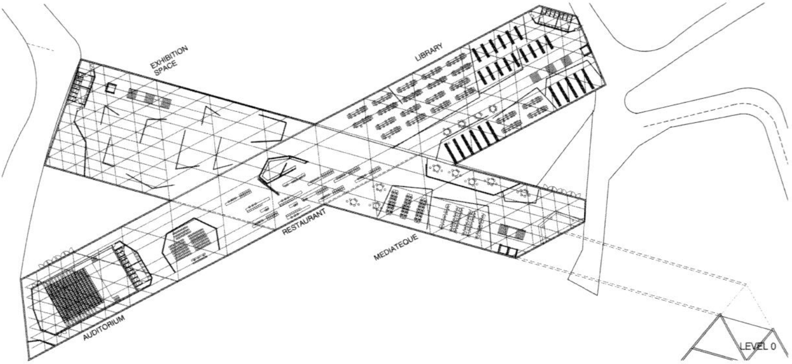
EXHIBITION SPACE
LIBRARY
RESTAURANT
MEDIATEQUE
AUDITORIUM
LEVEL 0

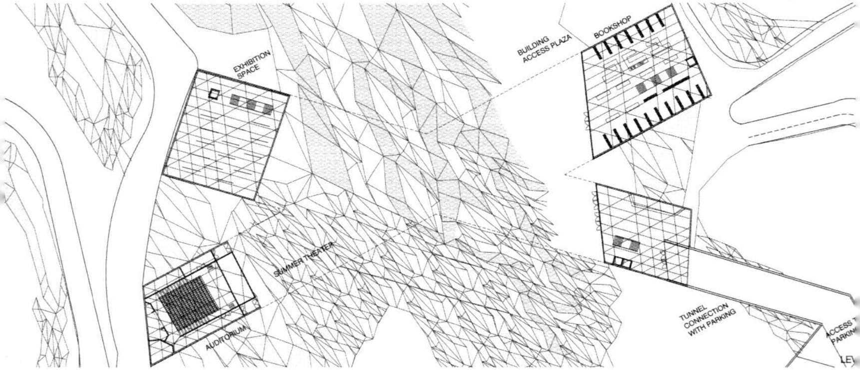
EXHIBITION SPACE
BUILDING ACCESS PLAZA
BOOKSHOP
SUMMER THEATER
AUDITORIUM
TUNNEL CONNECTION WITH PARKING

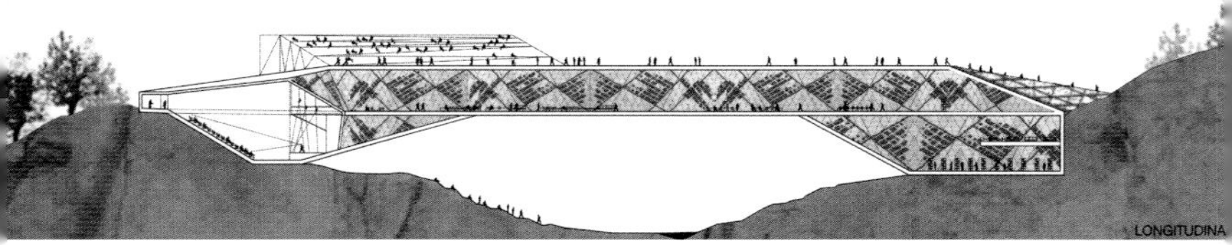
LONGITUDINA

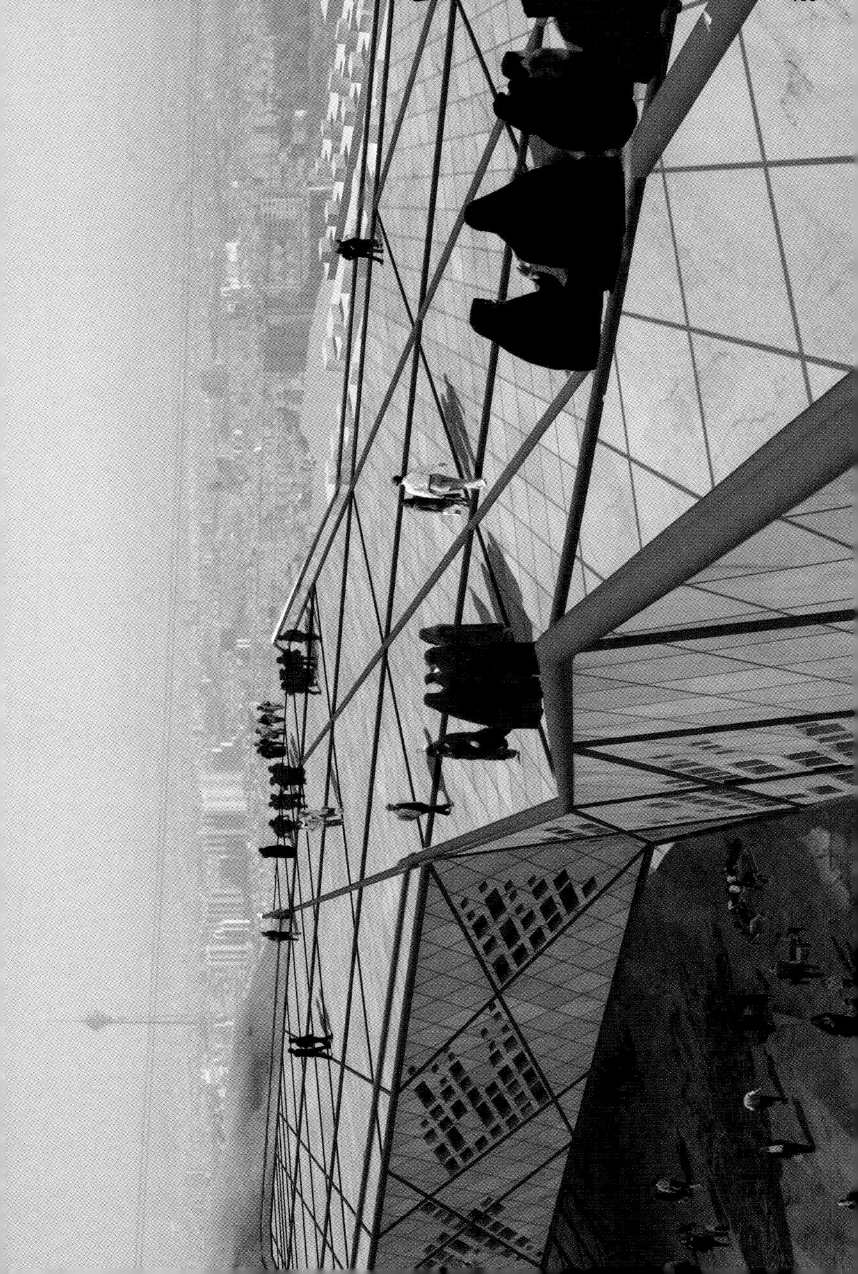

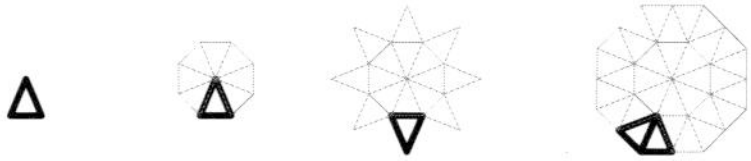

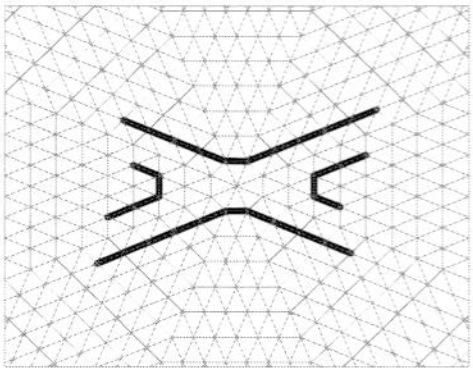

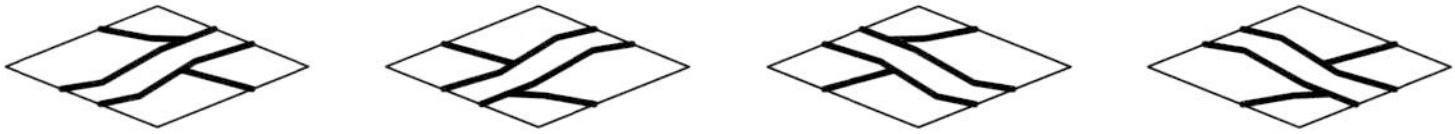

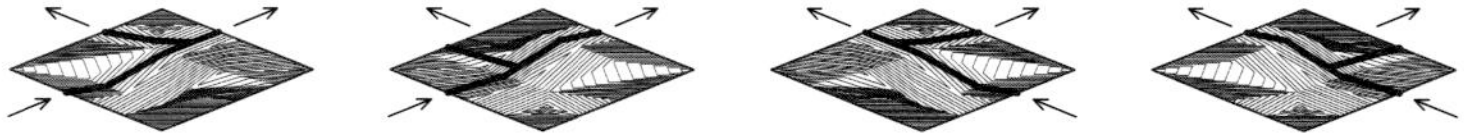

New Taiwan by Design

Taiwan. 2003—
Local partner:
J.M. Lin The Observer Design Group

1st Prize international competition

Measuring
/12

In 2003 the government of Taiwan decided to organize a series of architecture competitions in order to stimulate the improvement of tourist facilities in various parts of the island. The objective was to bring about a qualitative transformation of some of the most popular places, at a time when the phase of quantitative development of the island's economy and exports had been operating with evident success for a number of years. In our case, we decided to take part in the competitions for the design of two ports in the north of the island. These projects were to prompt us to reflect on the nature of human intervention in the coast, and specifically in the ports. Taiwan ranks 42nd in the world as a tourist destination in terms of number of visitors. In the main these visitors are travelling on business (37%) and come from the Asian region (45%). Achieving the proposed objective involves: understanding the current situation, analysing potential strengths, proposing a strategy. If we compare Taiwan with other island or coastal tourist destinations around the world (Hawaii, Cuba, Miami, Australia, Malaysia) we find that Taiwan has the following key conditions for success at the global level: good climate, good economy and trade, unique landscape, fine cuisine, tradition and culture, 3,000 million people within less than 3 hours by air and 4,000 million within less than 5 hours. What Taiwan lacks are major tourist attractions ready to cater for this incipient industry.

The keys to tourist development are:

- All tourist development starts with local national tourism.
- Tourism only attains full development when it combines with investment in property development.
- There is no relevant tourist business without a wide lodging offer.
- An intelligent environmental policy demands impacts concentration.
- The tourist industry develops on the basis of a critical mass of accumulation of people.
- Only with enough critical mass the time offer is developed and acquires enough quality and variety.
- Tourism is not organized in space, but in time. An adequate time architecture guarantees success.
- Public-sector investment is needed to stimulate private investment.
- Long term social sustainability of tourism, means that the nationals have a protagonical role in the touristic business as entrepreneurs.
- Tourism is about diversity and tolerance. It's not possible to impose tourists conducts different to those that make them happy, as long as these are socially acceptable.

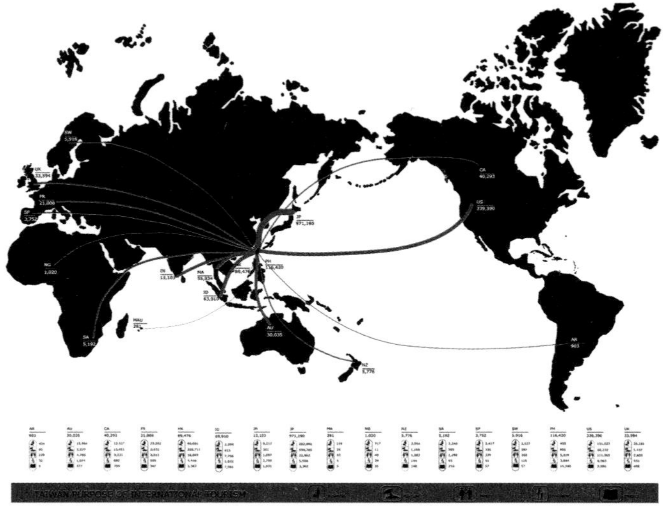

GEOGRAPHY

Global flow of tourists to Taiwan

GEOMETRY

Taiwan's ranking among tourist destinations

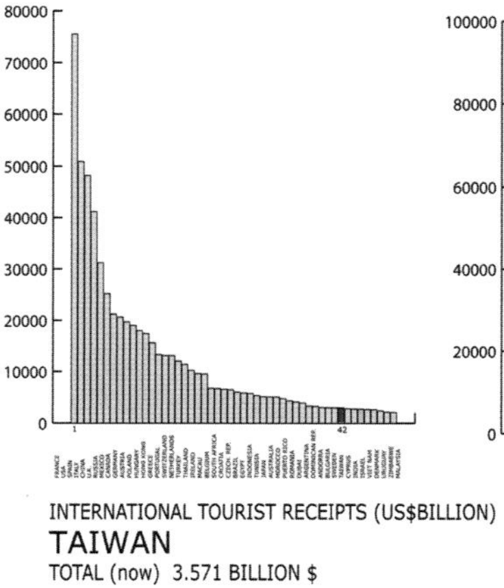

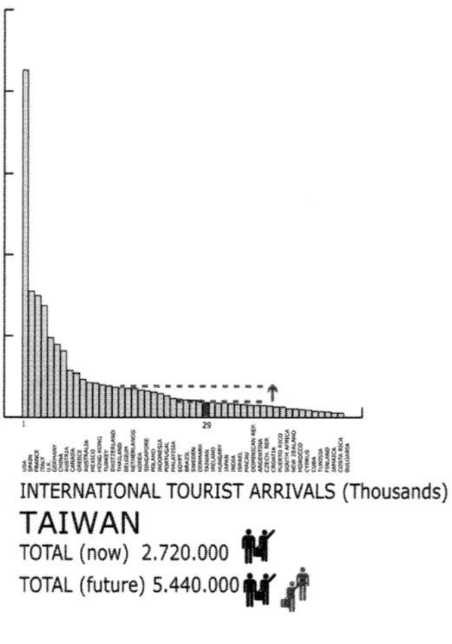

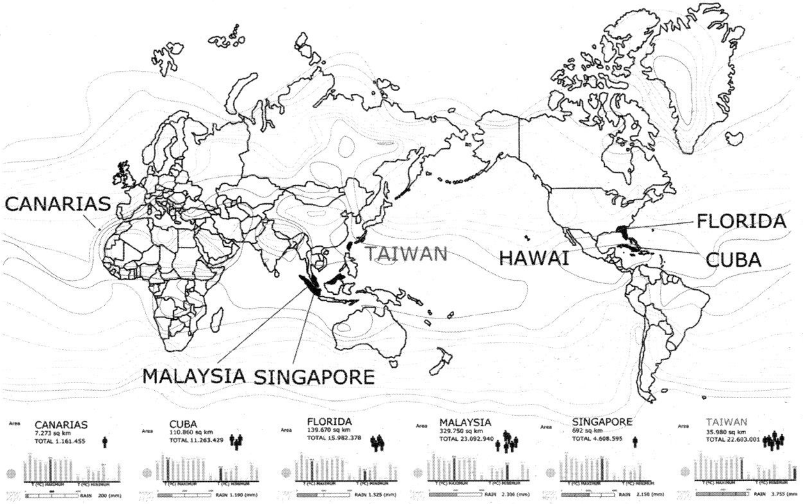

LOGIC

Strategic positioning in relation to competitors

STRUCTURE

Diversity of landscapes that structure tourist attractions

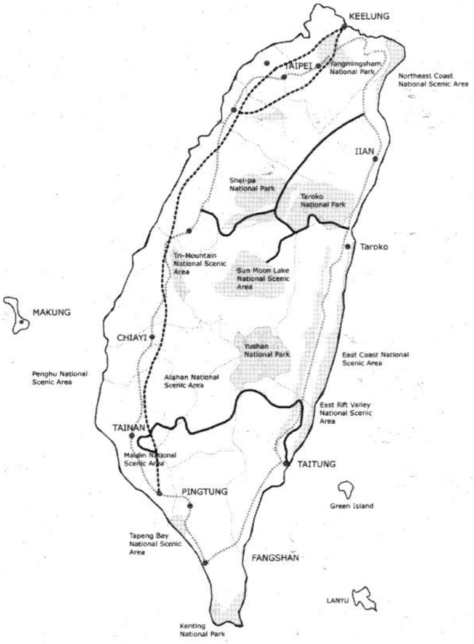

TAIWAN NATIONAL PARKS AND SCENIC AREAS

2 CATALOGUE OF ARTIFICIAL NATURES
Vicente Guallart Architecture. Barcelona. Spain

We evaluate the GEOGRAPHY of the place on multiple scales.
We acknowledge its GEOMETRY.
We discover its internal LOGIC: the nature of its nature.
And we develop STRUCTURES that will organize human activity.
Architecture.

海岸
COAST

凹凸地形
RELIEF

山
MOUNTAI

地理 GEOGRAPHY

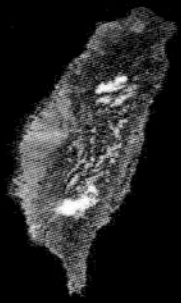

TAIWAN
Taiwan is an island with a surface area of 32,260 square kilometres and a coastal length of 1,566 kilometres. This is according to the National Geographic Society.

Landscape on the coast of Taiwan, with multiple folds.

Stratified mass

幾何 GEOMETRY

HOW LONG IS THE COAST OF TAIWAN?
Benoit Mandelbrot, the creator of Fractals would question this information The length of the coast always depends on the scale of measurement used.

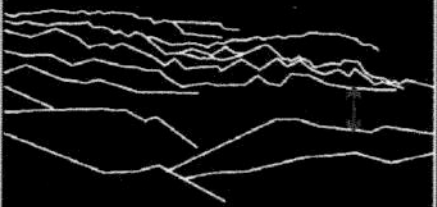

Profiles of the coast.

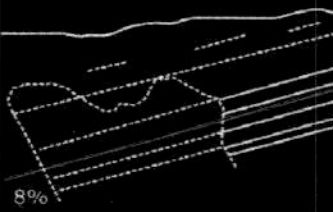

The strata iare organized in rel
the internal forces of the earth

邏輯 LOGIC

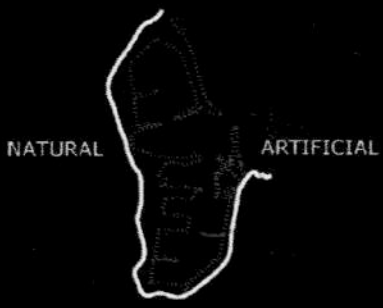

WHAT IS A PORT?
A port by definition is an artificial structure, which is situated between land and sea with two objectives:
1. To increase the **length** and breadth of the coastline
2. To create more **surface** area.

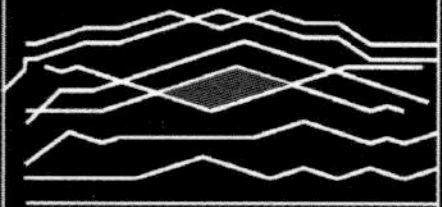

Overlapping profiles that generate voids at their points of intersection.

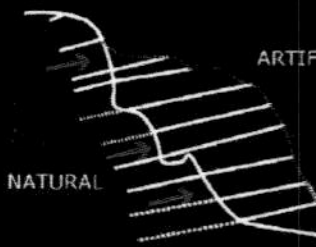

The geological void produce
mountain by a quarry c
regenerated by adopting the
stratification of the surro
massif.

結構 STRUCTURE

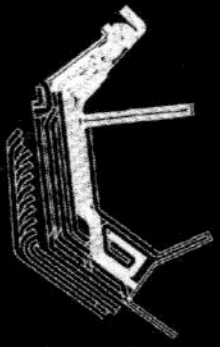

HOW TO CREATE A FLAT ORDER?
How does one organise a horizontal surface where the functions continually change according to the time and in where mobility is the basic concept?
We propose to stablish a linear pattern.

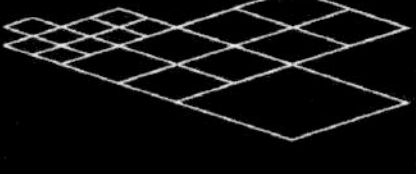

Self-resembling rhomboidal structure

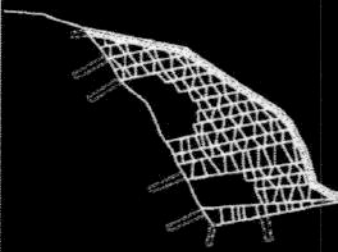

Reconstructed mountain-b
projecting from the earth, esta
itself vertically and horizontally

樹
TREE

ypical of tropical climates.

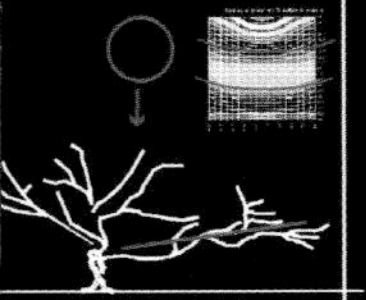

al structure with orientation of
anches in relation with the sun
on

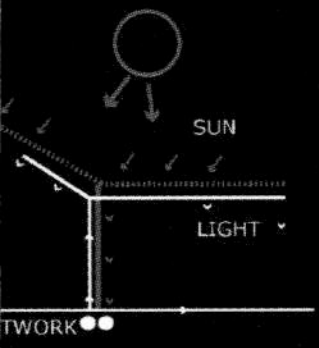

oltaic tree: the panels, like
capture the light of the sun
end it down to the roots. The
electricity.

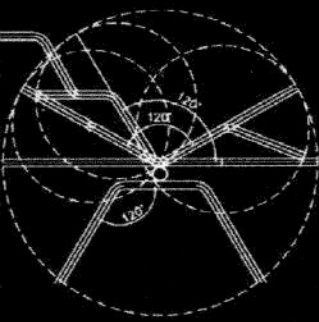

ure with photovoltaic panels
ed in relation to the angle of the
d the activities it accommodates
vide these with shade.

岩石
ROCK

Volcanic rock with beginnings of disintegration

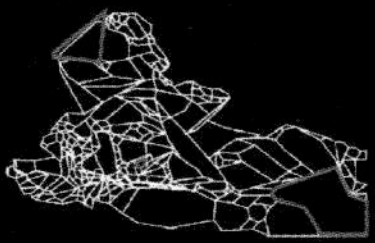

Reconstruction of the volume containing different degrees of fragmentation.

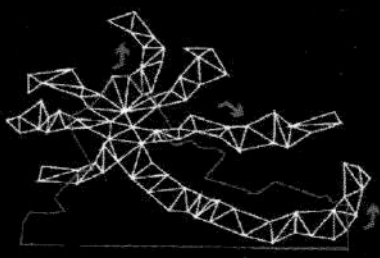

Surface deployed on the basis of triangular patterns.

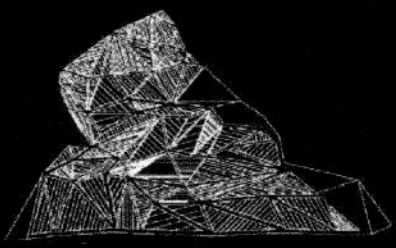

Wooden volume reconstructed on the basis of three-dimensional mimesis.

石
STONE

Volcanic stone, pumice.

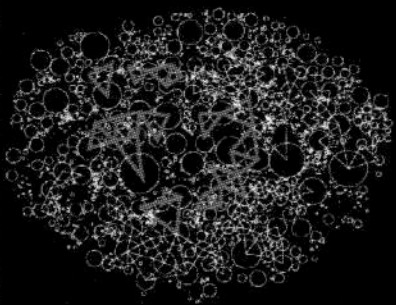

Circular pattern formed by gas escaping from the lava. The circles are related to a pattern of 180°.

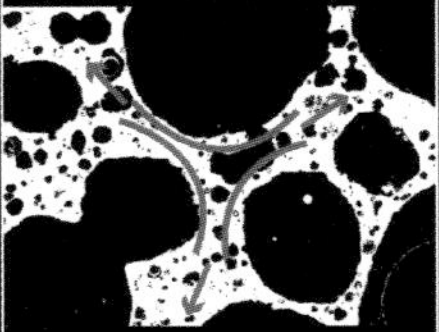

Microscopic detail of the stone. The minimum mass supports the maximum volume.

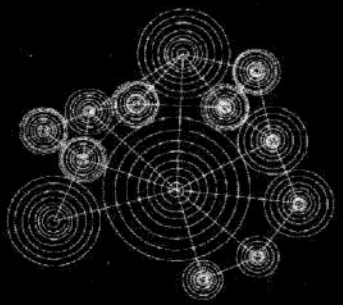

Free-standing umbrella structure with multiple dimensions facilitating ventilation between these and in section.

礦物
MINERAL

Microscopic detail of the metamorphic volcanic stone.

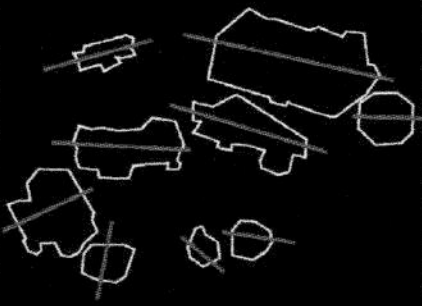

Freely organized polygons with lines that orient themselves in their vicinity.

Small linear systems that orient themselves around the mass attractors.

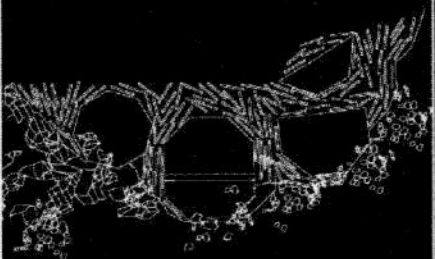

Large crystalline system containing water.

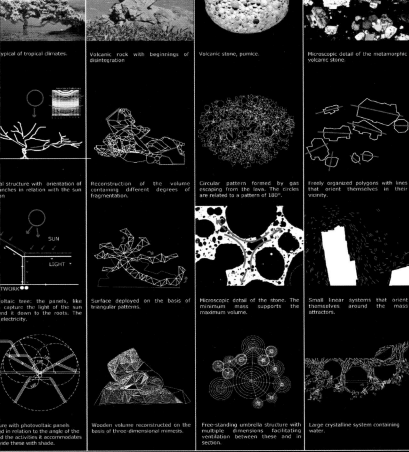

Batoutz Harbor

Taiwan. 2003—
Local partner:
J.M. Lin The Observer Design Group

1st Prize international competition

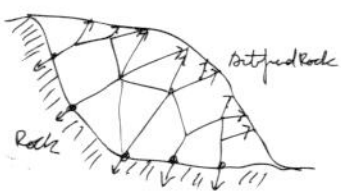

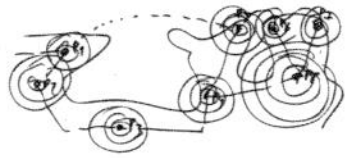

International tourist destination

Stay: four days

Batoutz is situated fifty minutes by car from Taipei, near Keelung, the city's traditional port. The size of the port, its proximity to the capital and its landscape all facilitate it conversion into an international tourist destination while conserving its fishing activity. For this to be achieved, what is needed in addition to quality tourist provision based on cuisine are facilities geared towards a Conventions and Trade and Culture tourism that will provide the impetus for the desired shift in scale.

The proposal:

A Facilities required
Fish market, seafood restaurant and traditional shops

B Proposed facilities
A hotel with panoramic views at the entrance of the port, Hotel-Spa-Convention Centre, reconstructing the mountain overlooking the port, a high-tech shopping mall and multi-screen cinemas, a traditional open-air market, an artificial sports complex.

C Facilities in development
The Ocean Museum and the park

The aim is to strike a balance between residential and leisure uses

The Port of Batoutz has potential for a wide-ranging and complex tourist development; the principal problem will consist in balancing housing with leisure uses, the variety and quality of which requires a critical mass of users bulk sufficient to make it viable. The proposal is based on the conviction that the successful development of tourist activity consists in making available a wide range of leisure uses throughout the course of the day, and these will have to be complemented by a sufficient level of accommodation to ensure a continuity of demand for the catering establishments and shops. Because the proposal is centred exclusively on the port area, it contains a limited development of the hotel capacity, which will need to be increased by means of interventions in the immediate periphery of the port. Once both phases have been concluded, the total accommodation will be not less than 10,000 m^2, of which at least 70% will be occupied by hotels.

Port Batoutz as a component of the network of coastal tourist nodes

The proposal is conceived from the conviction that Batoutz is the hub of a network of tourist destinations that extends all along the coast of Taiwan. These nodes will have to contain amenities that will satisfy the leisure needs of their own residents and at the same time complement the others, so that each of these, including Batoutz, will be able to add to its own extensive range of services and activities those provided by other destinations and by the capital of Taipei itself, places which tourists are likely to visit in the course of their stay. The provision thus configured will be sufficient to satisfy the spectrum of leisure needs for a minimum of 7 days, although the length of stay could be extended or the stay repeated in successive years if complemented with visits to other destinations. The loss of consumer revenue represented by the 'loss' of tourists making excursions outside of Batoutz would be compensated by the visit of other tourists staying in other resorts in the network.

The architecture of time: leisure spaces

If success in tourism is related to the quantity, variety and quality of the leisure provision, what is needed is a programme of uses that can satisfy the multiple demands that may be made by tourists, in such a way as to offer a range of functional alternatives all through the day. The organization of these sequences is known as 'the architecture of time'. The considerable size of Port Batoutz and its area of influence allows us to anticipate a wide spectrum of leisure provision that—although constituting no more than the embryo of what will be available once the subsequent phases of the project are implemented—will keep the visitor active, with at least 35 functions from 9 in the morning on, and with at least 10 functions during the night. These functions will cover all the needs for the use of time, enabling us to assert with confidence that the project fulfils all the functional requirements necessary for a satisfactory stay.

The organization of time in space

In order to give complete satisfaction with such a range of provision and meet the objective of satisfying the desires of the tourist, what is needed a spatial organization of uses that guarantee the functional efficiency of the system as a whole. To do this, it is essential to plan a distribution of facilities that takes due account of the potential and the limitations of each space. In the project that we are proposing we have organized 11 different spaces (Cultural Plaza, Fishing Area, Artificial Mountain, Shopping Centre, Traditional Open-air Market, Sports Centre, Museums, Leisure Area, Boat Access, Hotel Tower and Excursions), most of which contain a variety of establishments and options. The set of typical uses is estimated at 40 within the area, complemented by 5 proposed excursions: together these constitute one of the most important concentrations of tourist leisure provision in Taiwan.

How to Structure a Port

The construction of a port is one of the activities that makes most environmental impact on a territory, given that it changes its surface area, which is one of its basic characteristics. This being so, the question that a project for a port must resolve in architectural and landscaping terms is how to structure a very wide and largely unzoned horizontal platform accommodating functions that change over time for which the basic point of departure is the mobility of the various systems that operate there.

In recent years the traditional port activities centred on fishing, transport, industry and logistics have been joined by tourism and leisure uses, thanks to the exceptional conditions of climate, landscape and cuisine found in ports. The logic that should guide the laying out of a port is grounded in the necessary multiplicity of circulation systems, rhythms, timetables and qualities of the facilities required by the port's combination of activities. Our project proposes to establish a linear structuring sequence that defines a vibration between land and sea tracing dozens of possible coastlines. The resulting open system will order growth in keeping with the circulation of different functional groups (boats, buses, cars, bicycles crowds, individuals) and the implanting of functional attractors in the port.

This schema enables the process of developing the final project to take into account the negotiations between various conditions, demands and expectations of the various user groups and the economic criteria of the project's developers as these arise. Starting a project by setting a pattern and the keys that can be used to intervene in it makes it possible to create a tension throughout the construction period (usually prolonged over several years), thus ensuring that even though not all the buildings are completed, a sense of unity prevails throughout the process.

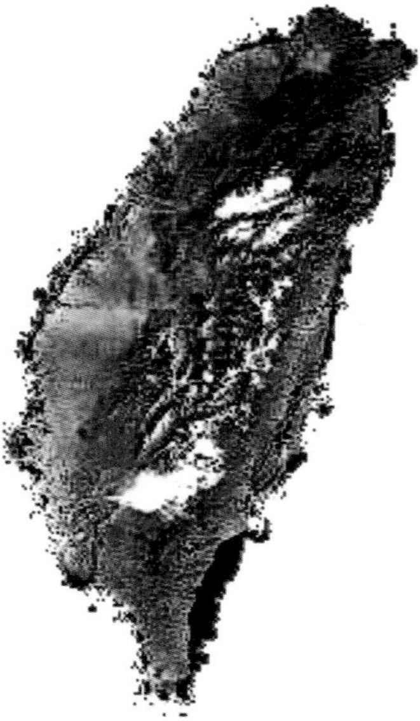

GEOGRAPHY

The island of Taiwan

GEOMETRY

The length of its coastline depends on the ruler it is measured with

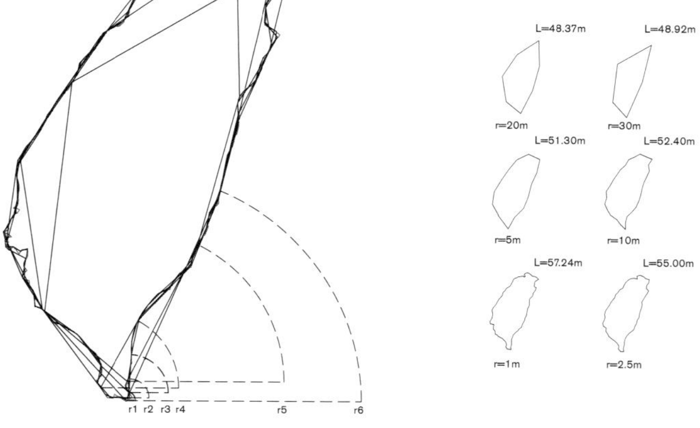

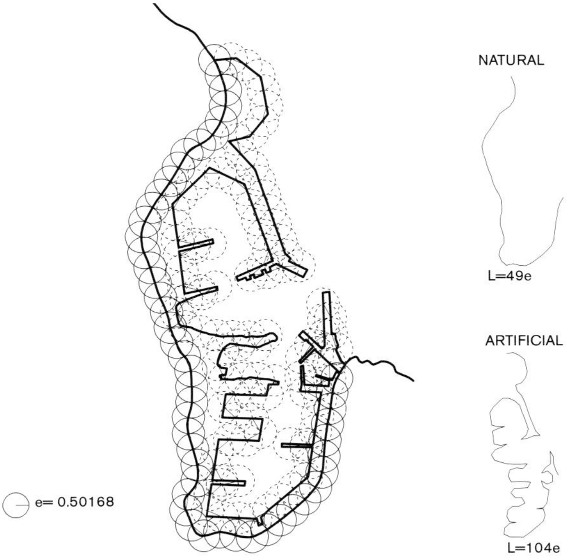

LOGIC

A port increases the length of the coast and the surface area of a territory

STRUCTURE

A pattern serves to structure the introduction of functions

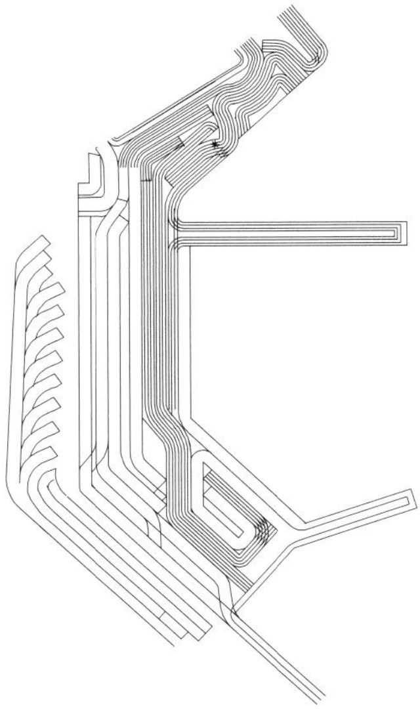

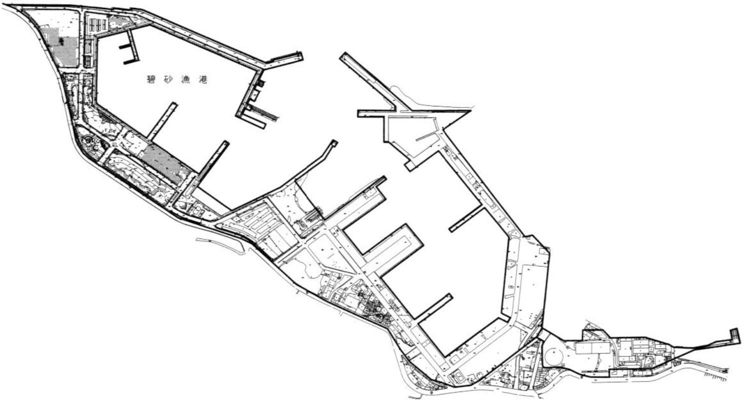

GEOGRAPHY

A port

GEOMETRY

Pattern every six metres

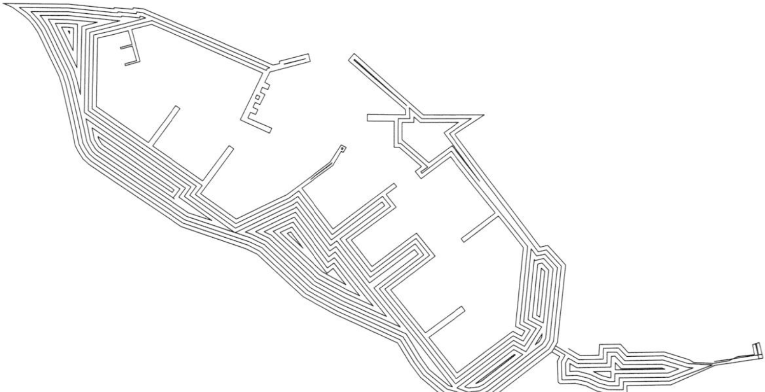

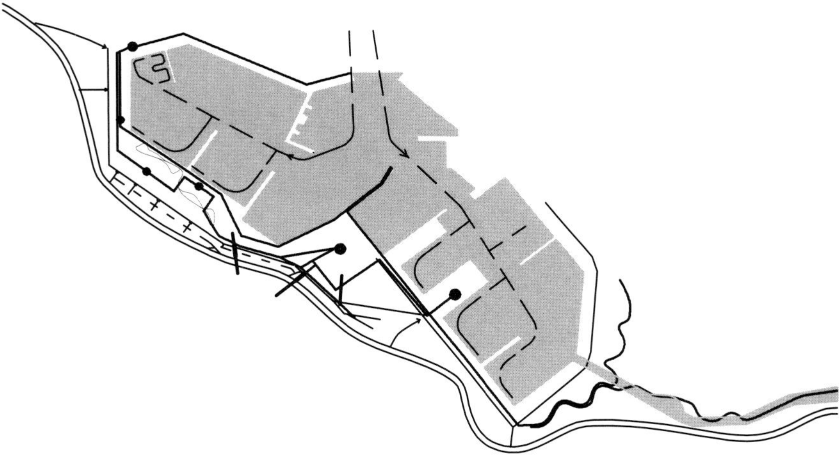

LOGIC

The functional nodes set up rhythms in the space

STRUCTURE

The ordering pattern is transformed with activity

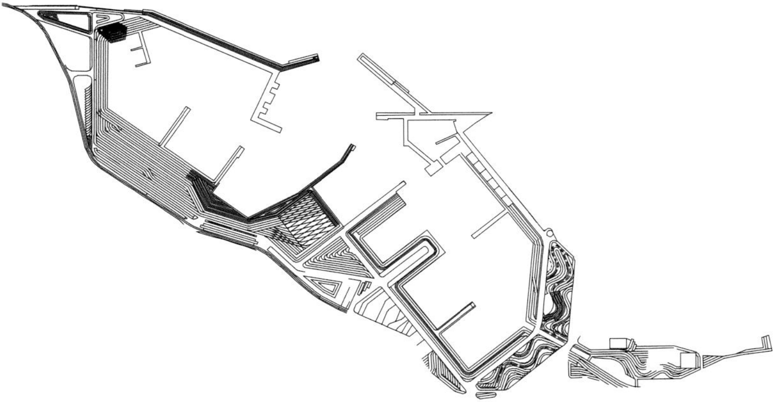

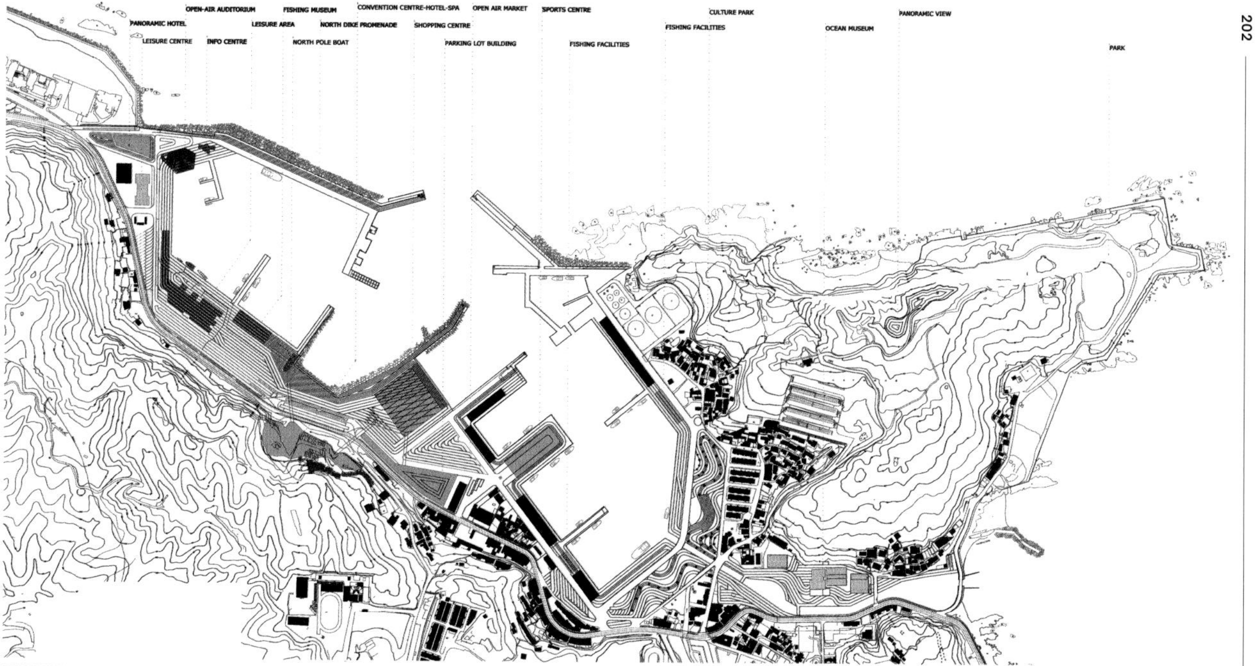

	USES	AREA	UNITS	DEVELOPER: PUBLIC	DEVELOPER: PRIVATE	PHASE 1	PHASE 2	PHASE 3	NATURE	9	10	11	12	13	14	15	16	17	18	19	20	21	22	23	24	1	2
A1	LEISURE AREA	5.180m2	1	X		X			RELIEF																		
	CAFÉS	660m2	15	X		X			RELIEF	X	X	X	X	X	X	X	X	X	X	X	X	X	X	X	X	X	X
	RETAIL FISH MARKET	430m2	15	X		X			RELIEF	X	X	X	X	X	X	X	X	X	X	X	X						
	STORES	1.600m2	42	X		X			RELIEF	X	X	X	X	X	X	X	X	X	X	X	X	X					
	FOOD PLAZA RESTAURANTS	600m2	13	X		X			RELIEF	X	X	X	X	X	X	X	X	X	X	X	X	X	X	X	X		
	RESTAURANTS	2.130m2	15	X		X			RELIEF	X	X	X	X	X	X	X	X	X	X	X	X	X	X	X	X		
A2	PHOTOVOLTAIC PERGOLA	180m	1	X		X			TREE	X	X	X	X	X	X	X	X	X	X	X	X	X	X	X	X	X	X
A3	OPEN-AIR AUDITORIUM	2.700m2	1000 P.	X		X			COAST															X	X	X	X
A4	INFO CENTRE	1000m2	1	X		X				X	X	X	X	X	X	X	X	X	X	X	X	X	X				
A5	NORTH DIKE PROMENADE	450m	1	X		X			COAST	X	X	X	X	X	X	X	X	X	X	X	X	X	X	X	X	X	X
A6	OCEAN TOURISM CRUISE	70m2	1	X		X																					
	NORTH COAST FAST FERRY		1	X		X				X	X	X	X	X	X	X	X	X	X								
	SUBMARINE (VISIT TO ISLAND)		1	X		X				X	X	X	X	X	X	X	X	X	X								
	BOAT HIRE		1	X		X				X	X	X	X	X	X	X	X	X	X								
	FISHING RENTAL EXPERIENCE		1	X		X				X	X	X	X	X	X	X	X	X	X								
A7	PARKING LOT		[illegible]	X		X			COAST	X	X	X	X	X	X	X	X	X	X	X	X	X	X	X	X	X	X

	USES	AREA	UNITS	DEVELOPER: PUBLIC	DEVELOPER: PRIVATE	PHASE 1	PHASE 2	PHASE 3	NATURE	9	10	11	12	13	14	15	16	17	18	19	20	21	22	23	24	1	2
A8	MUSEUMS		1	X		X																					
	VIRTUAL FISHING MUSEUM	2.800m2	1	X		X				X	X	X	X	X		X	X	X	X	X							
	NORTH POLE BOAT		1	X		X				X	X	X	X	X		X	X	X	X	X							
B1	PANORAMIC HOTEL				X		X																				
	HOTEL	50.684m2	[illegible]		X		X		STRATA	X	X	X	X	X	X	X	X	X	X	X	X	X	X	X	X	X	X
	TERRACE SWIMMING POOL	590m2	1		X		X		STRATA	X	X	X	X	X	X	X	X	X	X	X	X	X	X				
	RESTAURANT	1.890m2	4		X		X		STRATA					X	X	X							X	X	X		
	DISCOTHEQUE	301m2	1		X		X		STRATA															X	X	X	X
	KARAOKE	341m2	1		X		X		STRATA											X	X	X	X	X	X	X	X
	PANORAMIC VIEW ELEVATOR	1.650m2	1		X		X		STRATA	X	X	X	X			X	X	X	X	X	X	X	X				
B2	ARTIFICIAL MOUNTAIN		1		X		X		MOUNTAIN																		
	CONVENTION CENTRE	2.675m2	1500 p.		X		X		MOUNTAIN	X	X	X	X	X	X	X	X	X	X	X	X						
	HOTEL	12.770m2	[illegible]		X		X		MOUNTAIN	X	X	X	X	X	X	X	X	X	X	X	X	X	X	X	X	X	X
	SPA Thalassotherapy	2.165m2	1		X		X		MOUNTAIN	X	X	X	X				X	X	X	X	X						
	RESTAURANT	3500m2	4		X		X		MOUNTAIN					X	X	X						X	X	X			
	FITNESS CENTRE	1.073m2	1		X		X		MOUNTAIN	X	X	X	X				X	X	X	X	X						

	USES	AREA	UNITS	DEVELOPER: PUBLIC	DEVELOPER: PRIVATE	PHASE 1	PHASE 2	PHASE 3	NATURE	9	10	11	12	13	14	15	16	17	18	19	20	21	22	23	24	1	2
B3	SHOPPING CENTRE		1		X		X		MINERAL																		
	FASHION SHOPS	2.010m2	30		X		X		MINERAL	X	X	X	X	X	X	X	X	X	X	X	X	X					
	HIGH-TECH MARKET	3.795m2	54		X		X		MINERAL	X	X	X	X	X	X	X	X	X	X	X	X	X					
	CINEMAS	1.840m2	8		X		X		MINERAL							X	X	X	X	X	X	X	X	X	X		
	CAFÉ TERRACES AND MUSIC	2.687m2	19		X		X		MINERAL	X	X	X	X	X	X	X	X	X	X	X	X	X	X	X	X	X	
B4	PARKING LOT BUILDING	14.685m2	[illegible]		X		X		RELIEF	X	X	X	X	X	X	X	X	X	X	X	X	X	X	X	X	X	X
B5	SPORTS CENTRE		1		X		X		RELIEF																		
	ARTIFICIAL GOLF/BASEBALL	6.300m2	1		X		X		RELIEF	X	X	X	X	X	X	X	X	X	X	X	X						
	TENNIS-BASKETBALL-MINI FOOTBALL	3.315m2	4		X		X		RELIEF	X	X	X	X	X	X	X	X	X	X	X	X	X	X				
	FAMILY GAMES	6.366m2	1		X		X		RELIEF	X	X	X	X	X	X	X	X	X	X								
B6	FISHING FACILITIES	7.613m2	2	X			X		COAST	X	X	X	X	X	X	X	X	X	X								
B7	OPEN AIR MARKET		1	X			X		COAST	X	X	X	X	X	X	X	X	X	X	X	X	X	X	X	X	X	X
C1	CULTURAL PLAZA		1	X				X	COAST																		
	OCEAN MUSEUM	34.779m2	1	X				X	COAST	X	X	X	X	X			X	X	X	X	X						
	CULTURE PARK	16.000m2	1	X				X	COAST	X	X	X	X	X			X	X	X	X	X						
C2	LEISURE CENTRE	9.700m2	1	X				X		X	X	X	X	X	X	X	X	X	X	X	X	X	X				

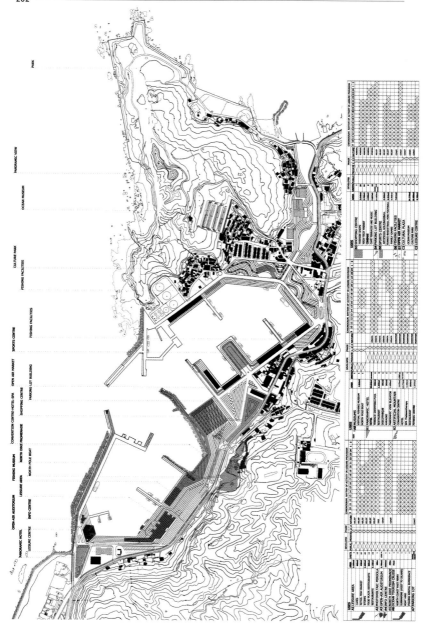

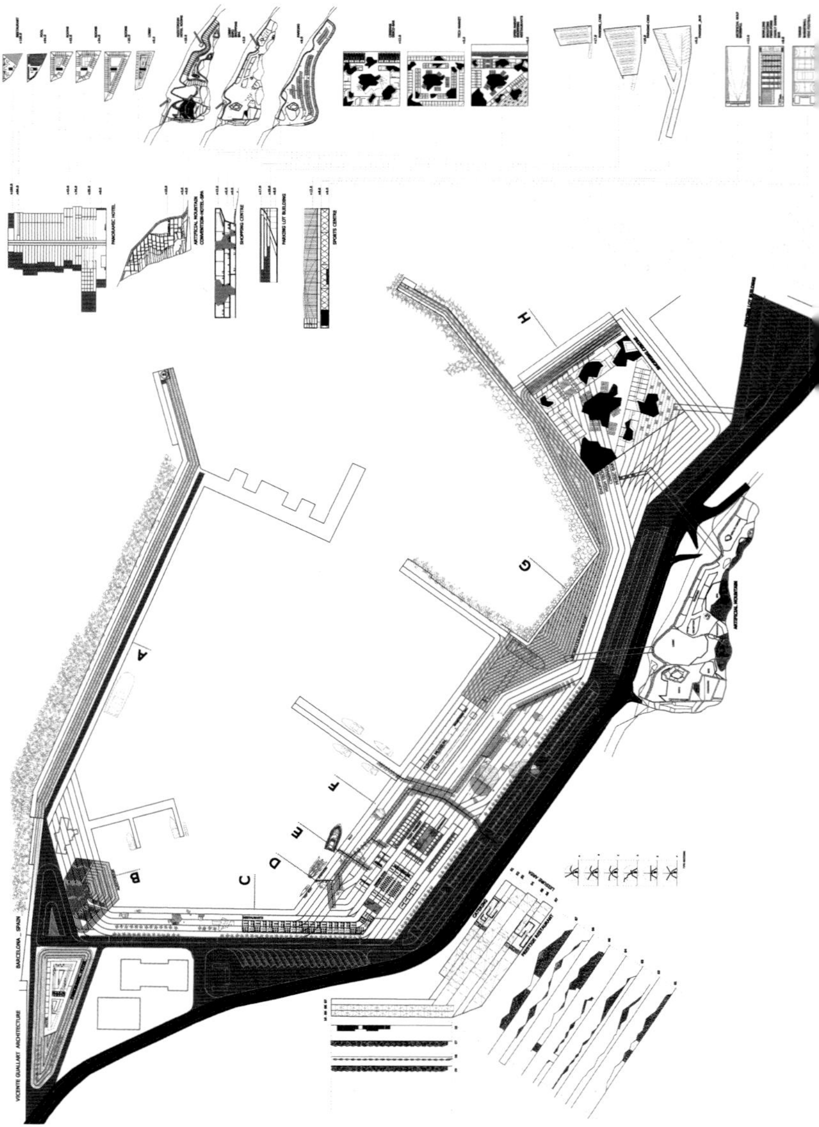
VICENTE GUALLART ARCHITECTURE
BARCELONA _ SPAIN
PANORAMIC HOTEL
ARTIFICIAL MOUNTAIN
CONVENTION-HOTEL-SPA
SHOPPING CENTRE
PARKING LOT BUILDING
SPORTS CENTRE
ARTIFICIAL MOUNTAIN
A
B
C
D
E
F
G
H

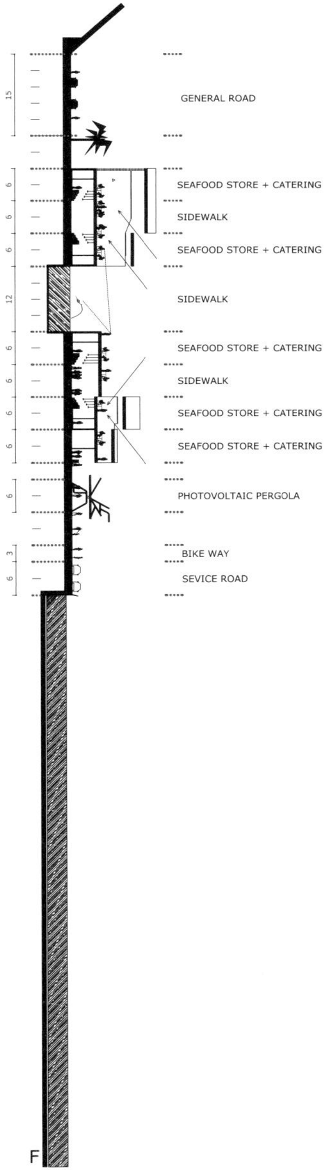
15
GENERAL ROAD
6
SEAFOOD STORE + CATERING
6
SIDEWALK
6
SEAFOOD STORE + CATERING
12
SIDEWALK
6
SEAFOOD STORE + CATERING
6
SIDEWALK
6
SEAFOOD STORE + CATERING
6
SEAFOOD STORE + CATERING
6
PHOTOVOLTAIC PERGOLA
3
BIKE WAY
6
SEVICE ROAD
F

Ocean Plaza

Taiwan. Project 2003—
Local partner:
J.M. Lin The Observer Design Group

1st Prize international competition

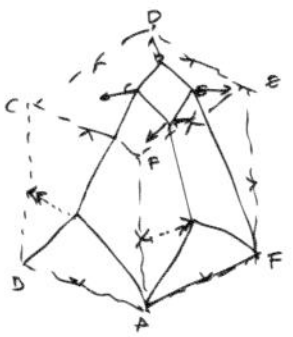

Parametrizing
/14

How Do You Build a Rock?

The project for the artificial rocks in Taiwan grew out of two traditions: on the one hand that of the Japanese Zen garden in which various natural rocks are surrounded by an expanse of raked gravel in such a way that both their form and their position generate tension; on the other, that of the large expanses of timber decking that are found in ports around the world, on which people can relax by the sea. In the Ocean Plaza in Batoutz we decided to create a garden of artificial rocks made of timber, modelled on the volcanic rocks that ring the port. But how do you generate a family of artificial rocks on the basis of neighbouring natural rock formations? We decided to look for a set of geometric rules common to all the rocks in a family. Having established that most rocks are more or less pyramidal, with inflections toward the centre of their edges, it was decided to start with a cube and define take 20 points on its surface that could be used to create pyramidal elements with triangulated surfaces similar to the original rocks.
The system was developed as follows: If we think of a cube as having 20 points, 8 correspond to its vertices (v), and the other 12 to the midpoints of its edges (m). If we want to generate a rock starting from this geometric basis, we have 6 sides (A, B, C, D, E, F), each of which has 8 points, of which the 4 midpoints on the edges (m4) are shared with the four adjacent sides and each of the 4 vertices (v4) is shared with another 2 sides. So if any one side is modified by joining the midpoints of the edges, five sides will be modified. At the same time we also have another relation of dependence, because when we look at the possible connections between the 20 basic points (20b) we find intersections, giving us the first generation of new points (pg1), 29 per side, with a resolution of 194 points in the first generation; 20b + 147 g1. We thus have a system with a number of initial classifications of the elements and the dependencies between them. Now we could take any of the avenues offered by new technologies. In this case we opted for one based on equations and conditions of connection, which promised to be particularly viable for the creation of new points of intersection.

The system starts with the data of the basic cube, these dimensions distort the cube in the 8v, starting always from the centroid of the bottom of the cube. Introducing here a new parameter—the angle between the axes of the centroid of our cube—in order to generate the first families, we can now explore the family of the right angle. The next step is to define the points to be modified; at this stage the points are only modified in terms of their connection. Using a spreadsheet, a series of formulas enables us to calculate the midpoint, the intersection between two lines, the lines between two midpoints and finally the midpoint of these new lines to generate new points (pg1) on the basis of the first set of connection relations, using in each case the formula that serves to find a new point. The resulting data are then interrelated with a 3D programme that recognizes the coordinates of each point and the activation of more or fewer points. Finally, in order to create more irregular configurations, new parameters of deformation are introduced, now with a polar system and based on the centroid. The result is a parametric rock that is configured in terms of its number of faces and connections, on the basis of a simple cube.

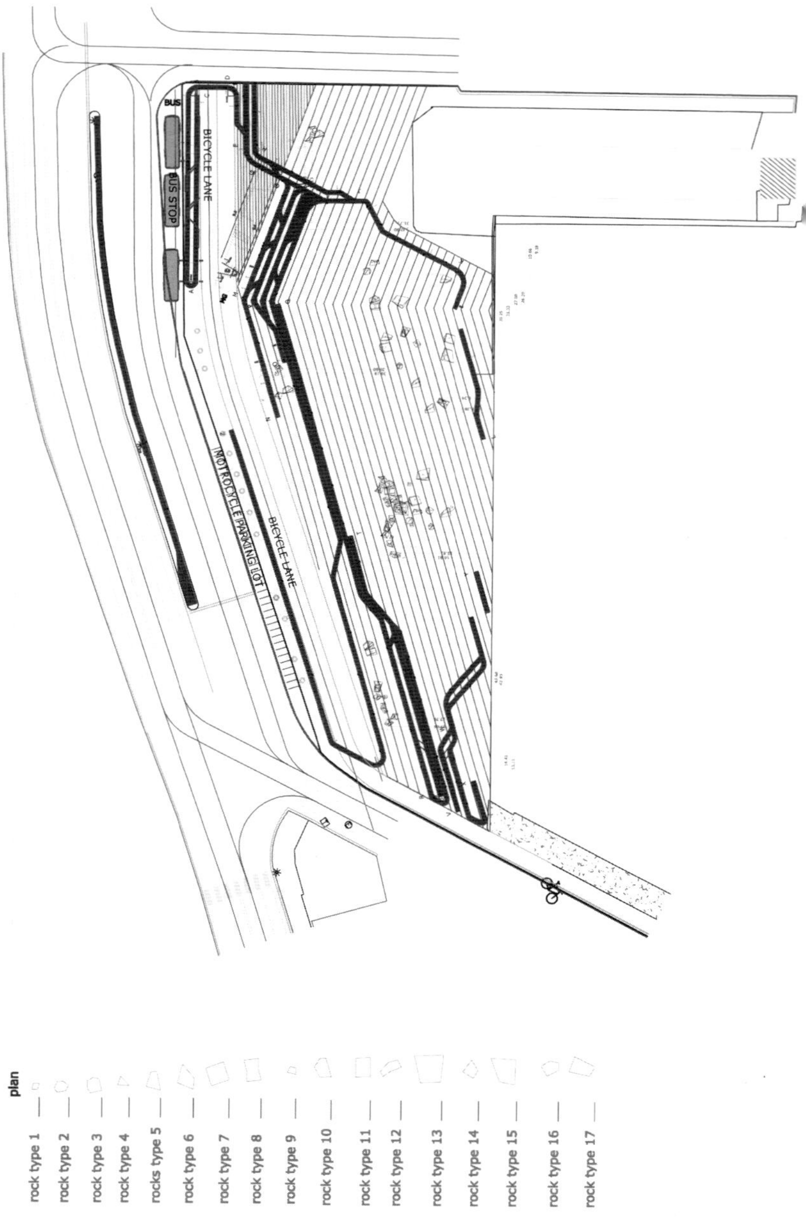
BUS
BICYCLE LANE
BUS STOP
MOTROCYCLE PARKING LOT
BICYCLE LANE
plan
rock type 1
rock type 2
rock type 3
rock type 4
rocks type 5
rock type 6
rock type 7
rock type 8
rock type 9
rock type 10
rock type 11
rock type 12
rock type 13
rock type 14
rock type 15
rock type 16
rock type 17

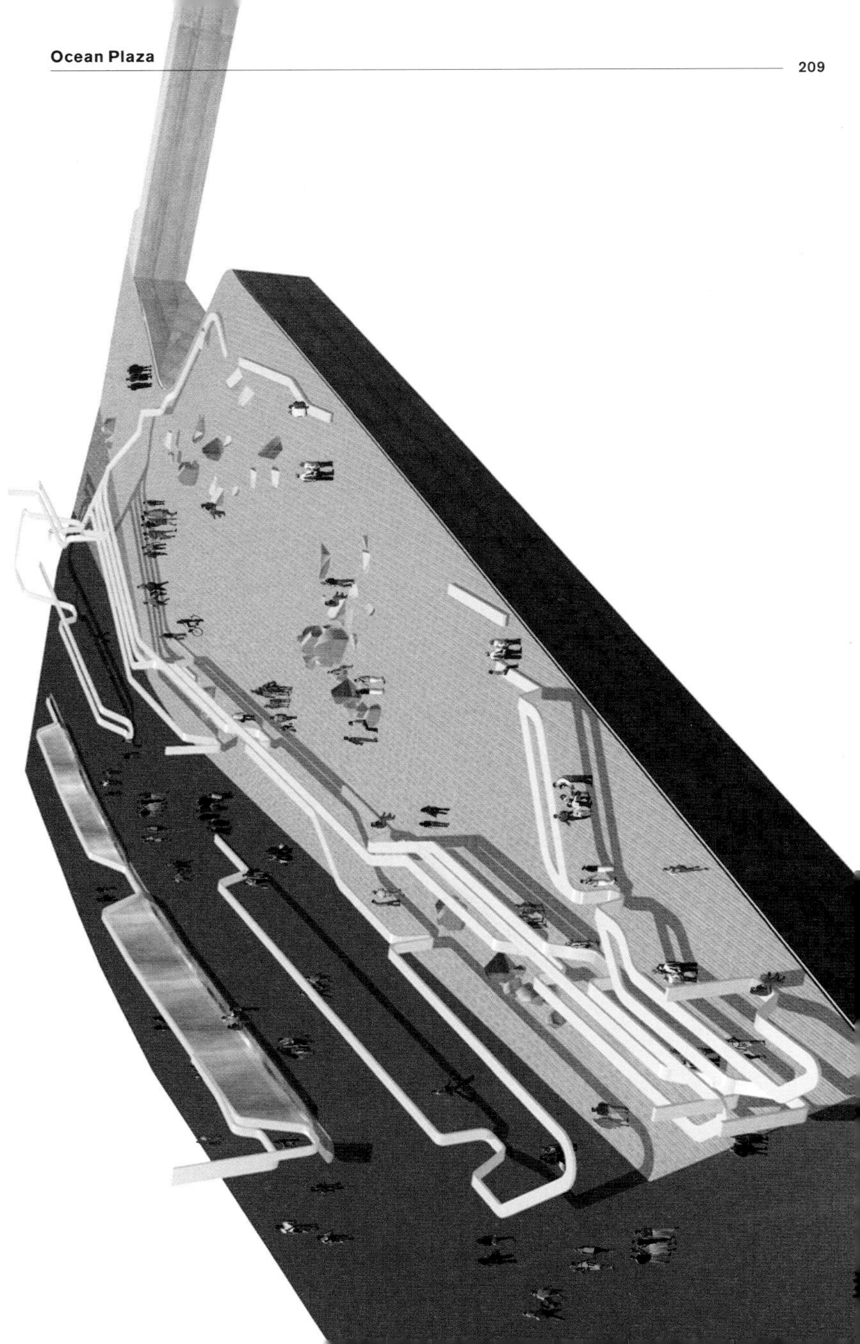

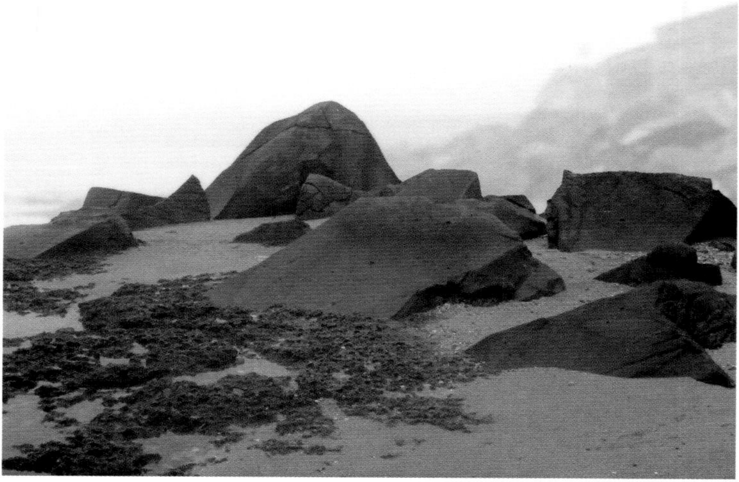

GEOGRAPHY

Self-organized volcanic Zen garden

GEOMETRY

Formal and relational diversity

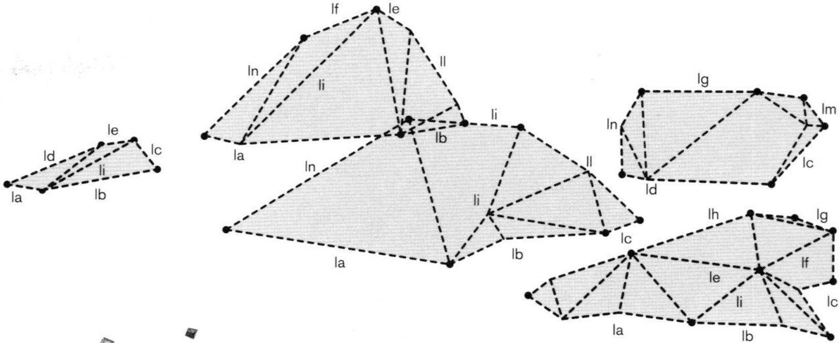

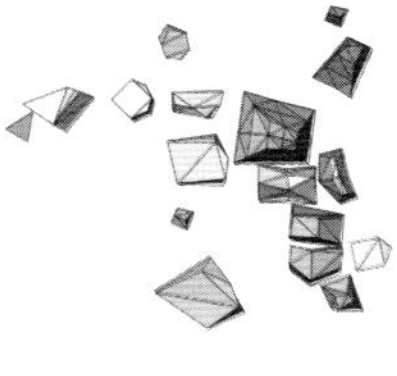

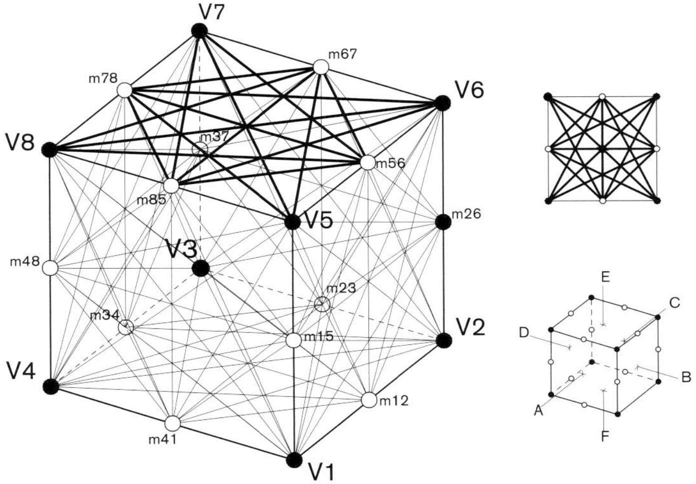

LOGIC

Specific parametric logic for reconstructing the rocks

STRUCTURE

An artificial rock

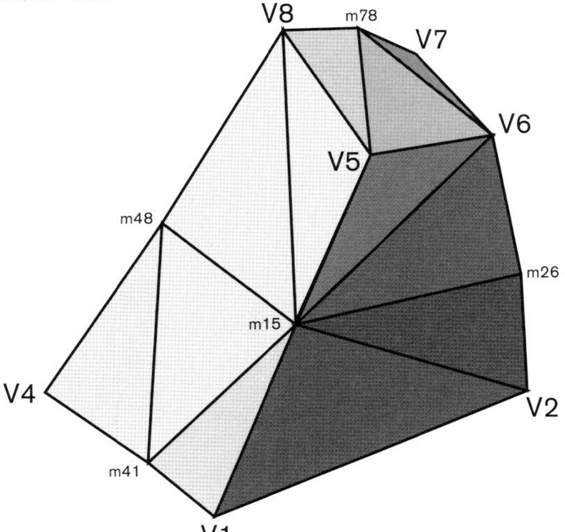

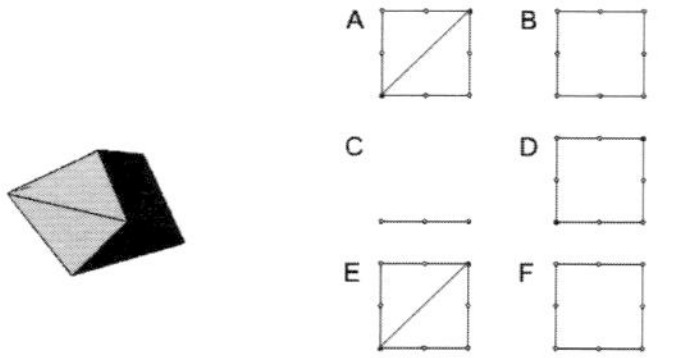

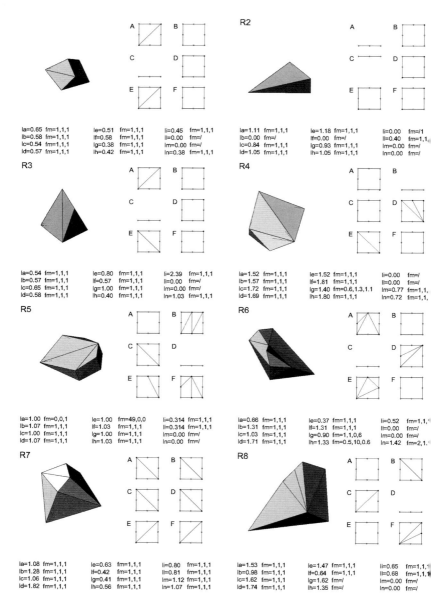

la=0.65 fm=1,1,1	le=0.51 fm=1,1,1	li=0.45 fm=1,1,1
lb=0.58 fm=1,1,1	lf=0.58 fm=1,1,1	ll=0.00 fm=/
lc=0.54 fm=1,1,1	lg=0.38 fm=1,1,1	lm=0.00 fm=/
ld=0.57 fm=1,1,1	lh=0.42 fm=1,1,1	ln=0.38 fm=1,1,1

R2

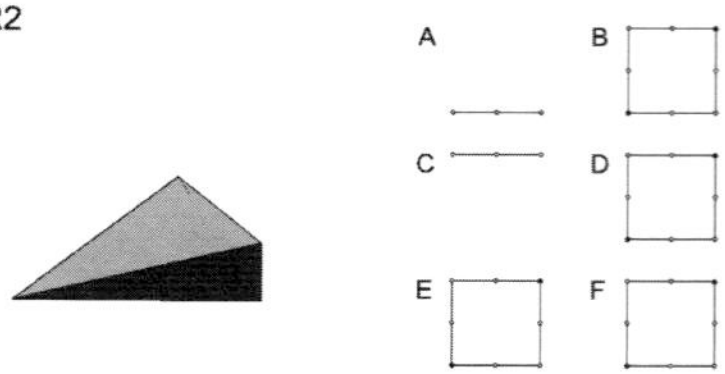

la=1.11 fm=1,1,1	le=1.18 fm=1,1,1	li=0.00 fm=/1
lb=0.00 fm=/	lf=0.00 fm=/	ll=0.40 fm=1,1,
lc=0.84 fm=1,1,1	lg=0.93 fm=1,1,1	lm=0.00 fm=/
ld=1.05 fm=1,1,1	lh=1.05 fm=1,1,1	ln=0.00 fm=/

R3

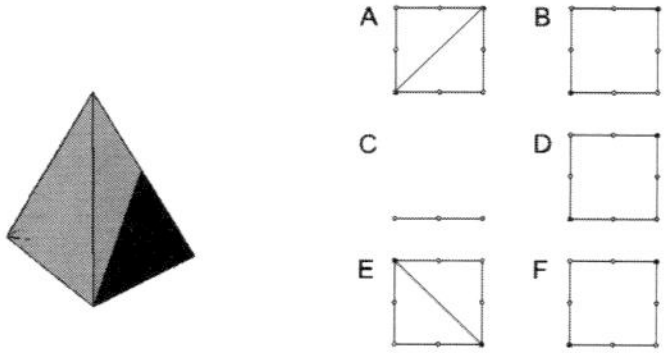

la=0.54 fm=1,1,1	le=0.80 fm=1,1,1	li=2.39 fm=1,1,1
lb=0.57 fm=1,1,1	lf=0.57 fm=1,1,1	ll=0.00 fm=/
lc=0.65 fm=1,1,1	lg=1.00 fm=1,1,1	lm=0.00 fm=/
ld=0.58 fm=1,1,1	lh=0.40 fm=1,1,1	ln=1.03 fm=1,1,1

R4

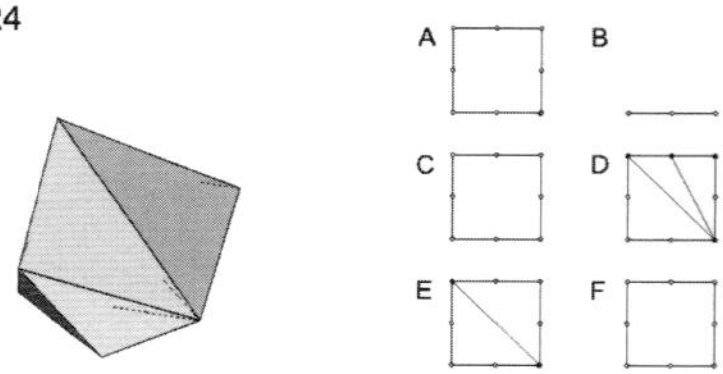

la=1.52 fm=1,1,1	le=1.52 fm=1,1,1	li=0.00 fm=/
lb=1.57 fm=1,1,1	lf=1.81 fm=1,1,1	ll=0.00 fm=/
lc=1.72 fm=1,1,1	lg=1.40 fm=0.6,1.3,1.1	lm=0.77 fm=1,1,
ld=1.69 fm=1,1,1	lh=1.80 fm=1,1,1	ln=0.72 fm=1,1,

R5

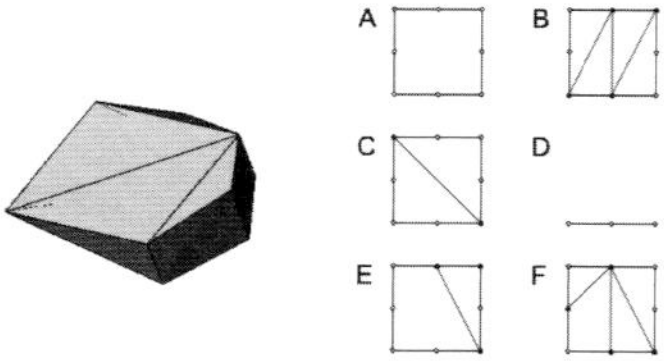

la=1.00 fm=0,0,1	le=1.00 fm=49,0,0	li=0.314 fm=1,1,1
lb=1.07 fm=1,1,1	lf=1.03 fm=1,1,1	ll=0.314 fm=1,1,1
lc=1.00 fm=1,1,1	lg=1.00 fm=1,1,1	lm=0.00 fm=/
ld=1.07 fm=1,1,1	lh=1.03 fm=1,1,1	ln=0.00 fm=/

R6

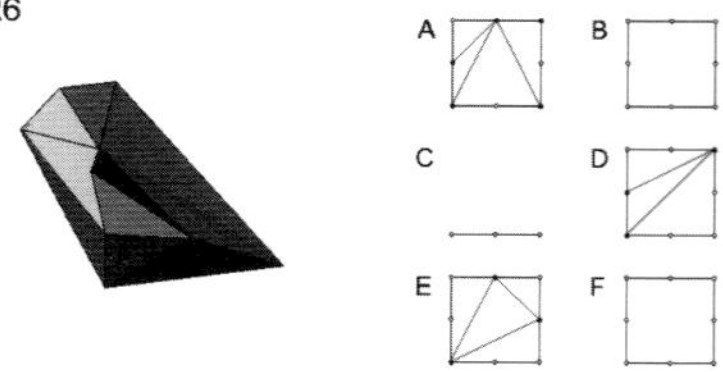

la=0.66 fm=1,1,1	le=0.37 fm=1,1,1	li=0.52 fm=1,1,
lb=1.31 fm=1,1,1	lf=1.31 fm=1,1,1	ll=0.00 fm=/
lc=1.03 fm=1,1,1	lg=0.90 fm=1,1,0,6	lm=0.00 fm=/
ld=1.71 fm=1,1,1	lh=1.33 fm=0.5,10,0.6	ln=1.42 fm=2,1.

R7

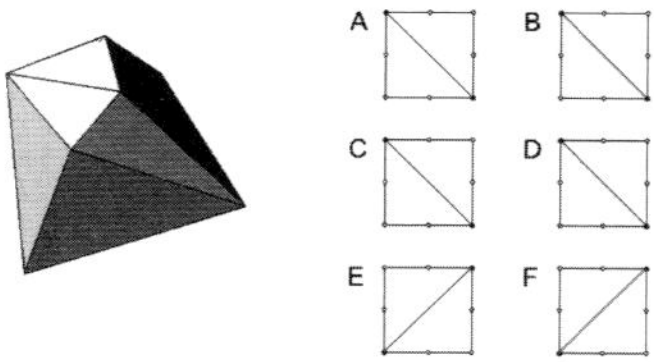

la=1.08 fm=1,1,1	le=0.63 fm=1,1,1	li=0.80 fm=1,1,1
lb=1.28 fm=1,1,1	lf=0.42 fm=1,1,1	ll=0.81 fm=1,1,1
lc=1.06 fm=1,1,1	lg=0.41 fm=1,1,1	lm=1.12 fm=1,1,1
ld=1.82 fm=1,1,1	lh=0.56 fm=1,1,1	ln=1.07 fm=1,1,1

R8

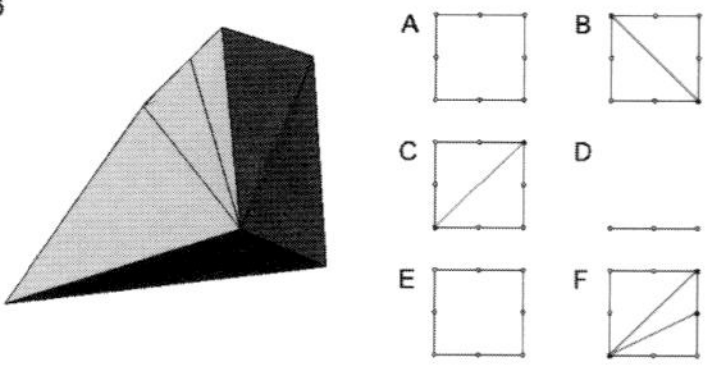

la=1.53 fm=1,1,1	le=1.47 fm=1,1,1	li=0.65 fm=1,1,
lb=0.98 fm=1,1,1	lf=0.64 fm=1,1,1	ll=0.68 fm=1,1,
lc=1.62 fm=1,1,1	lg=1.62 fm=/	lm=0.00 fm=/
ld=1.74 fm=1,1,1	lh=1.35 fm=/	ln=0.00 fm=/

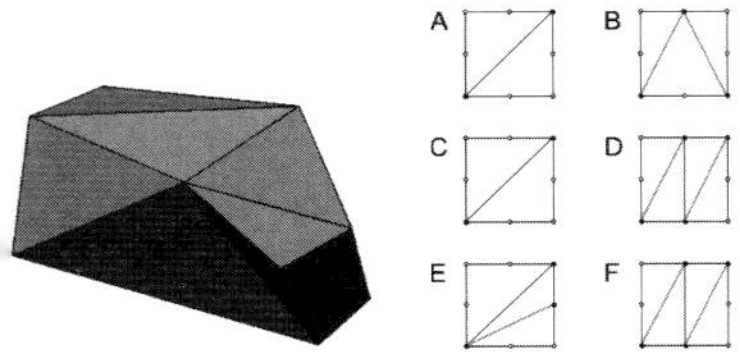

R10

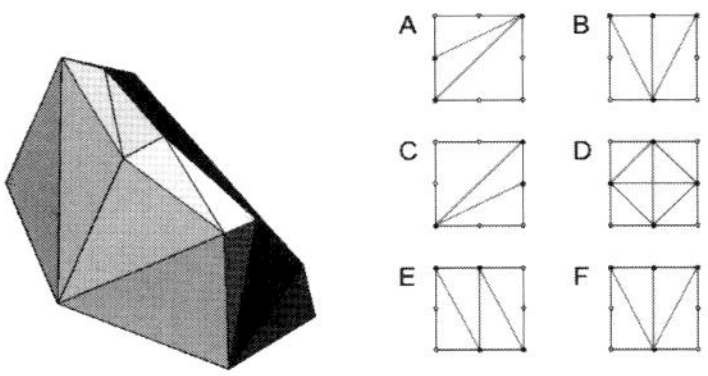

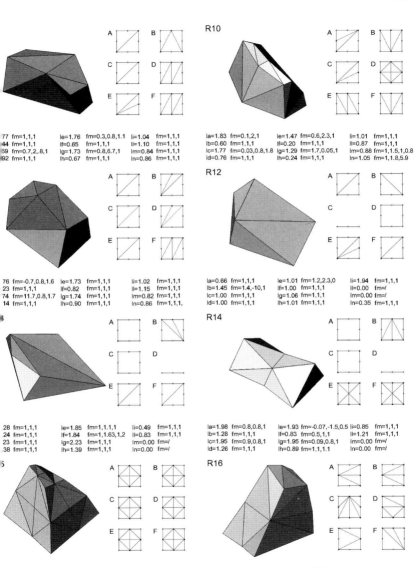

77	fm=1,1,1	le=1.76	fm=0.3,0.8,1.1	li=1.04	fm=1,1,1
44	fm=1,1,1	lf=0.65	fm=1,1,1	ll=1.10	fm=1,1,1
69	fm=0.7,2,.8,1	lg=1.73	fm=0.8,6.7,1	lm=0.84	fm=1,1,1
92	fm=1,1,1	lh=0.67	fm=1,1,1	ln=0.86	fm=1,1,1

la=1.83	fm=0.1,2,1	le=1.47	fm=0.6,2.3,1	li=1.01	fm=1,1,1
lb=0.60	fm=1,1,1	lf=0.20	fm=1,1,1	ll=0.87	fm=1,1,1
lc=1.77	fm=0.03,0.8,1.8	lg=1.29	fm=1.7,0.05,1	lm=0.88	fm=1,1.5,1,0.8
ld=0.76	fm=1,1,1	lh=0.24	fm=1,1,1	ln=1.05	fm=1,1.8,5.9

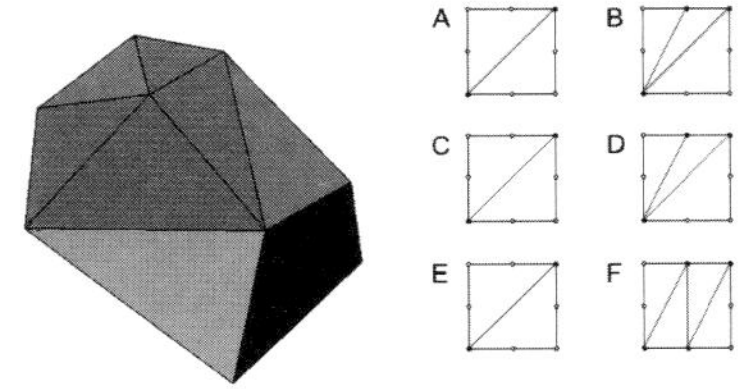

R12

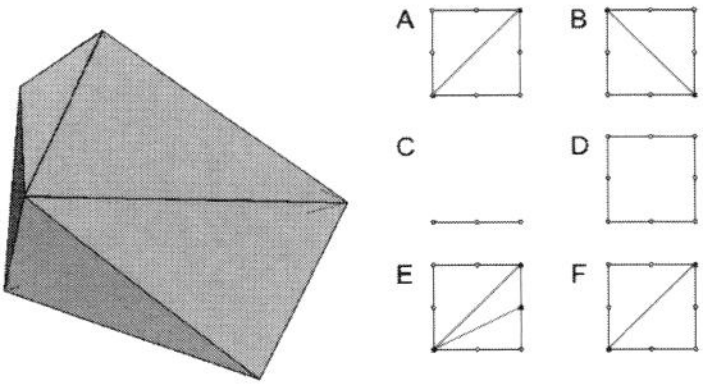

76	fm=-0.7,0.8,1.6	le=1.73	fm=1,1,1	li=1.02	fm=1,1,1
23	fm=1,1,1	lf=0.82	fm=1,1,1	ll=1.15	fm=1,1,1
74	fm=11.7,0.8,1.7	lg=1.74	fm=1,1,1	lm=0.82	fm=1,1,1
14	fm=1,1,1	lh=0.90	fm=1,1,1	ln=0.86	fm=1,1,1,

la=0.66	fm=1,1,1	le=1.01	fm=1.2,2.3,0	li=1.94	fm=1,1,1
lb=1.45	fm=1.4,-10,1	lf=1.00	fm=1,1,1	ll=0.00	fm=/
lc=1.00	fm=1,1,1	lg=1.06	fm=1,1,1	lm=0.00	fm=/
ld=1.00	fm=1,1,1	lh=1.01	fm=1,1,1	ln=0.35	fm=1,1,1

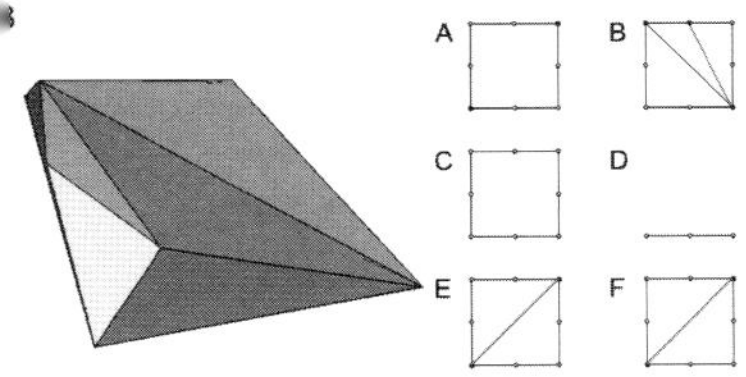

R14

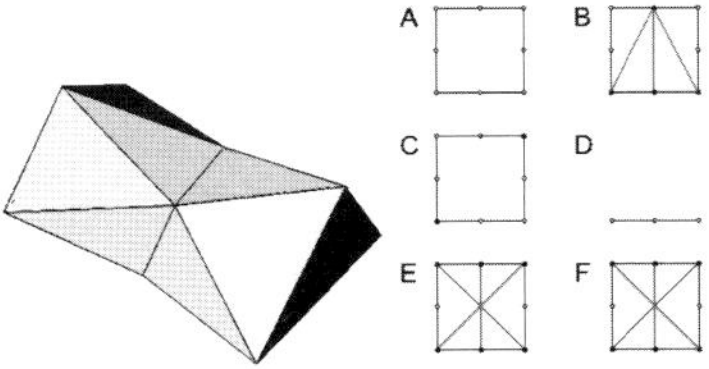

28	fm=1,1,1	le=1.85	fm=1,1.1,1	li=0.49	fm=1,1,1
24	fm=1,1,1	lf=1.84	fm=1,1.63,1,2	ll=0.83	fm=1,1,1
23	fm=1,1,1	lg=2.23	fm=1,1,1	lm=0.00	fm=/
38	fm=1,1,1	lh=1.39	fm=1,1,1	ln=0.00	fm=/

la=1.98	fm=0.8,0.8,1	le=1.93	fm=-0.07,-1.5,0.5	li=0.85	fm=1,1,1
lb=1.28	fm=1,1,1	lf=0.83	fm=0.5,1,1	ll=1.21	fm=1,1,1
lc=1.95	fm=0.9,0.8,1	lg=1.95	fm=0.09,0.8,1	lm=0.00	fm=/
ld=1.26	fm=1,1,1	lh=0.89	fm=1,1,1.1	ln=0.00	fm=/

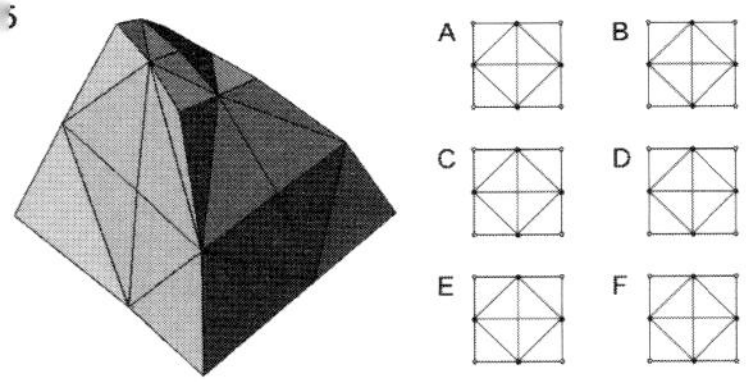

R16

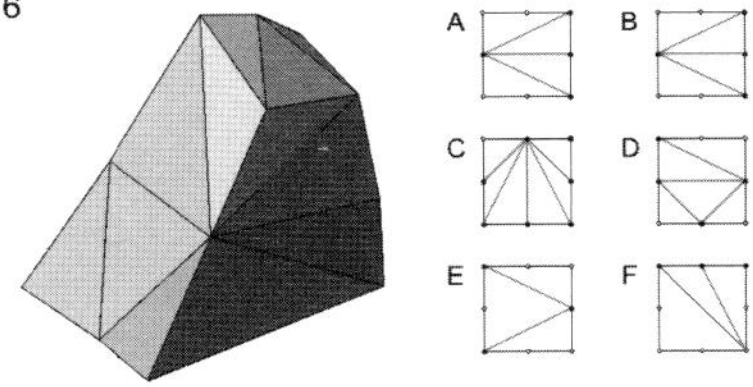

48	fm=2.5,1,1	le=0.61	fm=1,1.1,1	li=2.39	fm=1,1.1,0.9
81	fm=1.9,0.9,1	lf=1.06	fm=1,1,1	ll=2.43	fm=1.1,0.9,1
48	fm=0.5,1,1	lg=1.08	fm=1,1,1	lm=2.00	fm=1.2,1.1,1
52	fm=1,1,1	lh=1.00	fm=1,1,1.1	ln=1.69	fm=1.1,1,2.1,1

la=1.85	fm=1,1,1	le=0.74	fm=1,1,1	li=1.65	fm=0.9,0.9,1,1
lb=0.90	fm=1,1,1	lf=0.58	fm=1,1,1	ll=1.22	fm=0.5,1,1
lc=1.85	fm=0.5,1,1	lg=0.67	fm=1,1.2,1	lm=1.57	fm=0.9,1.1,0.9
ld=1.47	fm=1,1,1	lh=0.85	fm=1,1,1	ln=2.00	fm=1,1,1.1

R1

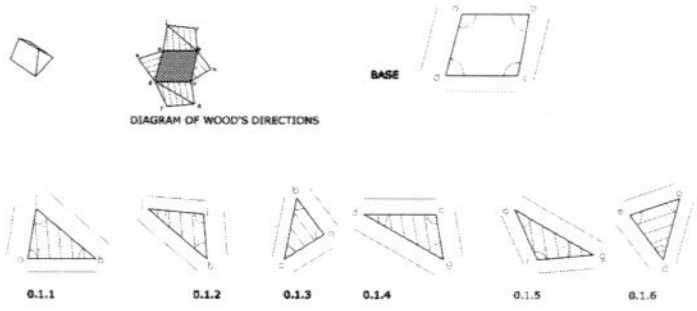

R2

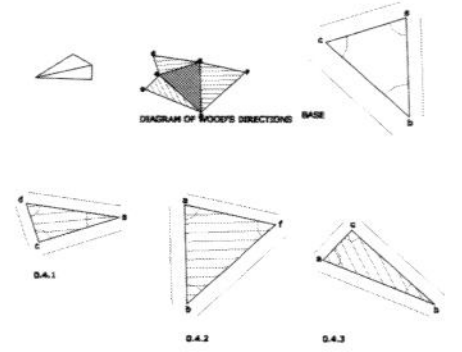

R3

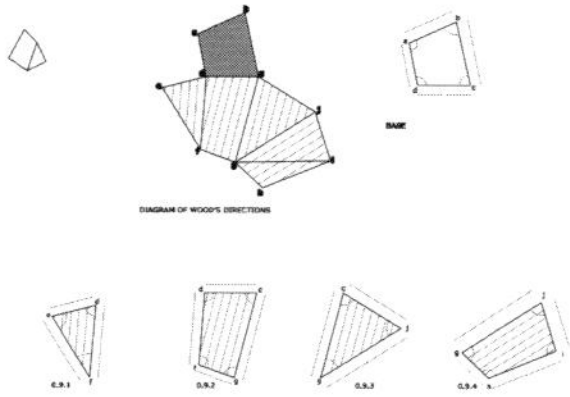

R4

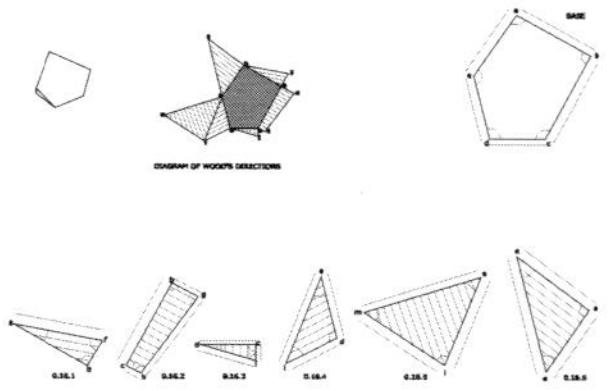

R5

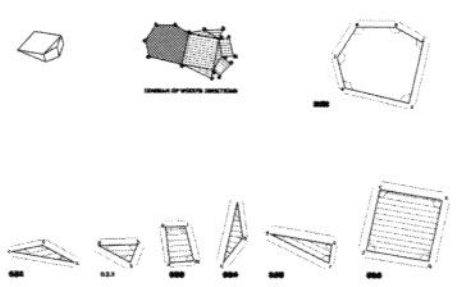

R6

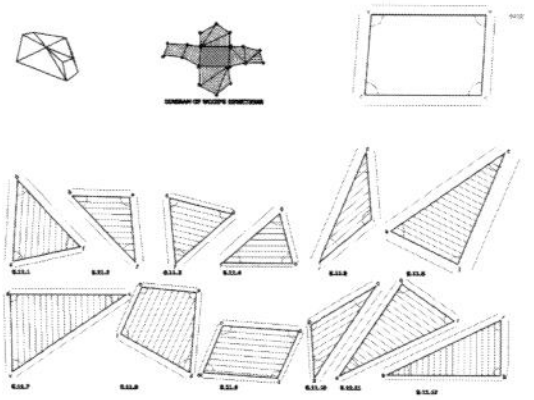

R7

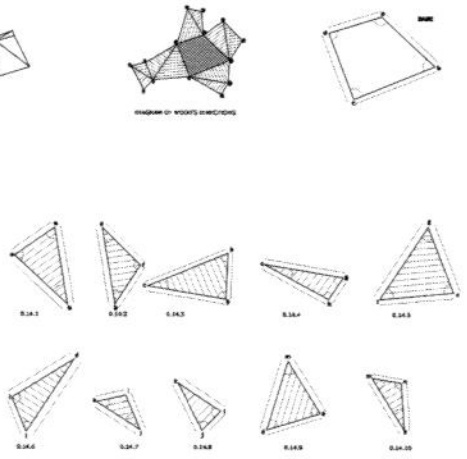

R8

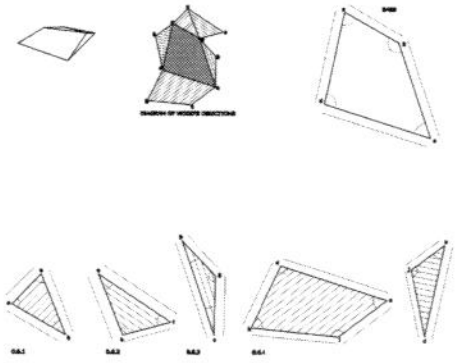

R9

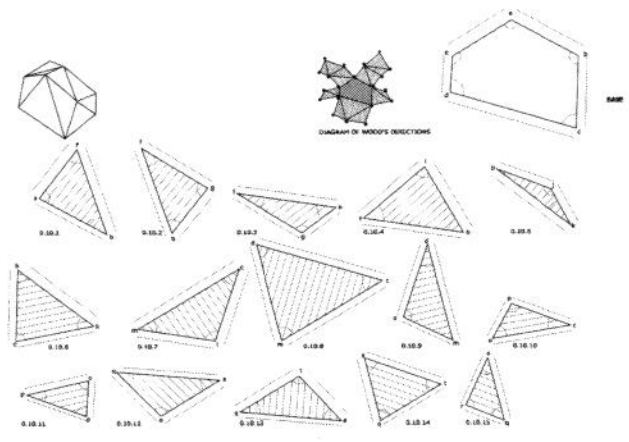

R10

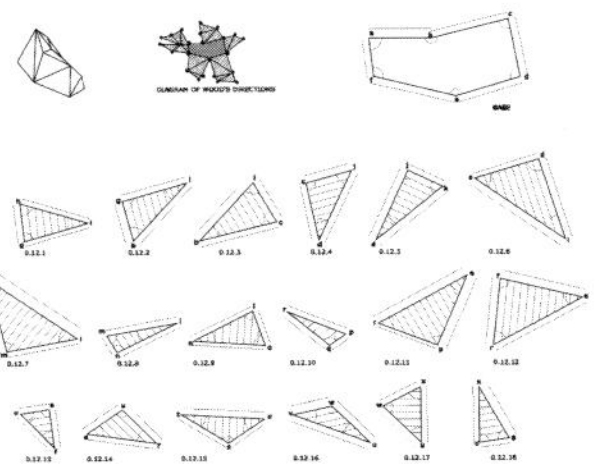

R11

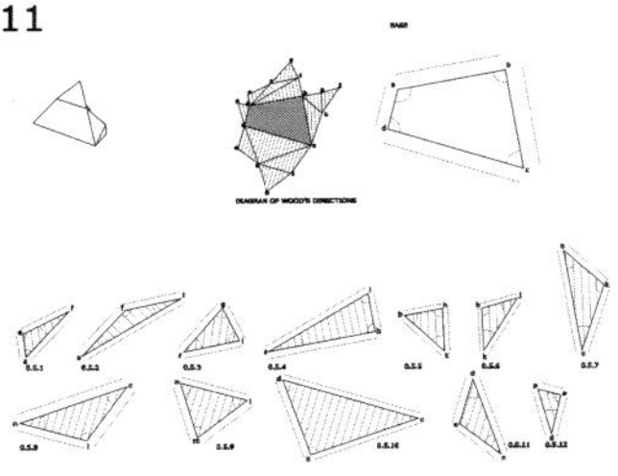

R12

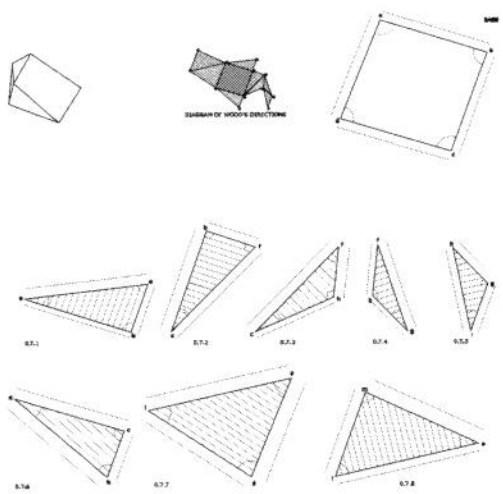

R13

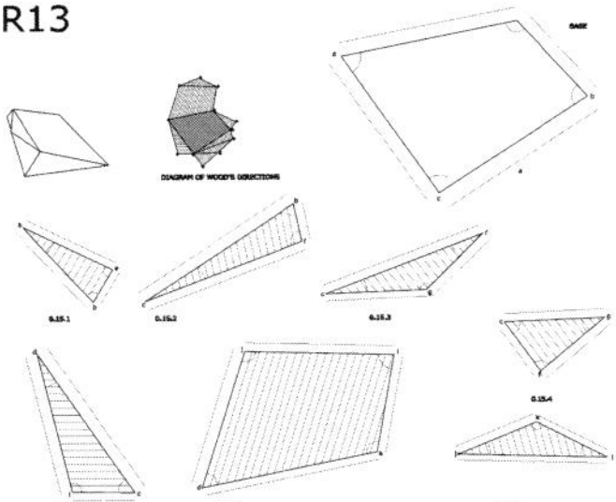

R14

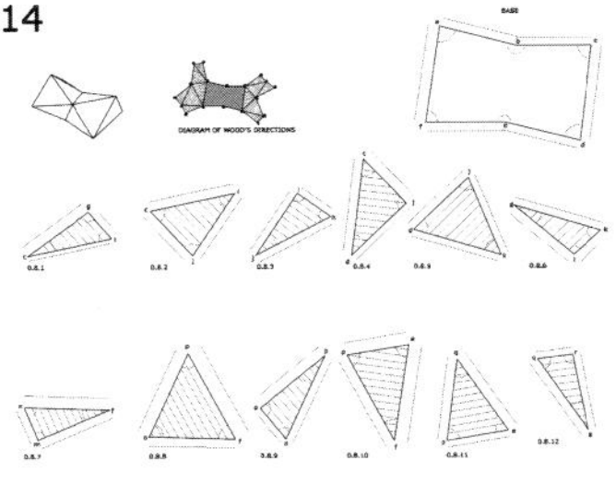

R16

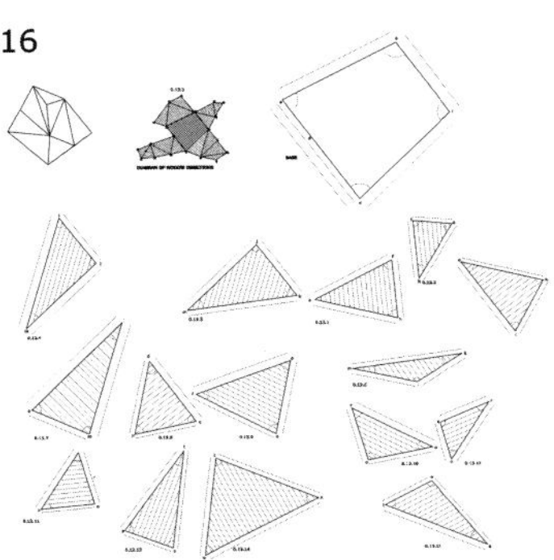

R16

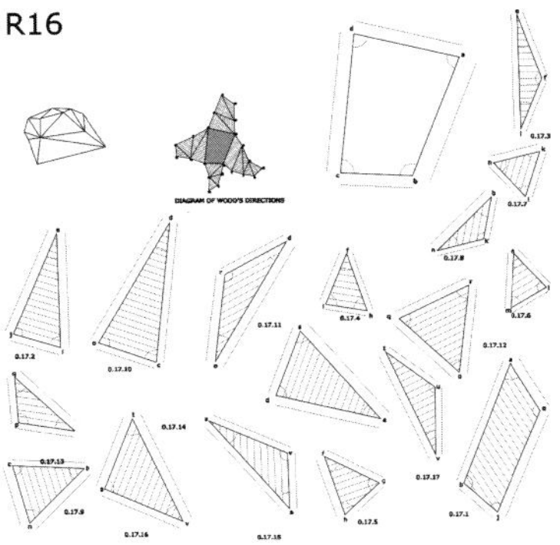

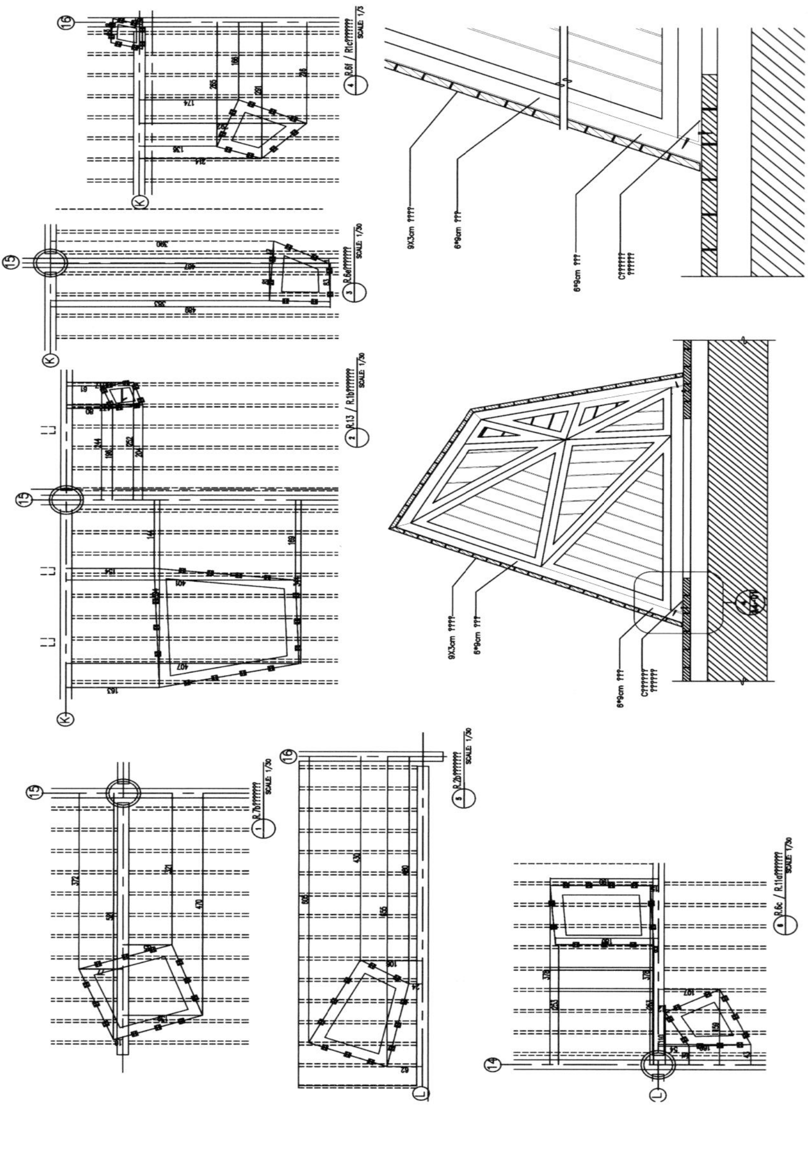

Fugee Port

Taiwan. Project 2003—
Local partner:
J.M. Lin The Observer Design Group

1st Prize international competition

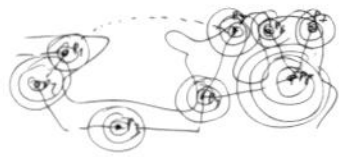

Excursion to the new taiwanese tradition.

Fugee is a small fishing port with a particular geographic meaning: is just by the side of the north cape of the Taiwan island. Taking into account the spatial limitations of the Port of Fugee, our proposal envisages a tourist operation designed to complement Taiwan's principal existing facilities, exploring the possibilities of Fugee's traditional productive specialization, its relationship to the sea and fishing, and developing other alternative uses of the space that are linked to the green space to the North-east.

The proposal is structured in three parts:

1 Port
Constructing a series of individualized roofs to create an interior micro climate that will protect the fish market, the restaurant and the shops. The roof, with water, will give shelter from the sun and help to purify the air of the smell of fish.

2 North Itinerary: Excursion to the north with three enclaves
Artificial seawater swimming pools (as in the Canary Islands) to enable a richer spectrum of leisure use of the port.
Panoramic belvedere viewing platform looking to the north, with a wooden deck and a scale model of Taiwan.
Bar close to the beach

3 Future
In the future a new prestige hotel by the port, beach hotels and a series of public amenities will encourage residence in this exceptional setting.

The port

In the port area the project envisages uses directly related to fishing, configuring the space as a focus for food and crafts, in this way rooting the proposal in the history of the Port of Fugee. The retail sale of fish will be complemented with the construction of a series of restaurants of different sizes and categories in order to respond to the different levels of demand; however, the aim is that Fugee should be identified as a major centre of gastronomic at the national level, through its specialization in seafood. At the same time, it is suggested that the souvenir shops should have special sections devoted to Taiwanese crafts where tourists can watch the craftsmen at work. The spectrum of uses will be active for 18 hours a day, alternating according to their nature.

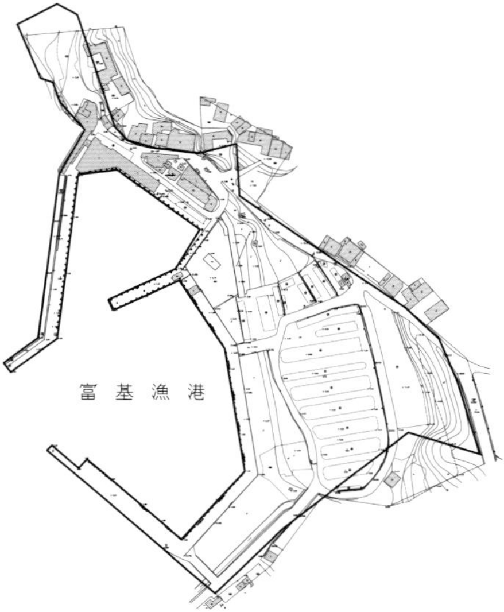

GEOGRAPHY

The port of Fugee

GEOMETRY

A generic schema

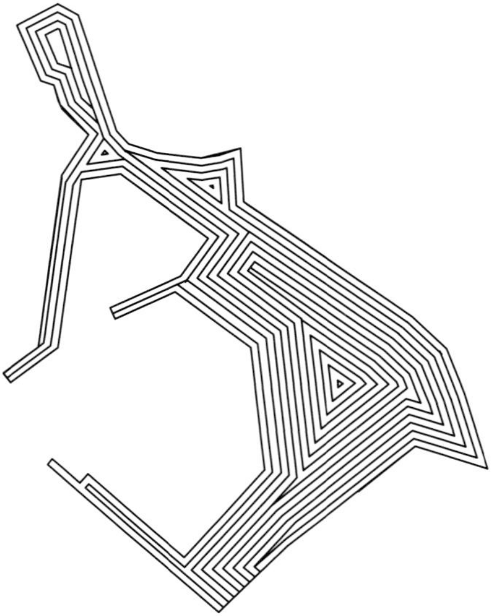

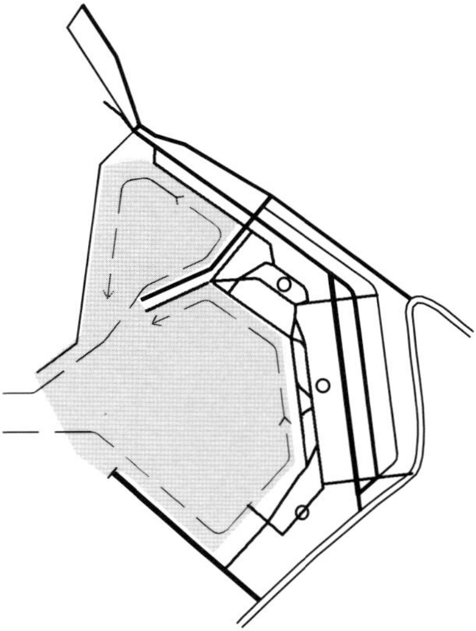

LOGIC

Flows and nodes in the space

STRUCTURE

A specific schema

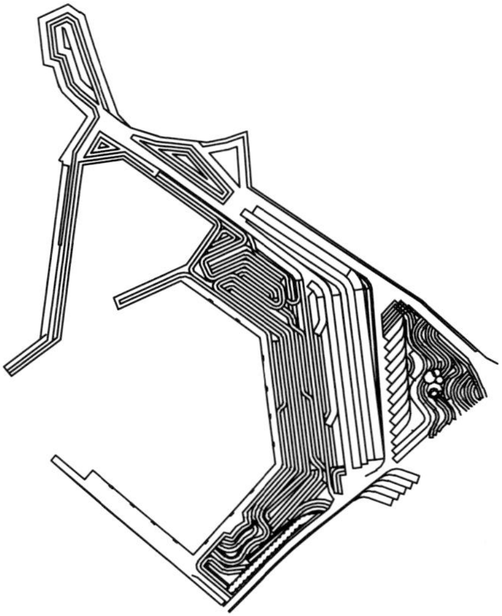

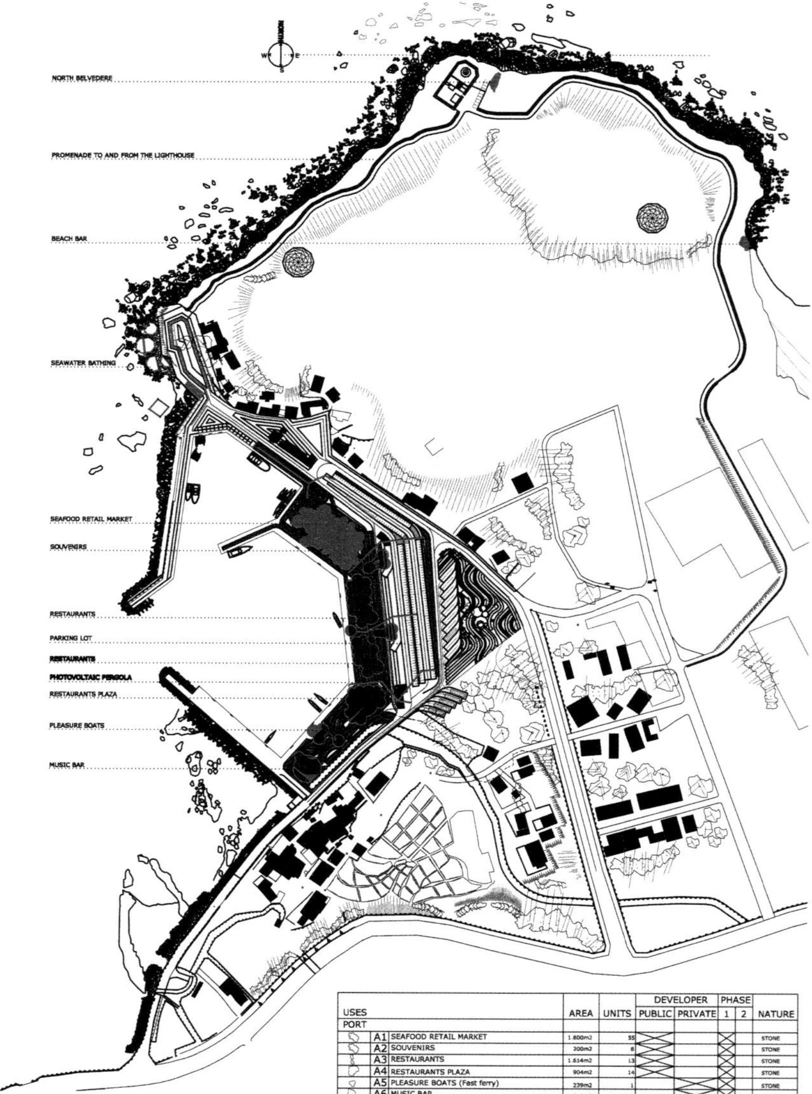

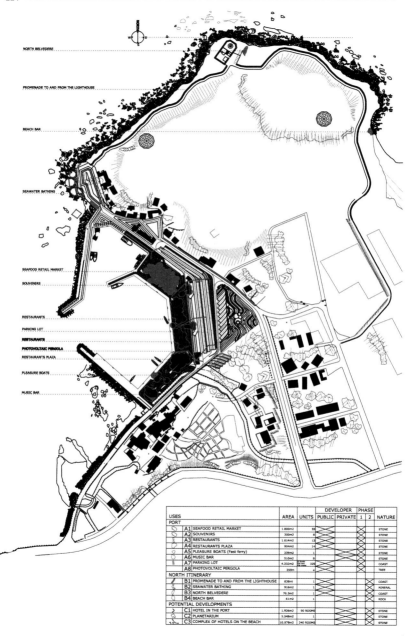

USES			AREA	UNITS	DEVELOPER PUBLIC	DEVELOPER PRIVATE	PHASE 1	PHASE 2	NATURE
PORT									
	A1	SEAFOOD RETAIL MARKET	1.800m2	55	X		X		STONE
	A2	SOUVENIRS	200m2	8	X		X		STONE
	A3	RESTAURANTS	1.614m2	13	X		X		STONE
	A4	RESTAURANTS PLAZA	904m2	14	X		X		STONE
	A5	PLEASURE BOATS (Fast ferry)	239m2	1		X	X		STONE
	A6	MUSIC BAR	510m2	8		X	X		STONE
	A7	PARKING LOT	4.232m2	325	X		X		COAST
	A8	PHOTOVOLTAIC PERGOLA	350m	4	X		X		TREE
NORTH ITINERARY									
	B1	PROMENADE TO AND FROM THE LIGHTHOUSE	838ml	1	X			X	COAST
	B2	SEAWATER BATHING	916m2	1	X			X	MINERAL
	B3	NORTH BELVEDERE	76.5m2	1	X			X	COAST
	B4	BEACH BAR	61m2	1		X		X	ROCK
POTENTIAL DEVELOPMENTS									
	C1	HOTEL IN THE PORT	1.926m2	90 ROOMS		X		X	STONE
	C2	PLANETARIUM	5.548m2	1		X		X	STONE
	C3	COMPLEX OF HOTELS ON THE BEACH	10.978m2	240 ROOMS		X		X	STONE

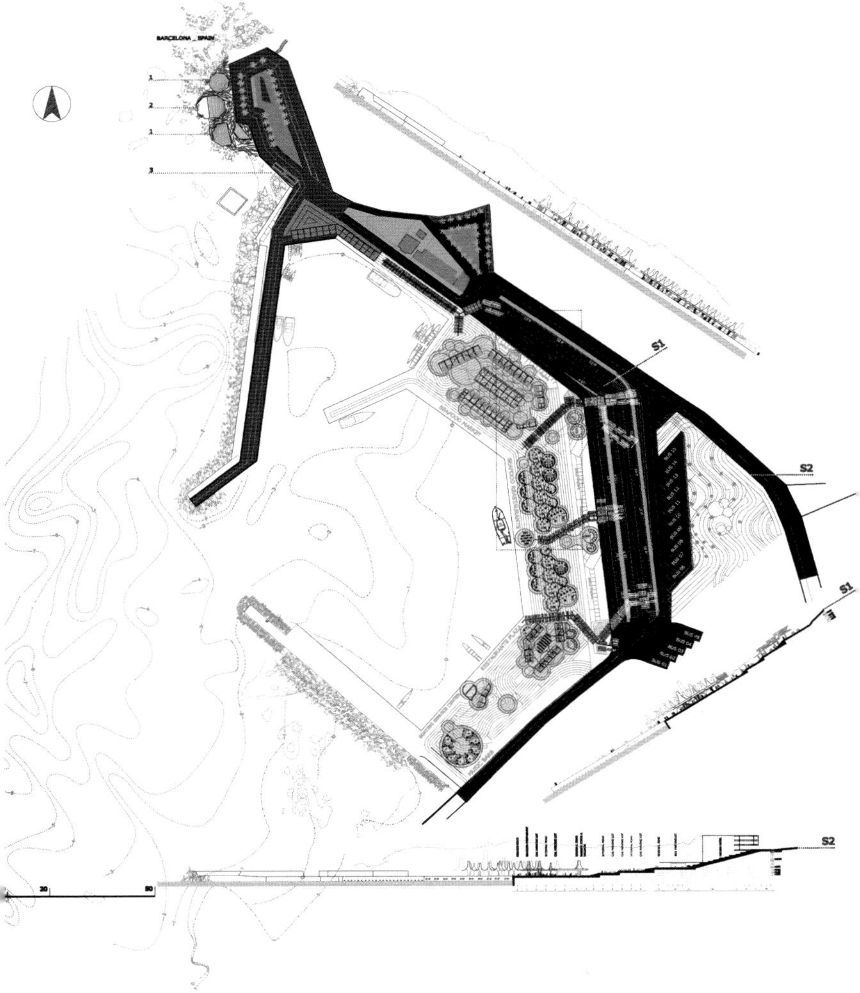
BARCELONA _ SPAIN
1
2
1
3
S1
S2
S1
S2
SEAFOOD MARKET
20
50

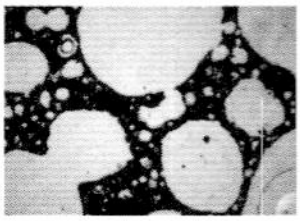

GEOGRAPHY

Volcanic rock created when gases are expelled and the material solidifies

GEOMETRY

The cavities in the rock have a 180° geometrical relationship

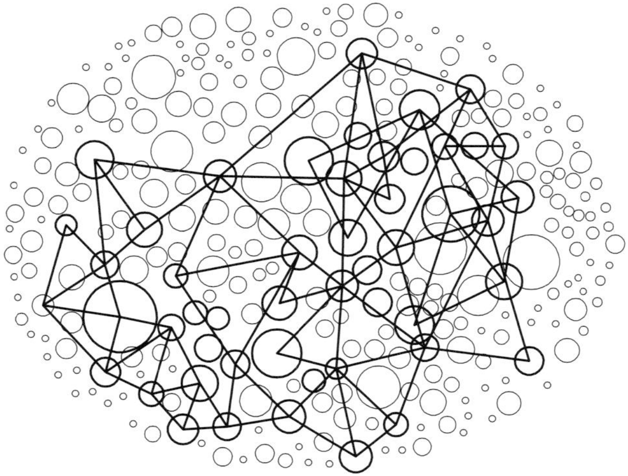

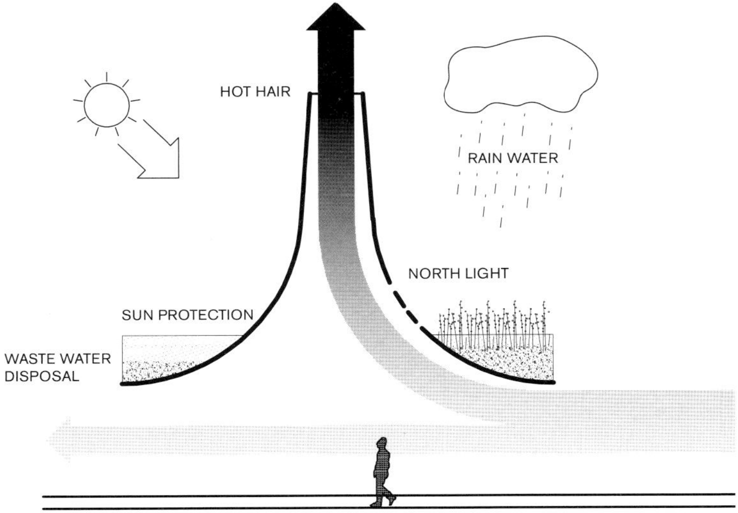

LOGIC

The roof stimulates air movement creating an artificial microclimate

STRUCTURE

Structural pattern based on the ordering principles of the rock

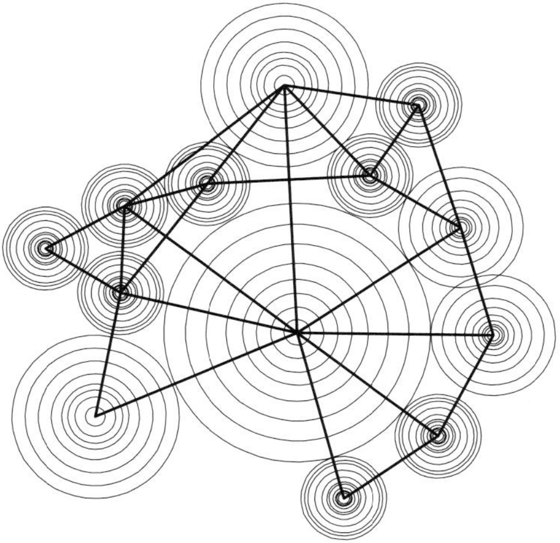

ON SALE

Roof with natural water treatment

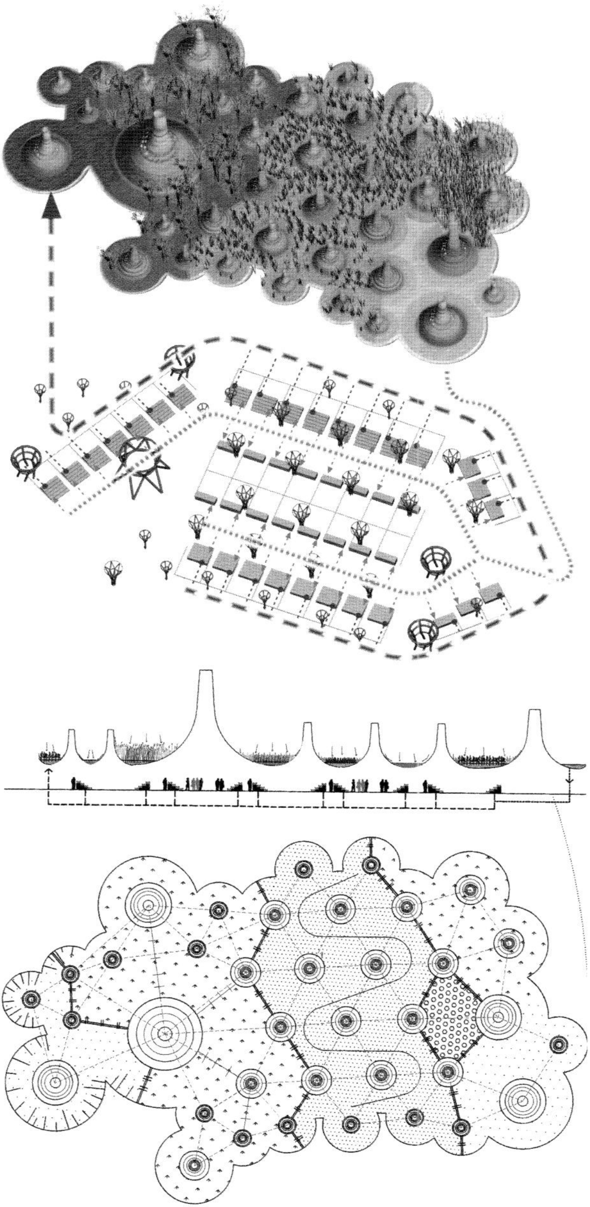

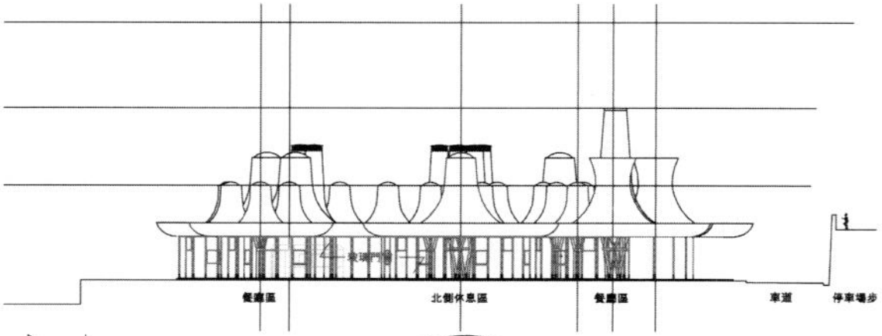
餐廳區
北側休息區
餐廳區
車道

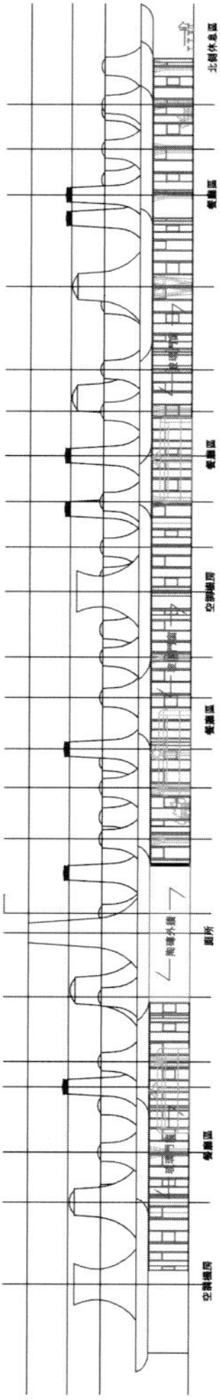

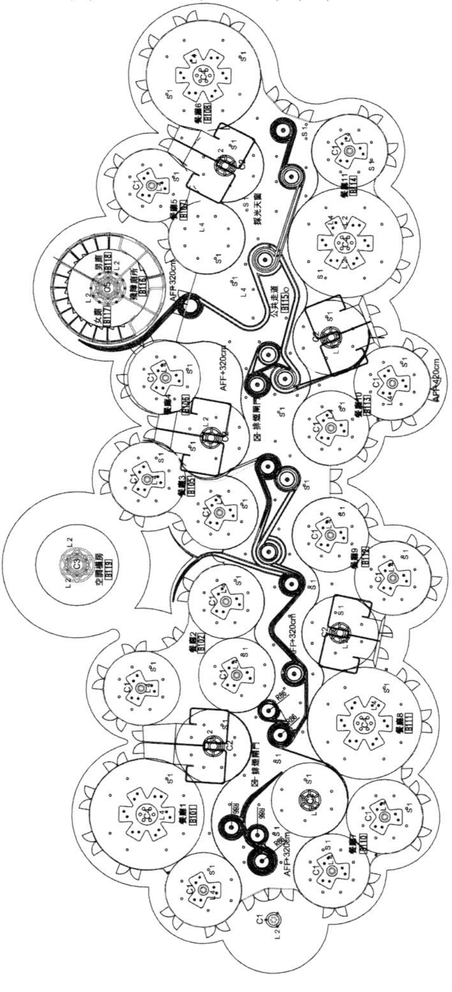

Market

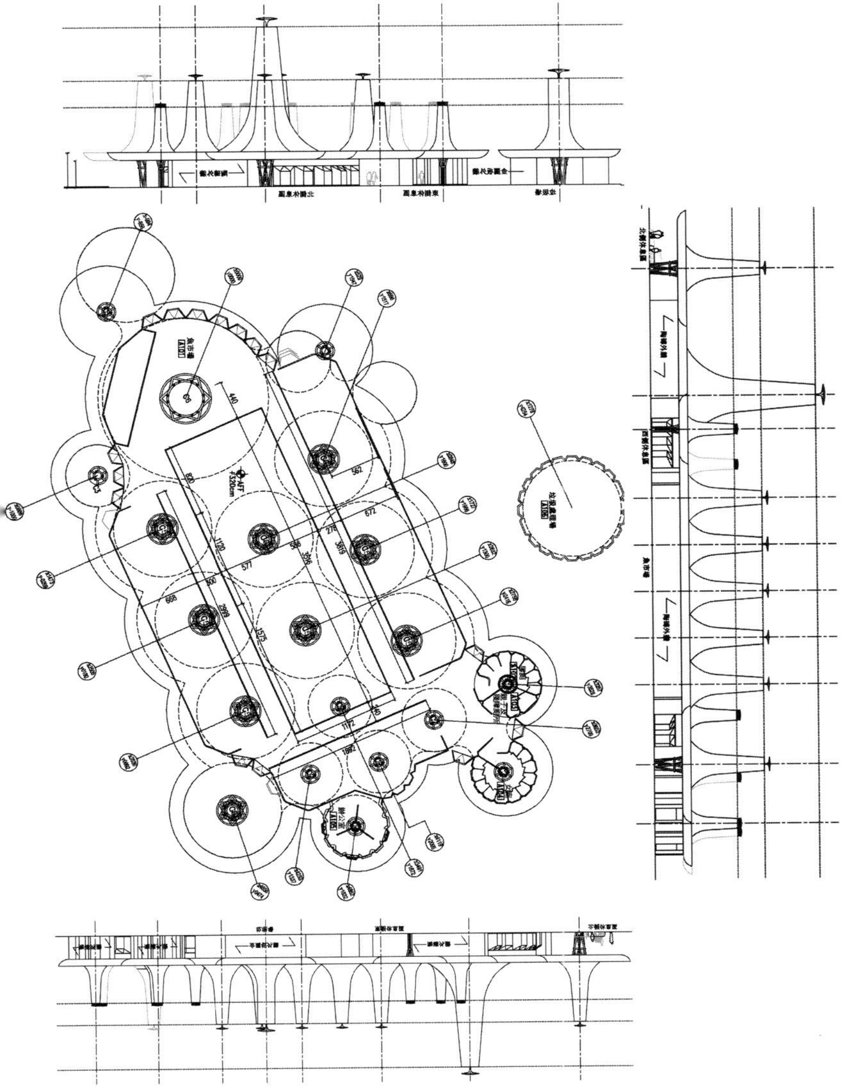

U1

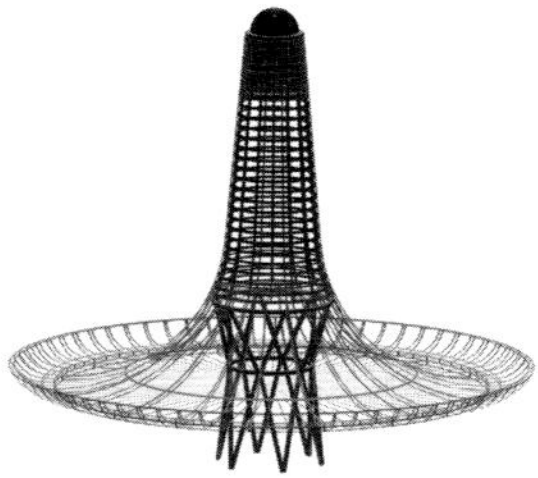

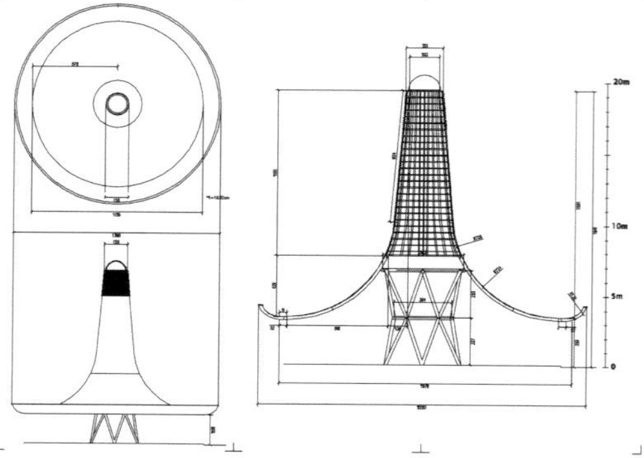

U2

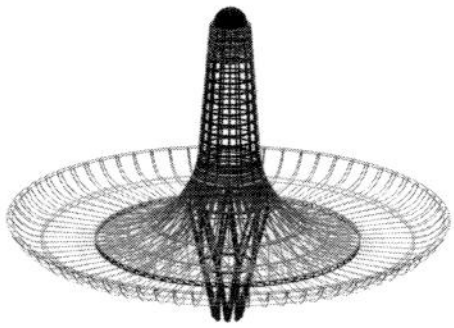

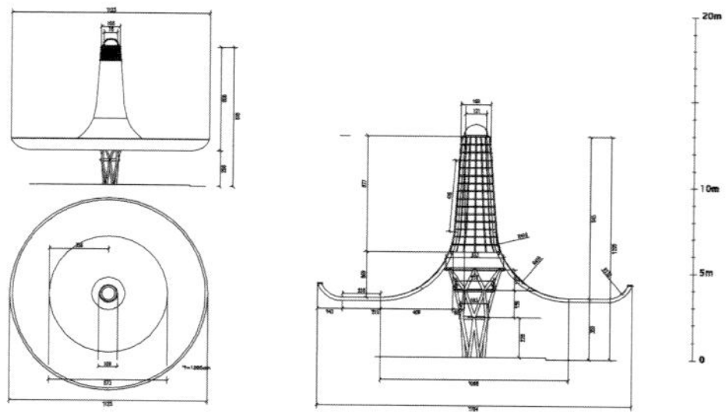

U3

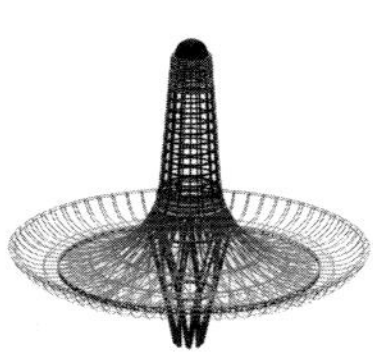

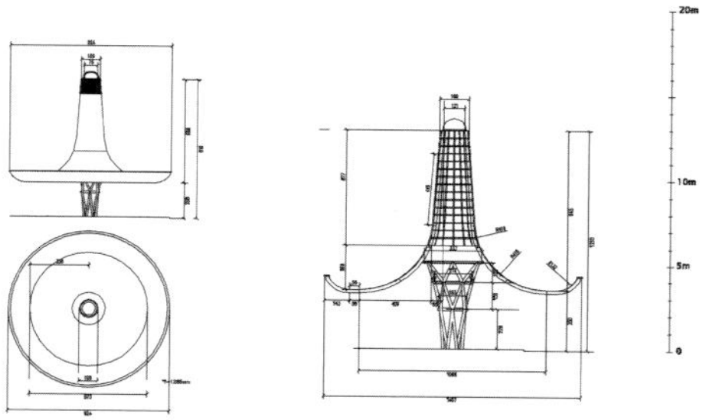

Umbrellas

U4

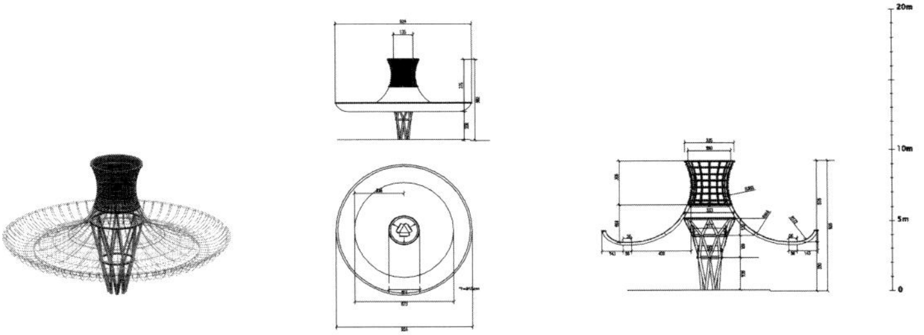

U5

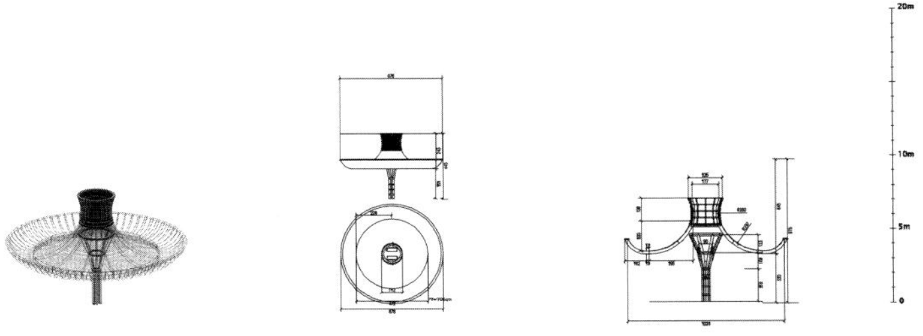

U6

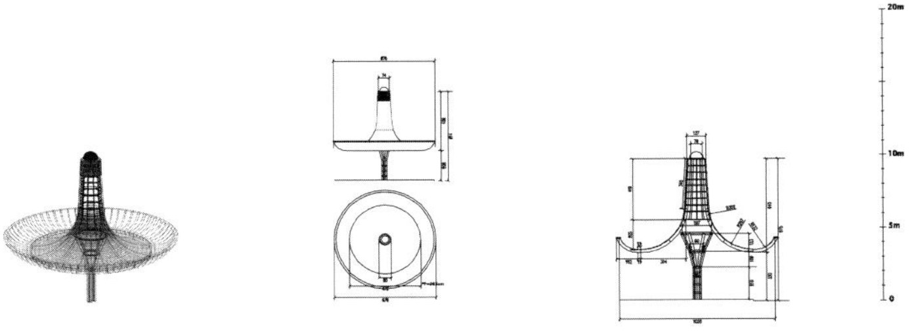

Insolation

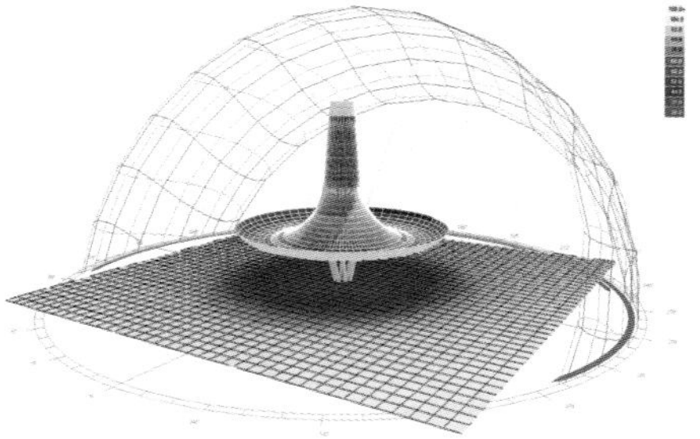

Insolation

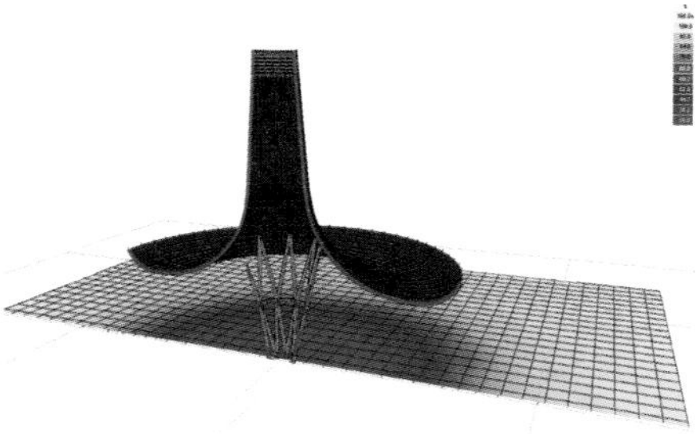

Wind analysis

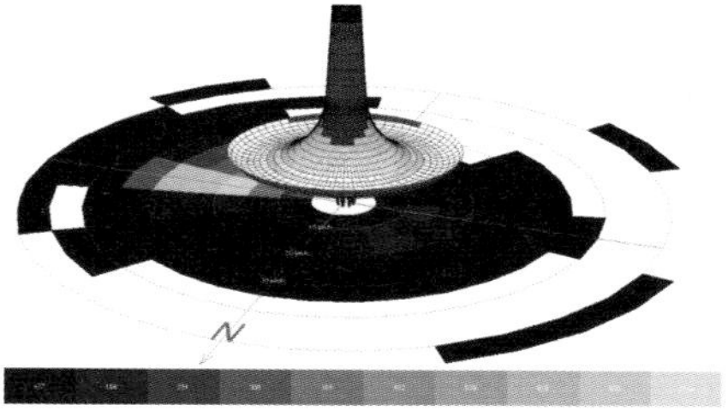

Study of shadows

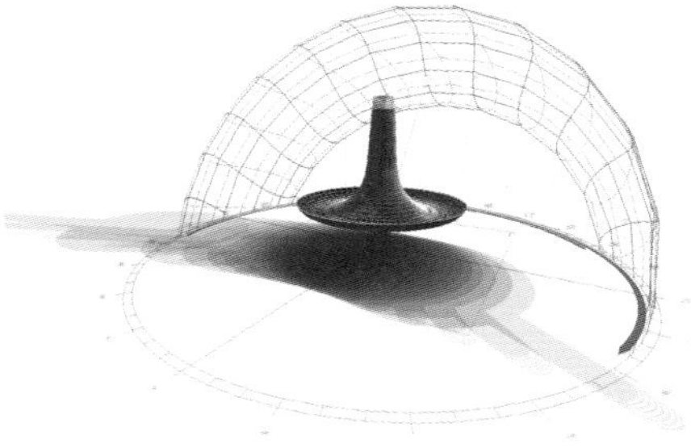

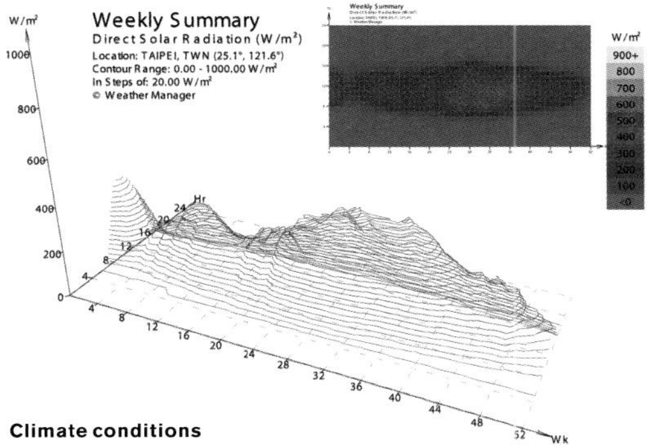

Climate conditions

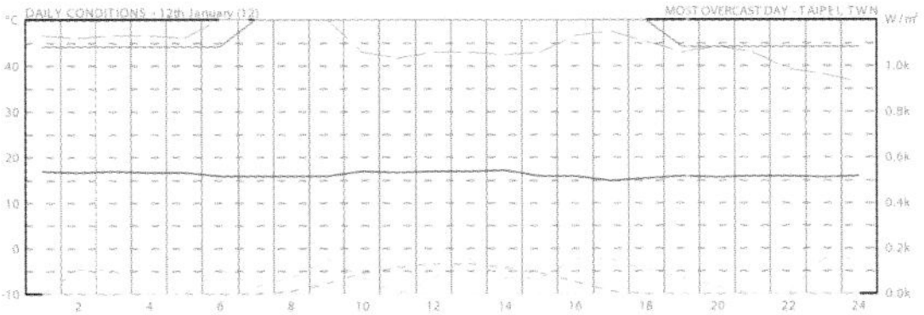

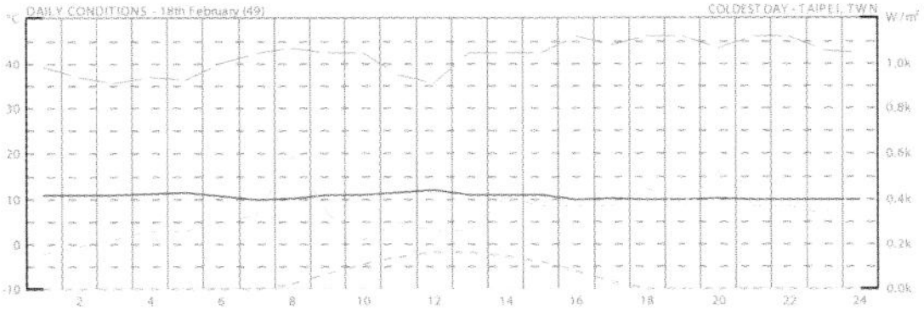

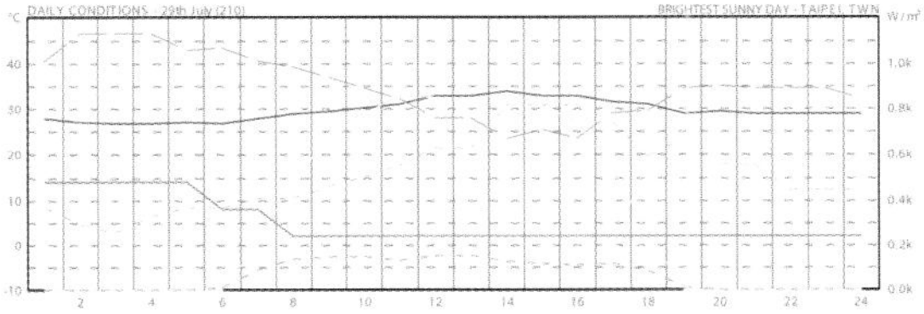

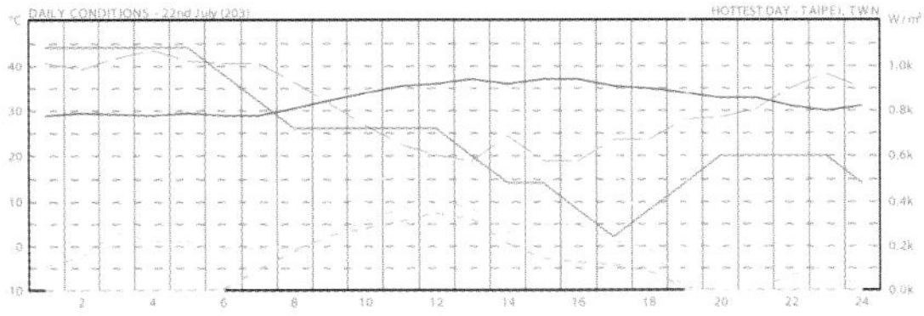

Prevailing winds

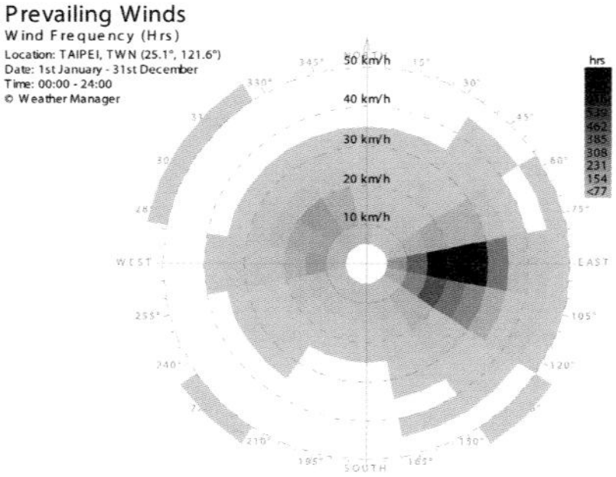

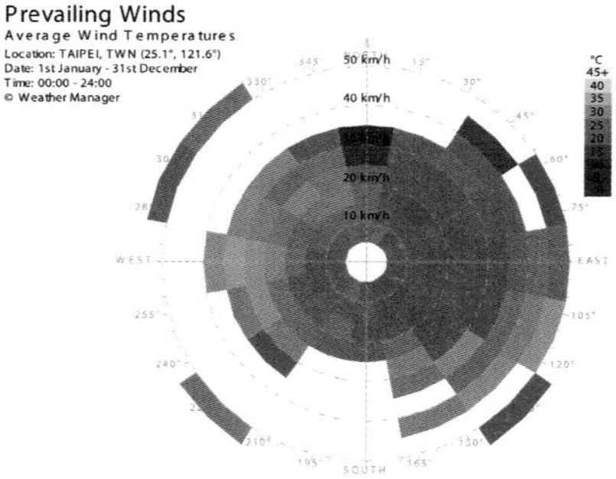

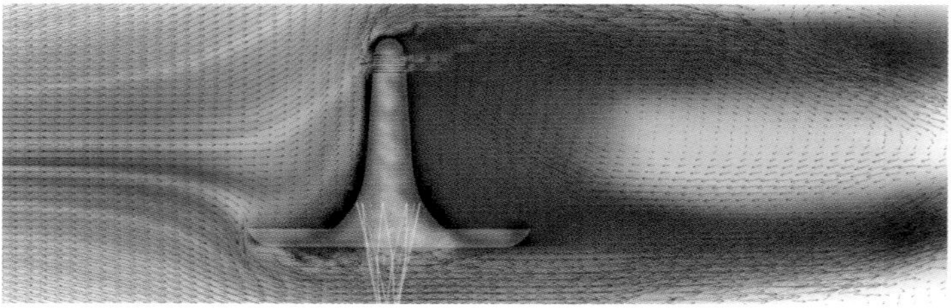

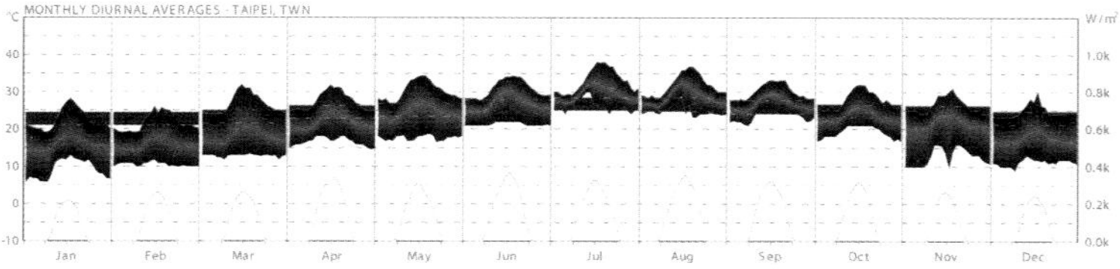

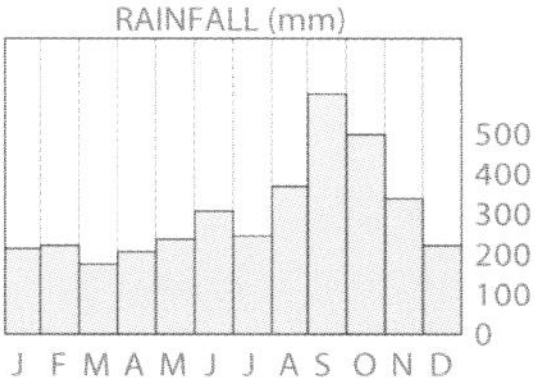
RAINFALL (mm)
500
400
300
200
100
0
J F M A M J J A S O N D

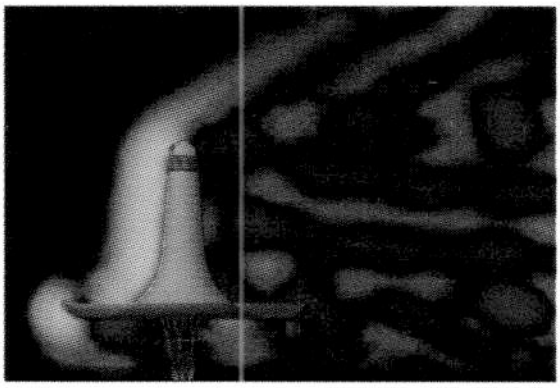

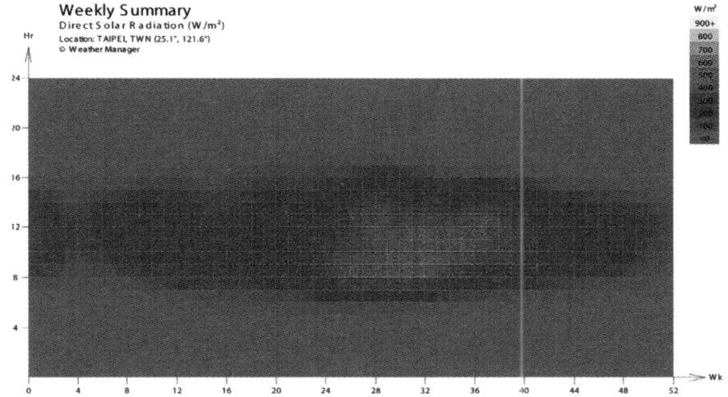
Weekly Summary
Direct Solar Radiation (W/m²)
Location: TAIPEI, TWN (25.1°, 121.6°)
© Weather Manager
Hr
Wk
W/m²
900+
800
700
600
500
400
300
200
100

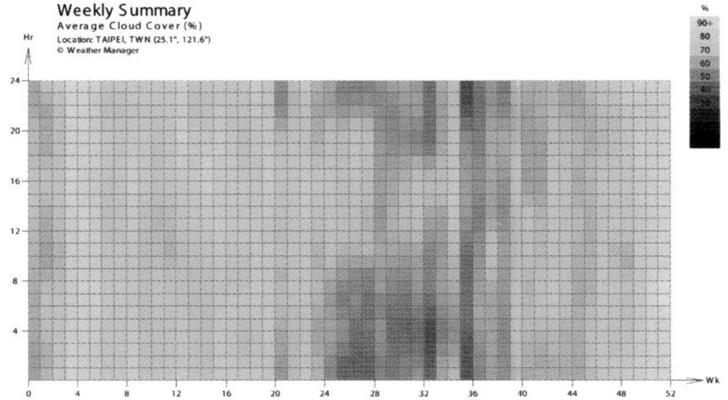
Weekly Summary
Average Cloud Cover (%)
Location: TAIPEI, TWN (25.1°, 121.6°)
© Weather Manager
Hr
Wk
%
90+
80
70
60
50
40

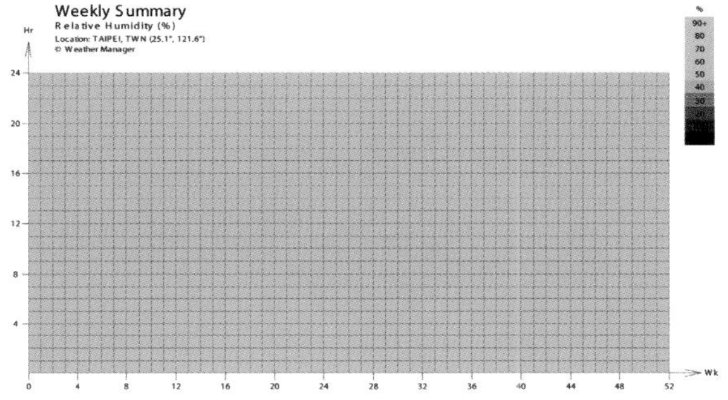
Weekly Summary
Relative Humidity (%)
Location: TAIPEI, TWN (25.1°, 121.6°)
© Weather Manager
Hr
Wk
%
90+
80
70
60
50
40
30

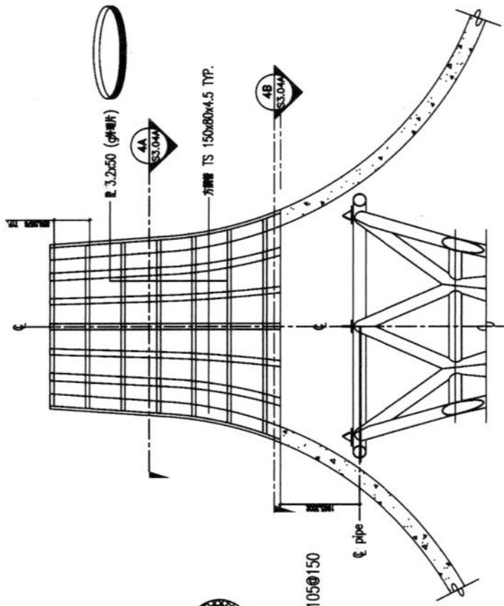
℘ 3.2x50
TS 150x80x4.5 TYP.
4A
S3.04A
4B
S3.04A
℄ pipe

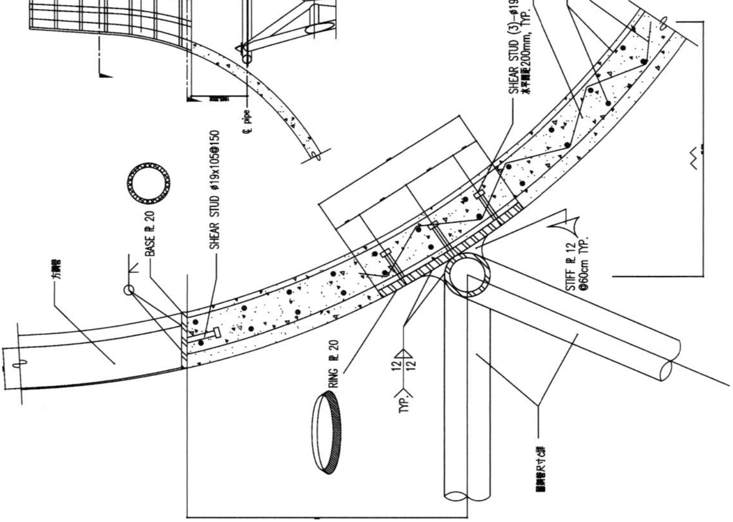
SHEAR STUD (3)-ø19x105
水平間距200mm, TYP.
#5@200mm (H)(V)
#5@200mm (V)
BASE ℘ 20
SHEAR STUD ø19x105@150
STIFF ℘ 12
@60cm TYP.
RING ℘ 20
TYP.
12
12

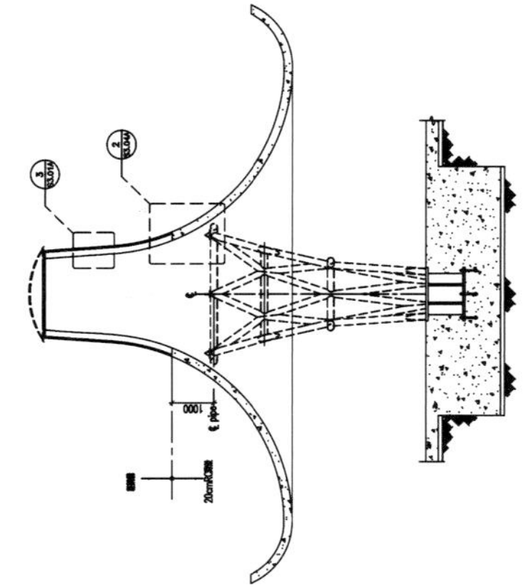
1000
℄ pipe

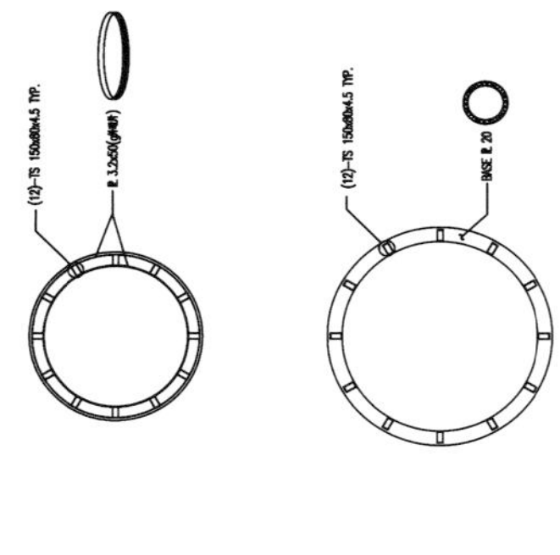
(12)-TS 150x80x4.5 TYP.
℘ 3.2x50
BASE ℘ 20

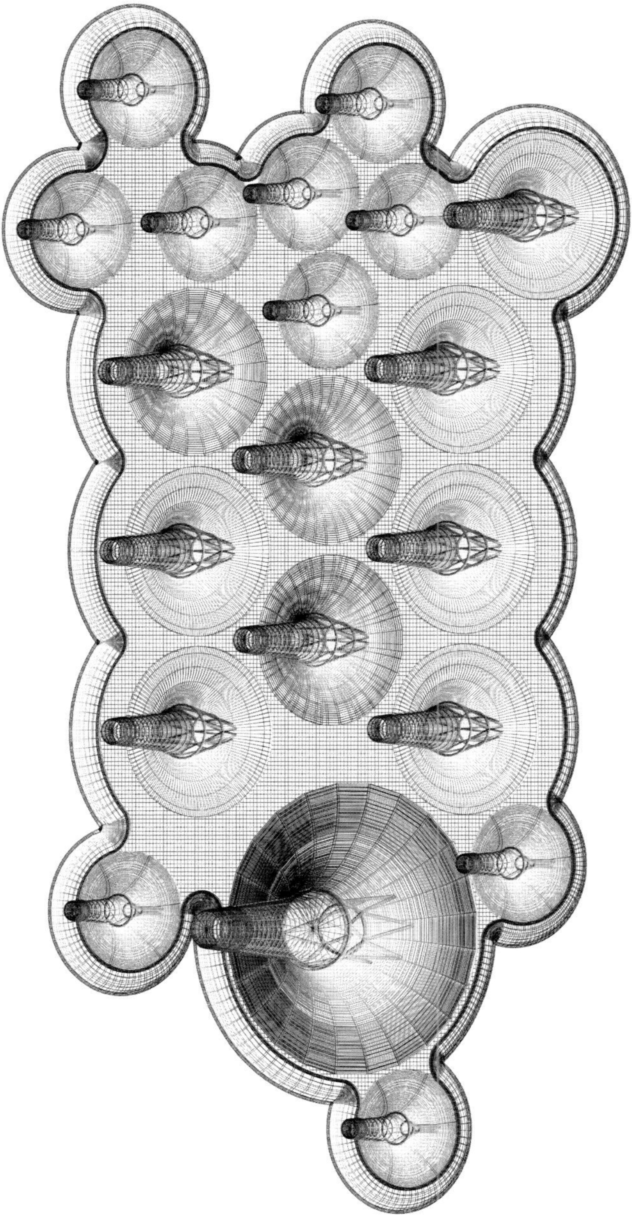

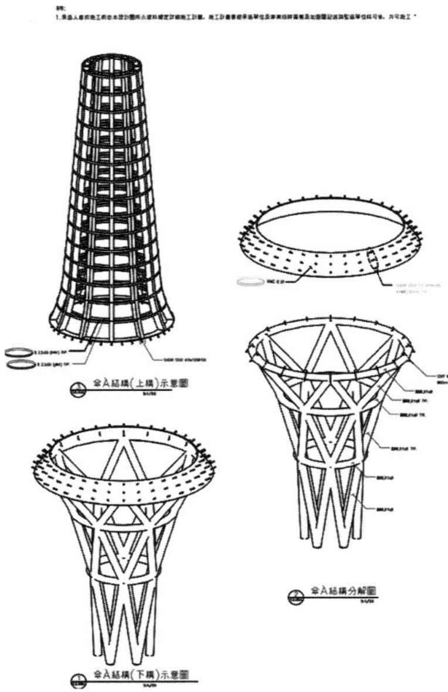
傘A結構(上構)示意圖
傘A結構分解圖
傘A結構(下構)示意圖

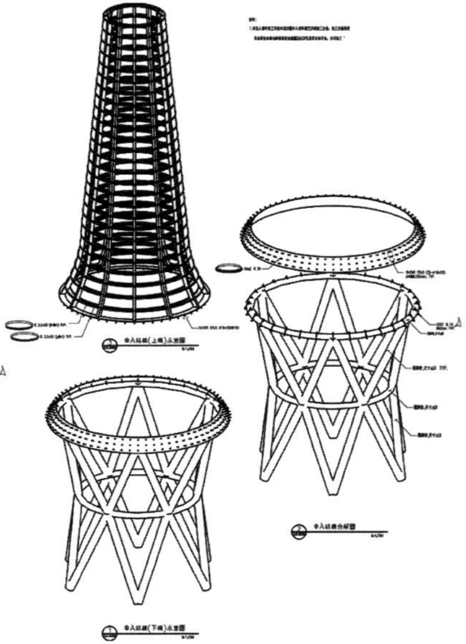
傘A結構(上構)示意圖
傘A結構分解圖
傘A結構(下構)示意圖

Structure

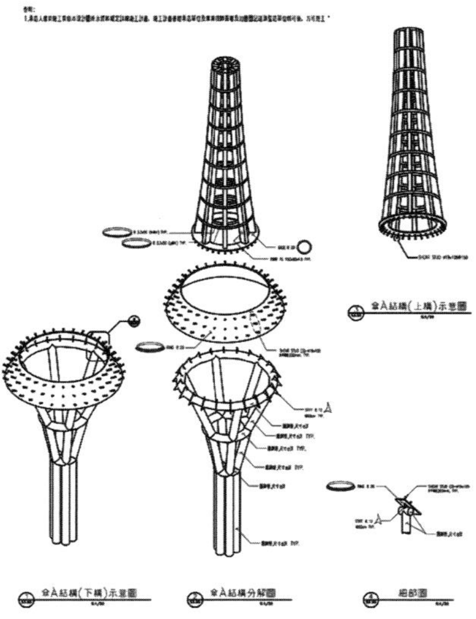
傘A結構(上構)示意圖
傘A結構(下構)示意圖
傘A結構分解圖
細部圖

Stress diagrams

餐廳區

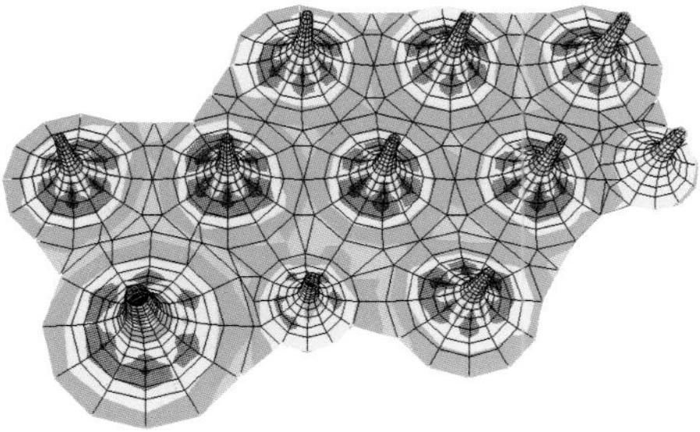

餐廳區

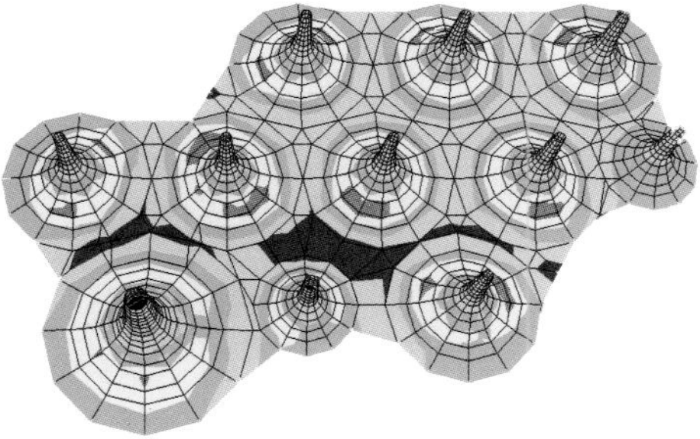

餐廳區

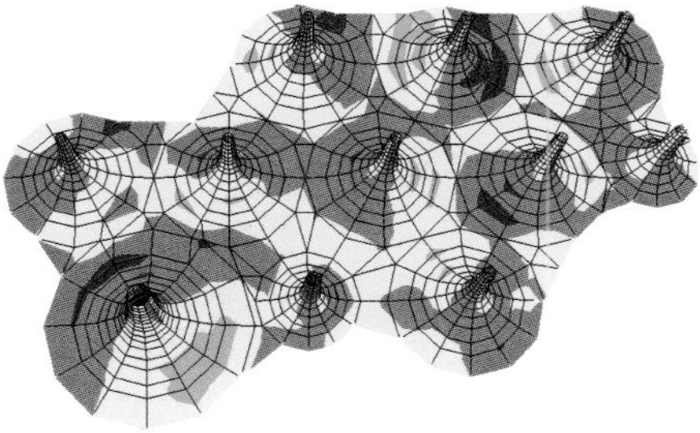

餐廳區

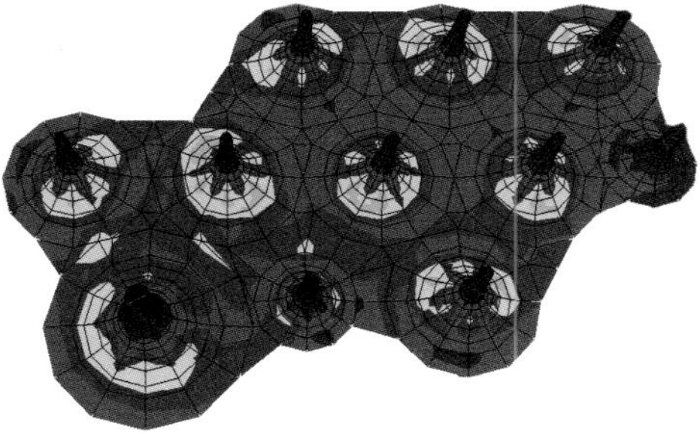

Keelung Port

Taiwan. 2003—
Local partner:
J.M. Lin The Observer Design Group

1st Prize international competition

Measuring
/12

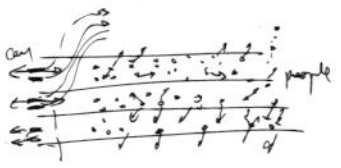

Humanizing
/27

Keelung is the port of Taipei, the capital of the island of Taiwan. Located 30 km to the north of the capital, it is one of the most important container ports in Asia. Keelung has all the vitality of a major port, with one of the most bustling night-time markets in the Far East and an extensive and multifarious central commercial area adjoining the port. The city nevertheless bears the traces of rapid economic growth. Its principal transportation infrastructures—roads, railway lines, and the port itself—continue to limit the creation of quality public spaces in the downtown area. In the light of this, the authorities invited projects as part of the plan to create new 'Gateways' in Taiwan, oriented toward defining the interaction between the port and the city.

In fact, the fundamental issue to be resolved by the various projects drawn up during the different phases of the competition and in the subsequent construction scheme was how to identify the characteristics of a new central public space for the city with which the citizens of Keelung could identify. Historically, Asian cities have a strong tradition of use of the public space and a dynamic inside-outside relationship that has generated numerous instances of cities, neighbourhoods and residential or commercial sectors of great urbanity. However, the economic development of recent years seems to have oriented urban development toward public spaces more in line with the American model, based on the habitability of air-conditioned interior spaces or urban mobility based on the car that makes the car park one of the fundamental interchanges in urban life. This makes it difficult to identify significant urban spaces created in the last few years that respond to the traditional dynamic occupation of the public space. Keelung is seeing the start of another process that is already present in most American, European and Australian cities, in which the port-city interaction is redefined in the interests of a greater public use of port spaces. In this way the historic port zones, which are normally in the proximity of central urban places, are ceded by the port to the city as a site for leisure and commercial uses, sports ports and even hotel and residential zones. Darling Harbour in Sydney, the Port of Boston or Port Vell in Barcelona are examples of such transformations.

A program to improve the urban quality of Keelung

Keelung has emerged with notable success from the quantitative phase of its urban development. The strength of its economy, the youth of its population and the sustained growth experienced in recent decades have given rise to a vital and dynamic city. But this is not enough. It is time now to move on to the qualitative phase, of improving the quality of life of the citizens, of reordering the most important spaces and of creating an innovative, cutting-edge urban image. To achieve this purpose, architecture alone is not sufficient: this is the moment for urbanism, for concerted action that will establish relationships between the different pieces that make up the central space of the city.

Specific Strategies

To create a symbolic and functional centrality. A city is defined internally and externally by the strength and quality of its central space. Our proposal offers the opportunity of creating a more powerful and complex urban centre than will come to constitute Keelung's symbolic space and serve to project an image of the city to the exterior.

To reinforce the urban structure connecting the East and West of the city with a civil axis.

A new and more effective link between the East and West zones of the city will assist in integrating the space of production and relation (East) with the access infrastructures (West), promoting the functional and economic complementarity of both, giving continuity to the canal and generating the axis of force that the city has historically lacked.

To obtain new spaces of public amenities

A city assumes its real significance for its citizens when it has a network of amenities that satisfies not only the basic needs but also the demand for sports, culture, contact and other analogous needs. The image of modernity is closely associated with these functions, which in Keelung are still only an incipient presence.

To reinforce relational uses.

The structural base of a city is, much more than its streets and buildings, the set of human relationships that are created and developed within it.

The city is an accumulation of complex functions and relationships between people, so that limiting it to commercial spaces implies a reductionist perception of the urban phenomenon. The new amenities and leisure spaces, the effective pedestrian link between the different urban sectors and the bridge itself constitute the bases on which centrality will be reinforced by the intensity and dynamism of the human relationships it accommodates.

To reorganize the transport area.
In the West zone of the area of intervention the three main transport infrastructures of the city converge. The solution that is envisaged for this space is not confined to embracing their existence as such, but seeks to facilitate the uses that these infrastructures induce and require, spatially organizing their satisfactory distribution and functional integration in the ways that are most convenient for the commuters and proposing cultural and leisure uses that will extend beyond the usual commuter timetable to avoid the risk of it losing its vitality and becoming marginalized.

To restructure the area of socio-cultural amenities
In the West zone there are a variety of cultural, administrative and commercial facilities whose integration is problematic, because of the difficulties in the way of pedestrian movement. At the same time there is a need to generate new uses and functions that will reinforce the relational contents of the public spaces, in order to provide a qualitatively richer urban framework for the citizens. This entails the restructuring of the area of amenities to the East of the port and the incorporation of new functions.

To extend the area of pedestrian connection
In spite of living from the sea and with the sea, the people of Keelung are confronted by major obstacles when it comes to enjoying it, in view of the impact of vehicular traffic on the seafront and the very limited space that has been reserved for pedestrian circulation. To overcome this obstacle we propose a solution that not only improves the flow of pedestrian circulation but also generates a space that, as in all of the best operations for the restructuring of city-port interfaces, permits the creation of a rest space where people can enjoy contemplating the sea and the bustling activity of the port.

First proposal

The solution proposed in the first phase of the competition posited the option of going beyond the original limits of the port to expand the city out over the water, creating a pedestrian bridge and a series of associated platforms. This would serve as an autonomous urban space, set apart from the traffic routes that skirt the edge of the sea, and reinforce the East-West axis of the city, connecting the train station with the municipal museum and the city hall. This solution also served to create a spacious maritime public plaza for water-related leisure activities. The bridge would have a metal structure on piles sunk into the seabed, with a central swing section to let masted boats into the central sheet of water. The municipal authorities considered the scheme to be very interesting, but it was sidelined because it exceeded the limits of actuation agreed with the port.

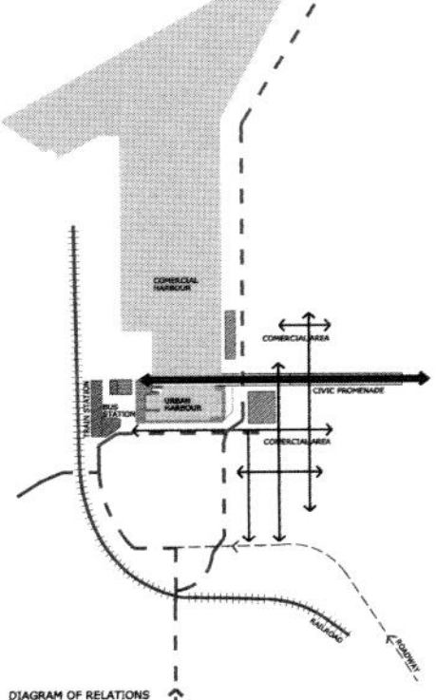

DIAGRAM OF RELATIONS

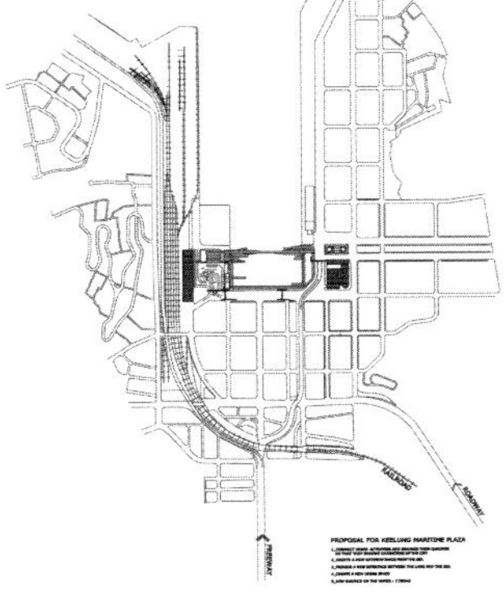

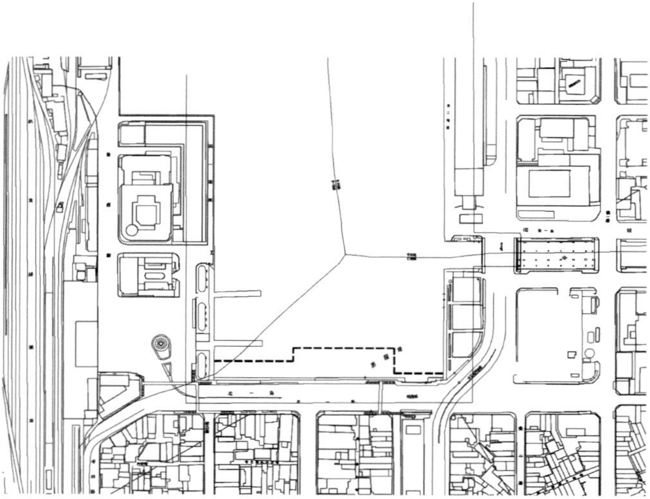

GEOGRAPHY

Interface between city and port in Keelung

GEOMETRY

Urban gridlock caused by port traffic

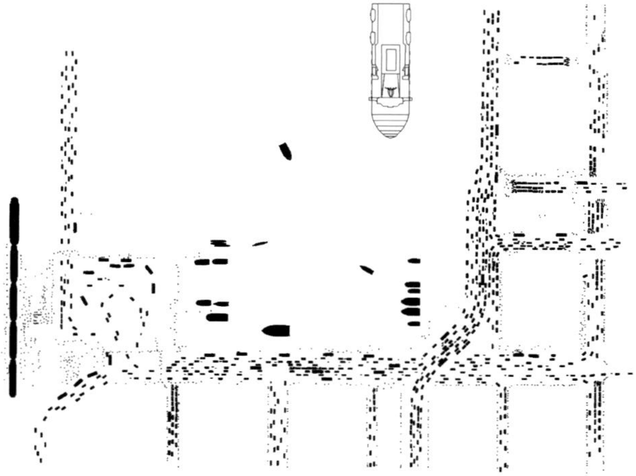

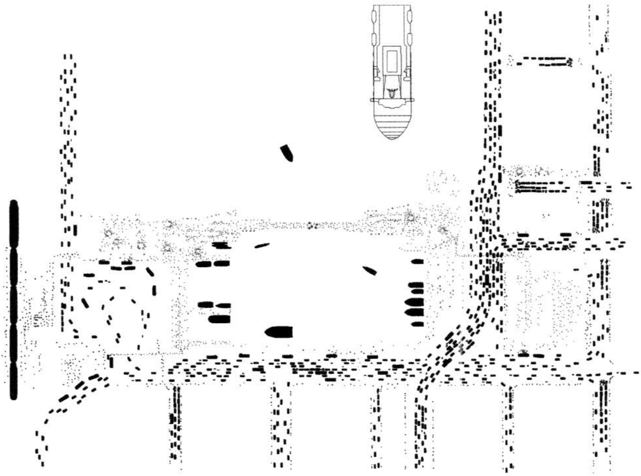

LOGIC

A new bridge makes a space for pedestrians in the port

STRUCTURE

New structure of the public space

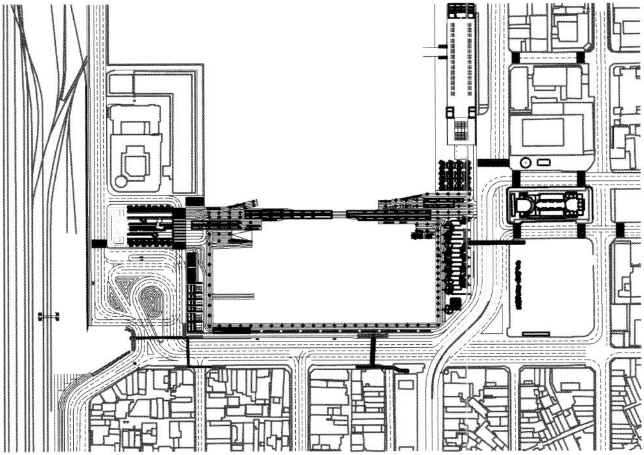

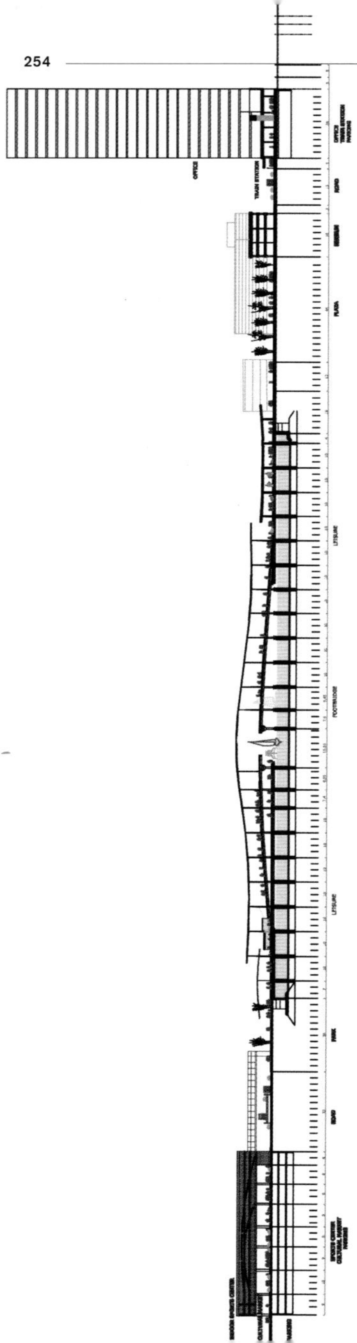
OFFICE
TRAIN STATION
ROAD
MUSEUM
PLAZA
LEISURE
FOOTBRIDGE
LEISURE
PARK
ROAD

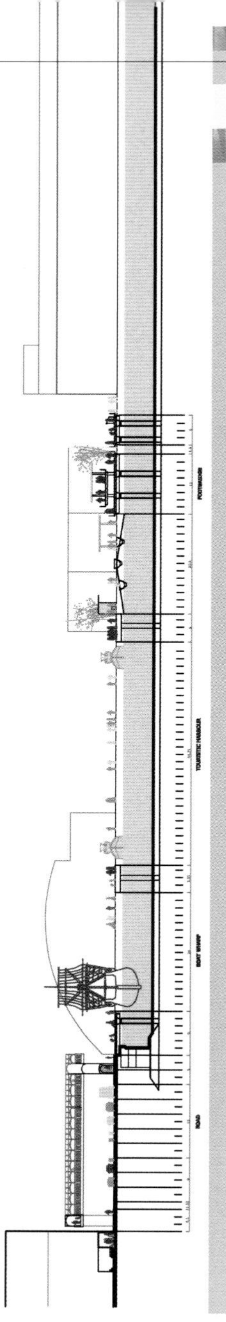
FOOTBRIDGE
TOURISTIC HARBOUR
BOAT WHARF
ROAD

Axonometry

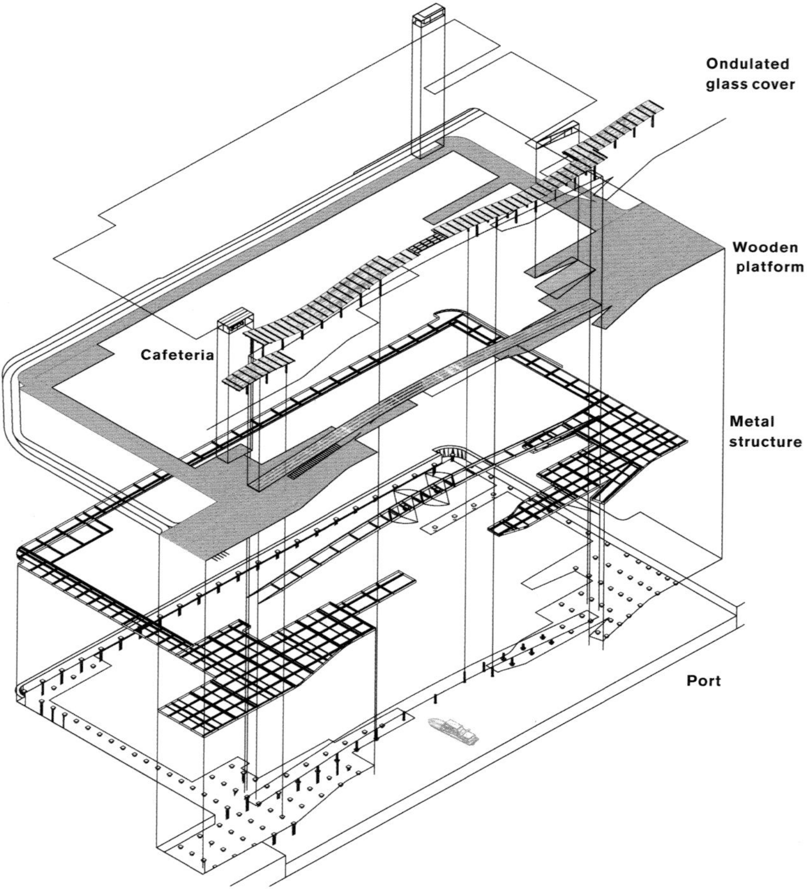
Ondulated
glass cover
Wooden
platform
Cafeteria
Metal
structure
Port

The second proposal, which won the competition, was confined to the line of actuation set by the port authority. Nevertheless, it raised the possibility of this line being a dynamic boundary by creating various floating timber platforms which could be separate from the principal platform to allow a more relaxed use of the public space on the basis of a fragment distributed by the sheet of water. These platforms would accommodate a tea house, a landing stage for kayaks and a small auditorium, making it possible to reconfigure the line of the coast according to the particular events to be held there.

The third proposal, on which the construction project is based, assumed a fixed coastline, centring the design on the creation of a dynamic line between the urban edge and the platform, reworking ideas developed in previous projects. In this case, having analysed the functioning of the various activities that come together here, the scheme proposes a pergola that provides a covered walkway extending from the commercial zone to the station, dynamically expanding this structure by way of the wooden platform. This pergola, created with a linear pattern like the tentacular fronds of a marine plant, is folded both vertically and horizontally to generate rest spaces on the seafront and to spell out the word K-E-E-L-U-N-G on the urban front. This new timber platform will thus act as an icon similar to those ferry terminals in which the name of the port is eye-catchingly displayed. The timber platform also has a garden of wooden 'rocks' that will be replicated in the Ocean Plaza in Batoutz. In this case, the traditional Oriental rock gardens is materially transformed to become folds in the surface of the public space, inviting people to relate to them physically in various ways; a similar appropriation has been made of the outcrops of volcanic rock on the neighbouring coast.

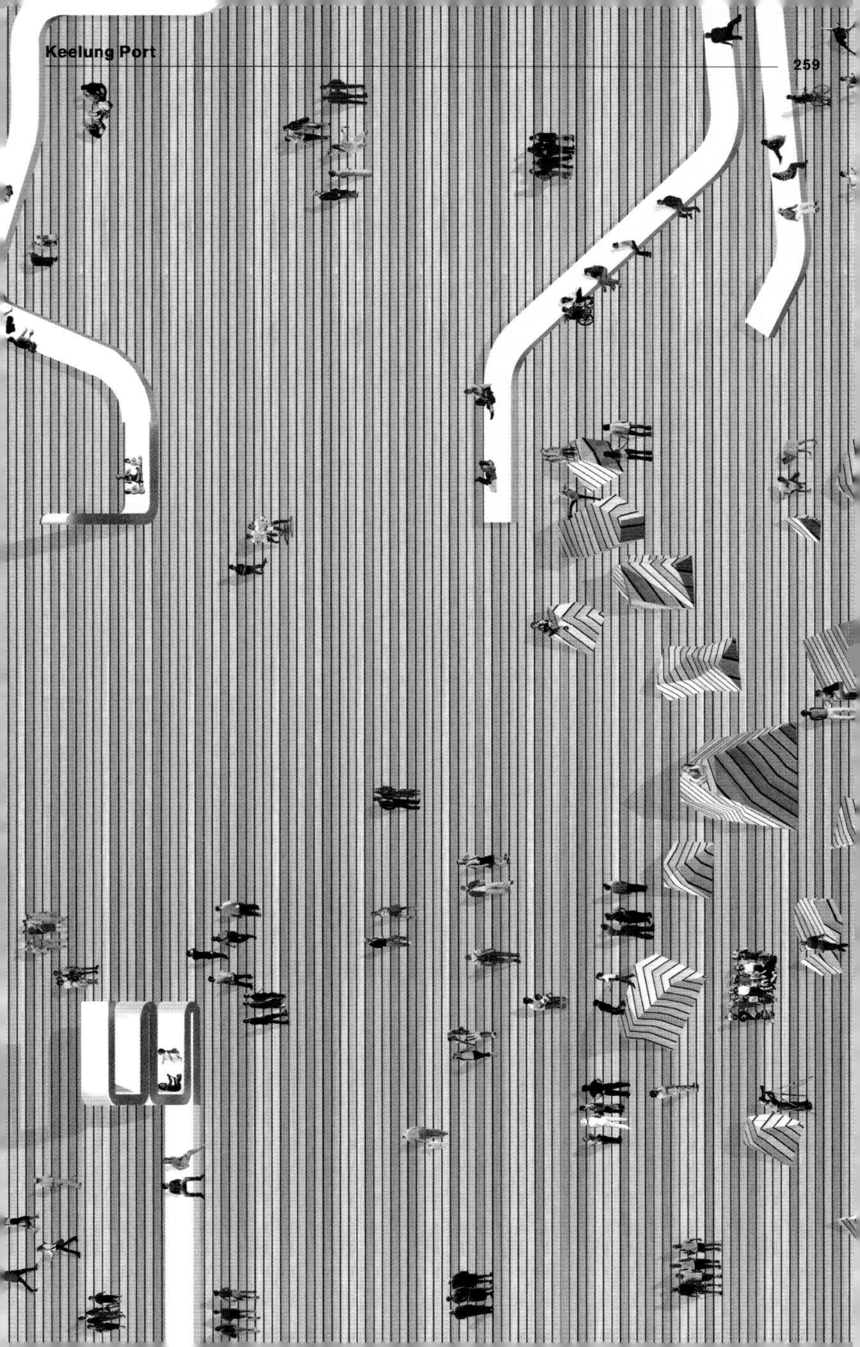

一般說明:

一、內港區平台　　鋼構雨遮及座椅C.1~C.17，依序詳A5-02至A5-14。

二、東碼頭　　鋼構雨遮及座椅C.18~C.36，依序詳A5-15至A5-17。

三、鋼構字樣　　W.1~W.6，詳A5-18/W,7，詳A4-06。

四、垂直立桿表　　S.1~S.33，依序詳A5-19至A5-22。

五、彩色玻璃色彩計畫　　詳A5-23至A5-25(含鋼構雨遮及座椅伸縮縫位置)。

六、日光燈具配置計畫　　詳A5-26至A5-28(含鋼構雨遮及座椅伸縮縫位置)。

七、欄杆表　　H.1~H.19，詳A5-29至A5-30。

八、石狀木構造物尺寸　　R.1~R.14，詳A6-02至A6-07。

九、石狀木構造物錨錠位置　　詳A6-08至A6-09。

十、得標廠商須提出配合色彩計畫之鋼構雨遮及座椅鑲嵌玻璃之顏色樣品，交予設計單位審核並經業主認可後，方可施作。

十一、內港區平台之鋼構雨遮結構完成面(TOS)相對於忠一路側新設人行道裝修完成面高程(+190)可分爲+375和+500兩種，本區雨遮結構完成面高度(TOS)需平整一致，不隨原木平台之百分之三洩水坡度而有所變化。

十二、東碼頭之鋼構雨遮結構完成面(TOS)以相對於+145之裝修完成面高程(TOF)設定，雨遮高程僅+375一種，本區雨遮結構完成面高度(TOS)需平整一致，不隨本區等高地形高程差異而有所變化。

十三、獨立之鋼構座椅椅面高程距離裝修完成面高程(TOF)爲45cm，並依相對於設置點之裝修完成面高程(TOF)而定。

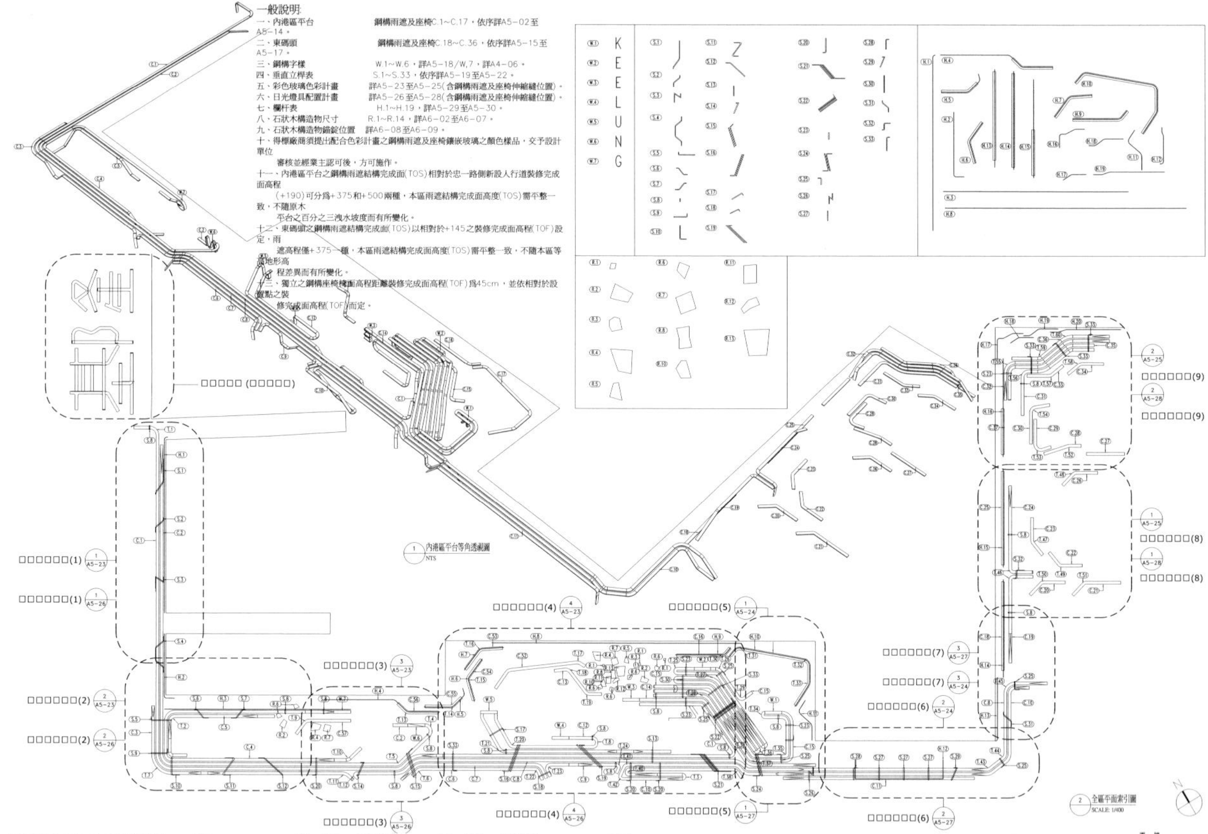

基隆海洋廣場新建工程

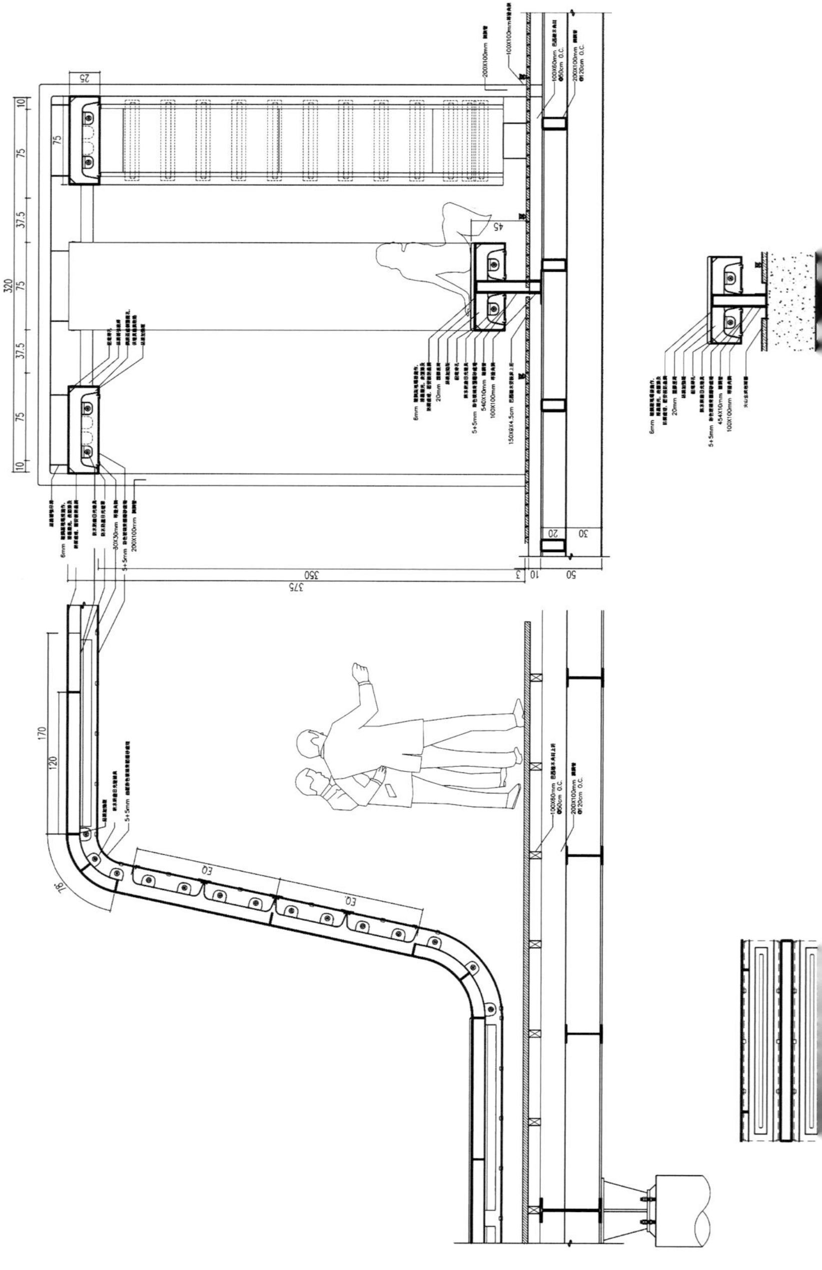

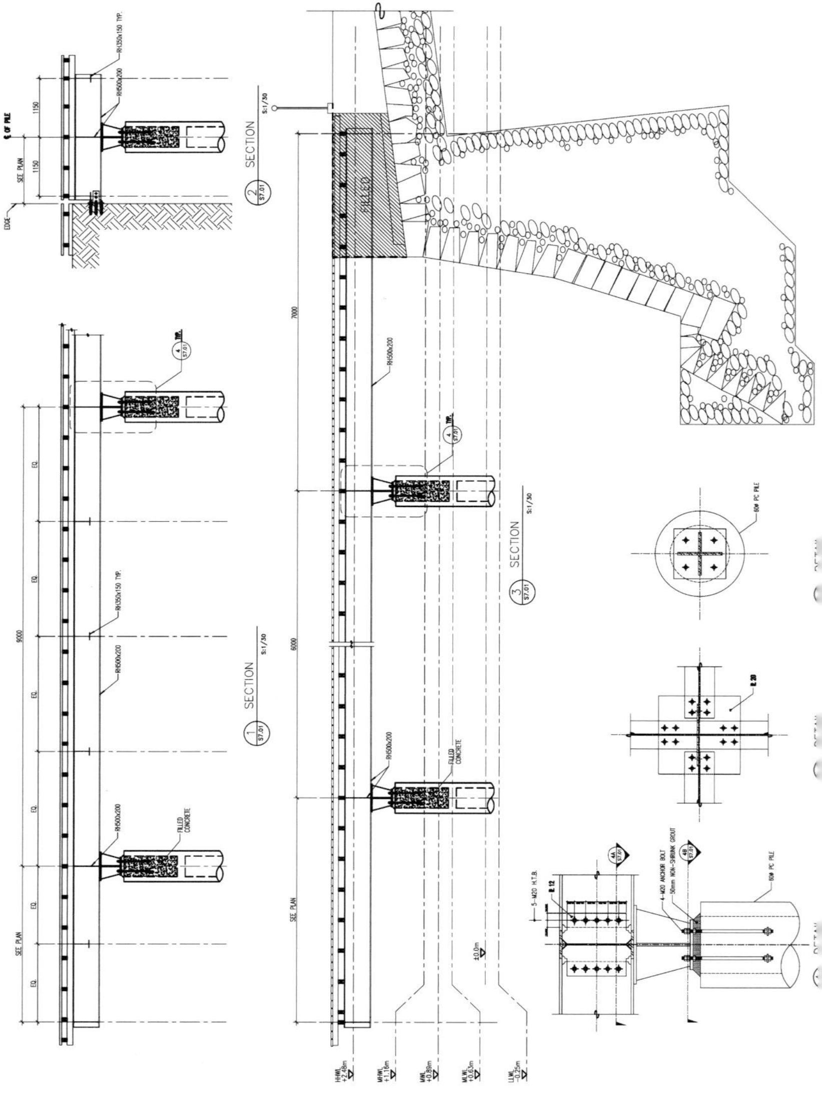

℄ OF PILE
SEE PLAN
1150
1150
EDGE
RH350x150 TYP.
RH500x200
4 S7.01 TYP.
9000
EQ.
EQ.
EQ.
EQ.
EQ.
EQ.
FILLED CONCRETE
1 S7.01 SECTION S:1/30
2 S7.01 SECTION S:1/30
FILLED
7000
6000
4 S7.01 TYP.
3 S7.01 SECTION S:1/30
±0.0m
HHWL +2.48m
MHWL +1.16m
MWL +0.89m
MLWL +0.63m
LLWL -0.25m
60Ø PC PILE
PL 20
5-M20 H.T.B.
PL 12
4A S7.01
4B S7.01
4-M20 ANCHOR BOLT
50mm NON-SHRINK GROUT
60Ø PC PILE

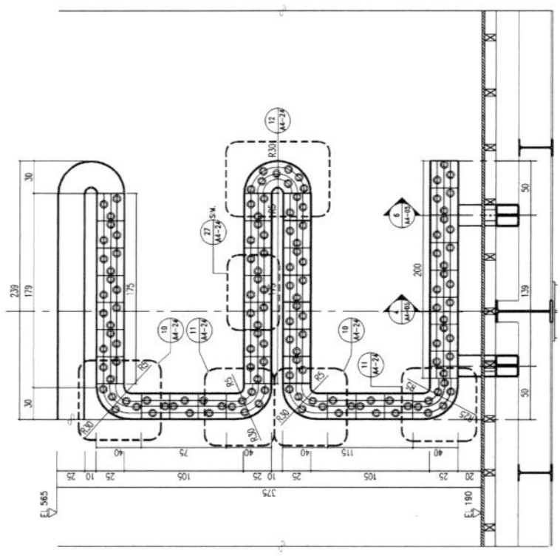

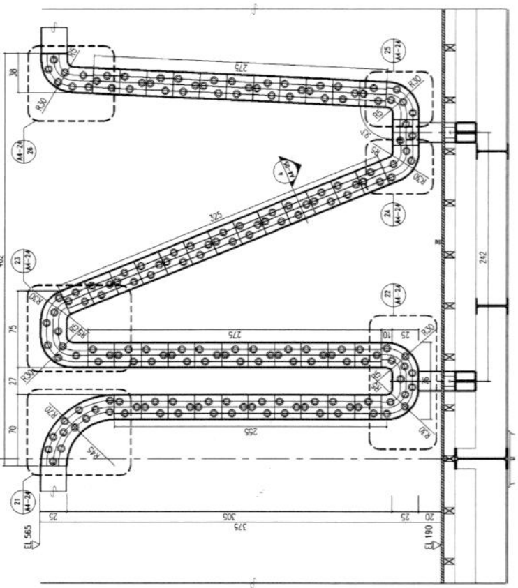

3 W.3立面详图

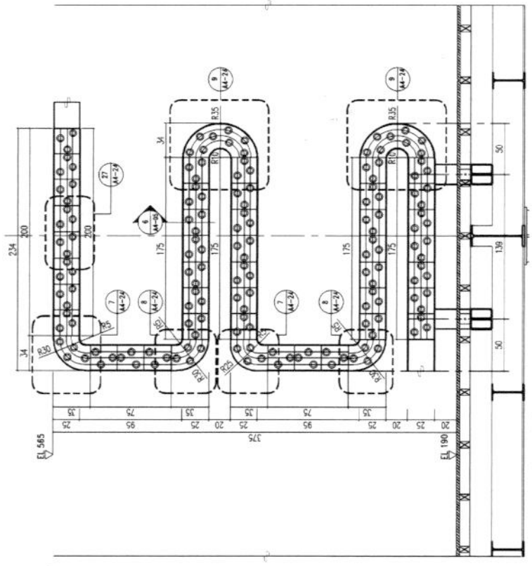

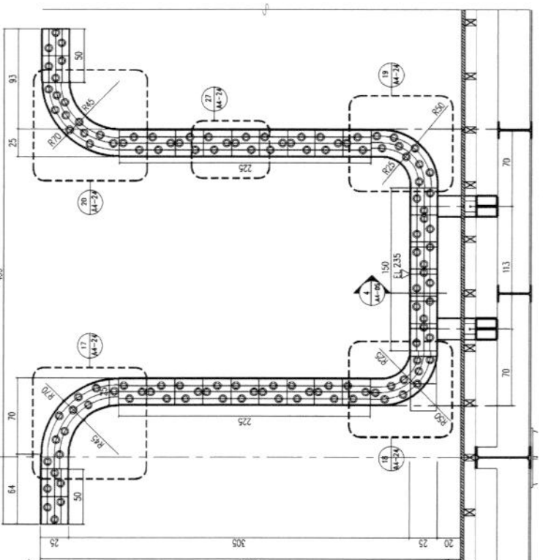

2 W.2立面详图

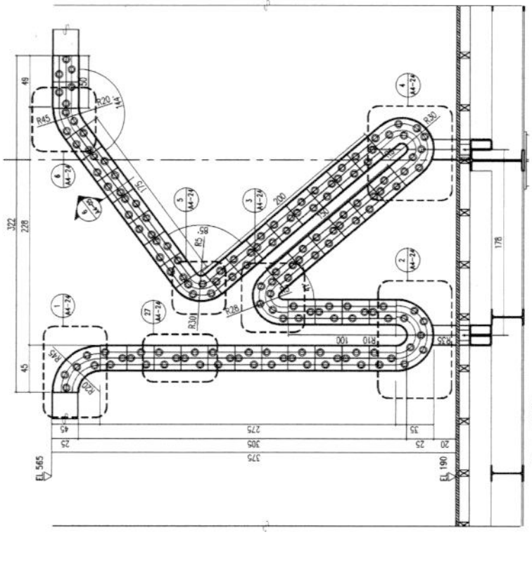

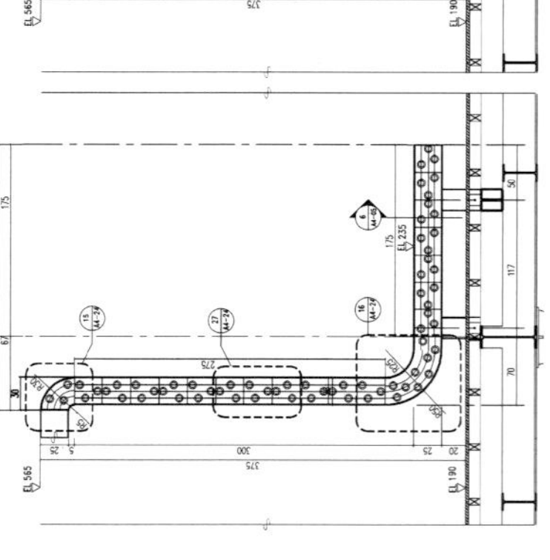

1 W.1立面详图

Vinaròs Micro-coasts

Vinaròs, Castellón. Spain. 2007
With Marta Malé-Alemany

1st Prize national competition

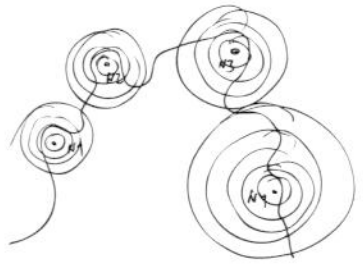

Vinaròs is a town on the Mediterranean coast of Spain, near the delta of the river Ebro, about halfway between Barcelona and Valencia. Its south shore is a succession of coves and promontories on a terrain composed of strata of easily fractured conglomerate rocks. The length of the coastline and the surface area of the municipality are constantly changing as a result of the action of the sea, which produces continual land slippage and erosion. This zone has been developed with detached houses on small plots.

This project can be taken to exemplify the way the scale of the gaze is the key to perceiving the logic to be acted on. At the intermediate scale the place is of very little interest in urbanistic or environmental terms, given the proximity of the residential developments to the coast. The coves and points appear at first sight to be far removed from the ideal 'virgin' state of what could be described as natural. On the small scale, however, it becomes clear that this sequence of coves and outcrops, micro-inlets, pools of seawater, stones eroded by the sea and rocks shaped by the tide has an exceptional beauty.

How big does a geographical feature have to be for it to have a name?

Our analyses have made it possible to map micro-places of more than sufficient identity to deserve a name, thus breaking with the logic that a territorial event has to be big to be beautiful or worth naming. Our project has consisted in establishing a mechanism with which to measure the coast, on the basis of the creation of hexagonal timber platforms with a constant length of side based on the scale of the human body. These micros-coasts are organized to form islands of variable size, located where there is rock in close proximity to the sea. The platforms are composed of just two different pieces, one flat, the other with a microtopography, which serve to generate surfaces that can be perfectly flat or partially or fully folded. Their positioning on the coast is determined by criteria of access to the sea and interaction with the dynamic line of the original coast.

Following their installation, people were quick to appropriate the new microcoasts and utilize them in a variety of ways. The relationship between the size, orientation and location of the platform and the number and social profile of the people using them is an interesting phenomenon in terms of the socialization of the space.

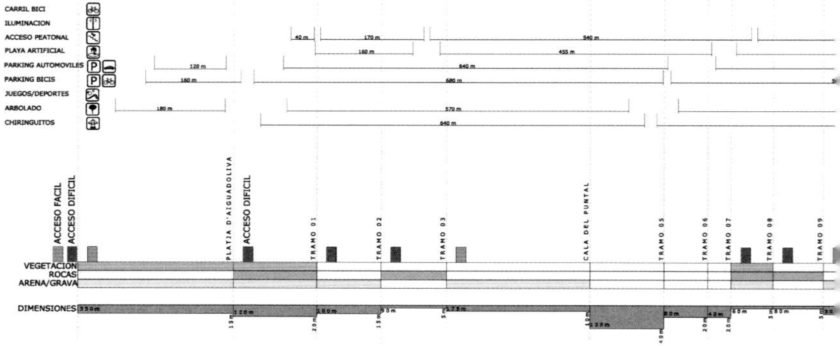
CARRIL BICI
ILUMINACION
ACCESO PEATONAL
PLAYA ARTIFICIAL
PARKING AUTOMOVILES
PARKING BICIS
JUEGOS/DEPORTES
ARBOLADO
CHIRINGUITOS
40 m
170 m
540 m
160 m
455 m
120 m
640 m
160 m
680 m
180 m
570 m
640 m
ACCESO FACIL
ACCESO DIFICIL
PLATJA D'AIGUADOLIVA
ACCESO DIFICIL
TRAMO 01
TRAMO 02
TRAMO 03
CALA DEL PUNTAL
TRAMO 05
TRAMO 06
TRAMO 07
TRAMO 08
TRAMO 09
VEGETACION
ROCAS
ARENA/GRAVA
DIMENSIONES

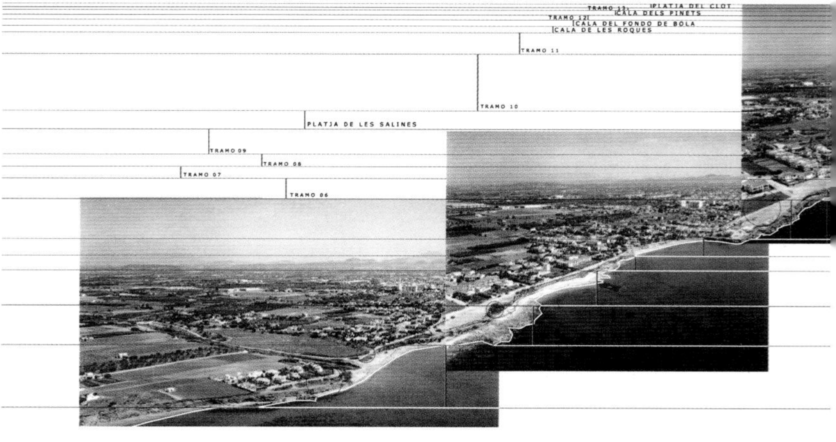
TRAMO 13
PLATJA DEL CLOT
CALA DELS PINETS
TRAMO 12
CALA DEL FONDO DE BOLA
CALA DE LES ROQUES
TRAMO 11
TRAMO 10
PLATJA DE LES SALINES
TRAMO 09
TRAMO 08
TRAMO 07
TRAMO 06

940 m
75 m
60 m
220 m
60m
335 m
115 m
510 m
320 m
600 m
335 m
1040 m
475 m
1580 m
PLATJA DE LES SALINES
TRAMO 10
TRAMO 11
CALA DE LES ROQUES
CALA DEL FONDO DE BOLA
TRAMO 12
CALA DELS PINETS
TRAMO 13
PLATJA DEL CLOT
240m
270m
170m
TRAMO 05
CALA DEL PUNTAL
TRAMO 03
TRAMO 02
TRAMO 01
PLATJA D'AIGUADOLIVA

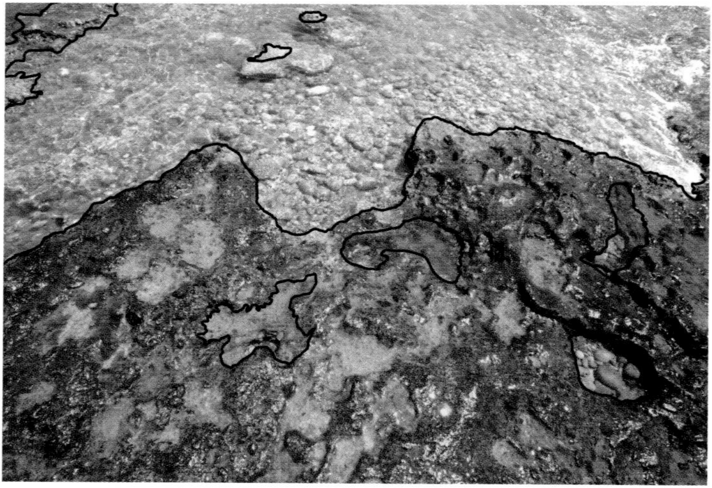

GEOGRAPHY

Mediterranean microcoast

GEOMETRY

Hexagonal pattern for measuring the coast

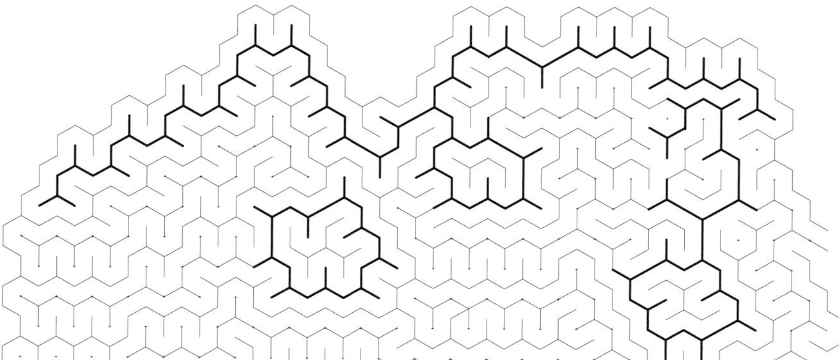

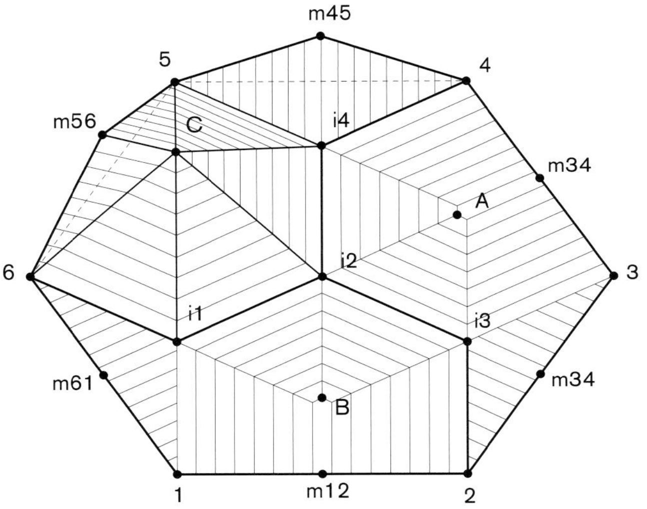

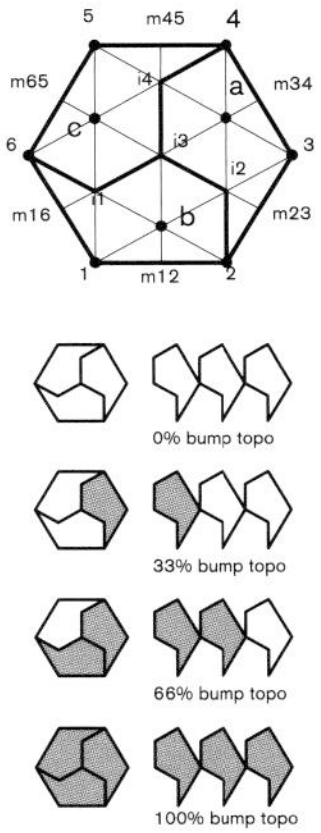

LOGIC

Microtopography

STRUCTURE

System of platforms for occupying the rocky coast

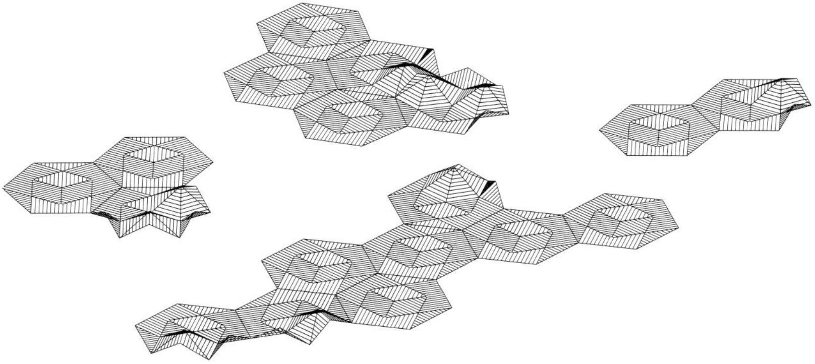

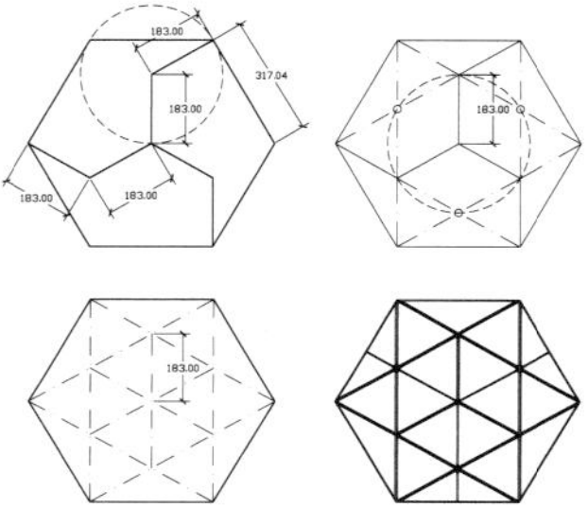
183.00
317.04
183.00
183.00
183.00
183.00
183.00

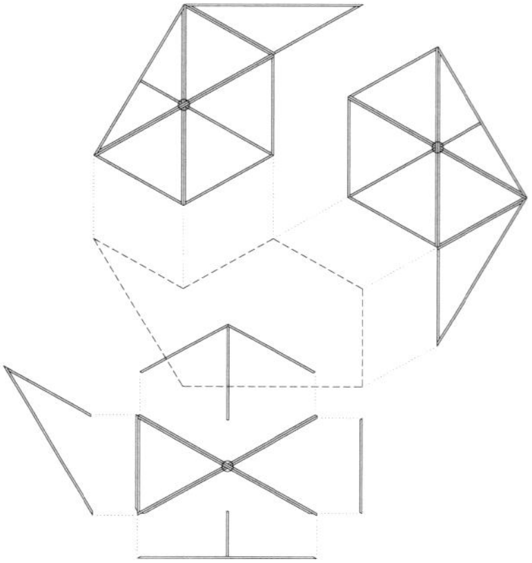

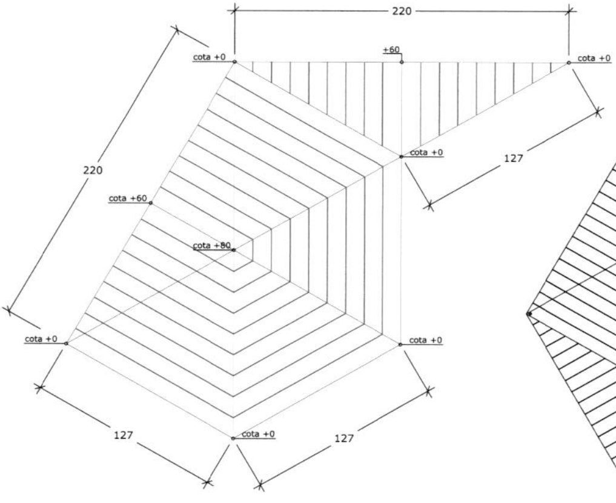
220
+60
cota +0
cota +0
cota +0
127
220
cota +60
cota +80
cota +0
cota +0
cota +0
127
127

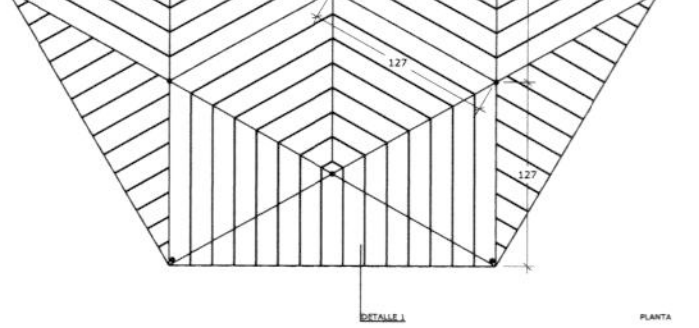
PIEZA 1
127
220
127
127
127
127
DETALLE 1
PLANTA

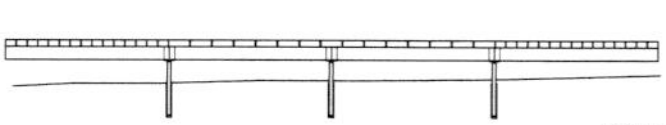
SECCIÓN E: 1/10

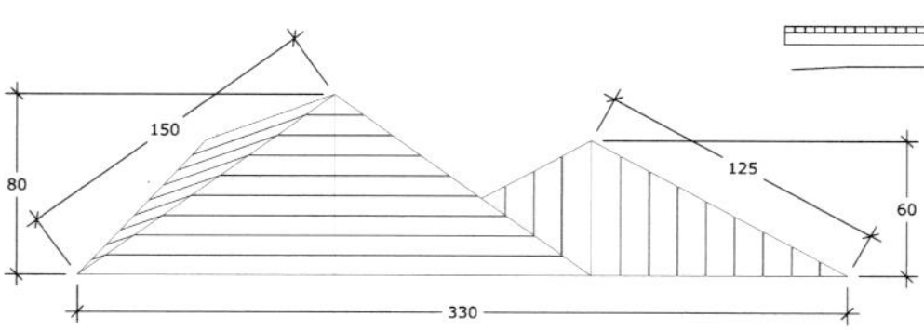
150
80
125
60
330

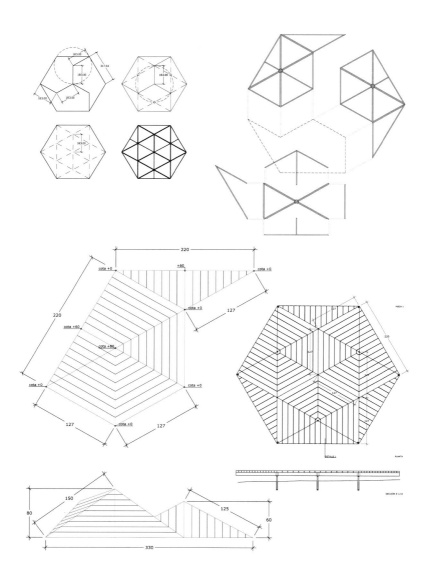

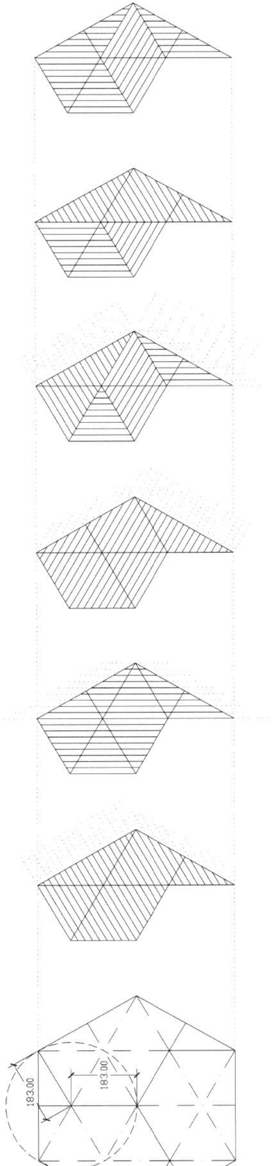
183.00
183.00

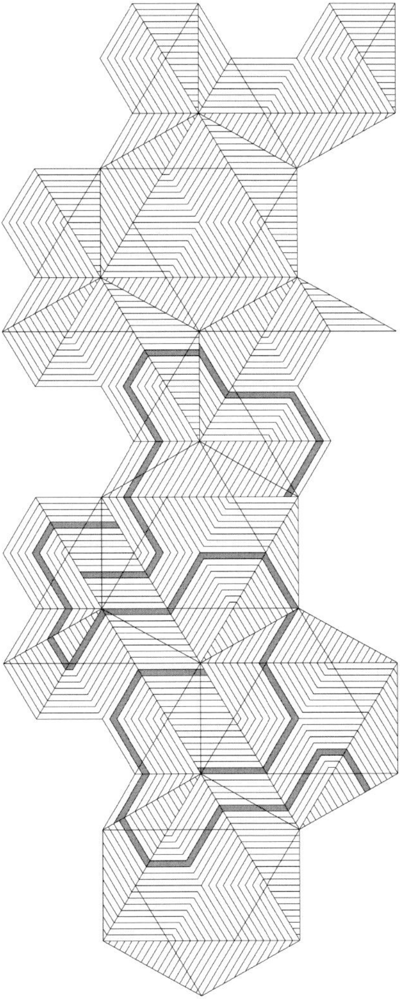

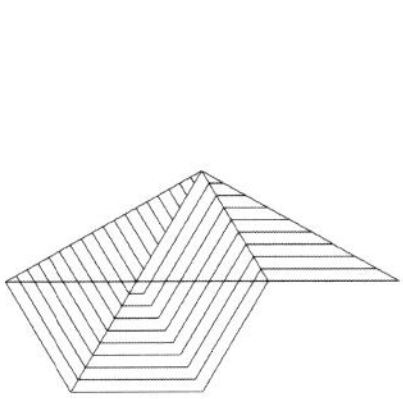

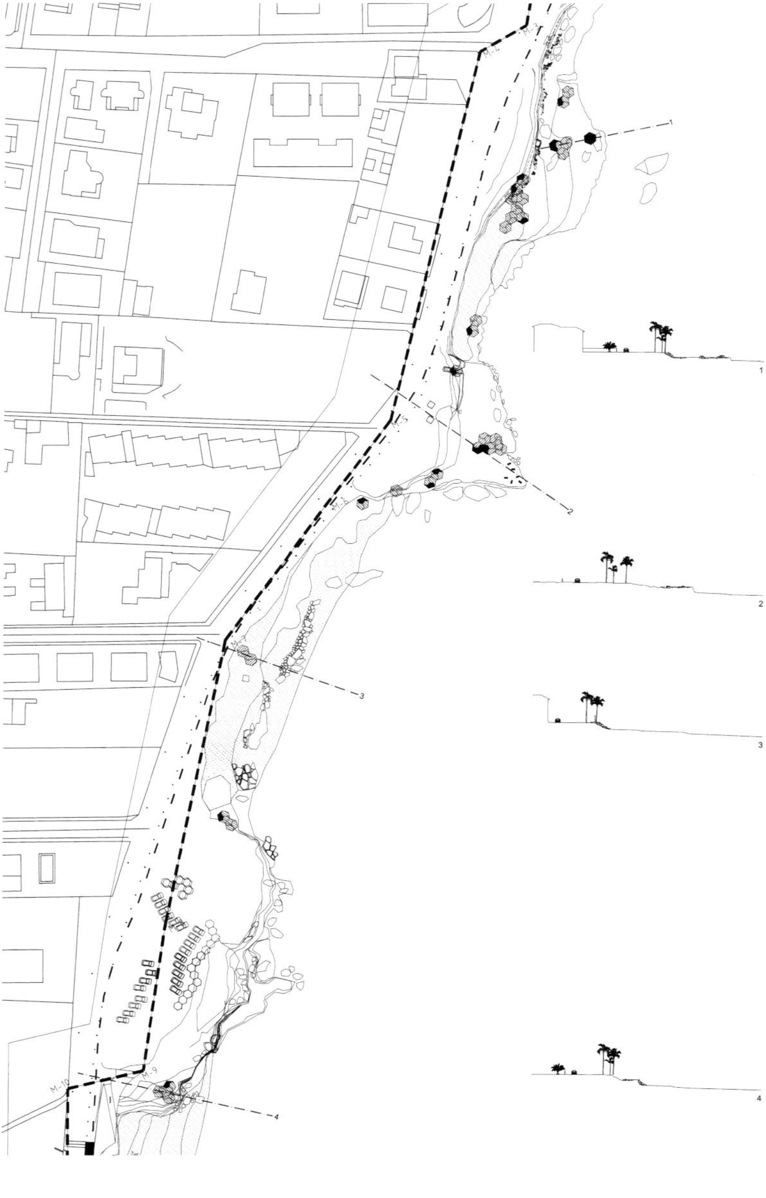
M-2
M-3
1
M-5
2
M-6
3
4
M-9
M-10
1
2
3
4

Cristóba de Mou- ra street

Barcelona. Spain. 1998

With Max Sanjulián

Biomimesis
/07

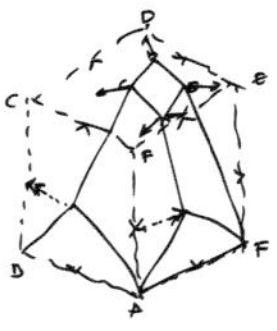

Parametrizing
/14

Re-urbanizing
/25

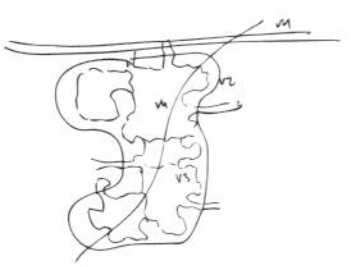

Multi-velocity
/26

Implementation of the Cerdà Plan for Barcelona, originally drawn up in the mid 19th century, will finally be completed in the 21st century. Cristóbal de Moura, a street that lies between the Gran Via and the Diagonal, on the right-hand side of the Eixample, is one of the last in the city to be urbanized. The orthogonal grid created by the engineer Cerdà is laid out between the sea and the hills, with a basic regular sequence of streets twenty metres wide set a hundred metres apart; every third street parallel to or perpendicular to the sea is wider and grander, constituting what are known as 'superblocks'. Cristóbal de Moura is one such street. Its ordering invites a reflection on how a street, whose basic parameters were defined by the conditions of life in an industrial economy, should be designed for the information society. In effect, most of the main processes of urban development in our cities are oriented toward the simple functional fitting out of a space in response to a generic way of living. Our project set out to map out how the design of a vital space can respond to the lifeways of the information society.

The scheme addresses various issues associated with new lifestyles that arise here and there in our cities: issues that, considered as an interrelated whole and integrated in a unitary design, can give rise to new kinds of urban space. People will work in or very close to their own homes, and will be related more by the type of technologies they utilize or the amount of space they need than by the fact of working for the same company. This has the double benefit of saving both energy and time spent in daily commuting. Public spaces should generate at least part of the energy they consume, and should accommodate urban orchards and gardens for growing fresh produce in the immediate vicinity of the housing.

There should be provision for sports activities in the public space immediately adjacent to people's homes, to allow them to exercise at any time to compensate for the intrinsically sedentary nature of telematic work and television-centred leisure time. Rainwater will be collected from at least 30% of the surface area, as an alternative to the sealing off of the soil and the reduction of the phreatic water level.

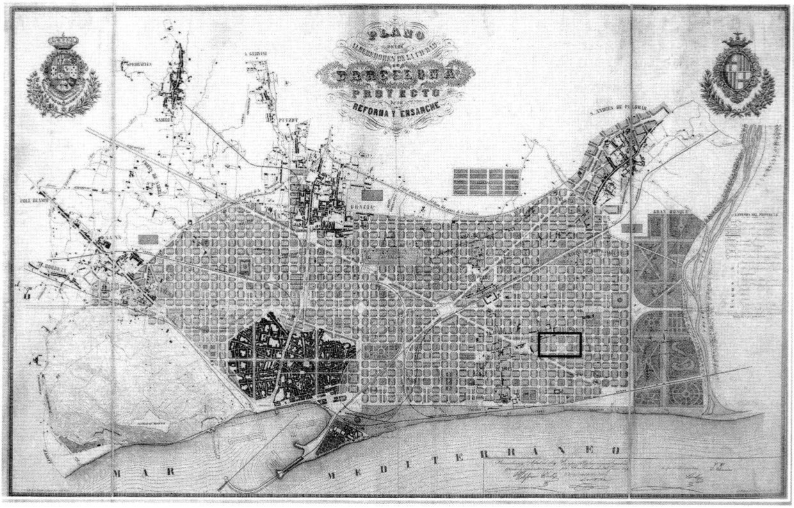

GEOGRAPHY

The Barcelona of the 1859 Cerdà Plan, completed in 2009

GEOMETRY

The city's 'superblock' macro structure

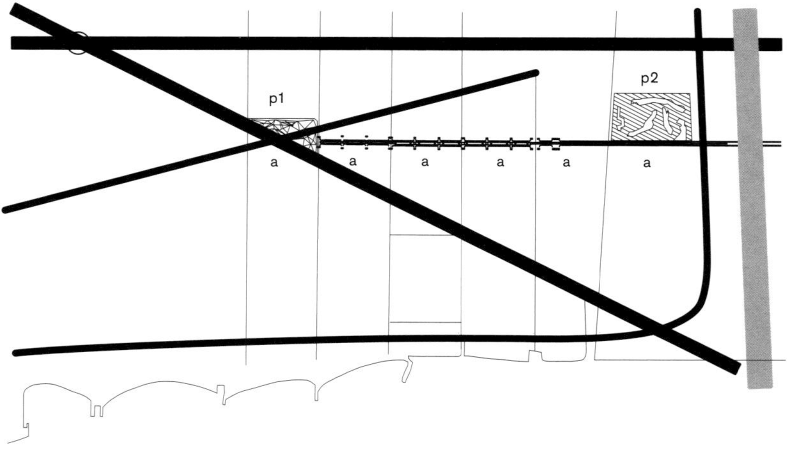

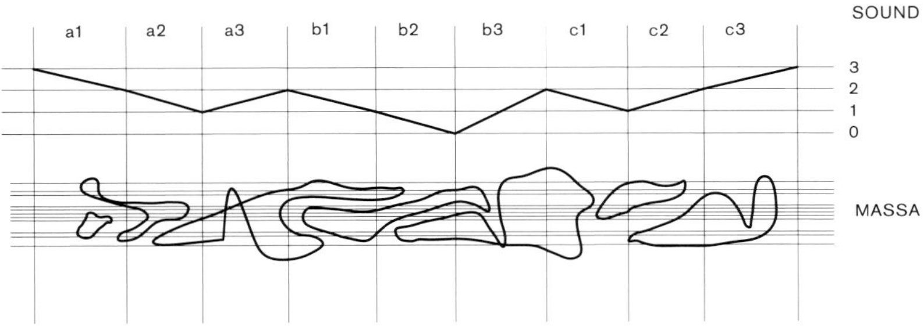

LOGIC

Urban rhythm related to noise and the distance between streets

STRUCTURE

A pattern of flows structures the urban space

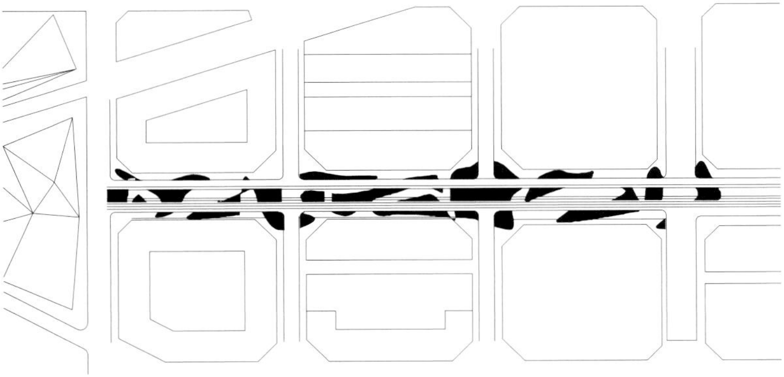

Our project proposed the creation of a linear pattern three metres wide as the initial basis for the organization of the different circulation systems that coexist in a public thoroughfare (pedestrians, cars, cyclists, joggers) by means of mobility lanes. This two-dimensional system is then overlaid by a structure based on the potential crossings between points on the street and the noise levels of the different lanes. The interaction between the linear pattern and the oriented amorphous mass determines position of the various sequences of trees and the permeability of the soil.

The importance of the soil is manifested in the design of a metal matrix which distributes water, electricity and information along linear channels. This matrix will be capable of emitting light and changing colour, spraying water vapour and supplying the various urban elements in need of connection, while at the same time serving to determine the degree of permeability of the soil.

The vegetation is organized on three levels, as it is in the typical Mediterranean market garden: the ground level is planted with grass and flowers, the intermediate level is occupied by orange trees and other fruit trees, and the upper level is occupied not by palms but by photovoltaic 'trees'.

This linear pattern accommodates a variety of elements. Sequentially ordered sport rocks allow people to exercise in the street, running and stopping according to previously established criteria. The rocks can be used for different types of exercises, making use of various urban elements (basically cars, barriers, rubbish bins, etc.) to support different parts of the body to perform an extensive range of exercises.

The urban avatar is a sculptural element with a function different from its form. It acts as a digital avatar similar to the adaptable personalities we assume when we operate on the Internet. In this case we designed urban elements in the form of wire-frame trees that can operate in functional terms as digital instruments by means of presence detectors, PA and lighting systems.

The urban icons and sculptural elements should reinforce the connection between the physical world and the digital realm. The town needs to know as much about the cars that drive around it and their destinations as their occupants know about the town. If the city authorities know where vehicles are going to they will be better able to manage circulation and redirect traffic flows. Though public spaces can be occupied temporarily by cars, they should be prepared for complete pedestrian use.

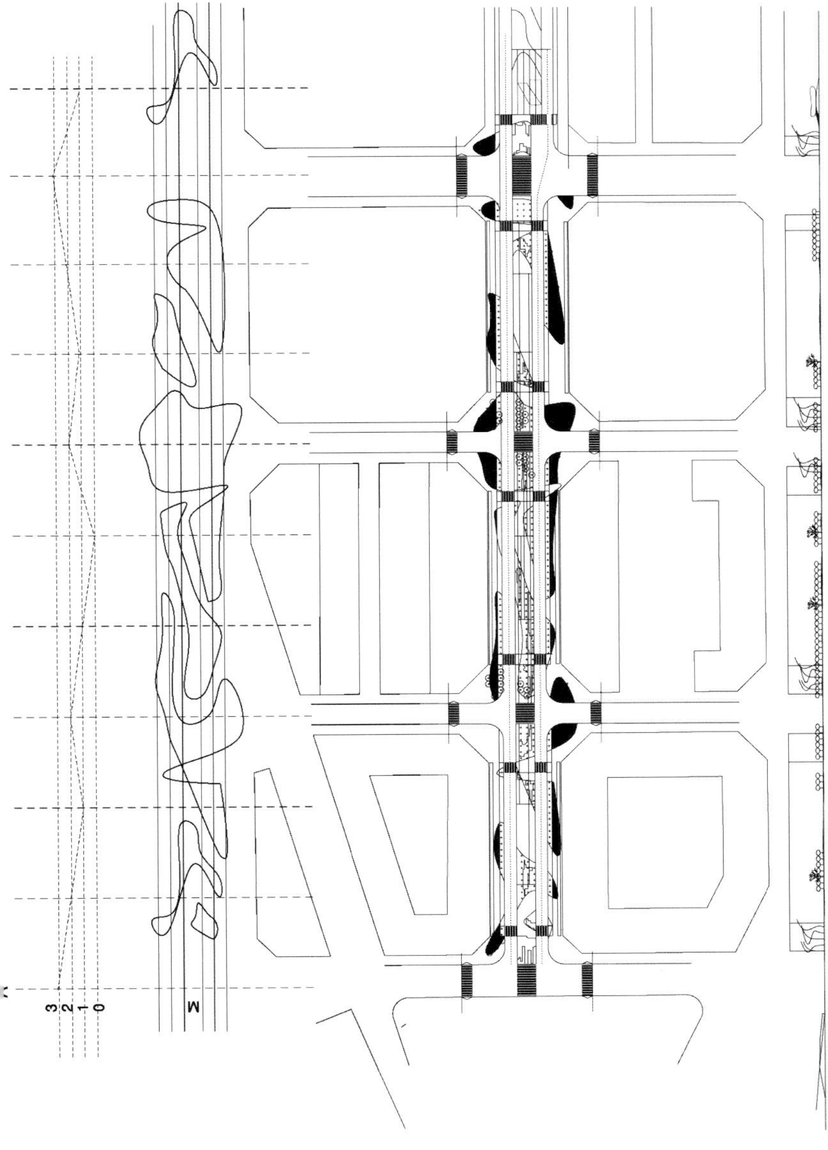
3
2
1
0
M

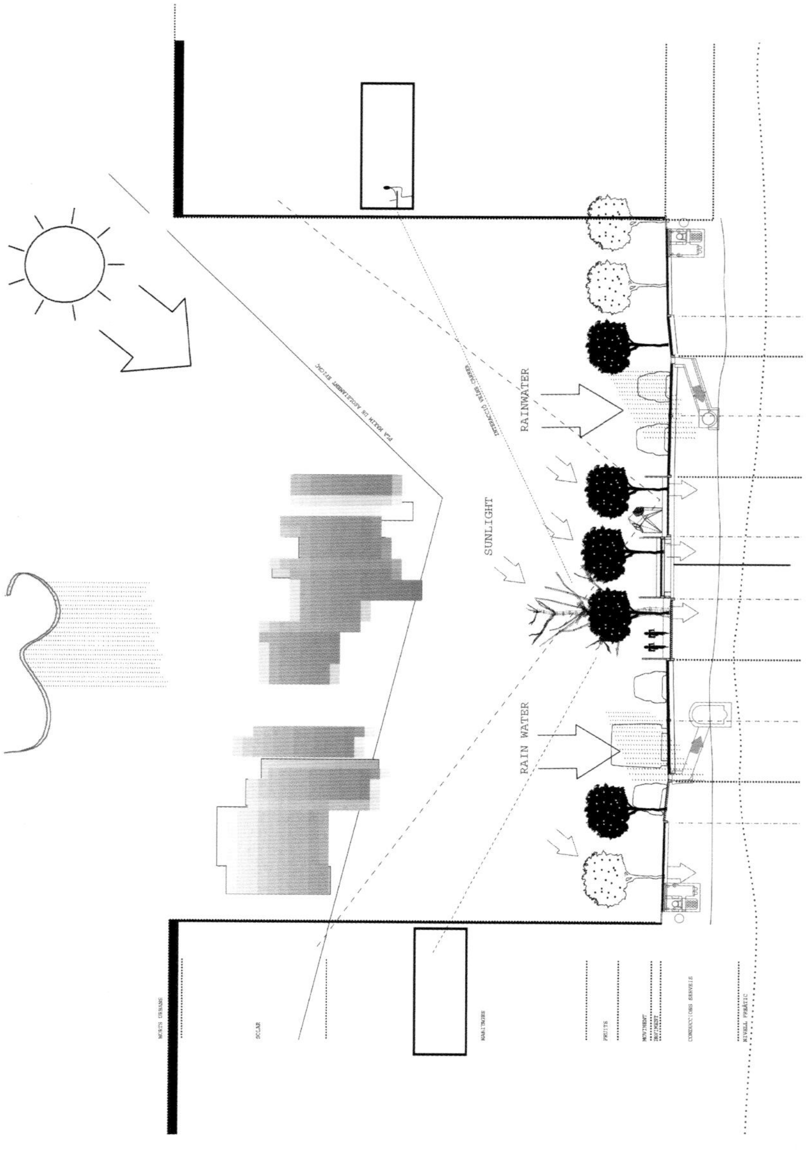
RAINWATER
SUNLIGHT
RAIN WATER
MURS URBANS
SOLAR
FRUITS
MOVIMENT
PAVIMENT
CONDUCCIONS SERVEIS
NIVELL FREÀTIC

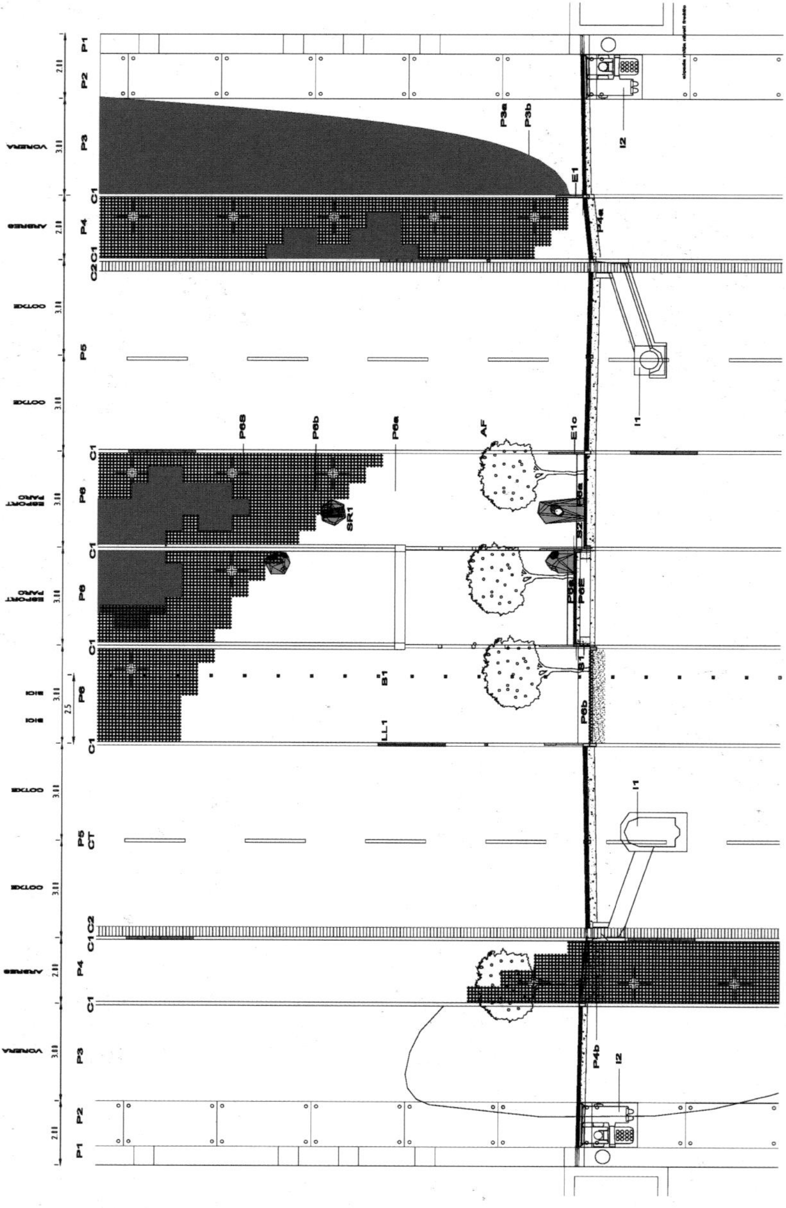
P1
P2
P3
P4
C1
C2
P5
CT
P6
VORERA
ARBRES
COTXE
ESPORT PARC
BICI
P3a
P3b
E1
P4a
P4b
I1
I2
P6S
P6b
P6a
AF
E1c
SR1
B1
LL1
P6E

The photovoltaic tree is an element that demonstrates the possibility of creating artificial elements that behave according to the logic of the natural world. In this case it is a matter of integrating photovoltaic panels—a purely technological element—into the urban space. However, considered in terms of their capacity to transform the sun's energy into electricity, these panels can be compared to the leaves of a tree. In the case of a photovoltaic tree, the fruit is light. We carried out a detailed analysis of the optimum positioning of these elements in the street to ensure the best insolation and energy yield, in addition to the urban function of creating shade for people to rest in. Like trees, these elements have a common pattern of form and growth and can be adapted to different environmental situations. We decided to limit the height of the tree to twelve metres, so as to be able to use standard metal bars, which can be bent into shape for specific needs. An analysis of the most appropriate insolation for the production of energy in a given latitude and longitude makes it clear that there is no need for the solar panels to have a single orientation; they can operate within a range that in Barcelona is between 30 and 70 degrees longitudinally and from -20 to +20 degrees of latitude. A family of elements adapted to the public space thus emerges. These structures also support lighting systems using optic fibre or LEDs. The most effective system at present is to supply all of the energy generated to the electricity network, given the incentives for the generation of energy by means of passive systems, and to consume the necessary amount at night, the net balance being always positive. In the centre of our cities, a new species emerges.

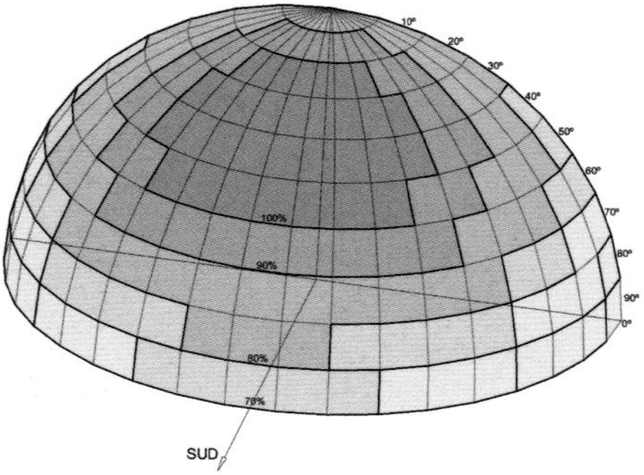

Insolation efficiency in relation to the orientation

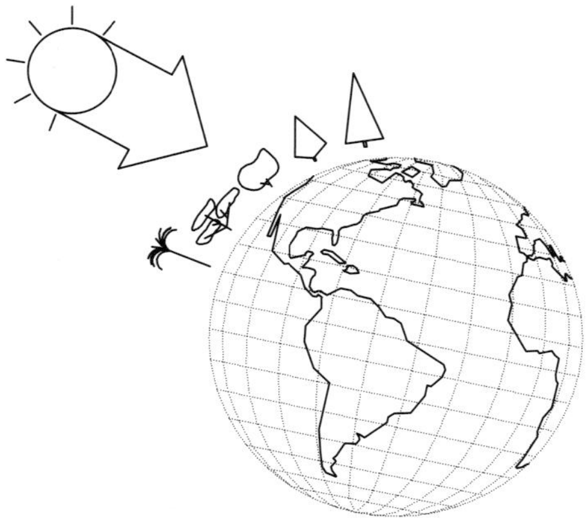

GEOGRAPHY

Trees are shaped by their environment

GEOMETRY

Metabolism of the tree

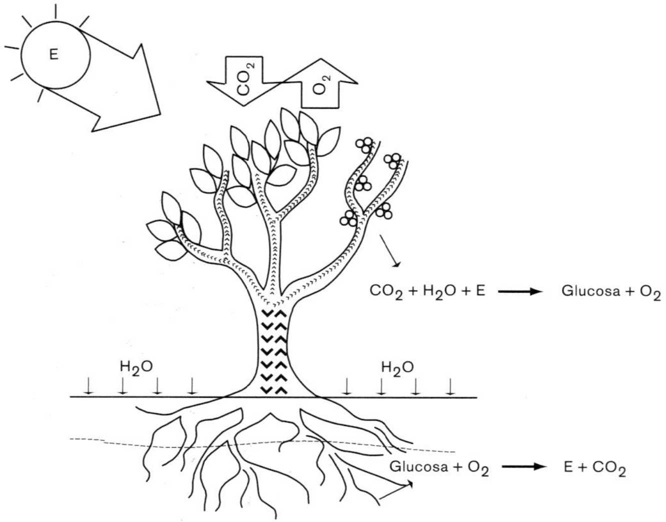

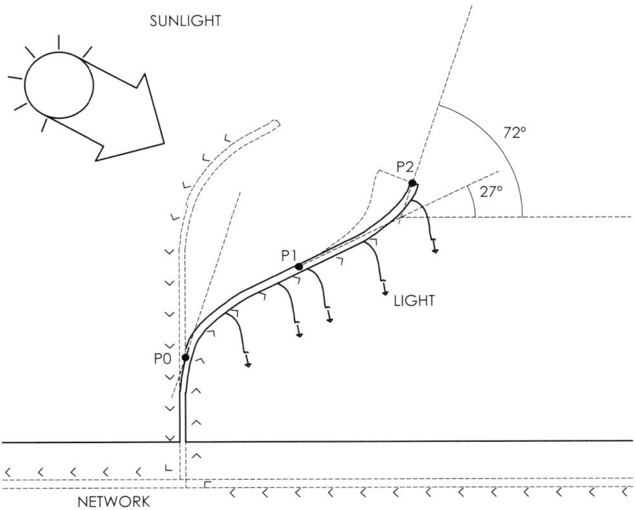

LOGIC

Photovoltaic tree, sharing the logic of exchanges of its natural counterpart

STRUCTURE

A structure that gives light and shade

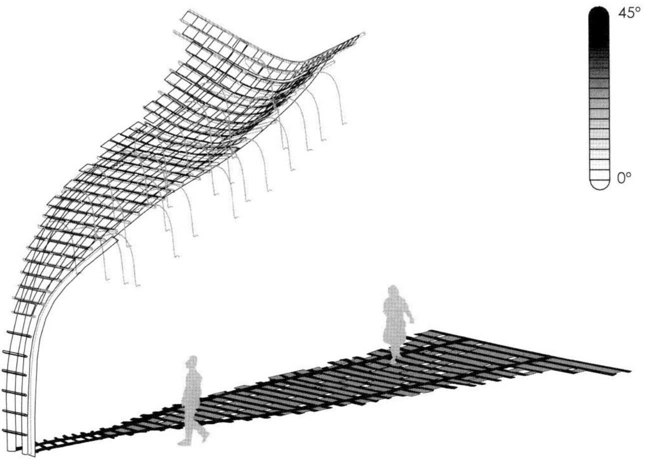

A1

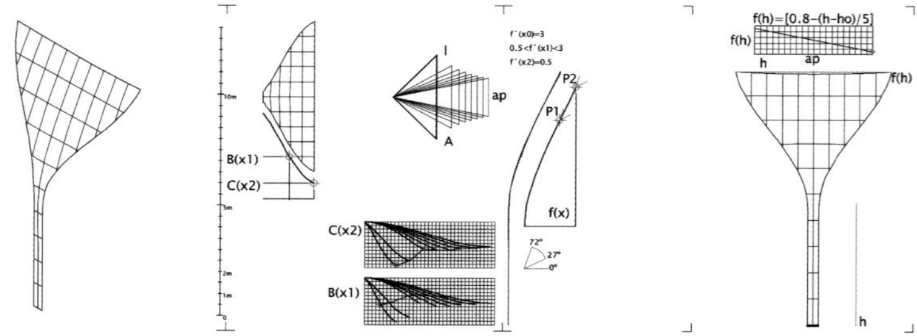
10m
5m
2m
1m
0
B(x1)
C(x2)
I
ap
A
f´(x0)=3
0.5<f´(x1)<3
f´(x2)=0.5
P2
P1
f(x)
72°
27°
0°
f(h)=[0.8-(h-ho)/5]
f(h)
h
ap
f(h)
h

A2

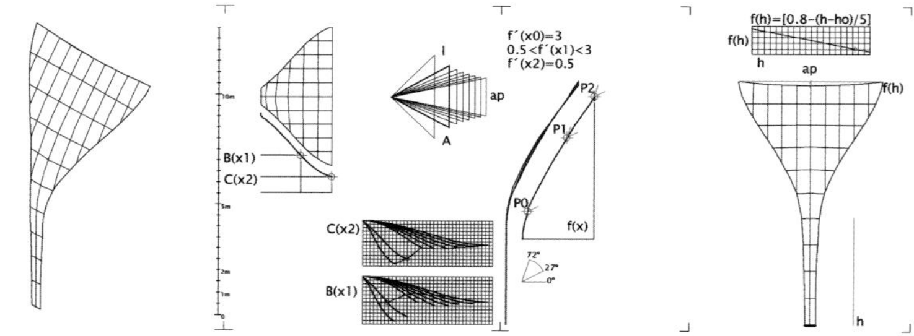
10m
5m
2m
1m
0
B(x1)
C(x2)
I
ap
A
f´(x0)=3
0.5<f´(x1)<3
f´(x2)=0.5
P2
P1
P0
f(x)
72°
27°
0°
f(h)=[0.8-(h-ho)/5]
f(h)
h
ap
f(h)
h

A3

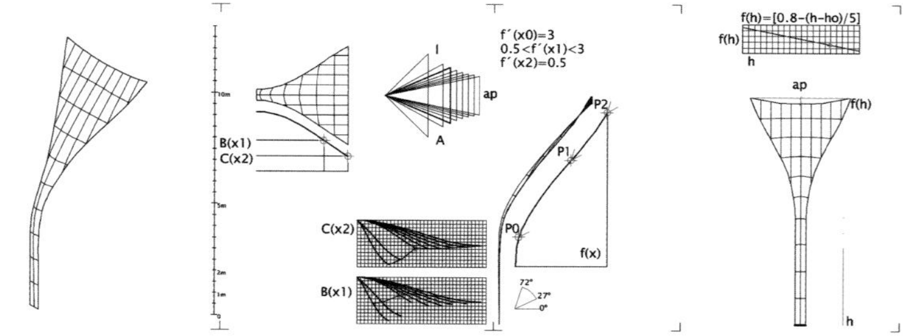
10m
5m
2m
1m
0
B(x1)
C(x2)
I
ap
A
f´(x0)=3
0.5<f´(x1)<3
f´(x2)=0.5
P2
P1
P0
f(x)
72°
27°
0°
f(h)=[0.8-(h-ho)/5]
f(h)
h
ap
f(h)
h

A4

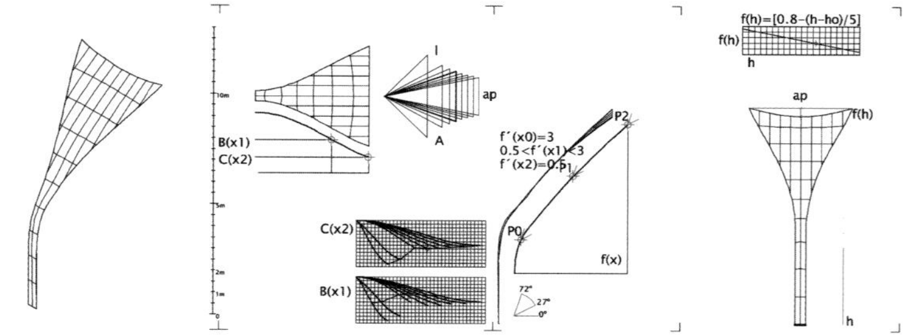
10m
5m
2m
1m
0
B(x1)
C(x2)
I
ap
A
f´(x0)=3
0.5<f´(x1)<3
f´(x2)=0.5
P2
P1
P0
f(x)
72°
27°
0°
f(h)=[0.8-(h-ho)/5]
f(h)
h
ap
f(h)
h

A5

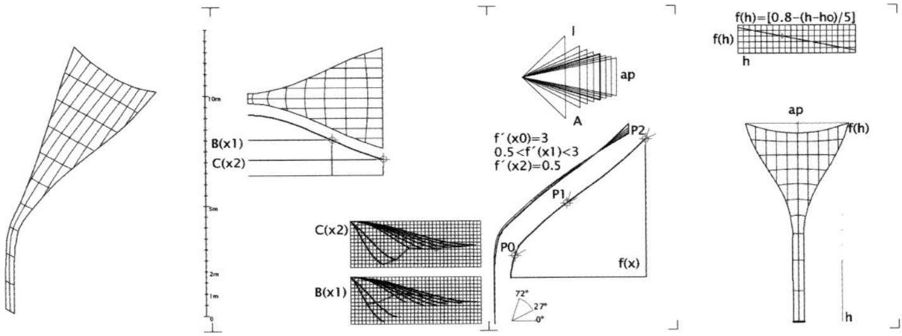
10m
B(x1)
C(x2)
5m
2m
1m
0
C(x2)
B(x1)
l
ap
A
f´(x0)=3
0.5<f´(x1)<3
f´(x2)=0.5
P2
P1
P0
f(x)
72°
27°
0°
f(h)=[0.8-(h-ho)/5]
f(h)
h
ap
f(h)
h

A6

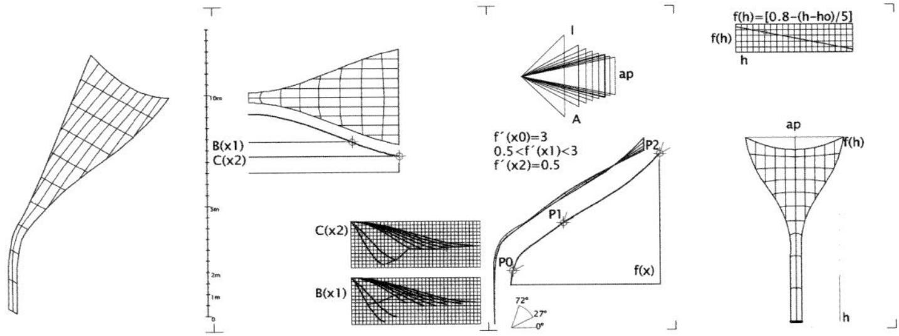
10m
B(x1)
C(x2)
5m
2m
1m
0
C(x2)
B(x1)
l
ap
A
f´(x0)=3
0.5<f´(x1)<3
f´(x2)=0.5
P2
P1
P0
f(x)
72°
27°
0°
f(h)=[0.8-(h-ho)/5]
f(h)
h
ap
f(h)
h

A7

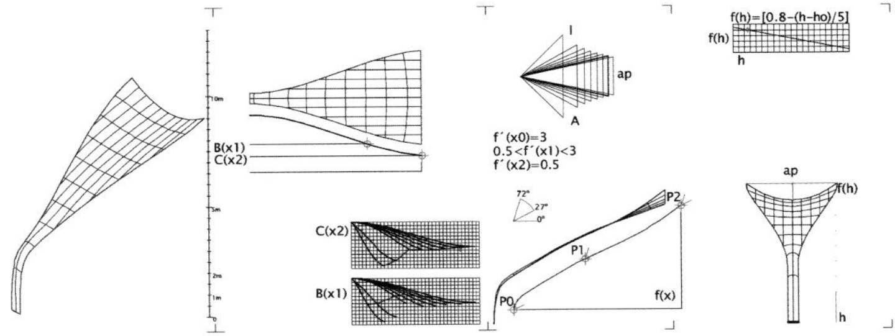
10m
B(x1)
C(x2)
5m
2m
1m
0
C(x2)
B(x1)
l
ap
A
f´(x0)=3
0.5<f´(x1)<3
f´(x2)=0.5
72°
27°
0°
P2
P1
P0
f(x)
f(h)=[0.8-(h-ho)/5]
f(h)
h
ap
f(h)
h

A8

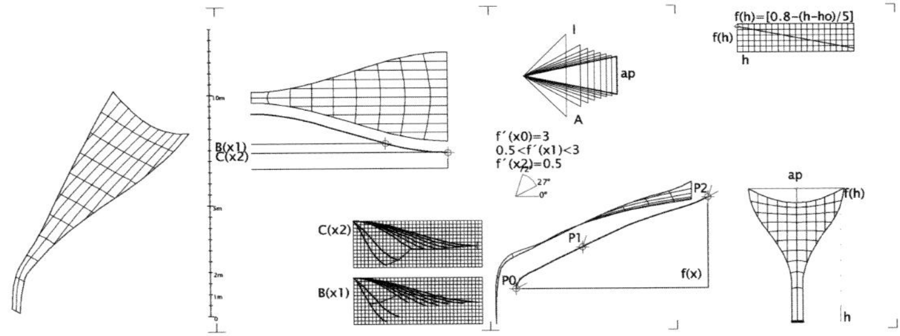
10m
B(x1)
C(x2)
5m
2m
1m
0
C(x2)
B(x1)
l
ap
A
f´(x0)=3
0.5<f´(x1)<3
f´(x2)=0.5
27°
0°
P2
P1
P0
f(x)
f(h)=[0.8-(h-ho)/5]
f(h)
h
ap
f(h)
h

Sport rocks

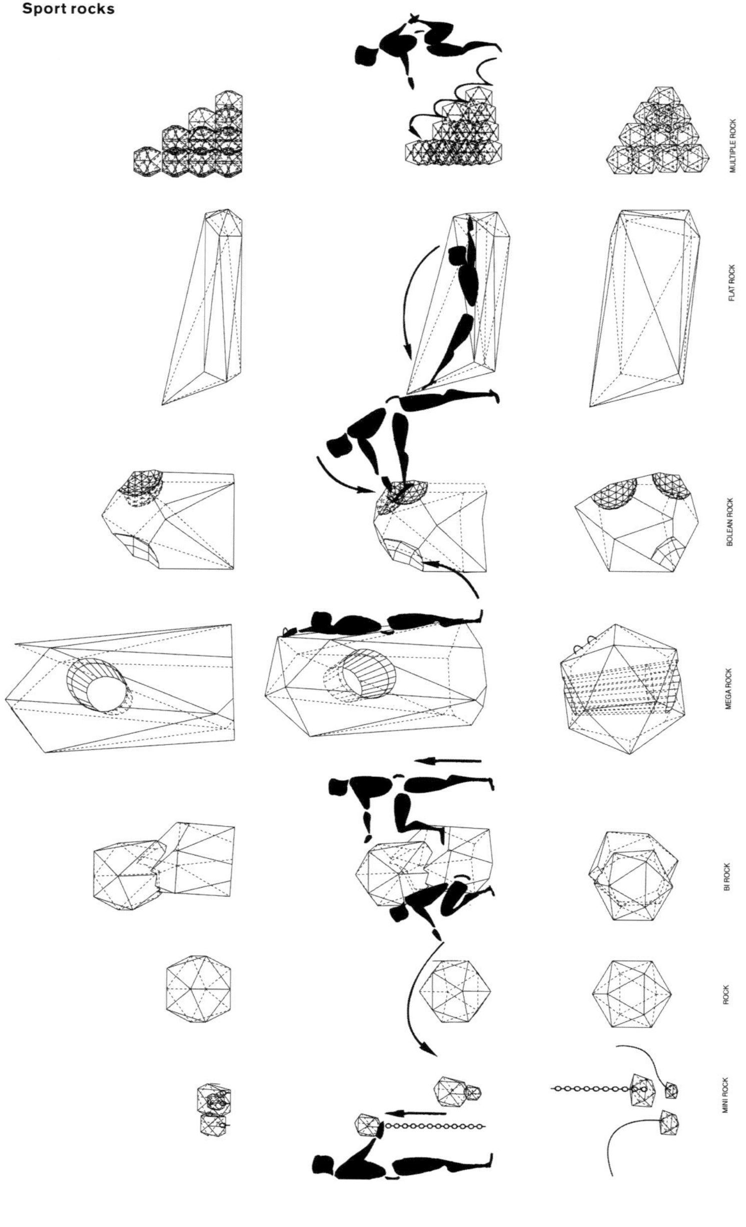
MULTIPLE ROCK
FLAT ROCK
BOLEAN ROCK
MEGA ROCK
BI ROCK
ROCK
MINI ROCK

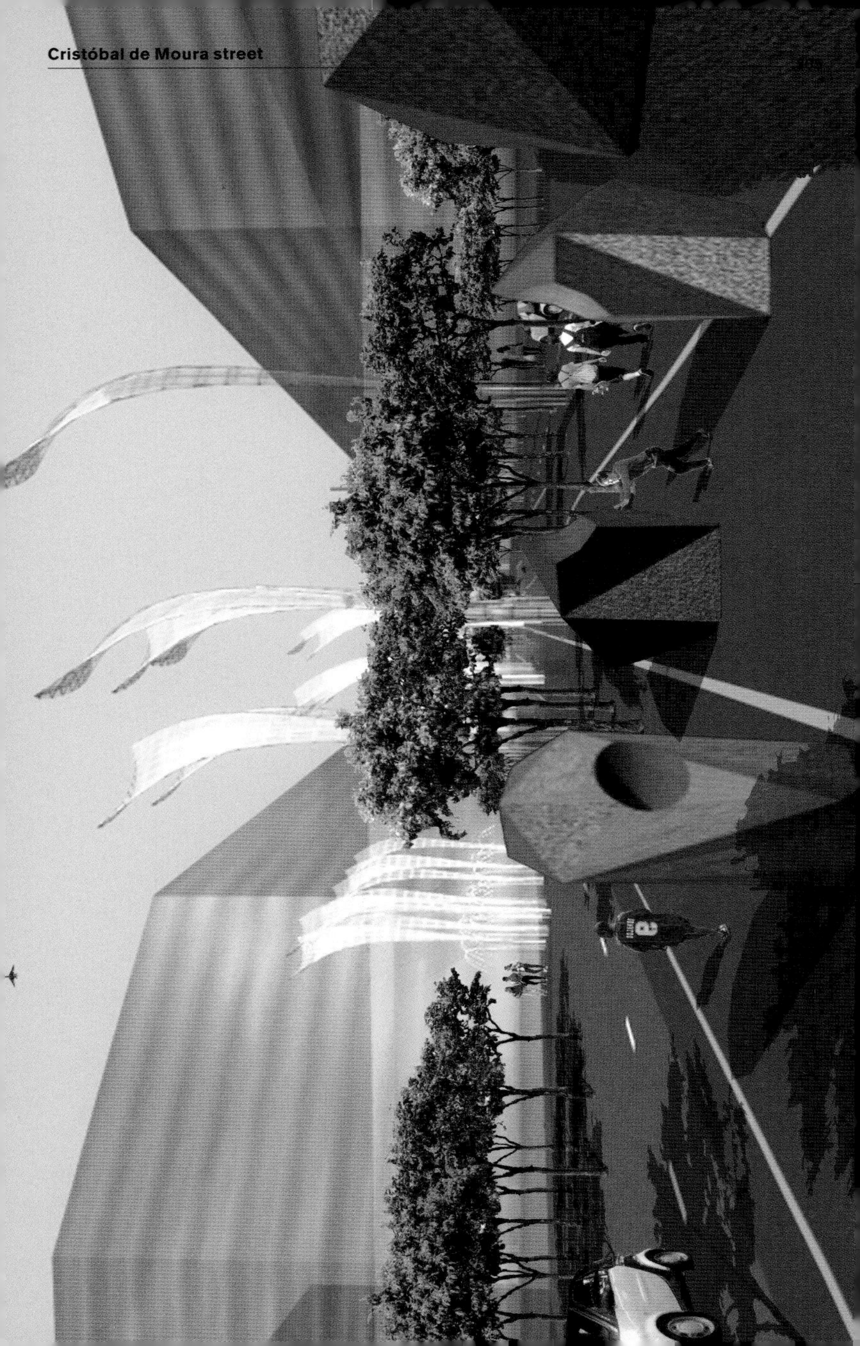

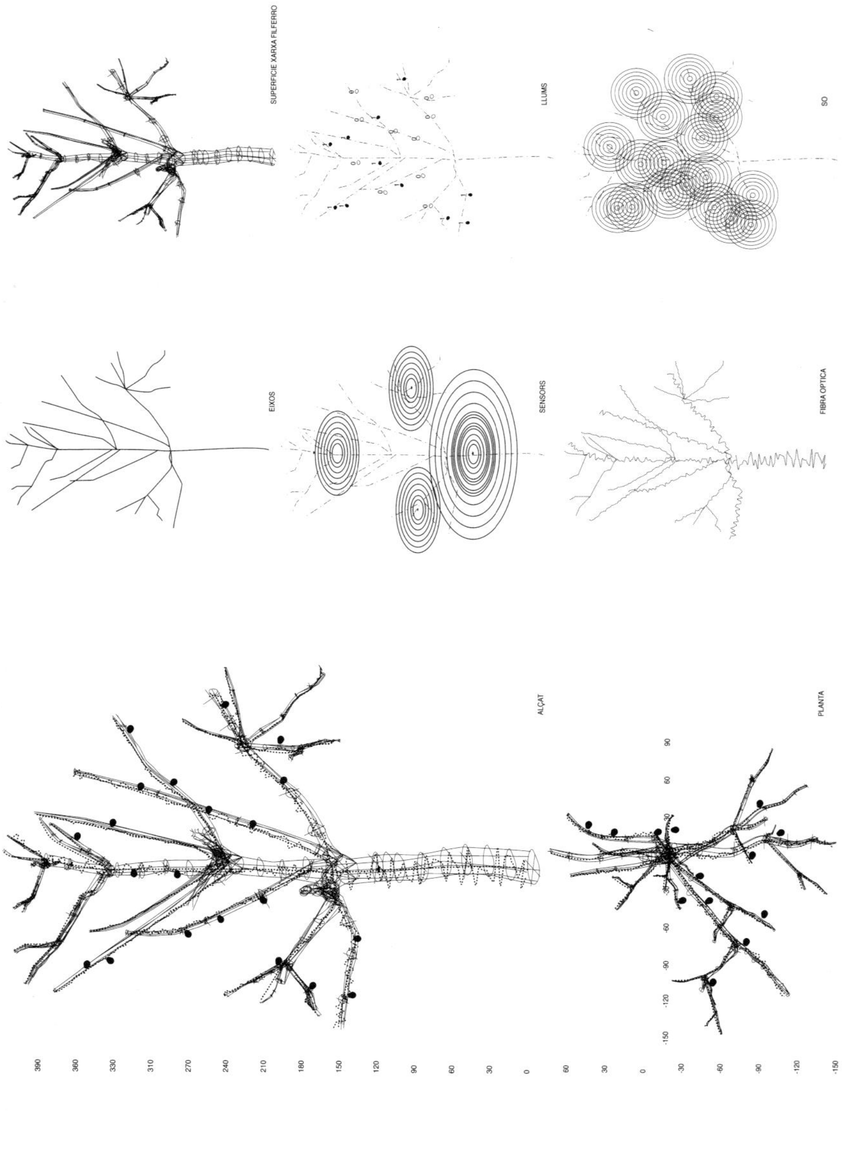
SUPERFICIE XARXA FILFERRO
LLUMS
SO
EIXOS
SENSORS
FIBRA OPTICA
ALÇAT
PLANTA
390 360 330 310 270 240 210 180 150 120 90 60 30 0
60 30 0 -30 -60 -90 -120 -150
90 60 30 -30 -60 -90 -120 -150

Vinaròs Promenade

Vinaròs, Castellón. Spain. 2007—

1st Prize national competition

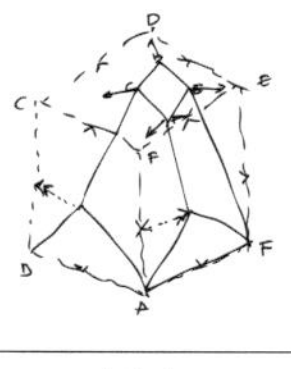

Parametrizing
/14

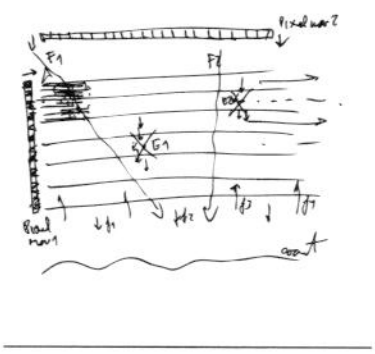

Automaton pattern
/15

Vinaròs is the most northerly town of the Valencia region. During the 20th century, urban growth made it necessary to delimit the town's relation with the sea by means of a seafront promenade that subsequently became a pole of attraction for the tourist boom that Spain began to experience in the 1960s. In fact Vinaròs did not undergo the processes of peripheral growth or the programmatic consequences of delocalization of its commercial activities typical of the 1980s, nor the massive influx of tourist hotels and franchises that occurred in neighbouring towns. As such it presents a very interesting urban type, in many respects having jumped directly from the 1970s to the 21st century.

Reform of the seafront promenade, as the interface between the centre of the town and the sea, offered a great opportunity for a public initiative to define the desired standards of urban quality for future growth. In fact the promenade is today a place of great urban vitality, occupied mainly by cars, which coexist with seafood restaurants, an open-air auditorium for orchestral and choral concerts and open-air film screenings, and the regular street markets and events throughout the year, frequented by people on their way to and from the beach. Social interaction in its pure state.

The main decision here was to transform the entire promenade into an area for pedestrian use, in order to take full advantage of the place's latent tourist and civic potential, restricting vehicle access for loading and unloading to certain times of the day, and allowing freer access out of season, when this is compatible with the reduced level of pedestrian activity. The structure of the town's road system is such that traffic in the part closest to the port could be routed behind the buildings on the streets parallel to the promenade. However, the absence of any such parallel streets in the central and northern sectors prompted the decision to construct a tunnel between the end of the promenade and the 250-place car park to be laid out beneath the central plaza. This car park will be connected with others in or under adjacent squares to create a real underground mobility network that allows cars to drive in from the outskirts to the centre of the town and park close to the beach and the seafront promenade. It was also decided to eliminate the concrete wall separating the beach from the promenade to enable the whole area to be perceived as a continuous space composed of a variety of materials, from the sand of the artificial beach to the cenia stone from a local quarry. Another significant decision was that the promenade, which at present has an irregular topography, should have a constant level that would set off its eight-hundred metre horizontal line against the natural line of the sea's horizon. This serves to resolve the difference in level between the beach and the promenade by means of a system of tiers that can be occupied in a variety of ways.

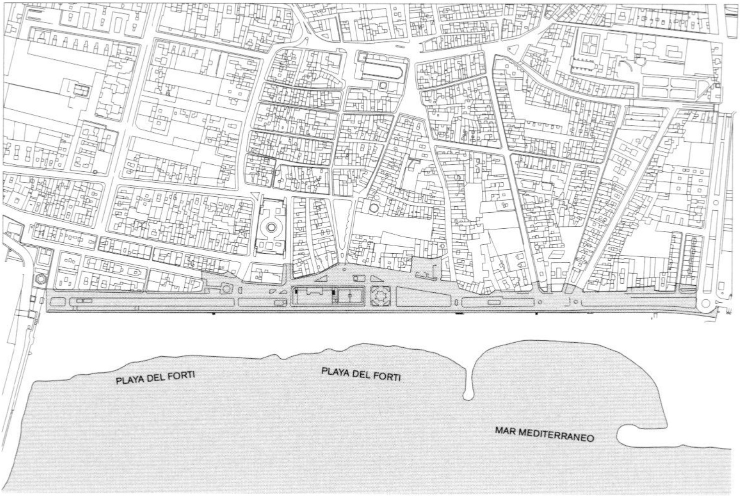

GEOGRAPHY

An urban centre on the Mediterranean

GEOMETRY

The coastline, roads and urban flows affect the promenade

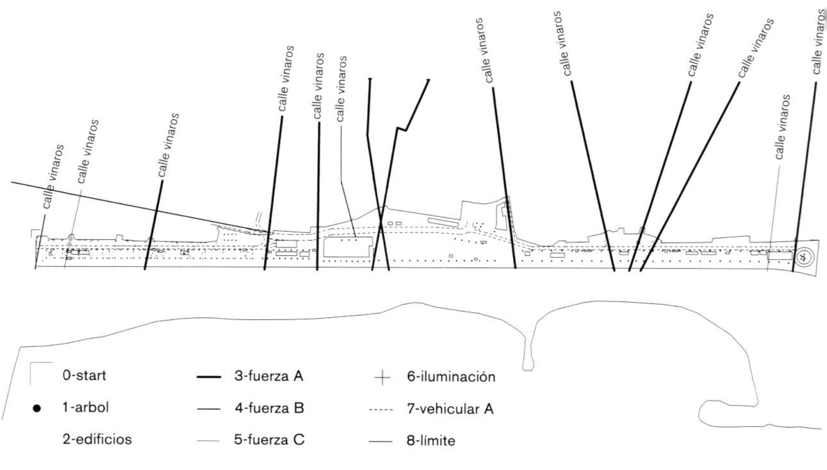

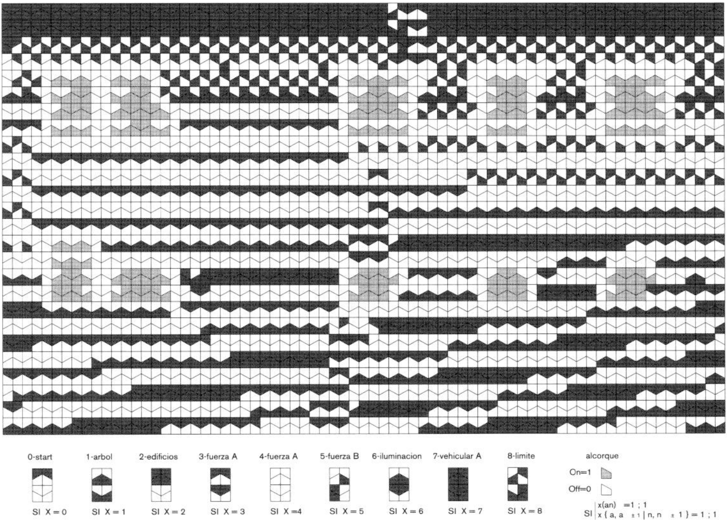

LOGIC

Cellular automaton based on a reading of the environment

STRUCTURE

An urban pattern that embodies the memory of the place

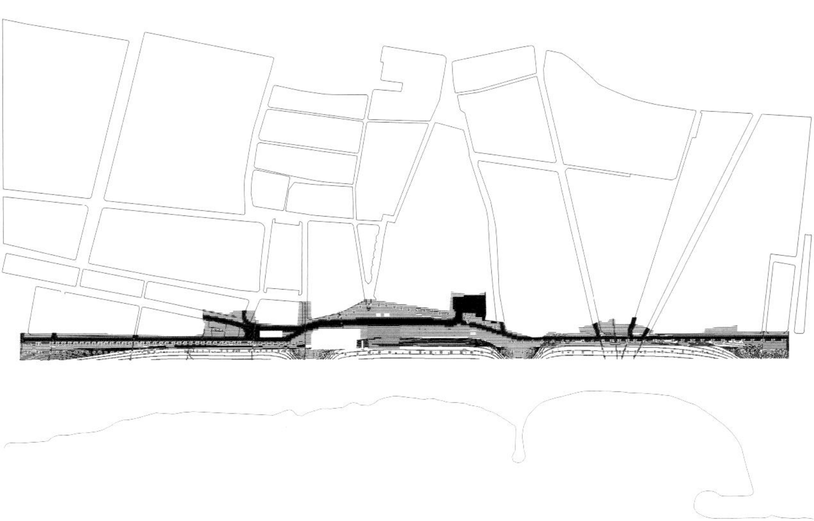

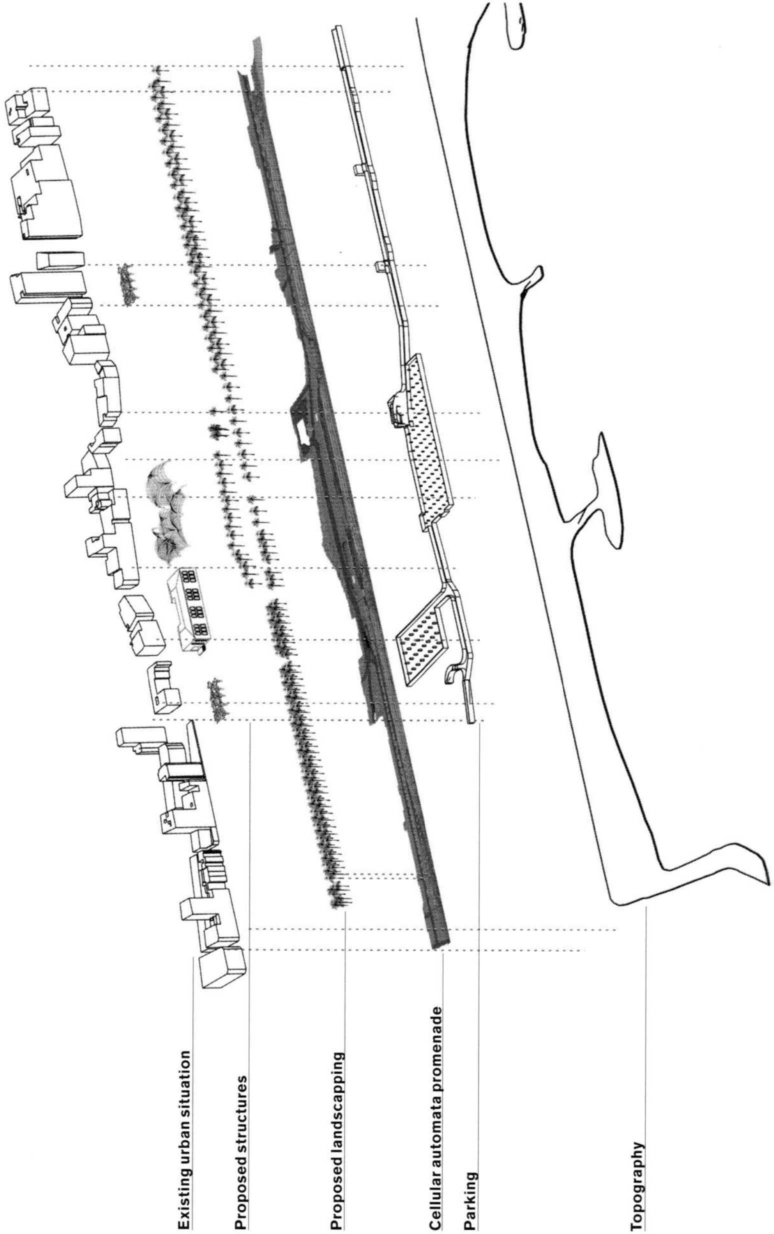

Existing urban situation
Proposed structures
Proposed landscapping
Cellular automata promenade
Parking
Topography

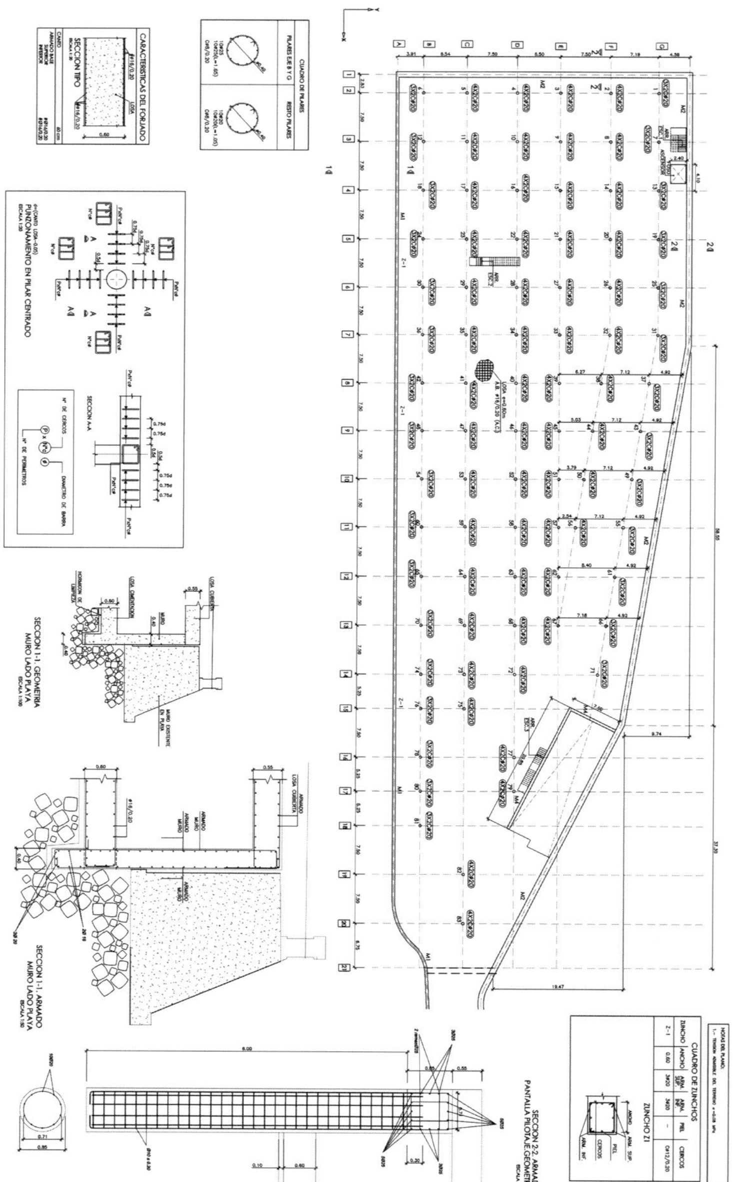
CARACTERISTICAS DEL FORJADO
SECCION TIPO
CUADRO DE PILARES
PILARES EJE B Y G
RESTO PILARES
PUNZONAMIENTO EN PILAR CENTRADO
SECCION A-A
SECCION 1-1. GEOMETRIA
MURO LADO PLAYA
SECCION 1-1. ARMADO
MURO LADO PLAYA
SECCION 2-2. ARMADO
PANTALLA PILOTAJE.GEOMETRIA
CUADRO DE ZUNCHOS
ZUNCHO Z1
NOTAS DEL PLANO:

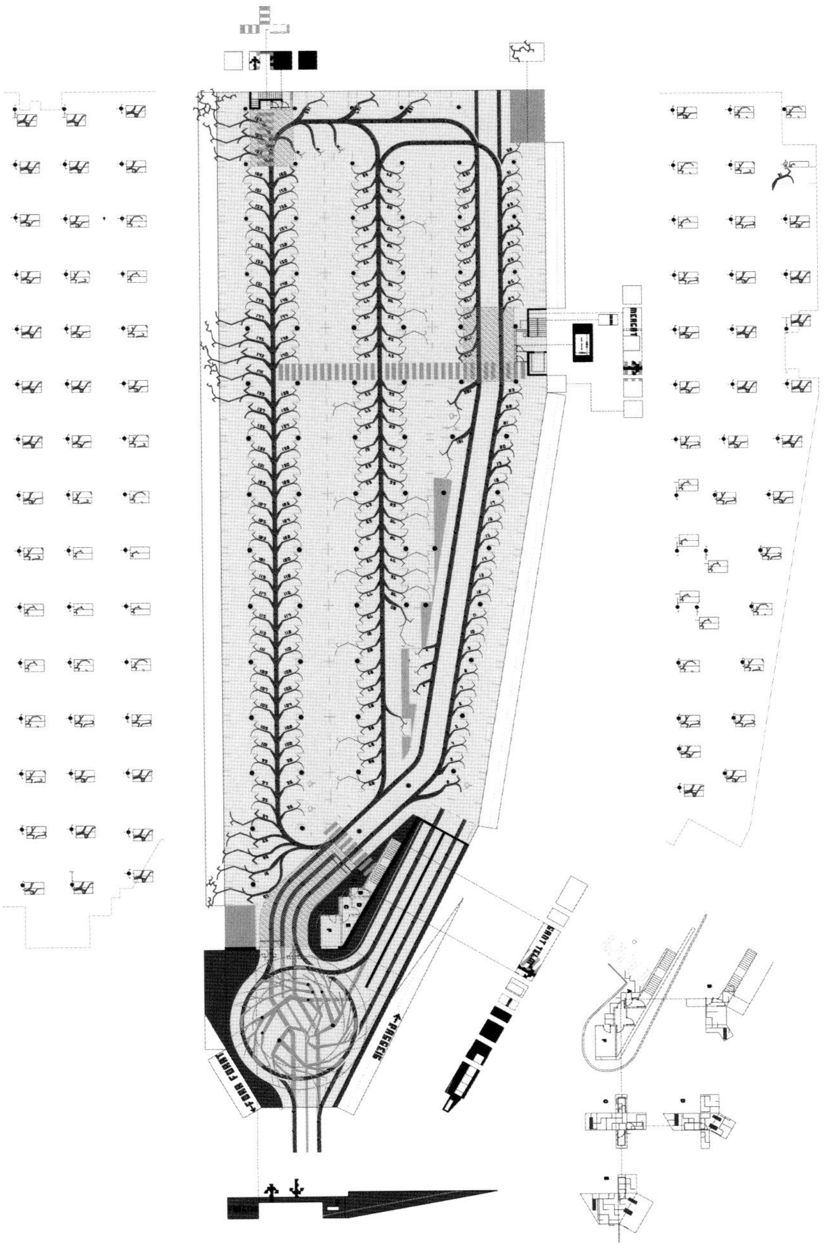
MERCAT
SANT TELM
←PASSEIG
←FORA FORAT

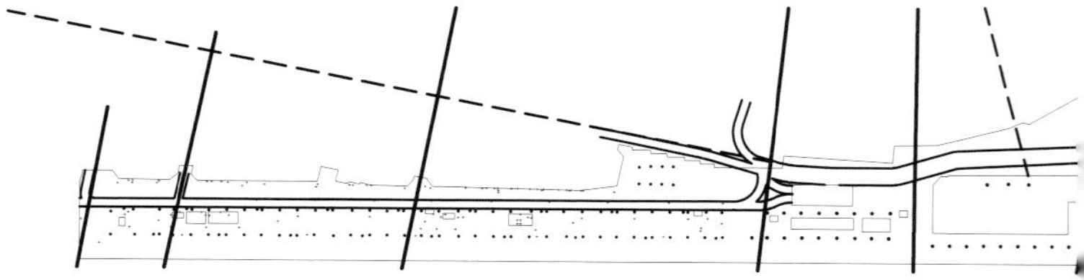

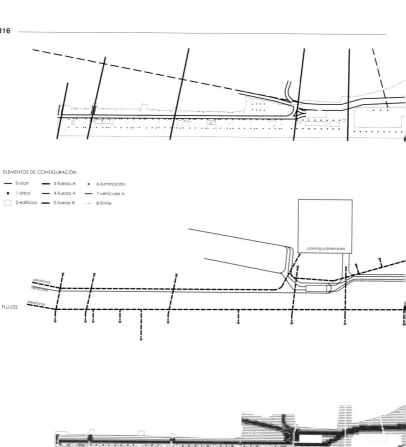

ELEMENTOS DE CONFIGURACÓN

- 0-start
- 1-árbol
- 2-edificios
- 3-fuerza A
- 4-fuerza A
- 5-fuerza B
- 6-iluminación
- 7-vehicular A
- 8-límite

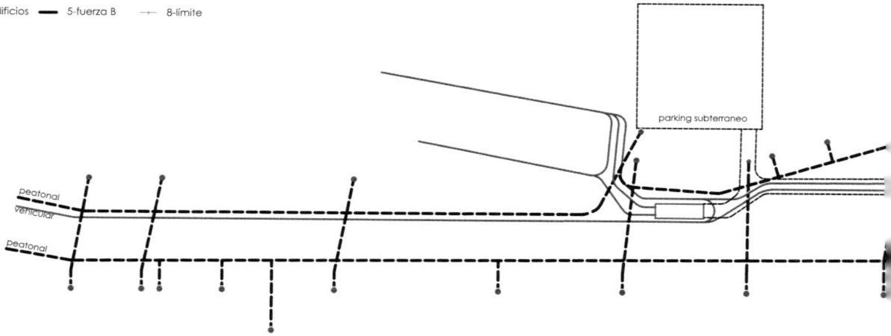

FLUJOS

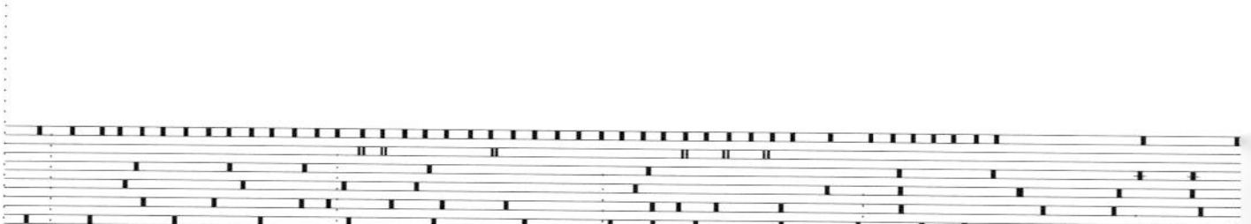

PATRÓN AUTÓMATA

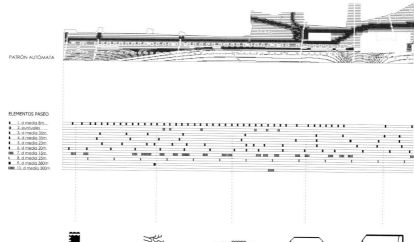

ELEMENTOS PASEO

1. d media 8m
2. puntuales
3. d media 35m
4. d media 35m
5. d media 23m
6. d media 20m
7. d media 15m
8. d media 25m
9. d media 380m
10. d media 300m

1 ALCORQUES   2 RAYAS   3 BAJADAS   4 LAVAPIÉS   5 BARANDILLAS

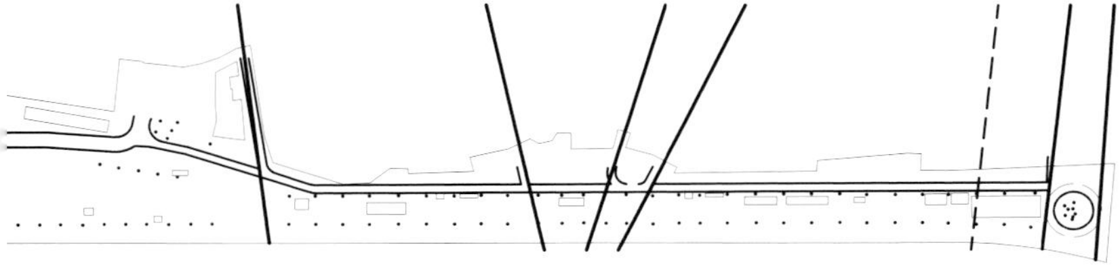

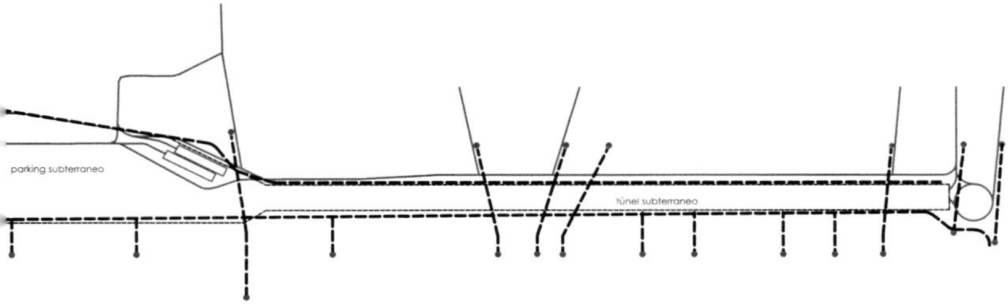
parking subterraneo
túnel subterraneo

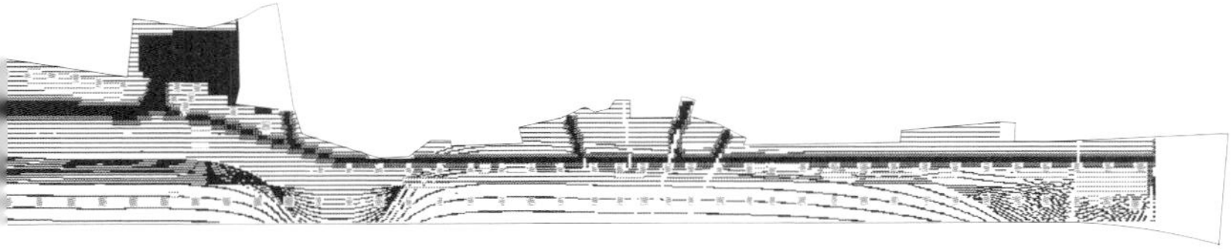

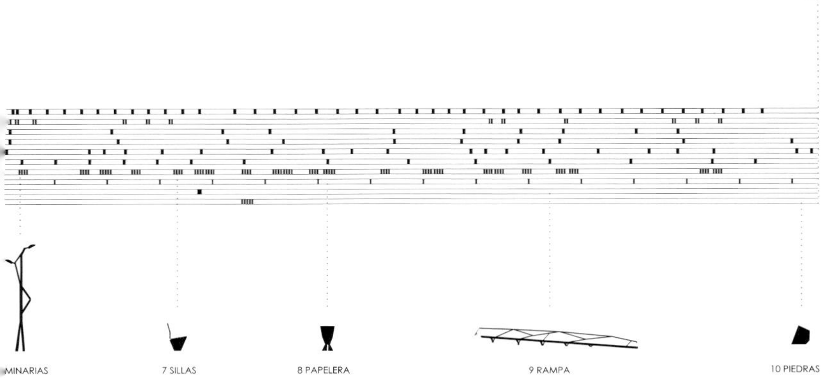
MINARIAS
7 SILLAS
8 PAPELERA
9 RAMPA
10 PIEDRAS

Malla patrón

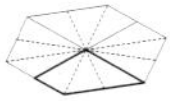

Agregación

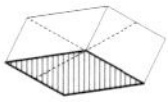

Solidificación-n1

Solidificación-n2

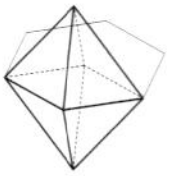

gen01

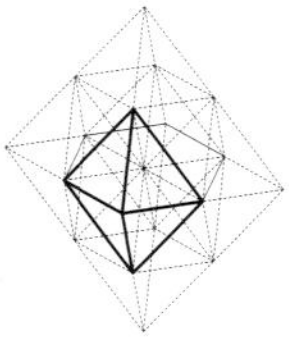

gen02

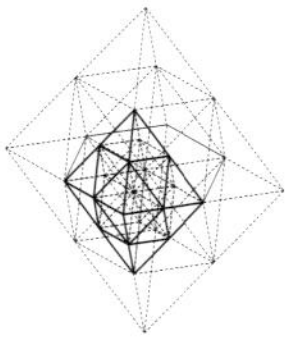

Estructura-gen01

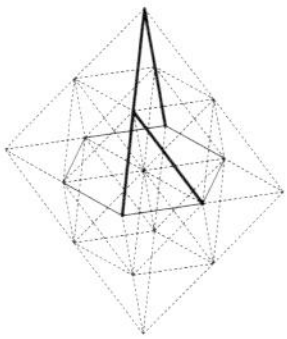

Estructura-gen02

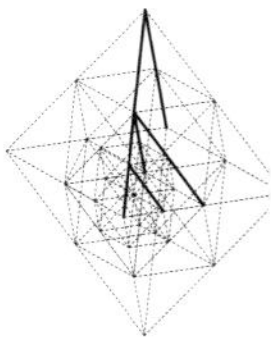

Crecimiento L01

01

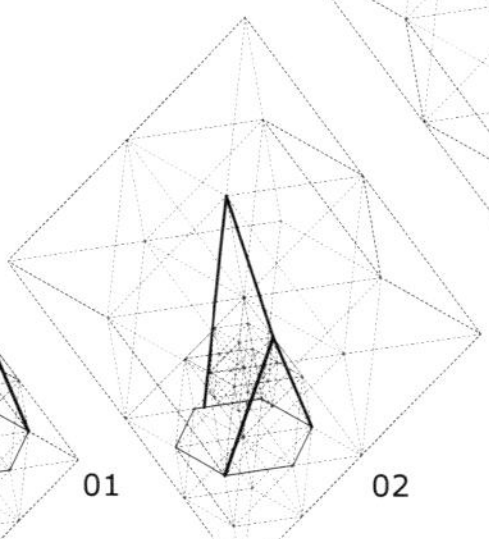

02

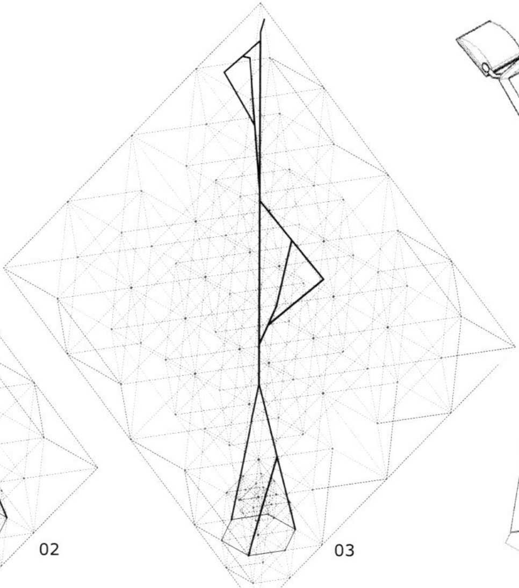

03

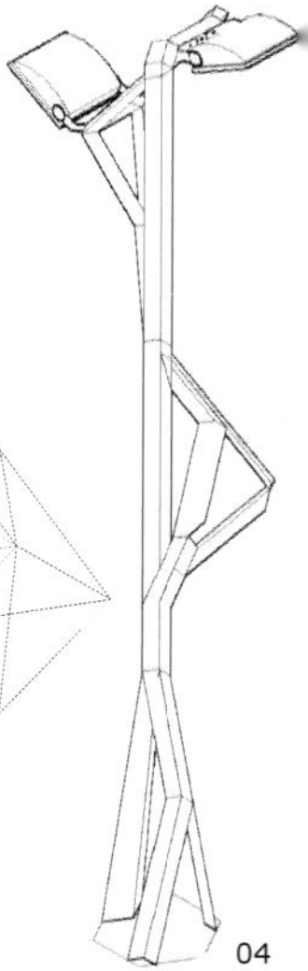

04

Sistema

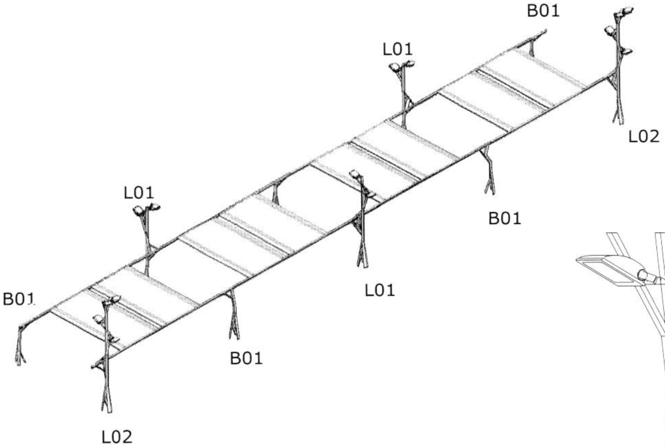

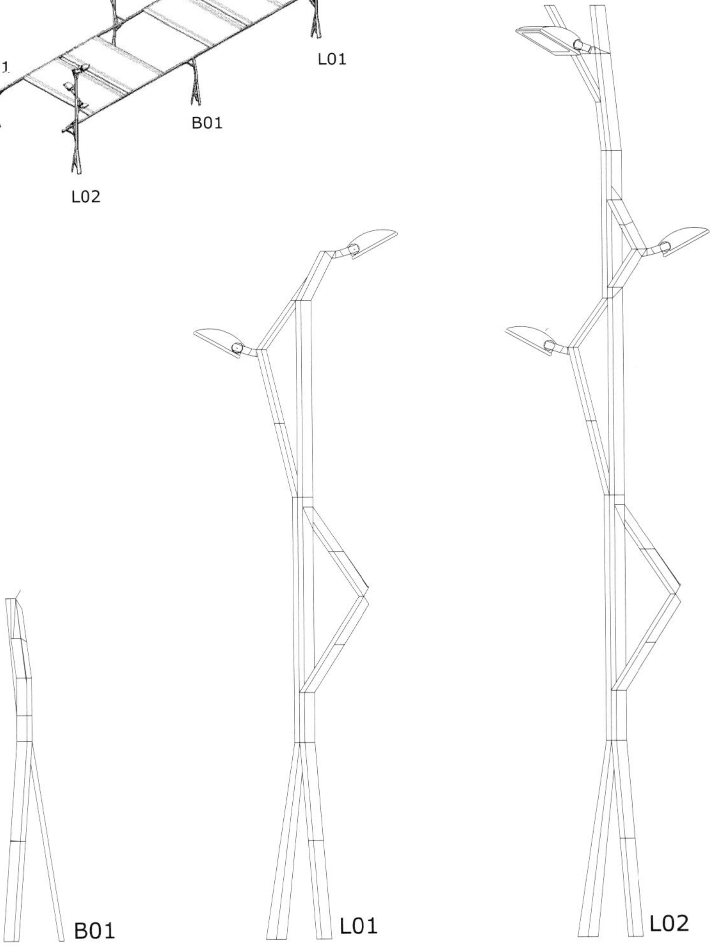

B-01

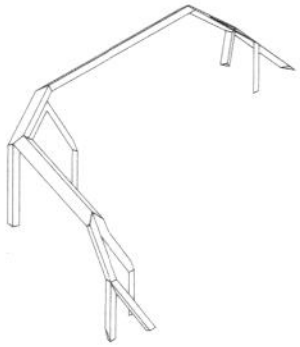

A1+U2+B1+U1+A2

B-02

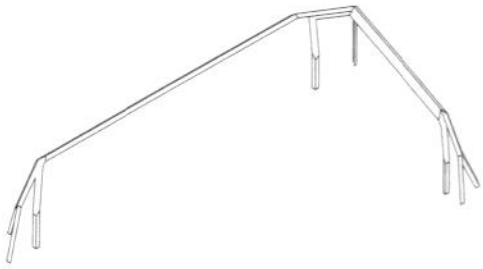

A1+U1+B2+U2+A1

B-03

B2+U2+A2

B-04

A1+U2+B1+U1+A2

B-05

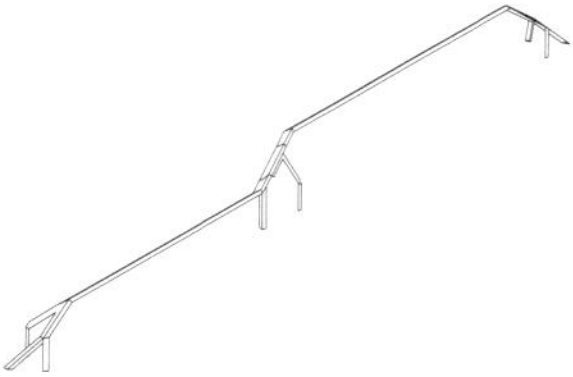

A2+U1+B1+U1+A2

B-06

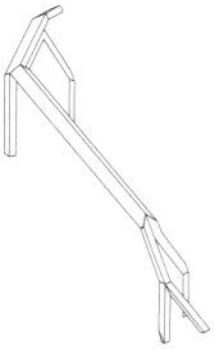

B1+U2+A1

B-07

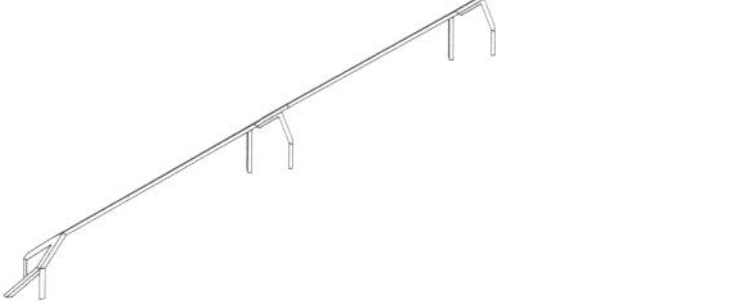

A2+U1+B1+U1+B1+U1+A2

B-08

A1+U1+B1+U1+A2

B-09

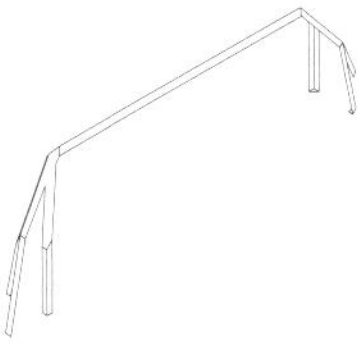

A1+U1+A1

B-10

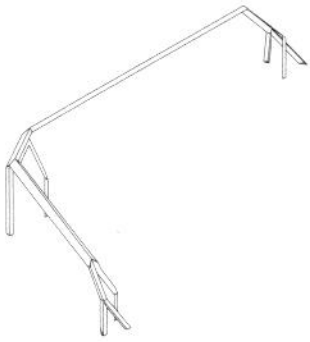

A1+U2+B1+U1+A2

B-11

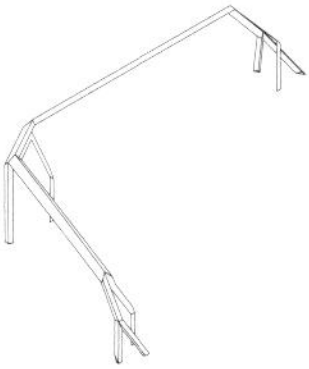

A1+U2+B1+U1+A2

B-12

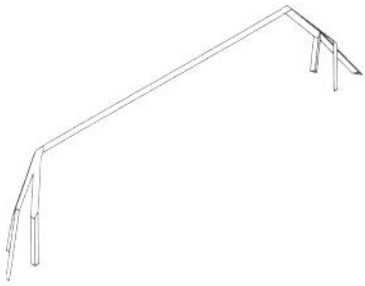

A1+U1+A2

B-13

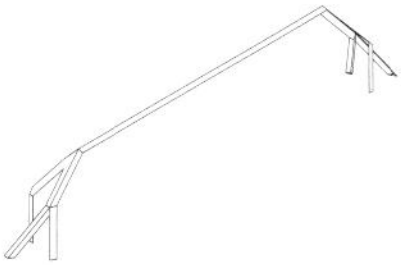

A2+U1+A2

B-14

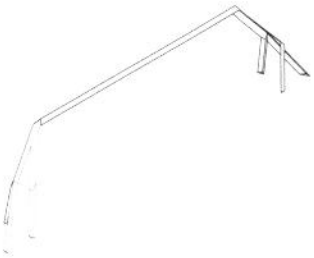

A1+U1+A2

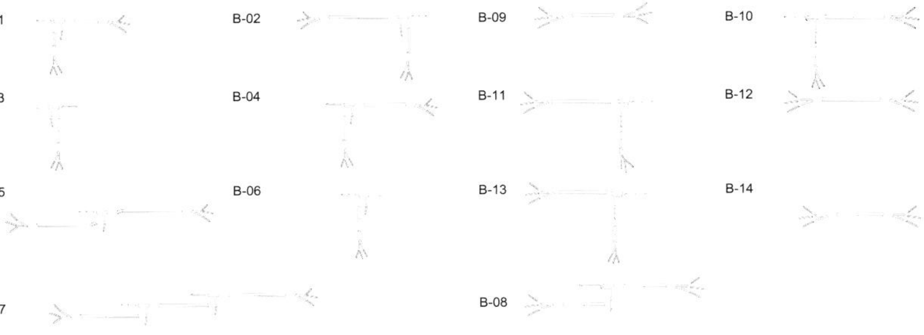

B-01 B-02 B-09 B-10
B-03 B-04 B-11 B-12
B-05 B-06 B-13 B-14
B-07 B-08

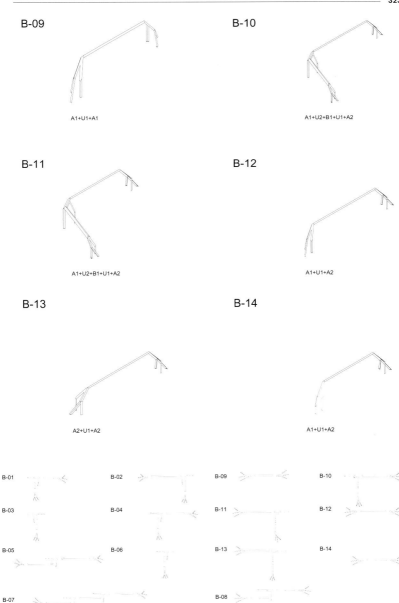

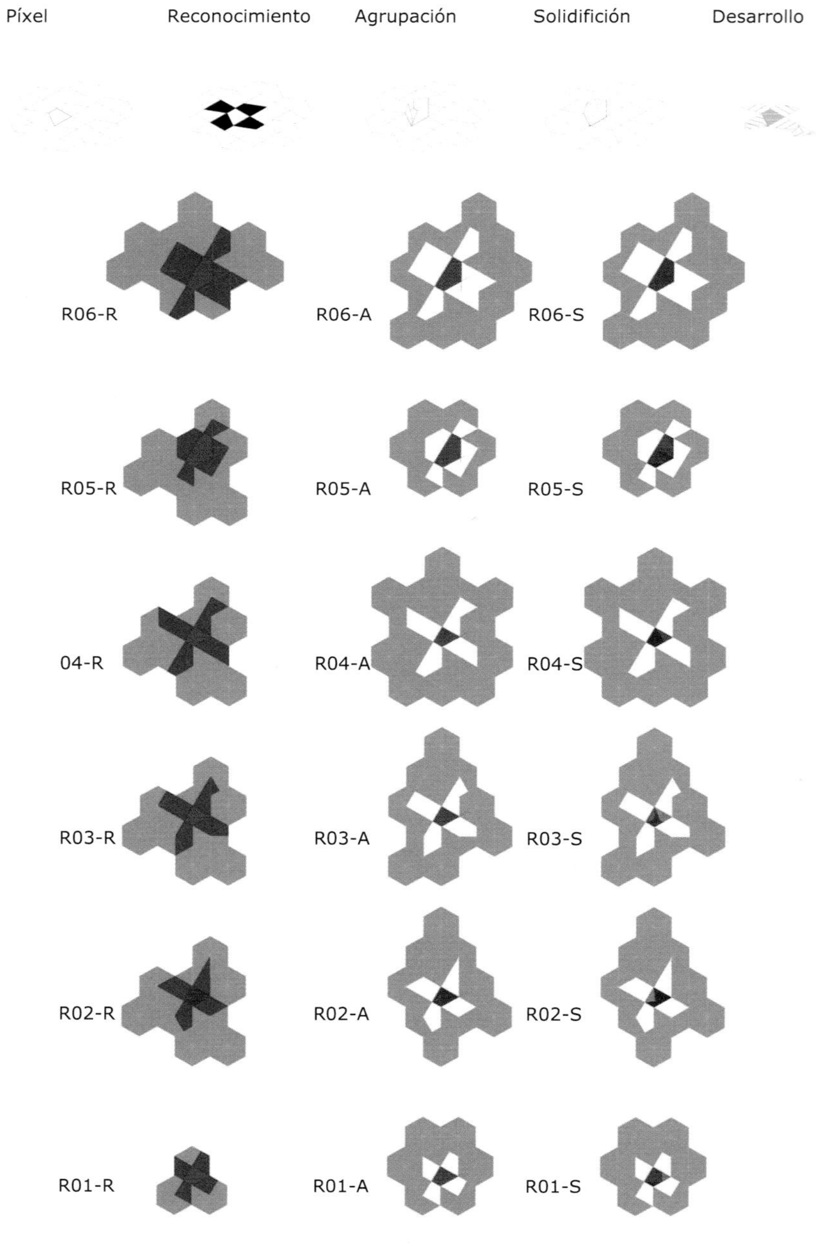
Píxel
Reconocimiento
Agrupación
Solidifición
Desarrollo
R06-R
R06-A
R06-S
R05-R
R05-A
R05-S
04-R
R04-A
R04-S
R03-R
R03-A
R03-S
R02-R
R02-A
R02-S
R01-R
R01-A
R01-S

R-01

b=1

L=1

g=1a

nc=8

R-02

b=1

L=1

g=1a

nc=8

R-03

b=2

L=2

g=1a

nc=9

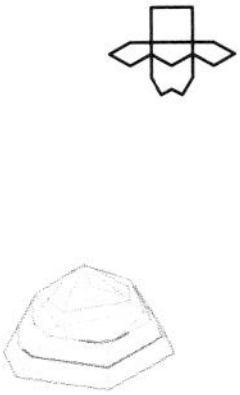

R-04

b=2

L=2

g=1a

nc=11

R-05

b=4

L=2

g=1a

nc=12

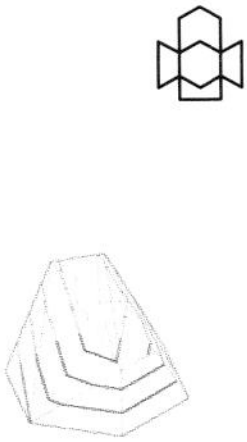

R-06

b=1

L=2

g=2a

nc=8

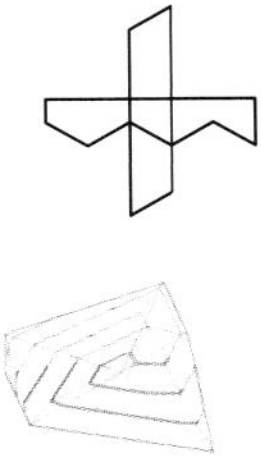

R-07

b=1

L=2

g=2a

nc=8

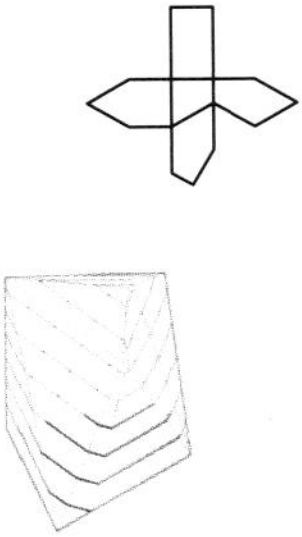

R-08

b=2

L=2

g=2a

nc=9

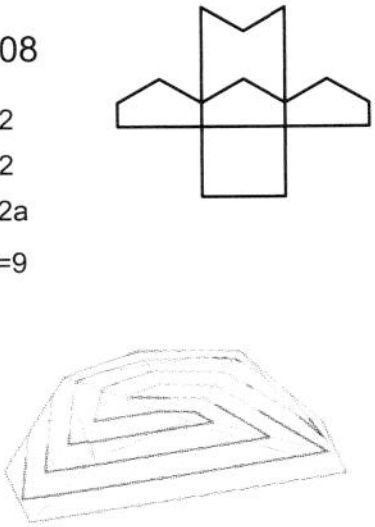

R-09

b=4

L=3

g=2a

nc=11

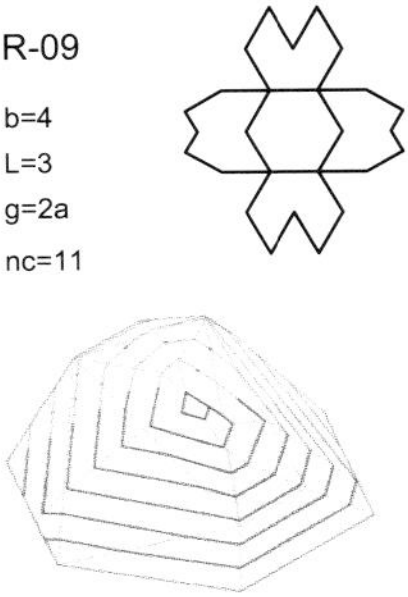

R-10

b=1

L=2

g=2a

nc=8

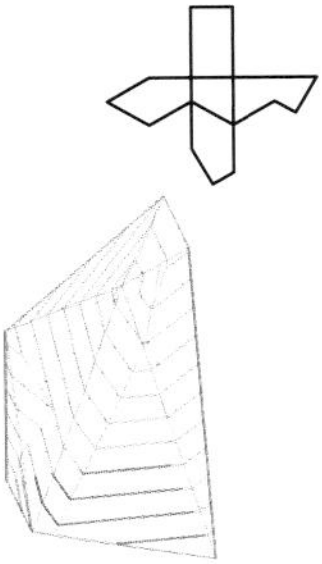

R-11

b=1

L=2

g=3a

nc=28

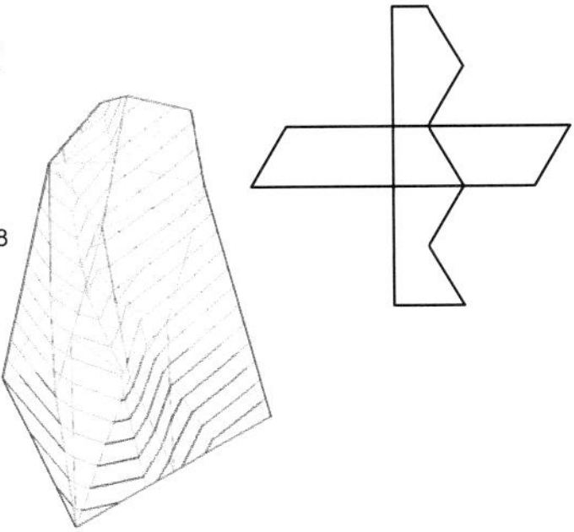

Píxel

Red celular autómata

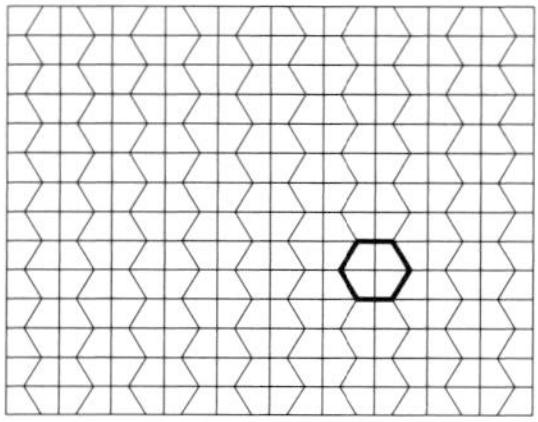

Cambio parámetros del píxel

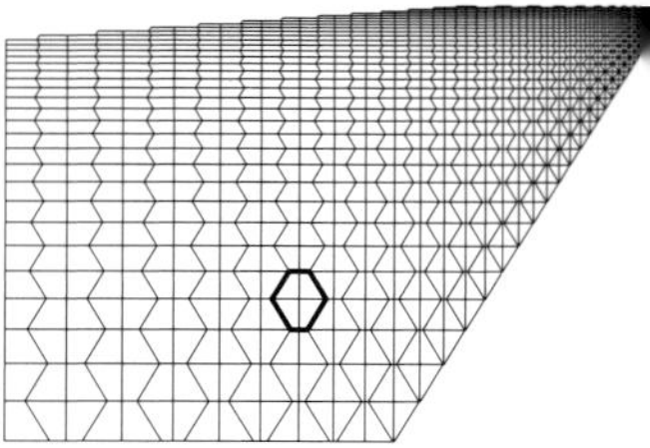

Nuevo píxel

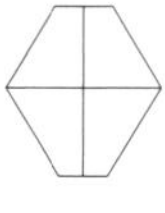

Parámetros

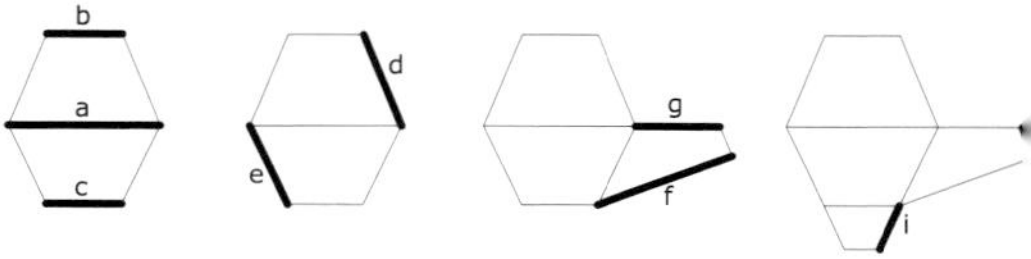

Familia

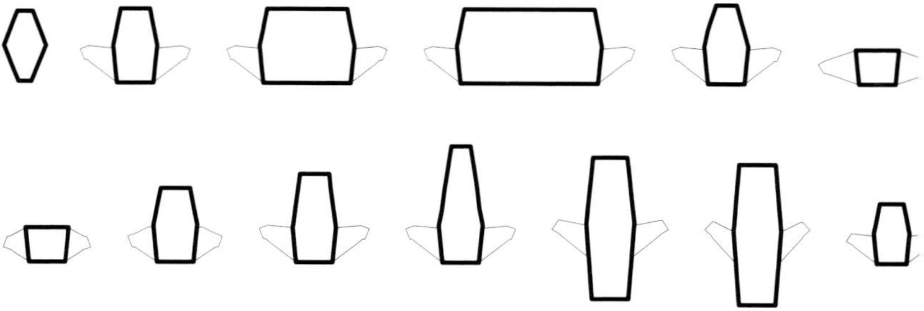

Plegado

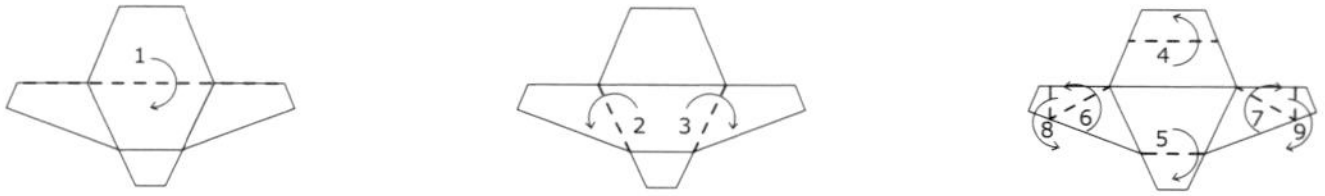

S-01

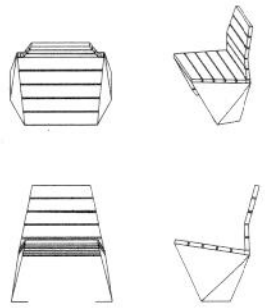

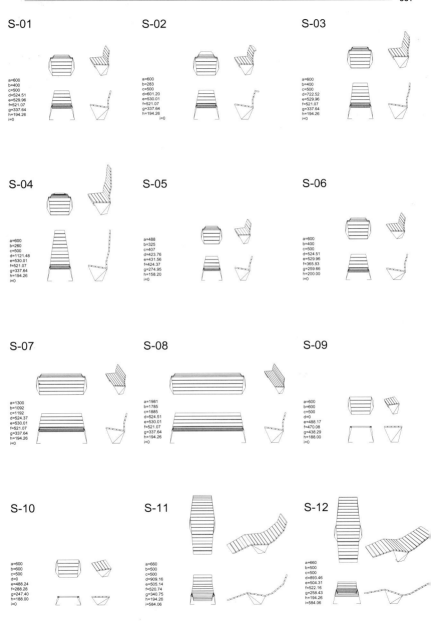

a=600
b=400
c=500
d=524.51
e=529.96
f=521.07
g=337.64
h=194.26
i=0

S-02

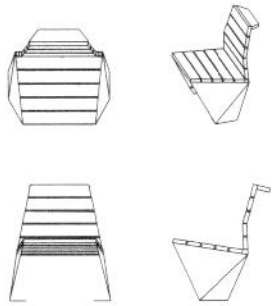

a=600
b=283
c=500
d=601.20
e=530.01
f=521.07
g=337.64
h=194.26
i=0

S-03

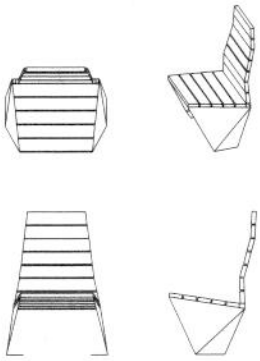

a=600
b=400
c=500
d=722.52
e=529.96
f=521.07
g=337.64
h=194.26
i=0

S-04

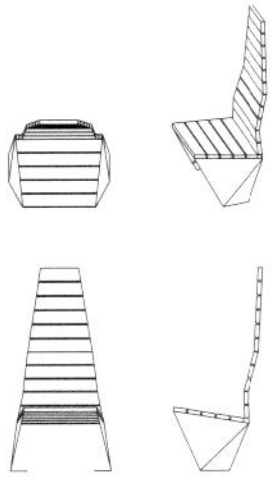

a=600
b=260
c=500
d=1121.48
e=530.01
f=521.07
g=337.64
h=194.26
i=0

S-05

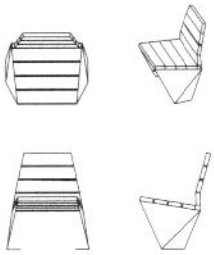

a=488
b=325
c=407
d=423.76
e=431.56
f=424.37
g=274.95
h=158.20
i=0

S-06

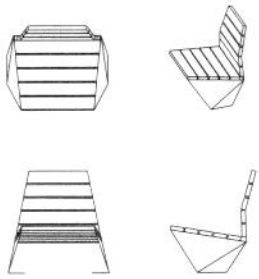

a=600
b=400
c=500
d=524.51
e=529.96
f=365.83
g=259.66
h=200.00
i=0

S-07

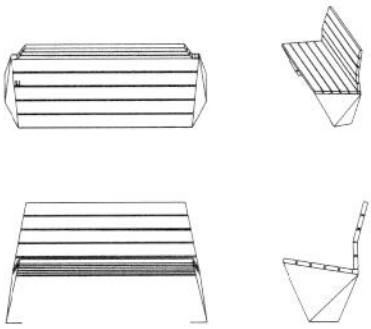

a=1300
b=1092
c=1192
d=524.37
e=530.01
f=521.07
g=337.64
h=194.26
i=0

S-08

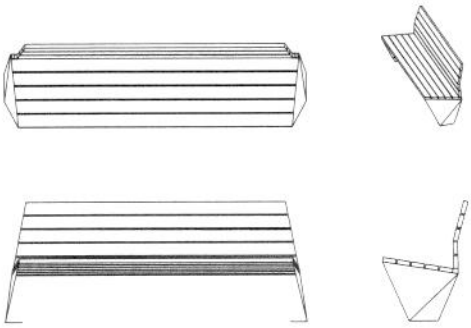

a=1981
b=1785
c=1885
d=524.51
e=530.01
f=521.07
g=337.64
h=194.26
i=0

S-09

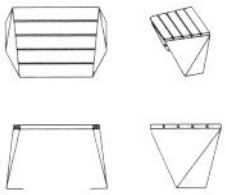

a=600
b=600
c=500
d=0
e=488.17
f=470.08
g=438.29
h=188.00
i=0

S-10

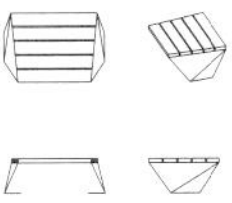

a=600
b=600
c=500
d=0
e=488.24
f=288.28
g=247.40
h=188.00
i=0

S-11

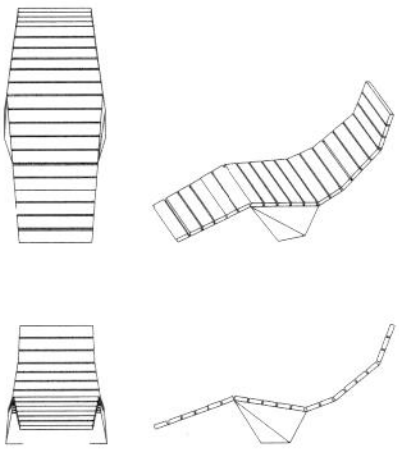

a=660
b=500
c=500
d=909.16
e=505.14
f=520.74
g=340.75
h=194.26
i=584.06

S-12

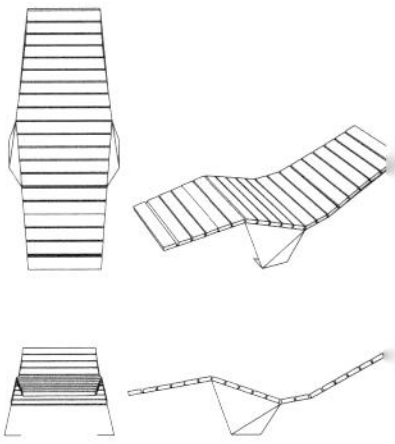

a=660
b=500
c=500
d=893.46
e=504.31
f=522.16
g=258.43
h=194.26
i=584.06

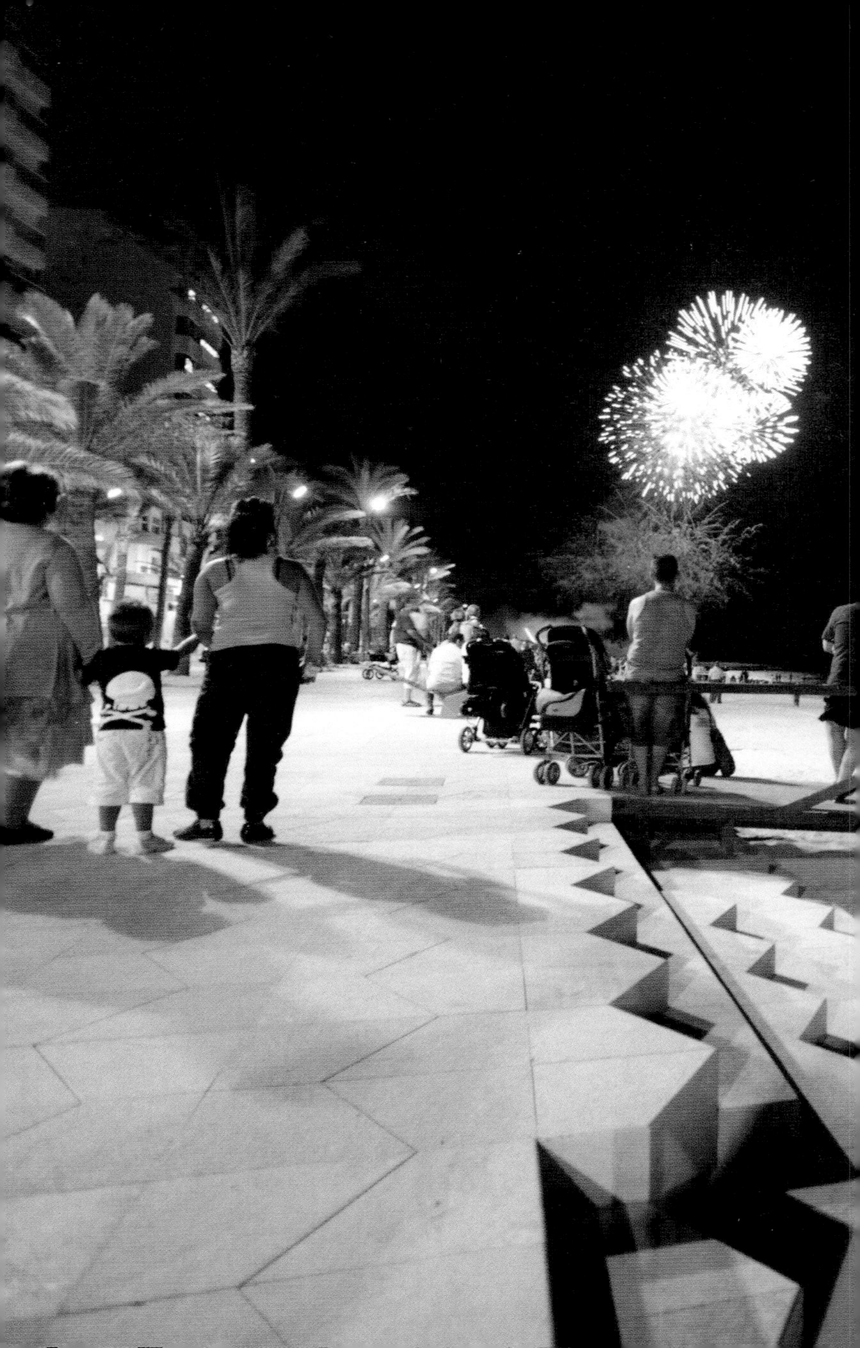

Vinaròs Sea Pavilion

Vinaròs, Castellón. Spain. 2007—

1st Prize national competition
witht KHO Ocio S.L

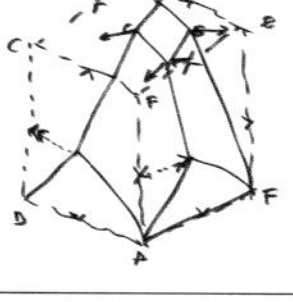

The Town Council of Vinaròs held a competition for the design and construction of a restaurant and leisure area at the north end of the town's Mediterranean seafront promenade.

We decided to develop a parametric arboreal system in which all of the units were self-similar: both the structures that rest on the ground and those that rise up to expel fumes or take in light.
The structures are of 3 mm painted galvanized steel, thin enough to be easily cut and folded to create a continuous hollow structural element. The openings in the structure are filled with glazed and opaque surfaces, on which the LED lights are mounted.

All of the structures have a hexagonal pattern that is deformed on a regular basis on the side facing the coast.

The process of fabricating these structures, involving the plasma cutting of some 1,736 different pieces, was an opportunity to experiment with the use of advanced manufacturing systems in which the architect directly produces the components of the project using parametric design and scripting programmes.

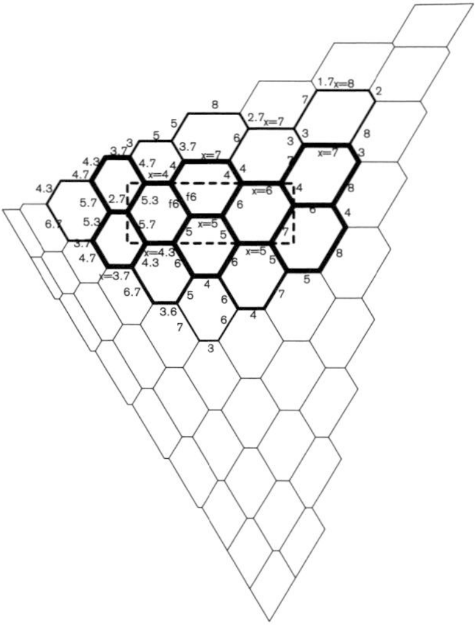

GEOGRAPHY

A generic parametric geography

GEOMETRY

A growing system

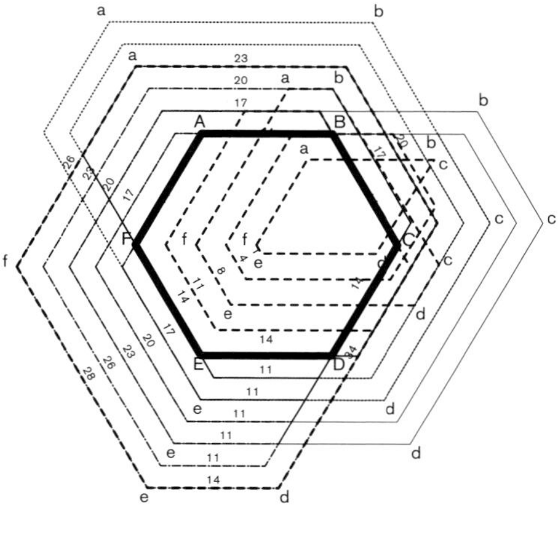

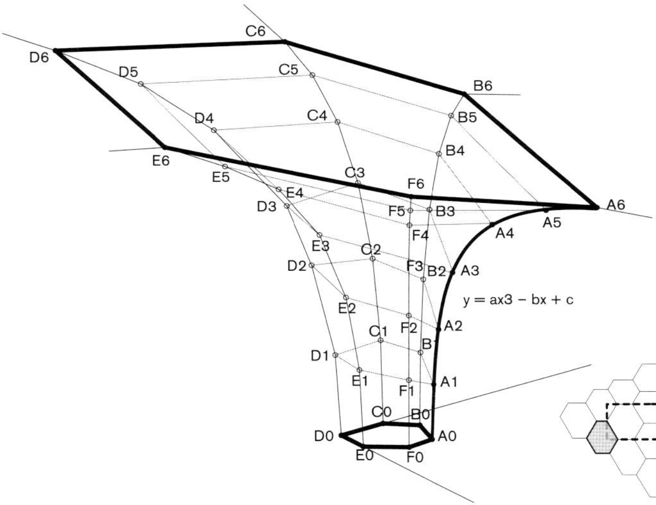

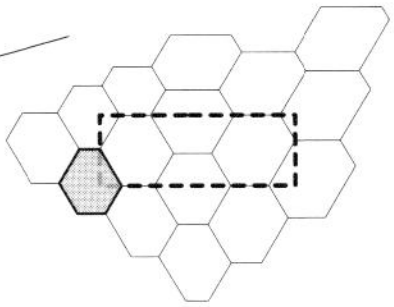

LOGIC

A logic of transformation

STRUCTURE

A structure of aggregation of similar units

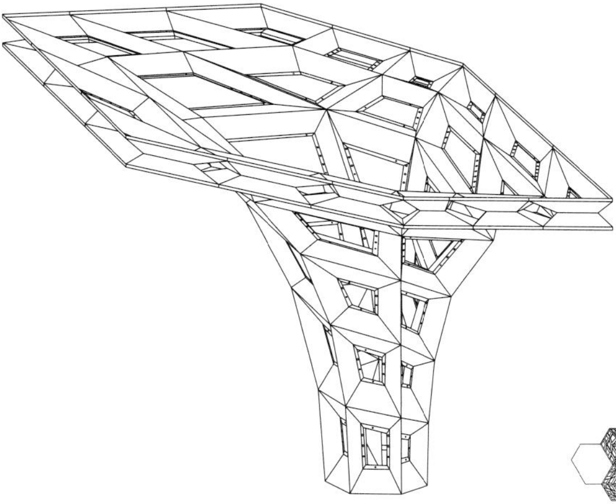

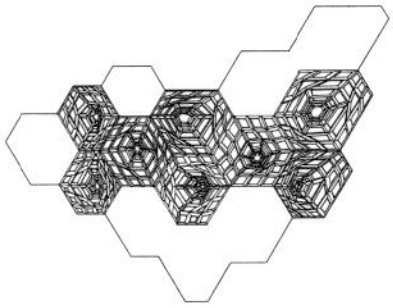

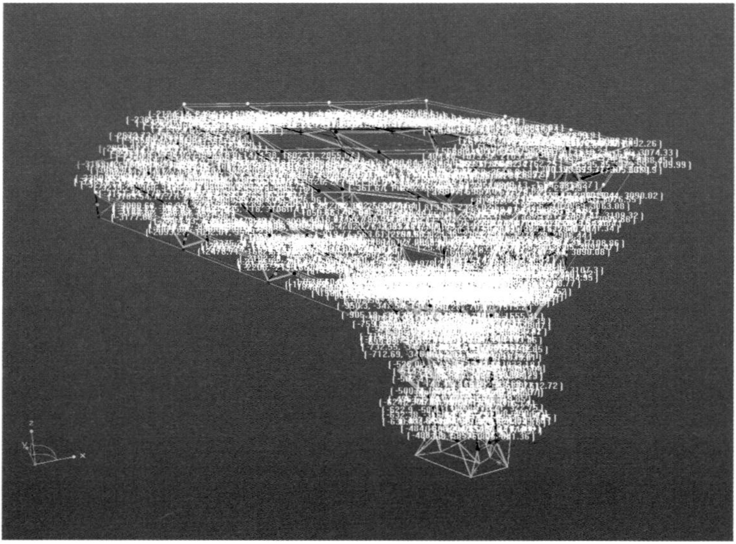

Relational parameters

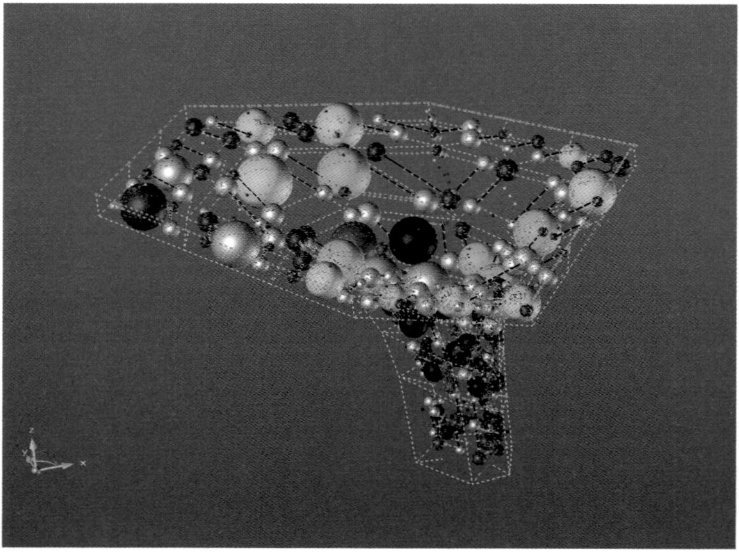

System nodes

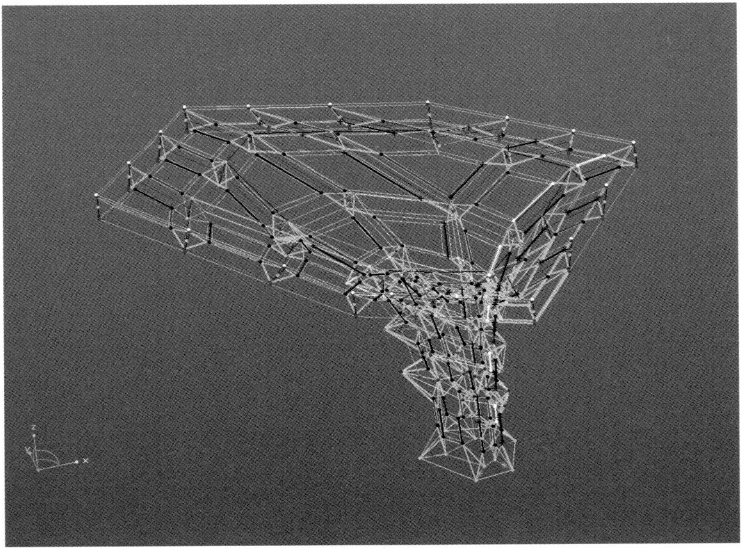

Generated structure

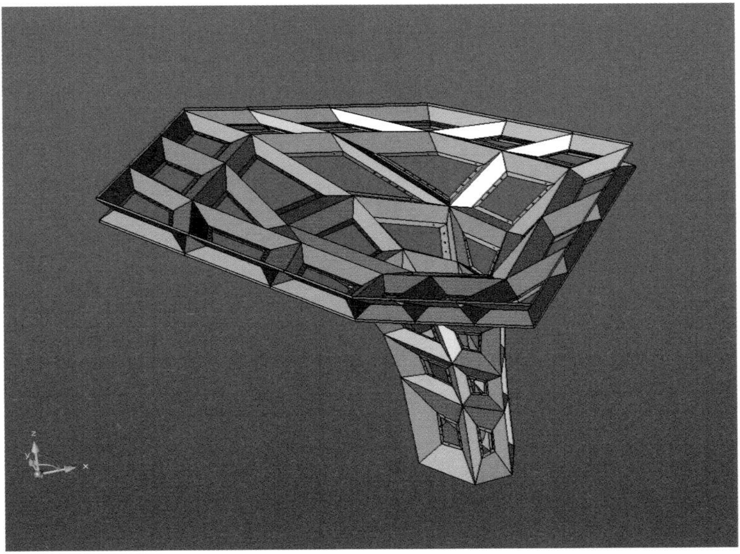

Materialization

Tree 01

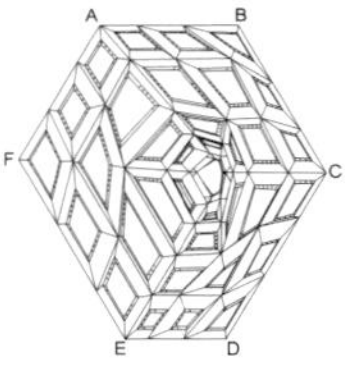

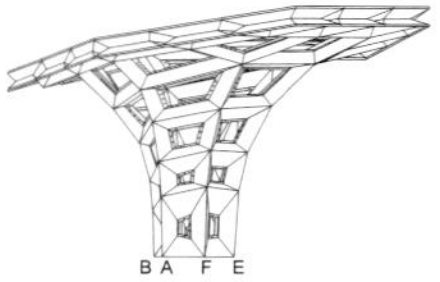

P-ab: 3,70
P-bc: 4,70
P-cd: 5,30
P-de: 2,70
P-ef: 5,70
P-fa: 4,30

Tree 02

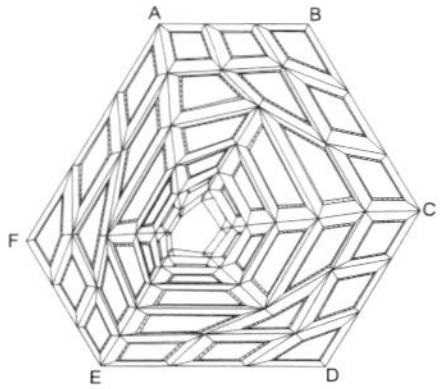

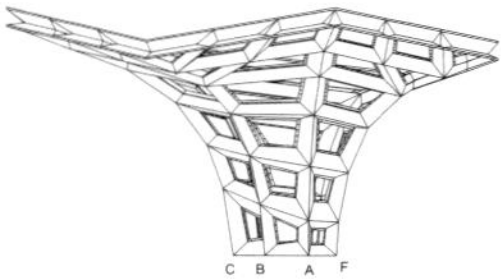

P-ab: 4,00
P-bc: 6,00
P-cd: 5,00
P-de: 6,00
P-ef: 4,00
P-fa: 7,00

Tree 03

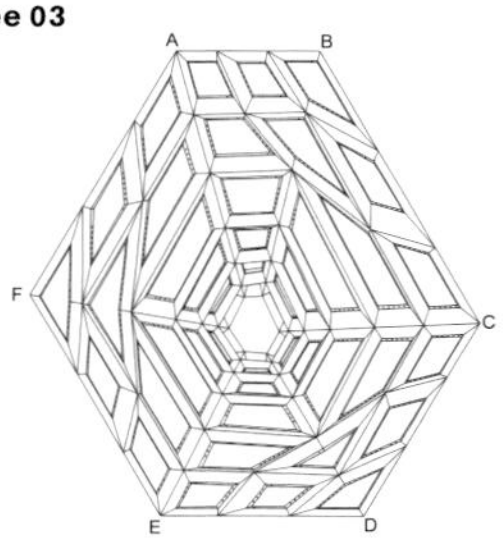

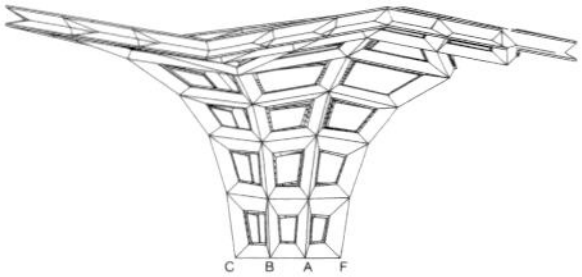

P-ab: 3,00
P-bc: 8,00
P-cd: 6,00
P-de: 4,00
P-ef: 7,00
P-fa: 7,00

Tree 04

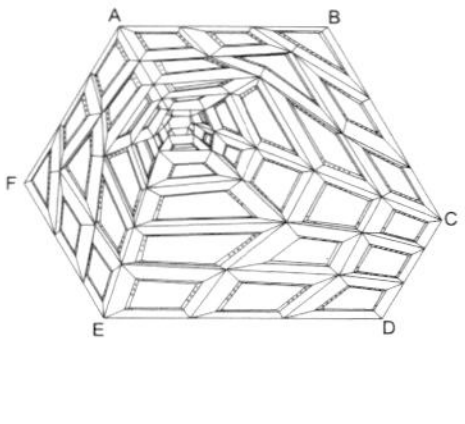

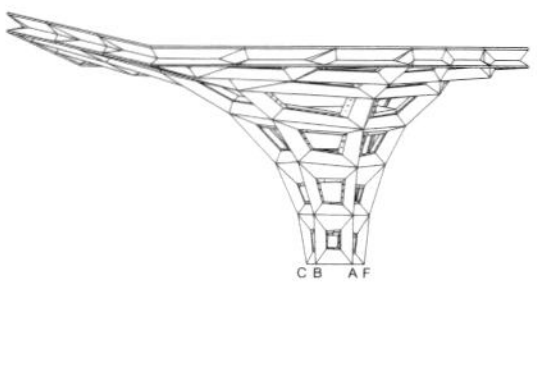

P-ab: 7,00
P-bc: 6,00
P-cd: 4,00
P-de: 8,00
P-ef: 5,00
P-fa: 5,00

Tree 05

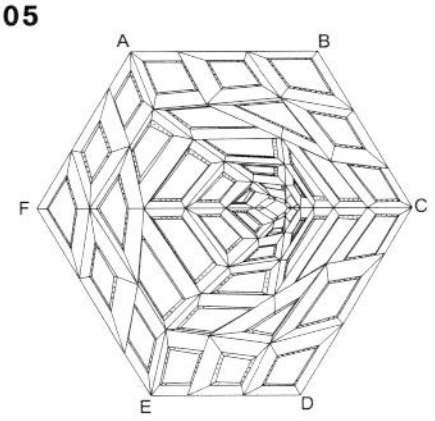

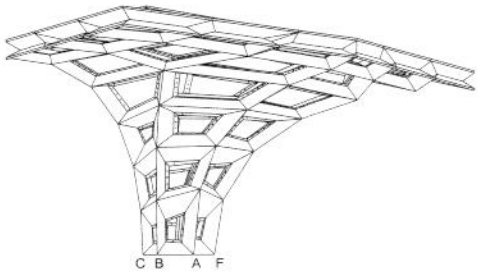

P-ab: 5,00
P-bc: 5,00
P-cd: 6,00
P-de: 4,00
P-ef: 6,00
P-fa: 5,00

Tree 06

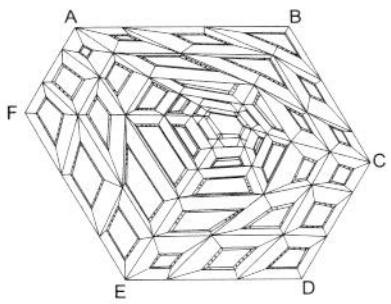

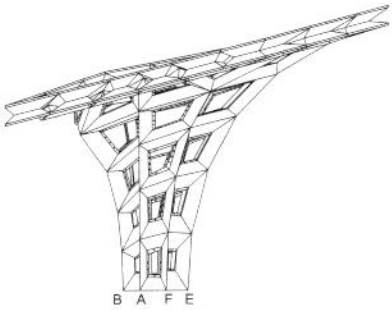

P-ab: 2,70
P-bc: 5,70
P-cd: 4,30
P-de: 3,70
P-ef: 4,70
P-fa: 5,30

Tree 07

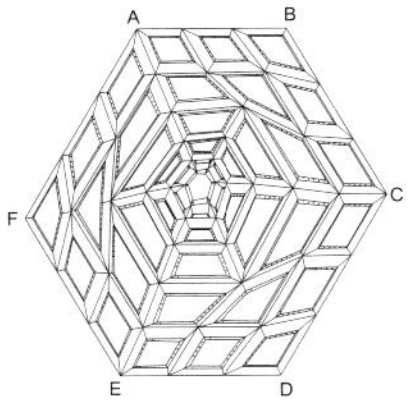

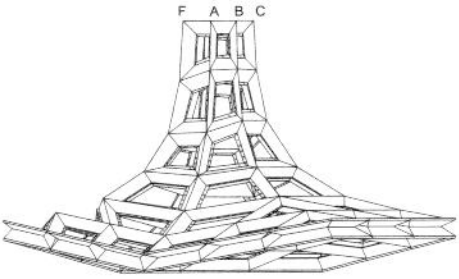

P-ab: 4,00
P-bc: 5,30
P-cd: 5,70
P-de: 4,30
P-ef: 5,00
P-fa: 6,00

Tree 08

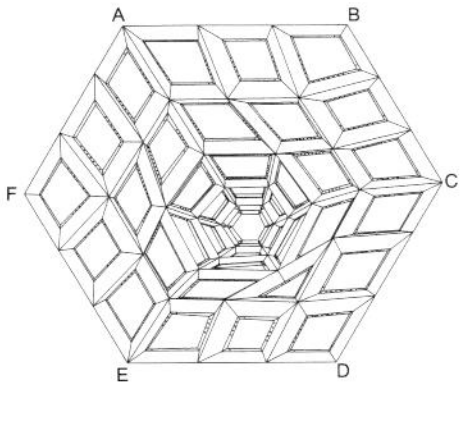

P-ab: 6,00
P-bc: 5,00
P-cd: 5,00
P-de: 7,00
P-ef: 4,00
P-fa: 6,00

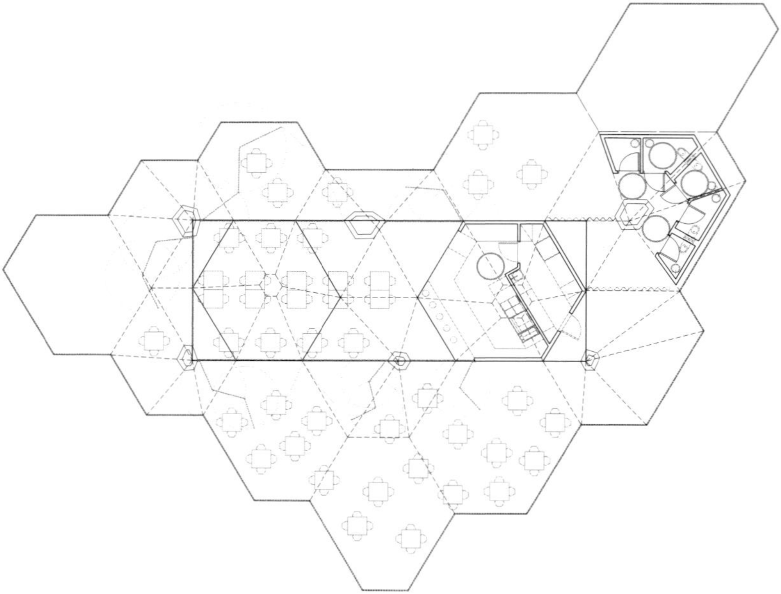

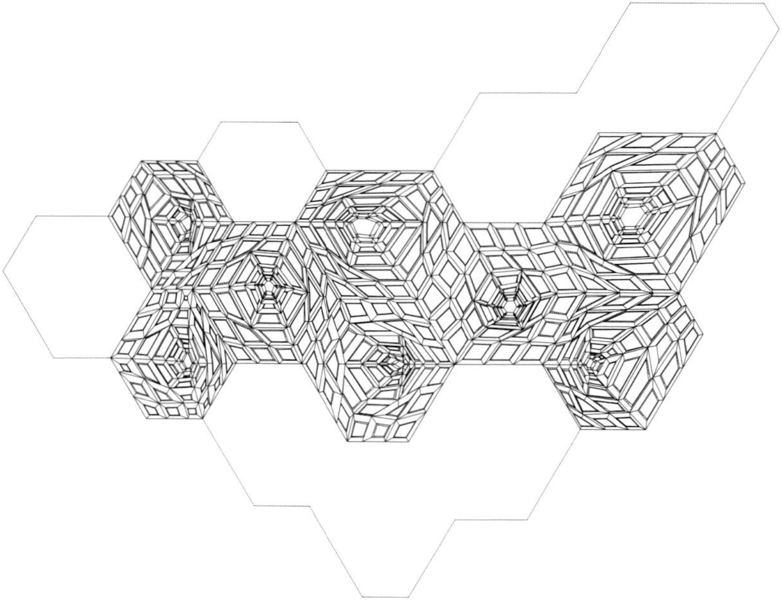

Apartments in Cambrils

Cambrils, Tarragona. Spain. 2002—2006

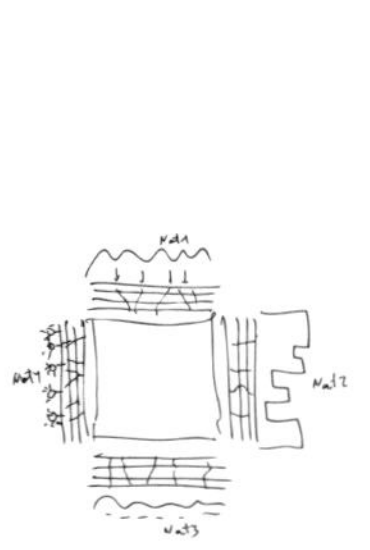

Reflecting
/16

Positioning
/20

Under pressure from the expansion of the urban across the territory, besieged on all sides by architecture and the real-estate business or by the banal, decontextualized condition of theme-park tourist resorts, the traditional locations for the architecture of tourism are losing their ephemeral, light and ludic quality.

This project, however, seeks to recover the festive character of the leisure spaces of the coast by invoking their own nature, history, landscape and culture without having to resort to external arguments.

The immediate seafront is a scarce resource, of great economic and landscape value. It offers an opportunity to propose once again an architecture for tourism in which the fundamental argument is the use and enjoyment of the water, in interaction with a unique landscape.

The first key strategy was to create a new interaction between the interior and exterior of the building that involves dissolving the boundary of the interior with the terrace, literally extending the interior spaces outward and thus attaching more value to the house. Various proposals have been developed to achieve this:

- the expansion of the bedrooms onto the terraces by way of expanses of glazing and curtains
- the extension of the living and dining areas onto the terrace
- the continuation of the bathrooms onto the terrace to allow open-air showering
- the articulation of the kitchen-to-terrace connection by means of a bar.

The second strategy was to locate the wet elements (such as kitchen and bathroom, usually concealed in urban dwellings) on the façade, facing the sea, so as to make these places where water is an essential presence ludic spaces in direct visual connection with the sea.

Finally, the façade of the building, constructed as a sequence of dynamic lightweight skins, is transformed by sunlight and the colour of the natural surroundings (dawn, the sea, the gardens, sunset, the mountains and the Camp de Tarragona landscape) — a fundamental argument in the building's relationship with the landscape in which it is set.

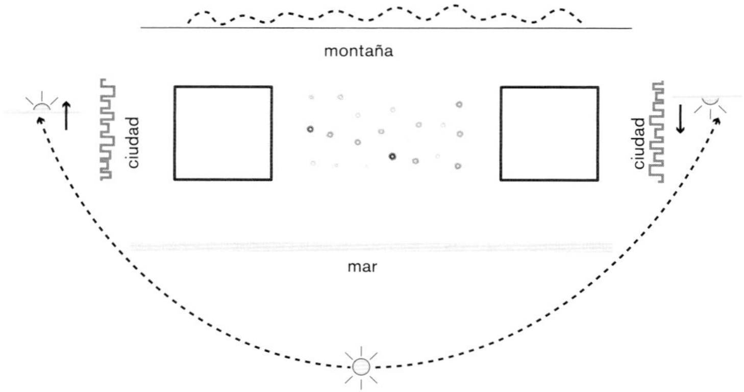

GEOGRAPHY

Two buildings in Camp de Tarragona, on the Mediterranean seafront

GEOMETRY

Chromatic quality of the surrounding landscapes

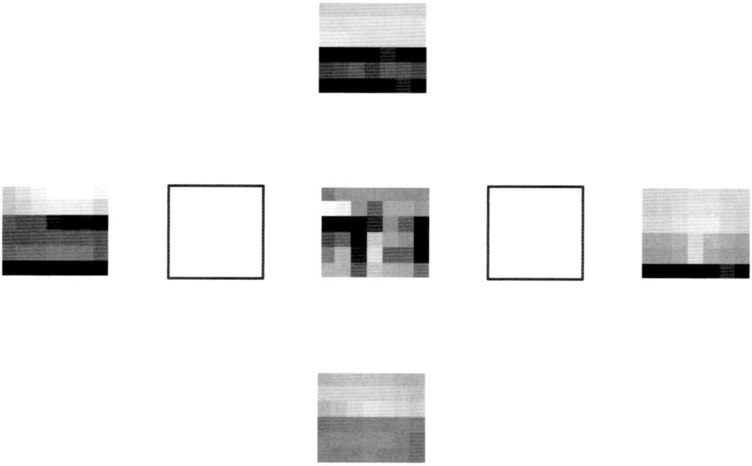

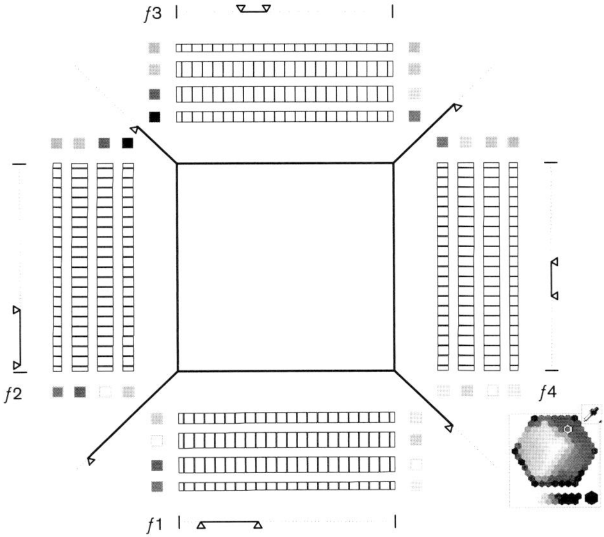

LOGIC

A machine for reading and ordering the light of its environment

STRUCTURE

A chromatic pattern constructed on the surrounding landscape

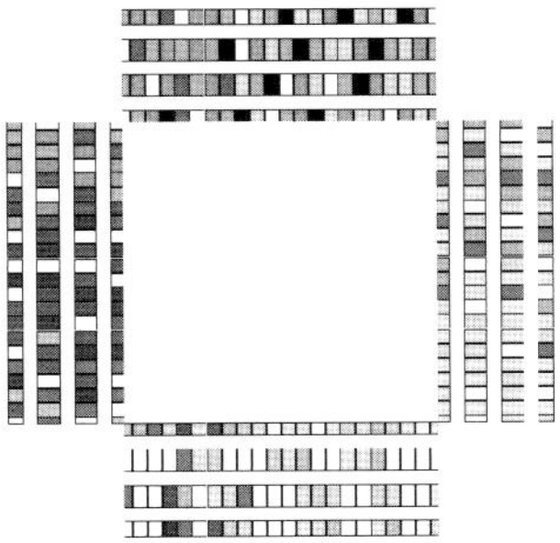

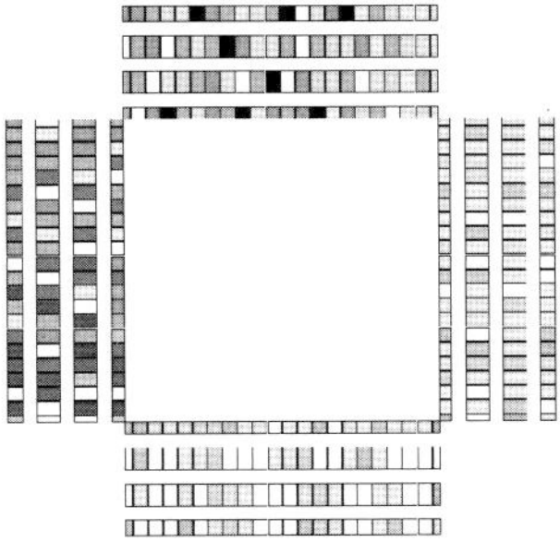

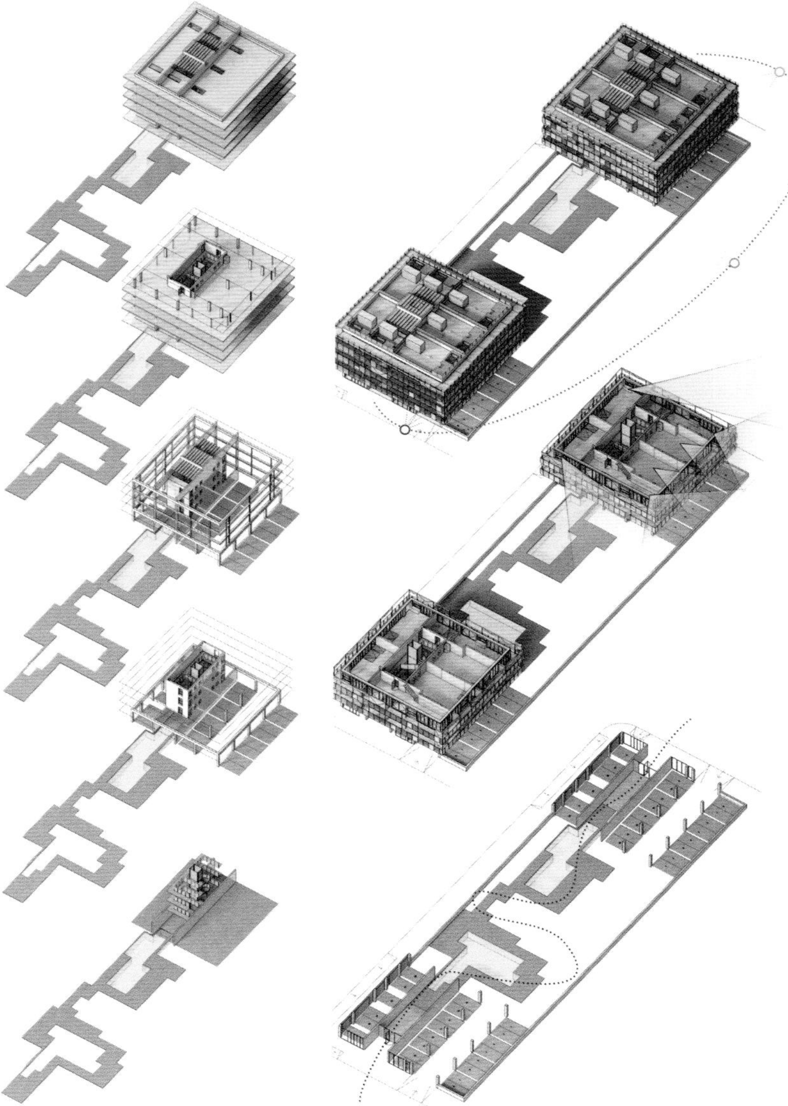

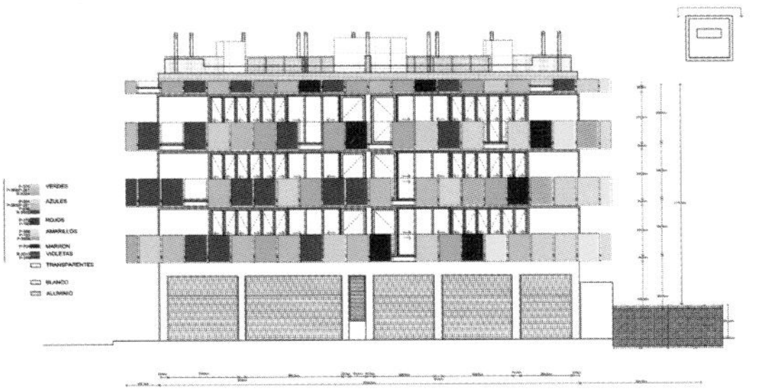
VERDES
AZULES
ROJOS
AMARILLOS
MARRON
VIOLETAS
TRANSPARENTES
BLANCO
ALUMINIO

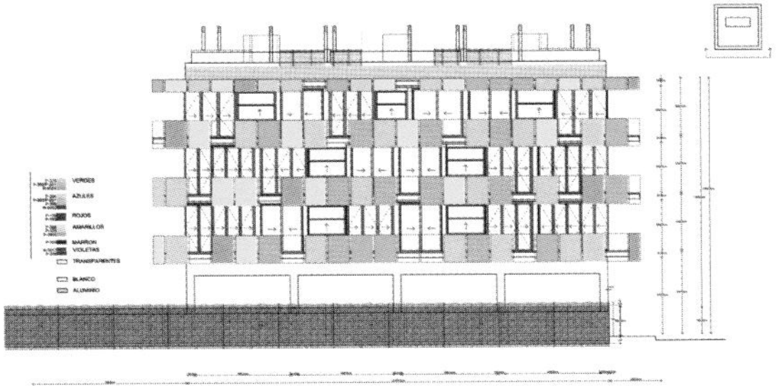
VERDES
AZULES
ROJOS
AMARILLOS
MARRON
VIOLETAS
TRANSPARENTES
BLANCO
ALUMINIO

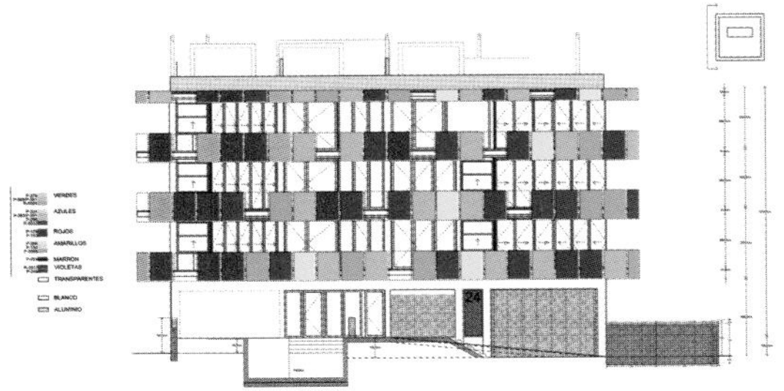
VERDES
AZULES
ROJOS
AMARILLOS
MARRON
VIOLETAS
TRANSPARENTES
BLANCO
ALUMINIO

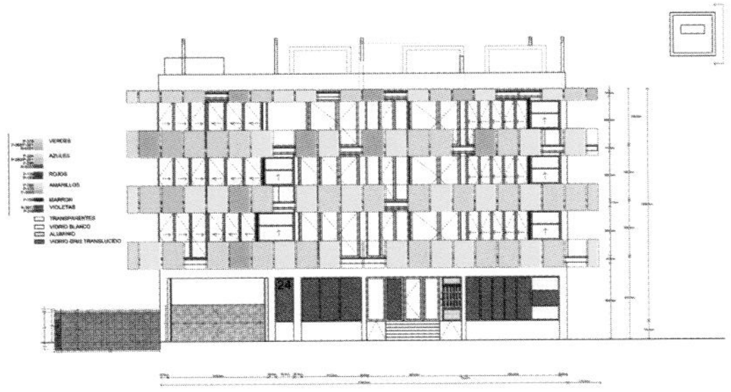
VERDES
AZULES
ROJOS
AMARILLOS
MARRON
VIOLETAS
TRANSPARENTES
VIDRIO BLANCO
ALUMINIO
VIDRIO GRIS TRANSLUCIDO

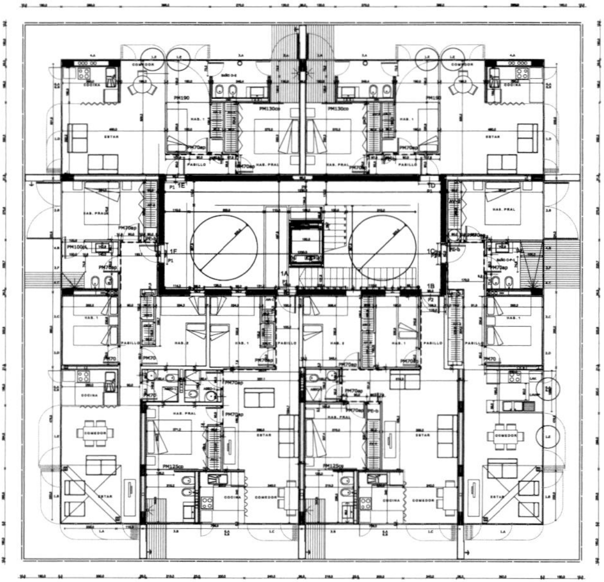

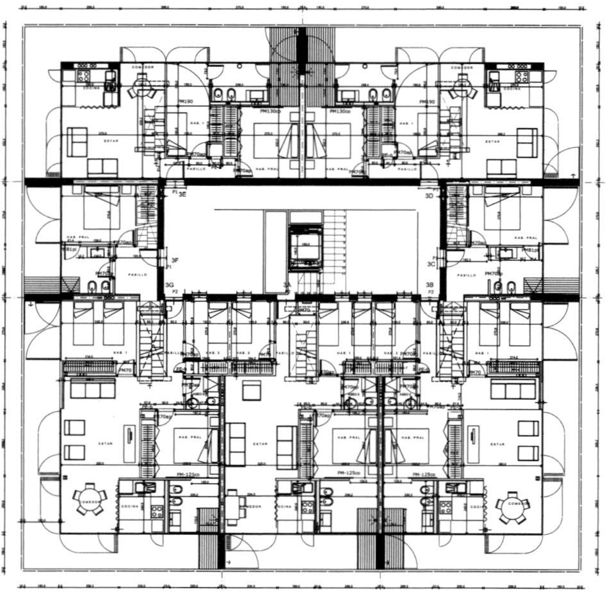

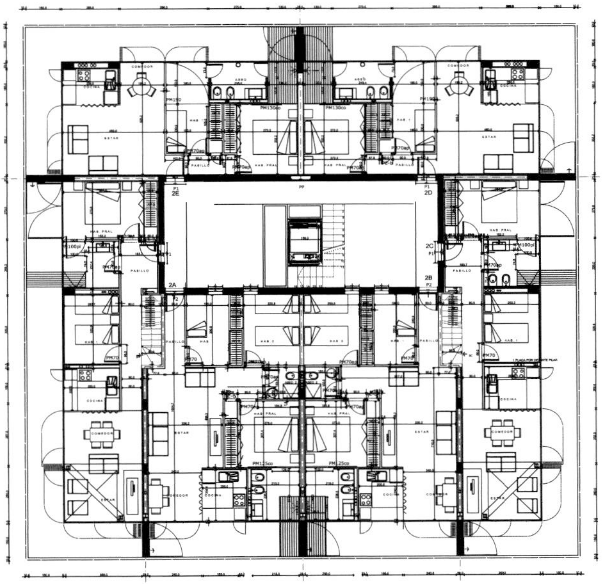

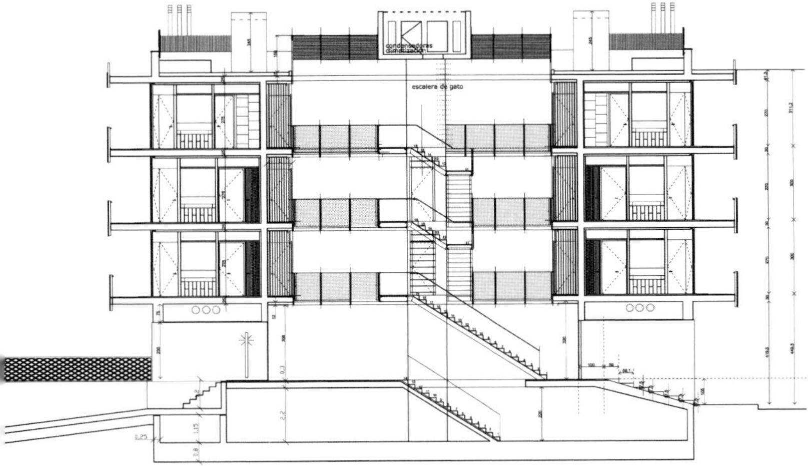
escalera de gato

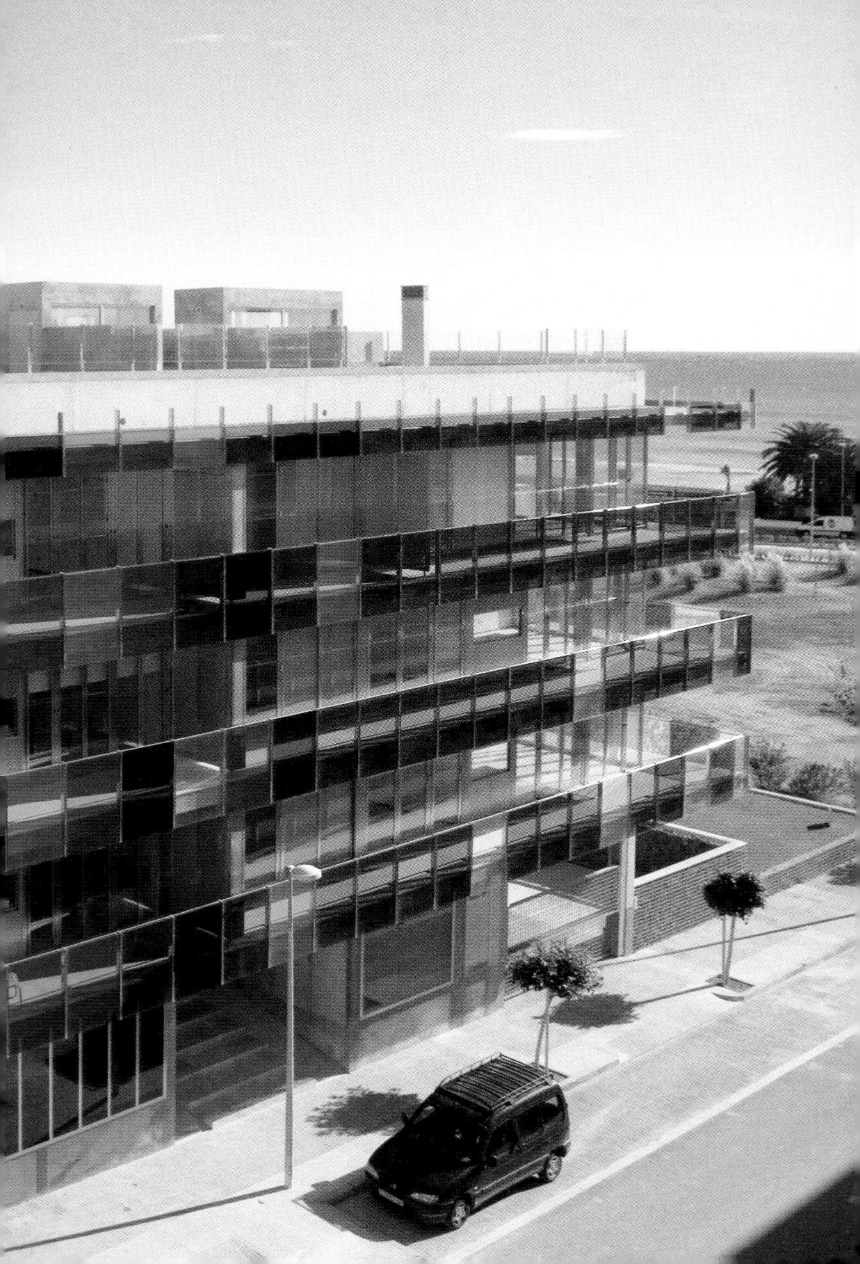

Hortal House

Comarruga, Tarragona. Spain. 2004

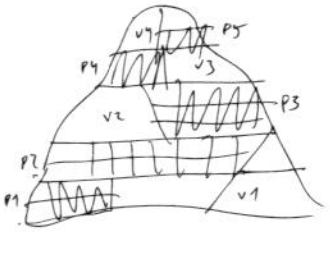

Accumulating
/11

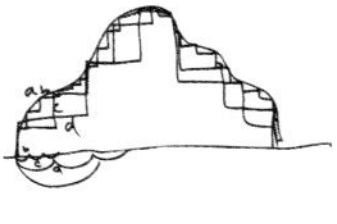

Resolution
/13

In a hilly area some three kilometres from the Mediterranean coast we built this villa anchored in the terrain, projecting itself towards the sea. The construction was conceived as a great concrete bracket, almost like a geographical feature that operates according to its own rules, in order to create a privileged position in its surroundings.

Given that buildings are far more expressive during construction than when they are completed, this building presents itself as deliberately unfinished, with the presence of the original texture of the concrete external walls, and the metal structure and the floor slabs forming the interior volume. Nevertheless, the openings in the wall have been given a more delicate finish, with stained glass windows, like gems incrusted in a massive rock, creating personalized landscapes in the interior.

The house responds to its environment with four different scales: to the West, fronting the access road, it is a single-storey volume defining a domestic scale (characteristic of a small house) with a pitched roof covered with rocks. To the North the volume rises up from the access ramp to the garage in a flat, compact form to create a place for mobility. To the South, the pool (which can be partially closed in) slides under the stepped bracket with a sun terrace around it. To the East, facing the sea, the villa is metallic and transparent, an almost urban building of three floors, with views of the sea.

We cannot say if this villa is a beautiful building or not. We would prefer to evaluate it using the same criteria with which we appraise a mountain or a rock: strong, hard, amorphous

GEOGRAPHY

Anthropisized lanscape

GEOMETRY

Elevated point over sea

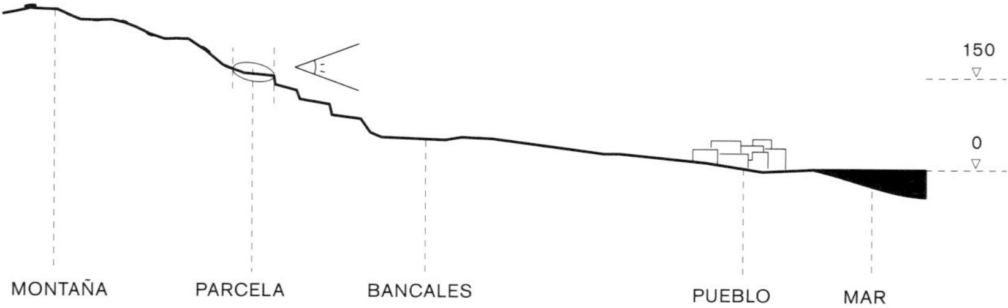

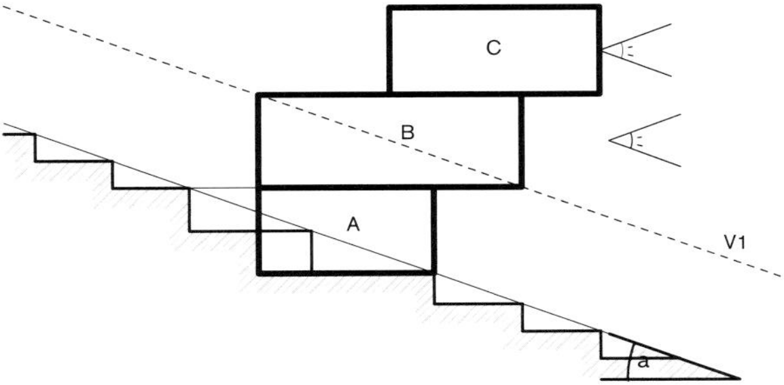

LOGIC

Spatial accumulation inverse to topography

STRUCTURE

Unfolded envelope in low resolution

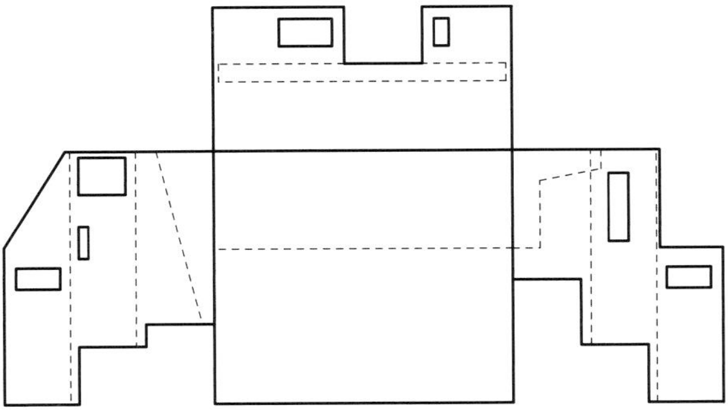

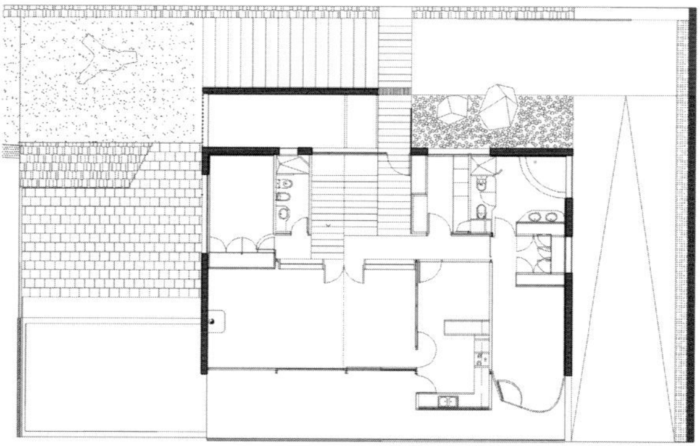

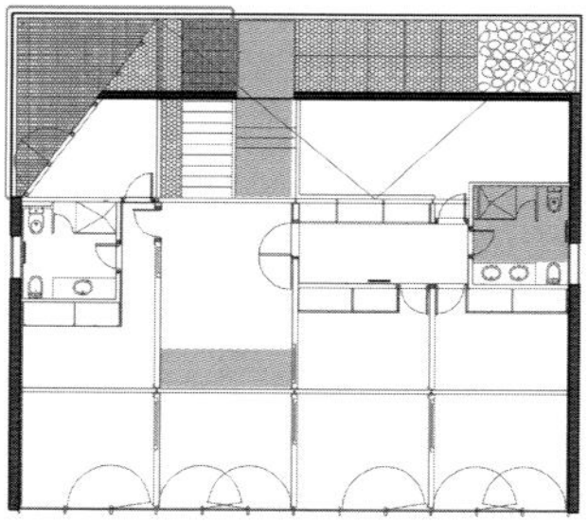

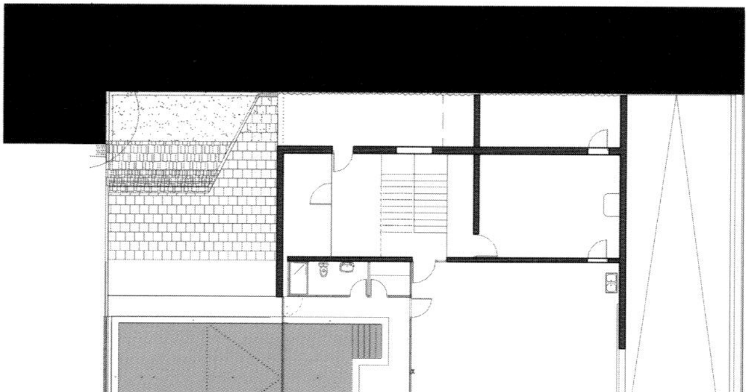

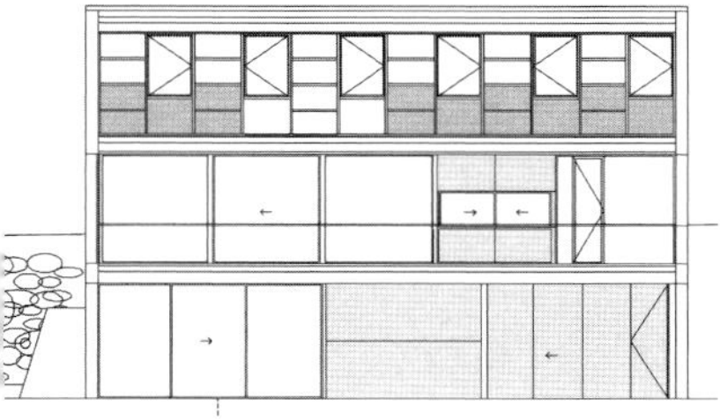

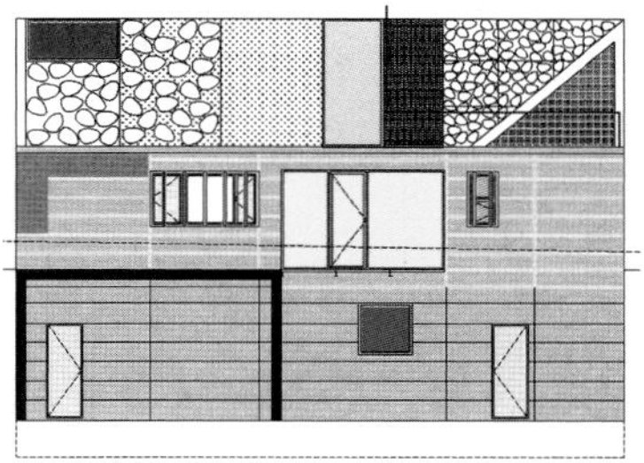

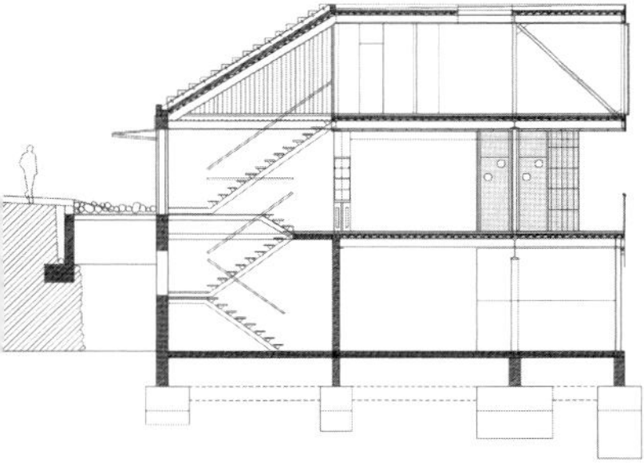

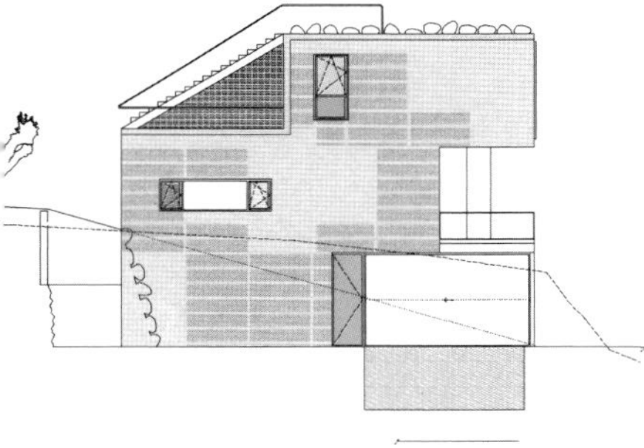

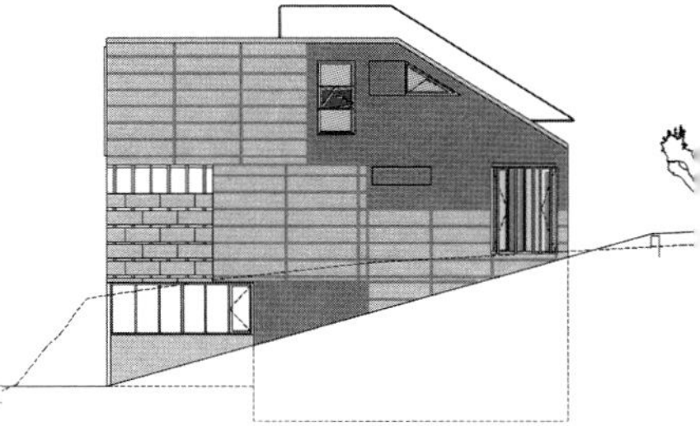

Avignon Expo 2000

Avignon. France. 2000
With Enric Ruiz Geli

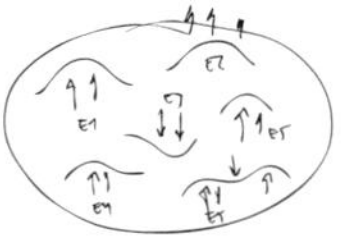

Bulging
/18

The exhibition *Beauty in Nature*, curated by Yves le Fur, was organized on the occasion of Avignon's year as European Capital of Culture in 2000. This exhibition presented objects of incredible naturalness in terms of various cultural, geological or scientific approaches; for example, 19th-century glass flowers from the Natural History Museum at Harvard.

In what setting can pieces of such incredible beauty be displayed?
We set out to use glass as a unifying element for the exhibition as a whole, creating 'cells' that grouped together all the members of a given family. These pieces were displayed against a black velvet background and lit with cold optical fibre in order to create a sense of weightlessness and 'enchantement' in space.

The project investigated the possibility of transforming or deforming the glass according to the logic of the elements it contained, thus creating autonomous entities designed on the basis of interaction with elements such as trees, pulmonary systems, radioactive rocks and pebbles, among others. The glass was shaped and moulded using the technical expertise of the glass manufacturers Cricursa, either through the deformation that occurs when a surface resting on a perforated metal plate is heated so that the glass deforms by its own weight, or by heating a sheet of glass until its advance is halted by its meeting with a rigid or double curved surface.

A micro mountain of glass finally protected the collection of glass flowers, making them the strangest piece in the exhibition. Eggs, stones and shells were protected by glass that simultaneously created an invisible halo around them and defined their magical beauty. On the basis of the research carried out for this exhibition, various architectural projects have made use of bulging techniques.

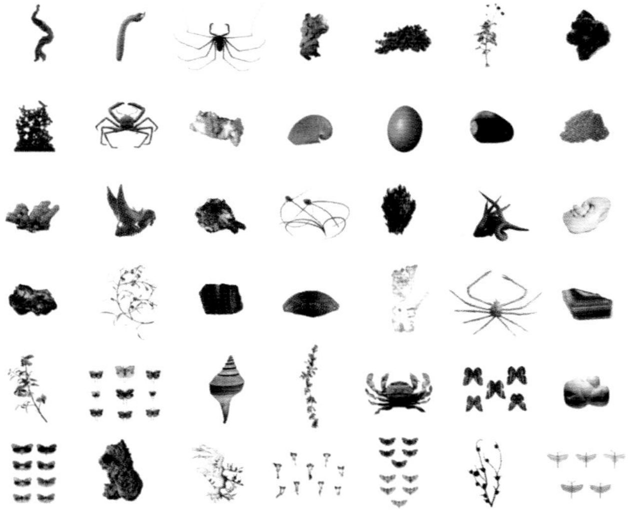

GEOGRAPHY

A collection of natural objects of great beauty

GEOMETRY

Organization of similar objects

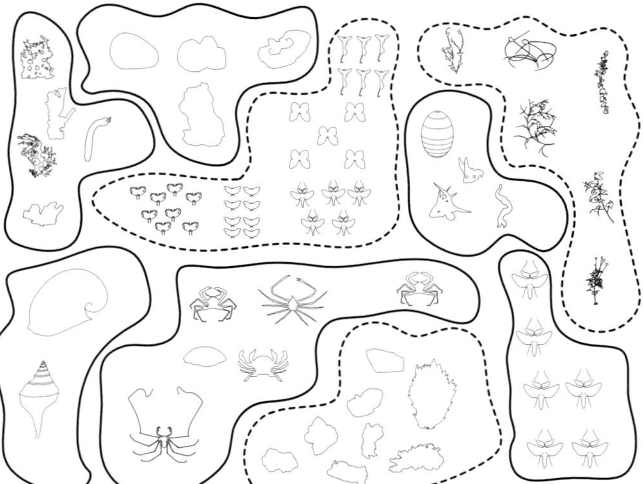

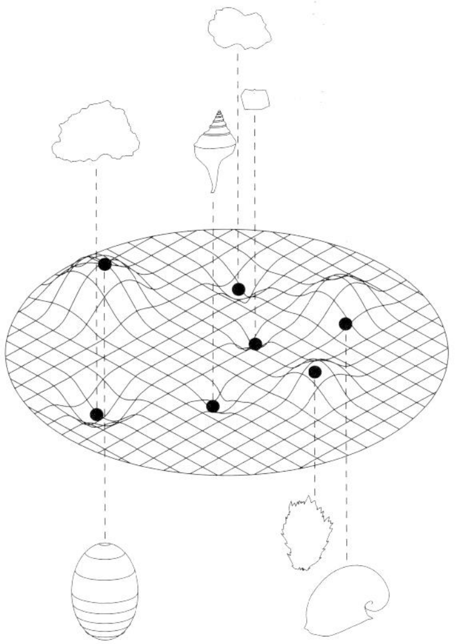

LOGIC

Deformation of the glass caused by the object's presence

STRUCTURE

An exhibition composed of crystalline environments

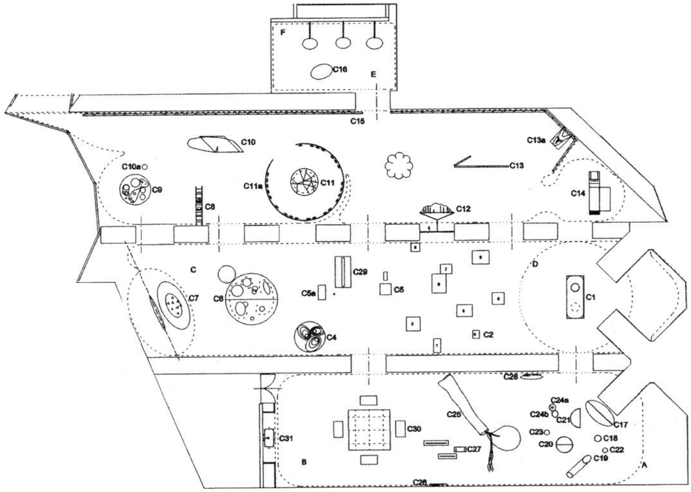

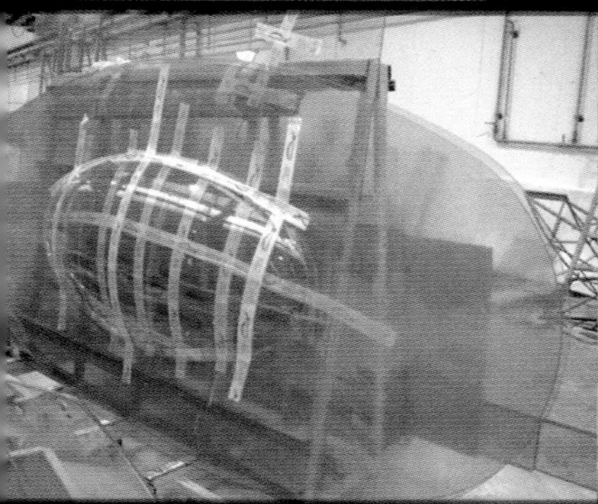

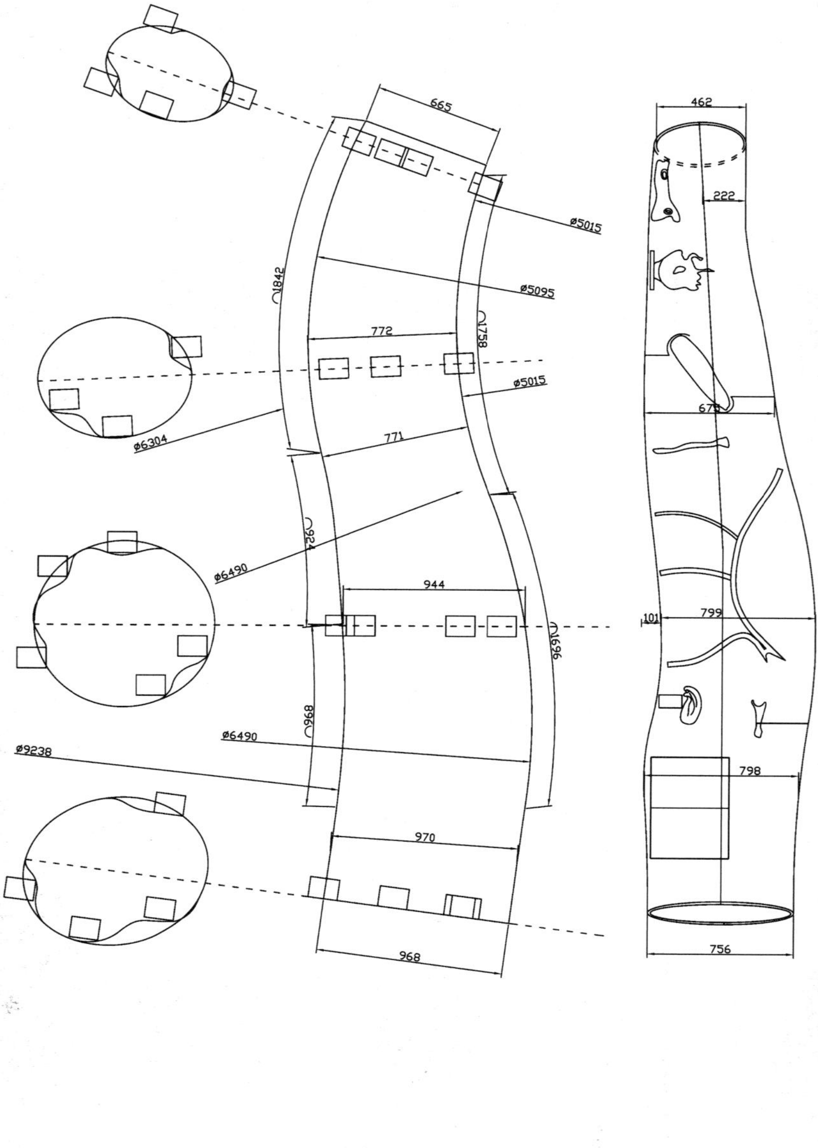
665
ø5015
ø5095
1842
772
1758
ø5015
ø6304
771
ø6490
924
944
1696
968
ø6490
ø9238
970
968
462
222
679
101
799
798
756

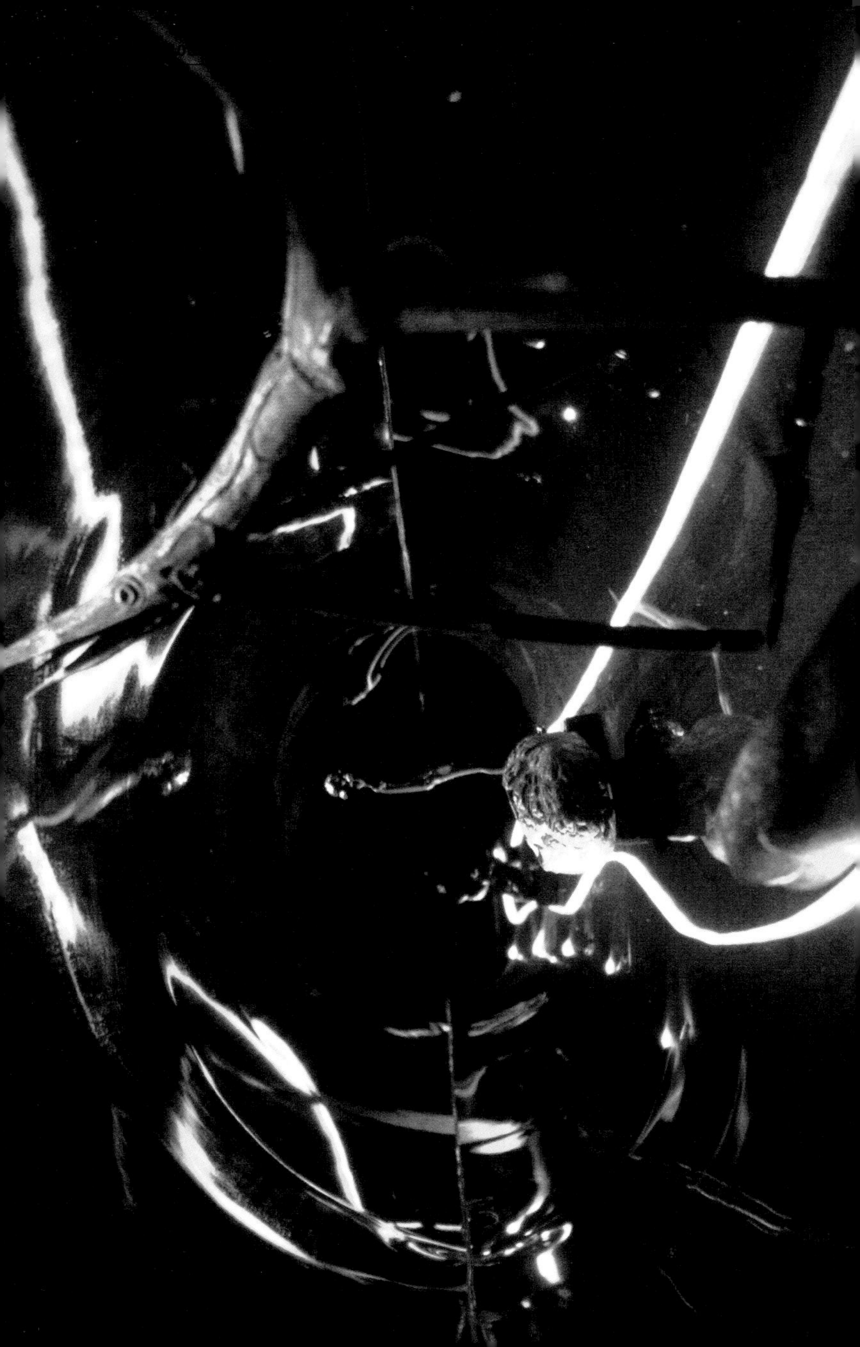

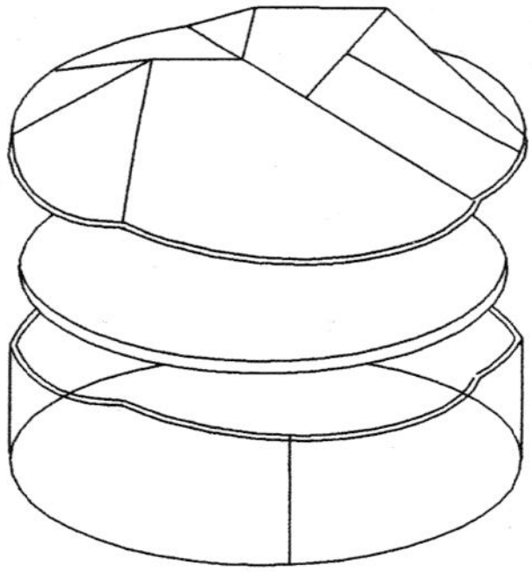

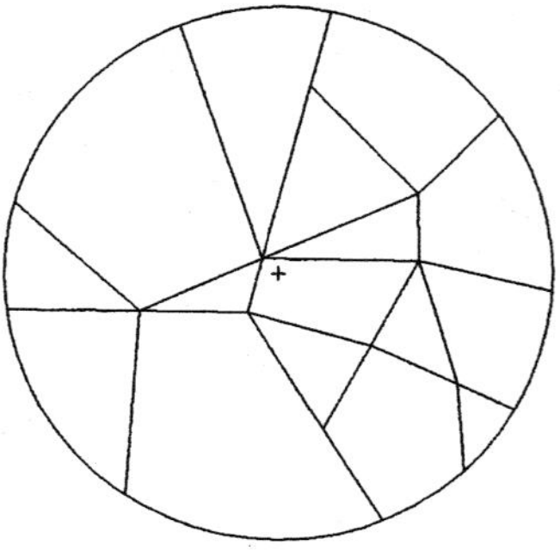

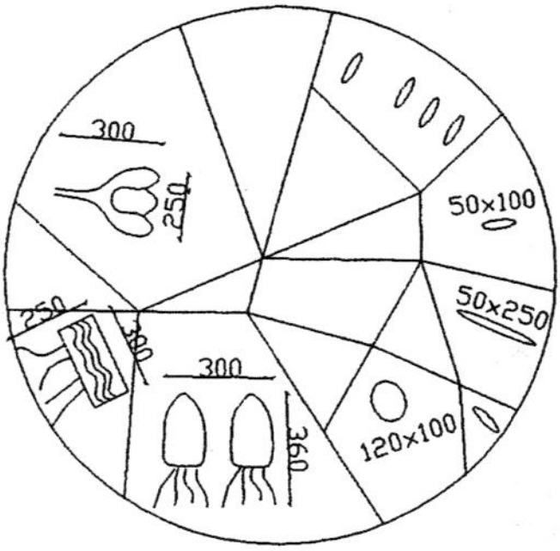
300
250
250
300
300
360
50×100
50×250
120×100

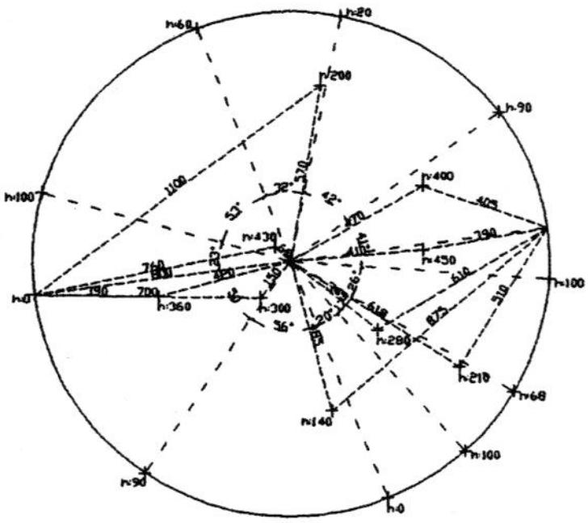

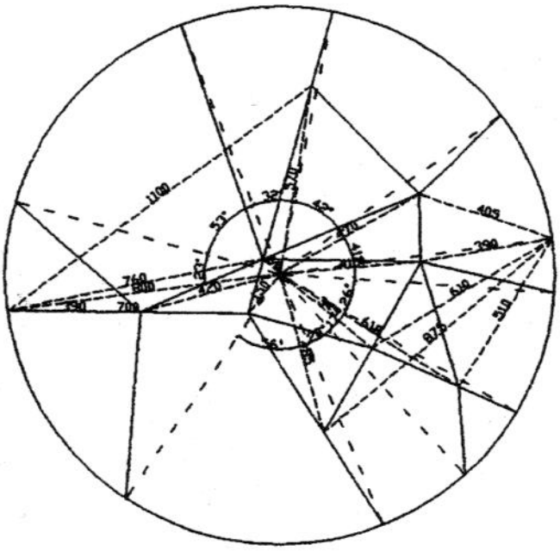

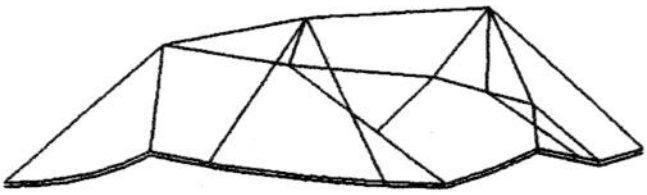

Clothing Museum

Valencia. Spain.
Project. 2004—2007
Construction. 2009—2010

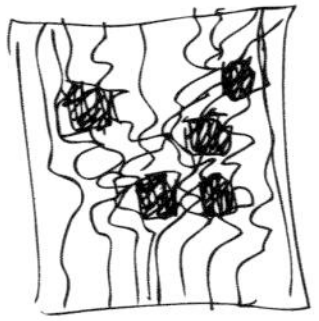

Valencia's new Museum of Clothing will be housed in the Palace of the Baron de Vallvert on del Mar street, in the heart of the city, a building constructed over several centuries. In the early years of the 20th century the Baron reformed the main façade, added new rooms, and notably increased the density of the central part of the building. He also acquired and incorporated into the building many antiquarian elements, including doors, windows and tiles, the outstanding historicist feature being the kitchen, its walls clad with 18th-century tiles, many decorated with human figures and culinary motifs. However, the reform was carried out with a very poor structural basis, and this has enabled the rapid development of the central part of the building.

The project proposes to maintain 50% of the building containing the principal rooms of the Baron's residence, and to create a new central space that will give the whole the scale of a museum. This new space defines its boundaries in terms of a geometric pattern used in Renaissance architecture (the basis of the building), which defines the system applied to the historic building. This pattern reads the traces of the existing building and creates a geometric grid, in such a way that the history of the building is recorded in the newly created space. This will be constructed with a structure of stainless steel and ceramic pieces whose size increases as in ascending order. The old timber beams of the roof will be recycled to floor from the top floor.

GEOGRAPHY

A historic building

GEOMETRY

The dating of the walls from the 15th century to the present

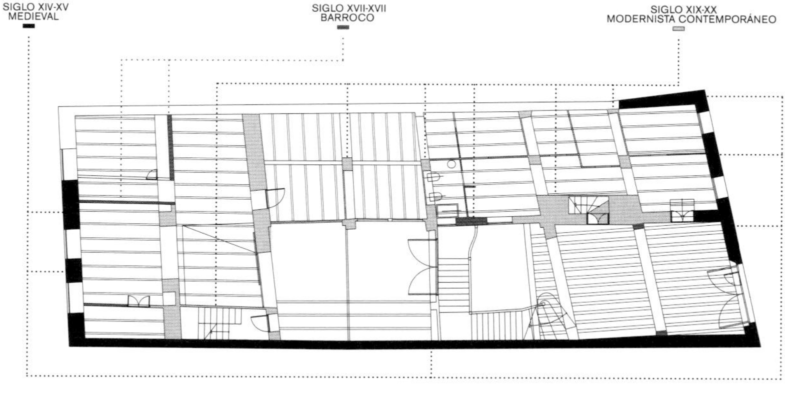

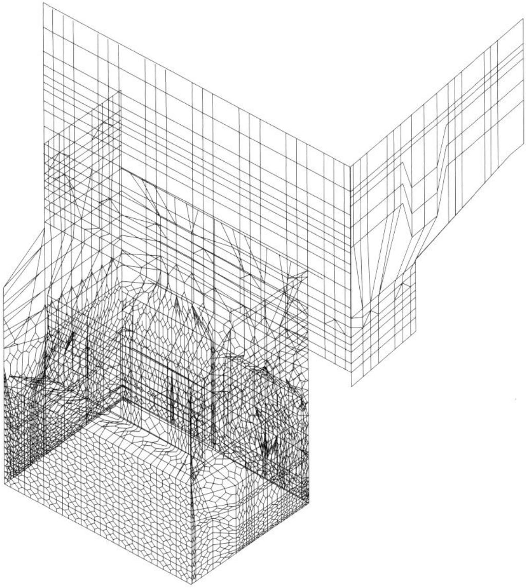

LOGIC

The mesh x-rays the building and fixes densities

STRUCTURE

The building within the building

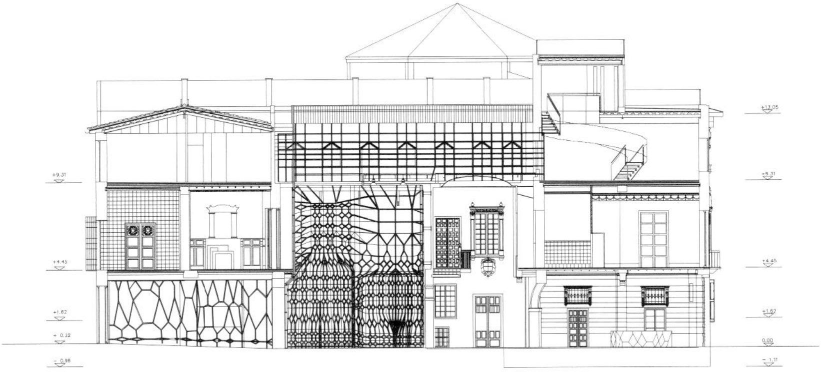

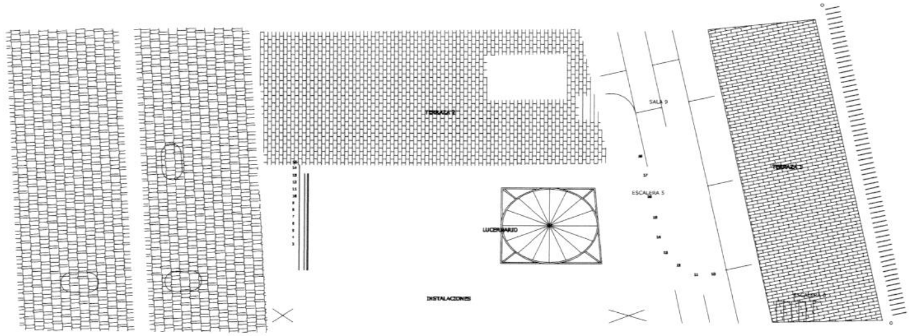

PLANTA TERCERA

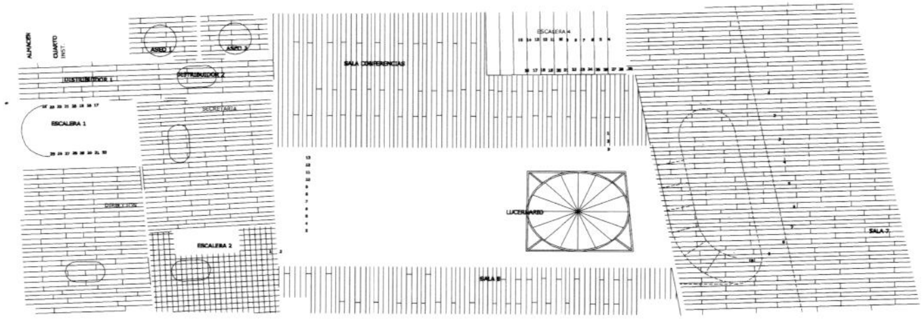

PLANTA SEGUNDA

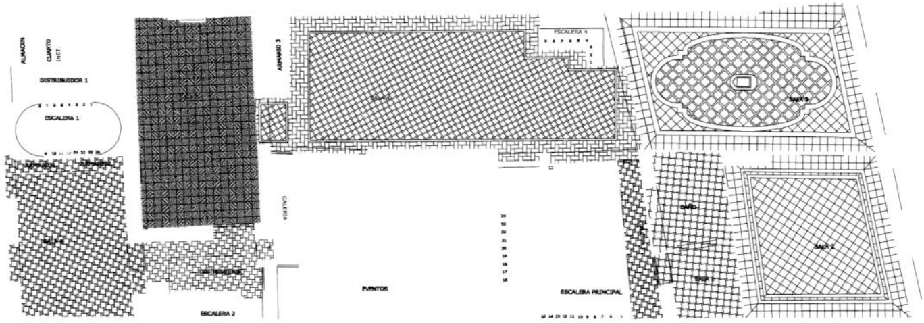

PLANTA PRIMERA

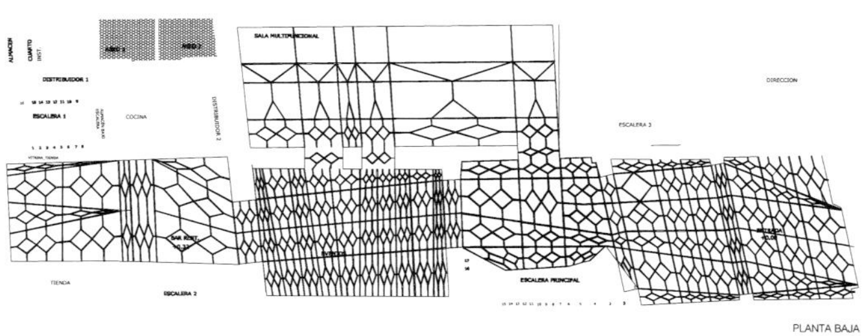

PLANTA BAJA

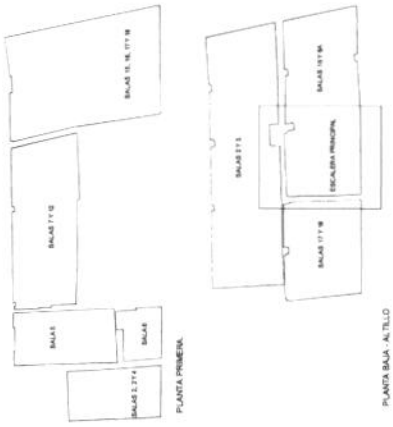

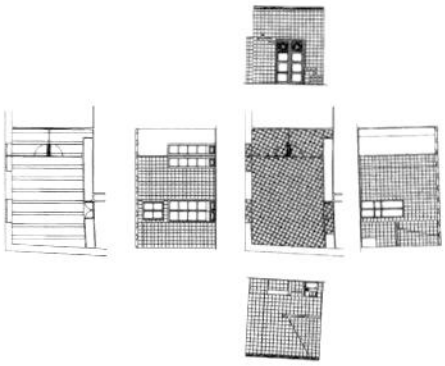

SALAS 2, 3 Y 4. PLANTA PRIMERA

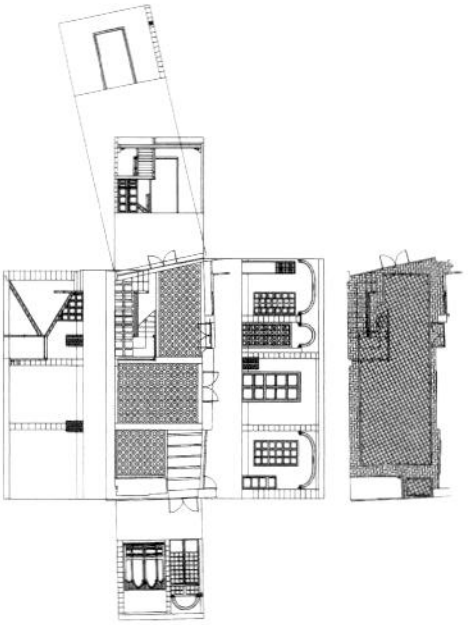

SALAS 7 Y 12. PLANTA PRIMERA

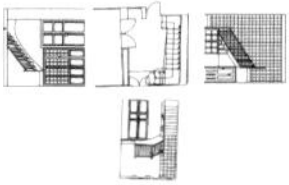

SALA 6. PLANTA PRIMERA

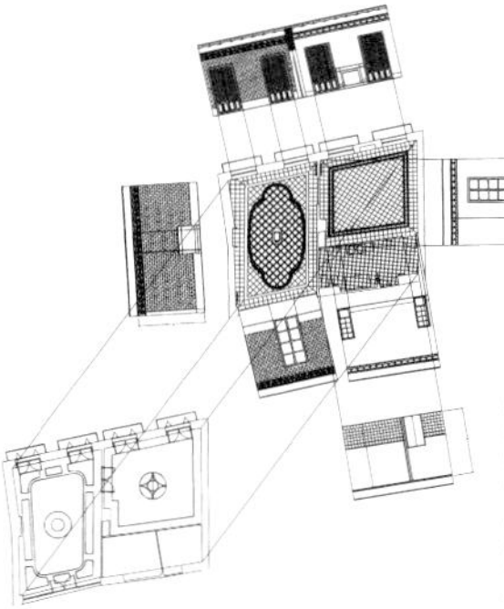

SALAS 15, 16, 17 Y 18. PLANTA PRIMERA.

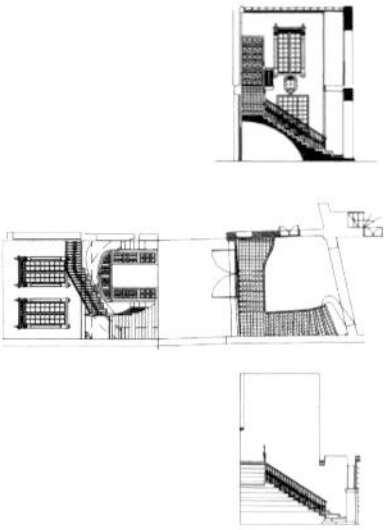

ESCALERA PRINCIPAL. PLANTA BAJA.

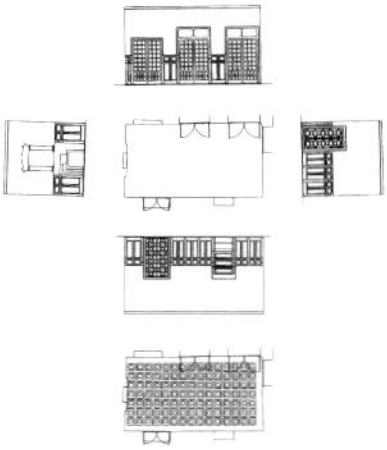

SALA 5. PLANTA PRIMERA

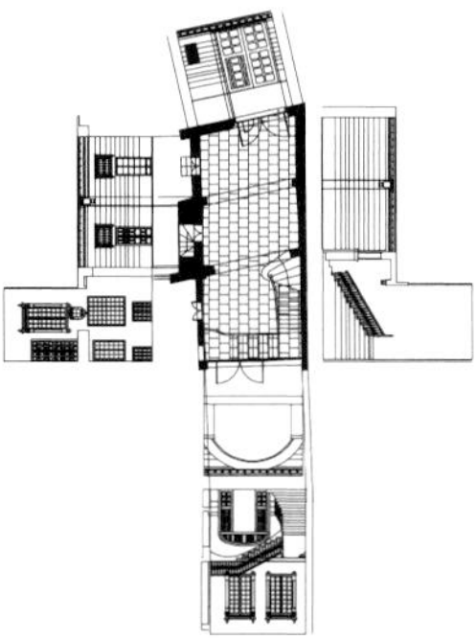

SALAS 15 Y 6A. PLANTA BAJA

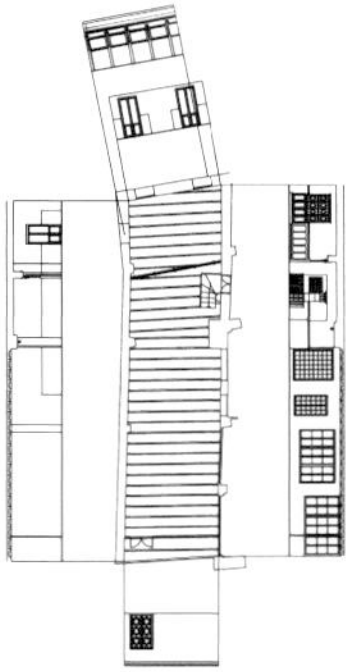

SALAS 2 Y 3. PLANTA ALTILLO

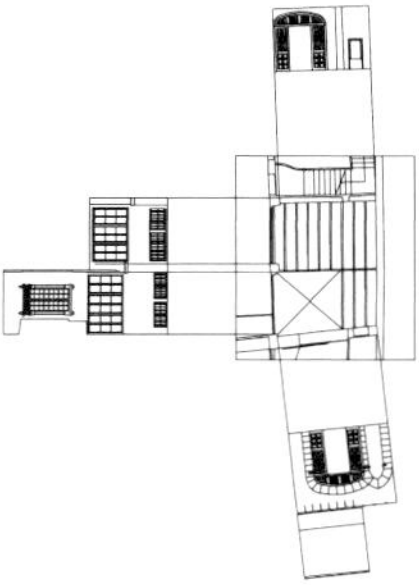

SALAS 17 Y 8. PLANTA BAJA

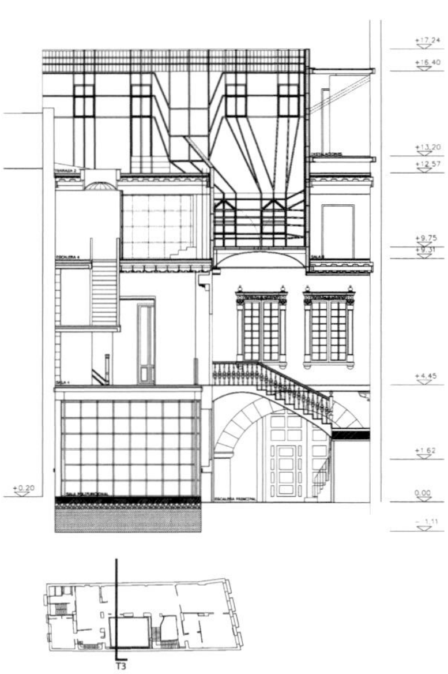
+17.24
+16.40
+13.20
+12.57
+9.75
+9.31
+4.45
+1.62
+0.20
0.00
– 1.11
T3

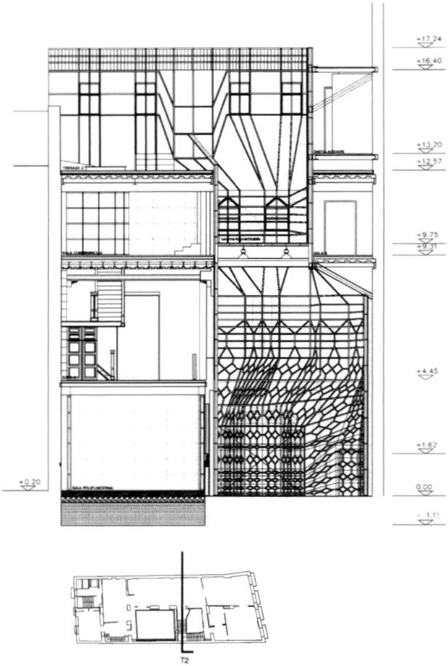
+17.24
+16.40
+13.20
+12.57
+9.75
+9.31
+4.45
+1.62
+0.20
0.00
– 1.11
T2

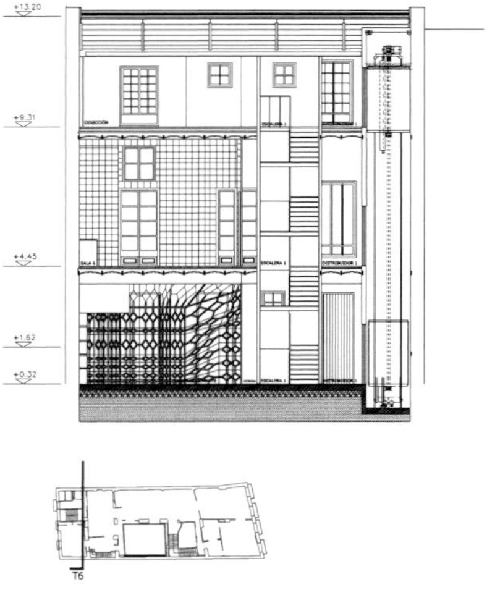
+13.20
+9.31
+4.45
+1.62
+0.32
T6

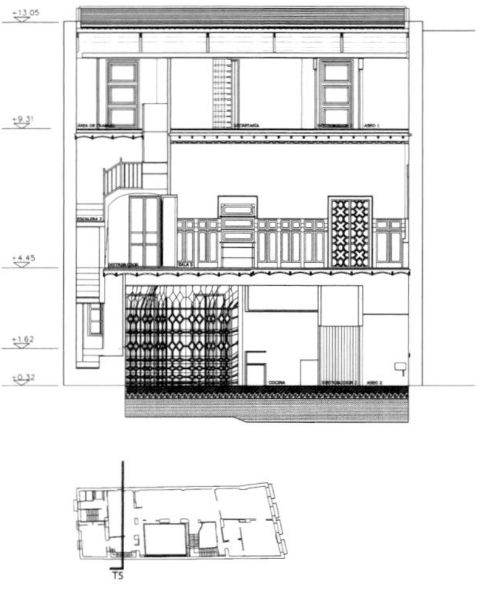
+13.05
+9.31
+4.45
+1.62
+0.32
T5

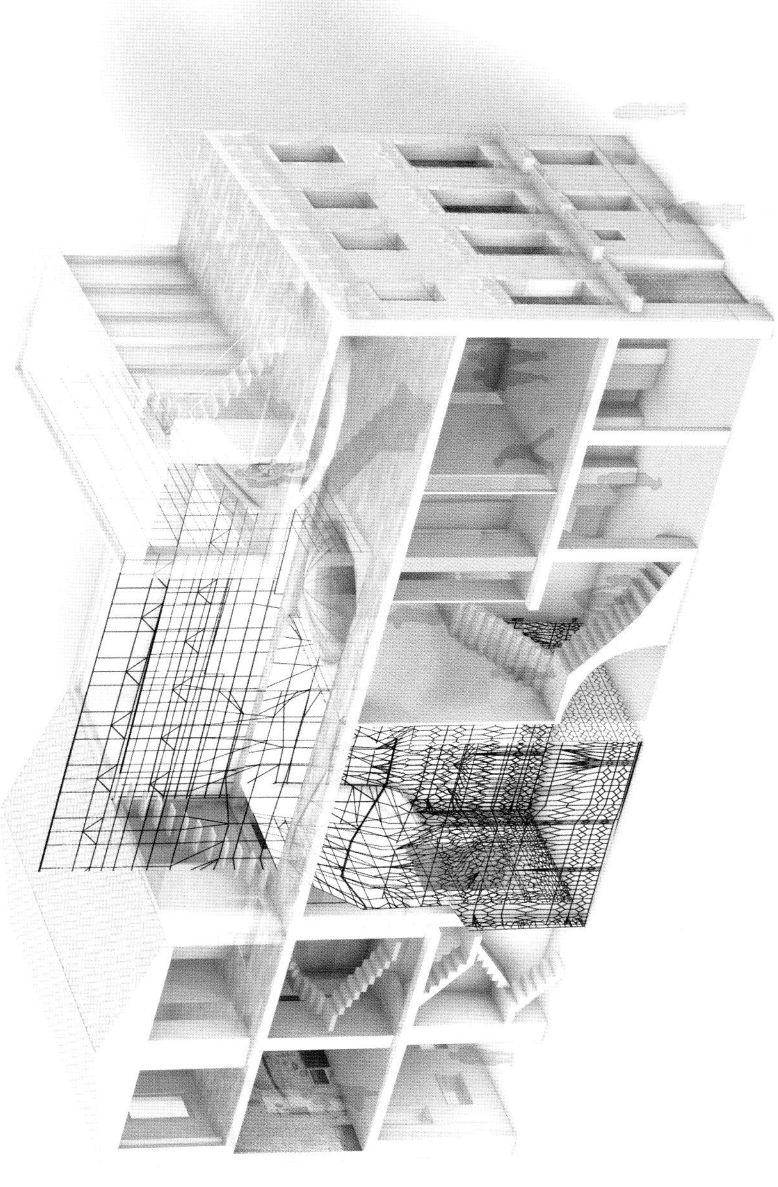

Arab Wall

Valencia. Spain. 1998

Positioning
/20

The Roman city of Valencia was founded in the year 138 BCE. It was occupied by the Moors more or less continuously from 711 until 1238, when it was definitively reconquered by the Christian King James I. In each of these successive phases the city was surrounded by a new wall as it expanded beyond its previously delimited bounds, until the last wall was demolished in 1858, and there is little trace of their presence in the historic city today. In the case of the Arab wall, what remains are a few towers in the midst of later constructions built in the last five hundred years.

This project set out to give new value to a discontinuous element that appears sporadically in the historic city centre. In the 1980s there was a move to demolish all of the later constructions around these Arab remains in order to create squares in which the ruins would stand out as iconic elements. Then the architect Ignasi de Solà-Morales carried out a restoration of the Roman wall in Barcelona in which he proposed that the vision should always be lateral, as it was for the inhabitants of the 19th-century city, who built very close to the wall because of the acute shortage of space. In our case we regarded the intervention as a cultural act, transforming the little that remained of the built heritage into something that could be called the 'urban edition' by articulating the various historic remains in itineraries and visits that draw on the logic of the guided tour more than on that of the urban space as such. We also decided that since very little of the wall remained, we should treat the foundations of other stretches of wall or of adjacent buildings as significant remnants of the built heritage, part of the DNA of the wall that deserved to be valorized. We therefore applied geometric logic to estimate the probable position of the missing towers, the foundations of which we felt sure we would find. However, the project was transformed when we discovered an old print of King James I attacking the Arab wall with his Christian troops, who had laid siege to the city for months. The king had tried to destroy the very wall that we were attempting to conserve almost eight centuries later. This led us to conclude that we ought to look at the wall from in front, encamped outside it like the Christian king, and transform it into a place to be in and not just to visit, to create a new wall, a wooden lattice that would act as a filter screening the backs of the neighbouring apartment buildings, and bombard this with images and sound, the media that connect us with contemporary culture.

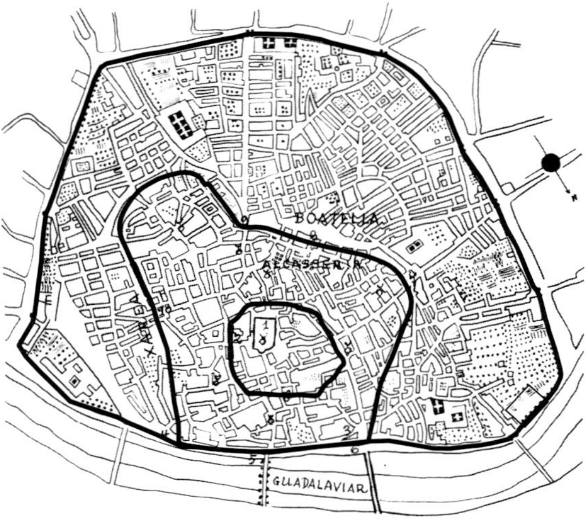

GEOGRAPHY

Walls in the centre of Valencia: roman, arab, christian

GEOMETRY

Sequence of towers (existing and inferred)

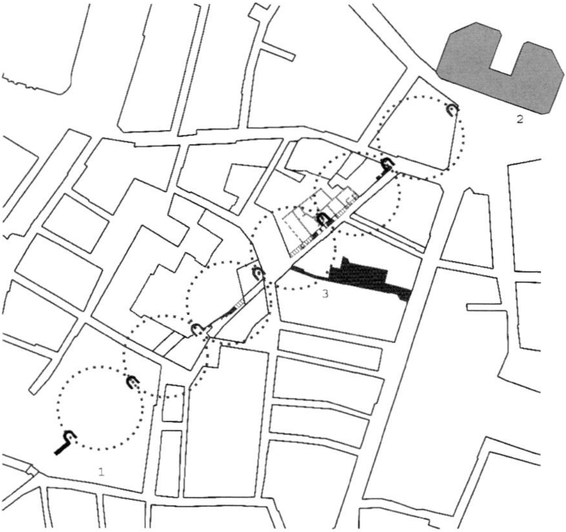

LOGIC

The king James I looks frontally at the Arab wall, and attacks it

STRUCTURE

The wall protecting the wall, in an urban patio

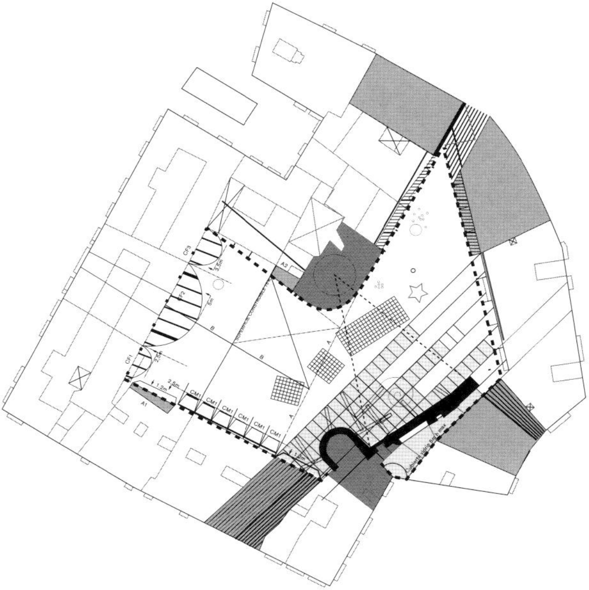

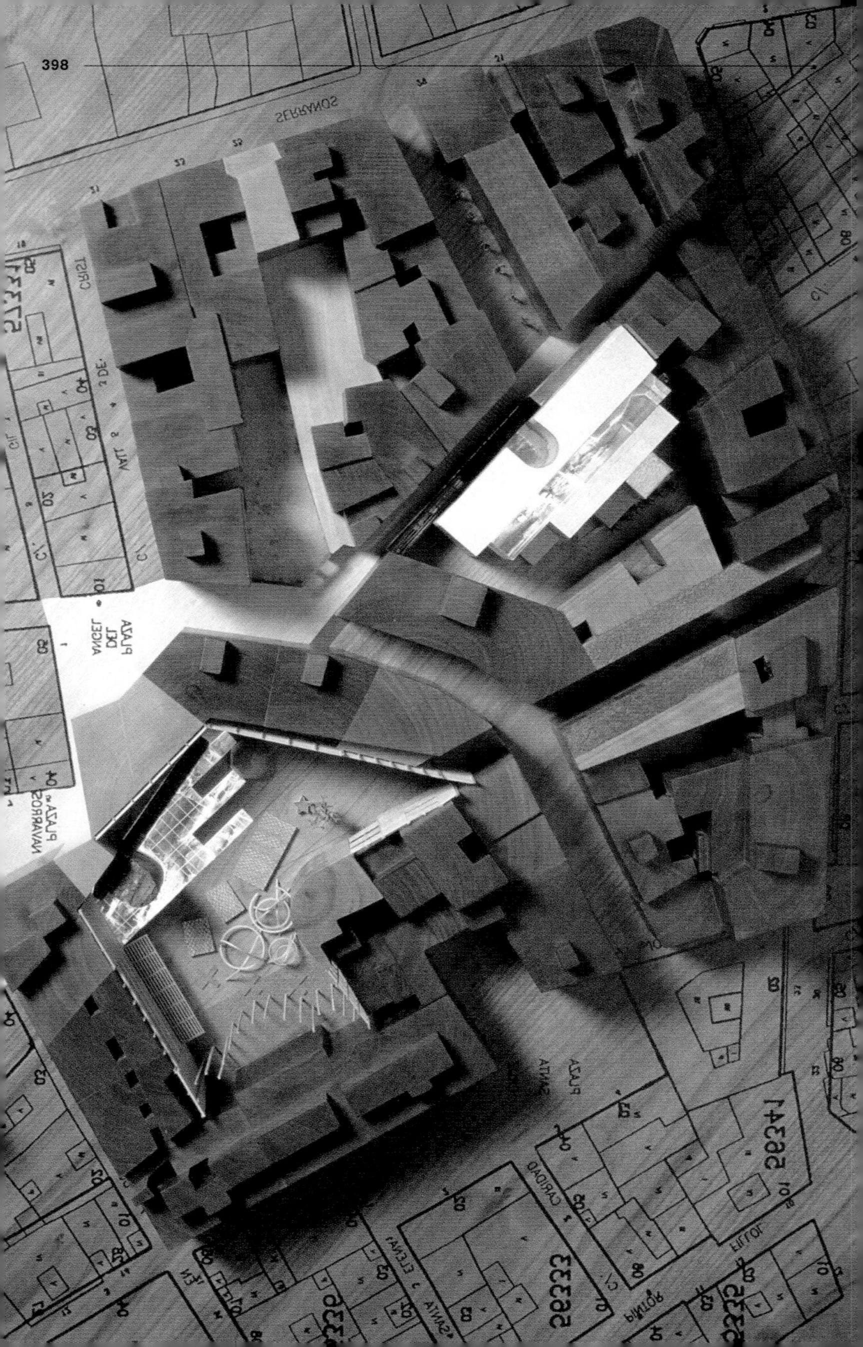

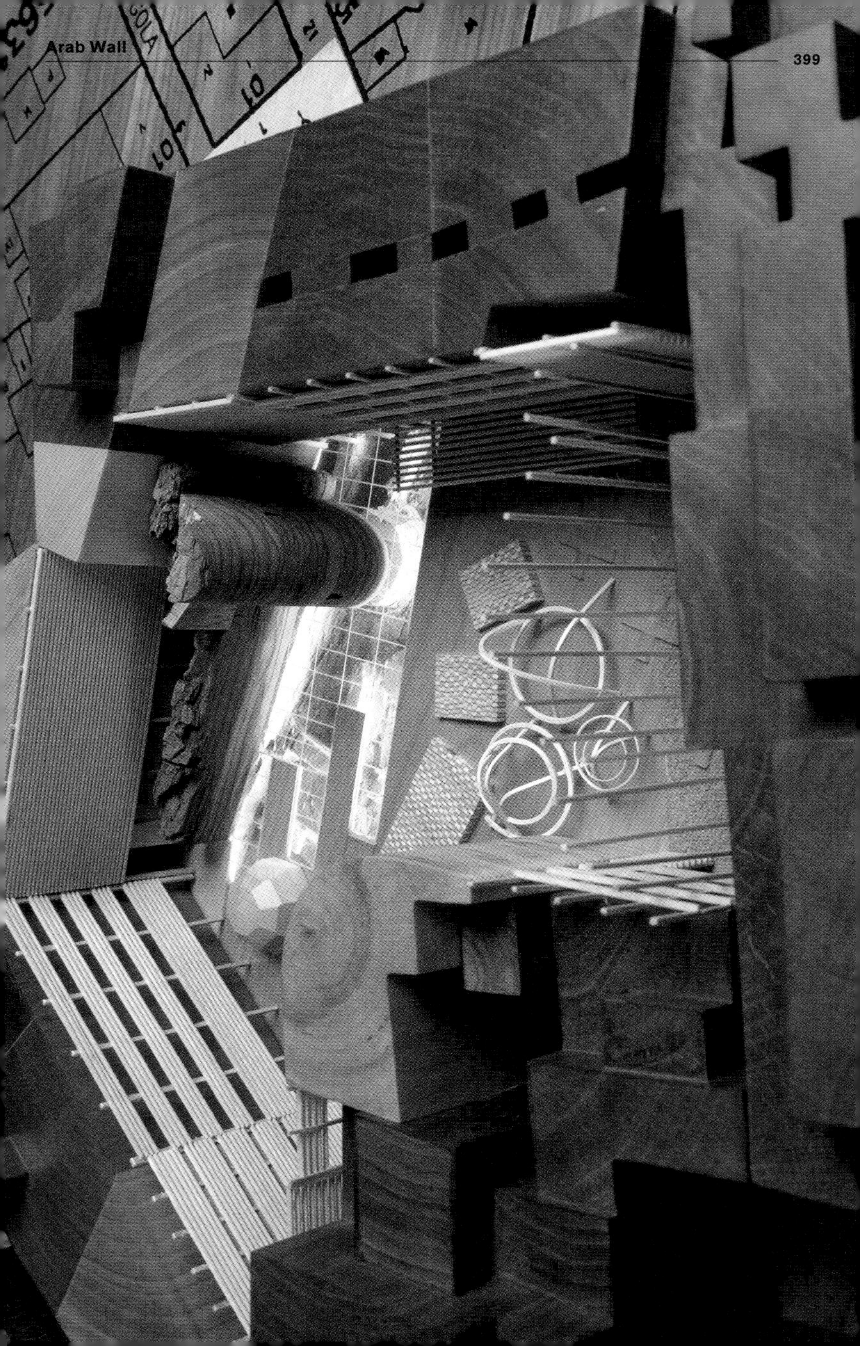

New Settle- ments

El Perelló, Tarragona. Spain.
Study 2003

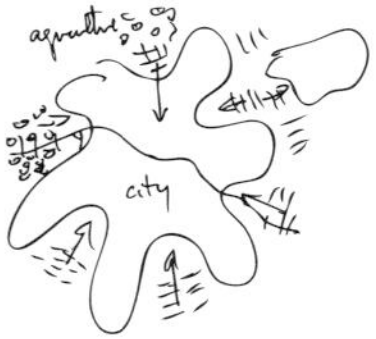

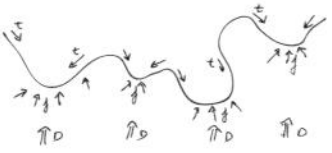

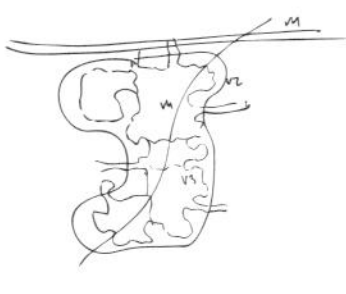

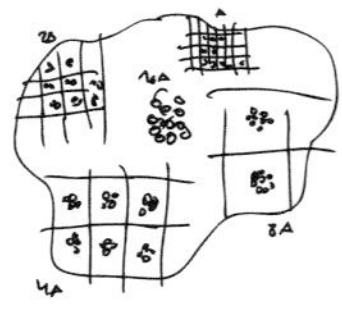

This study, commissioned by the mayor of El Perelló, a town on the Mediterranean coast, posits a new model for inhabiting rural areas that seeks to ensure a permanent human presence without urbanizing the space or destroying its landscape values. We were asked to integrate 400 homes into a particular 400 hectare site, between the historic centre and the coast, thus doubling the current population of 1200 people. The conventional doctrine of growth by grouping would have these houses create a stretch of new town next to the existing core, but in various parts of the Mediterranean coast it is permitted to build a house on a one-hectare plot, this traditionally being the minimum unit of cultivation, sufficient to support a family.
We analysed a number of strategies for occupation of the territory in terms of these two limits, assessing the impact of clusters of 2, 4, 16, 32, 64 and 256 houses, and using the existing rural tracks as the only road layout.

We asked ourselves at what point the group of houses would be large enough to constitute a new settlement that would compete with the existing one, and to what extent the grouping of a certain number of houses would leave enough land unbuilt to allow the area to be considered as still possessing genuine landscape value.

The final proposal defined nuclei of 16 houses built in a compact form on the high points of the landscape, thus creating constructions close in size to the traditional local farmsteads. Given their proximity to major towns and cities along the coast, these houses could be occupied on a permanent basis by information workers who want to get away from the frenetic pace of urban living during certain periods of the week.

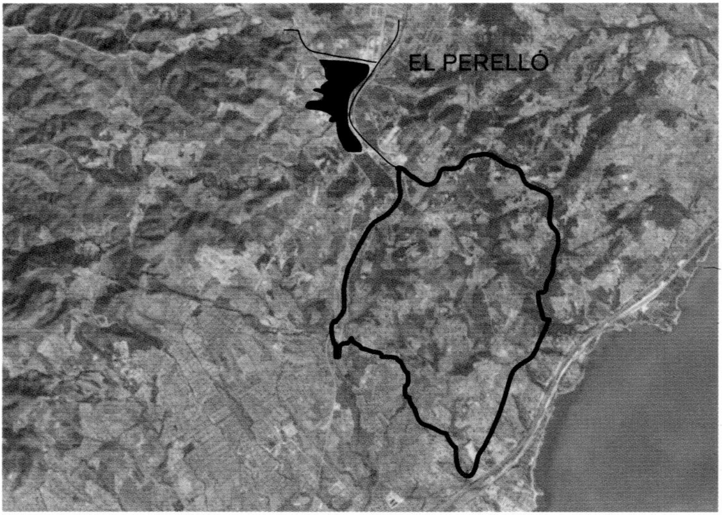

GEOGRAPHY

A small town not far from the Mediterranean coast

GEOMETRY

Potentially habitable area between the town and the sea

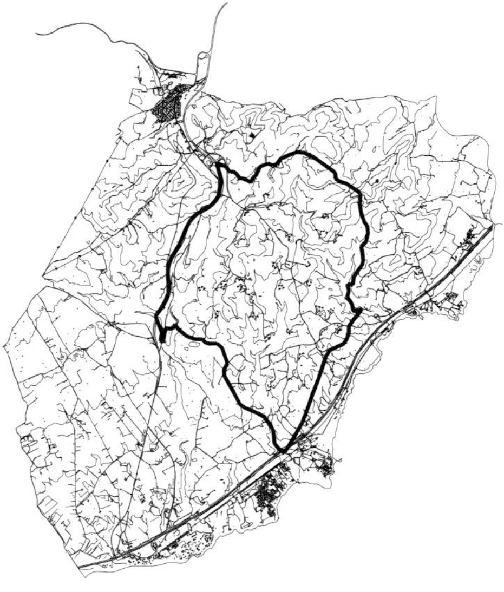

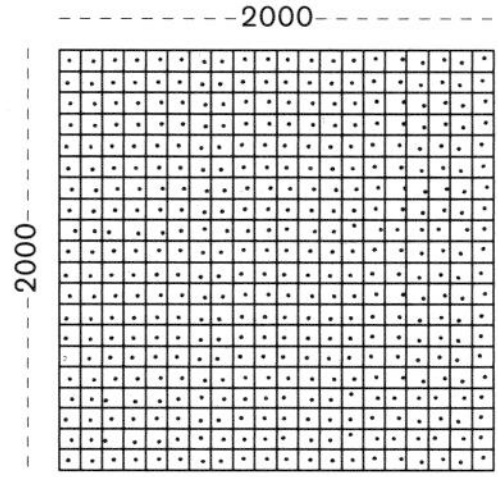

400 de 1v/1 ha

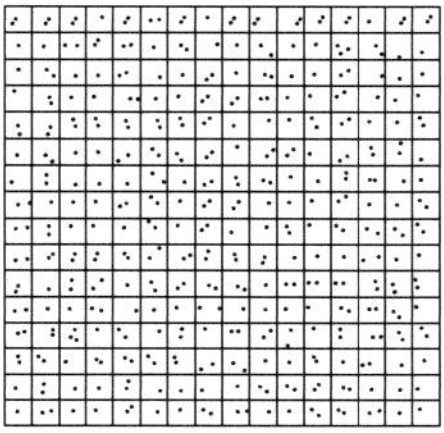

256 1-2v/1.56 ha

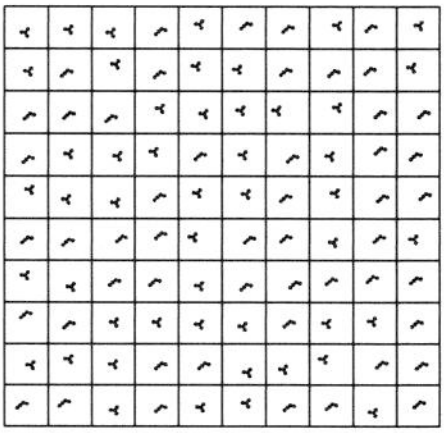

100 de 4v/4 ha

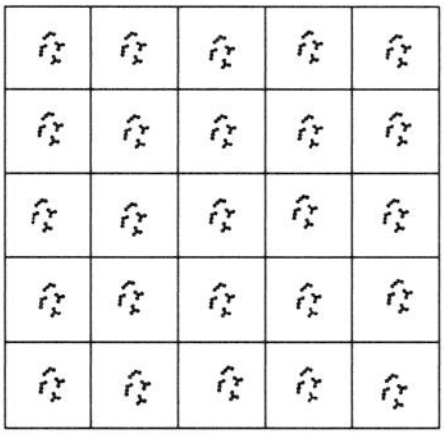

25 de 16v/16 ha

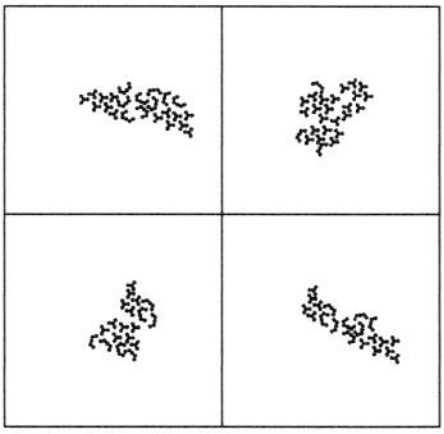

4 de 100v/100 ha

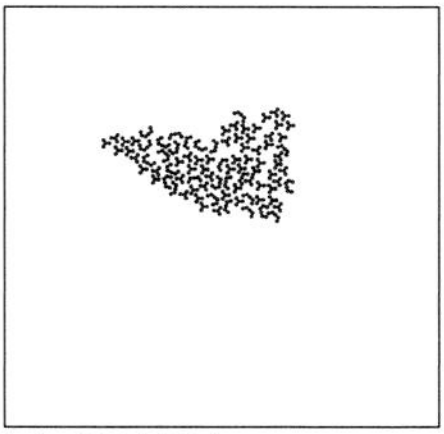

1 de 400v/400 ha

LOGIC

400 homes on 400 hectares with various grouping systems

STRUCTURE

25 clusters of 16 homes populate the territory

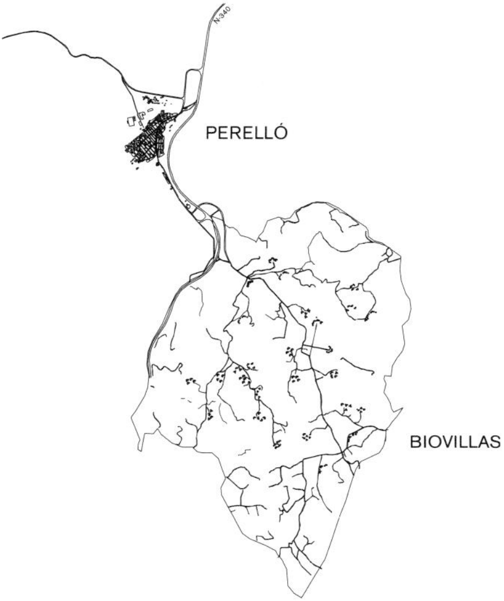

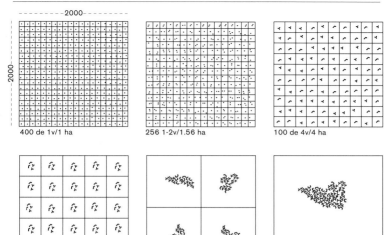

Biocli-matic Villages

Chinchilla, Albacete. Spain. 2007

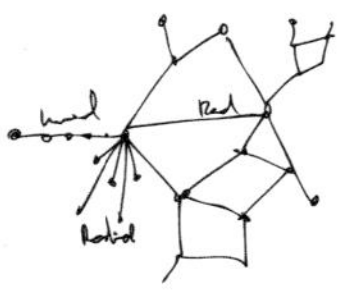

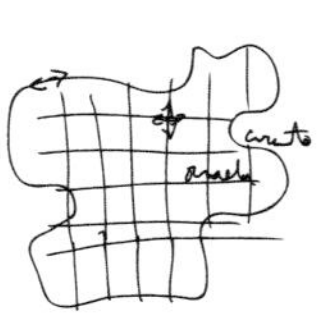

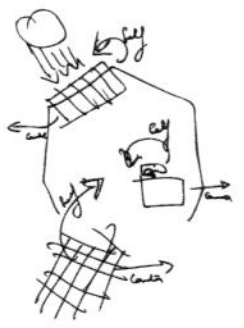

This is a project of a new neighbourhood in the Albacete metropolitan area, with 2,800 subsidized homes, cultural facilities and technology incubators. The project grew out of research into the creation of self-sufficient habitats for a new generation of citizens who want homes at an affordable price in a complete urban setting in which they can live, work and relax, in keeping with the lifestyles of the society information.

The district is intended for young people from the Albacete metropolitan area, the whole of Castilla-La Mancha and even from Madrid or Valencia, whose way of life is centred on networking or teleworking, taking advantage of Albacete's excellent communications thanks to the AVE advanced passenger train. The new district, laid out on 100 hectares near Chinchilla station, will be organized in sections defined by the circulation systems, which will also include pedestrian, cycle, sports and agriculture circuits. There will be more than 20 hectares of green space, sports facilities and agricultural plantations.

The houses are organized in 'villages' with self-sufficient management systems and energy production, urban allotments, homes and workplaces. There will also be business incubators and offices for innovative companies, especially in the fields of new technologies, sustainability and logistics.

The district will use on an experimental basis, for the first time in Europe, a domestic hydrogen micro-network, connecting buildings with different functions (homes, offices and cultural amenities) in such a way that each generates hydrogen cleanly and can share it with other units when needed. This will mark the beginning of the introduction of hydrogen networks, which the European Union has identified as the future of energy. The district will also have its own hydrogen-fuelled transport, thereby implementing the introduction of a public hydrogeneration system on the A-31, one of Spain's busiest motorways. In addition, a high-speed Intranet will connect all of the homes, enabling the residents to organize themselves by way of the neighbourhood web, an innovative browser that will promote social interaction.

From an urban perspective, an advanced neighbourhood is a compact nucleus developed on the basis of an integral project, with sufficient density and critical mass to generate the kind of social and economic relations associated with a city. As a result, the advanced district enjoys functional autonomy, generously equipped as it is with amenities that enhance the quality of life and accommodating a productive tertiary sector that provides jobs. A place to live in, not just to sleep in.

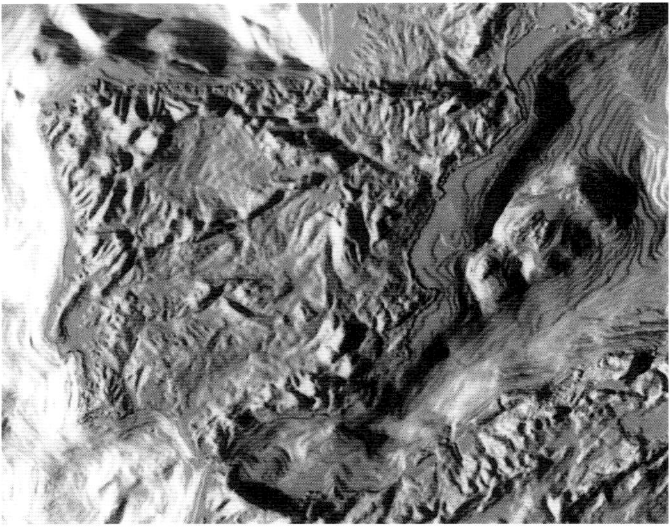

GEOGRAPHY

The physical geography of Spain

GEOMETRY

Provincial Iberia

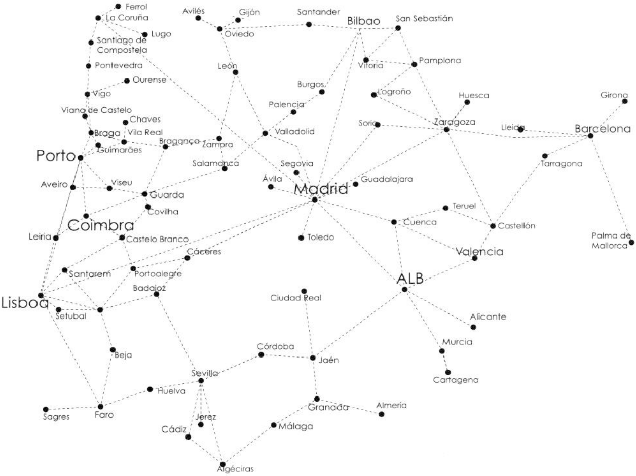

LOGIC

Territorial network of poles of attraction and specialized nodes

STRUCTURE

Centre, intermediate logistic ring and coast

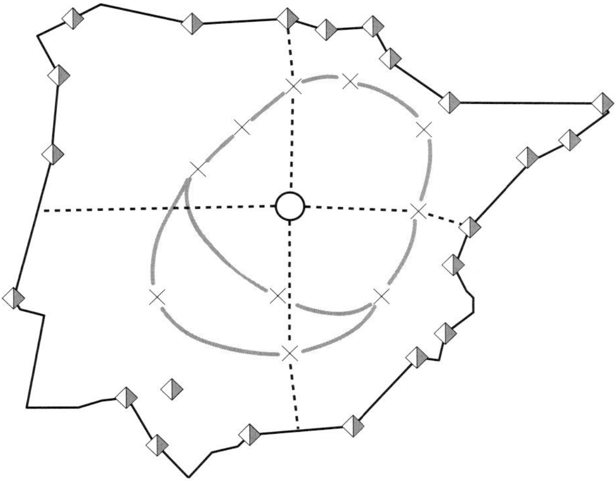

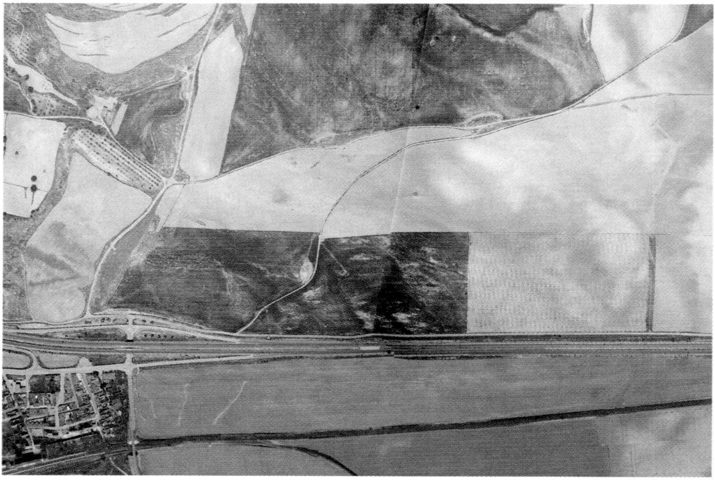

GEOGRAPHY

A moor in front of a motorway

GEOMETRY

100 ha of barren land

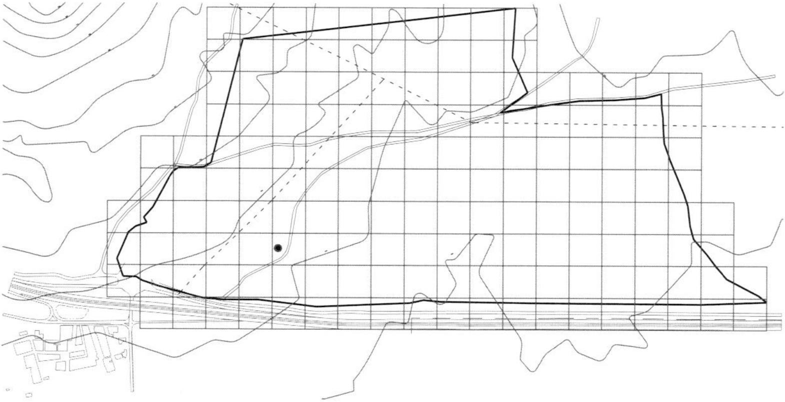

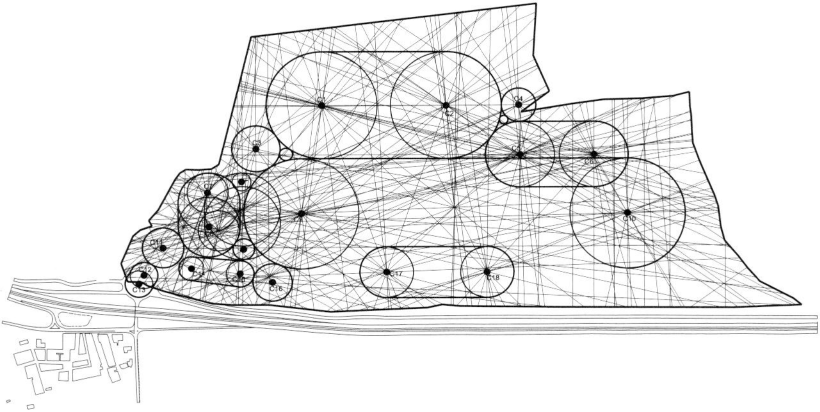

LOGIC

Foundation in the territory by means of circuits

STRUCTURE

The circuit replaces the mesh as a structure of implantation

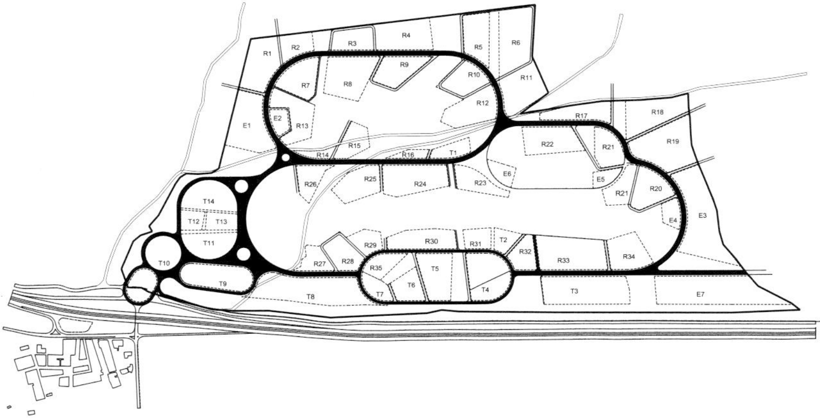

Transportation network

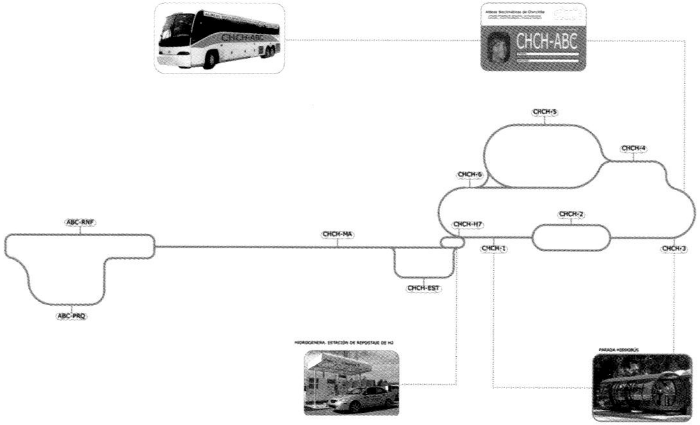

Energy network

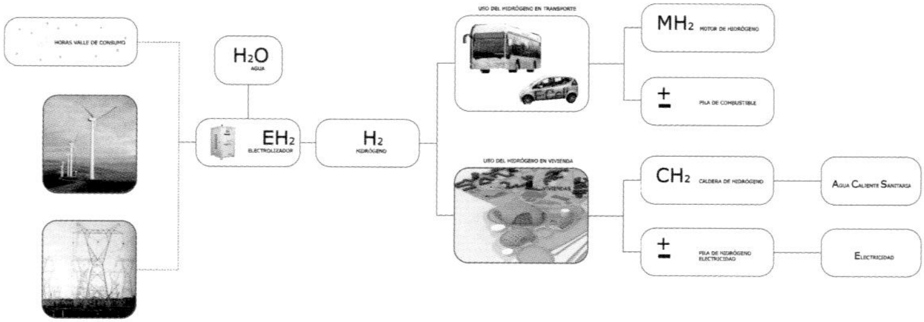

Information network

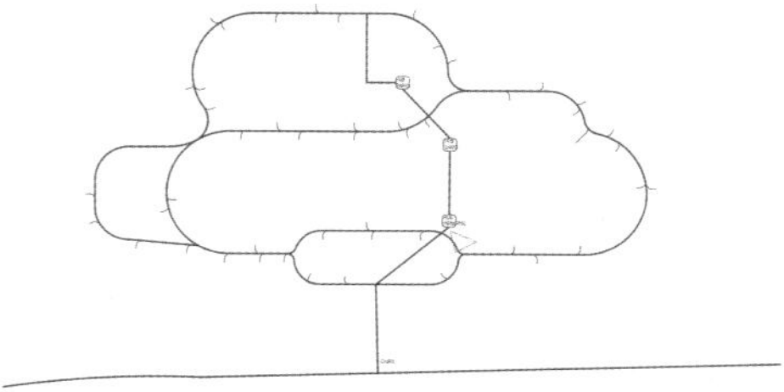

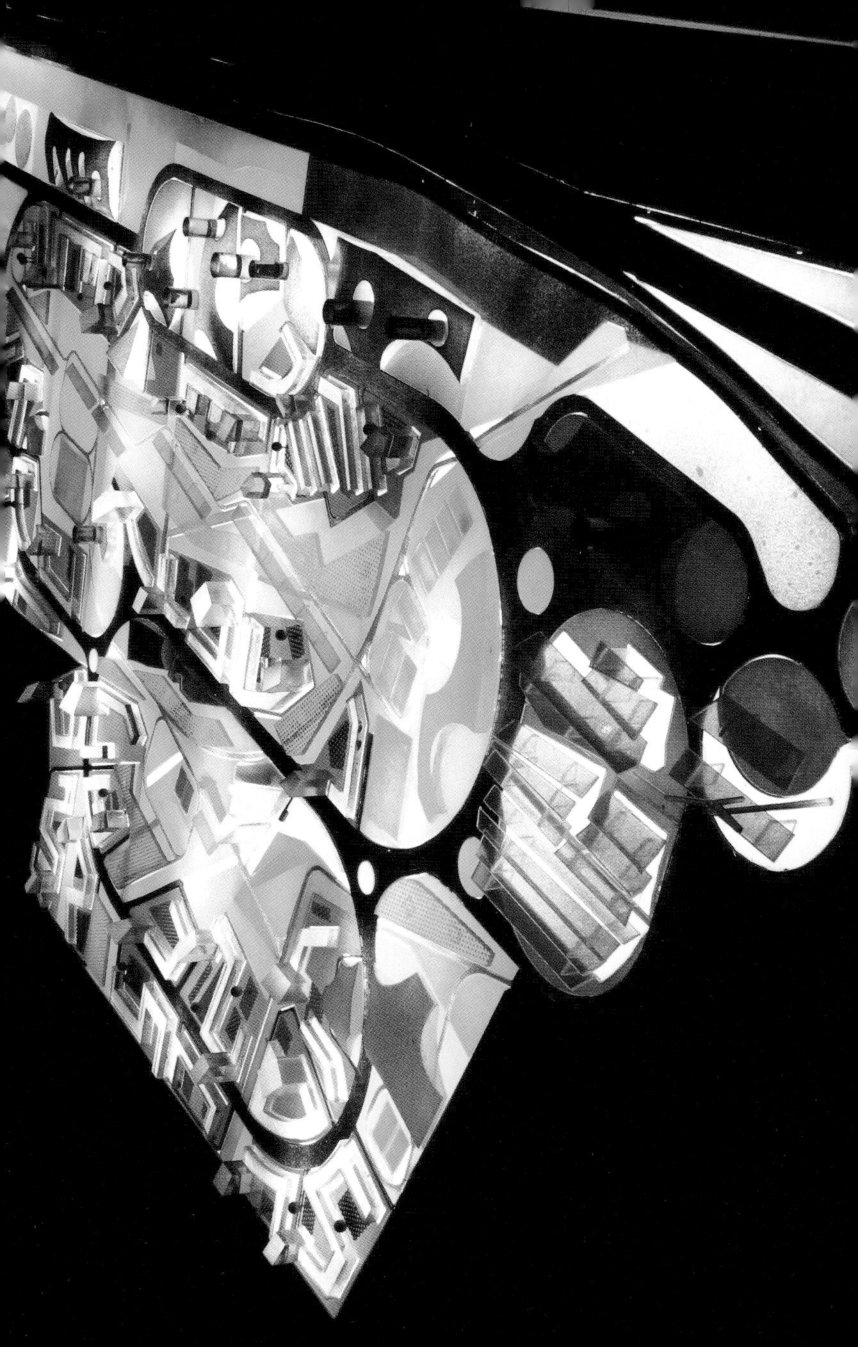

Eco tropical Neighbourhood

Motril. Spain. 2007
With Ángel Gijón

1st Prize national competition

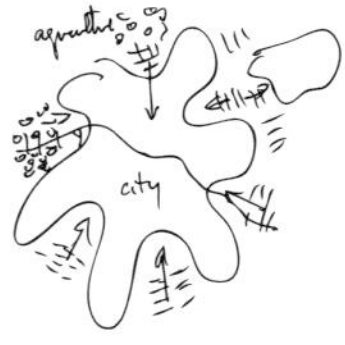

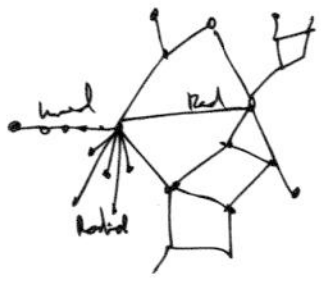

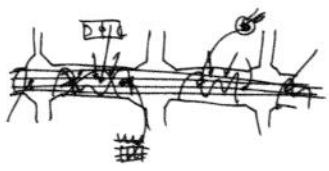

Motril, capital of the Costa Tropical area, in the province of Granada, is experiencing a major process of urban development as a result of its strategic geographical location on the Mediterranean coast between Málaga and Almería. Its role as the port of Granada, its position between the sea and the mountains, and the arrival of the Autovía del Mediterráneo motorway make the town a key site for the development of the region.

In the case of the MOT-3 project addressed by the present Plan, this is a key site for the development of the town. In its configuration, Motril gives a very clear message in terms of the models of urban growth that it wishes to promote, and especially with regard to the relationship between the population nuclei and the surrounding natural environment. This relationship between growth and interaction with the environment is the key issue to be resolved by urban planning at the start of the 21st century.

Concentric Growth or Radial Permeability

MOT-3 poses the choice between concentric growth and radial permeability on the northern edge of Motril. The approved general plan posited that a large environmentally protected area should be created between the port and the urban nucleus in the form of a sugar cane plantation and a park route. This large-scale green facility connects up with the town's Parque de los Pueblos de América and the Rambla de los Álamos avenue, which runs east to the sports centre and the municipal cemetery.

The MOT-3 sector is capable of opening up the town to the north, to the hills and the Sierra, reproducing in a symmetrical (but initially on a smaller scale) the environmental sugar cane plantation and giving concrete physical form to the sea-Motril-mountain environmental relationship.

The scheme thus identifies the opportunity to transform the green zones of a residential sector into a park, which would become the town's primary network, thereby benefiting at the local scale the residents of the new neighbourhoods adjoining this major amenity, and at the global scale benefiting the municipality as a whole by ensuring its openness to the natural networks around it.

Transfer of Traces

In the light of the foregoing reflections the design team decided to transfer the traces of the existing paths and plots and conserve the open spaces in their present state. This is the basis not only for an environmental continuity in the territory, but also for a cultural continuity, in preserving the lines of tracks that in many cases date from ancient times and—small though they are—have served to structure the use of the territory.

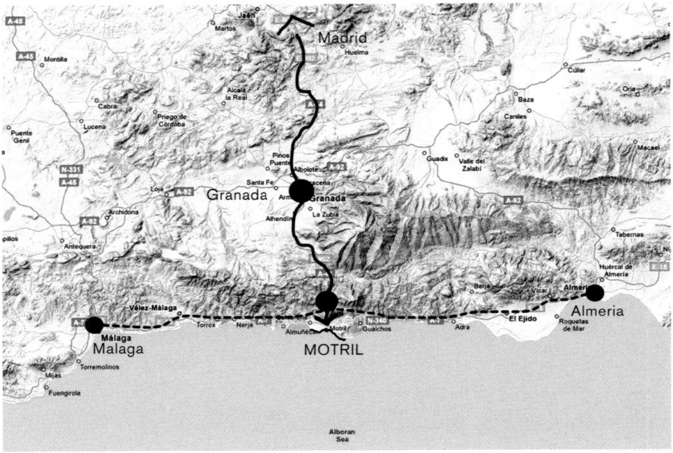

GEOGRAPHY

Strategic position of Motril, between three major cities

GEOMETRY

Urban growth by rings

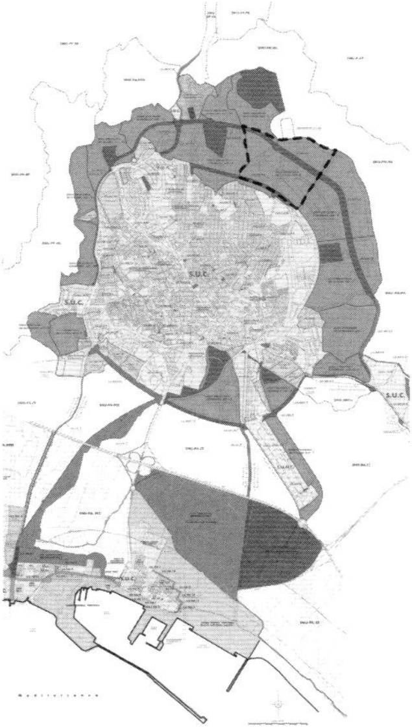

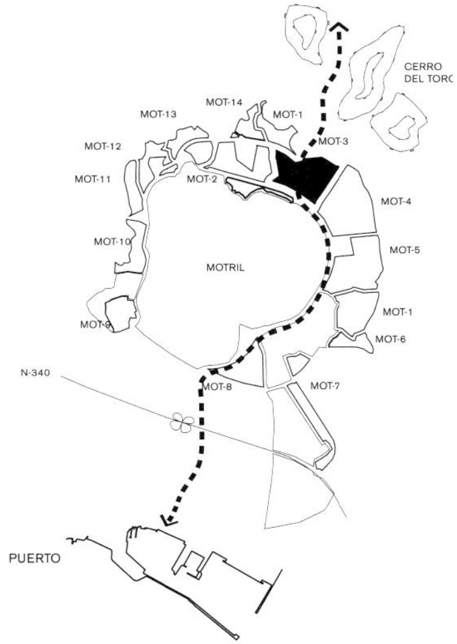

LOGIC

Development of the urban periphery, keeping the city open

STRUCTURE

Plot divisions based on agricultural holdings

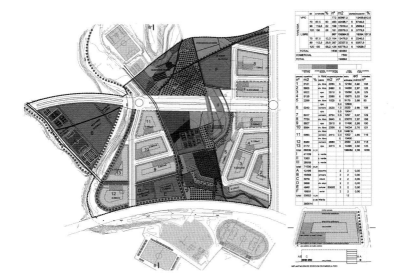

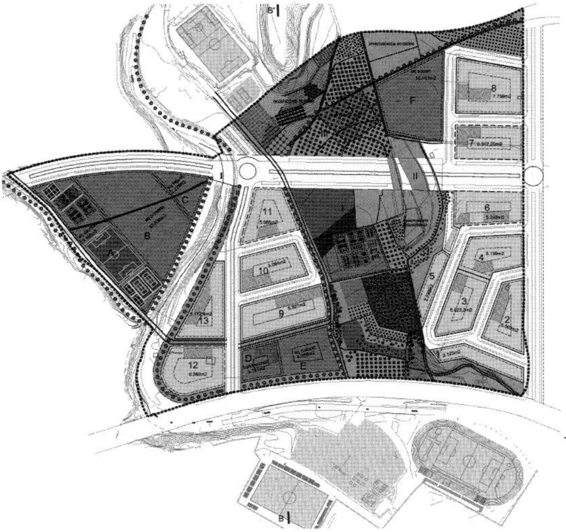

			construidos	%	nº	m2	plantas	ocupación	%
VIVIENDA	VPO				772	80997,3		13459,8	42,5
		70	87,5	50	463	40496,7	6	6749,8	
		90	112,5	22	158	17819,4	6	2969,9	
		120	150	28	151	22679,3	6	3779,8	
	LIBRE				867	109584,6		18264,1	57,5
		70	87,5	12,3	154	13476,9	6	2246,5	
		90	112,5	29,5	287	32327,5	6	5387,9	
		120	150	58,2	425	63778,3	6	10629,7	
	TOTAL				1636	190582			
COMERCIAL						7500			
TOTAL						198082			

parcela nº	superficie m2	%	v. libre usos	ocupación m2	plantas nº	techo edificable	ed m2/m2	viviendas nº
1	3121		viv. libre	2030	6	12180	3,90	105
2	5003		viv. libre	2460	6	14880	2,97	128
3	5022		vpo	2510	6	15060	3,00	129
4	5139		vpo	2595	6	15570	3,03	134
5	2299		viv. libre	1528	6	9170	3,99	80
6	5240		vpo		5,0	12600	2,89	108
			comerc	2520	1,0	2520		
7	5317		vpo		5,5	15047	3,07	129
			comerc	2724	0,5	1297		
8	7759		viv. libre	3845	6	23070	2,97	198
9	5927		vpo	2915	6	17490	2,95	150
10	5094		viv. libre	2339	6	14034	2,76	121
11	5085		viv. libre		5,6	13487,8	2,85	116
			comerc	2415	0,4	1002		
12	6360		viv. libre		5	13400	2,53	115
			comerc	2680	1	2680		
13	5172		vpo	2415	6	14490	2,80	125
total	66539	21,77				198082	2,98	1636
I	41139		z. verde					
II	1363		z. verde					
III	28508		z. verde					
total	71030	23,24						
A	13186		deportivo		2	2	0,00	
B	15568		primaria		2	2	0,00	
C	3279		infantil		2	2	0,00	
D	9698		viv. alquil.		2	2	0,00	
E	4940		cultural	53602	2	2	0,00	
F	10931		social		2	2	0,00	
total	53602	17,54				12		
		37,38	viario					
	305614							

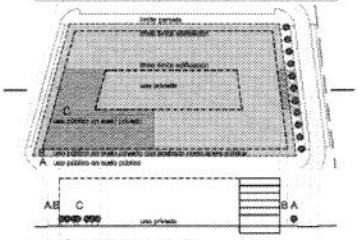

IMPLANTACIÓN DE EDIFICIOS EN PARCELA TIPO

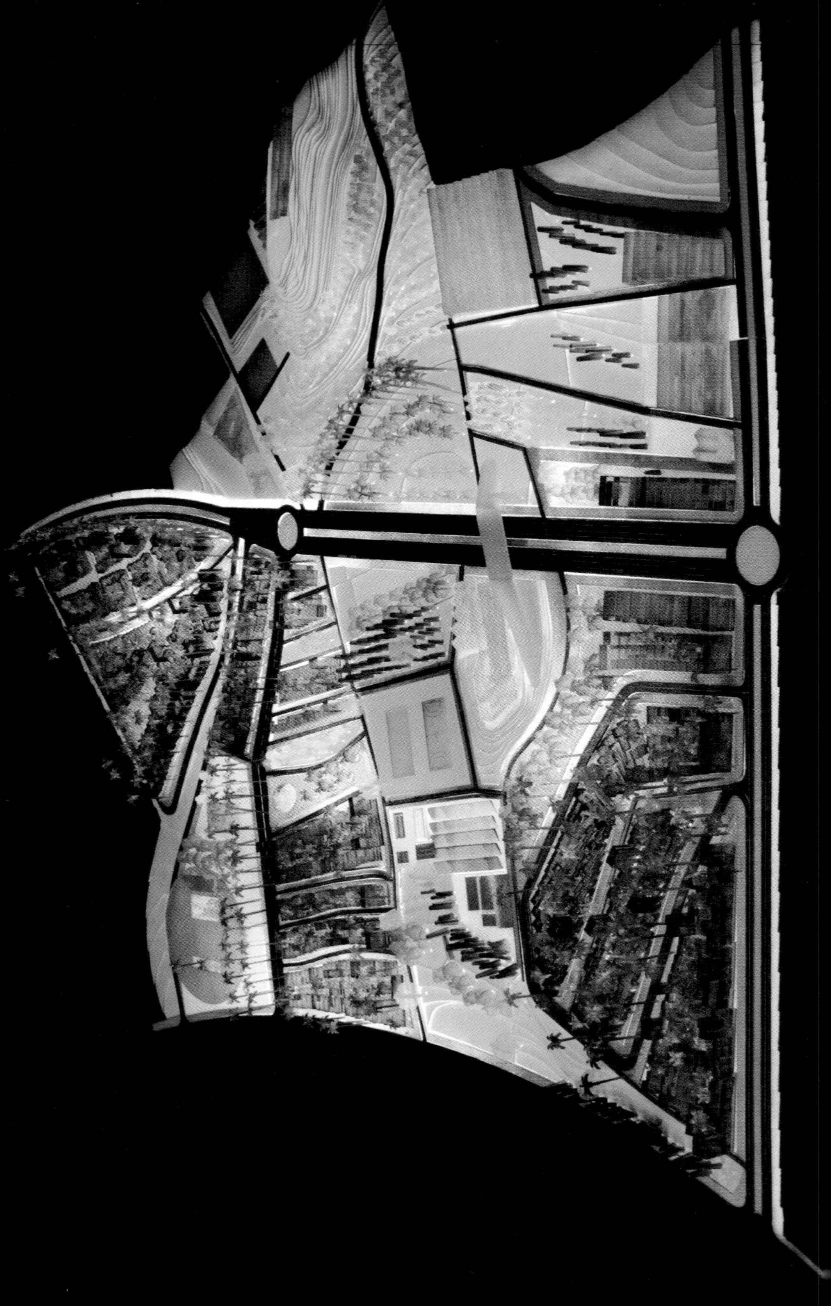

Socio-polis I

Valencia. Spain. 2002—2003
2nd Valencia Biennale

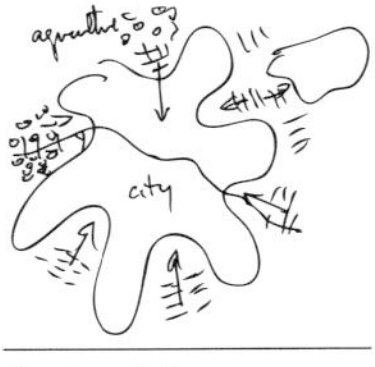

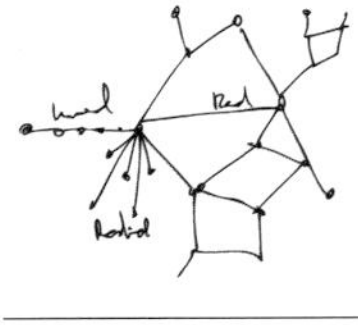

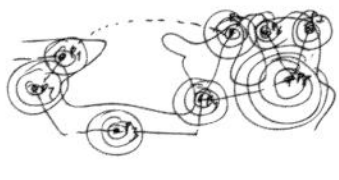

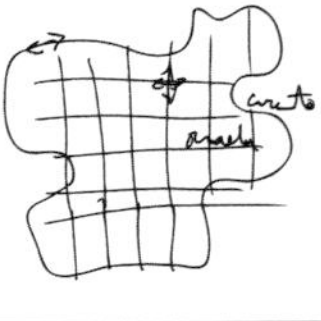

Researching in order to act

The Sociopolis project came into being to explore the possibility of creating a 'shared habitat' that would encourage a greater social interaction between its inhabitants, proposing new housing typologies in keeping with the new family conditions of our time, in a setting of high environmental quality.

The question to be answered was simple: if we live in the age of knowledge, and if in order to act the world has to invest in research, should we not devote part of our production of public housing to researching and developing new kinds of buildings that respond to our present needs and prefigure future situations? This elementary question has been formulated dozens of times, but only very rarely has there been sufficient cultural and political support for the response to be affirmative. In Valencia it was decided to make the Biennial of the Arts an opportunity for generating a project that would provide a basis for this universal reflection.

The social aspect of housing

The concept of social housing consists of two parts: Housing and Social. Traditionally the responsibility for building such homes (ranging from housing for disadvantaged sectors of the population to the subsidized housing that is more common in our time) rests with the same department responsible for constructing roads and other infrastructures. There is thus a tendency to attach far more importance to problems of production or budget than to social problems. The departments responsible for 'social action' devote much of their efforts to meeting the demands of the European model of welfare society, but in most cases make no attempt to situate these policies in their spatial dimension.

Nevertheless, the present project had an eminently social impetus, impelled by bodies that work with groups at risk of social exclusion and are concerned with generating forms of housing that respond to the new social needs. There is at present a shortage of affordable housing for young people, for elderly people (many of them living alone) who require some degree of public support, for people who have arrived from other regions or countries, and for people involved in specific social programmes. Taken together, these constitute a sizable portion of our society.

Inhabiting the huerta

The project, as a piece of generic research, was located on a site on the edge of the city of Valencia, in the huerta, in order to address a common situation in the process where urban growth comes face to face with the natural environment. The Valencian huerta has for centuries been an area of arable cultivation, with an important network of irrigation channels of Arab origin tha takes water from the river Turia and effectively structures the territory.
In the European urban tradition, whenever the city has grown, nature (and agriculture with it) has disappeared. The urban and the rural have been two opposed concepts.

However, Valencia and many other Mediterranean territories have a different history. For the Arabs, the huerta was their garden, a productive fertile territory that they inhabited, in which they built their palaces and which always incorporated the surrounding landscape. The monasteries and the mediaeval city learnt from this culture, developing the concept of the hortulus.

The rurban project

One way of breaking out of the city-country dichotomy is to generate places of transition between the two, to create 'rurban' territories with a view to integrate the culture of the huerta into the city, guaranteeing that certain values of the same are assumed as own of our culture and our time.

In the Valencia of the 21st century, at a moment in time when cities and territories are seeking to assert their differential characteristics in the face of globalization, the fact of having a landscape and a culture of the huerta in the city can be a key differential factor in favour of urban and cultural progress.

In the post-industrial era a new techno-agricultural society is emerging, in which as citizens of the planet we participate in its culture and economy through the information technologies, we travel to distant places by high-speed transport systems, but at the same time we affirm the quality of the local, of the immediate habitable environment; of a new intelligent balance between what we generate and what we consume.

The New Housing Project

The first decades of the 20th century established many of the characteristic features of housing that are still with us today: new standards of hygiene, the incorporation of electricity (and the appliances associated with it), the standardization of furniture and regulations governing housing requirements have combined to provide more or less decent housing for most citizens of the western world.

This situation has tended to consolidate routine approaches to the construction process, and given little impetus to innovative discourse in relation to housing. The information society poses new challenges and generates new opportunities:

How do we avoid the total isolation of the individual in their environment, and achieve a greater social cohesion? How do we promote greater environmental quality, integrating nature into habitable environments? How do we use the new information technologies to build better and live better? How do we integrate new functions into the home? How do we foster a supportive habitat?

New family units

The traditional family of two parents and one or more children now accounts for less than 50% of households in many regions of Spain. Increasing international—and especially intra-European—mobility, the emancipation of young people and the delay in starting to have children, higher life expectancy and the improvement in the quality of life of senior citizens are factors that condition the way people group together to occupy a house. We are now seeing the emergence of the concept of the virtual family, in which people of various generations who are not blood relatives behave to some extent as a family, sharing resources or activities.

Sociopolis thus proposes an open-ended organization of residential units, facilitating multiple configurations within a single building and enabling each house to be as individual as the people who live in it.

Accessible neighbourhood

More than 8% of the population has some kind of disability. Also, as people leave longer they have a greater mobility problem merely because of physical reasons. The children born in 2004 will live an average of 100 years. The matter of accessibility to everyplace in the city (houses, public spaces, working places, etc.), independently of their physical condition is a key issue to consider on the future neighbourhoods. It's not about disabled people having access to their own houses, but of being able to access and engage normally in any activity.

GEOGRAPHY

An agricultural area on the urban periphery of Valencia

GEOMETRY

Structure of land parcelling

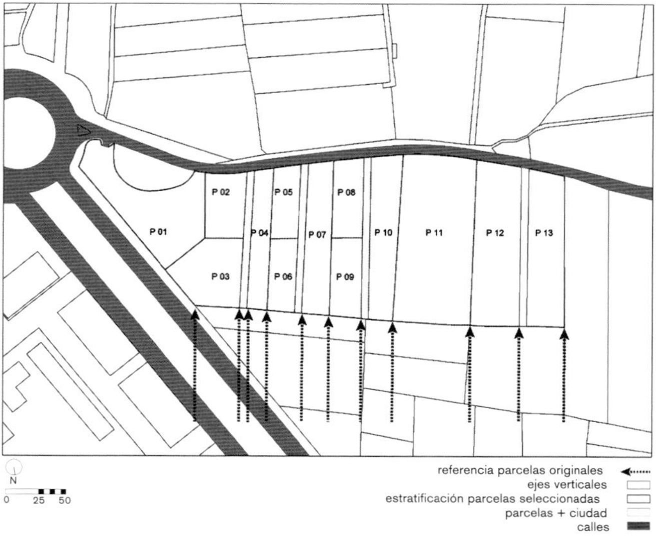

Solar

40,029.2 m2

Area Parcelas

Parcela 01	4762.0
Parcela 02	1748.2
Parcela 03	2670.5
Parcela 04	1830.3
Parcela 05	1331.9
Parcela 06	1331.0
Parcela 07	2682.6
Parcela 08	1623.7
Parcela 09	1623.7
Parcela 10	3086.1
Parcela 11	8499.7
Parcela 12	5088.6
Parcela 13	3751.8

Total 40,029.2 m2

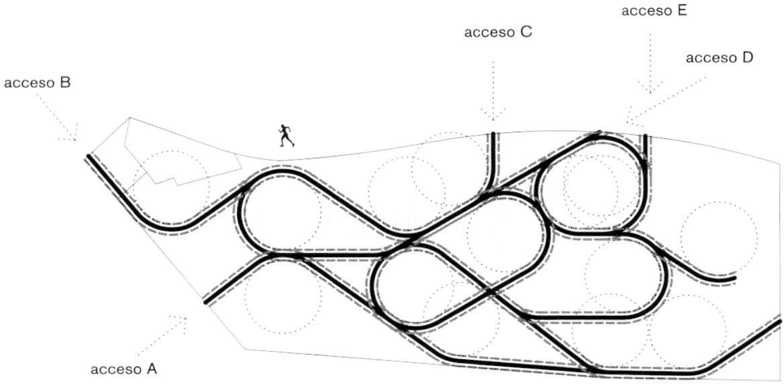

LOGIC

No urbanization: the sports circuit as internal circulation system

STRUCTURE

Urban structure superimposed on agricultural structure

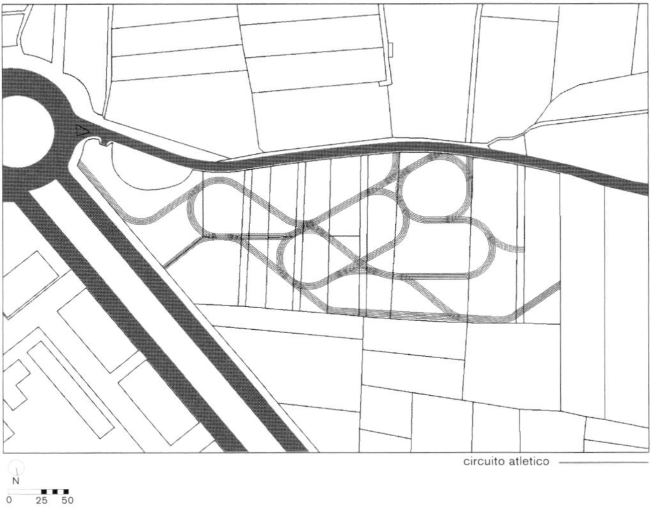

Areas / Parcelas

Parcela 01	4762.0 m2
Parcela 02	1748.2 m2
Parcela 03	2670.5 m2
Parcela 04	1830.3 m2
Parcela 05	1331.0 m2
Parcela 06	1331.0 m2
Parcela 07	2682.6 m2
Parcela 08	1623.7 m2
Parcela 09	1623.7 m2
Parcela 10	3086.1 m2
Parcela 11	8499.7 m2
Parcela 12	5088.6 m2
Parcela 13	3751.8 m2
Total	40,029.2 m2

Areas / Ejes Vehiculares

Eje 01	675.4 m2
Eje 02	741.7 m2
Eje03	787.9 m2

Areas / Ejes Protección

Eje 01	787.9 m2
Total	2992.9 m2

Areas / Tipo Huerta

Arbol frutal 100%	6837.5 m2
Arbol frutal 50%	15487.9 m2
Huerta de hortaliza 50%	1748.2 m2
Huerta de hortaliza 100%	14124.9 m2
Huerta de producción	1830.3 m2

Circuito

Pista de atletismo
5 lineas @ 1.22 mts
Radio de Giro
23.57 mts

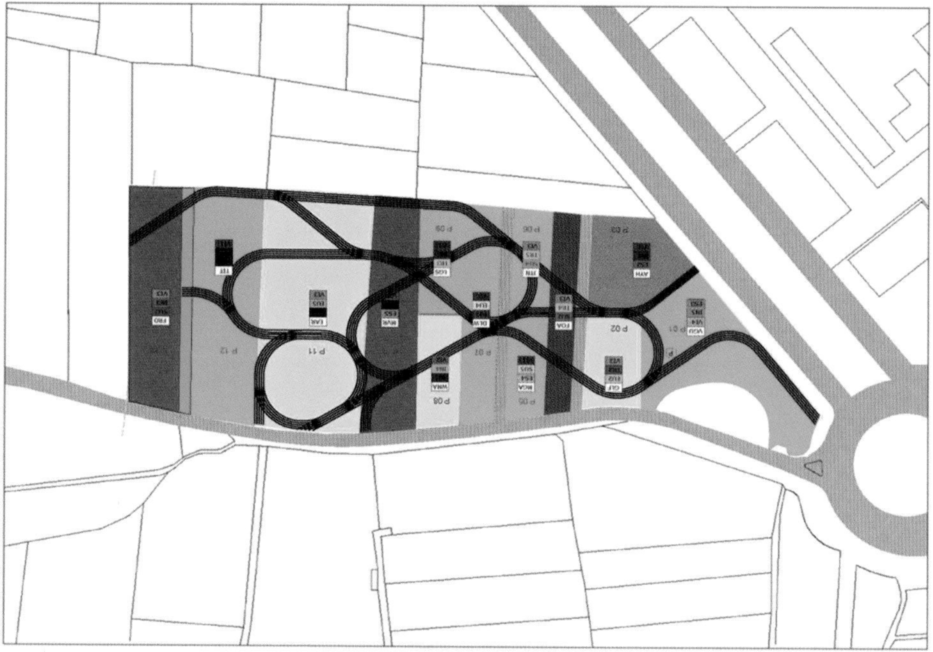

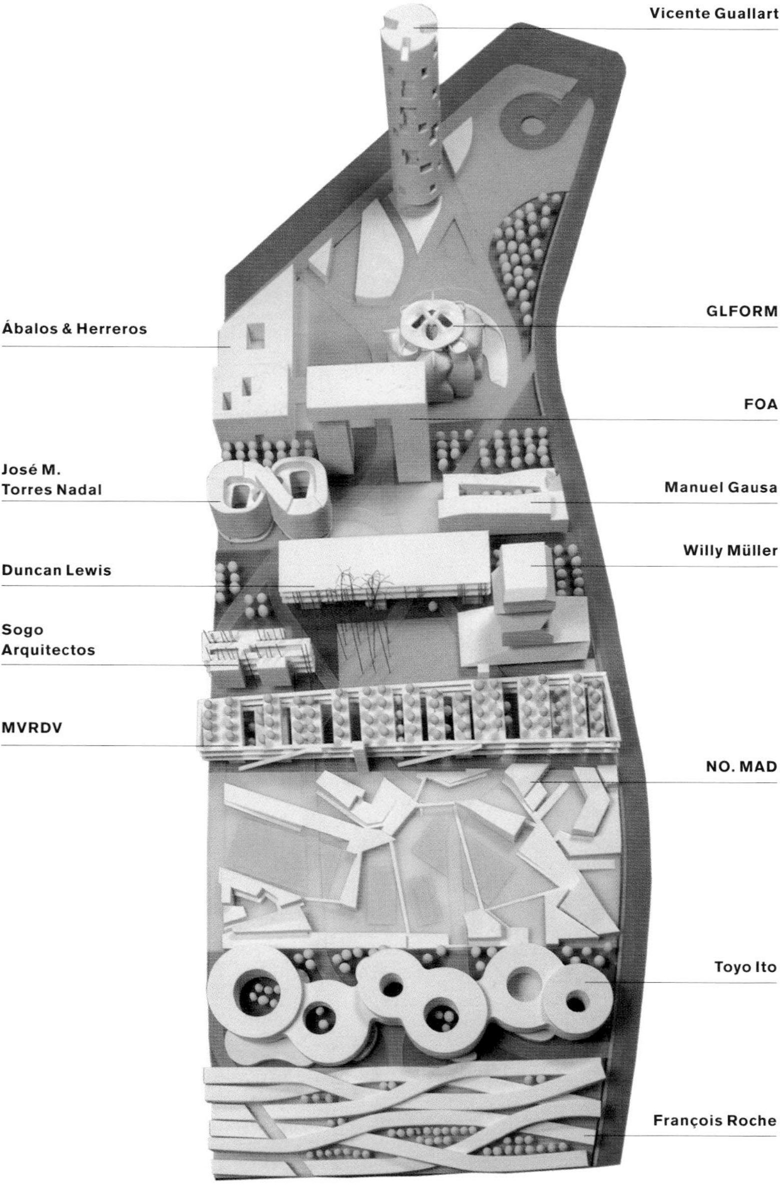
Vicente Guallart
GLFORM
Ábalos & Herreros
FOA
José M.
Torres Nadal
Manuel Gausa
Willy Müller
Duncan Lewis
Sogo
Arquitectos
MVRDV
NO. MAD
Toyo Ito
François Roche

Socio-polis Master-plan

Valencia. Spain. 2005—2010

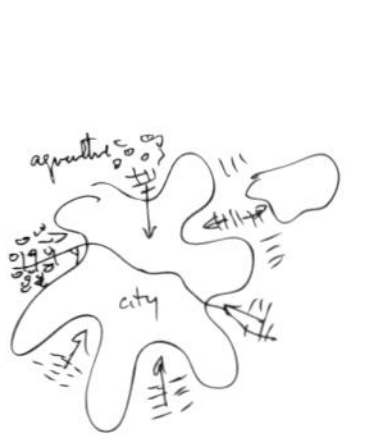

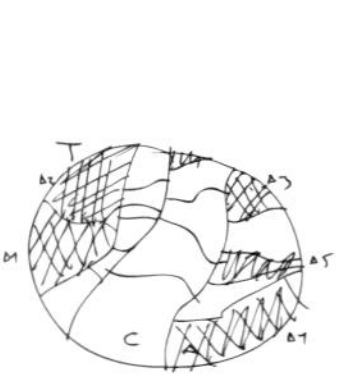

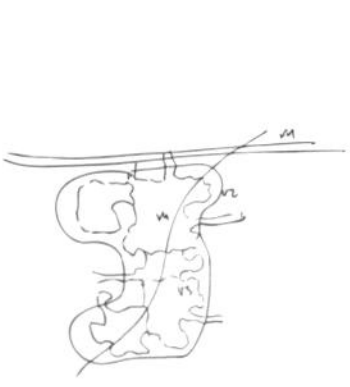

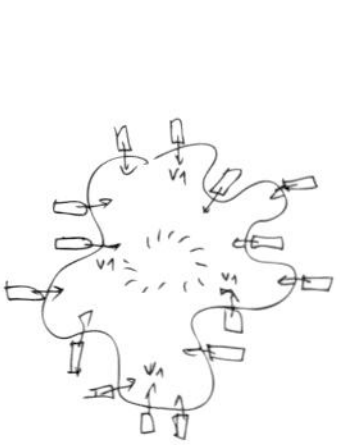

Sociópolis was presented at the Valencia Bienniale in 2003, as a project in which 13 international architecture firms took part. The project put forward a model of new urban development in which housing and multifunctional amenities were integrated in an agricultural environment, a continuation and updating of the model constituted by the Mediterranean hortulus.

Following the presentation of the project it was decided to construct a first neighbourhood of 3,000 homes in the La Torre district to the south of the city of Valencia, on a 350,000 m^2 site on the banks of the new course of the diverted River Turia; the same principles would be followed, but on a larger scale.

In this project the urban transformation is guided by a commitment to ensuring the maximum protection for the existing huerta (one of the traditional agricultural zones surrounding the city of Valencia) irrigated with waters from the River Turia by way of channels originally dug by the Arabs some 800 years ago. The new urban development reinforces the protection of the landscape and the environment while at the same time fulfilling a much-needed social function, making housing available at a controlled price to a great number of people.

Within the neighbourhood has four well-conserved historic farmhouses, and around these will be the focal points for 'urban farm' zones cared for by the local residents.

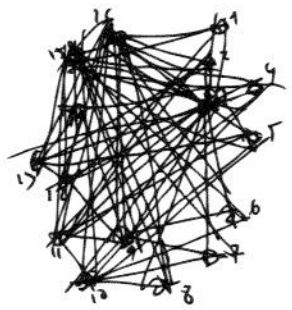

Emergence
/35

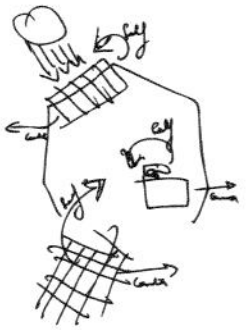

Self-sufficiency
/36

Sociopolis is essentially based on two premises: the first is that the question of habitability cannot be resolved simply by building homes, but must be addressed simultaneously at various scales, from the residential cell to the city; the second is that urbanity is a phenomenon that can have multiple formalizations, and that there is a need today to reformulate its principles in response to the need for interaction between the urban and the rural in order to create new habitable landscapes.

The idea of 'urbanity' is sometimes confused with the urban form with which the European city has taken shape. However, globalization has brought us into contact with diverse formalizations of the urban phenomenon in different parts of the world in which we can recognize social interaction, functional hybridization, compactness and diversity, without these adopting the form of the compact city familiar in the West.

Urbanism is a discipline founded in the 19th century which studies how people occupy the territory. According to the discipline's original principles, cities develop through the laying out of a rational system of roads and buildings, usually superimposed on agricultural territory, that allows human life to be organized around it. This kind of occupation of the territory, as it took place in the industrial era (subsequently reformulated on the basis of motorways and isolated construction) included the precise definition of the volumetries buildings were required to conform to.

In contrast to an urbanism of the peripheries we now propose an interactive, non-linear urbanism capable of interacting with its environment on an appropriate scale, in which the analysis of the functional and environmental conditions of the site serves to develop ad hoc responses. We need to start from global strategies of urban growth and development and formalize these in each case according to the specific conditions of the place. The basic structure of cities and territory is already made. The essential thing now is to define the places of encounter between the natural and the artificial. (It is probably also the time to establish new settlements in the territory that avoid expanding the periphery of an unstructured city.)

Sociopolis promotes urbanity without a traditional urban form. It foments social relations, hybridization, interaction, functional mixicity and the creation of green zones and amenities while proposing the construction of an open interface between the city and the huerta, the irrigated agricultural land outside Valencia. Part of the tension that supports the huerta is due to the 'red line' that delineates what is city and what is country. Sociopolis proposes to create an urban space that will act as a pre-park to an open metropolitan space which should include a considerable part of the huerta.

To this end it avoids proposing an abstract layout that would extend the poor adjacent urban structure, and instead bases its development on the conservation of most of the agricultural structure (and its associated historic irrigation channels) in the allocated sector through the implantation of circuits that are specialized according to their speed.

The neighbourhood will also promote social interaction and a sense of community by means of sports facilities such as a soccer pitch, an athletics circuit, games areas and a skating rink.

All of the proposed buildings are oriented toward the central landscaped zone, which has a surface area of 120,000 m^2, with direct access from the peripheral traffic circuit running round the complex.

In addition to residential blocks and towers the neighbourhood will have amenity buildings accommodating a hybrid programme, around which the public life of the neighbourhood will be organized. The public buildings will have rental housing intended for young people under thirty and elderly people, and at the same time all of the buildings will fulfil their public vocation by means of programmes that encourage social relations, such as an arts centre, a kindergarten, a sports zone, a social centre, a youth centre and studios for artists.

The architects participating in the project include Vicente Guallart, Abalos & Herreros, Manuel Gausa, Eduardo Arroyo, José María Torres Nadal, Sogo Arquitectos, Willy Muller, Antonio Lleyda / Eduardo de la Peña, Toyo Ito, MVRDV, Greg Lynn FORM, Duncan Lewis, José Luis Mateo, Kim Young-Joon, JM Lin, Jose Maria Lozano and Maria Colomer.

Valencia 2007

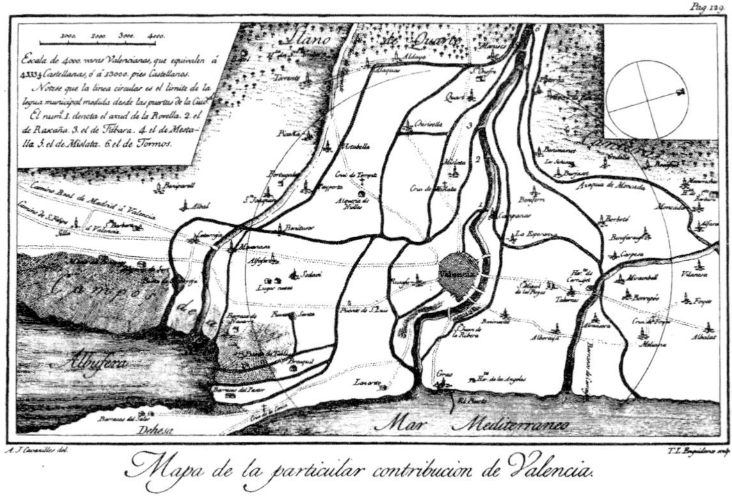

GEOGRAPHY

The founding of the city on the River Turia

GEOMETRY

System of eight irrigation channels watering the entire territory

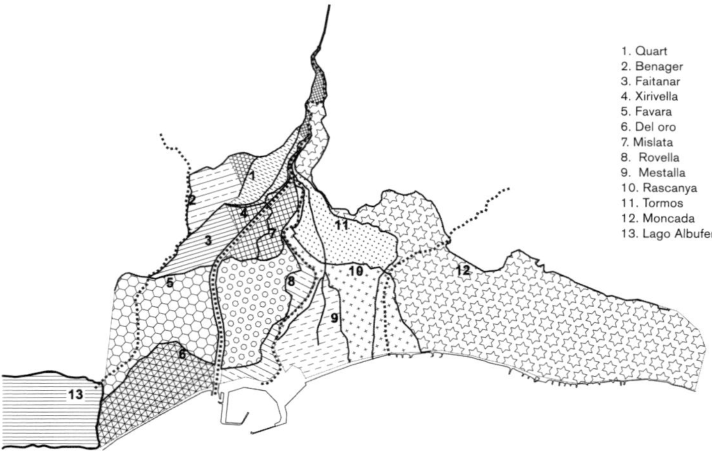

1. Quart
2. Benager
3. Faitanar
4. Xirivella
5. Favara
6. Del oro
7. Mislata
8. Rovella
9. Mestalla
10. Rascanya
11. Tormos
12. Moncada
13. Lago Albufera

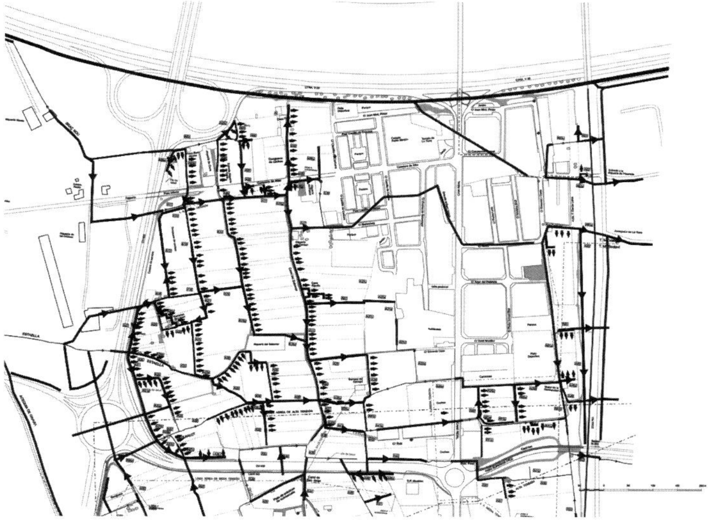

LOGIC

Network of irrigation channels as a basic system of urban development

STRUCTURE

Proposed circulation structure for the sector, at different speeds

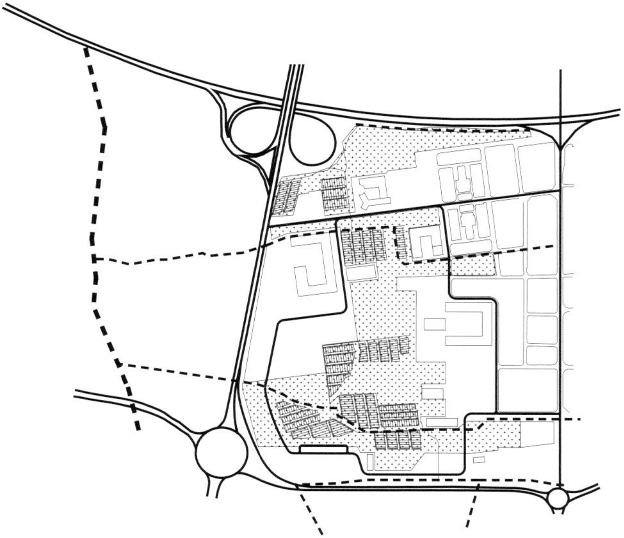

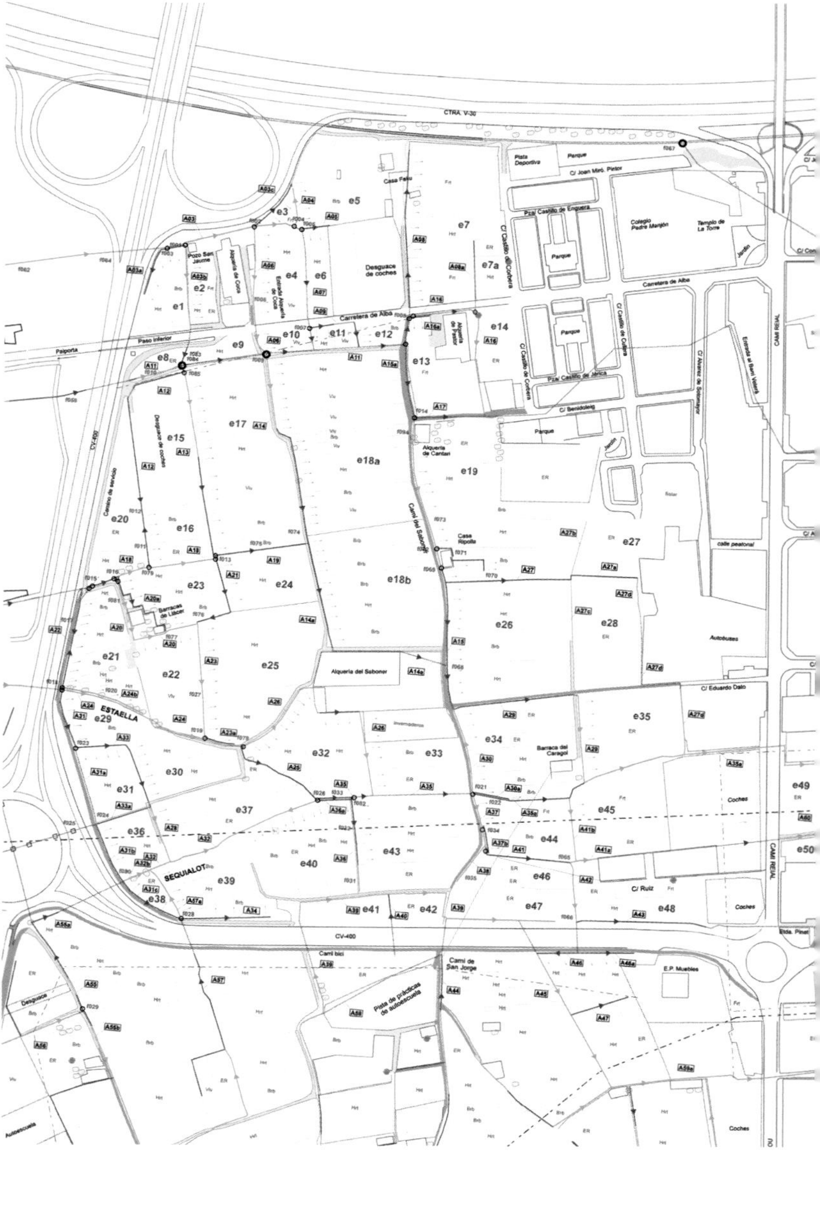
CTRA. V-30
Parque
Pista Deportiva
C/ Joan Miró, Pintor
Casa Felíu
Pza/ Castillo de Enguera
Colegio Padre Manjón
Templo de La Torre
Jardín
C/ Castillo de Corbera
Parque
Desguace de coches
Pozo Sant Jaume
Alquería de Coca
Entrada Alquería de Coca
Carretera de Alba
Paso inferior
Palporta
Alquería de Pastor
C/ Castillo de Cofera
Pza/ Castillo de Jérica
C/ Alvarez de Sotomayor
Entrada al Barri Velard
CAMI REIAL
C/ Benidoleig
Parque
Alquería de Cantarí
Desguace de coches
Centro de servicio
CV-400
Camí del Saboner
Casa Ripollà
calle peatonal
Barracas de Llàcer
Autobuses
Alquería del Saboner
C/ Eduardo Dato
ESTAELLA
Invernadero
Barraca del Caragol
Coches
SEQUIALOT
C/ Ruiz
CV-400
Camí bici
Camí de San Jorge
E.P. Muebles
Desguace
Pista de prácticas de autoescuela
Autoescuela
Coches
e1
e2
e3
e4
e5
e6
e7
e7a
e8
e9
e10
e11
e12
e13
e14
e15
e16
e17
e18a
e18b
e19
e20
e21
e22
e23
e24
e25
e26
e27
e28
e29
e30
e31
e32
e33
e34
e35
e36
e37
e38
e39
e40
e41
e42
e43
e44
e45
e46
e47
e48
e49
e50

f033

Acequia A35 (Estaella, tras la confluencia con el Seuialot). A la derecha se observa A36a, un pequeño regador cubierto.

f034

Acequias A37 (derecha) y A37b (regador).

f041

Partidor al E de la vía de tren, en el Horno de Alcedo.

f042

Partidor bajo trapa en A61a (Braç Nou), para desvío de agua a A61.

f035

a

f036

Acequia continuación deA61a, junto alAssagador de LaTorre.

f043

Acequia de Favara. Partidor junto al nuevo cauce del Turia.

f044

Acequia de Favara. Partidor inicio del Braç Nou.

f037

Acequia continuación de A62a, junto a la Entrada de la Alquería de Pioxarrota.

f038

Acequia continuación de A52. Junto al paso elevado a Sedaví.

f045

Acequia continuación de A48, en la zona del Horno de Alcedo, al otro lado de la vía del tren

f046

Acequia continuación de A61, en la zona del Horno de Alcedo, al otro lado de la vía del tren

f039

Acequia y partidor al E de la vía de tren, en el Horno de Alcedo.

f040

Acequias y partidor al E de la vía de tren, en el Horno de Alcedo.

f047

Acequia de Favara. Partidor inicio del Sequialot.

f048

Acequia de Estaella. Partidor que divide el agua hacia A18 (brazo secundario, izquierda), A24 (brazo principal, centro) y un regador, al W de la CV-400.

f017

Acequia A22. Obsérvese el uso de las pequeñas compuertas manuales para el riego de solamente algunas parcelas de la escala.

f018

Entrada de la acequia de Estaella (A24) en la zona de actuación. Confluencia de A24 (izquierda, bajo losa) con A22 (arriba), A31 (abajo, oculta bajo losa) y A24b (derecha). El partidor en A24-A24b permite desviar el agua hacia A22 y A31. Se observa entre la vegetación la boquerea de entrada de A24b, que toma agua desde A22.

f025

a

f026

Confluencia de Estaella (A25, continua como A35) y el Sequialot (A32). La parada en A25 permite desviar el agua hacia A32 para regar las parcelas de "e40"ambién permite que tome agua A36a, un pequeño regador cubierto que riega la parcela más oriental de "e40".

f019

Confluencia de A23 (ramal que llega por la izquierda, de fábrica) y A24 (Estaella, de tierra, derecha). A23 vierte en este punto los sobrantes a A24. Para regar "e25" desde A23 se hace parada a la llegada a A24 (en la foto, abierta). El pequeño regador de fábrica paralelo a Estaella (A23a) sirve para regar el extremo sur de "e25". La boquera en extremo inferior izquierda de la imagen corresponde al drenaje de "e37".

f020

Pequeño regador (A24b) de tierra, de construcción muy rudimentaria, para regar el extremo Sur de "e21".

f027

Acequia A23. Obsérvese la existencia de varias paradas, en la imagen abiertas, para el riego de determinadas parcelas (de "e25") a lo largo del regador

f028

Confluencia entre A57 (izquierda), A31 c (arriba), A57a (derecha) y A34 (abajo). La parada realizada al principio de A57a (abierta en la imagen) permite que el agua procedente de A57 o de A31c se desvíe hacia A34.

f021

Confluencia de A35 (derecha, emerege bajo camino del Saboner), A35a (izquierda centro, continuación de A35), A30 (abajo), A37 (arriba) y A30a (regador cubierto, izquierda, paralelo a A35a). Se pueden realizar diferentes paradas para desviar el agua parcial o totalmente a las distintas acequias.

f022

Como f021, con otro punto de vista, confluencia de A35 (frente, emerege bajo camino del Saboner), A35a (abajo, continuación de A35), A30 (derecha), A37 (izquierda) y A30a (regador cubierto, derecha, paralelo a A35a).

f029

La acequia A56 (izquierda, emerge bajo el camino), brazo que toma agua de la Acequia de Favara (f047), se divide aquí en A55 (arriba derecha) y A55a (abajo izquierda). La parada para desciar en uno u otro sentido se realiza en la confluencia.

f030

Acequia A38, parcialmente derruida. Junto a la valla discurre A41.

f023

Confluencia de A31 (derecha), A33 (abajo) y A31a (izquierda, cubierta). En la foto está montada la parada para desviar el agua que viene de A31 hacia A33.

f024

Confluencia de A31a (salida tubo, a la derecha), A33a (derecha), A31b (izquierda) y una tubería procedente de la rotonda de la CV-400.

f031

Acequia A36. Obsérvese como el último tramo está en desuso y parcialmente derruido.

f032

Acequia A36. Obsérvese la existencia de pequeñas compuertas manuales para realizar el riego de solamente algunas parcelas a lo largo del regador

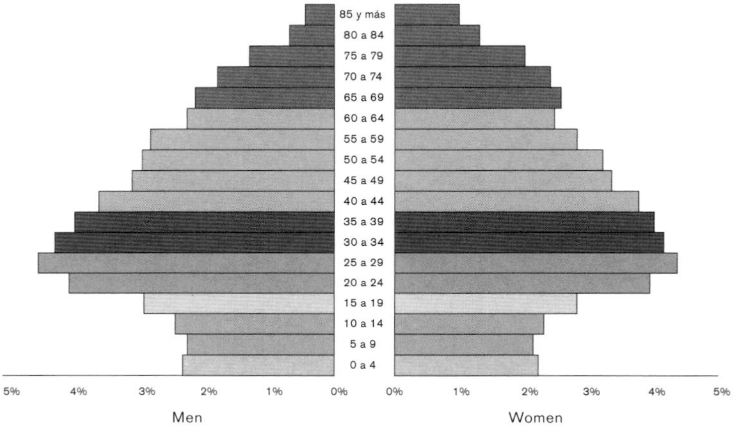

GEOGRAPHY

The population mushroom

GEOMETRY

Residential units reflecting the new types of family unit

Generational composition of spanish houses

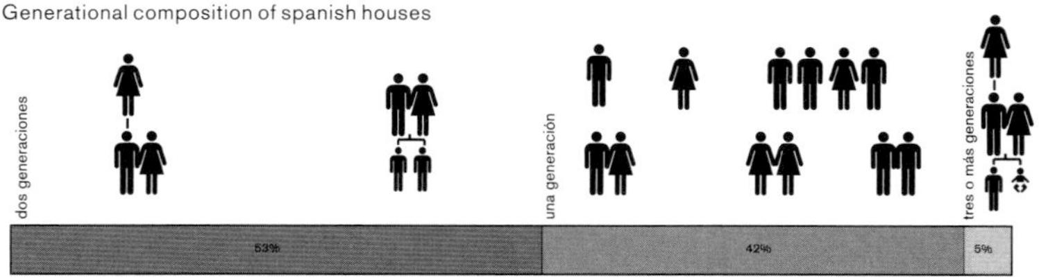

Spanish housing typology

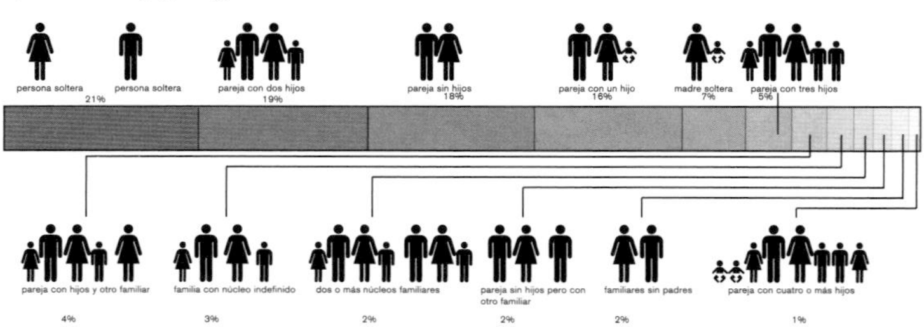

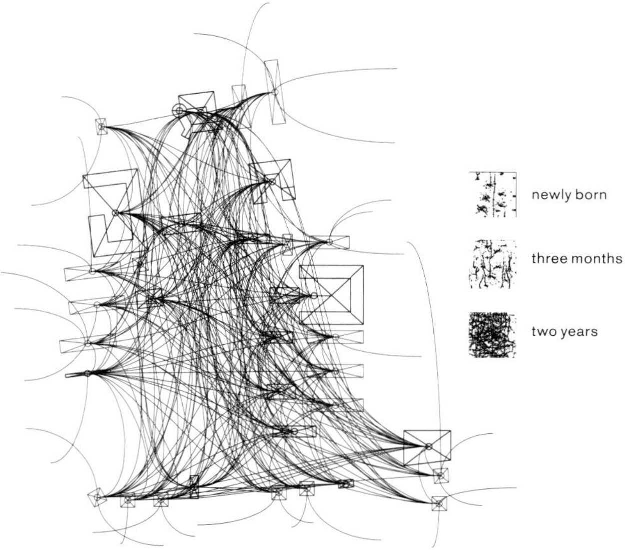

LOGIC

An urban synapse, the interaction of housing and amenities

STRUCTURE

Amenities grouped around the road circuit

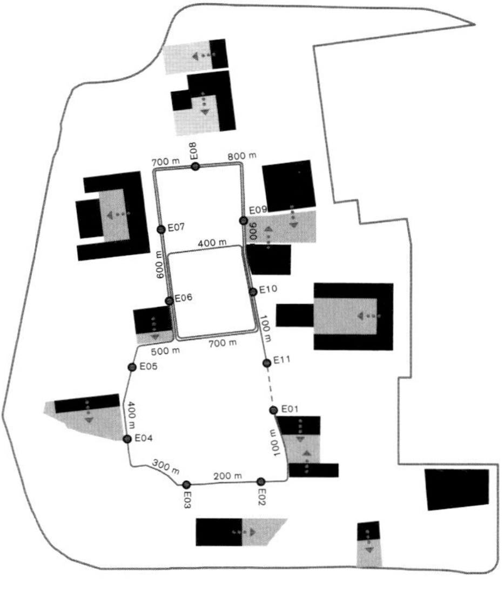

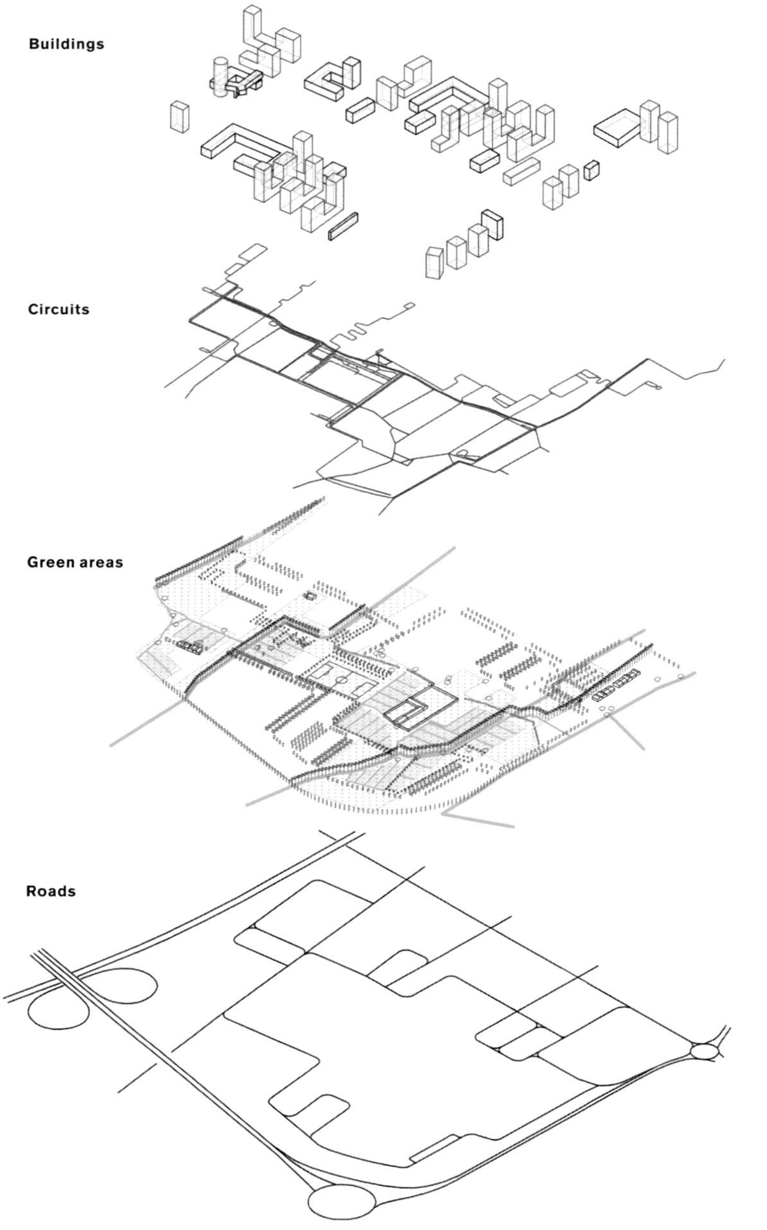
Buildings
Circuits
Green areas
Roads

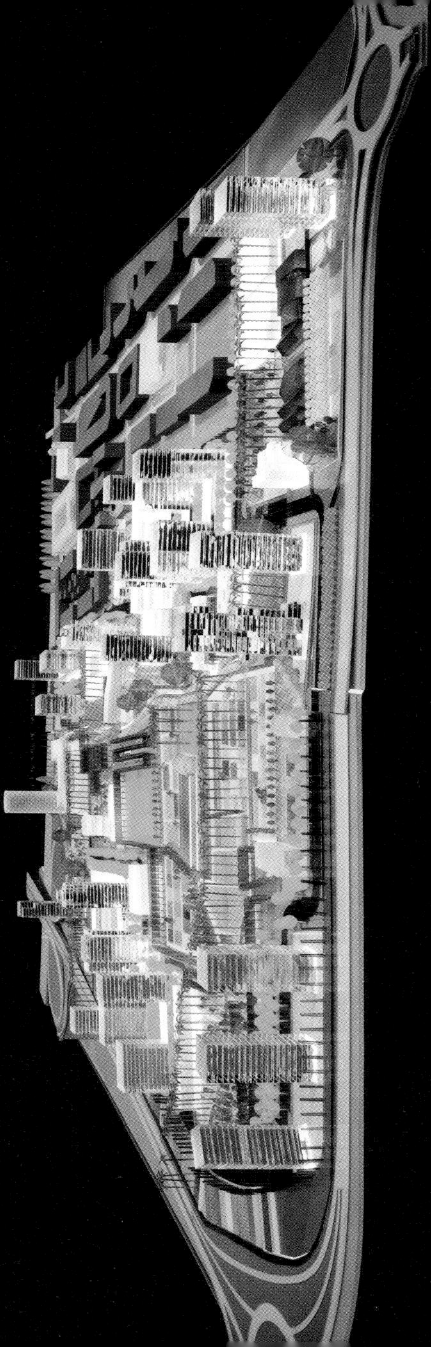

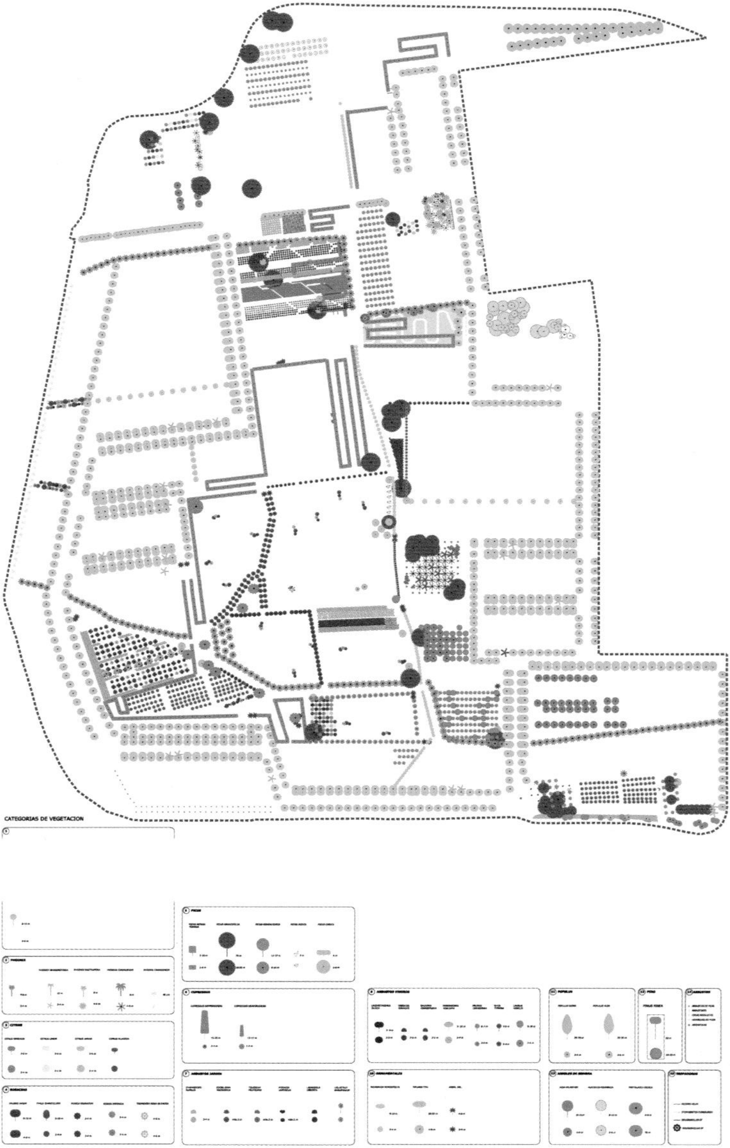
CATEGORIAS DE VEGETACION

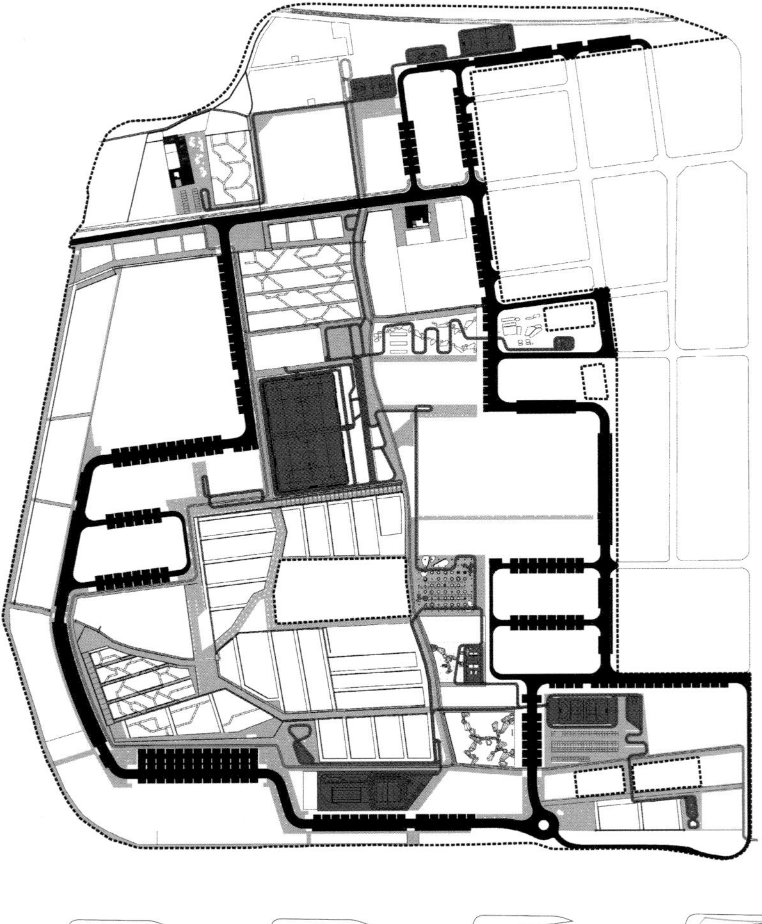

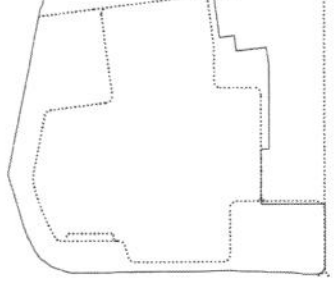

Cars

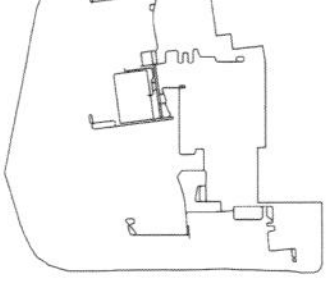

Sports

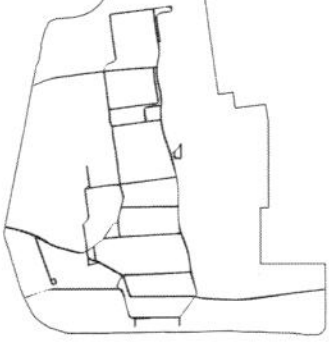

Pedestrians

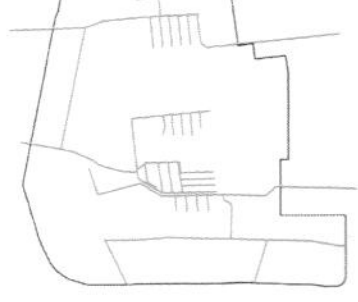

Irrigation

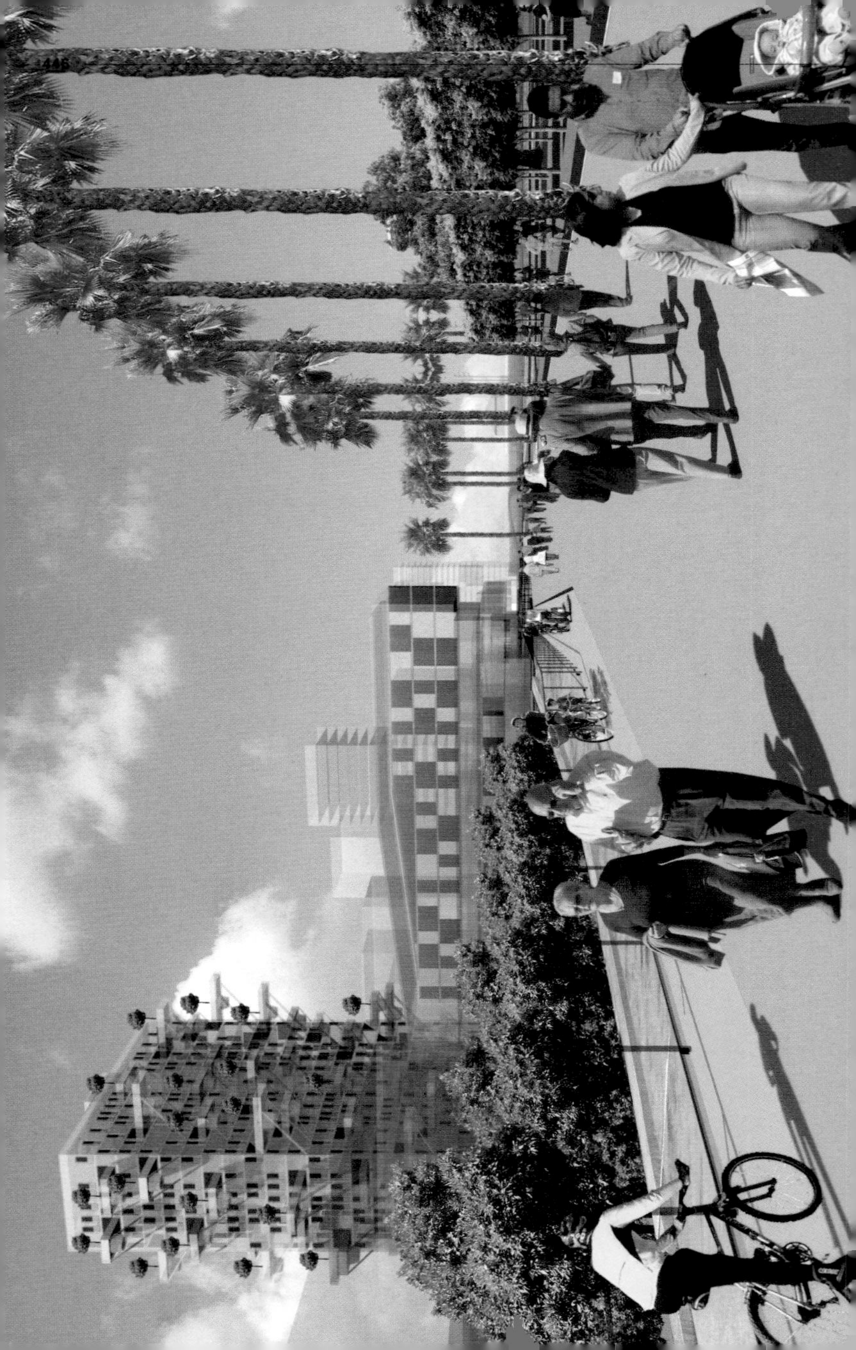

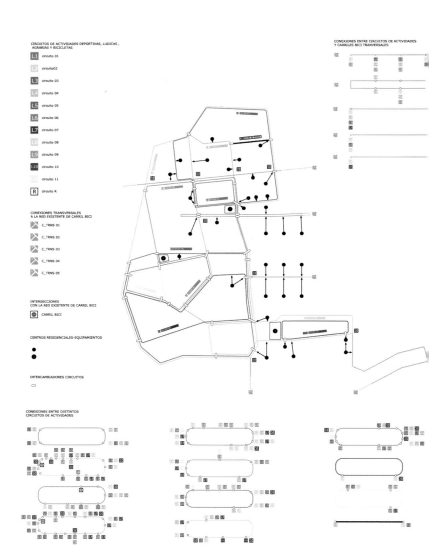

CIRCUITOS DE ACTIVIDADES DEPORTIVAS, LUDICAS , AGRARIAS Y BICICLETAS

L1 circuito 01

L2 circuito02

L3 circuito 03

L4 circuito 04

L5 circuito 05

L6 circuito 06

L7 circuito 07

L8 circuito 08

L9 circuito 09

L10 circuito 10

L11 circuito 11

R circuito R

CONEXIONES TRANSVERSALES A LA RED EXISTENTE DE CARRIL BICI

C_TRNS 01

C_TRNS 02

C_TRNS 03

C_TRNS 04

C_TRNS 05

INTERSECCIONES CON LA RED EXISTENTE DE CARRIL BICI

CARRIL BICI

CENTROS RESIDENCIALES-EQUIPAMIENTOS

INTERCAMBIADORES CIRCUITOS

CONEXIONES ENTRE CIRCUITOS DE ACTIVIDADES Y CARRILES BICI TRANVERSALES

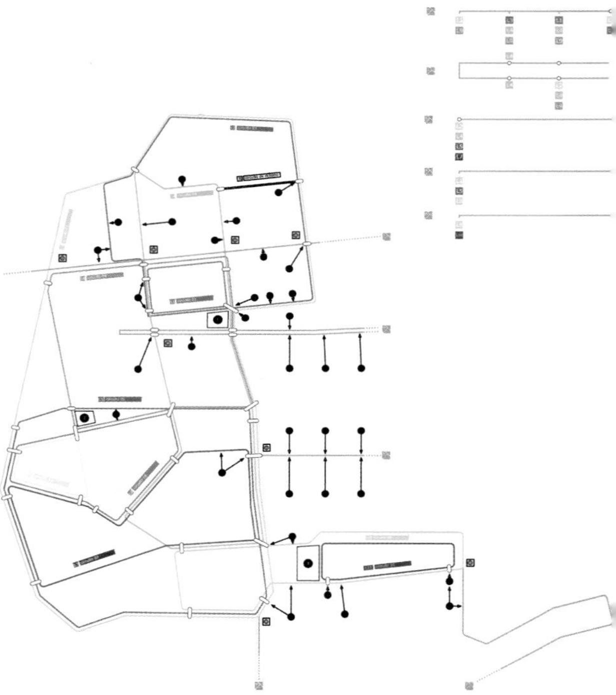

CONEXIONES ENTRE DISTINTOS CIRCUITOS DE ACTIVIDADES

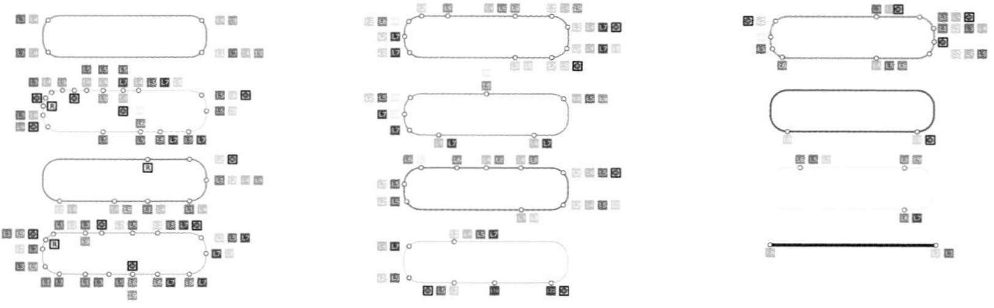

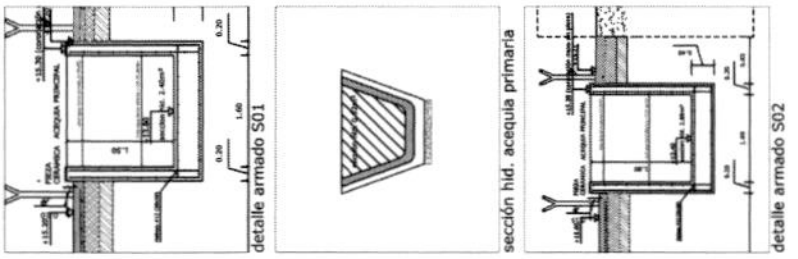
detalle armado S01
sección hid. acequia primaria
detalle armado S02

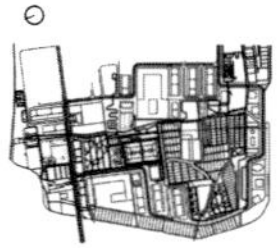

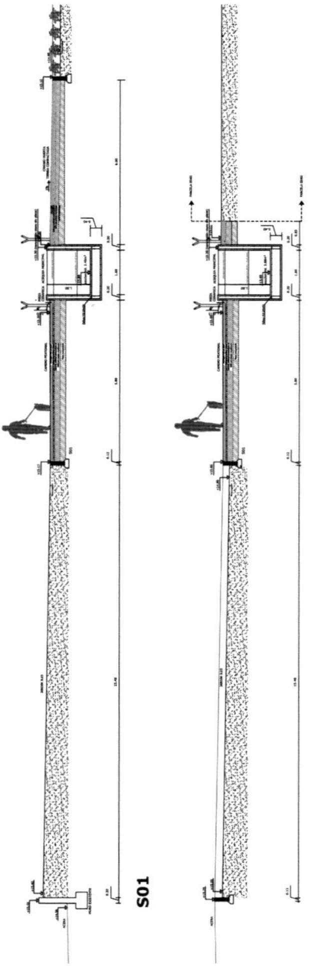

S01

S02

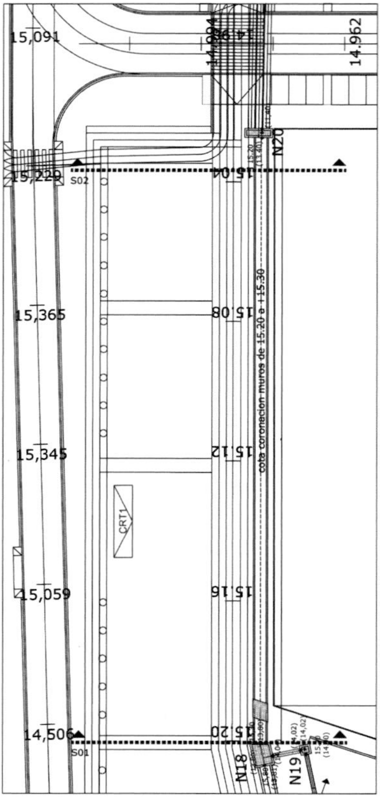
15,091
14,994
14,962
15,229
S02
15,04
N20
15,365
15,08
cota coronacion muros de 15.20 a +15.30
15,345
15,12
CRT1
15,059
15,16
14,506
S01
15,20
N18
N19

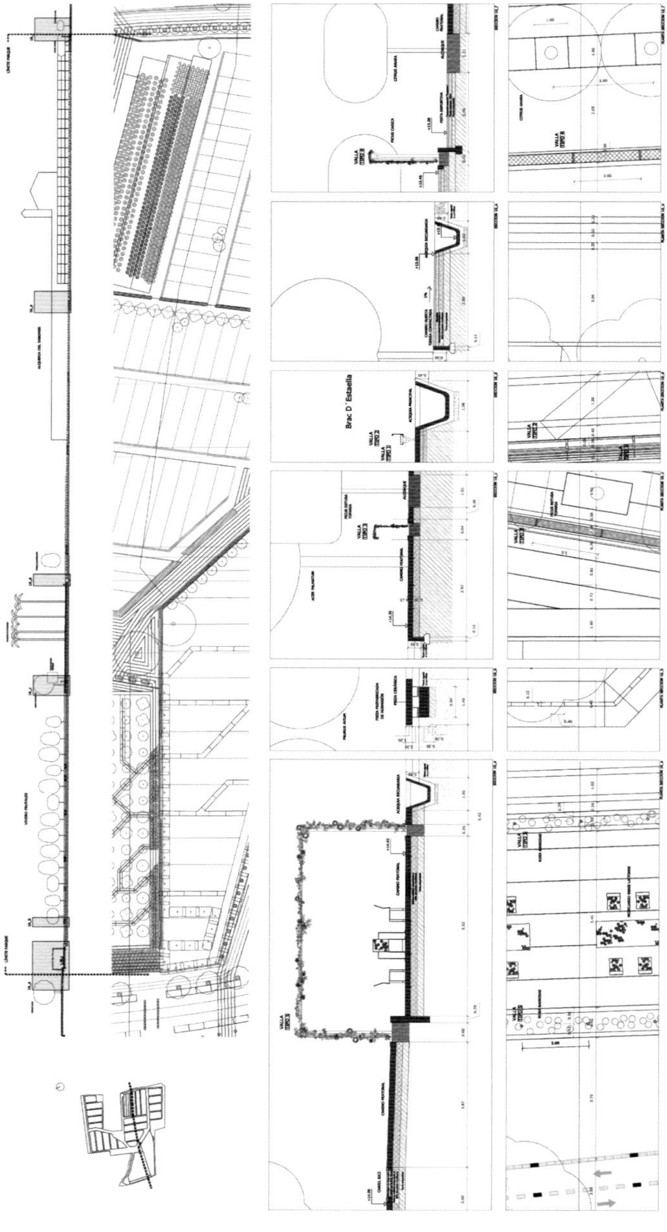
Brac D' Estella

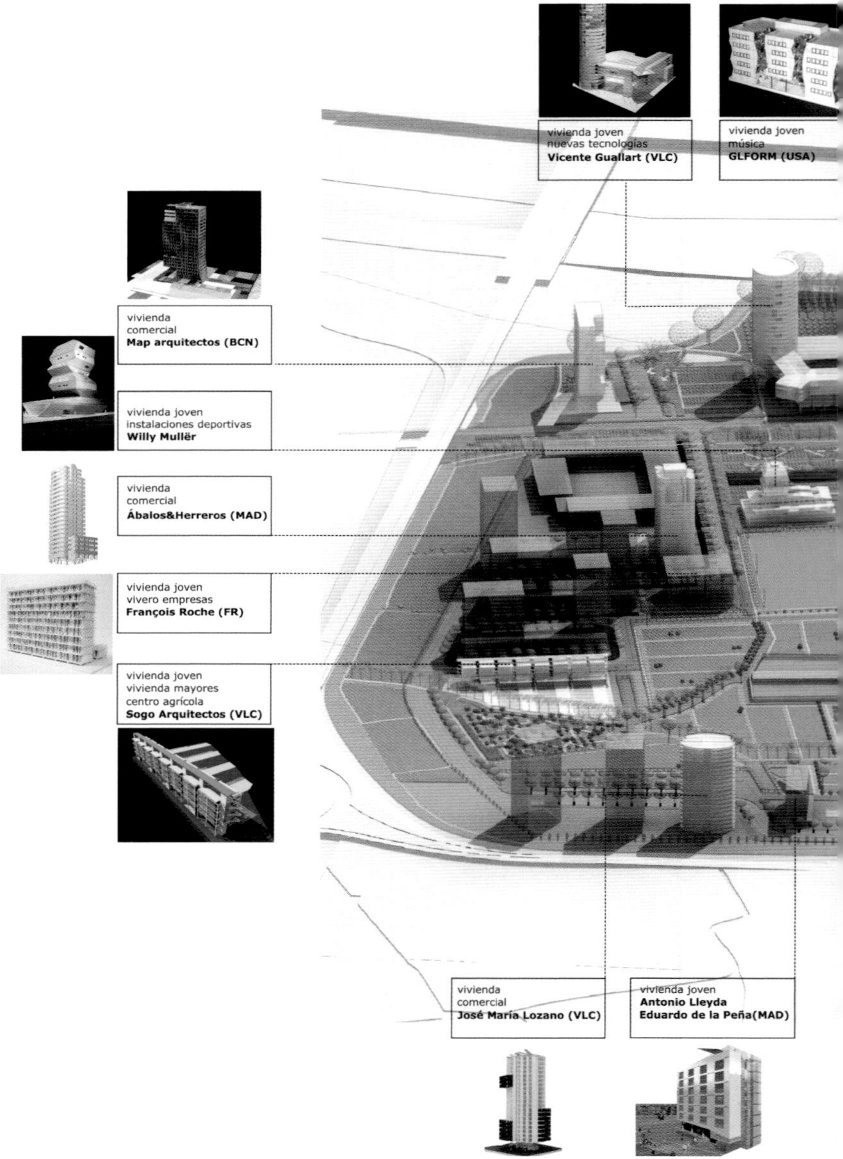
vivienda joven
nuevas tecnologías
Vicente Guallart (VLC)
vivienda joven
música
GLFORM (USA)
vivienda
comercial
Map arquitectos (BCN)
vivienda joven
instalaciones deportivas
Willy Mullër
vivienda
comercial
Ábalos&Herreros (MAD)
vivienda joven
vivero empresas
François Roche (FR)
vivienda joven
vivienda mayores
centro agrícola
Sogo Arquitectos (VLC)
vivienda
comercial
José María Lozano (VLC)
vivienda joven
Antonio Lleyda
Eduardo de la Peña(MAD)

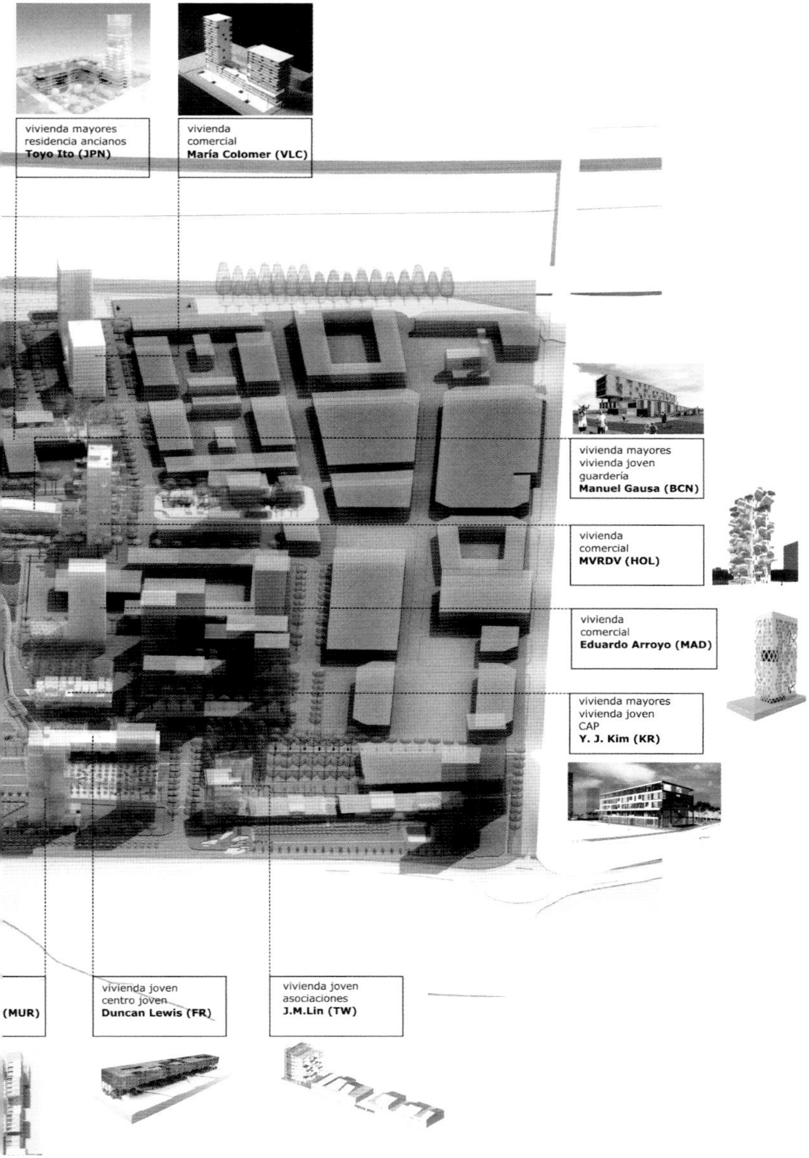
vivienda mayores
residencia ancianos
Toyo Ito (JPN)
vivienda
comercial
María Colomer (VLC)
vivienda mayores
vivienda joven
guardería
Manuel Gausa (BCN)
vivienda
comercial
MVRDV (HOL)
vivienda
comercial
Eduardo Arroyo (MAD)
vivienda mayores
vivienda joven
CAP
Y. J. Kim (KR)
(MUR)
vivienda joven
centro joven
Duncan Lewis (FR)
vivienda joven
asociaciones
J.M.Lin (TW)

Sharing Tower

Valencia. Spain. 2005—2011

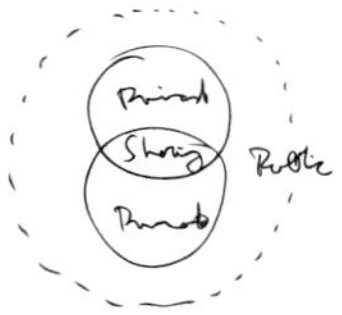

Sharing
/34

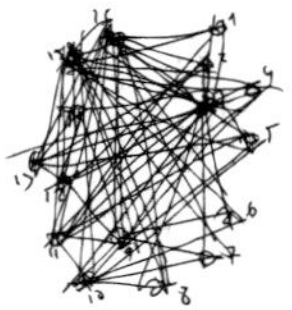

Emergence
/35

According to the Factor Four principle, we should be seeking to obtain twice the benefit with half the space, or with half the resources, in order to enhance the efficiency of our environment. This means that we need to construct more efficient homes and buildings that enable their occupants to share resources. The functions of the home—sleeping, washing, storing food, cooking, eating, washing clothes and relaxing—are organized around specific objects—bed, shower, fridge, cooker, table, washing machine, television. It is not logical for every small apartment to have all of the appliances required for these functions, which in many cases are in use only 10% of the time.

The alternative is to establish dynamic relations between apartments on the same floor, sharing spaces in groups of two, four or eight. This can allow a 25 m^2 apartment to have an effective area of 75 m^2. At the same time, the communal use of the space encourages social interaction.
The project area, on the boundary between agricultural land and the city, has an underground car park that serves as a speed interchanger between the urban city and the garden city proposed by Sociopolis: between an environment for driving around and the pedestrian city, between the fast city and the slow city.

The network society makes it possible to share resources so that people can do more with less. Between the public and the private space there is a shared space. The physical resources contained in the home should provide for the individual functions of the act of dwelling; each individual should have at least these resources in a minimum area of 25 m^2. If resources are shared by two, four or eight people, each of them will have a larger usable area at their disposal. Each person has the use of the sum of his or her individual space plus the collective space.

When it comes to sharing resources, there may be incompatibilities between certain activities because of different individuals' preferences in terms of how things look, sound and smell. In a sequence of different floors the sharing of resources can be organized according to the residents' compatibilities, with each floor functioning like a large house whose communal space is accessible from each personal space. The skin of the building is constructed like an X-ray of its internal functioning.

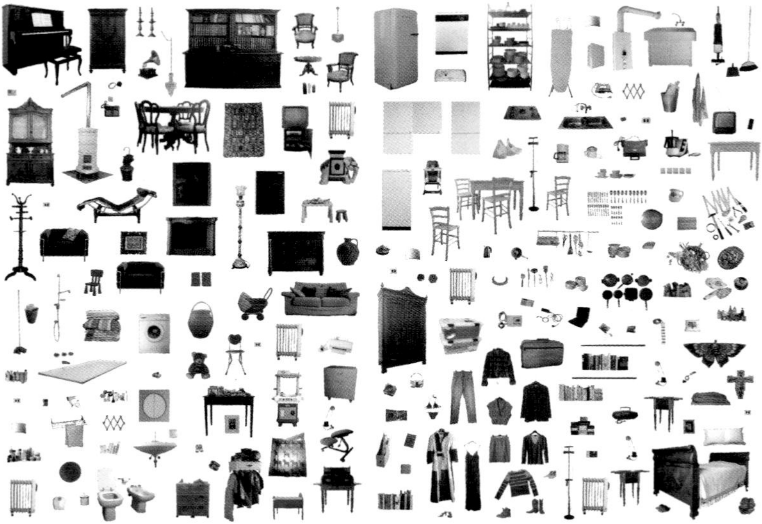

GEOGRAPHY

The objects in the home let people inhabit the space

GEOMETRY

Clusters of homes contain similar objects (and uses)

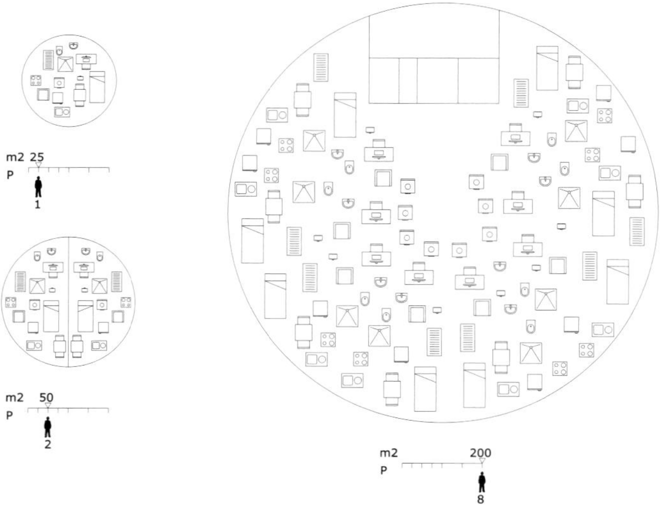

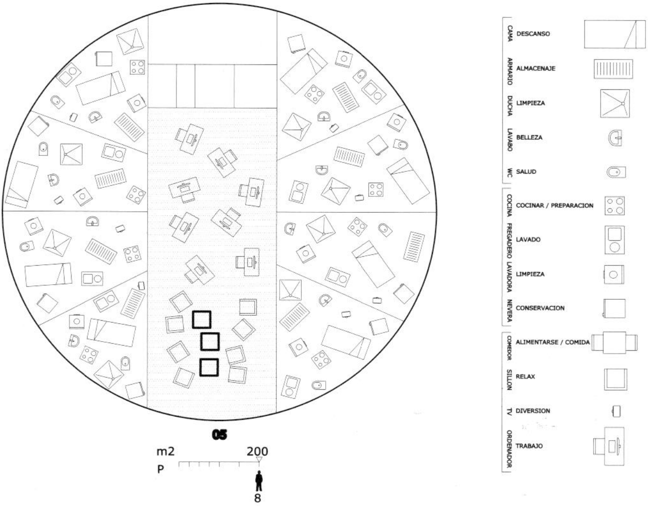

LOGIC

Shared spaces with the basic elements of habitability

STRUCTURE

Accumulation of configurations of shared macro-housing

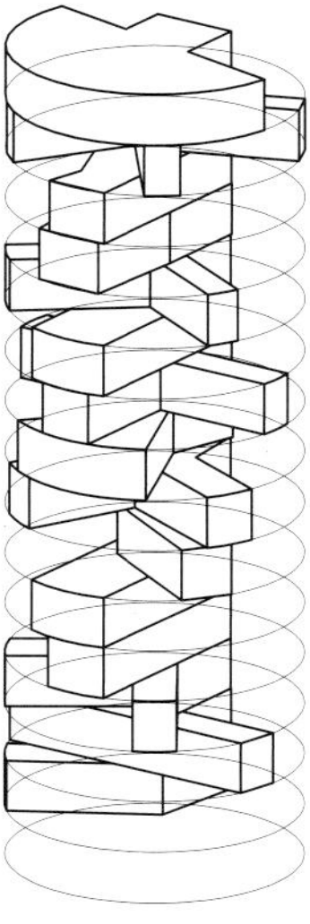

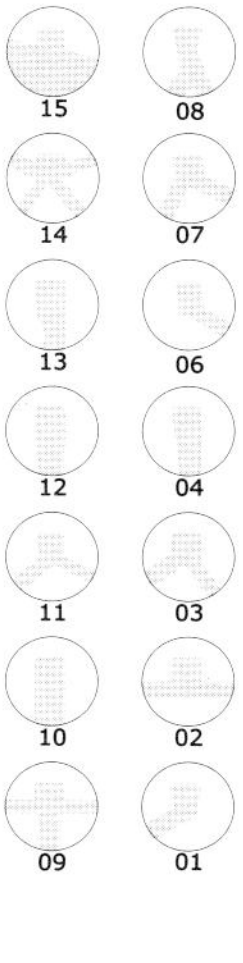

la sociedad en red
permite compartir recursos
para conseguir

"mas con menos"

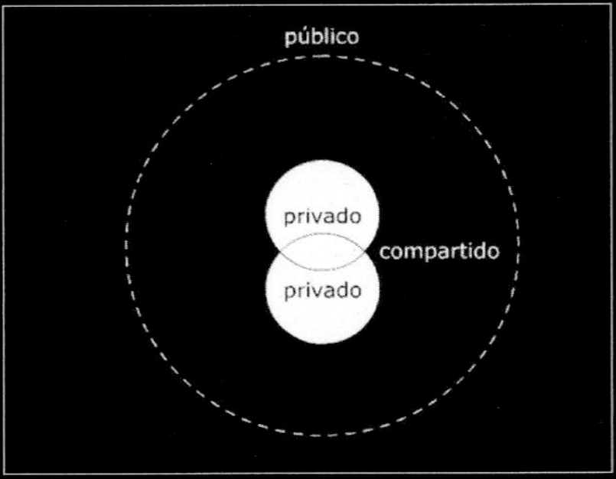

los recursos físicos que contiene un vivienda
permiten el desarrollo de funciones individuales
propias del hecho de habitar

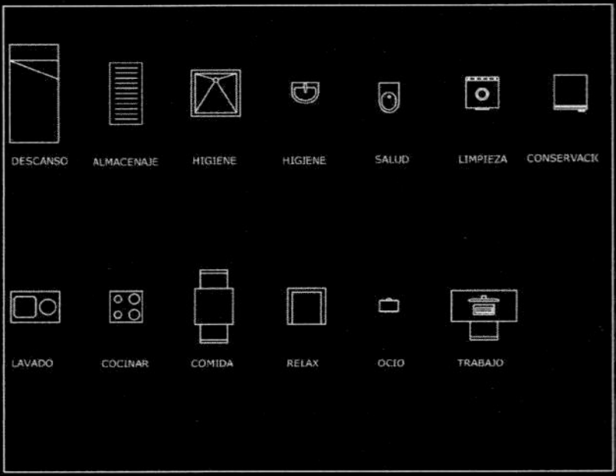

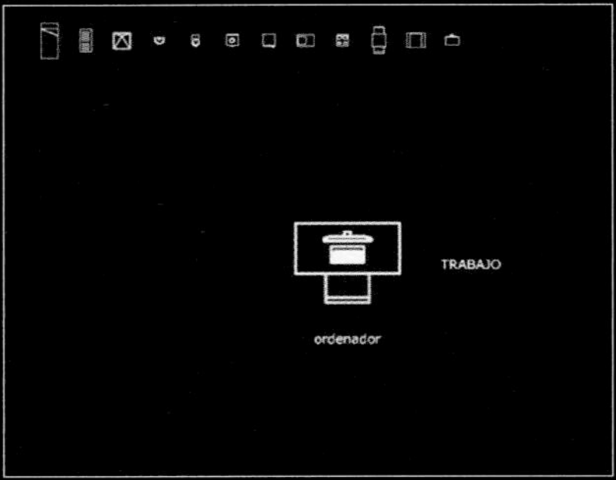

cada persona debería disponer al menos de estos recursos
en una superficie mínima de 25 m2

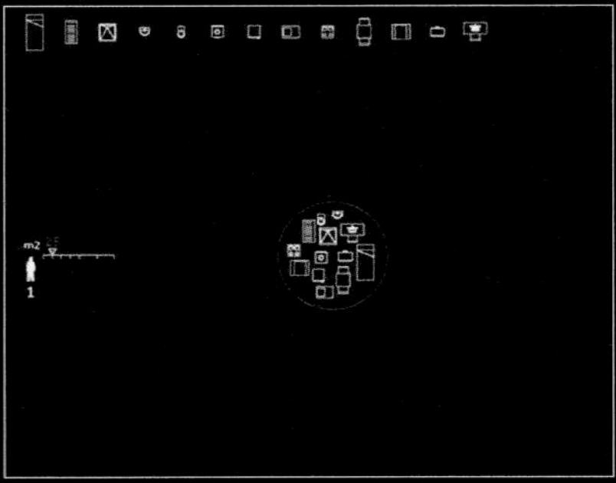

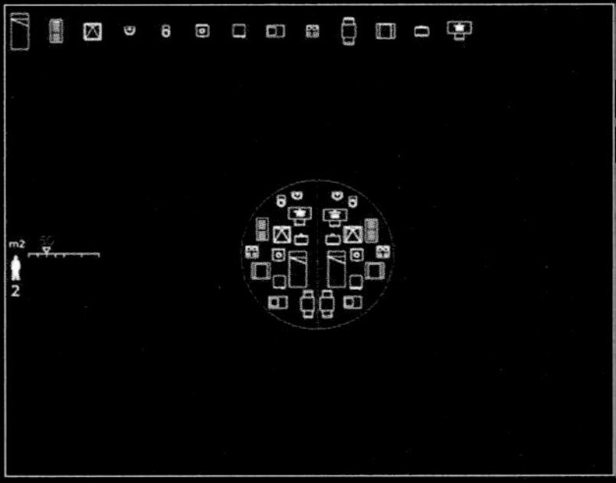

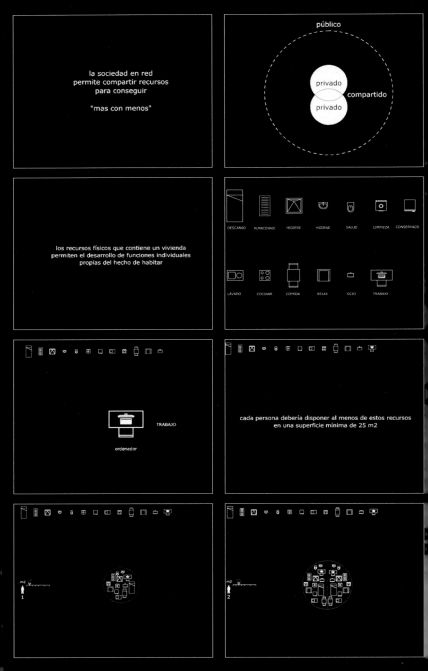

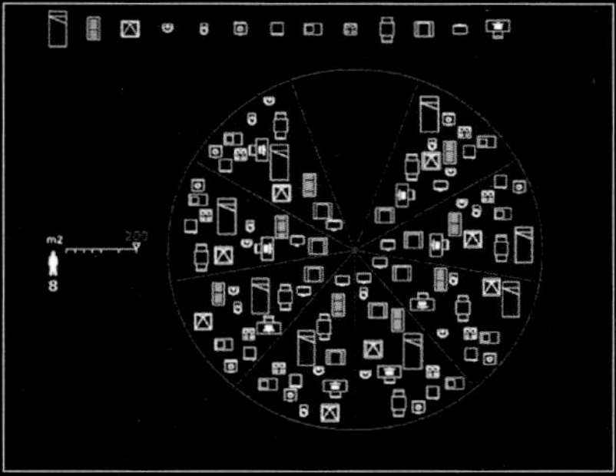

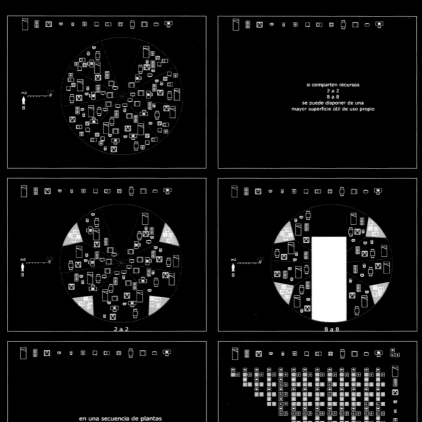

si comparten recursos
2 a 2
8 a 8
se puede disponer de una
mayor superficie útil de uso propio

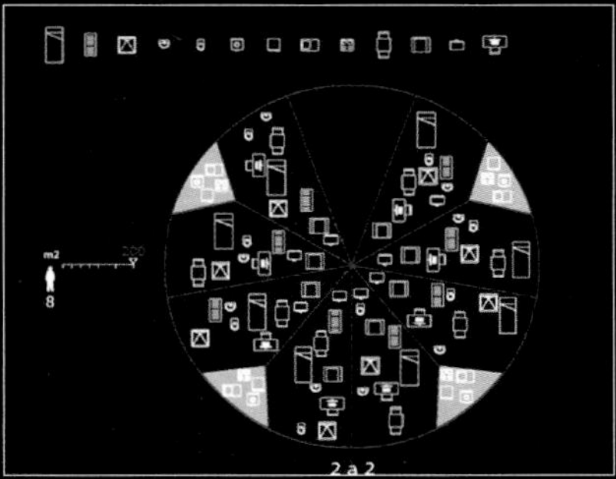

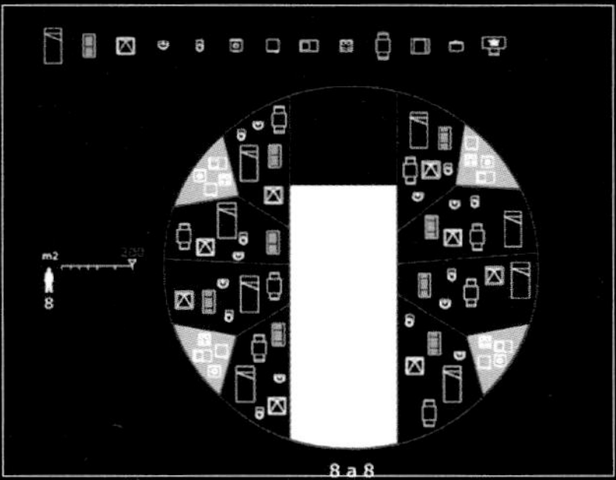

en una secuencia de plantas
se pueden definir diferentes recursos a compartir
que no produzcan incompatibilidades entre personas

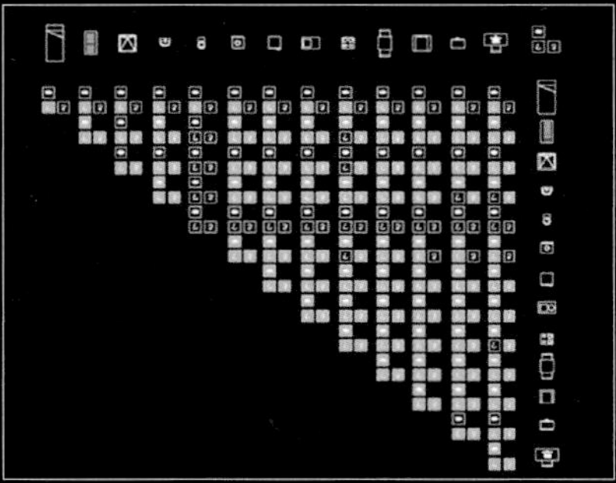

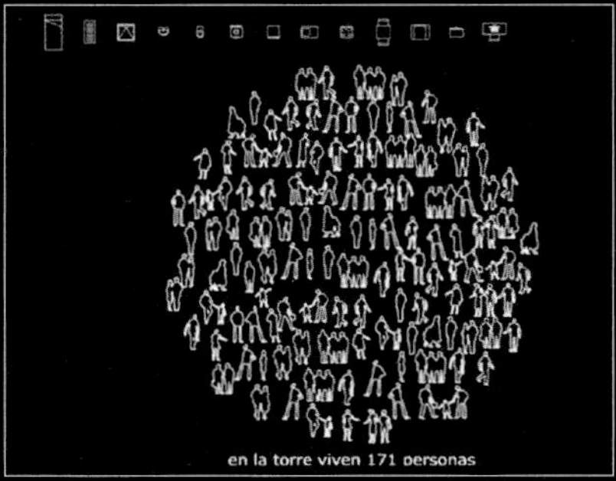

cada persona posee 15 m2
cada persona comparte 75 m2
cada persona disfruta 90 m2

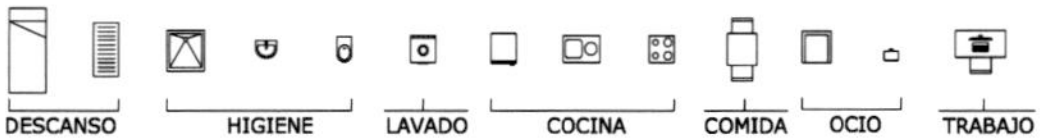
DESCANSO
HIGIENE
LAVADO
COCINA
COMIDA
OCIO
TRABAJO

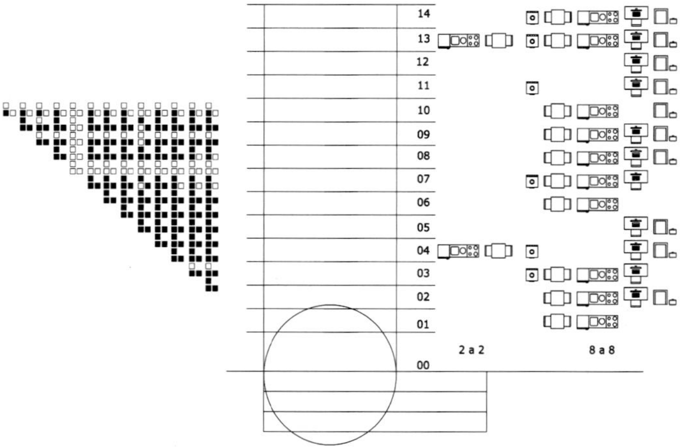
14
13
12
11
10
09
08
07
06
05
04
03
02
01
00
2 a 2
8 a 8

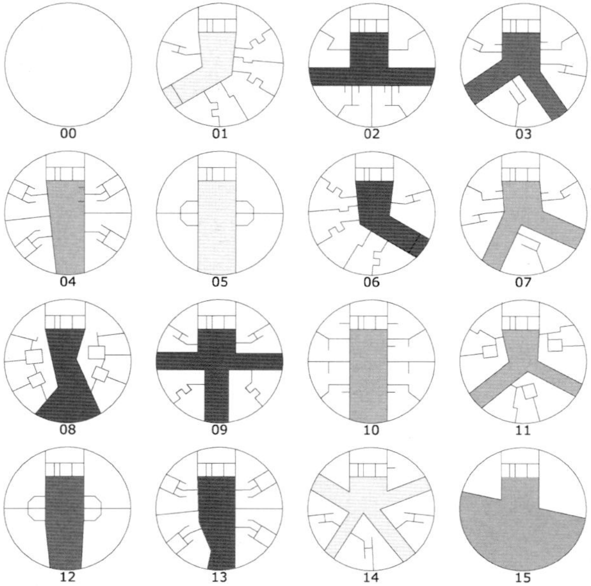
00
01
02
03
04
05
06
07
08
09
10
11
12
13
14
15

m2 255

P 12

1A	20.42m2
1B	19.84m2
1C	21.76m2
1D	27.80m2
1E	25.76m2
1F	16.15m2
1G	27.02m2
1H	23.55m2
COCINA +	
COMEDOR	52.02m2
TOTAL	255 m2

m2 255

P 14

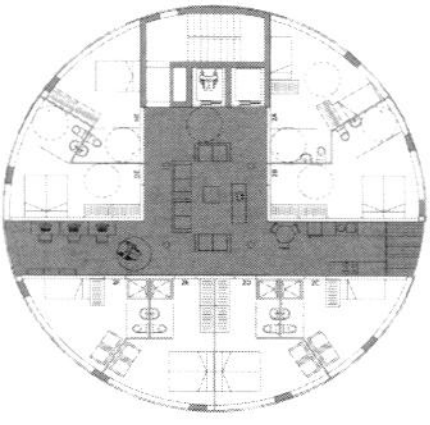

2A	21.25m2
2B	24.32m2
2C	17.08m2
2D	20.49m2
2E	20.40m2
2F	17.08m2
2G	24.32m2
2H	21.25m2
ESTAR + TV	
COCINA	
COMEDOR	
TRABAJO	71.26m2
TOTAL	255 m2

m2 255

P 12

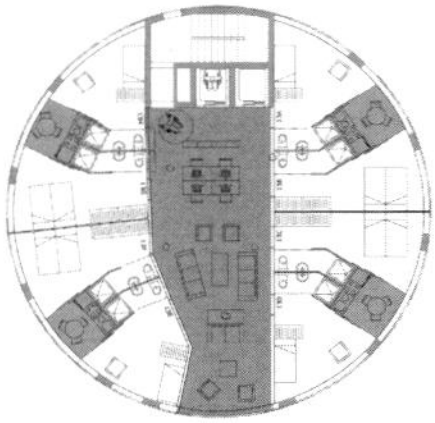

13A	29.85m2
13B	22.03m2
13C	22.03m2
13D	29.85m2
13E	20.65m2
13F	21.79m2
13G	21.3m2
13H	18.64m2
TRABAJO	
ESTAR	62.38m2
TOTAL	255 m2

m2 255

P 60

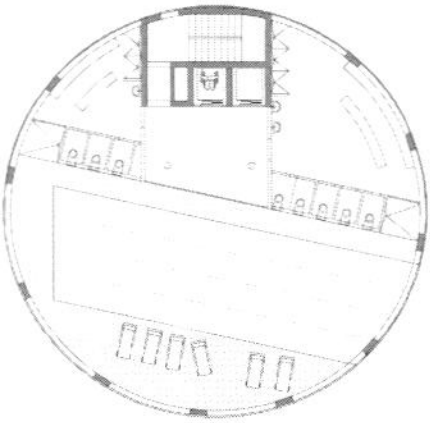

PISCINA	71.74m2
SOLARIUM	44.48m2
VESTUARIOS	44.07m2
ASEOS	13.60m2
ASEOS	17.26m2
ZONA COMÚN	21.05m2
TOTAL	255 m2

m2 255

P 14

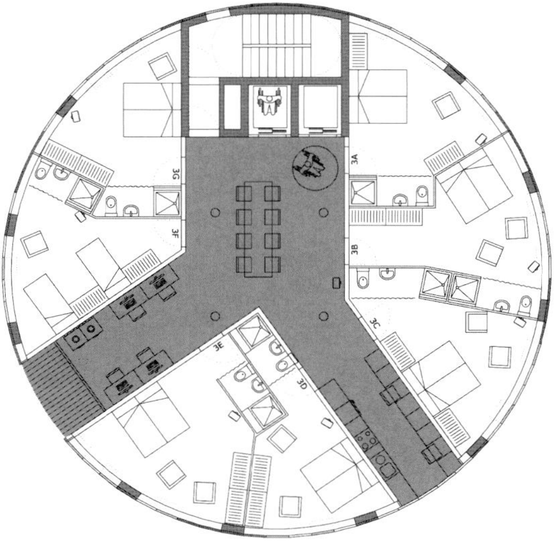

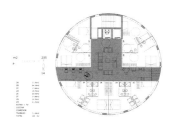

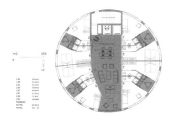

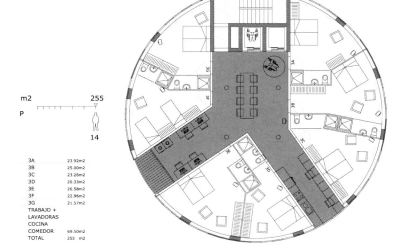

3A	23.92m2
3B	25.00m2
3C	23.26m2
3D	20.33m2
3E	26.58m2
3F	22.96m2
3G	21.57m2
TRABAJO +	
LAVADORAS	
COCINA	
COMEDOR	69.50m2
TOTAL	255 m2

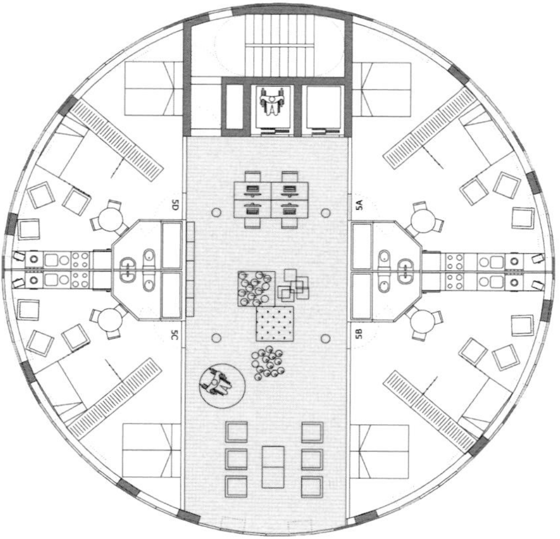

m2 255

P

12

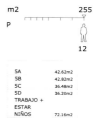

5A	42.62m2
5B	42.82m2
5C	36.48m2
5D	36.20m2
TRABAJO + ESTAR NIÑOS	72.16m2
TOTAL	255 m2

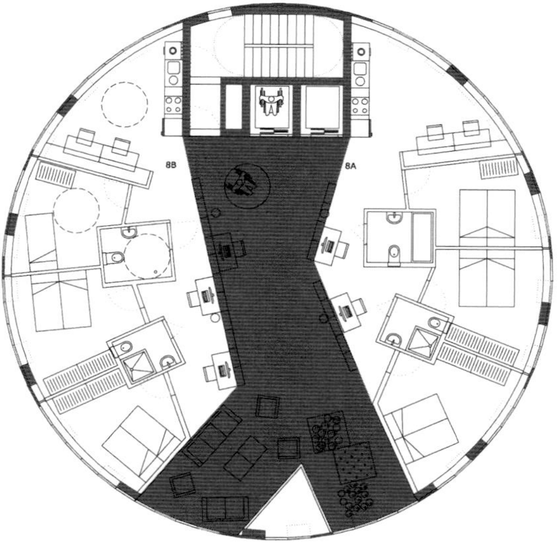

m2 255

P

11

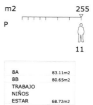

8A	83.11m2
8B	80.65m2
TRABAJO NIÑOS ESTAR	68.72m2
TOTAL	255 m2

m2 255

P 12

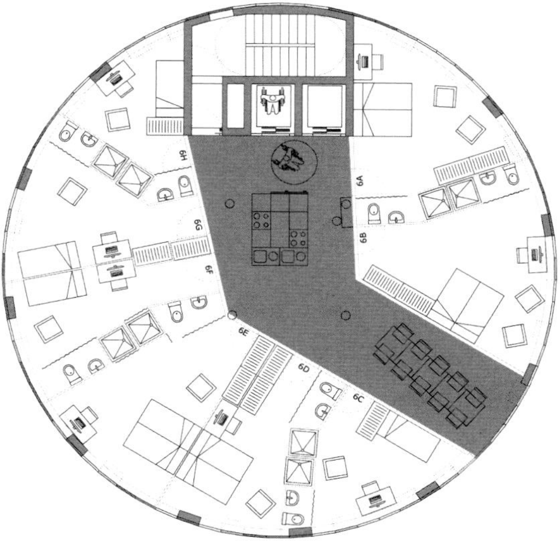

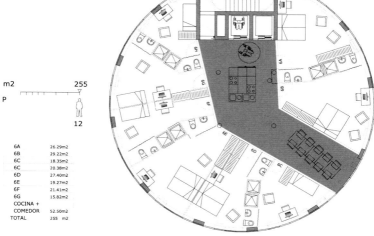

6A	26.29m2
6B	29.22m2
6C	18.35m2
6C	20.38m2
6D	27.40m2
6E	19.27m2
6F	21.41m2
6G	15.82m2
COCINA + COMEDOR	52.50m2
TOTAL	255 m2

m2 255

P 13

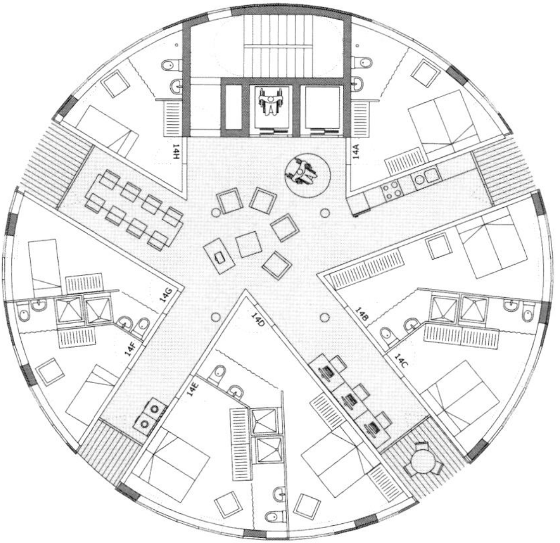

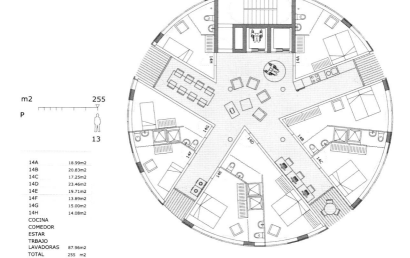

14A	18.99m2
14B	20.83m2
14C	17.25m2
14D	23.46m2
14E	19.71m2
14F	13.89m2
14G	15.00m2
14H	14.08m2
COCINA COMEDOR ESTAR TRBAJO LAVADORAS	87.96m2
TOTAL	255 m2

Sharing Tower 2005–

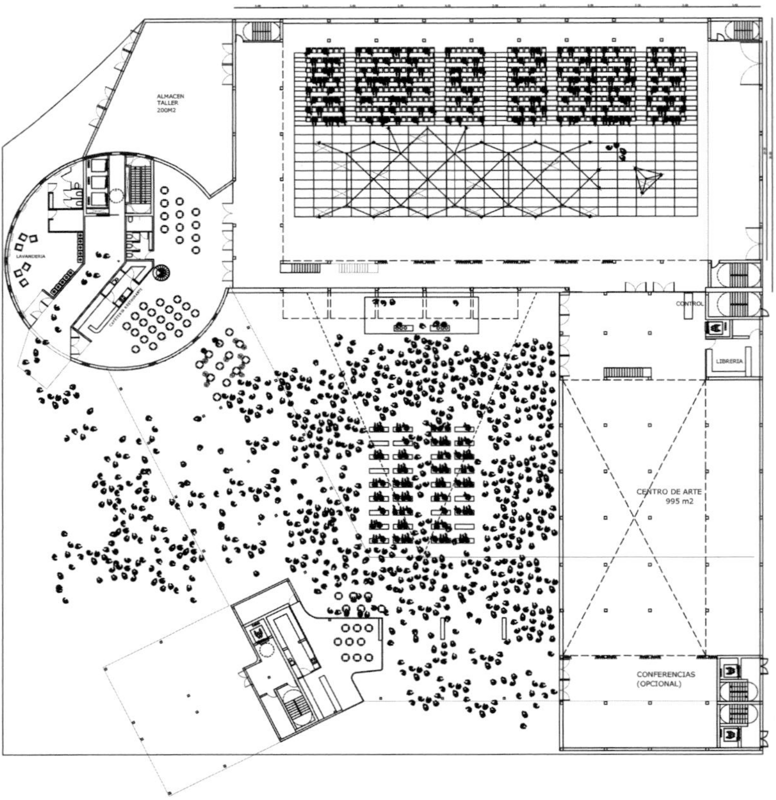

Uni-versity Hou-sing

Gandía. Spain. 2007—

1st Prize national competition

With Visoren

Multiscalar
/33

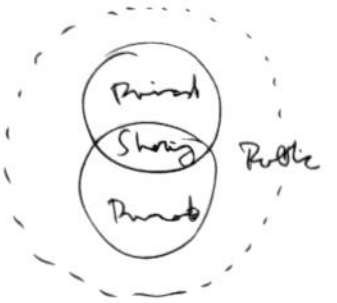

Sharing
/34

This project was developed in Gandia, a town with a population of 75,000 to the south of Valencia. The aim was to develop a hybrid project that would function essentially as a student residence while meeting the requirements of social housing, with the corresponding standards and characteristics. The proposed programme includes 102 apartments for young people, 40 apartments for senior citizens, and a civic and social centre for the town council.

The most interesting question from a programmatic point of view is the provision of shared spaces in the apartments for young people, which is in effect a new version from the traditional residence for young people. In Spain the national Housing Plan clearly establishes that apartments can be built with an area of between 30 and 45 m^2, with up to 20% of shared space, but does not specify where or how this should be located.

The fact is that the idea of sharing spaces is fully compatible with the goals of social and environmental sustainability, grounded as it is on the principle of 'doing more with less': that is, offering people more resources through the mechanism of sharing.

Recent analyses have identified a minimum of thirteen basic functions related to the fact of dwelling. Some of these are clearly private (sleeping, bathing, etc), while others can have a semi-public or shared nature: eating, relaxing, digital working, washing clothes, etc. These resources can be shared within a single dwelling, between two dwellings, between individuals on the same floor or two adjoining floors, on the scale of a whole building or between different buildings in the same neighbourhood. The key, then, is to choose the scale at which we want to share resources so as to create a particular model of habitability or another.

If we construct 102 apartments of 45 m^2 each, which may share 20% of their floor area, we can have up to 918 m^2 of shared space. This could be in the form of 51 shared spaces of 18 m^2 (each apartment in a pair contributing 9 m^2), or a single space of 918 m^2. Our proposal puts forward an interesting and innovative model with which to define three scales of habitability:

— A first, individual scale of 36 m^2, comprising the kitchen, bathroom and rest area in a loft-style apartment.
— A second, intermediate scale of 108, 72, 36, 24 and 12 m^2, shared by 18, 12, 6, 4 or 2 people, on every second floor. This comprises a spacious living area and contact and work areas.
— A third and larger scale of 306 m^2, shared by all 102 people and located on the ground floor, which will include a lounge, a laundry, Internet access and a library.

GEOGRAPHY

100 young people will inhabit a university hall of residence

GEOMETRY

The traditional residence has individual accommodation units and services

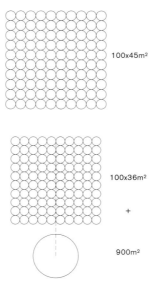

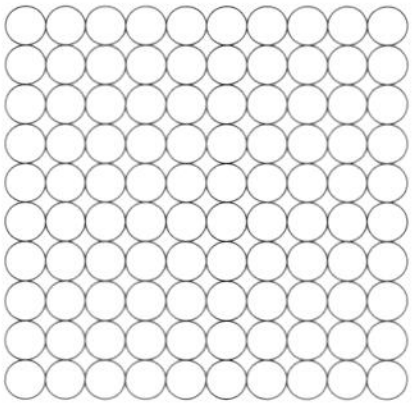

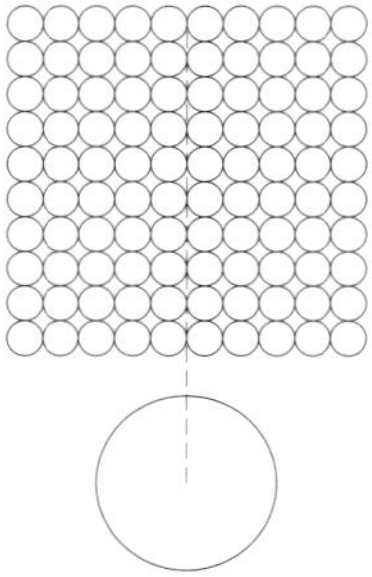

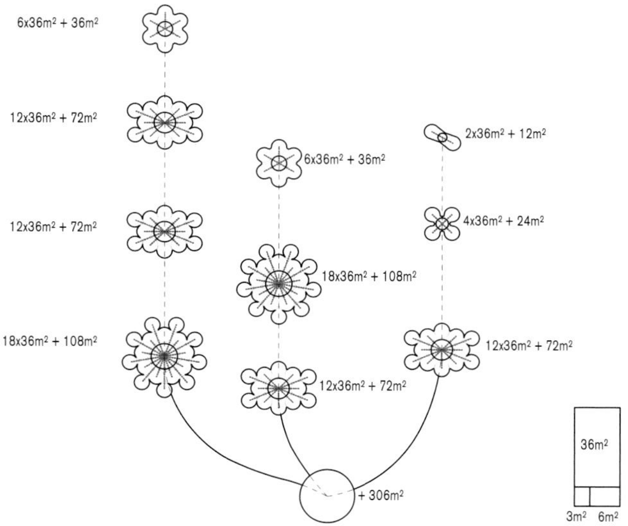

LOGIC

Grouping of accommodation units in communities with three degrees of privacy

STRUCTURE

Structure of grouping of the accommodation units

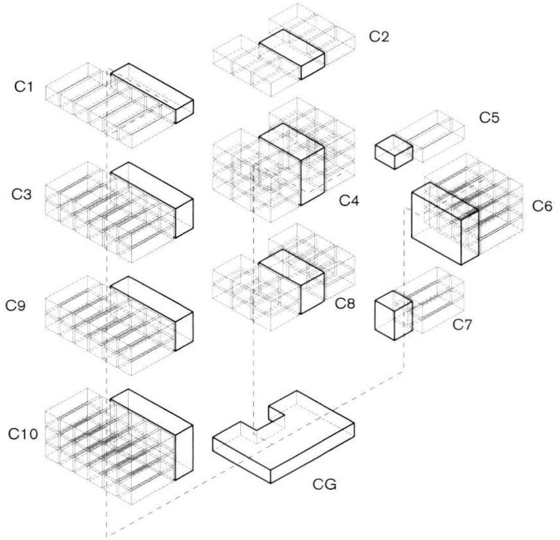

1:1 prototype

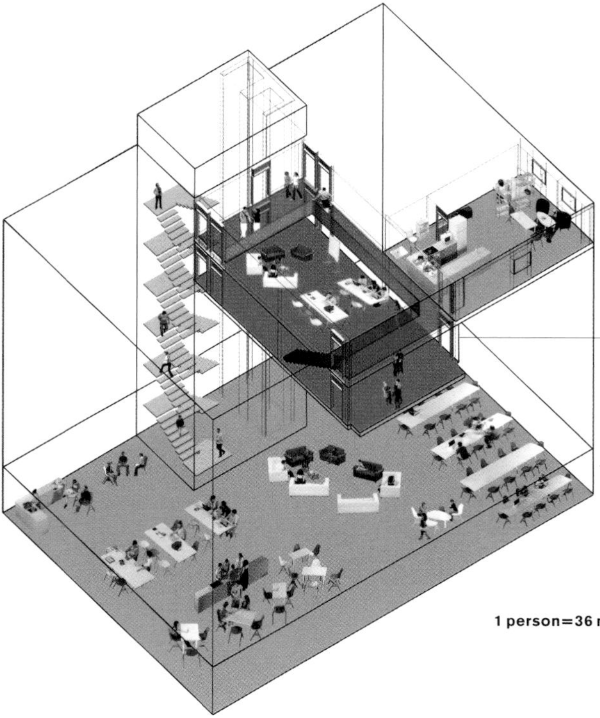

Block 2

Private space
1 person
36 m²

Shared space A
12 persons
72 m²

Shared space B
100 personas
300 m²

1 person = 36 m² + 72 m² + 300 m² = 408 m²

Block 1
Private = 1728 m²
Shared A = 288 m²

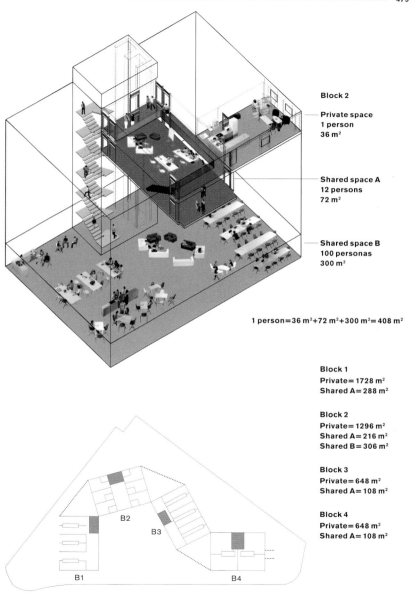

Block 2
Private = 1296 m²
Shared A = 216 m²
Shared B = 306 m²

Block 3
Private = 648 m²
Shared A = 108 m²

Block 4
Private = 648 m²
Shared A = 108 m²

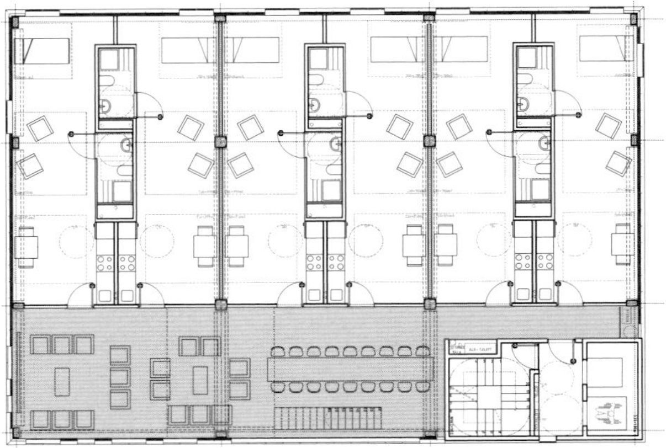

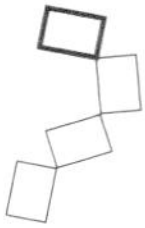

12 type A shared accommodation units

12 type B shared accommodation units

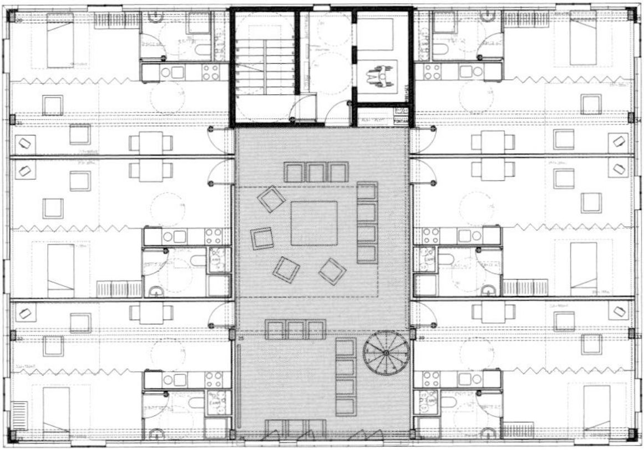

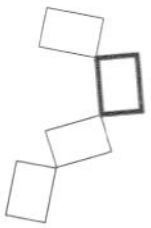

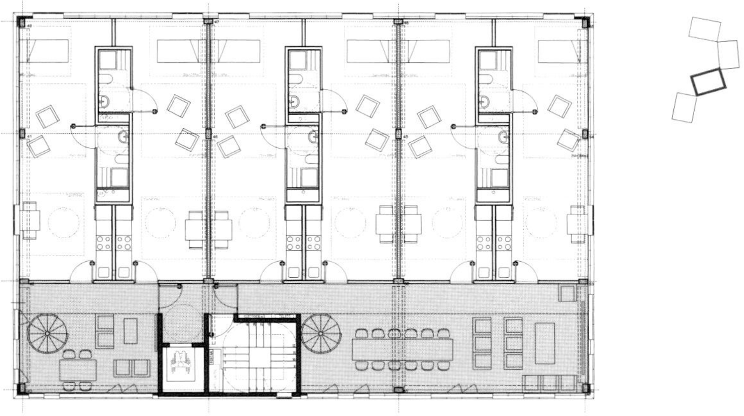

4 individual and 8 shared accommodation units

4 apartments for senior citizens

Kim Hyng Yoon Editing Co.

Seoul, South Korea. 2002
Local partner: Yong Joon Kim, YO2

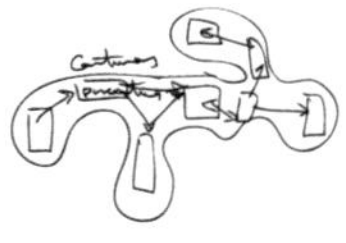

Discontinuity
/32

The project for the headquarters of the Kim Hyng Yoon company is sited in Paju Book City, a publishing city developed in the last few years near the border between South and North Korea on the basis of a master plan and urban design guidelines drawn up by Florian Beigel, Seung H-Sang, Min Hyun-Shik and Kim Young Joon.

The complex accommodates the entire spectrum of firms involved in the process of book production, from design and editing to printing, binding and distribution.

The criteria for the design of the buildings was very strict with regard to the implantation, but allowed absolute freedom in terms of internal organization. We envisioned the building in terms of the company chairman taking visitors on a tour. We imagined them entering on the ground floor and arriving on the roof by way of a single itinerary. We studied the Oriental way of working, in which the composition of small groups is essential to the organization of the work of the company as a whole.

The project is therefore structured as a sequence of platforms that divides the building not into four floors, but twenty-four. This served to create relational interior landscapes linking the different groups working in the building. The structural core has a central staircase which reproduces on the micro scale the overall structure of the building and provides access to the platforms. The building is constructed as a concrete block with solid floor slabs and façade and a single continuous strip window like the skin of a carefully peeled orange.

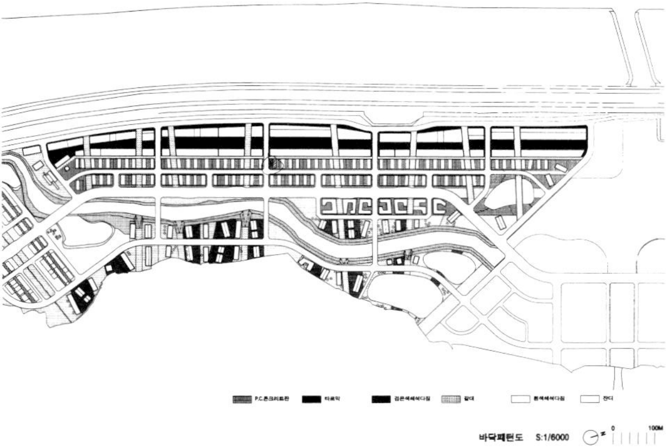

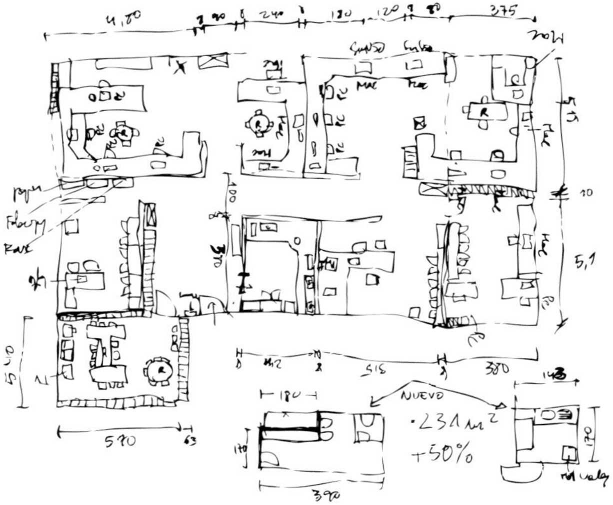

GEOGRAPHY

Social geography in a Korean design firm

GEOMETRY

Organization in terms of working groups

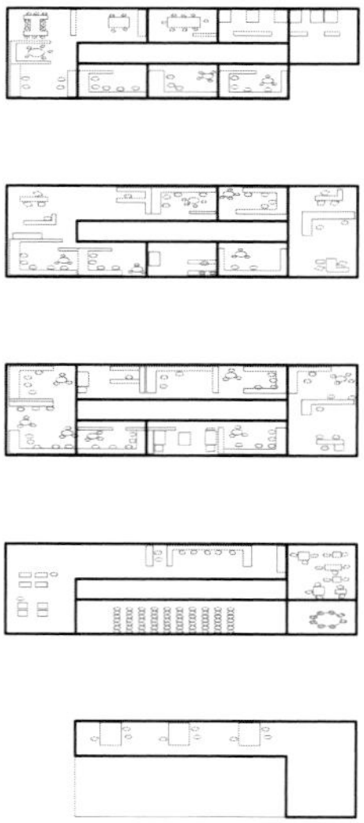

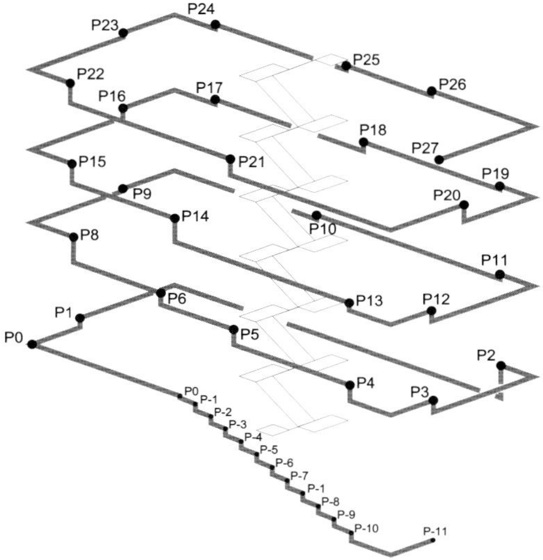

LOGIC

A building organized in terms of a sequence of levels

STRUCTURE

Self-similar structure with central nucleus and platforms

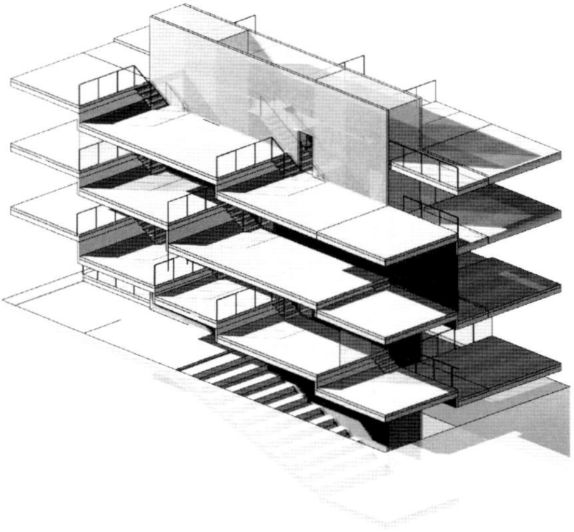

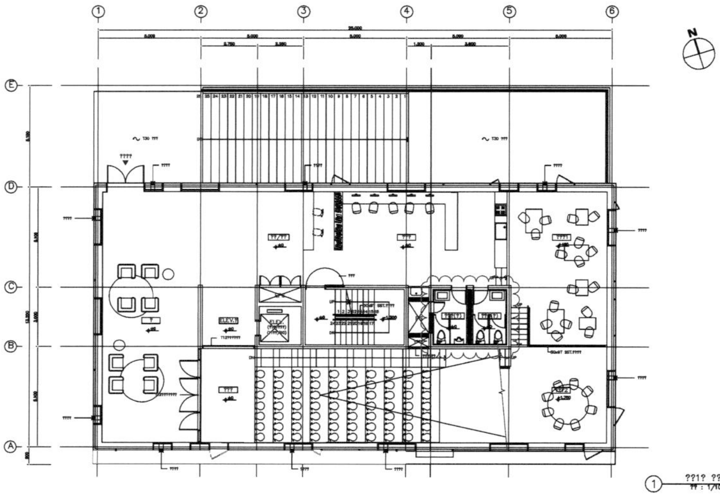

1 ??1? ???
?? : 1/100

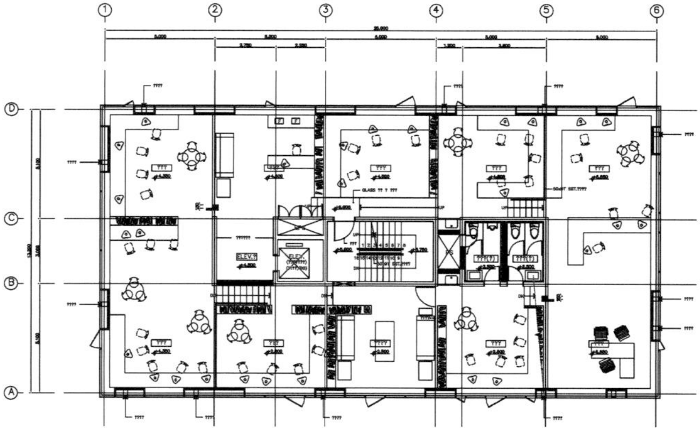

1 ??2? ???
?? : 1/100

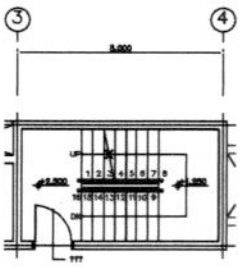

2 +2,500?? ?? ???
?? : 1/100

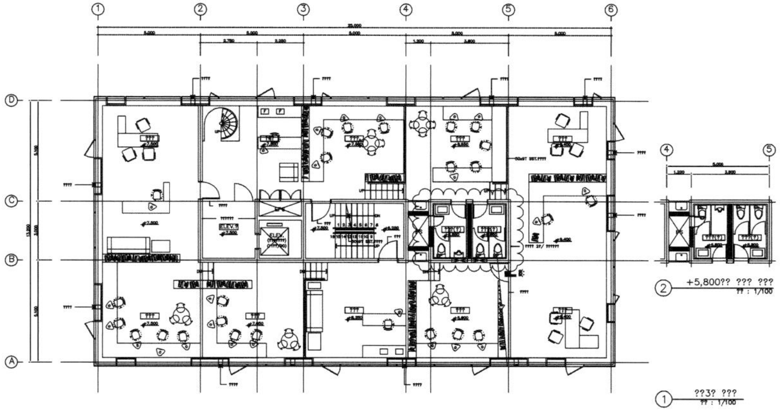
+5,800?? ??? ???
?? : 1/100
??3? ???
?? : 1/100

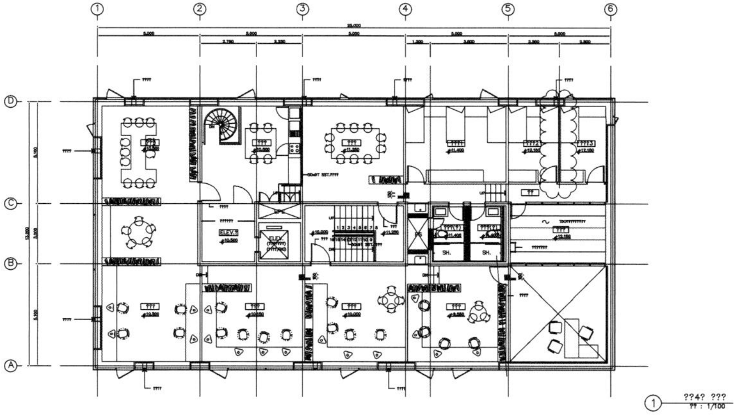
??4? ???
?? : 1/100

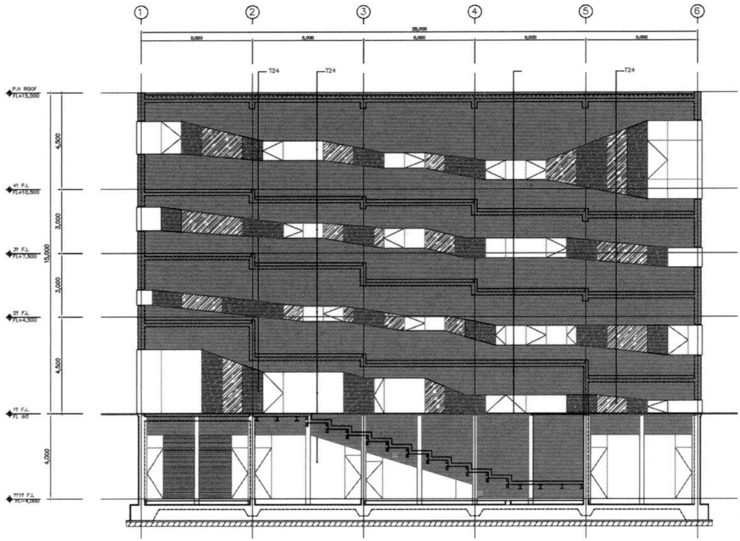

1
2
3
4
5
6
25,000
5,000
T24
P.H ROOF
FL+15,000
4F F.L
FL+10,500
3F F.L
FL+7,500
2F F.L
FL+4,500
1F F.L
FL ±0
15,000
4,500
3,000
4,000

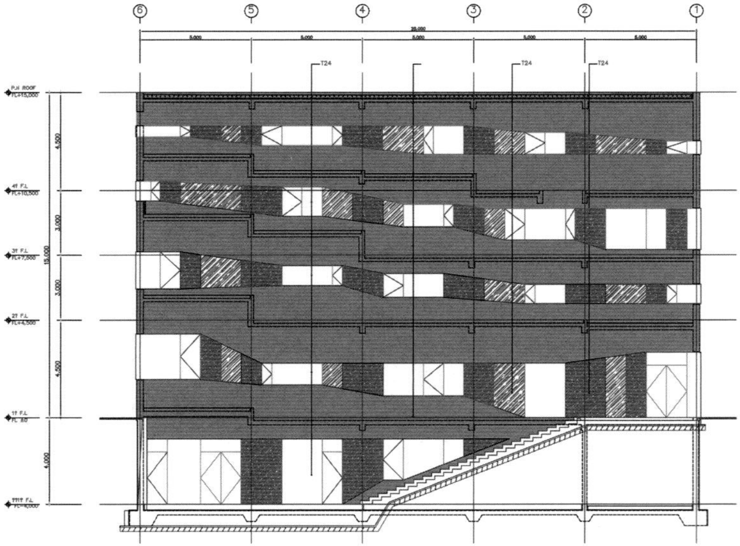

6
5
4
3
2
1
25,000
5,000
T24
P.H ROOF
FL+15,000
4F F.L
FL+10,500
3F F.L
FL+7,500
2F F.L
FL+4,500
1F F.L
FL ±0
15,000
4,500
3,000
4,000

Web Hotel

MACBA, Barcelona. Spain. 1998

Hypermedia
/37

Re-informing
/38

The Web hotel project was our contribution to the exhibition *Fabrications*, which was organized simultaneously in SFMoMA, the Wexner in Columbus, Ohio, the MoMA in New York and the MACBA in Barcelona. The curator in Barcelona, Xavier Costa, invited four architects to intervene in the plaza in front of the museum.

In our case, we decided to construct an element at the scale of a building, situated in front of the museum, covering an historicist building. We decided to construct a hybrid hotel whose façade was in Barcelona and whose rooms were on the Internet. The rooms could be configured on a website, changing the textures of the furnishings and the arrangement of objects inside them, using the VRML format.

When a person entered one of the virtual rooms, that room's light was really turned on in Barcelona. In this way a connection was made between the two worlds, transforming computer signals into electrical signals. A webcam in Barcelona relayed the image of the manipulation to the Internet visitor, thus closing the circle between an action in cyberspace and a reaction in the physical world.

GEOGRAPHY

A hybrid world between the physical and digital

GEOMETRY

The square in front of the MACBA in Barcelona

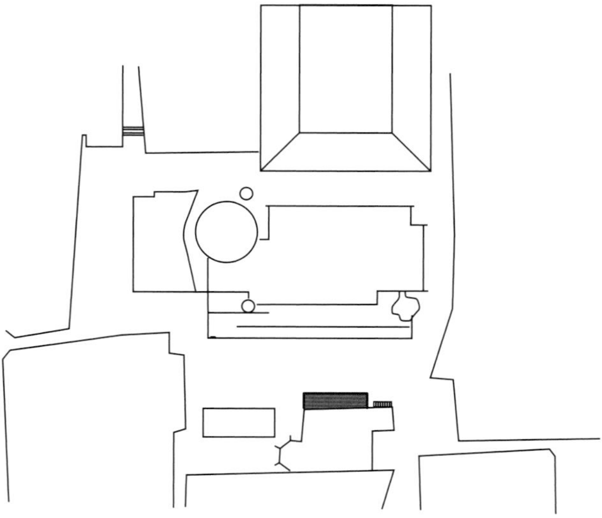

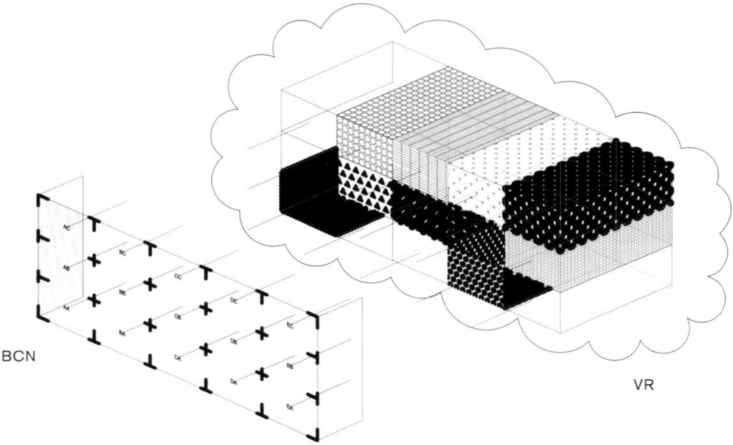

LOGIC

A hotel with a physical façade and virtual rooms

STRUCTURE

Façade. Lights. Server. Modem. Internet. Server. Web. Webcam

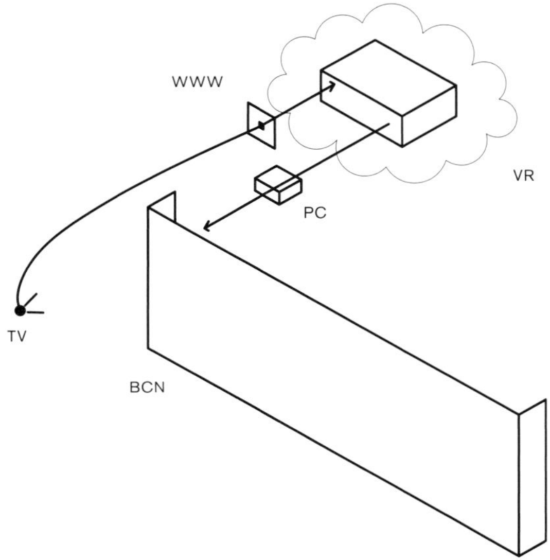

ca
ba
cc
bc

Media House

Barcelona. Spain. 2000
With Metápolis, MIT Center for Bits and Atoms, I2Cat
Elisava Master Interface

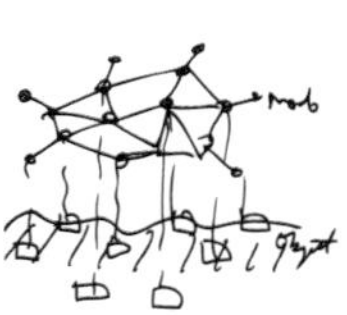

Hypermedia
/37

Re-informing
/38

The Media House Project is the fruit of a strategic alliance between the Massachusetts Institute of Technology's Media Lab's Consortium, Things that Think, the Metápolis group from Barcelona and the Fundació Politècnica de Catalunya, with the collaboration of the consortium I2CAT and the Elisava Design School. The purpose is to unite their respective potential in order to build a prototype of an informational house.

This Project enables the testing of the progression of information Technologies beyond that of computers and integrates them into everyday life, literally looking to build computers from the components of buildings, in such a way that the logical intelligence of a structure can grow with its physical form.

The Technologies that Media Lab are developing include techniques to distribute the work of some central servers to a wide number of small micro servers, to dramatically reduce costs and also the complex task of equipping them with Internet access, so that it is possible to integrate them into the simplest of the existing elements in "intelligent spaces".

The Metapolis Architects have developed an informative structure, which incorporates in just one element the physical structure, the electrical network, and the data network, which enables a dynamic and configurable link between the entities (people, objects, space, limits, networks and contents) and that which create an inhabitable environment.
The house is the computer, the structure is the network.

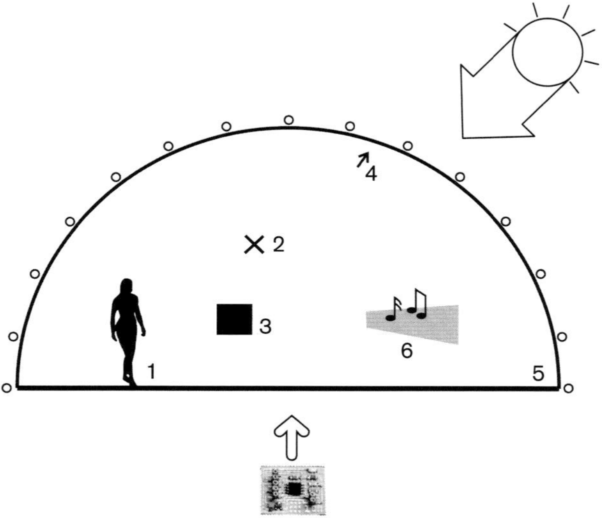

GEOGRAPHY

People, space, objects, boundaries, networks and contents

GEOMETRY

Data to define each category in a habitable environment

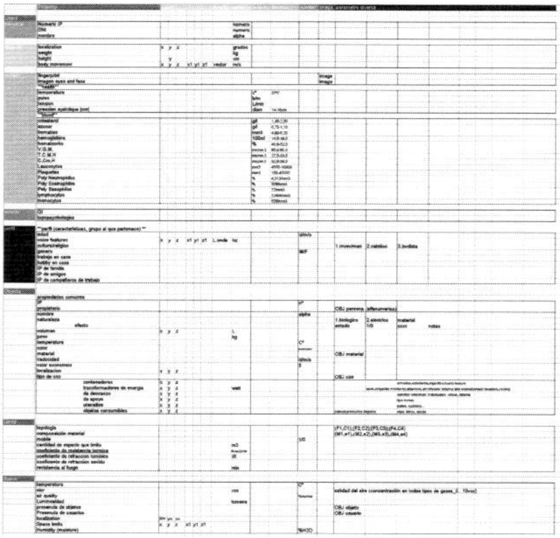

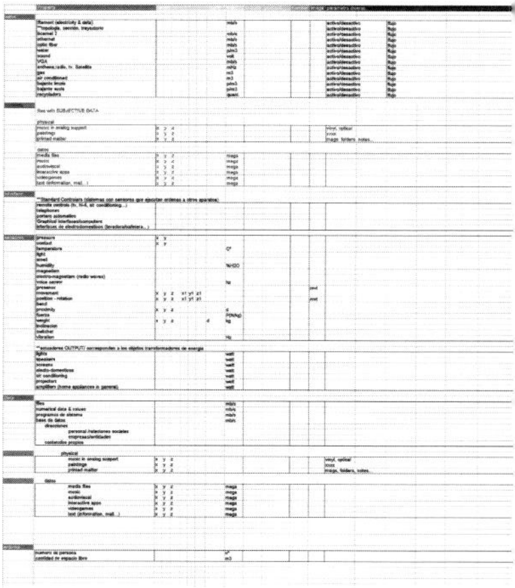

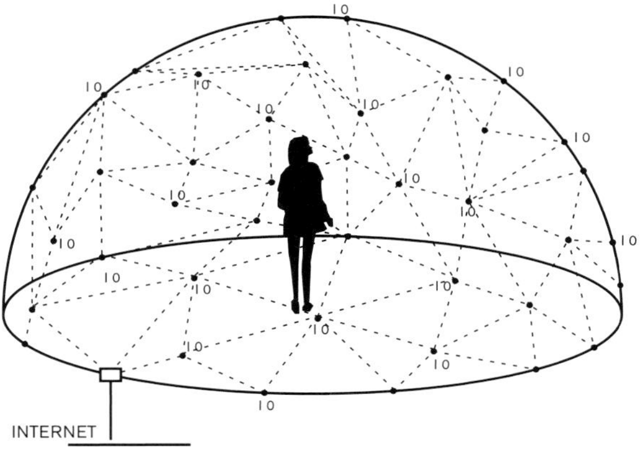

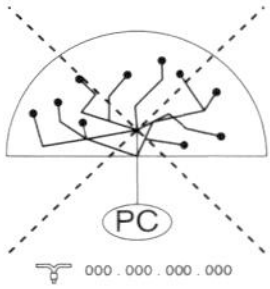

LOGIC

The intelligence of the space derives from the relations between micro servers

STRUCTURE

Physical space and the digital space are related by sensors and interactors

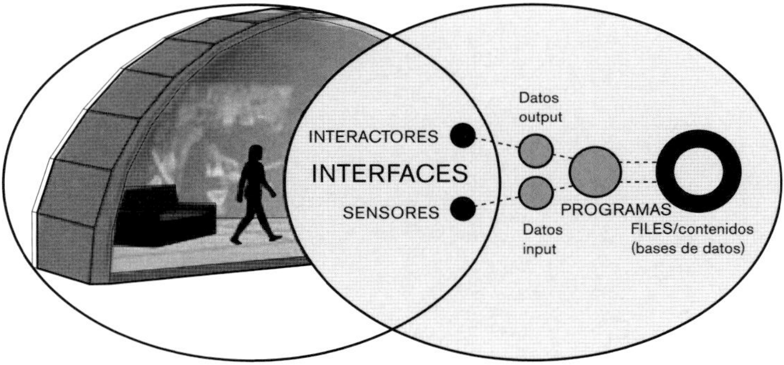

PHYSICAL AREA DATA

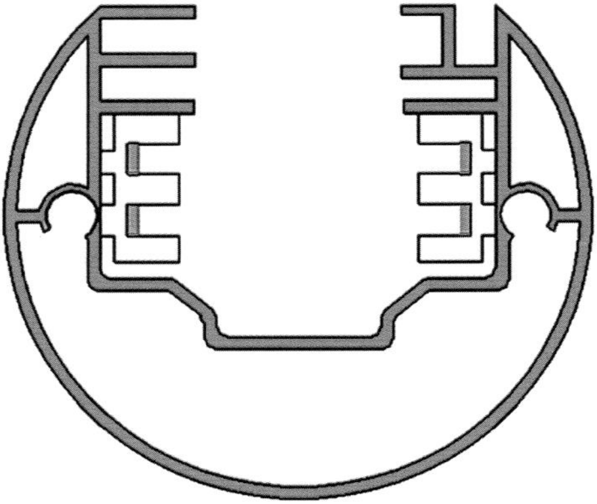

TIPO A

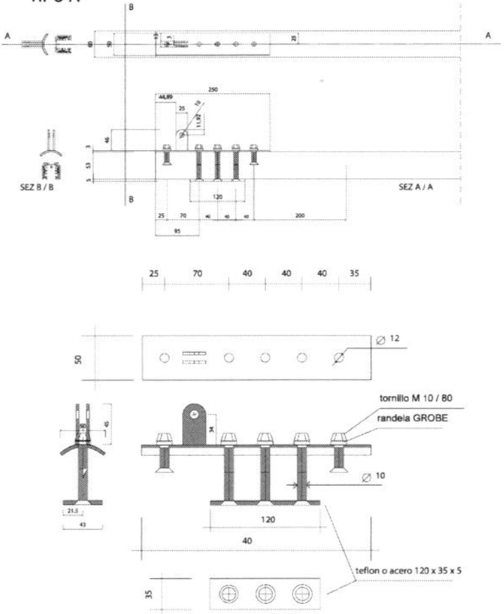
A
B
250
44,89
25
SEZ B / B
SEZ A / A
120
25 70 40 40 40 200
95
25 70 40 40 40 35
50
Ø 12
tornillo M 10 / 80
randela GROBE
Ø 10
120
40
teflon o acero 120 x 35 x 5
35

TIPO B

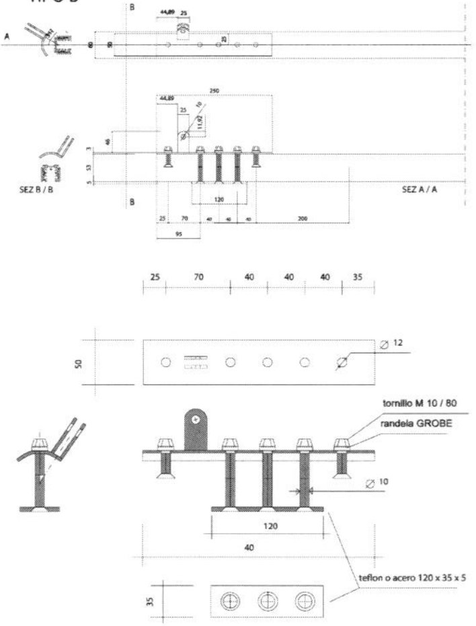
A
B
44,89
25
250
SEZ B / B
SEZ A / A
120
25 70 40 40 40 200
95
25 70 40 40 40 35
50
Ø 12
tornillo M 10 / 80
randela GROBE
Ø 10
120
40
teflon o acero 120 x 35 x 5
35

NUDO A

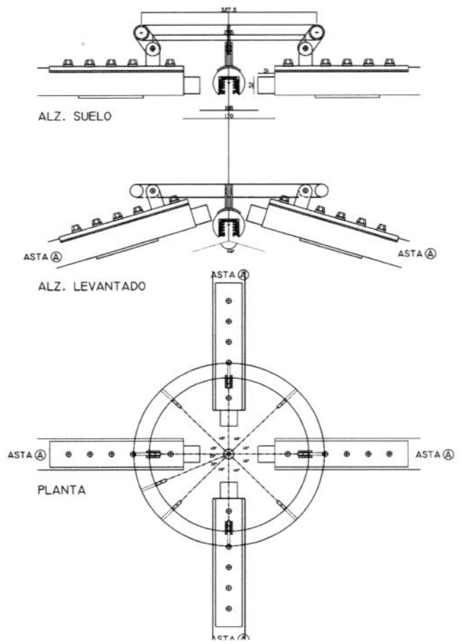

NUDO B

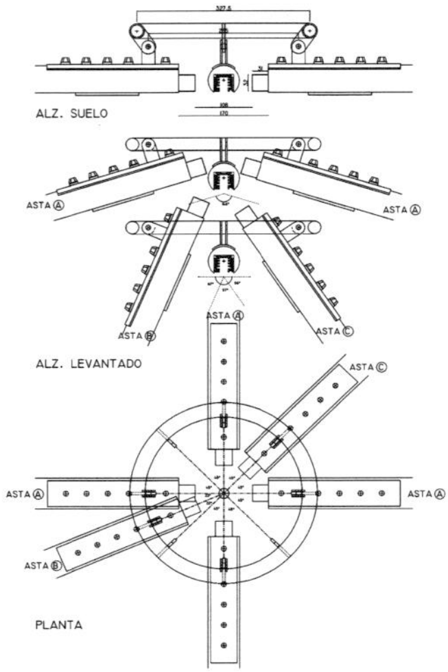

NUDO C

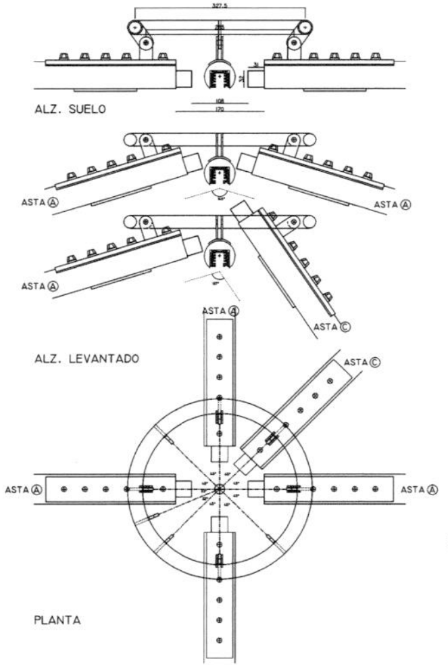

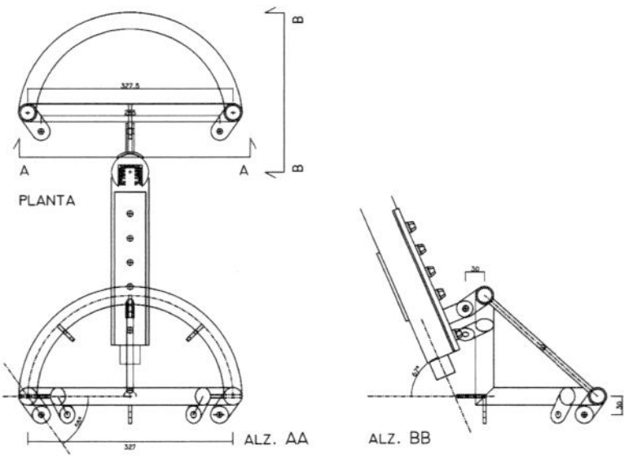

PIE P1

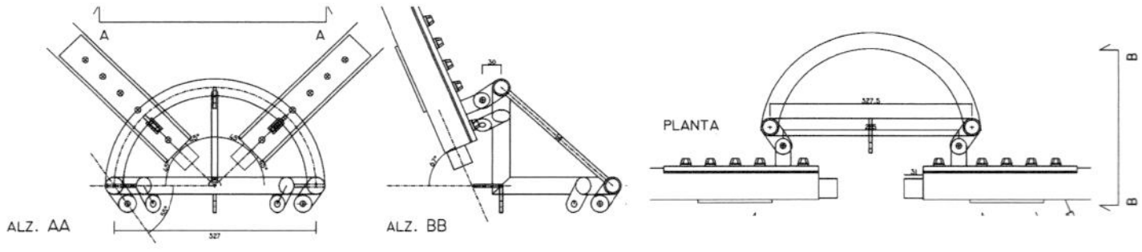

PIE P2

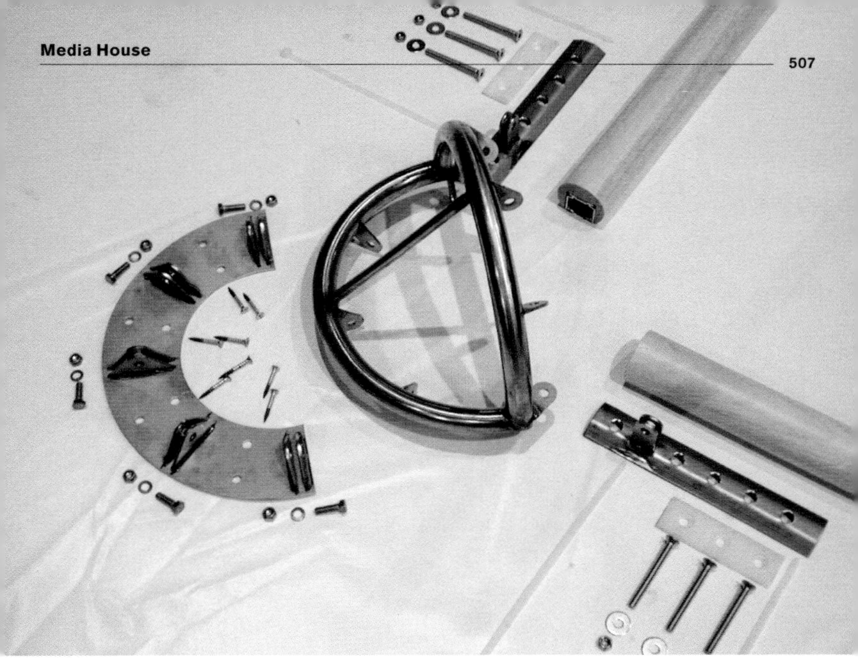

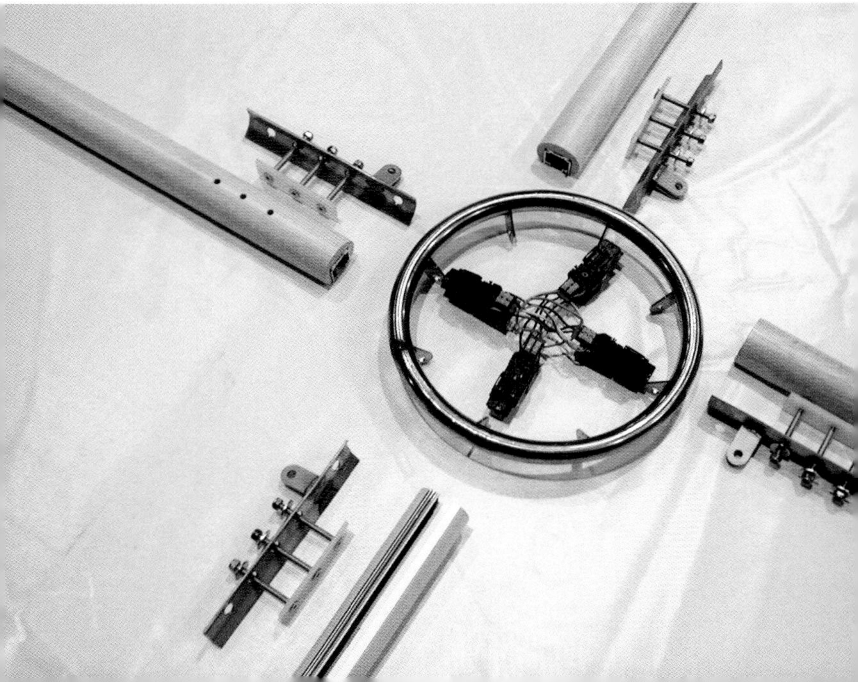

Structure

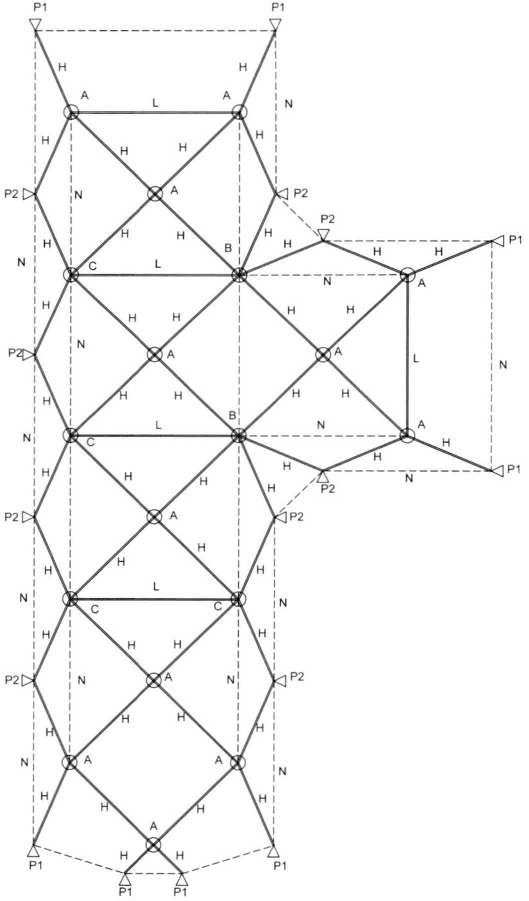

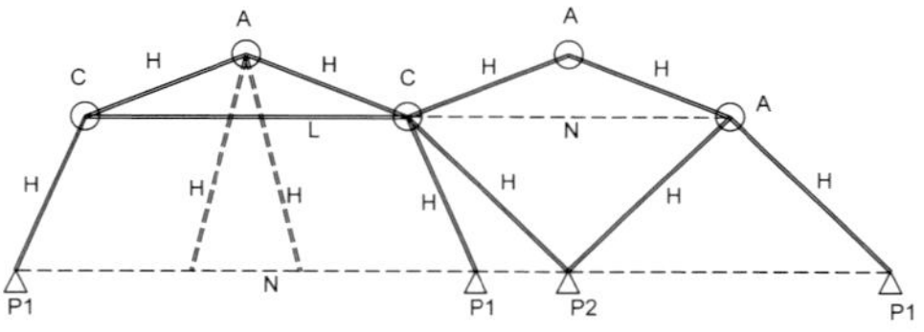

Technical plant. Mercat de les flors

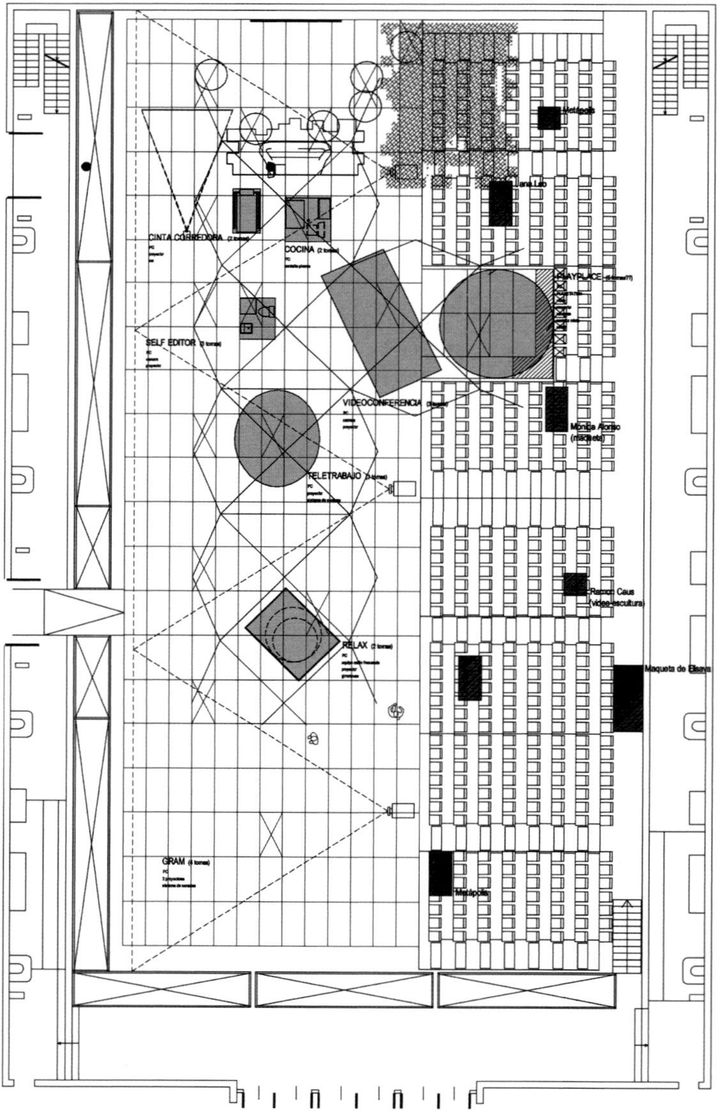

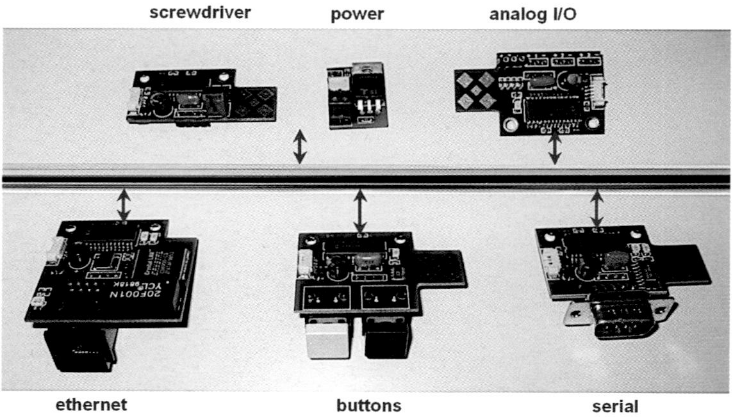
screwdriver
power
analog I/O
ethernet
buttons
serial

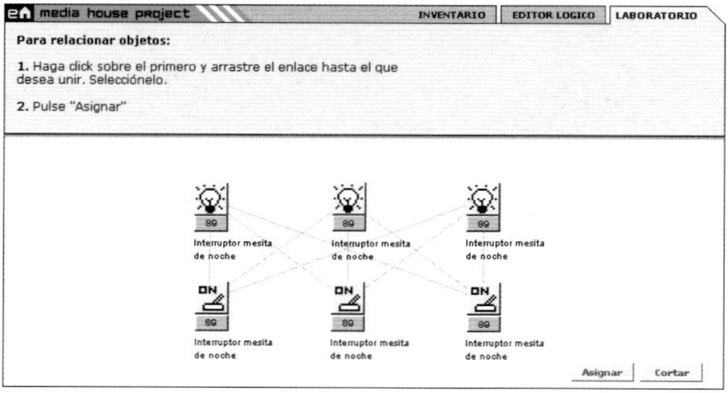
media house project
INVENTARIO
EDITOR LOGICO
LABORATORIO
Para relacionar objetos:
1. Haga click sobre el primero y arrastre el enlace hasta el que desea unir. Selecciónelo.
2. Pulse "Asignar"
89
Interruptor mesita de noche
89
Interruptor mesita de noche
89
Interruptor mesita de noche
ON
89
Interruptor mesita de noche
ON
89
Interruptor mesita de noche
ON
89
Interruptor mesita de noche
Asignar
Cortar

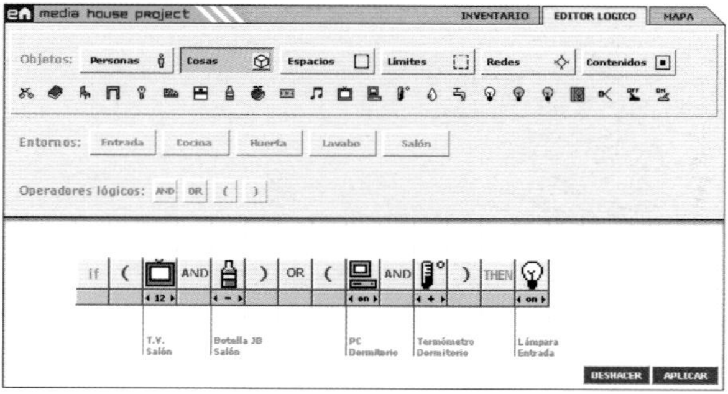
media house project
INVENTARIO
EDITOR LOGICO
MAPA
Objetos:
Personas
Cosas
Espacios
Límites
Redes
Contenidos
Entornos:
Entrada
Cocina
Huerta
Lavabo
Salón
Operadores lógicos:
AND
OR
(
)
If
(
AND
)
OR
(
AND
)
THEN
12
on
on
T.V. Salón
Botella JB Salón
PC Dormitorio
Termómetro Dormitorio
Lámpara Entrada
DESHACER
APLICAR

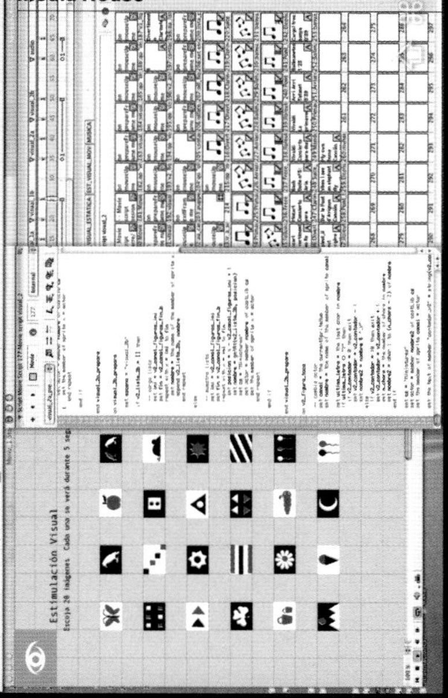
Estimulación Visual
Escoja 20 imágenes Cada uno se verá durante 5 segundos

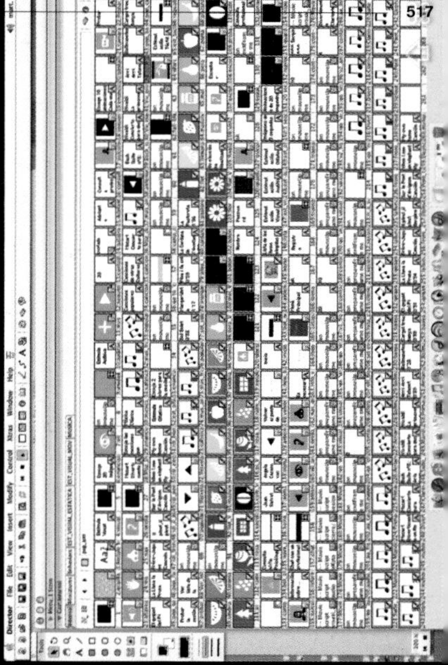

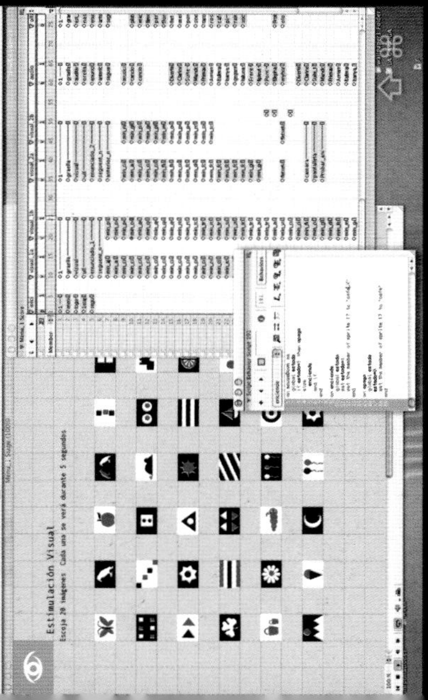
Estimulación Visual
Escoja 20 imágenes Cada uno se verá durante 5 segundos

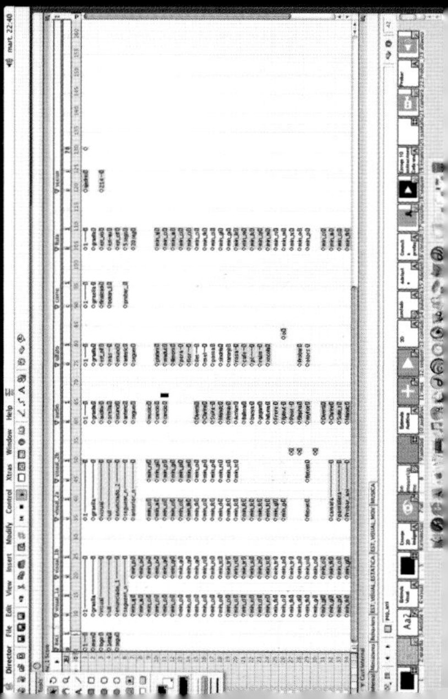

Hyper habitat

Reprogramming the World

Venice. Italy. 2008
XI Venice Bienniale
With IaaC, MIT Center for Bits and Atoms, Bestiario.

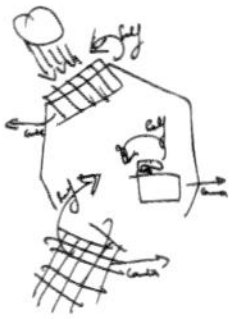

Self-sufficiency
/36

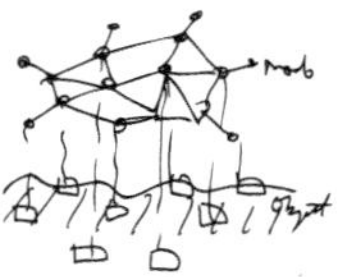

Hypermedia
/37

Re-informing
/38

The 2008 Venice Biennale was curated by Aaron Betsky on the theme 'Out There: Architecture Beyond Building'. For our contribution we decided to set up an international consortium involving Guallart Architects, the Institute for Advanced Architecture of Catalonia, The Center for Bits and Atoms at MIT and Bestiario.

Our project, entitled 'Hyperhabitat: Reprogramming the World', sought to take the idea of the multiscale habitat to the limit. Hyperhabitat is a model for defining the physical world in terms compatible with the digital world using the principles of a network. This serves to define a multiscale structure that can use the same principles to link any element of the physical world capable of having a digital identity, so that the world can be reprogrammed by identifying new relational systems composed of local and global systems.

Network

If a digital network is composed of nodes, connections, environments, protocols and contents and the people that operate them, the physical world can be defined in terms of the same layers, thus making the physical world and the digital world mutually compatible.

Any object, any house, building, neighbourhood, city or region, and any place with an identity in the physical world has the potential to be related to other nodes on any scale, in such a way that this interaction has logical principles with the potential to reprogramme the world.

Reprogramming

The history of civilization is the history of a succession of societies capable of managing more information using less energy; societies capable of being more efficient in everything, and therefore able to act with less energy expenditure, in turn making them capable of doing more. In our own time, information networks make it possible to reprogramme the world via multiple interrelated nodes that transcend the traditional hierarchical structure based on the management of the collective by public structures and promote processes of emergence based on peer-to-peer relations.

Objects

The industrial world transforms spaces into objects. And the digital world allows relationships between objects of different genealogies. The history of the 20th century is the history of the transformation of functions into passive mechanisms, organized in physical spaces by means of domestic appliances, and mechanisms that have made it possible to create running machines, washing machines, refrigerators and new windows on the world by means of electronic elements.

We expect our homes to satisfy certain basic functions of habitability in the form of basic objects—bed, cooker, toilet, wardrobe, etc. Now these objects/functions can have a digital identity that connects them with the genealogy of the material production of the world and allows them to establish new functionalities.

Foundation

In Venice we want to found a system capable of reprogramming the world by defining new relations between the elements that compose it. To do so we will initiate a participatory process of uploading the physical world onto the Internet at www.hyperhabitat.net and invite people all over the world to propose new relations between its component parts.

We intend to map any object, structure or place in the world using a system that orders any activity according to 21 categories, classified initially as homes, amenities, workplaces and services and eleven levels of use (from the individual to the planetary) and invite people to propose relations between them.

Multiscale

The world is constructed on the basis of multiscale networks with various layers of activity—there are nodes posited in terms of a single person (a home) and others that are open to hundreds, thousands or millions of people. Refrigerators can exist at the scale of a single home because there are central macromarkets at the scale of a million to supply them.

A crucifix is part of a network of religious identity that manifests itself at the personal, neighbourhood, city and national levels and has its highest expression in the Vatican, which represents a thousand million people.

Venice

In Venice we reproduced at 1:1 scale all the objects on one floor of a university hall of residence being constructed by Visoren in Gandia (Valencia) on the basis of ideas developed for the Sociopolis Sharing Tower in Valencia. Some of the objects used by the residents are intended for individual use (scale 1) and others for communal use (scale 10).

Internet 0

Every object in the home will have a micro-server that uses the Internet 0 protocol developed by The Center for Bits and Atoms. So every physical object can have an identity in the digital world and enter into relation with other objects on an economic, social or environmental level. The ultimate aim of providing physical elements with an informational identity is to make the system more efficient and thus to save energy.

Keyboard

The Venice installation will be a keyboard with which to interact with the world. Each of the objects in the installation is in fact a representation of a generic object (from a bed to a book, from a ball to a crucifix) that might be found in a typical home.

The installation objects give access to the network of real objects that people around the world have posted up on the Internet to provide connections and interactions with actual physical objects.

Relating

Our ability to operate and interact with networks and nodes at any scale reflects the ability of matter—the constructed—to carry information and establish local and global relationships.

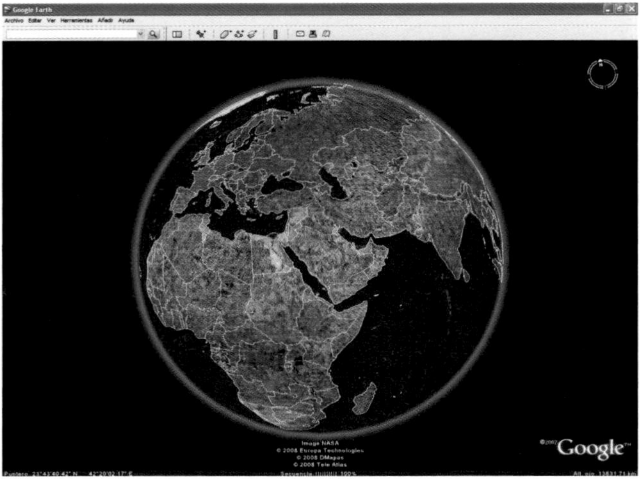

GEOGRAPHY

The world as seen on Google Earth

GEOMETRY

The world as a sequence of multiscalar nodes, networks and environments

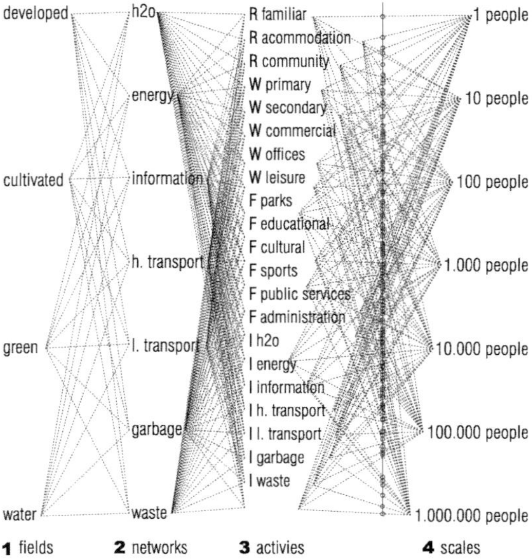

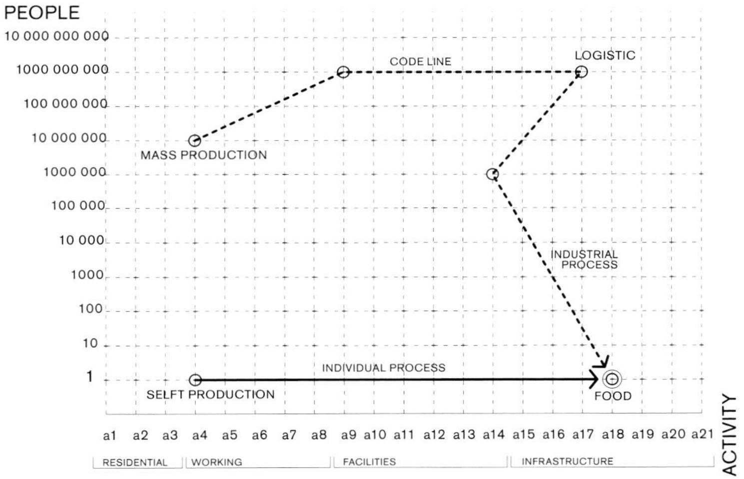

LOGIC

Reprogramming the world with more ordered information

STRUCTURE

A home as a keyboard with which to interact with the world

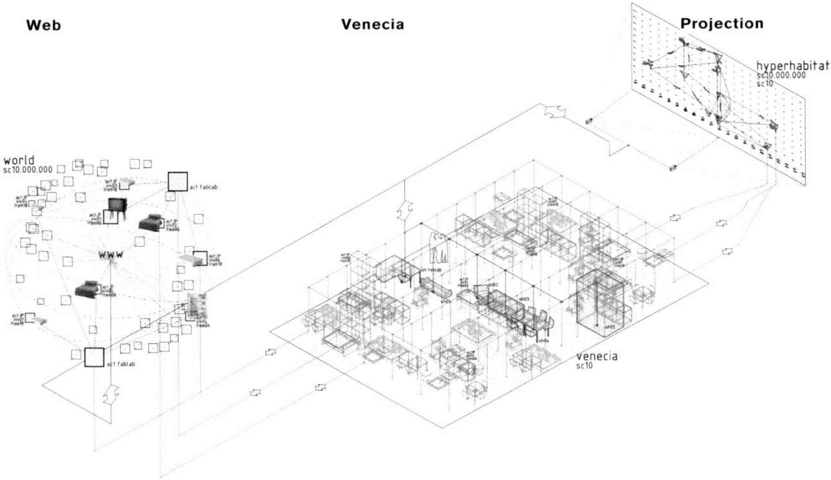

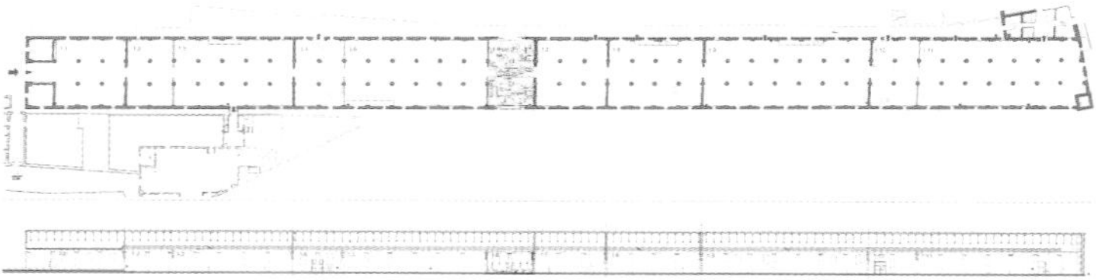

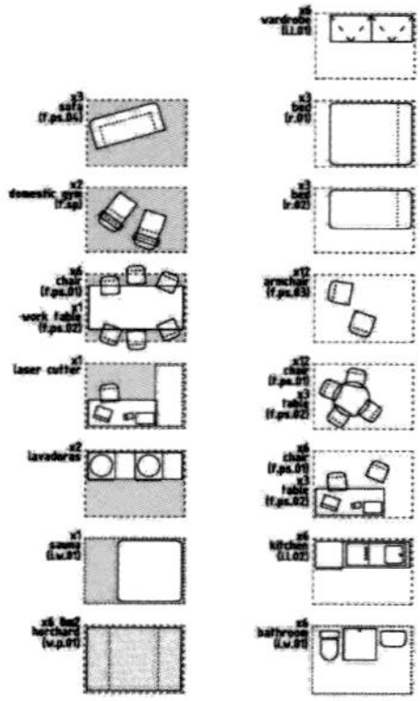

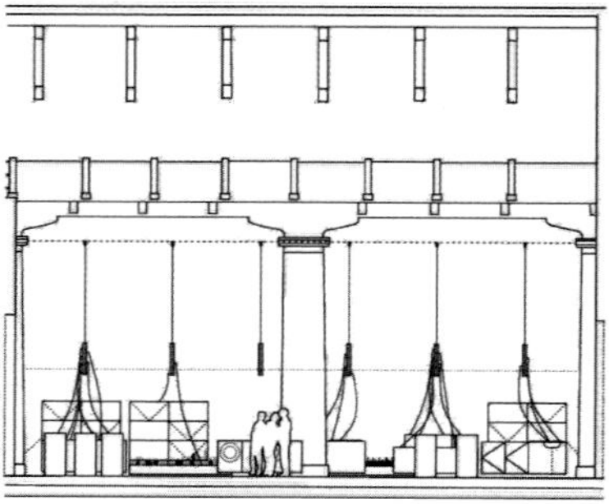

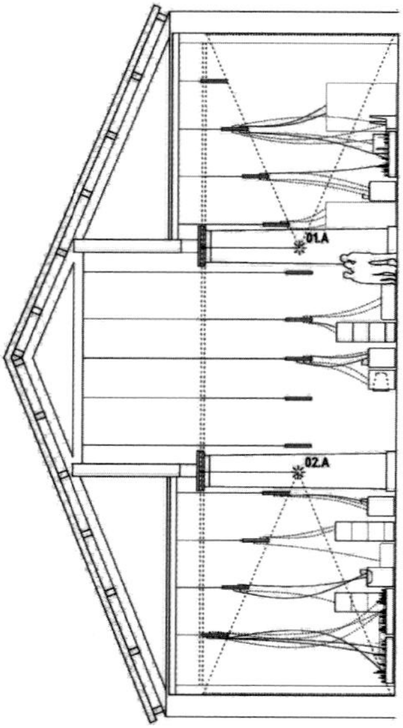

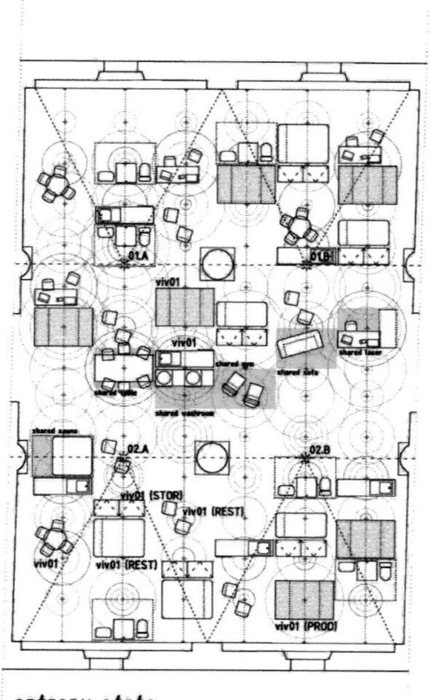

entropy state

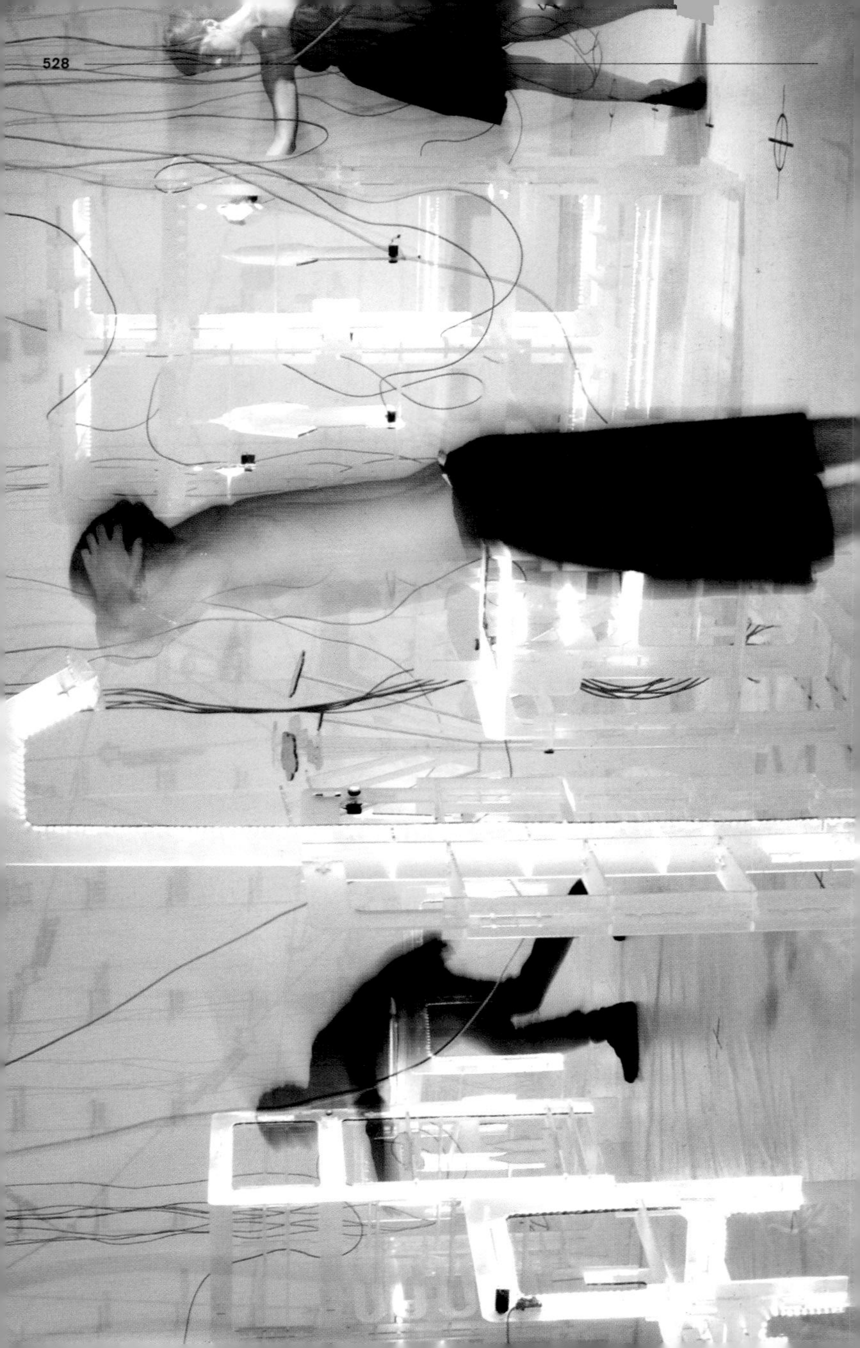

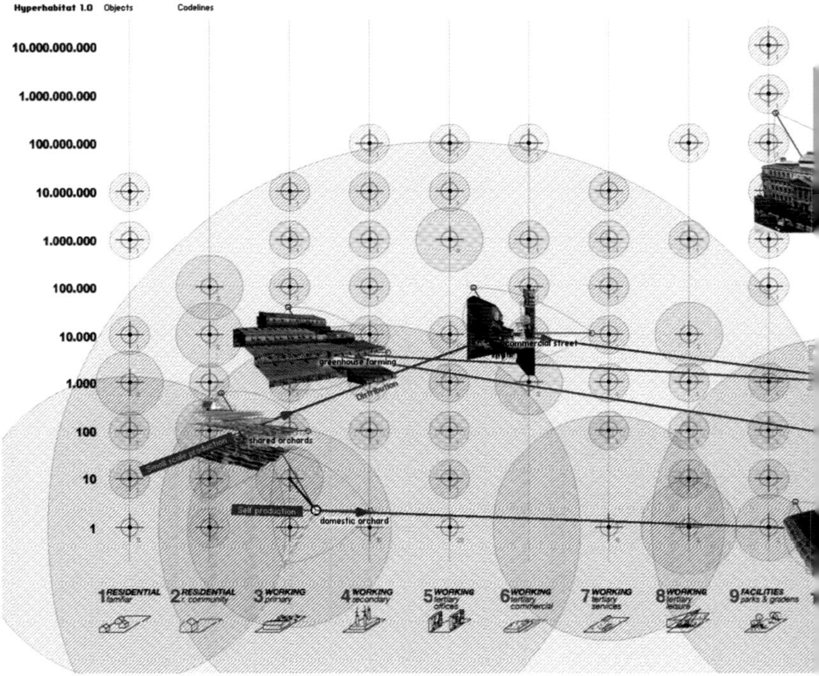

Relational map

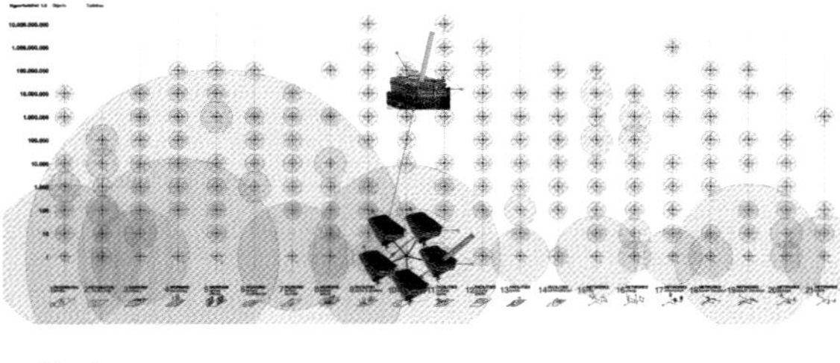

Books

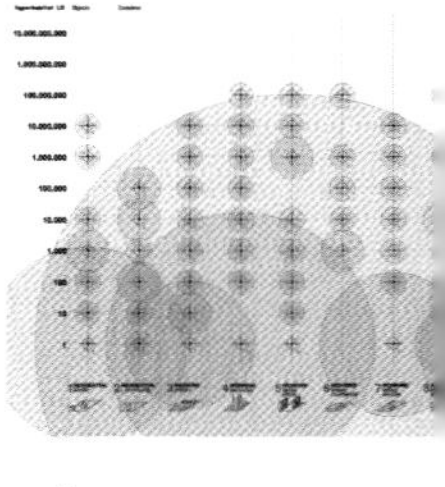

Energy

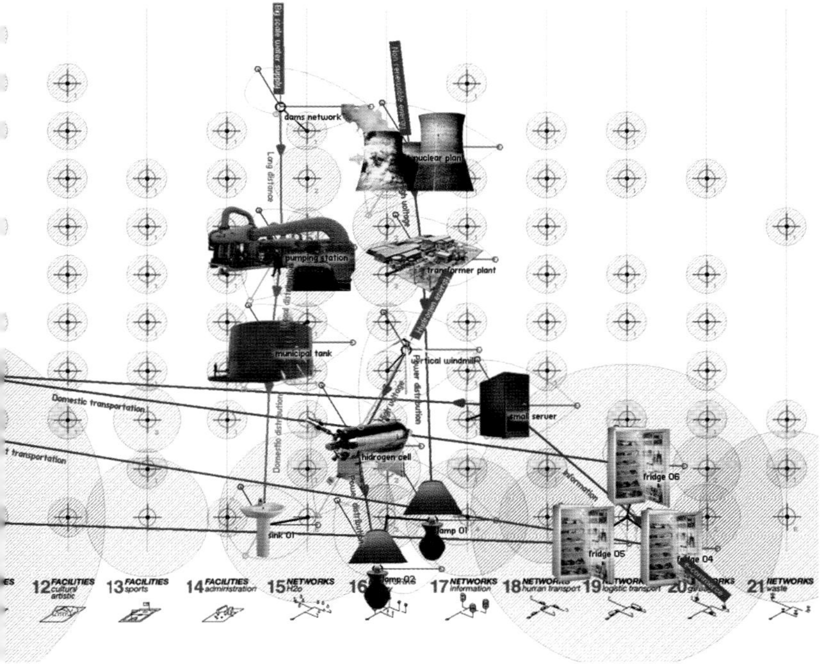
Big scale water supply
Non renewable energy
dams network
Long distance
nuclear plant
High voltage
pumping station
transformer plant
municipal tank
vertical windmill
Power distribution
Domestic transportation
Domestic distribution
small server
hidrogen cell
fridge 06
information
sink 01
lamp 01
fridge 05
fridge 04
lamp 02
12 FACILITIES cultural artistic
13 FACILITIES sports
14 FACILITIES administration
15 NETWORKS H2o
17 NETWORKS information
18 NETWORKS human transport
19 NETWORKS logistic transport
21 NETWORKS waste

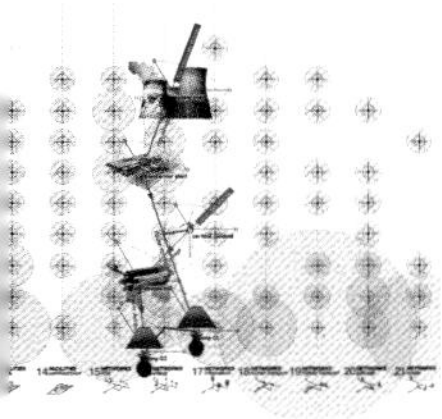

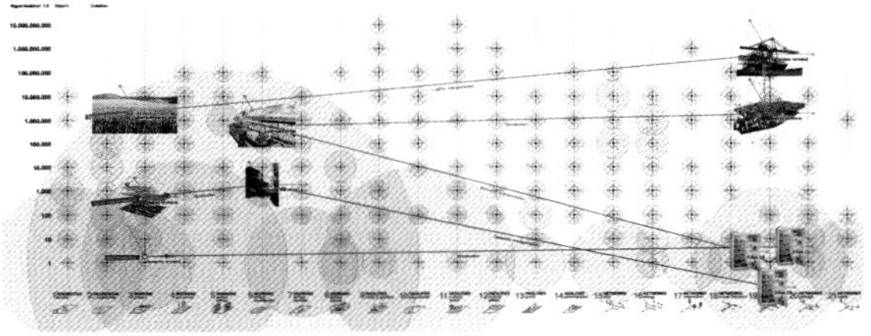

Food

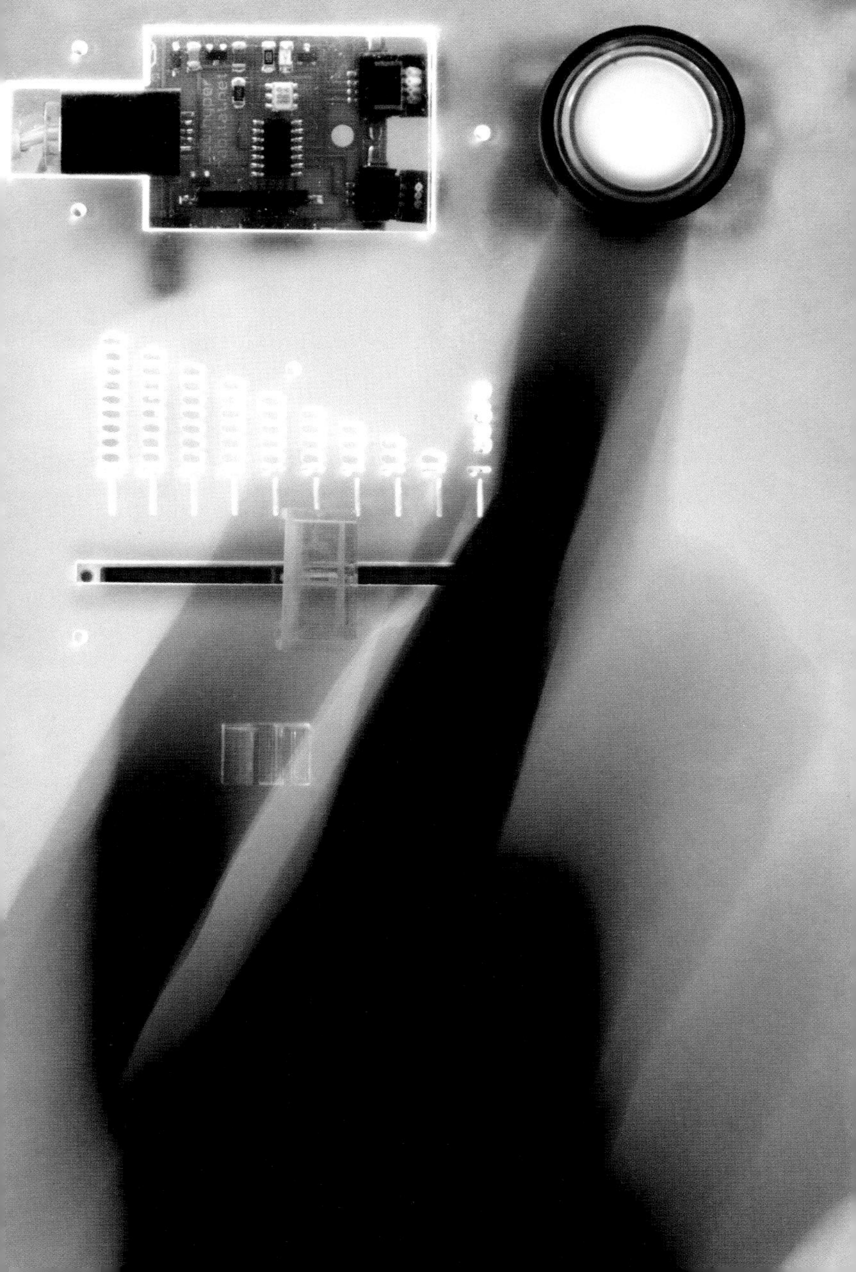

Can the planet withstand another 20th century?

The architecture of the 21st century will be the first that is part of natural history. The machineries of consumption and appropriation of the environment and its resources are pushing the global habitat toward collapse from exhaustion. The direct consequence of an age in which economic growth inevitably entailed physical growth.

Architecture and the city are the interface that we have provided ourselves with in order to interact with the world. At the local and the global scale.

Is it possible to define a general theory of multiscalar habitability on which we can live our lives in the decades to come?

We make the world fit for us to inhabit by means of functional nodes linked by networks that structure a once natural environment. A networked world. Architecture is the functional precipitation of activities in a place. Ordered crystals, condensers of micro worlds. Condensation of knowledge.

If recent history has been constructed on the basis of centralized systems of energy, information or production, the new history will be constructed on the basis of distributed, decentralized systems, by way of operational nodes—people, things, places, territories—that cooperate freely in order to be more efficient.

What is the architecture for distributed systems like?

As in all mutations, the saturation of the city's vital systems leads to their reprogramming on the basis of principles that are closer to those of information systems than the simple accumulation of inorganic matter.

Time and, with it, speed serve to define the rhythm of interaction between people and their environment. A new material in project design.

More ordered information creates a world that is more specific, not more generic. A world capable of accumulating history inside itself. What makes us human beings, not bacteria, is that our cells have managed to conserve information about their history through each mutation.

To construct anywhere on the planet is to submit the site to structural changes, which should be the product of the emerging relationships with the place, like a geological process of saturation or erosion.

More connected information generates more nature.

The re-programming of the world occurs when a fine informational rain is capable of drenching every element on the planet, endowing it with a digital identity, enabling it to interact with other elements by means of decentralized relational protocols.

In this way we create living organisms, never again inert, that react to specific geographies and mutate, where appropriate, in response to external influences. Rather than being a client node in a network, then, architecture is an entity that tends toward the connected self-sufficiency characteristic of natural systems.

Buildings as trees. Cities as forests.

Are architects, architects of information architecture? The citizens, instead of being the consumers of information, are its creators. The citizens, instead of being the consumers of architecture, can be its constructors.

Is architecture an iconic or a systemic activity?

Finally, every object we design and construct on the planet forms part of a functional network that connects the different scales of habitability.

1, 10, 100, 1,000, 10,000, 100,000, 1,000,000, 10,000,000, 100,000,000, 1,000,000,000, 10,000,000,000 people organize themselves by programming their relationship with the other scales by way of relational systems whose structure defines the cultural values of each society. From a book to the Library of Congress; from a lamp to a nuclear power station; from a crucifix to the Vatican. Any object, any building is ultimately the physical representation of an information node.

The construction of a dwelling, a block or a city is part of the same project of multiscalar habitability.

To change the history of the world is to change the history of the scalar relations between the functional networks of habitability.

Architecture can remain in the realm of fashion, as an activity that acts on the surface of things, or it can lead this structural transformation through which we can help to write a new history of the world.

Editorial Coordination:
Guillermo Iván López Domínguez
Collaborators: Fernando Meneses, Daniela Frogheri, Daniel Bas, Javier Alonso.
English translation: Graham Thomson

Hypercatalunya
Exhibition Date: 2003
Client: Generalitat de Catalunya, Institut Català del Sòl
Architecture: Guallart Architects
Main architects: Vicente Guallart, María Díaz, Lucas Cappelli
Collaborators: Leonardo Novelo, Lucas Jagodnik, Horacio Suaya, Sonia Sosa, Diego Dragotto, Carla Molinari
3D images: Tobias Laarman, Lucas Cappelli
Images: Laura Cantarella
IaaC Research: Luis Falcón, Ivan Llach, Raquel Palacios, Marina Guasch
Advisors:
Crystallographic Advisor: Albert Soler

Denia Mountain
Project Date: 2002
Client: Ayuntamiento de Denia
Site: Denia (Alicante)
Architect: Vicente Guallart
Façade geometry: Max Sanjulián
Auditorium: Jordi Mansilla
Collaborators: Ivan Llach, Moon Puig, Nacho Alonso, Natxo Solsona, Miquel Moragues, Raquel Colacios, Barbara Oelbrant, Guillem Augé, Ana Verges , Carlo Mezzino, Li-An Tsien, Inés Rivaya
Images: Laura Cantarella
Advisors:
Crystallographic advisor: Albert Soler
Acustic advisor: Higini Arau
Structure: Robert Brufau
Lawyer: Albert Cortina
Models: Christine Bleicher, Susanne Schulte
Polyurethane Model: Luis Fraguada, Monika Wittig
Photography: Luis Fraguada, Monika Wittig

Wrocław Expo
Competition Date: 2007
Client: Wrocław City Council
Site: Wrocław, Polonia
Architecture: Guallart Architects
Main architects: Vicente Guallart, María Díaz
Collaborators: Enrico Crobu, Asaduzzaman Rassel, Marian Albarrán, Fernando Meneses, Daniela Frogheri, Andrea Imaz, Rainer Goldstein, Ana Cabellos.
3D images: Lucas Cappelli, Gaëtan Kohler, Néstor David Palma.
Work models: Christine Bleicher, Laure-Hélène Pélissot, Filipa Barraquero
Methacrylate model: Fabián Asunción, Diego Gutiérrez, Ángel Gaspar, Juan Robledo, Rafael DeMontard
Lights: Toño Saeinz
Photography of model: Nuria Díaz (construction), Adrià Goula (final images)

Expo Shanghai 2010
Competition Date:2007
Client: Sociedad estatal para exposiciones internacionales, SEEI Spain
Site: Shanghai
Architecture: Guallart Architects
Main architects: Vicente Guallart, María Díaz, Fernando Meneses, Daniela Frogheri
Collaborators: Marian Albarrán, Ana Cabellos, Marta Vélez, Andrea Imaz, Rainer Goldstein, Ricardo Guerreiro
3D Images: Enrique Ramírez, Néstor David Palma, Ricardo Guerreiro
Models: Christine Bleicher, Laure-Hélène Pelis-sot, Filipa Barraquero, Gerardo Galaviz
Metallic Model: Lluquet
Software: Oriol Ferrer

Cultural Gate to Alborz
Date: 2008-
Client: Development of Cultural Environment Co.
Local partner: Bonsar Architecture Studio
Site: Tehran, Iran

Architecture: Guallart Architects
Main architects: Vicente Guallart, María Díaz
Collaborators: Fernando Meneses, Daniela Frogheri, Luis Fraguada, Andrea Imaz, Marcin Siekaniec, Katarzyna Z bczyk, Iwona Tajer, Pilar Díaz Rodríguez, Karen Kemp, Shahrzad Rahmani, Guillermo I. López Domínguez
Images: Solène Couet, Romain Lelièvre, Cyril Breton

New Taiwan by Design

Batoutz Port and Ocean Plaza
Project Date: 2003
Construction Date: 2008-
Main architects: Vicente Guallart, Maria Díaz
Local Architects: J.M. Lin The Oberver Design Group
Images: Laura Cantarella, Sabine Mayer
3D: Lucas Cappelli + Uoku.com-net artchitects; Lucas Jagodnik, Julieta Serena, Mariano Castro, Horacio Suaya
3D images: YLAB Tobias Laarmann
3D images Ocean Plaza: Néstor David Palma
Models: Fabián Asunción, Soledad Revuelto, Ángel Luis Gaspar, María José Bizama, Ruth Martín
Ocean Plaza Model: Theodora Christoforidou, Fotis Vasilakis, Andrea Imaz, Daniela Frogheri, Fernando Meneses
Collaborators: Christine Bleicher, Ester Rovira, Maria Osa, Kika Estarella, Ekhiñe Nieto, Michael Strauss, Rodrigo Landáburu, Melissa Magallanes, Carlos Valdés, Ricardo Guerreiro
Parametric Rocks Video: Oriol Ferrer
Advisors:
Tourism: José Miguel Iribas.
Sustainability: Rafael Serra Florensa. UPC.
Solar Energy: Oscar Acebes. TFM.
Structure: Willy Muller, WMA.
Port Engeneering: Vicente Cerdá, UPV
Crystallographic advisor: Albert Soler
Photography of rocks: Universitat de Barcelona.
Chinese translation: Lin Yi.
Chinese culture: Li-An Tsien

Fugee Port

Competition date: 2003
Project date: 2006
Client: Taipei County Government.
Site: Fugee Port, Taiwan
Architecture: Guallart Architects & J.M.Lin, The Observer Design Group
Main architects: Vicente Guallart, María Díaz

v. 1
Collaborators: Christine Bleicher, Ester Rovira, Maria Osa, Kika Estarella, Francisco Nieto, Michael Strauss, Rodrigo Landáburu, Melissa Magallanes, Carlos Valdés, Andreas Allen
3D: Lucas Cappelli + Uoku.com-net architects; Lucas Jagodnik, Julieta Serena, Mariano Castro, Horacio Suaya
3D images: YLAB Tobias Laarmann
Images: Laura Cantarella, Sabine Mayer

v. 2
Collaborators: Christine Bleicher, Amaya Coello, Ignacio Toribio, Francesco Moncada, Massimo Tepedino, Rainer Goldstein, Gawel Tyrala, Wobciech Szubinski, Torsten Altmeyer, Francis Holding, Inti Vélez, Mariano Arias, Katharina Schendl , Moritz Treese, Csíkva´ri Gergely

v. 3
Collaborators: Rainer Goldstein, Fernando Meneses, Daniela Frogheri, Marian Albarrán, Ana Cabellos, Marta Vélez, Andrea Imaz, Enrico Crobu
Models: Fabián Asunción, Soledad Revuelto, Ángel Luis Gaspar, María José Bizama, Ruth Martín, Christine Bleicher, Ricardo Guerreiro
3D images: Néstor David Palma

Advisors:
Sociologist: José Miguel Iribas.
Sustainability: Rafael Serra Florensa. UPC.
Solar energy: Oscar Acebes. TFM.
Crystallographic: Albert Soler
Chinese translation: Lin Yi.
Taiwanese traditions: Li-An Tsien.

Keelung Port
Date: 2003
Main architects: Vicente Guallart, Maria Diaz
Local partner: J.M. Lin The Observer Design Group
Collaborators: Dirk Barchstaedt, Christine Bleicher, Magnus Lundstrom, Rodrigo Landáburu, Melissa Magallanes, Ester Rovira, Manuel Shvartzberg Michael Strauss, Ricardo Guerreiro
Work models: Christine Bleicher
Models: Fabián Asunción, Soledad Revuelto, Ángel Luis Gaspar, María José Bizama, Ruth Martín
3D: Lucas Cappelli + UokU.com net-architects. Lucas Jagodnik, Julieta Serena, Mariano Castro, Horacio Suaya, Martin Eschoyez, Franco Cappelli.
Images: Laura Cantarella, Sabine Mayer
3D images: Néstor David Palma, Lucas Cappelli + UokU.com net-architects. Lucas Jagodnik, Julieta Serena, Mariano Castro, Horacio Suaya, Martin Eschoyez, Franco Cappelli.
Advisors:
Tourism: Jose Miguel Iribas.
Sustainability: Rafael Serra Florensa. UPC.
Solar energy: Oscar Acebes. TFM.
Structure: Willy Muller, WMA.
Port engineering: Vicente Cerdá, UPV
Crystallographic advisor: Albert Soler
Pictures of rocks: Universitat de Barcelona.
Chinese translation: Lin Yi.
Chinese culture: Li-An Tsien.

Vinaròs Microcoasts
Construction date: 2004
End of construction: 2006
Client: Vinarós City Council, Generalitat Valenciana and Tourism Ministry
Site: South Coast, Vinaròs.
Architecture: Guallart Architects
Main architects: Vicente Guallart, Marìa Díaz
Geometry: Marta Malé Alemany
Collaborators: Rainer Goldstein, Christine Bleicher, Wobciech Szubinski, Csikvari Gergely, Marta Vieira Baptista, Julia Futò, Moritz Treese, Massimo Tepedino, Amaya Coello, Ignacio Toribio, Francesco Moncada, Gawel Tyrala, Diego Martin
Photography: Laura Cantarella, Nuria Díaz
Models: Christine Bleicher, Theodora Christoforidou, Fotios Vasilakis, Gabriella Castellanos, Daniela Frogheri, Fernando Meneses, Andrea Imaz, Marta Vélez, Laure-Hélène Pelissot, Filipa Barraquero, Asaduzzaman Rassel
Construction: Binaria
Wooden Platforms: Gestalt

Cristóbal de Moura Street
Date: 1998
Client: City of Barcelona
Site: C/ Cristóbal de Moura (Barcelona)
Architecture: Vicente Guallart, Max Sanjulián

Vinaròs Promenade
Competition Date:2004
Beginning of construction: 2007
Client: Vinaros City Council, Generalitat Valenciana and Tourism Ministry
Site: Paseo marítimo, Vinaròs, Castellón
Architecture: Guallart architects
Main architects: Vicente Guallart, Maria Diaz

v. 1
Collaborators:Amaya Coello, Ignacio Toribio, Francesco Moncada, Massimo Tepedino, Rainer Goldstein, Gawel Tyrala, Wobciech Szubinski, Torsten Altmeyer
3D: Lucas Cappelli + Uoku.com-net architects; Lucas Jagodnik, Julieta Serena,Mariano Castro, Horacio Suaya
Images: Laura Cantarella

v. 2
Collaborators: Fernando Meneses, Daniela Frogheri, Marian Albarrán, Ana Cabellos, Marta velez, Andrea Imaz, Rainer Goldstein,

Diego Martin, Ricardo Guerreiro
3D images: Néstor David Palma, Asaduzzaman Rassel
Models: Christine Bleicher
Methacrylate model: Fabián Asunción, Diego Gutiérrez, Soledad Revuelto
Cellular Automata animation: Oriol Ferrer
Geometry and urban furniture: Daniela Frogheri y Fernando Meneses
Consultants:
Engineering: PGI Grup
Structures: VALTER
Technical architect: Estudi alegret, SL
Construction:
Constructor: Ferrovial
Stones: Mármoles Tarragona, SA
Fabrication of urban furniture: Lluquet

Vinaròs Sea Pavillion
Date: 2007-
Architecture: Guallart Architects
Main architects: Vicente Guallart, Maria Díaz
Collaborators: Daniela Frogheri, Fernando Meneses, Luis Fraguada, Andrea Imaz, Theodora Christoforidou, Fotios Vasilakis
Models: Christine Bleicher
Construction: Lluquet

Cambrils Apartments
Project date: 2002
End of construction: 2006
Client: Inmondial S.L. & Pellicer y Fills S.A.
Site: Cambrils, Tarragona
Architecture: Guallart Architects
Main architects: Vicente Guallart, Maria Díaz
Collaborators: Barbara Oelbrant, Pilar Basque, Cristina Dorado
3D images: Daniel Ibáñez, Rodrigo Rubio
Photography: Laura Cantarella, Luis Ros, Nuria Diaz
Models: Christine Bleicher, Salvador Gil
Consultants:
Structure: BIS Arquitectes
Engineering: Ingeniería ambiental
Technical architect: Estudi alegret, SL
Construction:
Crystallographic advisor: Cricursa
Painter: Salvador Sarrió
Tinted glass: CRICURSA, Alex Sesplugues
Aluminum: Aluminios DUCA
Wood: José Díaz
Carpentry: CARRE
Installations: Instal.lacions VINYOLS, Jordi Pedret
Interior divisions: ESTRUDEC
Acclimatization: AMBIT
Metal: MASDEU
Garden: De la Rosa
Awning: TOLDYSOL
Construction: Bertomeu Iglesias, S.L.

Hortal House
Date: 2000
Construction: 2001-2004
Client: Miguel Hortal and family
Site: Comarruga (Tarragona)
Architecture: Vicente Guallart
Collaborators: Pilar Gasque, Bárbara Oelbrandt
Models: Christine Bleicher
Technical architect: Ton Feliu
Structural Engineering: BIS arquitectes, David García
Construction: José Jiménez
Tinted glass: CRICURSA, Alex Sesplungues
Metallic construction: Carlos Jurado
Aluminum: ALUMIER
Carpentry: José Rivero
Installations: MEFISA, Miguel Hortal
Photography: Vicente Guallart, Luis Ros, Laura Cantarella

Avignon Expo 2000
Project date: 1999
Exhibition date: 2000
Client: Mission 200 en France. Ministère de la Culture
Site: Avignon Space Jean Laurent, France
Curator: Jean de Loissy, Yves Le Fur
Exhibition design: Vicente Guallart, Enric Ruiz

Collaborator: Joulie Roualt
Producer: Alain Thuleau
Illumination: Philips
Glass: Cricursa
Execution: BEC
Photographer: Giovanni Zanzi

Fashion Museum
Date of project: 2006
Client: Generalitat Valenciana, Fundación Barón de Vallbert
Architecture: Guallart Architects
Main architects: Vicente Guallart, María Díaz
Collaborators: Marian Albarrán, Ana Cabellos, Fernando Meneses, Daniela Frogheri, Marta Vélez, Andre Imaz, Rainer Goldstein, Ricardo Guerreiro
3D images: Gaëtan Kohler
Models: Christine Bleicher

Arab Wall
Project date: 1998
Client: Oficina Riba
Site: Valencia
Architecture: Guallart Architects
Main architect: Vicente Guallart
Model: Adria Maines

New Settlements
Date: 2003
Site: El Perelló
Client: Generalitat de Catalunya
Architecture: Guallart Architects
Main architects: Vicente Guallart, María Díaz
Collaborators: Pilar Basque, Bárbara Oelbrant.

Bioclimatic Villages
Project date: 2007
Client: Promohogar
Site: Chinchilla de Monte Aragón, Albacete
Architecture: Guallart Architects
Main architects: Vicente Guallart, María Díaz
Collaborators: Marian Albarrán, Ana Cabellos
Models: Fabian Asunción, Ángel Gaspar, Rafael DeMontard
Images: Nestor David Palma
3D: Lucas Cappelli + UokU.com - net architects; Lucas Jagodnik,
Mariano Castro, Horacio Suaya, Martín Escoyez
Photography of models: Adrià Goula, Daniel Ibáñez
Consultants:
Program: José Miguel Iribas
-Asociación de Jóvenes Empresarios de Castilla La Mancha (AJE)
-CLM Energía

Eco Tropical Neighbourhood
Project date:2007
Client: Empresa pública del suelo de Andalucía
Site: Motril, Granada
Architecture: UTE Guallart architects & Angel Gijón
Collaborators: Marian Albarrán, Ana Cabellos, Marta Vélez, Andrea Imaz, Rainer Goldstein, Fernando Meneses, Daniela Frogheri
Engineering: Grupo Medina
Environment and landscape: Gestión Técnica Medioambiental
Urbanist lawyer: José Antonio Martín Estebané
Model: Fabián Asunción, Rafael DeMontard, Salvador Gil
Photography of the model: Adrià Goula

Sociopolis
Project date: 2005
Beginning of construction: 2006
Client: Generalitat Valenciana, Instituto Valenciano de Vivienda S.L. (IVVSA)
Site: La Torre Sector, Valencia
Architecture: Guallart architects
Main architects: Vicente Guallart, Maria Diaz

V1
Coordination: Gerardo Solera, José Olagüe
Collaborators: Margarita Flores, Amaya Coe-

llo, Ignacio Toribio, Christine Bleicher, Melissa Magallanes, Francesco Moncada, Massimo Tepedino, Ana Inácio, Manuel Shvartzberg, Mirko Usai, Francis Holding

V2
Collaborators: Christine Bleicher, Amaya Coello, Ignacio Toribio, Francesco Moncada, Massimo Tepedino, Rainer Goldstein, Gawel Tyrala, Wobciech Szubinski, Torsten Altmeyer, Francis Holding, Inti Velez, Mariano Arias, Katharina Schendl , Moritz Treese, Csíkva´ri Gergely, Javier Moreno, Rubén Beltrán, Xavier Salat, Mareike Richter, Alejandra de Diego

V3
Coordination in Valencia: Alejandra de Diego
Collaborators: Fernando Meneses, Daniela Frogheri, Marian Albarrán, Ana Cabellos, Marta Vélez, Andrea Imaz, Rainer Goldstein, Ricardo Guerreiro

Images: Laura Cantarella
3D: Lucas Capelli, UokU.com net architects: Lucas Jagodnik, Julieta Serena, Mariano Castro, Marín Eschoyez
Models: Fabián Asunción, Soledad Revuelto, Ángel Luis Gaspar, María José Bizama, Ruth Martín, Rafael DeMontard, Salvador Gil, Omar, Guillermo
Models: Christine Bleicher
Photography of the model: Adrià Goula
Consultants:
Sociologist: Jose Miguel Iribas
Landscape: Manuel Colominas, Agricultural Engineer
Study of environmental impact: Javier Obartí, EVREN
Urbanist lawyer: Maria Ángeles García Capdepón
Digital neighborhood: David Iribas
Re division project: Nebot Arquitectos
Construction:
Technical direction: IVVSA _ Maria Jesús Rodríguez
Direction of technical engineering: IVVSA _ Fernando Esteve
Project coordination: IVVSA _ Carlos Llopis, Javier Soriano
Urbanization engineering: IDOM
Construction company: UTE Ortiz e Hijos & Franjuan

Sharing Tower
Project date: 2006
Client: Instituto Valenciano de Vivienda S.L. (IVVSA)
Site: La Torre Sector, Valencia
Architecture: Guallart Architects
Main architects: Vicente Guallart, Maria Díaz
Models: Fabian Asuncion

v. 1
Collaborators: Cristina Dorado, Leonardo Novelo, Sonia Ayala, Martín Osuna, Andreas Allen
3D: Lucas Cappelli + UokU.com - net architects; Lucas Jagodnik, Mariano Castro, Horacio Suaya, Martín Escoyez
Images: Laura Cantarella
Models: Fabian Asunción, Soledad Revuelto, Angel Luis Gaspar, Rafael DeMontard
Photography: Adrià Goula

v. 2
Collaborators: Julia Futo, Gaultier Le Romancer, Teresa Benito, Marta Vieira, Marinella Giuliano, Valentina Racheli, Cristina Balet, Alejandra de Diego
Models: Christine Bleicher

v. 3
Collaborators: Marian Albarran, Ana Cabellos, Marta Velez, Andrea Imaz, Rainer Goldstein
Models: Fabian Asunción, Soledad Revuelto, Angel Luis Gaspar
Photography of models: Adrià Goula

Consultants:
Engineering: Grupo JG
Structures: VALTER

University Housing

Project housing: 2007
Client: VISOREN
Site: Gandia
Architecture: Guallart Architects
Main architects: Vicente Guallart, María Díaz
Collaborators: Andrea Imaz, Rasa Mizaraité, Lina Savickaité, Daniela Frogheri, Fernando Meneses, Ricardo Guerreiro, Katarzyna Klimek
Images, 3D: Asaduzzaman Rassel, Lina Savickaité, Rasa Mizaraité, Néstor David Palma Models: Christine Bleicher, Katarzyna Klimek, Marta Carraro, Antonio Berton

Kim Hygn Yoon Editing Co.
Project date: 2001 (V1) 2004 (v2)
End of construction:2006
Client: Kim Hyng Yoon Editing Co
Site: Paju Book City. Seúl. Corea.
Architecture: Guallart Architects
Local Architect: Young Joon Kim, YO2

V. 1
Main architects: Vicente Guallart, Max Sanjulián
Collaborators: Pilar Gasque

v. 2
Main architects: Vicente Guallart, Maria Díaz
Collaborators: Esther Rovira, Magnus Lundstrom,
Images, 3D: Lucas Cappelli + UokU.com (net architects); Lucas Jagodnik, Mariano Castro, Horacio Suaya, Martín Eschoyez.
Photography: Sr. Kim Hun

Web Hotel

Date: 1998
Site: Barcelona
Client: MACBA
Architect: Vicente Guallart
Artistic direction: Nuria Díaz
Collaborators: Max Sanjulián, Quim Gil, Roger Cabezas

Media House

Date: 2001
Site: Mercat de les flors, Barcelona
Metapolis:
Media House Directors: Vicente Guallart, Enric Ruiz-Geli, Willy Müller
Structure: Max Sanjulián
gRAm: Susana Noguero
Structural typologies: Maurizio Bonizzi, Giovanni Franceschelli, Silvia Banchini, Roberto Secchi
Nodes and integration: Michel Oltramare
Housing X-Ray: Laura Cantarella
Furniture concepts: Mekhala Otramare
I'm a robot: Sophie Cornanguer
Web: Jorge Pasalagua
3D models: Rupert Maurus
Web interface: AREA·, Federico Joselevich, Chema Lungobardo, Sebastián Puiggros, Elisa Lee, Manel Ruíz
Data visualization: innothna, Julio Hardisson, Daniel Bravo, Carles Ballvé
Lighting: Toni Rueda
Project Consultants:
Architects: Robert Brufau, Jaume Adreriu
UPC: Ramón Sagüesa
Bert Bongers
Kitchen and Garden: Paco Guzmán
Chromotherapy: Mónica Alonso
Videoconferencing: Jana Leo
MIT Media Lab:
Massachussets Institute of Technology
The Center For Bits and Atoms:
Director: Neil Gershenfeld
Microservers: H. Shrikumar
Interfaces RS 485: Matt Hancher
Elisava
Director of the Interfaces masters course: Nuria Díaz
Play place: Jaime Colom
New Baby: Karina Cocho
New kid: Marina Turró
Web house: Fabiola López, Joao Esteves, Marta Pimienta
Humanhouse interface: Enric Gili
Media Kitchen: Marcos Gonzalez, Susana Juan

Self editor: Yoel Lenti
Chromaroom: Ignacio Mondine, Miguel Sola
Chromotherapy: Estela Ocampo
Project tutors: M. Angeles García, psychologist; José Manuel Berenguer, Orquesta del Caos; Sergi Jordà, UPF; Carlos Silva, TechnoMedia; Sergio Schvarstein, MM Factory
I2Cat, Internet 2 a Catalunya
Director: Sebastià Sallent
UPC: Artur Serra, Rosa María Martin, Anna Agustí, Josep Paradells
Prous Science: Josep Prous
UPC: Jesús Alcober, Cristina Cervelló, Josep Mangues
Prous Science: Jesús Salillas
Hospital de Sant Pau: Pablo López

Hyperhabitat: Reprogramming the World

A project by: Guallart Architects, Institute for Advanced Architecture of Catalonia, The Center for Bits and Atoms, Bestiario
Institutional partners: Ministerio de Vivienda, Ajuntament de Barcelona, Ajuntament de Gandía
Development partners: Visoren, Proinosa, Construcciones Riera
Collaborators: Schneider, Irpen, Luz Negra, Mefisa
Guallart Architects: Vicente Guallart, María Díaz
Institute for Advanced Architecture of Catalonia: Daniel Ibáñez, Rodrigo Rubio, Marta Malé Alemany, Areti Markopoulou, Laia Pifarré
MIT's Center for Bits and Atoms: Neil Gershenfeld, Kenny Cheung, Luis Lafuente Molinero
Fab Lab Network: Víctor Viña, Tomás Diez
Bestiario: Andrés Ortiz, Santiago Ortiz, José Aguirre, Daniel Aguilar
Nitropix Web Projects: Lucas Cappelli, Emilio DeGiovanni, Esteban Lesta, Roberto Lascano, Roxana DeGiovanni
with Schneider Electric: David Kopp
and Cisco: Kerry Lynn
Architects collaborating with installation: Vagia Pantou, Christian Zorzen, Alessio Carta, Francisca Aroso, Luis Fernando Odiaga, Maria Papaloizou, Stefania Sini, Daniel Bas, Melissa Mazik, Georgia Voudouri, Hemant Purohit, Renu Gupta, Luciano Bertoldi, Peerapong Suntinanond, Ifigenia Arvaniti, Georgios Machairas
Ismini Koronidi, Javier Olmeda Raya, Anastasia Fragoudi, Alexandra Theodorou, Higinio Llames, Susana Tesconi, Nuria Sanz, Panagiota Papachristodoulou, Luis Casado (electrician), Martinez (electrician)
Photography: José Morraja
Stylist: Letizia Orue

PUBLISHED BY ACTAR
Barcelona/New York
www.actar.com

GRAPHIC DESIGN
Ulises Chamorro @ Actar Pro

TRANSLATION
Graham Thomson

DIGITAL PRODUCTION
Oriol Rigat, Carmen Galán

PRINTING
Ingoprint SA

DISTRIBUTION
ACTAR D
Roca i Batlle 2-4
08023 Barcelona
T +34 93 4174993
F +34 93 4186707
office@actar-d.com
www.actar-d.com

ACTAR–D USA
158 Lafayette St., 5th Floor
New York, NY 10013
T +1 212 9662207
F +1 212 9662214
officeusa@actar-d.com
www.actar-d.com

ISBN 978-84-95951-61-8
DL B-4813-2009

© of the edition, ACTAR, 2008
© of the works, their authors
© of the photographs, their authors

All rights reserved

Printed and bound
in the European Union